The Global Information Technology Report

2002–2003

Readiness for the Networked World

Soumitra Dutta
Bruno Lanvin
Fiona Paua

INSEAD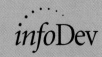

WORLD
ECONOMIC
FORUM

COMMITTED TO
IMPROVING THE STATE
OF THE WORLD

*info*Dev

New York • Oxford
Oxford University Press
2003

The Global Information Technology Report 2002–2003: Readiness for the Networked World (GITR) is published by the World Economic Forum where it is a special project within the framework of the Global Competitiveness Programme. The *GITR* is the result of a collaboration between the World Economic Forum and INSEAD, France.

At the World Economic Forum:

Professor Klaus Schwab
President

Dr. Peter K. Cornelius
Director

Jennifer Blanke
Economist

Fiona Paua
Economist

Emma Loades
Manager

At INSEAD:

Professor Soumitra Dutta
Roland Berger Professor of e-Business and
Information Technology

Dean for Executive Education

Amit Jain
Research Program Manager
eLAB@INSEAD

Gauri Goel
Research Associate
eLAB@INSEAD

Michele Hibon
Senior Research Fellow

At the World Bank:

Bruno Lanvin
Manager of the Information for Development
Program (infoDev)

Heini Shi
Program Officer, infoDev

A special thank you to Mitchell & Company Graphic Design for their excellent work on the report cover.

Thank you to Pearl Jusem and her team at DBA Design for the great interior graphic design and layout.

The terms *country* and *nation* as used in this report do not in all cases refer to a territorial entity that is a state as understood by international law and practice. The term covers well-defined, geographically self-contained economic areas that may not be states but for which statistical data are maintained on a separate and independent basis.

This Report contains material reprinted with permission from World Information Technology and Services Alliance (WITSA), 1401 Wilson Boulevard, Suite 1100, Arlington, VA 22209, USA. Prior written consent from the original data provider must be obtained for third-party use of this material.

Oxford University Press

Oxford   New York
Auckland   Bangkok   Buenos Aires   Cape Town
Chennai   Dar es Salaam   Delhi   Hong Kong   Istanbul
Karachi   Kolkata   Kuala Lumpur   Madrid   Melbourne
Mexico City   Mumbai   Nairobi   São Paulo   Shanghai
Singapore   Taipei   Tokyo   Toronto

Copyright © 2003
by the World Economic Forum
and INSEAD

Published by
Oxford University Press, Inc.
198 Madison Avenue
New York, New York 10016
http://www.oup.com

ISBN 0–19–516169–6

9 8 7 6 5 4 3 2 1

Printed in the United States of America
on acid-free paper

Contents

Preface

Professor Klaus Schwab
World Economic Form

The *Global Information Technology Report 2001–2002*, which was the first and most comprehensive assessment of the networked readiness of countries, was released last year at a time when the technology sector was reeling from its peak and the global economy was entering a period of diminishing growth expectations. This year, we present the second in the series, the *Global Information Technology Report 2002–2003*, against the backdrop of continued consolidation in the technology sector and the prevailing heightened uncertainty in the global economy. What we want to do with the *Report* is not just to provide a yearly "snapshot" of networked readiness, but to establish a process whereby governments and other decision makers can evaluate progress on a continual basis.

The rationale for releasing this *Report* at this particular time has never been more compelling. At a time when economic growth is stalling in many parts of the world, the *Report* reiterates that the use and application of information and communication technologies (ICT) remain among the most powerful engines of growth. Moreover, at a time when powerful ethnic, religious, and socioeconomic schisms are emerging, it is more important than ever to use ICT to provide tools with which people can connect and communicate.

ICT continue to offer the best hope for developing countries to accelerate their development processes. With much of the attention focused on the undoing of the technology bubble, the gains being made, particularly in developing countries, are often overlooked. Despite recent scant coverage in the media, there continues to be progress in the technology sector. This is manifested in increasing rates of technological diffusion in many developing countries, as well as in rapidly expanding rates of innovation in the advanced countries. Recognizing the importance of benchmarking performance and disseminating best practices, this *Report* monitors the progress in networked readiness that is undoubtedly occurring in various parts of the world, and reveals the obstacles that prevent countries from fully capturing the benefits of ICT.

The *Report* is both timely and relevant, and this fact is crucial because it captures the experiences of the technology sector; these lessons are too costly and important to be missed or ignored. The experiences of businesses have stressed the necessity of a sustainable business model and the need for prudence when allocating resources to technology investments. Meanwhile, the lessons for governments include, among others, the importance of assessing the appropriateness of the choice of technologies; and the affirmation that it is the development of the individual, through education and skills development, that must lie at the core of any successful long-term strategy towards a knowledge-based economy. These and other lessons are distilled and synthesized in this *Report*, which draws on the expertise of scholars and practitioners, as well as that of policymakers and business leaders.

At a time of uncertainty in the global economy, it is often difficult to look ahead towards recovery. In this regard, we commend the contributors to this *Report* for their vision and commitment to produce a valuable resource for policymakers and business leaders engaged in the task of promoting networked readiness. We especially thank the editors of the *Report*, Soumitra Dutta of INSEAD, Bruno Lanvin of the infoDev Program of the World Bank, and Fiona Paua of the World Economic Forum, for their leadership role in this project; thanks also to Dr. Peter K. Cornelius, who has been charged with heading the Global Competitiveness Programme under which this *Report* is published. Finally, we also thank the Global Digital Divide Initiative Task Force and secretariat for their continuing commitment to addressing many of the obstacles mentioned in this *Report*.

Executive Summary

Soumitra Dutta, INSEAD
Bruno Lanvin, infoDev
and
Fiona Paua, World Economic Forum

Since the first quarter of 2000, a profound shift has occurred in the field of information and communication technologies (ICT). Share prices of technology companies have fallen to a small fraction of their peaks and the sector has undergone massive consolidation, with many companies falling into insolvency. As the dust settles and the technology bubble dissipates, it is clear that many important lessons can be learned from what has transpired in the sector. Amid the prospect of prolonged deceleration of economic growth, it is more important than ever to understand the contributions of ICT to economic growth and productivity.

It is within this context that we publish the *Global Information Technology Report 2002–2003*, the second such report. With the rapid changes in the technology sector, dramatic shifts in the global economic and political landscape, and policy innovations in respective national contexts, there is an ever-increasing need to continue to benchmark performance and monitor progress across nations.

As in the first edition, this year's *Report* is the most comprehensive assessment of networked readiness, covering eighty-two of the leading economies of the world. Building upon and refining the previous methodology, distilling the strengths of other measures of readiness, and benefiting from a greater array of data sources, this *Report* introduces an enhanced analytical framework that is used to examine networked readiness for three important stakeholders—the individual, business, and government—within a nation's economic and policy context.

The findings of the *Report* are presented in three sections: essays, country profiles and data tables. The essay section draws upon the expertise of scholars, practitioners, policymakers and business leaders, and is divided into two parts. The first part is an exposition of the components of and the analytical framework underlying the Networked Readiness Index, while the second part consists of regional and country case studies that apply the analytical framework, highlight the policy challenges, and emphasize best practices and lessons learned. The Country Profiles Section provides a detailed snapshot of each country's networked readiness relative to other countries. The *Report* concludes with data tables, which contain rankings of countries for every variable covered in the *Report*.

The ranking of countries in the Networked Readiness Index 2002–2003 is presented in the first chapter by Soumitra Dutta and Amit Jain. This chapter describes how the Index was designed and constructed after a thorough and extensive investigation of the relationship between networked readiness and key variables such as gross domestic product per capita, ICT expenditure, and Internet usage. The Index is a composite of three components: the environment for ICT offered by a given country or community; the readiness of a community's key stakeholders (individuals, businesses, and government) to use ICT; and finally, the use of ICT by these stakeholders.

The succeeding chapter is an exposition of the first component of the Networked Readiness Index, the networked environment. The second chapter, "Crafting the Environment for Networked Readiness," by José María Figueres-Olsen and Fiona Paua, emphasizes the importance of ensuring that an appropriate and effective policy framework is in place. The chapter addresses the question: what needs to be in place in terms of the environment—market conditions, regulatory framework, and the network infrastructure—to enable individuals, businesses, and governments to participate in and benefit more fully from the networked economy? Recognizing the complexity of the task and that there is no simple blueprint to be followed, the chapter draws on lessons gleaned from the policy experiences of various countries and, where available, highlights best practices.

The third, fourth, and fifth chapters discuss the three dimensions of analysis, individuals, businesses and governments, respectively. The third chapter, "Ready for the Networked Future? The Role of the Individual in the Networked Society," by Dirk Reiter, Helmut Meitner, and Carsten Rossbach, focuses on the capability of individual citizens to capture the benefits of ICT. In examining usage and barriers to uptake and making clear analytical distinction between enablers, incentives, and value-chain components, the chapter concludes by proposing six items for the "agenda for the networked future."

"ICT: A Critical Enabler of Managerial Innovation," is the fourth chapter, in which Scott Beardsley, Ingo Beyer von Morgenstern, Luis Enriquez, Stefan Mytilineos, and Jürgen Wunram analyze the relationship between ICT investment and productivity improvements and conclude that ICT is a critical enabler of productivity. The authors identify the key source of productivity improvement to be managerial innovation, and the key stimuli of managerial innovation to be broader economic forces such as competition, structural change for industries, and regulation. Recognizing the complexity of ICT implementation, the authors also caution that in many cases, ICT has failed to deliver performance improvements.

Bruno Lanvin, in his chapter, "Leaders and Facilitators: The New Roles of Governments in Digital Economies," brings the roles of governments into perspective. The emergence of a global digital economy challenges many of the traditional roles of governments; the examples of the most "network ready" economies show that governments have to accept new responsibilities and roles, both as leaders and as facilitators of their respective countries' integration

in the global information economy. Surveying a vast array of governmental practices and strategies, varying from the highly successful to the disastrous, the chapter identifies the ways in which ICT have changed the potential and actual roles and functioning of governments, as well as the ways in which governments have most successfully contributed to the enhancement of national network competitiveness.

The succeeding chapters present case studies that highlight the application of the Framework in assessing the networked readiness of various regions and selected countries. The sixth chapter, "ICT in Africa: A Status Report" by Mike Jensen, assesses the networked readiness of Africa. Recognizing the diversity of the region, the chapter contains a comprehensive analysis of ICT diffusion and use in the different countries of the region. Most important, the chapter highlights the key ICT initiatives in the region, and identifies areas for policy action.

The seventh chapter, "Networked Readiness: Latin America's Last Train," by Lionel C.Carrasco, Rossana Fuentes-Berain, and Roberto Martínez Illescas, emphasizes how imperative it is for the region to promote networked readiness. Citing the political, regulatory, and infrastructure challenges, as well as the need for more content, both traditional and transactional, the chapter identifies possible actions, strategies, and models that could be embraced by the three main stakeholders.

In the chapter, "ICT Challenges for the Arab World," Soumitra Dutta and Mazen Coury discuss ongoing developments in ICT in the Arab world. After reviewing the ICT-awareness of Arab governments by looking into their strategic plans and operational five-year plans, Dutta and Coury observe the uneven levels of awareness of and importance given to ICT both in stated national strategies and demonstrated success in implementation. To cap their analysis, the two authors outline specific policy recommendations that range from the need to create a common Arab ICT strategy to the importance of stimulating Arabic content.

The ninth chapter, "ICT: Pockets of Leadership in East Asia" by Arnoud De Meyer, analyzes the networked readiness of East and Southeast Asian nations, with the exception of Japan and China. Capturing the diversity of the state of the ICT sectors of these countries, the analysis divides the nine countries covered into three main groups, with the first group consisting of the leaders in networked readiness: Singapore, Taiwan, Korea, and Hong Kong. The second group is comprised of Malaysia and Thailand, while the third group is composed of the Philippines, Indonesia, and Vietnam. The chapter identifies areas of outstanding performance as well as the potential for growth in these countries in several areas, including outsourcing, broadband usage, SMS, e-government, and IT applications in health care and port management.

"Driving the e-Economy: Contrasting Approaches in the United States, Europe, and Japan," by Mark Melford, Constantijn van Oranje-Nassau, and Soumitra Dutta, contains detailed international comparisons of the selected governments' progress in driving their respective e-agendas. The authors examine the common challenges and widely contrasting approaches of governments in the United States, Europe, and Japan. It also traces regional developments and identifies best practices as part of its assessment of the networked readiness of these three countries at the level of the individual, business, and government.

The eleventh chapter is a country case study on China, "Born Global: The Impact of the WTO Process on China's ICT Competitiveness," by Bruno Lanvin, Pamela Mar, Christine Zhen-Wei Qiang, and Frank-Jürgen Richter. The authors discuss China's networked readiness in the context of its accession to the World Trade Organization (WTO). According to the authors, China's preparation and implementation of its WTO commitments could provide the catalyst for China to become a center of innovation, content creation, and research and development. On the other hand, the government is facing difficult trade-offs, and enterprises need to redefine their core competencies while constantly assessing and responding to changing market circumstances, including the evolving regulatory framework. During this process, China will likely be regarded as an intellectual and political leader of a progressive trend to strengthen the development aspects of the trade liberalization process.

The final chapter is a country case study on India, by N.R. Narayana Murthy and Sukumar S., "Influence of ICT on the Development of India's Competitiveness." The case study is an in-depth and comprehensive examination of the technological progress achieved in specific sectors of India's economy as well as the challenges India faces on the path of ICT expansion. The authors note that while the Indian ICT industry and the country's ICT professionals have been on the cutting edge of technological evolution, a vast majority of the people have neither the access nor the awareness and education to derive benefits from advancing technology. The authors also observe, however, that some of the sociotechnical innovations created in the country hold promise, not only to influence conditions in India, but also to help reduce the digital gap in many other developing countries.

Part 3 contains detailed country profiles for each of the eighty-two countries included in the assessment. This section is followed by a presentation of the data tables and the statistical methodology used to compute the Networked Readiness Index. Taken together, these last two sections of the *Report* allow the reader to gain a deeper understanding of the networked readiness of a particular nation.

The essays, along with the last two data-oriented sections of the *Report*, are all intended to serve as a guide to national leaders as they craft the appropriate policy framework that will enable individuals, businesses, and governments to fully capture the benefits of ICT. Beyond the scope of the *Report*, however, lies perhaps an even greater challenge, and that is the translation of policy into action and from action, to visible outcomes. We hope that with this second edition of the *Global Information Technology Report*, we have contributed to the establishment of a process for benchmarking progress in networked readiness throughout the world.

Part 1
The Networked Readiness Index
Framework

Chapter 1

The Networked Readiness of Nations

Soumitra Dutta and Amit Jain

INSEAD

Overview

INSEAD has long recognized the fundamental role of information and communication technology (ICT) as a catalyst for organizational transformation and change. Therefore, gaining a better understanding of the economic and business impact of ICT has been identified as a key research priority, giving rise to a multitude of research streams. The Networked Readiness Index 2002–2003 discussed in this chapter is the product of one such research effort.

ICT forms the "backbone" of several industries, such as banking, airlines, and publishing, and is an important value-adding component of consumer products, such as television sets, cameras, cars, and mobile telephone sets. ICT is today a dominant force in enabling companies to exploit new distribution channels, create new products, and deliver differentiated value-added services to customers. ICT is also an important catalyst for social transformation and national progress. Disparities in the levels of ICT readiness and usage could translate into disparities in levels of productivity, and hence could influence a country's rate of economic growth. Understanding and leveraging ICT is critical for nations striving for continued economic progress.[1]

Over the past few years, numerous attempts have been made to measure the comparative levels of ICT development of nations. The multitude of these efforts and the diversity of the organizations conducting them only help underline the importance of ICT as a key factor contributing to a nation's development, and as a cohesive force for integrating a nation into the global economy. The speed with which technological forces affect us and the rapidity of the ensuing changes requires a mechanism for measurement that not only accounts for factors enabling the spread and usage of ICT, but that also explicitly considers the roles played by the major stakeholders—individuals, businesses, and governments.

This chapter presents the Networked Readiness Index (NRI) that has been used to assess the comparative progress of eighty-two countries along different dimensions of progress in ICT. The discussion is divided into five main sections. First, we shall discuss previous attempts to measure the ICT competitiveness of countries and communities. Following this, there is a discussion on the Networked Readiness Framework and the procedure used to arrive at the NRI results. Third, the results of the research and analysis are presented; that is, the relative ranking of nations based on their degrees of networked readiness. Fourth, we take a closer look at the three indexes (and their constituent subindexes) composing the NRI, and at how various countries have fared on each of these dimensions. Finally, the fifth section investigates the relationship between networked readiness and key variables such as gross domestic product (GDP) per capita, ICT expenditure, and Internet usage, in addition to presenting some of the challenges that were faced while conducting the study.

Previous Efforts to Measure ICT Competitiveness

The task of capturing a nation's competitiveness in a single index score remains a significant challenge. Prior measurement approaches varied significantly with the type of organization in which they were developed, and the aims, objectives, methodology and results the measurement produced (see Table 1). Table 2 gives a detailed analysis of leading past efforts at measuring the ICT competitiveness of nations, and presents information about the countries/communities covered in each approach, the strengths and weaknesses of the approach, and a general description of the methodology. The Networked Readiness Index Framework (NRI Framework) proposed in this chapter builds upon these prior frameworks and research.

Table 1. **Previous Approaches**

Type of organizations	• Private sector • Government sector • Academic institutions
Objectives	• Policymaking and evaluation tool for countries • Measure state of internet acceptance (or e-readiness) in a country or community • Measure the growth of internet in the world
Results	• Comparative analyses of countries • Identification of lacunae and fortes of independent communities • Stages of ICT development of a country

The private sector, governmental organizations (including transnational consortia) and academic institutions have been the key drivers in developing ICT measurement efforts. Naturally then, one would expect the subject of the analysis to vary, based on the intended application of the agency formulating it. We see that reports like the Global Technology Index and McConnell's Ready? Net. Go! are rooted in the private sector and are meant to be guides for other businesses. The APEC e-Commerce Assessment Guide, developed by the Asia-Pacific Economic Cooperation (APEC) e-Commerce Steering Group, has significant representation from both the business community and governmental organizations; the APEC assessment acts as a policy guide for governments, based on input from the business community. This translates into the report having a significant emphasis on metrics falling within the purview of the government: aspects such as basic infrastructure, current policy indicators, laws and taxation. On the other hand, Mosaic's Global Diffusion of the Internet comes from the academic world and presents a more balanced framework; they include business-related measures like organizational infrastructure, and government-related measures like connectivity infrastructure.

The objectives of the different approaches also vary significantly. There have been two main motivations for assessing networked readiness in the past: first, as a policymaking and evaluation tool for countries, and second, as a measure of the state of Internet acceptance in a country or community. One would add a word of caution here. The different tools have often sought to measure the "readiness" of different communities and the factors that contribute to this readiness. The definition of readiness itself, however, varies from one study to the other. This fact is important, because the measurement and assessment of the factors are consistent with the study's definition. Hence, while APEC's readiness guide and McConnell's Ready? Net. Go! both define readiness as the level of preparation of a community to participate in the increasingly networked world, the Computer Systems Policy Project (CSPP) defines it as the level of development of a community to ensure that e-commerce can thrive and deliver real value to a community. Other agencies, such as the Center for International Development (CID) at Harvard University, have extended the concept of readiness to include the potential of a community to participate in ICT developments.

The methodology used in prior research also varies. Studies such as the APEC e-Commerce Readiness Assessment Guide and Global Diffusion of the Internet rely upon questionnaire-based data. Others, such as the CID study, are a hybrid of survey questionnaires and hard data. Only recently has there been a move to incorporate impact metrics in any of these studies. This is understandable, because ICT have only recently had widespread impact, moving beyond the initial elite users such as academia and the military. Now, not only has a level of maturity been reached in terms of the technology to enable a networked world, but also, all the key stakeholders have come around to accepting and exploiting productivity advantages enabled by ICT. Hence, an important indicator of ICT competitiveness in the future will be the impact of ICT on the citizens, businesses, and government of a nation. Some of the older models, such as the CSPP and APEC models, are primarily readiness-based analyses. As a reflection of the development of thought in this direction, agencies such as the Economist Intelligence Unit (EIU) and the CID have incorporated impact metrics into their frameworks.

The results produced by the different tools fall into three main categories: (1) those that look to provide a comparative analysis amongst the various countries (i.e., the 2002 Global Technology Index); (2) those that are designed

Table 2. **Key Efforts to Measure ICT Competitiveness**

Intended Application	Countries Covered	Strengths and Weaknesses	Overall Analysis
APEC e-Commerce Readiness Assessment Guide, 2000 by the Asia-Pacific Economic Cooperation (APEC) Electronic Commerce Steering Group			
To help member governments develop policies to promote the balanced development of e-commerce	The report does not include the study of any one country but provides a guide for analysis. It has been used for evaluating various countries, such as Hong Kong and Malaysia	**Strengths** 1. Fairly comprehensive readiness assessment 2. Provides a toolkit that is easily reusable by the member states for self-assessment **Weaknesses** 1. There is no hard data-based analysis 2. Assessment is based on soft data or opinions of individuals 3. Impact analysis of ICT has not been done 4. Relative rankings of the different countries are not available 5. There is no overall guide for interpreting the results	This tool was created with the influence of the industry, in order to help in guiding the policymaking efforts of governments. It is comprehensive in its coverage of the readiness factors, with little analysis of the impact of past initiatives. It examines six broad indicators for e-commerce, and these are developed into a series of questions that provide direction to desirable e-commerce policies and for the removal of barriers to electronic trade. The six indicators are: 1. Basic infrastructure and technology 2. Access to necessary services 3. Current level and type of use of the Internet 4. Promotion and facilitation activities 5. Skills and human resources 6. Positioning for the digital economy The guide does not provide a comparative assessment of nations. It is a questionnaire-based self-assessment guide for the use of member countries on a one-off basis. Its output is a good guide for macro-level policy making but not for businesses looking for guidance on the relative e-competitiveness of nations.
Global Diffusion of the Internet, 2001 by The Mosaic Group			
The framework is designed to assess the state of Internet diffusion in a country. It is useful for business stakeholders wanting to make use of and invest in the Internet, for policymakers debating how to positively (or negatively) influence its use and development, and for researchers studying the large-scale diffusion of complex interrelated technologies.	Mosaic has studied about 25 countries—mainly developing countries in Asia, the Middle East, and central Europe, apart from some NRI leaders such as Finland and Hong Kong	**Strengths** 1. Provides a good picture of the state of diffusion of Internet in a given community or country 2. Addresses the perspective of all stakeholders, including individuals, businesses, and government. 3. Outputs results in the form of an easy-to-understand Kiviat diagram **Weaknesses** 1. Lacks overall e-competitiveness analysis 2. Focuses only on Internet penetration and not on ICT in general 3. Methodology remains primarily qualitative.	It has been formulated by Mosaic, a group that has roots in academia. The framework analyzes the diffusion of the Internet in a country along six main lines: 1. Pervasiveness—level of use by individuals 2. Sectoral absorption— level of use by organizations in the sectors academic, commercial, health, and government. 3. Connectivity infrastructure—quality and robustness of the underlying network infrastructure. 4. Organizational infrastructure—the number and robustness of the organizations (e.g., ISP) providing the infrastructure. 5. Geographic dispersion—how geographically dispersed are the organizations providing infrastructure ? 6. Sophistication of use—how intense has the adoption of the technology been? The framework is more balanced and addresses all stakeholders: individuals, businesses and government. It is particularly useful for the study of a given community. While the framework might be useful for policymaking, it makes comparative analysis of nations complex. The report relies on a questionnaire as its primary source of data.

Table 2. **Key Efforts to Measure ICT Competitiveness (continued)**

Intended Application	Countries Covered	Strengths and weaknesses	Overall Analysis
Ready? Net. Go! By McConnell International, 2001			
The framework is designed to assess a country's e-readiness, or capacity to participate in the global digital economy. It aims to evaluate who is e-ready: which countries are enabling businesses, governments, and citizens to flourish in the networked economy.	The 2001 report covers 53 countries. While the emphasis is on developing countries, no geographic region is predominant.	**Strengths** 1. Provides a qualitative reference guide for the comparative e-competitiveness of nations. 2. Is rich in examples of the way in which ICT has been promoted or used across the world, which can serve as guide to policymaking. **Weaknesses** 1. Does not provide an overall assessment of a country in terms of its e-readiness.	McConnell International is a consulting firm helping clients with technology policy and strategy. Clients include governments, nongovernmental organizations (NGOs), multinational organizations, and private sector firms. It analyzes a country's e-readiness on the following dimensions: 1. Connectivity—whether networks are easy and affordable to access and use 2. e-Leadership—the role that government and businesses play to promote the use of networked technologies in a country, and whether e-readiness is a national priority 3. Information security—can the processing and storage of networked information be trusted? 4. Human capital—are the right people available to support e-business and to build a knowledge-based society? 5. e-Business climate—how easy it is to do e-business today? The report is a good tool for business leaders trying to assess the global state of development of the Internet. However, it is difficult to gain an understanding of the relative level of e-readiness of countries studied.
2002 Global Technology Index (GTI) by Dr. Howard Rubin, Metricnet.com, 2002			
The index is meant to be a measure of the economic dynamism and strength, as well as the technological capabilities and potential, of a country.	This report covers more than 50 countries spread over all the important commercial zones of the world. It has an even mix of developing and developed countries.	**Strengths** 1. Provides a comprehensive and overall score for each country 2. Ranks the various countries using subcriteria to assist those interested in specific areas of competence for a market **Weaknesses** 1. Methodology used is not explicitly explained, such as how the overall index is computed 2. Analysis is largely readiness-driven	Metricnet.com is a data collection and distribution service and is a division of the META group. The 2002 Global Technology Index is one of many such reports available at metricnet.com. The data for this report however are driven by statistics from independent data sources such as the CIA, IMD, and the NUA Internet surveys. The five factors used to measure the GTI are: 1. Knowledge jobs 2. Globalization 3. Economic dynamism and competition 4. Transformation to a digital economy 5. Technological innovation capacity This Global Technology Index produces a set of indexes ranking the nations according to their competitiveness. The framework has been kept largely unchanged from the previous report, making it easy to track the movement of countries in the rankings.

Table 2. **Key Efforts to Measure ICT Competitiveness (continued)**

Intended Application	Countries Covered	Strengths/ Weaknesses	Overall Analysis
International Survey of e-Commerce by The World Information Technology and Service Alliance (WITSA), 2000			
This report seeks to determine: 1. What factors are most important for the deployment of e-business 2. The degree of business and consumer use of e-commerce.	Contributions from the 27 member countries are used, and there is a good mix of developing and developed countries.	**Strengths** 1. Addresses the key issues and concerns on the ICT policymaker's agenda 2. Attempts to provide a more detailed analysis of the eight key global issues identified, each of which are applicable to any nation **Weaknesses** 1. Lacks country-based analysis. 2. Lacks comparative overall ranking of nations 3. Survey-based; lacks basis in hard data and related analysis	WITSA is a consortium of 38 IT-industry associations that are often involved in policy-influencing activities. This cross-national perspective is reflected in this survey; it has no special focus, but highlights eight global issues in the development of e-business. 1. Trust, security and privacy 2. Technology 3. Workforce issues 4. Public policy 5. Taxation 6. Business process 7. Costs 8. Consumer attitudes The report is not meant to provide an understanding of country-specific readiness measures for e-commerce. The results are important for policymakers looking to understand the primary concerns around the development of e-business. Given that WITSA consists of industry associations, most of the factors that have been considered for this survey are policy issues falling under the purview of governments rather than of private businesses.
Negotiating the Digital Divide by Center for International Development and Conflict Management (CIDCM), University of Maryland			
The project focuses on analyzing the development of the Internet in developing countries, particularly in African countries.	Ghana, Senegal, Kenya. Reports for China and Brazil are also underway.	**Strengths** 1. Aim is to augment knowledge of Africa 2. Focuses on the process of Internet diffusion, and pays special attention to the roles and interactions of institutions and individuals **Weaknesses** 1. Focus is only on Internet-related technologies and skills 2. Does not allow for intercountry comparisons	This framework is the work of CIDCM, an academic institutution involved in conflict management and preventive diplomacy. This project, in partnership with the U.S. Agency for International Development, is designed not only to assess the advancement of the Internet, but also to enable it, with a particular focus on the sub-Saharan African region. CIDCM seeks a re-usable model; however, the individual studies are nation specific. The guidelines for employing the framework recommend a combination of questionnaires and statistical data analysis. It identifies the deployment of the Internet as being divided into four stages: Pre-commercial, Commercial, Competitive, and Consolidated. It also considers the ease and speed of negotiations of the different actors, such as individuals, businesses, governments, and NGOs. A toolbox has been developed to apply the framework to new studies.

Table 2. Key Efforts to Measure ICT Competitiveness (continued)

Intended Application	Countries Covered	Strengths/ Weaknesses	Overall Analysis
Readiness for Living in the Networked World by the Computer Systems Policy Project (CSPP)			
The CSPP self-assessment tool is designed to help determine how prepared a community or country is to participate in the networked world.	The report does not examine any given country, but presents a tool that is generally applicable.	**Strengths** 1. Breaks down the analysis for each of the 23 indicators into four stages of development according to the indicator's performance 2. Tool is fairly easy to use **Weaknesses** 1. Demarcates stages for each category, but does not advise how to move between stages 2. Focused on readiness with a limited analysis of impact	The CSPP is a public policy advocacy group, and is comprised of chairpersons and chief executive officers of leading U. S. information technology companies. The report presents a series of 23 questions under 5 distinct groups 1. The network (infrastructure) 2. Networked places (access) 3. Networked applications and services 4. Networked economy 5. Network world enablers The report proposes analyzing each of the 23 indicators by classifying a country in one of four categories, or stages of development. Categories range from the stage one community with a minimum of the necessary technology and applications, to the stage four community, which has advanced technology and ubiquitous applications. The framework itself does not compare different communities; rather, it presents an assessment based on the given inputs for the various questions.
Readiness for the Networked World by Information Technologies Group, Center for International Development (CID) at Harvard University			
The guide is intended to be a tool for government policymakers to assess the state of networked readiness of a community. It is targeted at communities in developing countries seeking to define a strategy to participate in the networked world.	The Global Information Technology Report 2001–2002 builds upon this approach to conduct analysis leading to the evaluation of a mix of 75 developed and developing countries.	**Strengths** 1. Breaks down analysis into four stages of development for each of the 19 indicators, according to its performance on the same. 2. Tool is simple and easy to use **Weaknesses** 1. Demarcates stages for each category, does not advise how to move between stages 2. Focused on readiness with a limited analysis of impact	This framework builds on the earlier CSPP framework, and has been developed in an academic institution. It represents a more balanced approach. The CID report looks at 19 different categories of indicators, which fall into 5 distinct groups: 1. Network access 2. Networked learning 3. Networked society 4. Networked economy 5. Network policy The report proposes analyzing each of the 19 indicators by classifying a country in one of four categories, or stages of development. The framework itself does not compare different communities and just presents an assessment based on the given inputs for the various questions.

to identify lacunae and fortes of independent communities (i.e., McConnell's Ready? Net. Go!); and (3) those that identify the stage of development of a country (the CID and CSPP studies). While all categories are important for different aspects of policymaking, reports such as the 2002 Global Technology Index present a better understanding of the overall and relative development of countries, and reports such as McConnell's Ready? Net. Go! are good representations of the policymakers' view of the state of affairs in a particular community. A report that does not fit either of these categories is the World Information Service and Technology Alliance (WITSA) International Survey of e-Commerce, which provides information about generic challenges in establishing and furthering e-business without a focus on specific markets.

The Networked Readiness Framework 2002–2003

Influences on the NRI Framework

In the *Global Information Technology Report 2001–2002*, CID defined the Networked Readiness Index as "the potential and degree of preparation of a community to participate in the Networked World." While we concur with this definition, we would like to extend it to include the potential and preparation of a community within its encompassing environment. By adding this, we separate environmental factors within which stakeholders, such as individuals, businesses, and governments, operate from the potential and preparedness of these same stakeholders.

The CID Networked Readiness Index (Figure 1) is divided into two overall measures: network use and enabling factors. The former "measures the extent of current network connectivity" while the latter "measures a country's capacity

Figure 1. **The Networked Readiness Index Framework 2001–2002**

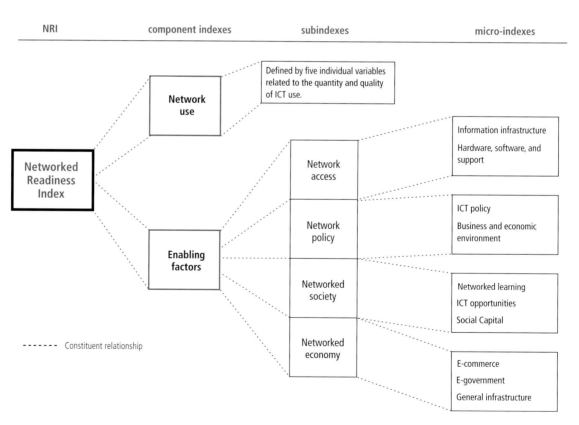

| NRI | component indexes | subindexes | micro-indexes |

Network use — Defined by five individual variables related to the quantity and quality of ICT use.

Networked Readiness Index

Enabling factors

Network access — Information infrastructure; Hardware, software, and support

Network policy — ICT policy; Business and economic environment

Networked society — Networked learning; ICT opportunities; Social Capital

Networked economy — E-commerce; E-government; General infrastructure

------- Constituent relationship

Source: Global Information Technology Report 2001-2002, Information Technologies Group, Center for International Development at Harvard University

Figure 2. The IAP Framework

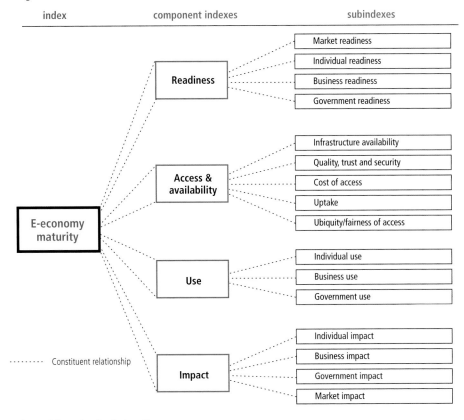

index | component indexes | subindexes

Readiness
- Market readiness
- Individual readiness
- Business readiness
- Government readiness

Access & availability
- Infrastructure availability
- Quality, trust and security
- Cost of access
- Uptake
- Ubiquity/fairness of access

Use
- Individual use
- Business use
- Government use

Impact
- Individual impact
- Business impact
- Government impact
- Market impact

E-economy maturity

- - - - - Constituent relationship

Source: Information Age Partnership

The IAP model (Figure 2) introduces an explicit distinction between the three key players in a nation—individuals, businesses, and government—within the context of the market. We have chosen to retain this distinction in our definition of the NRI Framework. The EFQM's European Quality Model (Figure 3) is structured into two layers—enablers and impact—each of which is further broken into constituent layers focusing on leadership, processes, and results. The NRI Framework (Figure 4) that we have employed in this report has a similar structure and constitution.

Both the IAP and the EFQM-TQM frameworks are consistent with the CID model in that they also break up the analysis into impact and enabling factors. This structure is important in order to extend the basis of a community assessment

to exploit existing networks and create new ones" (Kirkman et al 2002). The enabling factors are further broken up into several constituent subindexes such as network access, policy, society and economy. The strength of CID's model lies in the fact that it takes a step forward by defining a fairly comprehensive and well-developed framework, and that it is a simple and well-structured model.

While the CID model serves as a reference point, two other efforts have had an important bearing on the NRI Framework: The Information Age Partnership (IAP) from the United Kingdom, and the European Foundation for Quality Management (EFQM) version of the Total Quality Management (TQM) model. It is interesting to observe TQM models, as they are widely used by corporations globally to evaluate and benchmark their achievements with respect to TQM. Although measuring ICT readiness is different from measuring TQM achievements, the measurement framework and principles used within TQM provide valuable lessons for our study.

from that of their current participation in the networked world to the potential future impact that the community can make on the networked world. However, the key refinement of our model is the explicit realization that this analysis of potential needs to be further broken up to study the role of the individual, business, and government operating within an overall environment. These three key dimensions have been recognized explicitly in the past by models such as the IAP, and implicitly by some of the models outlined in the earlier part of this chapter.

Figure 3. The EFQM Excellence Model

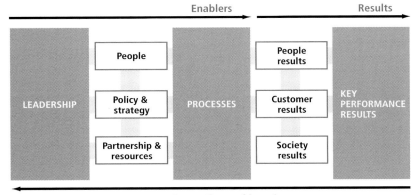

Enablers | Results

LEADERSHIP
- People
- Policy & strategy
- Partnership & resources

PROCESSES

- People results
- Customer results
- Society results

KEY PERFORMANCE RESULTS

Innovation and learning

Source: European Foundation for Quality Management

The NRI Framework

The Networked Readiness Index Framework 2002–2003 represents an effort to untangle the underlying complexity behind the role of ICT in a nation's development. The Framework and its components not only provide a model for computing the relative development and use of ICT in countries, but also allows for a better understanding of a nation's strengths and weaknesses with respect to ICT.

Figure 4 depicts the structure of the NRI Framework. The NRI Framework is based upon the following premises:

1. There are three important stakeholders to consider in the development and use of ICT: individuals, businesses, and governments;

2. There is a general macroeconomic and regulatory environment for ICT in which these stakeholders play out their respective roles;

3. The degree of ICT (and hence the impact of ICT) on the three stakeholders is linked to the degree of their readiness (or capability) to use and benefit from ICT.

The NRI is defined as "the degree of preparation of a nation or community to participate in and benefit from ICT developments." As shown in Figure 4, the Index is a composite of three components: the environment for ICT offered by a given country or community; the readiness of the community's key stakeholders (individuals, businesses, and governments) to use ICT; and finally, the usage of ICT amongst these stakeholders. A discussion in greater detail on the structure of the Framework is presented in the section titled, Disaggregating the Networked Readiness Index.

Figure 4. **The Networked Readiness Index Framework 2002–2003**

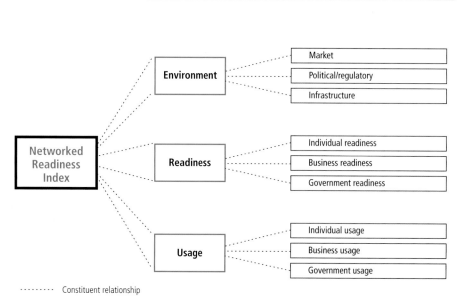

Constituent relationship

Source: INSEAD

NRI Results for 2002–2003

The overall results for the Networked Readiness Index 2002–2003 are presented in Table 3.[2] Finland comes out with the top rank, followed by the United States. Finland has performed well across all the component indexes of the NRI Framework. Singapore, Sweden, and Iceland occupy 3rd, 4th, and 5th place, respectively. Canada gets the 6th place, followed by the United Kingdom, Denmark, and Taiwan with almost equal NRI scores. Germany comes in 10th place. Of note also are:

1. Israel, with its rapidly developing e-business sector and large technically-skilled workforce, has a current rank of 12;

2. Korea, with its very high Internet penetration and one of the highest usages of broadband in the world, is ranked 14th;

3. Estonia is the leader amongst the Eastern European countries, with a rank of 24.

One sees in the top twenty-five rankings the following regional groupings:

1. The Americas. Two countries—the United States and Canada;

2. Western Europe. Fourteen countries, led by Scandinavia;

3. Asia and Oceania. Seven countries, led by Singapore;

4. The Middle East and North Africa. One country—Israel;

5. Central and Eastern Europe. One country—Estonia.

Furthermore, one can observe the following:

1. The top-ranked South American countries are Brazil (29th), Chile (35th), and Argentina (45th). As a block, Latin America fares poorly in the NRI rankings. Secondary analysis leads us to believe that this is partially explained by the relatively low levels of governmental readiness of these countries.

2. In Asia, India with its immense pool of trained IT manpower is ranked 37th, and Thailand follows at rank 41; China is ranked 43rd.

3. Russia comes in with an overall ranking of 69.

4. There are few countries from Africa and Central Asia that are included in the rankings. This is due to limitations in obtaining reliable data from these nations (see last section for more details on limitations of the research).

Table 3. **The Networked Readiness Index**

Country	Score	NRI Rank
Finland	5.92	1
United States	5.79	2
Singapore	5.74	3
Sweden	5.58	4
Iceland	5.51	5
Canada	5.44	6
United Kingdom	5.35	7
Denmark	5.33	8
Taiwan	5.31	9
Germany	5.29	10
Netherlands	5.26	11
Israel	5.22	12
Switzerland	5.18	13
Korea	5.10	14
Australia	5.04	15
Austria	5.01	16
Norway	5.00	17
Hong Kong SAR	4.99	18
France	4.97	19
Japan	4.95	20
Ireland	4.89	21
Belgium	4.83	22
New Zealand	4.70	23
Estonia	4.69	24
Spain	4.67	25
Italy	4.60	26
Luxembourg	4.55	27
Czech Republic	4.43	28
Brazil	4.40	29
Hungary	4.30	30
Portugal	4.28	31
Malaysia	4.28	32
Slovenia	4.23	33
Tunisia	4.16	34
Chile	4.14	35
South Africa	3.94	36
India	3.89	37
Latvia	3.87	38
Poland	3.85	39
Slovak Republic	3.85	40
Thailand	3.80	41

Country	Score	NRI Rank
Greece	3.77	42
China	3.70	43
Botswana	3.68	44
Argentina	3.67	45
Lithuania	3.65	46
Mexico	3.63	47
Croatia	3.62	48
Costa Rica	3.57	49
Turkey	3.57	50
Jordan	3.51	51
Morocco	3.50	52
Namibia	3.47	53
Sri Lanka	3.45	54
Uruguay	3.45	55
Mauritius	3.44	56
Dominican Republic	3.40	57
Trinidad and Tobago	3.36	58
Colombia	3.33	59
Jamaica	3.31	60
Panama	3.30	61
Philippines	3.25	62
El Salvador	3.17	63
Indonesia	3.16	64
Egypt	3.13	65
Venezuela	3.11	66
Peru	3.10	67
Bulgaria	3.03	68
Russian Federation	2.99	69
Ukraine	2.98	70
Vietnam	2.96	71
Romania	2.66	72
Guatemala	2.63	73
Nigeria	2.62	74
Ecuador	2.60	75
Paraguay	2.54	76
Bangladesh	2.53	77
Bolivia	2.47	78
Nicaragua	2.44	79
Zimbabwe	2.42	80
Honduras	2.37	81
Haiti	2.07	82

We would like to emphasize that while rankings are useful as relative indicators of a nation's ICT excellence, there are several limitations to the analytic process. For one, caution should be exercised while comparing countries that are closely ranked. Countries ranked closely together can show very small variation in index scores. Costa Rica (index = 3.57, rank = 49) and Turkey (index = 3.57, rank = 50) even have the same overall score. In this case, Costa Rica had an overall index score marginally higher than that of Turkey, but it was at the 3rd decimal place. Additionally, small differences in the index may be outside the limits of statistical significance because a number of missing observations were estimated using analytic techniques such as regression and clustering.

Also, only eighty-two countries were considered in our analysis because of limitations in the availability of data from reliable sources. Ranking other countries remains a challenge for the future. Any overall ranking on a global basis needs to account for these missing countries, and any inferences drawn on the current rankings should be done with this taken into consideration.

Interpreting the results

The NRI permits business leaders and public policymakers to investigate the reasons leading to a nation's ranking and relative performance. It captures key factors relating to the environment and the readiness and usage of the three stakeholders in ICT (individuals, businesses, and governments), and can be used to understand the performance of a nation or even a region with regards to ICT development. The component index and subindex rankings serve to identify key areas where a nation is under- or overperforming. For example, relative imbalances in development across the three component indexes of environment, readiness, and usage could be identified.

In order to supplement the NRI analysis, one is strongly encouraged to consult the chapters in this Report addressing in detail the ICT issues across different geographic regions. Additionally, in the country section of the Report, key statistics relating to the eighty-two countries can be found, and towards the end of the Report there are listings of the variables used during the current analysis to compute the ranking results.

Box 1. **Comparing the Networked Readiness Index**

Country	2002–2003	2001–2002
Finland	1	3
United States	2	1
Singapore	3	8
Sweden	4	4
Iceland	5	2
Canada	6	12
United Kingdom	8	10
Denmark	7	7
Taiwan	9	15
Germany	10	17

Comparisons with results 2001–2002
One should exert restraint while comparing the NRI results for 2002-2003 to that of the previous year—2001–2002. The NRI Framework 2002–2003 is an evolution of the model used to compute the Index last year. Further, the variables used to compute the NRI vary due to the model differences. For example, variables related to the readiness and adoption of ICT by governments is given a higher importance in the NRI Framework

Finally, the complexity of ICT-related issues in a nation can become obscured by the numerical figure of its NRI. A country such as India, for example, shows enormous geographic and demographic divides in ICT usage. India has one of the largest ICT workforces in the world. One can find intense ICT usage in technology clusters such as Bangalore and Gurgaon (near New Delhi), or amongst the upper middle bracket of incomes. The other side of the story is that large parts of the country lack even telephone connectivity. In Singapore, on the other hand, there is high usage of ICT across all stakeholders—individuals, businesses, and governments.

Disaggregating the Networked Readiness Index

The NRI provides a quick and relative benchmark of the overall success of a country in participating in and benefiting from ICT. While this is useful, one may need to gain further insights into the areas in which a nation over- and underperforms, and to understand the key drivers determining a country's ranking. One can do so by looking at the component indexes: environment, readiness, and usage. (See Table 3 for the overall results of each component index.) Further insight may be gained by looking at the subindexes composing each component index. The final level of detail can be obtained by having a close look at the sixty-four variables comprising the subindexes, which are presented at the end the report. Figure 5 gives a schematic diagram of the relationships between the various indexes, and how they add up to form the NRI. The technical appendix to the chapter provides details on the computation of the NRI.

Figure 5. **Disaggregating the Networked Readiness Index**

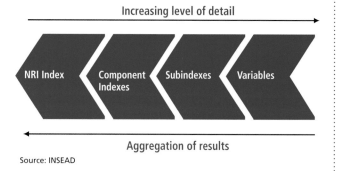

Source: INSEAD

Environment

The environment component index is designed to measure the conduciveness of an environment that a country can provide for the development and usage of ICT. As can be seen from Table 4, the top countries with regards to the environment are the United States, Finland, and Iceland, and the results are consistent with the overall index. An

exception is Israel, which has a rank of 12 on the overall NRI and that of 5 for environment. The primary driver for Israel's excellent rank is the country's policy and regulatory environment for ICT, both of which reflect the high priority given to ICT by the government.

Table 5 presents the detailed ranking results and scores of each of the three subindexes comprising the environment:

Market. This entails the assessment of whether or not there are appropriate human resources and ancillary businesses to support a knowledge-based society. The forces that play an important role in determining the market environment for ICT are varied and include measures such as availability of funding and skilled labor, and the level of development of the corporate environment. The leader for this subindex is the United States, followed by Finland, the United Kingdom, and Sweden. It is noteworthy that Israel is also ranked high (at 5th place).

Political/regulatory. The priorities of a nation are reflected in its policies and laws, and these in turn influence its rate of growth and direction of development. This component of the NRI measures the impact of a nation's

Table 4. Networked Readiness Index Component Indexes

Country	Environment Score	Environment Rank	Country	Readiness Score	Readiness Rank	Country	Usage Score	Usage Rank
United States	5.83	1	Singapore	6.41	1	Finland	5.85	1
Finland	5.58	2	Finland	6.34	2	Singapore	5.58	2
Iceland	5.32	3	United States	6.06	3	Sweden	5.53	3
Canada	5.30	4	Sweden	5.95	4	United States	5.49	4
Israel	5.27	5	Canada	5.87	5	Iceland	5.36	5
Sweden	5.26	6	Iceland	5.86	6	Denmark	5.32	6
United Kingdom	5.24	7	Taiwan	5.82	7	Taiwan	5.22	7
Singapore	5.22	8	Israel	5.81	8	Korea	5.22	8
Germany	5.18	9	Switzerland	5.73	9	Netherlands	5.17	9
Netherlands	5.12	10	United Kingdom	5.72	10	Canada	5.17	10
Denmark	5.05	11	Denmark	5.62	11	Germany	5.14	11
Austria	4.95	12	Korea	5.60	12	United Kingdom	5.08	12
Switzerland	4.94	13	Japan	5.56	13	Norway	4.94	13
Australia	4.89	14	Germany	5.56	14	Australia	4.88	14
Taiwan	4.88	15	Netherlands	5.51	15	Switzerland	4.87	15
Ireland	4.86	16	France	5.51	16	Hong Kong SAR	4.80	16
France	4.85	17	Hong Kong SAR	5.46	17	Belgium	4.66	17
Luxembourg	4.81	18	Austria	5.44	18	Austria	4.64	18
Japan	4.79	19	Australia	5.35	19	Israel	4.60	19
Norway	4.78	20	Ireland	5.31	20	France	4.55	20
Hong Kong SAR	4.71	21	Estonia	5.29	21	Estonia	4.51	21
New Zealand	4.66	22	Norway	5.29	22	Japan	4.51	22
Belgium	4.64	23	Belgium	5.20	23	Ireland	4.50	23
Italy	4.61	24	New Zealand	5.12	24	Italy	4.40	24
Spain	4.58	25	Czech Republic	5.04	25	Spain	4.38	25
Korea	4.50	26	Spain	5.03	26	Brazil	4.32	26
Portugal	4.28	27	Tunisia	5.01	27	New Zealand	4.32	27
Estonia	4.28	28	Hungary	5.00	28	Portugal	4.15	28
Malaysia	4.24	29	Malaysia	4.95	29	Czech Republic	4.08	29
Hungary	4.24	30	Luxembourg	4.93	30	Slovenia	4.04	30
Czech Republic	4.18	31	Italy	4.78	31	Luxembourg	3.90	31
Brazil	4.17	32	Slovenia	4.75	32	Chile	3.88	32
Chile	4.04	33	Brazil	4.72	33	Argentina	3.84	33
India	3.98	34	Chile	4.50	34	Poland	3.79	34
Tunisia	3.98	35	China	4.50	35	South Africa	3.73	35
Slovenia	3.89	36	Thailand	4.49	36	Hungary	3.67	36
Slovak Republic	3.86	37	Portugal	4.41	37	Mexico	3.67	37
South Africa	3.86	38	Latvia	4.41	38	Malaysia	3.64	38
Greece	3.79	39	Slovak Republic	4.38	39	Latvia	3.54	39
Thailand	3.68	40	India	4.35	40	Turkey	3.53	40
Latvia	3.66	41	Lithuania	4.33	41	Tunisia	3.50	41
Botswana	3.66	42	Sri Lanka	4.29	42	Greece	3.39	42
Jordan	3.64	43	Costa Rica	4.23	43	India	3.33	43
Namibia	3.61	44	South Africa	4.23	44	Croatia	3.33	44
Lithuania	3.57	45	Poland	4.20	45	Slovak Republic	3.30	45
Dominican Republic	3.56	46	Botswana	4.16	46	Uruguay	3.25	46
Poland	3.56	47	Greece	4.13	47	Thailand	3.24	47
Croatia	3.52	48	Croatia	4.02	48	Botswana	3.22	48
Morocco	3.50	49	Morocco	4.01	49	Costa Rica	3.18	49
Trinidad and Tobago	3.49	50	Jamaica	3.99	50	Venezuela	3.13	50
China	3.49	51	Namibia	3.98	51	China	3.12	51
Uruguay	3.48	52	Mexico	3.97	52	Lithuania	3.05	52
Argentina	3.47	53	Jordan	3.95	53	El Salvador	3.01	53
Mauritius	3.43	54	Mauritius	3.91	54	Philippines	2.99	54
Sri Lanka	3.39	55	Vietnam	3.90	55	Mauritius	2.99	55
Turkey	3.38	56	Dominican Republic	3.88	56	Panama	2.98	56
Philippines	3.33	57	Bulgaria	3.84	57	Morocco	2.98	57
Costa Rica	3.30	58	Trinidad and Tobago	3.80	58	Colombia	2.94	58
Colombia	3.30	59	Turkey	3.79	59	Jordan	2.93	59
Mexico	3.24	60	Russian Federation	3.78	60	Peru	2.85	60
Panama	3.22	61	Colombia	3.76	61	Namibia	2.83	61
Jamaica	3.20	62	Indonesia	3.72	62	Trinidad and Tobago	2.79	62
Venezuela	3.10	63	Panama	3.71	63	Dominican Republic	2.76	63
Egypt	3.06	64	Argentina	3.70	64	Indonesia	2.76	64
Indonesia	3.01	65	Uruguay	3.61	65	Egypt	2.76	65
El Salvador	3.01	66	Ukraine	3.58	66	Jamaica	2.75	66
Peru	2.95	67	Egypt	3.57	67	Sri Lanka	2.68	67
Russian Federation	2.88	68	Peru	3.50	68	Ecuador	2.62	68
Bulgaria	2.87	69	El Salvador	3.48	69	Ukraine	2.58	69
Ukraine	2.77	70	Philippines	3.43	70	Nigeria	2.56	70
Romania	2.75	71	Romania	3.35	71	Nicaragua	2.50	71
Nigeria	2.69	72	Venezuela	3.11	72	Paraguay	2.50	72
Vietnam	2.61	73	Guatemala	2.89	73	Guatemala	2.45	73
Guatemala	2.55	74	Zimbabwe	2.87	74	Bangladesh	2.40	74
Bolivia	2.41	75	Ecuador	2.85	75	Bulgaria	2.38	75
Zimbabwe	2.41	76	Paraguay	2.85	76	Bolivia	2.38	76
Bangladesh	2.37	77	Bangladesh	2.81	77	Vietnam	2.37	77
Ecuador	2.32	78	Honduras	2.66	78	Russian Federation	2.30	78
Paraguay	2.28	79	Bolivia	2.62	79	Honduras	2.25	79
Honduras	2.20	80	Nicaragua	2.62	80	Haiti	2.19	80
Nicaragua	2.19	81	Nigeria	2.61	81	Zimbabwe	1.97	81
Haiti	1.83	82	Haiti	2.19	82	Romania	1.88	82

Table 5. Environment Subindexes
Environment Subindex = 1/3 Market + 1/3 Political/Regulatory + 1/3 Infrastructure

Market Country	Score	Rank	Political/Regulatory Country	Score	Rank	Infrastructure Country	Score	Rank
United States	6.08	1	Singapore	5.86	1	Iceland	5.94	1
Finland	5.92	2	Israel	5.84	2	United States	5.75	2
United Kingdom	5.56	3	Finland	5.76	3	Luxembourg	5.59	3
Sweden	5.56	4	United States	5.67	4	Japan	5.46	4
Israel	5.36	5	Canada	5.62	5	Sweden	5.23	5
Germany	5.16	6	Netherlands	5.44	6	Germany	5.22	6
Taiwan	5.12	7	Malaysia	5.41	7	Canada	5.20	7
Netherlands	5.11	8	Ireland	5.37	8	Australia	5.15	8
Canada	5.08	9	Iceland	5.31	9	Denmark	5.13	9
Singapore	4.93	10	United Kingdom	5.28	10	Switzerland	5.09	10
France	4.93	11	Austria	5.28	11	Finland	5.05	11
Ireland	4.91	12	Denmark	5.19	12	France	4.89	12
Switzerland	4.88	13	Australia	5.18	13	Singapore	4.89	13
Norway	4.86	14	Germany	5.15	14	United Kingdom	4.87	14
Denmark	4.84	15	Luxembourg	5.03	15	New Zealand	4.86	15
Austria	4.78	16	India	5.00	16	Netherlands	4.80	16
Iceland	4.70	17	Sweden	4.99	17	Austria	4.78	17
Japan	4.63	18	Hong Kong SAR	4.98	18	Hong Kong SAR	4.77	18
Korea	4.59	19	Spain	4.95	19	Taiwan	4.71	19
Italy	4.53	20	Belgium	4.91	20	Norway	4.70	20
Belgium	4.43	21	Italy	4.85	21	Spain	4.62	21
New Zealand	4.42	22	Switzerland	4.85	22	Israel	4.61	22
Hong Kong SAR	4.38	23	Taiwan	4.82	23	Belgium	4.57	23
Australia	4.35	24	Tunisia	4.81	24	Italy	4.43	24
Brazil	4.21	25	Portugal	4.81	25	Korea	4.39	25
Spain	4.17	26	Norway	4.78	26	Ireland	4.31	26
Estonia	4.12	27	France	4.73	27	Czech Republic	4.15	27
India	4.12	28	New Zealand	4.70	28	Estonia	4.12	28
Hungary	4.10	29	South Africa	4.61	29	Slovenia	4.11	29
Chile	4.00	30	Estonia	4.58	30	Portugal	4.10	30
Czech Republic	3.97	31	Hungary	4.54	31	Hungary	4.07	31
Portugal	3.95	32	Brazil	4.52	32	Greece	4.04	32
Luxembourg	3.79	33	Korea	4.50	33	Argentina	3.97	33
Tunisia	3.76	34	Czech Republic	4.42	34	Chile	3.93	34
Malaysia	3.65	35	Slovenia	4.31	35	Uruguay	3.86	35
Costa Rica	3.63	36	Botswana	4.30	36	Slovak Republic	3.79	36
Slovak Republic	3.61	37	Japan	4.28	37	Brazil	3.78	37
Poland	3.58	38	Namibia	4.27	38	Croatia	3.76	38
Lithuania	3.45	39	Thailand	4.25	39	Lithuania	3.72	39
South Africa	3.45	40	Chile	4.21	40	Malaysia	3.67	40
Latvia	3.38	41	Slovak Republic	4.20	41	Latvia	3.58	41
Thailand	3.36	42	Mauritius	4.16	42	Namibia	3.58	42
Botswana	3.33	43	Jordan	4.14	43	Jordan	3.56	43
Greece	3.30	44	Trinidad and Tobago	4.13	44	Mauritius	3.54	44
Colombia	3.29	45	Morocco	4.05	45	Turkey	3.52	45
Slovenia	3.25	46	Philippines	4.05	46	South Africa	3.52	46
Dominican Republic	3.25	47	Greece	4.04	47	Poland	3.48	47
Jordan	3.23	48	Latvia	4.03	48	Dominican Republic	3.42	48
Morocco	3.23	49	Dominican Republic	4.00	49	Thailand	3.42	49
China	3.20	50	Turkey	3.97	50	Trinidad and Tobago	3.42	50
Sri Lanka	3.11	51	Jamaica	3.96	51	Peru	3.40	51
Uruguay	3.09	52	China	3.91	52	Tunisia	3.38	52
Panama	3.08	53	Sri Lanka	3.85	53	China	3.36	53
Argentina	3.04	54	Croatia	3.77	54	Botswana	3.36	54
Croatia	3.03	55	Indonesia	3.70	55	Mexico	3.32	55
Namibia	2.98	56	Nigeria	3.70	56	Panama	3.32	56
Trinidad and Tobago	2.93	57	Mexico	3.64	57	Morocco	3.22	57
Russian Federation	2.91	58	Poland	3.61	58	Sri Lanka	3.21	58
Vietnam	2.90	59	Lithuania	3.56	59	Bulgaria	3.20	59
Philippines	2.90	60	Venezuela	3.54	60	Costa Rica	3.17	60
Indonesia	2.85	61	Colombia	3.48	61	El Salvador	3.16	61
Mexico	2.75	62	Uruguay	3.48	62	Colombia	3.13	62
Ukraine	2.74	63	Argentina	3.40	63	Venezuela	3.08	63
Zimbabwe	2.72	64	Egypt	3.39	64	Egypt	3.08	64
El Salvador	2.71	65	Bangladesh	3.36	65	Philippines	3.05	65
Egypt	2.70	66	Panama	3.26	66	Guatemala	3.01	66
Jamaica	2.70	67	El Salvador	3.16	67	Jamaica	2.93	67
Venezuela	2.69	68	Costa Rica	3.11	68	Bolivia	2.87	68
Turkey	2.65	69	Ukraine	3.06	69	Russian Federation	2.85	69
Bulgaria	2.63	70	Romania	3.06	70	India	2.84	70
Mauritius	2.58	71	Peru	2.97	71	Ecuador	2.83	71
Romania	2.58	72	Vietnam	2.94	72	Romania	2.61	72
Peru	2.47	73	Zimbabwe	2.89	73	Paraguay	2.57	73
Paraguay	2.24	74	Russian Federation	2.88	74	Ukraine	2.49	74
Bangladesh	2.16	75	Bulgaria	2.77	75	Indonesia	2.48	75
Nigeria	2.16	76	Honduras	2.65	76	Nigeria	2.21	76
Guatemala	2.12	77	Nicaragua	2.59	77	Honduras	2.10	77
Nicaragua	2.12	78	Guatemala	2.50	78	Vietnam	1.99	78
Bolivia	2.01	79	Bolivia	2.36	79	Nicaragua	1.86	79
Haiti	1.97	80	Ecuador	2.22	80	Zimbabwe	1.63	80
Ecuador	1.90	81	Paraguay	2.03	81	Bangladesh	1.60	81
Honduras	1.84	82	Haiti	1.97	82	Haiti	1.55	82

Box 3. CASE STUDY: Broadband Rollout in Japan

Japan's incumbent telecom service provider NTT had invested heavily in ISDN with the result that Japan had the world's highest ISDN penetration in 1999. NTT planned to upgrade ISDN to FTTH as the next generation high-speed network. However, Tokyo Metallic convinced Ministry of Post & Telecom (MPT) to open up the NTT infrastructure for DSL service.

Action: MPT swiftly enacted policies to un-bundle local loops of NTT, and in this way to allow other operators. NTT upgraded all exchanges for ADSL. However it continued to provide ISDN to its users. Other operators joined Tokyo Metallic in providing DSL service, which began to take away share from NTT's ISDN subscribers. NTT was thus forced to offer DSL service itself. Yahoo! marked its entry in September 2001 with a DSL offering at half the price of NTT, driving the prices further down.

Result: Japan today has one of the world's most competitive and cheapest broadband services. The uptake has grown exponentially since DSL was introduced.

polity, laws, and regulations, and their implementation for the development and use of ICT. The leaders from the political/regulatory perspective are Singapore, Israel, Finland, the United States, and Canada, not a surprising result given that these governments are known for their strong support of and emphasis on ICT. Box 2 presents a case study of Canada, highlighting how government policy can be used aggressively to promote networked readiness.

Infrastructure. Infrastructure is defined as the level of availability and quality of the key access infrastructure for ICT within a country. A quality ICT-access infrastructure facilitates the adoption, usage, and impact of these technologies, which in turn promotes investment in infrastructure. Infrastructure thus plays a critical role in influencing the networked readiness of a nation. The countries ranked at the top for this component are Iceland, the United States, Luxembourg, Japan, and Sweden. One notes that India is at 70th place for infrastructure—a very low rank compared to its overall position of 34 in environment—which is perhaps an indication of the heterogeneous proliferation of ICT across different socioeconomic and geographic segments in the country. Box 3 presents a case study of how steps were taken to develop infrastructure and service offerings in Japan by promoting competition within the telecommunications industry. As a consequence of these activities, Japanese consumers can today access one of the most competitively priced broadband services in the world.

Readiness

The readiness of a nation measures the capability of the principal agents of an economy (citizens, businesses, and governments) to leverage the potential of ICT. Such capability becomes manifest in a nation's community in the presence of a combination of factors, such as the relevant skills for using ICT in individuals, access and affordability of ICT for corporations, and local government usage of ICT for its own services and processes. As shown in Table 4, Singapore ranks highest on overall readiness, in spite of placing 11th in business readiness. Singapore is supported by a very strong performance in government readiness, reflecting the fact that ICT is a top-priority item on the government's agenda. Third-ranked United States, on the other hand, has high scores in business readiness. Second-placed Finland shows a consistent performance across all three readiness subindexes, and illustrates the basic concept behind the NRI that a nation's readiness is determined by the degree to which technology permeates across all three stakeholders of the community—individuals, businesses, and government.

Detailed results for each of the subindexes used for measuring readiness (listed below) can be found in Table 6.

Individual readiness measures the readiness of a nation's citizens to utilize and leverage ICT. Factors that are used to measure this include literacy rates, mode and locus of access to the Internet, and the degree of connectivity of individuals. The top three positions on individual readiness go to Finland, Singapore, and Iceland. Korea, at 6th place, has an exceptional score on individual readiness—the country has both high penetration of the Internet in general, and one of the highest penetrations of broadband in the world.

Business readiness measures the readiness of a cross section of businesses to participate in and benefit from ICT. The aim is to focus not just on the largest corporations, but to also include small- and medium-sized businesses and their willingness to exploit ICT and invest in the ICT skills of their employees. Not surprisingly, the United States has 1st place for business readiness; it is followed by Finland, Israel, and Sweden. Also noteworthy is India's ranking of 27 for business readiness compared to its position of 70 for individual readiness; this indicates a growing digital divide between the different ICT stakeholders in the country.

Government readiness measures the readiness of a government to employ ICT. It is reflected in the policymaking machinery and internal processes of the government, and in the availability of government services online. If the polity of a nation decides to make ICT a priority, this becomes visible in the short- and long-term policy measures and laws that help encourage ICT deployment and use. It is also apparent in the government

Table 6. **Readiness Subindexes**
Readiness component index = 1/3 Individual Readiness + 1/3 Business Readiness + 1/3 Government Readiness

Individual			Business			Government		
Country	Score	Rank	Country	Score	Rank	Country	Score	Rank
Finland	6.71	1	United States	6.65	1	Singapore	7.00	1
Singapore	6.38	2	Finland	6.45	2	Taiwan	5.86	2
Iceland	6.38	3	Israel	6.34	3	Finland	5.86	3
Canada	6.30	4	Sweden	6.30	4	Tunisia	5.56	4
Sweden	6.29	5	Germany	6.30	5	Israel	5.54	5
Korea	6.27	6	Switzerland	6.28	6	Canada	5.47	6
United States	6.13	7	Japan	6.03	7	United States	5.41	7
Australia	6.07	8	Iceland	5.94	8	United Kingdom	5.36	8
United Kingdom	6.06	9	Taiwan	5.91	9	Iceland	5.27	9
Denmark	6.06	10	France	5.88	10	Sweden	5.27	10
Netherlands	6.05	11	Singapore	5.85	11	Hong Kong SAR	5.26	11
Hong Kong SAR	6.03	12	Canada	5.83	12	Ireland	5.24	12
Austria	6.01	13	Denmark	5.77	13	Estonia	5.15	13
Belgium	6.00	14	United Kingdom	5.72	14	China	5.14	14
Norway	5.99	15	Netherlands	5.66	15	Korea	5.12	15
New Zealand	5.92	16	Austria	5.63	16	Switzerland	5.08	16
Switzerland	5.84	17	Belgium	5.54	17	Denmark	5.04	17
Estonia	5.78	18	Korea	5.41	18	Malaysia	4.94	18
France	5.77	19	Ireland	5.29	19	Japan	4.91	19
Germany	5.76	20	Norway	5.29	20	France	4.87	20
Japan	5.75	21	Australia	5.24	21	Netherlands	4.81	21
Taiwan	5.68	22	Luxembourg	5.12	22	Hungary	4.74	22
Czech Republic	5.67	23	Hong Kong SAR	5.08	23	Australia	4.74	23
Israel	5.54	24	Brazil	5.03	24	Austria	4.66	24
Slovenia	5.52	25	Czech Republic	5.01	25	Sri Lanka	4.66	25
Hungary	5.47	26	Spain	5.00	26	Spain	4.65	26
Spain	5.45	27	India	5.00	27	Germany	4.61	27
Italy	5.41	28	Estonia	4.95	28	Luxembourg	4.61	28
Ireland	5.39	29	New Zealand	4.93	29	Norway	4.58	29
Slovak Republic	5.17	30	Italy	4.93	30	New Zealand	4.50	30
Malaysia	5.12	31	Costa Rica	4.79	31	Czech Republic	4.45	31
Luxembourg	5.07	32	Hungary	4.78	32	Brazil	4.37	32
Croatia	5.03	33	Malaysia	4.78	33	India	4.18	33
Latvia	5.02	34	Slovenia	4.75	34	Chile	4.18	34
Portugal	5.01	35	South Africa	4.66	35	Lithuania	4.16	35
Poland	4.93	36	Tunisia	4.64	36	Portugal	4.14	36
Argentina	4.92	37	Chile	4.59	37	Jamaica	4.06	37
Panama	4.91	38	Thailand	4.56	38	Belgium	4.06	38
Thailand	4.88	39	Slovak Republic	4.54	39	Thailand	4.04	39
Greece	4.87	40	Latvia	4.39	40	Morocco	4.01	40
Lithuania	4.81	41	China	4.38	41	Italy	4.00	41
Tunisia	4.81	42	Greece	4.36	42	Slovenia	3.99	42
Bulgaria	4.79	43	Poland	4.31	43	Vietnam	3.99	43
Chile	4.75	44	Botswana	4.27	44	Botswana	3.86	44
Brazil	4.75	45	Namibia	4.25	45	Latvia	3.82	45
Costa Rica	4.72	46	Egypt	4.22	46	South Africa	3.69	46
Turkey	4.68	47	Turkey	4.20	47	Mexico	3.68	47
Russian Federation	4.68	48	Morocco	4.18	48	Namibia	3.63	48
Romania	4.49	49	Mexico	4.13	49	Jordan	3.48	49
Trinidad and Tobago	4.45	50	Mauritius	4.09	50	Croatia	3.47	50
Jordan	4.43	51	Portugal	4.09	51	Slovak Republic	3.44	51
Colombia	4.37	52	Indonesia	4.07	52	Mauritius	3.40	52
Botswana	4.34	53	Lithuania	4.03	53	Poland	3.37	53
South Africa	4.33	54	Dominican Republic	4.02	54	Dominican Republic	3.34	54
Sri Lanka	4.32	55	Argentina	3.97	55	Bulgaria	3.25	55
Uruguay	4.30	56	Jordan	3.94	56	Colombia	3.25	56
Dominican Republic	4.29	57	Sri Lanka	3.91	57	Costa Rica	3.18	57
Ukraine	4.25	58	Jamaica	3.90	58	Greece	3.17	58
Mauritius	4.23	59	Panama	3.80	59	Trinidad and Tobago	3.15	59
Indonesia	4.20	60	Trinidad and Tobago	3.78	60	Uruguay	3.07	60
Mexico	4.10	61	Peru	3.73	61	Russian Federation	2.95	61
Egypt	4.08	62	Ukraine	3.72	62	Indonesia	2.88	62
Philippines	4.08	63	Vietnam	3.72	63	El Salvador	2.88	63
Namibia	4.07	64	Russian Federation	3.71	64	Philippines	2.87	64
Peru	4.01	65	Colombia	3.66	65	Ukraine	2.77	65
Jamaica	4.00	66	El Salvador	3.58	66	Peru	2.76	66
El Salvador	3.99	67	Croatia	3.56	67	Nigeria	2.71	67
Vietnam	3.98	68	Venezuela	3.51	68	Nicaragua	2.55	68
China	3.96	69	Bulgaria	3.48	69	Bangladesh	2.53	69
India	3.87	70	Uruguay	3.47	70	Turkey	2.48	70
Venezuela	3.84	71	Guatemala	3.42	71	Romania	2.42	71
Morocco	3.84	72	Zimbabwe	3.41	72	Egypt	2.41	72
Guatemala	3.69	73	Philippines	3.35	73	Panama	2.41	73
Bolivia	3.63	74	Paraguay	3.34	74	Ecuador	2.30	74
Paraguay	3.61	75	Bangladesh	3.25	75	Argentina	2.20	75
Zimbabwe	3.60	76	Romania	3.15	76	Honduras	2.01	76
Ecuador	3.23	77	Ecuador	3.02	77	Venezuela	1.96	77
Honduras	3.06	78	Nigeria	2.95	78	Bolivia	1.84	78
Nicaragua	2.84	79	Honduras	2.91	79	Zimbabwe	1.61	79
Haiti	2.75	80	Nicaragua	2.47	80	Paraguay	1.60	80
Bangladesh	2.66	81	Bolivia	2.40	81	Guatemala	1.58	81
Nigeria	2.18	82	Haiti	2.29	82	Haiti	1.52	82

itself using ICT and equipping its people to do the same. Singapore leads on government readiness, followed by Taiwan and Finland. Of note is Estonia, which at 13th in government readiness, an indication of the government's push in ICT; government readiness is one of the factors contributing to Estonia's overall rank of 24.

Usage

The usage component is a measure of the level of impact that ICT has had on the principal stakeholders in the NRI Framework—that is, individuals, businesses, and governments. The assessment of usage includes changes in behaviors and lifestyles, and changes in other economic and noneconomic factors brought about by the adoption of ICT. Finland, Singapore, and Sweden are the top three performers with regards to overall usage, as shown in Table 4. One can observe variances in country performance across the three subindexes, reflecting uneven effects across the three principal stakeholders. For example, Germany is ranked high for business usage (1st), but relatively low for individual (17th) and government (20th) usage. Another notable example is Estonia, with high government readiness (13th) and usage (8th), but relatively low positions for individual (28th) and business (31st) usage. Table 7 shows detailed results and scores for each of the three subindexes (listed below) used for measuring usage:

Individual usage gives an indication of the level of adoption and usage of ICT by a nation's citizens. This information is generated by assessing the deployment of connectivity-enhancing technologies such as telephones and Internet connections, the levels of Internet usage, and money spent online. Individual usage rankings differ significantly from rankings of individual readiness. The top performers in individual usage are Korea, Finland, Denmark, the Netherlands, and Sweden. Korea and the Netherlands stand out, as they are ranked significantly lower for both the overall NRI and overall usage.

Business usage measures the level of deployment and use of ICT across all businesses in a nation. Business usage is measured by factors such as the level of business-to-business and business-to-consumer e-commerce, the use of ICT for activities such as marketing, and levels of online transactions. The top five performers are Germany, Sweden, the United States, Finland, and Iceland.

Government usage is the level of use of ICT by the government of a given country. The government, besides making ICT a priority, can also benefit from the usage of ICT itself. This usage can help the government streamline services to its citizens and improve its overall functioning. Factors used to measure this usage include the volume of transactions that businesses have with governments and the presence of government services online. The top-ranking countries on

> ### Box 4. CASE STUDY: Health Industry in France
>
> In 1996, the French government launched the Sesam-Vitale program to control health expenditures (10 percent of GDP). The objective of the program was to fully replace the paper-based system of reporting doctor visits with an electronic system. The program was expected to help better understand expenditure, to improve efficiency and to enhance quality of healthcare.
>
> **Action:** A card (Carte Vitale) with an embedded microchip has been handed out to individuals covered by healthcare insurance. Healthcare Professionals (HCP) and pharmacists received similar identification cards. During a visit to a doctor, the visitor's card is inserted into a dedicated terminal, which automatically records the visit. Information at the end of the day is transmitted via Internet to the appropriate organization.
>
> **Results:** About 41 percent of HCPs currently transmit forms online. About 80 percent of doctors possess PC (compared to 10–15 percent in 1995). Individuals get automatically reimbursed within 5 days versus several weeks before. Net annual savings to government: Euro 150–200m.

this measure are Finland, Singapore, Iceland, Taiwan, and Sweden. Of note is Estonia at 8th place, reflecting the fact that the country's government is "walking the talk"—both promoting ICT in the country, and also using ICT for its own functioning. Box 4 presents the case of Carte Vitale and shows how the French government has benefited from the use of ICT in the health care sector.

Understanding Networked Readiness

More than a single measure

The degree of a nation's networked readiness is the result of a multitude of effects. Our research started with a set of more than 130 different variables or indicators for evaluating networked readiness, and these were narrowed down by statistical analysis to a set of sixty-four variables. These sixty-four variables were grouped under the nine subindexes of the NRI Framework. This provides us with an opportunity to study some of the interrelationships across the variables and the components/subindexes of the NRI Framework.

GDP and networked readiness

Any attempt to use a single measure to approximate networked readiness would be a simplification. One of the most intuitive and appealing measures that one may be tempted to use as a proxy is the GDP per capita of a country. A closer look at the NRI results would show that Estonia,

Table 7. **Usage Subindexes**
Usage component index = 1/3 Individual Usage + 1/3 Business Usage + 1/3 Government Usage

Individual			Business			Government		
Country	Score	Rank	Country	Score	Rank	Country	Score	Rank
Korea	5.19	1	Germany	6.19	1	Finland	6.73	1
Finland	4.90	2	Sweden	5.96	2	Singapore	6.72	2
Denmark	4.87	3	United States	5.95	3	Iceland	6.46	3
Netherlands	4.81	4	Finland	5.93	4	Taiwan	6.23	4
Sweden	4.64	5	Iceland	5.58	5	Sweden	5.98	5
Japan	4.62	6	Netherlands	5.51	6	United States	5.94	6
United States	4.57	7	Singapore	5.49	7	Canada	5.91	7
Luxembourg	4.57	8	United Kingdom	5.42	8	Estonia	5.75	8
Singapore	4.53	9	Denmark	5.40	9	Denmark	5.69	9
United Kingdom	4.51	10	Switzerland	5.39	10	Brazil	5.49	10
Canada	4.46	11	Norway	5.23	11	Hong Kong SAR	5.39	11
Norway	4.46	12	Korea	5.20	12	Australia	5.35	12
Belgium	4.39	13	France	5.14	13	United Kingdom	5.32	13
Taiwan	4.38	14	Canada	5.14	14	Korea	5.26	14
Switzerland	4.28	15	Hong Kong SAR	5.08	15	Netherlands	5.18	15
Australia	4.24	16	Australia	5.06	16	Norway	5.14	16
Germany	4.17	17	Argentina	5.05	17	Austria	5.11	17
Slovenia	4.13	18	Taiwan	5.05	18	Ireland	5.09	18
Iceland	4.05	19	Brazil	5.03	19	Israel	5.09	19
Israel	3.99	20	Spain	5.03	20	Germany	5.08	20
Ireland	3.97	21	Italy	5.01	21	Chile	4.96	21
Austria	3.96	22	Belgium	4.96	22	Switzerland	4.95	22
Hong Kong SAR	3.91	23	Japan	4.90	23	Tunisia	4.89	23
New Zealand	3.79	24	Austria	4.85	24	France	4.83	24
France	3.68	25	Poland	4.72	25	India	4.80	25
Portugal	3.66	26	Israel	4.72	26	Portugal	4.79	26
Italy	3.62	27	Czech Republic	4.71	27	Spain	4.72	27
Estonia	3.44	28	South Africa	4.69	28	Hungary	4.68	28
Greece	3.43	29	New Zealand	4.54	29	Belgium	4.63	29
Spain	3.39	30	Ireland	4.45	30	New Zealand	4.62	30
Czech Republic	3.14	31	Estonia	4.35	31	Italy	4.58	31
Latvia	3.11	32	Mexico	4.31	32	Malaysia	4.48	32
Uruguay	3.02	33	Venezuela	4.01	33	China	4.44	33
Hungary	2.91	34	Portugal	3.99	34	Czech Republic	4.38	34
Slovak Republic	2.84	35	Chile	3.98	35	Mexico	4.26	35
Argentina	2.78	36	Malaysia	3.95	36	Thailand	4.20	36
Turkey	2.74	37	Slovenia	3.94	37	South Africa	4.19	37
Chile	2.71	38	Turkey	3.89	38	Poland	4.07	38
Lithuania	2.63	39	Botswana	3.80	39	Slovenia	4.05	39
Trinidad and Tobago	2.62	40	Costa Rica	3.76	40	Latvia	4.03	40
Poland	2.58	41	Croatia	3.74	41	Japan	4.01	41
Croatia	2.54	42	India	3.71	42	Turkey	3.97	42
Malaysia	2.50	43	Tunisia	3.65	43	Lithuania	3.96	43
Brazil	2.44	44	Slovak Republic	3.63	44	Botswana	3.93	44
Mexico	2.43	45	Thailand	3.60	45	Croatia	3.71	45
Venezuela	2.40	46	El Salvador	3.60	46	Argentina	3.69	46
Bulgaria	2.37	47	Indonesia	3.59	47	Mauritius	3.67	47
Jamaica	2.35	48	Philippines	3.58	48	Jordan	3.65	48
South Africa	2.31	49	Luxembourg	3.56	49	Greece	3.57	49
Panama	2.29	50	Latvia	3.48	50	Costa Rica	3.57	50
Mauritius	2.28	51	Jordan	3.44	51	Colombia	3.56	51
Costa Rica	2.21	52	Morocco	3.44	52	Luxembourg	3.56	52
Ukraine	2.18	53	Panama	3.43	53	Morocco	3.55	53
El Salvador	2.14	54	Hungary	3.43	54	Namibia	3.50	54
Colombia	2.08	55	Ecuador	3.40	55	Slovak Republic	3.43	55
Peru	2.06	56	Uruguay	3.36	56	Philippines	3.42	56
Philippines	1.98	57	Peru	3.31	57	Dominican Republic	3.40	57
Russian Federation	1.97	58	Namibia	3.24	58	Uruguay	3.37	58
Paraguay	1.96	59	Nicaragua	3.23	59	Egypt	3.34	59
Tunisia	1.96	60	Nigeria	3.18	60	El Salvador	3.29	60
China	1.95	61	Egypt	3.17	61	Sri Lanka	3.26	61
Romania	1.95	62	Colombia	3.17	62	Panama	3.24	62
Morocco	1.93	63	Greece	3.17	63	Jamaica	3.23	63
Thailand	1.92	64	Honduras	3.13	64	Peru	3.19	64
Botswana	1.91	65	Bolivia	3.10	65	Indonesia	3.16	65
Nicaragua	1.91	66	Dominican Republic	3.06	66	Vietnam	3.09	66
Bolivia	1.86	67	Bangladesh	3.05	67	Nigeria	2.99	67
Dominican Republic	1.84	68	Haiti	3.04	68	Venezuela	2.96	68
Guatemala	1.79	69	Guatemala	3.02	69	Trinidad and Tobago	2.84	69
Sri Lanka	1.78	70	Mauritius	3.01	70	Ukraine	2.84	70
Egypt	1.76	71	Sri Lanka	3.00	71	Russian Federation	2.80	71
Ecuador	1.76	72	China	2.98	72	Paraguay	2.73	72
Namibia	1.74	73	Trinidad and Tobago	2.89	73	Ecuador	2.70	73
Jordan	1.71	74	Paraguay	2.80	74	Bangladesh	2.70	74
Honduras	1.68	75	Ukraine	2.72	75	Bulgaria	2.61	75
Zimbabwe	1.65	76	Jamaica	2.65	76	Guatemala	2.53	76
Indonesia	1.53	77	Vietnam	2.56	77	Nicaragua	2.37	77
Nigeria	1.51	78	Lithuania	2.55	78	Haiti	2.20	78
India	1.47	79	Zimbabwe	2.40	79	Bolivia	2.18	79
Bangladesh	1.47	80	Bulgaria	2.16	80	Honduras	1.94	80
Vietnam	1.44	81	Russian Federation	2.12	81	Romania	1.89	81
Haiti	1.32	82	Romania	1.82	82	Zimbabwe	1.87	82

Figure 6. **GDP PPP per Capita versus Network Readiness Index, Partial Log Regression**

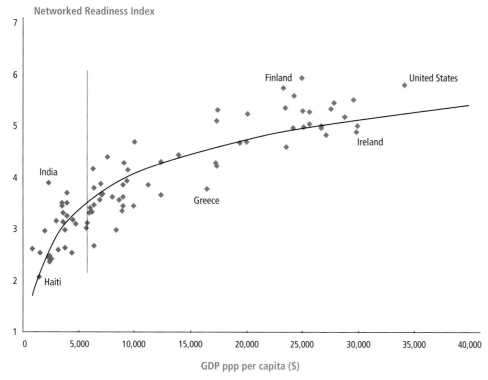

Source: Technology Management Department, INSEAD

with a GDP per capita of US$10,066, has an NRI score of 4.69 and is ranked 24th overall; however, Mauritius, with a very similar GDP per capita of US$10,017 has a score of 3.44 and an overall ranking of 56. There is thus a wide spread in the NRI score for a given GDP purchasing power parity (PPP) per capita; this is but one of many such examples.

Nevertheless, one could look at the relationship between the NRI and GDP in order to obtain a better understanding of trends, and also to identify over- and underperformers with respect to the trend. Figure 6 gives a plot between GDP PPP per capita and the Networked Readiness Index. The partial log regression plot presents a possible trend. One would immediately notice the following:

1. For a given GDP PPP per capita, there is a spread in the NRI scores around the regression plot as presented above

2. The impact of GDP seems to be very high at low GDP values, and the NRI score increases rapidly with small increases in GDP

3. Around a GDP per capita of US$9,000, the curve tapers off and the effect of increasing GDP is much less pronounced.

Countries widely distanced from the regression plot could be examples of underperformers or overperformers. Thus, Luxembourg, with a very high GDP per capita, has a moderate NRI score, whereas Finland with about half the GDP per capita of Luxembourg leads the NRI ranking.

Similarly, India would be overperforming on its NRI score with respect to its GDP per capita.

ICT expenditure and networked readiness

Plotting ICT spending versus NRI gives a similar trend to that of GDP PPP per capita versus NRI. It is notable, however, that there is a very large spread in the NRI score (see Figure 7) at a given ICT expense (as a percentage of GDP); this raises the question of whether or not the ICT dollar is effectively promoting networked readiness. For example, Spain spends less on ICT (as a percentage of GDP) than Vietnam, but has a significantly higher score on the NRI. This emphasizes the importance of other variables (such as market and regulatory factors); these variables play a significant role in determining the degree of networked readiness of a nation. Notable observations from Figure 7 include:

1. The United States, Finland, and Spain are among the leading overperformers

2. Romania, Vietnam, Columbia, and New Zealand are among the leading underperformers

3. New Zealand, with the highest ICT expenditure (percentage of GDP), has a modest NRI score of 4.70.

Internet users per 100 and readiness component index

One could be tempted to use the number of Internet users in a country as a proxy estimate of the networked readiness

Figure 7. **ICT Spending (Percent GDP) versus Networked Readiness Index, Partial Log Regression**

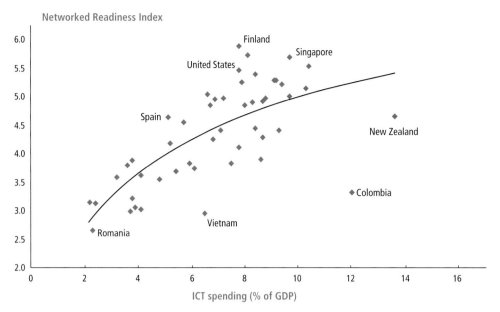

Source: Technology Management Department, INSEAD

Figure 8. **Number of Internet Users per 100 versus Readiness Component Index, Partial Log Regression**

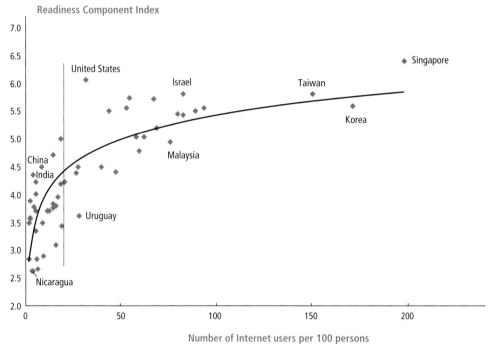

Source: Technology Management Department, INSEAD

of a country. Figure 8 shows a plot between the number of Internet users per 100 persons (number of Internet accounts) and the readiness component index. One would thus see the existence of a possible relationship between these, represented by the partial logarithmic regression plot. One sees that readiness scores increase sharply from 0 to 20 Internet users per 100, and much more gradually thereafter. The relatively flat curve at above 20 to 30 Internet users per 100 persons implies the importance of other factors beyond this point in influencing the degree of readiness of a nation, factors such

as the quality of connectivity, speed of connectivity, and the availability of online services, among others. Interesting observations that can be made from analyzing this plot are:

1. Singapore, with one of the highest Internet users per 100 persons ratio, outperforms the trend line with the highest readiness component index scores. Apart from a high concentration of businesses and the presence of a skilled workforce, Singapore benefits from a strong government push in ICT.

Figure 9. **Readiness Component Index versus Usage Component Index, Partial Polynomial Regression**

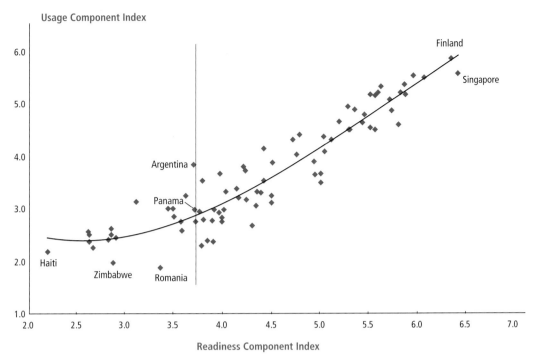

Source: Technology Management Department, INSEAD

2. Korea, with the second highest number of Internet users, performs relatively moderately on the readiness component index—the country is at 12th place, despite having one of the best broadband penetration in the world. Korea shows higher readiness on the individual dimension compared with their business and government readiness.

3. India and China, with relatively low numbers of Internet users, have relatively higher readiness scores; this is probably because of the regional and demographic digital divides in these countries.

4. A number of South American countries, such as Nicaragua and Uruguay, are only just starting to witness the propagation of the Internet; this is reflected in lower readiness scores.

Is there a threshold for usage to take off?

One would expect the readiness and usage scores of a nation to move hand in hand. A country having a high degree of readiness would be able to transform this ICT capability into usage statistics, and hence show a high score on the usage component index. For example, Singapore and Finland have among the highest readiness component index scores, and this readiness is translated into real ICT usage and represented by high usage scores (see Figure 9).

A closer look at the trend of readiness versus usage at lower values of readiness will reveal that usage remains rather flat with initial increases in readiness. This leads us to believe

that there is a threshold to readiness; a country needs to have a certain level of readiness with regards to ICT before there can be effective usage of and a consequent impact from ICT. A certain critical mass in terms of numbers of users, or the availability of narrowband and broadband services or of services online, is essential before these indicators are reflected in real usage metrics. Thus it can be determined that:

1. Haiti, with a readiness score of 2.19 and a low usage score of 2.19, must develop its readiness before usage starts increasing significantly;

2. Romania is a significant underperformer below the threshold level, and while it has a readiness score of 3.35, this does not result in a correspondingly higher usage level;

3. Panama and Argentina are at the threshold level; Argentina, however, is a significant overperformer, with a usage level of 3.84.

Research Challenges

Finding the facts. Even the best-planned frameworks can face seemingly insurmountable obstacles to their implementation because of the lack of reliable data. The overriding aim in our research and analysis has been to provide a scientific and credible interpretation of reality. Thus, the first step in our research has been to collect the most complete and high-quality set of data relating to ICT. We used two types of data in our research: soft data, which are subjective data gathered from questionnaires (such as the Executive Opinion Survey); and hard data, which are driven by statistics collected by reputable independent agencies (such as the World Bank and the International Telecommunication Union). Both these sets of data play a crucial role in the overall analysis. The soft data are critical in determining the opinion of the decision makers and influencers who are intimately familiar with a nation's economy. On the other hand, the hard data captures fundamental elements related to the development of infrastructure, human capital, and ICT.

Absence of key usage metrics. Key ICT, such as mobile telephony and the Internet, are still undergoing rapid development. Owing to this dynamism, accurate usage metrics are difficult, if not impossible, to obtain and/or are not up to date. In the absence of such usage metrics, one has to devise ways to best estimate the development of a country's ICT. For example, metrics on cost savings on high-speed Internet access and usage, on key measures of policy and regulation, and on the use of ICT by governments, remain elusive.

Selection of countries. Availability of objective and reliable data are critical while preparing a report of this type. To ensure quality information, we have restricted the study to eighty-two countries. Availability of data has, in fact, been a key factor in selecting the countries that form part of this study. As a consequence, regions suffering from a chronic lack of reliable statistics, such as Africa and Central Asia, are underrepresented in the NRI.

Ensuring statistical significance. Once solid and reliable facts had been accumulated, a comprehensive statistical analysis was conducted. Following the classic steps of any such analysis, correlation and factor analyses were conducted to drop closely correlated or interrelated variables. Following this, missing data in the dataset were estimated using regression and clustering techniques. The variables were then classified along the lines of the NRI Framework.

Data estimation. Despite our best efforts to collect data from all major international sources, it has been necessary at times to cope with incomplete sets of data for the countries under consideration. In order to compensate for this, statistical procedures, mainly regression and clustering techniques, have been used to estimate missing data. Control procedures and checks have been devised to ensure that estimations were reasonable and not overly favorable or disadvantageous in their representation of the concerned country.

Calculating the NRI. In order to calculate the Index, the data were first transformed on a scale of one to seven to give each piece of information equal weight. Next, each subindex was computed as a mathematical average of the variables composing it. The same approach was used to calculate the component indexes. Finally, the NRI was computed as an average of the three component indexes. The detailed statistical procedures followed can be found in the Networked Readiness Index: Methodology section of this report.

Summary

Measuring a country's networked readiness remains a significant challenge, and any framework or model representing networked readiness remains, at best, a simplified representation of reality. The NRI Framework attempts to interpret the underlying complexity of the development and use of ICT in an intuitive and easy-to-comprehend model. The overall NRI is a summary measure of a nation's ability to participate in and benefit from ICT. The NRI provides guidance to business leaders and public policymakers to enhance the impact of ICT on all key stakeholders—individuals, businesses, and governments.

The essence of networked readiness extends beyond any single metric; that said, there are over- and underperforming countries—countries that have put ICT on the national agenda and have strived to make it an area of excellence, and others that have not done so. The former countries have succeeded in going beyond individual measures of national income or national ICT spending to provide an optimal environment for ICT development, thus promoting high levels of readiness and usage for all three key stakeholders. Finland, Singapore, and Korea are such leaders; these three could serve as role models for other nations in their quest for ICT excellence. The NRI allows a nation to benchmark its ICT performance and determine the effectiveness of policy. It also permits a country to learn from the policy and performance of other countries with similar profiles, and to identify best practice.

ICT is the key to the evolution of our practices in many domains, such as education, work, personal relations, work effectiveness, and national productivity. An interesting characteristic of ICT, such as that of the Internet and mobile communications, is that overall value increases nonlinearly with the number of connected individuals and organizations. Increasing developing countries' levels of participation in ICT not only creates benefits for these countries; it also increases the overall potential of all connected stakeholders to realize value.

Endnotes

1. United Nations Development Programme (2001); Schwab et al (2002).

2. A NRI ranking of nations was presented for 2001 to 2002 in Kirkman et al (2002). The Networked Readiness Index 2002–2003 ranking cannot be directly compared with this earlier ranking, as the underlying framework and variables used in our research differ from those used in the earlier research by Kirkman et al.

3. For example, Israel with an overall ranking of 12, does well on environment (where it is ranked 5th) and readiness (8th) dimensions, as compared to the usage dimension where it is ranked 19th. See Table 4.

References

Asia-Pacific Economic Cooperation (APEC). 2000. The APEC e-Commerce Readiness Assessment Guide. APEC Readiness Initiative.

Bridges.org. 2001. Comparison of e-Readiness Assessment Models. October 2001. Online. http://www.bridges.org/ereadiness/tools.html.

Center for International Development, Information Technologies Group, Harvard University. Ongoing. Readiness for the Networked World: A Guide for Developing Countries. Online. http://www.readinessguide.org.

Computer Systems Policy Project (CSPP). Readiness For Living in the Networked World: A Self-Assessment Tool for Communities. Online. http://www.cspp.org.

European Foundation for Quality Management. The EFQM Excellence Model. Online. http://www.efqm.org/model_awards/model/excellence_model.htm.

International Telecommunication Union (ITU). 2001. World Telecommunication Indicators. Geneva: International Telecommunication Union.

Kirkman, G. S., P. K. Cornelius, J. D. Sachs, and K. Schwab, eds. 2002. The Global Information Technology Report 2001–2002: Readiness for the Networked World. New York: Oxford University Press for the World Economic Forum.

McConnell International and World Information Service and Technology Alliance (WITSA). 2001. Ready? Net. Go! Partnerships Leading the Global Economy. Online. http://www.witsa.org/papers/e-readiness2.pdf.

Organisation for Economic Co-operation and Development (OECD). 2001. Science, Technology and Industry Outlook: Drivers of Growth: Information Technology, Innovation, and Entrepreneurship. Paris: Organisation for Economic Co-operation and Development.

Rubin, H. 2002. 2002 Global Technology Index. Online. http://www.metricnet.com.

Schwab, K., M. Porter, J. D. Sachs, P. K. Cornelius, and J. McArthur, eds. 2002. The Global Competitiveness Report 2001–2002. New York: Oxford University Press for the World Economic Forum.

Wolcott, P., L. Press, W. McHenry, S. Goodman, and W. Foster. 2001. "A Framework for Assessing the Global Diffusion of the Internet," Journal of the Association for Information Systems 2(Article 6).

World Bank. 2002. World Development Indicators 2001. Online. http://www.worldbank.org/data/wdi/index.htm

World Information Technology and Services Alliance (WITSA). 2000.

International Survey of e-Commerce 2000. Online. http://www.witsa.org/papers/ecomsurv.pdf

United Nations Development Programme (UNDP). 2001. Human Development Report: Making New Technologies Work for Human Development. New York: Oxford University Press.

Technical Appendix: Constructing the Networked Readiness Index

The Networked Readiness Index 2002–2003 separates environmental factors from ICT readiness and usage, and hence there are three component indexes each for environment, readiness, and usage. Starting from a set of more than 130 ICT-related variables, we have divided these variables among the nine subindexes. We then eliminated variables based on analytic procedures such as correlation analysis, and Cronbachs Alpha test. The detailed statistical procedures that we followed can be found in the Networked Readiness Index: Methodology section of this report. Our final NRI computation is based on a set of sixty-four variables.

Definitions of the Networked Readiness Index, component indexes and subindexes

The Networked Readiness Index is defined as follows:

Networked Readiness Index = 1/3 Environment + 1/3 Networked Readiness + 1/3 Network Usage

A. Environment component index is defined as follows:

Environment = 1/3 Market + 1/3 Political/Regulatory Factors + 1/3 Infrastructure

1. Market subindex is defined by the following data variables:

    i. Venture capital availability
    ii. State of cluster development
    iii. Competition in the telecommunications sector
    iv. Availability of scientists and engineers
    v. Brain drain
    vi. Public spending on education (percentage of GDP)
    vii. Domestic software companies in international markets
    viii. Domestic manufacturing of IT hardware
    ix. ICT expenditure (percentage of GDP)

2. Political/regulatory subindex is defined by the following data variables:

    i. Effectiveness of law-making bodies
    ii. Legal framework for ICT Development
    iii. Subsidies for firm-level research and development
    iv. Government restrictions on Internet content
    v. Prevalence of foreign technology licensing

3. Infrastructure is defined by the following variables:

    i. Overall infrastructure quality
    ii. Local availability of specialized IT services
    iii. Number of telephone mainlines (per 1,000 people)
    iv. Number of telephone faults (per 100 main lines)
    v. Number of telephone mainlines per employee
    vi. Number of fax machines (per 1,000 people)
    vii. Local switch capacity (per 100,000 people)
    viii. Ease of obtaining new telephone lines
    ix. Waiting time for telephone mainlines (in years)
    x. Number of secure Internet servers

B. The readiness component index is defined as follows:

Readiness = 1/3 Individual Readiness + 1/3 Business Readiness + 1/3 Government Readiness

1. Individual readiness is defined by the following variables:

    i. Sophistication of local buyers' products and processes
    ii. Availability of mobile Internet access
    iii. Availability of broadband access
    iv. Public access to the Internet

    v. Secondary school enrollment (percentage net)

   vi. Total adult illiteracy rate (in percent)

  vii. Quality of math and science education

 viii. Cost of local call (US$ per three minutes)

   ix. Cost of off-peak local cellular telephone call (US$ per three minutes)

    x. Cost of residential telephone subscription (US$ per month)

2. Business readiness is defined by the following variables:

    i. Firm-level technology absorption

   ii. Firm-level innovation

  iii. Capacity for innovation

  iv. Business Intranet sophistication

   v. Quality of local IT training programs

  vi. Cost of business telephone subscription (US$ per month)

3. Government readiness is defined by the following variables:

    i. Government prioritization of ICT

   ii. Government procurement of advanced technology products

  iii. Competence of public officials

  iv. Government online services

C. The Usage component index is defined as follows:

Usage = 1/3 Individual Usage +1/3 Business Usage + 1/3 Government Usage

1. Individual usage is defined by the following variables:

    i. Use of online payment systems

   ii. Number of radios (per 1,000 people)

  iii. Number of television sets (per 1,000 people)

  iv. Number of cable television subscribers (per 1,000 people)

   v. Number of mobile telephones (per 1,000 people)

  vi. Number of Internet users (per 100 people)

  vii. Number of narrowband subscriber lines (per 100 people)

 viii. Number of broadband subscriber lines (per 100 people)

   ix. Household spending on ICT (US$ per month)

2. Business usage is defined by the following variables:

    i. Use of Internet for coordination with customers and suppliers

   ii. Businesses using e-commerce (in percent)

  iii. Use of Internet for general research

  iv. Sophistication of online marketing

   v. Presence of wireless e-business applications

  vi. Use of email for internal correspondence (in percent)

  vii. Use of email for external correspondence (in percent)

 viii. Pervasiveness of company Web pages

3. Government usage is defined by the following variables

    i. Use of Internet-based transactions with government

   ii. Government online services

  iii. Government success in ICT promotion

Chapter 2

Crafting the Environment for Networked Readiness

José María Figueres-Olsen and Fiona Paua

World Economic Forum

In the aftermath of the bursting of the technology bubble, one thing remains constant: information and communication technologies (ICT) have been and continue to be a powerful engine for economic and social development. ICT provide tools that accelerate growth and enhance productivity. The benefits of ICT must thus be harnessed to improve living standards worldwide, for only then can there be a feasible chance for achieving extreme poverty eradication and the other goals of the United Nations Millennium Declaration.

For ICT to serve as an engine for development, it is absolutely critical that an effective policy framework is in place; such a framework will enable an economy to fully capture the benefits of the technologies. The environment—market conditions, regulatory framework, and the network infrastructure—forms the foundation of a country's Networked Readiness. Setting the "right" environment is difficult, however, for it requires policy coherence among various areas, ranging from labor and education policies to telecommunications and capital market reforms. The task also entails flexibility in adapting to rapidly-changing technologies and shifting global capital and trade patterns. In addition, there is no simple blueprint that can be followed—a particular policy mix that is suitable for one country may not be applicable to another because of any one of a myriad of complex variables, ranging from varying geographic terrain to differing and dynamically evolving economic, political, and institutional contexts. The onus is, therefore, on national policymakers and business leaders to tailor and craft their respective policies to create an environment that best facilitates their country's Networked Readiness.

This chapter is intended to serve as a guide to policymakers and business leaders who are seeking to establish a solid foundation for promoting Networked Readiness. Existing national strategies are assessed and lessons gleaned from the varying policy experiences of countries in the course of their attempts at fostering the most appropriate and effective foundation for promoting Networked Readiness. This chapter, which covers in its analysis eighty-two of the world's leading economies, also seeks to highlight best practices, where available, and provide an indication of the range of policy options and initiatives.[1] Building on the findings of the Networked Readiness Index (2002–2003), this chapter applies the analytical framework outlined in the *Report* for assessing the readiness of a country's environment. Accordingly, the chapter is divided into three parts, corresponding to the three components of the environment subindex: market conditions, regulatory framework, and infrastructure.[2]

The first part addresses the following question: what needs to be in place, in terms of the market environment, to enable individuals, businesses, and governments to participate and benefit more fully in the networked economy? The conditions of the three key resource factors in a networked economy—human resources, capital markets, and technology—are also assessed.

Box 1. The Framework

PART I: MARKET ENVIRONMENT

HUMAN RESOURCES

Education

Infrastructure-related: computerization and networking of schools and libraries

Content-related: training of educators and integration of ICT in the curriculum

Government expenditures in education

Labor

Certification

Skills development

Skills matching

Reversing brain drain

CAPITAL

Early-stage financing: access to venture capital

Later-stage financing: access to capital markets

TECHNOLOGY

Technological Diffusion

Role of trade in technology transfer

Role of foreign direct investment in technology transfer

Technological Innovation

Financing: grants, subsidies, tax concessions, loans

Academia-business collaboration

Industry clusters

Ease of patent registration

PART II: LEGAL AND REGULATORY FRAMEWORK

LEGAL FRAMEWORK

Basic legal framework: property rights, contract law

Revising and creating relevant legislation: e-commerce

Harmonization with international law

REGULATORY FRAMEWORK

Regulatory capacity

Degree of regulation

Regulatory process

Licensing/auctions

Standards setting

Dispute resolution: interconnection

PART III: INFRASTRUCTURE

Market Structure: Privatization, Liberalization

Pricing

International: cost of connecting to international gateways, accounting rates, Internet telephony

Domestic: choice or regulatory pricing regime, metered vs. non-metered, issue of subsidies

Universal Service/Access

Content: local content, content regulation, taxation, privacy, and consumer data protection

Network Quality: network service and support, quality of service monitoring, security

Supporting Infrastructure: electricity, postal systems, customs, transport logistics

Financial Infrastructure: payment gateway, identification, authentication

In the second part a similar question is posed, but this question pertains to the type of legal and regulatory environment that needs to be in place. After first assessing the legal framework, both basic as well as technology-specific legislation, the regulatory framework is examined, including the institutional capacity and structure as well as specific regulatory issues that have a direct impact on the development and use of the network infrastructure.

In the third and final part, the state of the infrastructure is analyzed and the range of policies needed to facilitate the development of efficient networks discussed. The access, availability, and quality of telecommunications and Internet communications networks, as well as supporting infrastructure such as transport, postal, and energy, is also examined.

Despite the seemingly discrete schematic divisions, it is worth noting that the underlying factors are interconnected, with implications that overlap the three components. It is thus important to have a comprehensive overview as well as a detailed analysis of each of these three components.

Combined, these three components depict a country's environment and whether that environment enables it to capture fully the benefits of participating in the networked world. Using these three components, the five countries with the best environments are (in descending order) the United States, Finland, Iceland, Canada, and Israel. At the opposite extreme, countries that require the most improvement in their network environments are (in descending order) Honduras, Nicaragua, and Haiti.

Part I: The Market Environment

There are three resource factors that a country needs most to participate and benefit fully in a networked world: human resources, capital, and technology. Without human resource development, a country's citizens would be unable to use and adapt technologies and create new ones. Similarly, the ability of governments, businesses, and individuals to engage in activities and projects involving technological creation and innovation would be impaired without the breadth and depth of financial markets that allow for access to capital with reasonable costs and conditions. Moreover, countries also need environments that are conducive to technological diffusion, which is the process of adopting and adapting technologies developed abroad, and to innovation, the process of creating new technologies.

The succeeding discussion delves deeper into the factors that define a country's market environment. It also examines the performance of successful countries in this regard, particularly countries that have scored well in the market subindex. These countries include the United States, Finland, the United Kingdom, Sweden, and Israel.

Box 2. **On Visions and National Strategies**

The revolutionary gains ushered in by information and communications technologies (ICT) have compelled the highest levels of governments to craft a national ICT strategy. As early as 1991, Singapore, among the front-runners, launched a national ICT strategy, outlined in *IT2000 Plan: A Vision of an Intelligent Island*. The United States announced its national information initiative two years later, in 1993, with the publication of *The National Information Infrastructure: Agenda for Action*. Later that same year, the European Union (EU) published a *White Paper on Competitiveness*, which highlighted that there is a close link between the sophistication of a country's information infrastructure and its economic prosperity. Within a span of five years, Canada, Japan, and most of the European countries followed suit with respective national initiatives.

The last five years have also witnessed the unveiling of national ICT strategies in many developing countries. Policies outlined in Malaysia's *Vision 2020*, of which *Multimedia Super Corridor Project* is a component, have fortified the country's position as one of the leading exporters of electronic products. India's *1998 Action Plan* has catalyzed the Internet expansion in the country. Moreover, Jordan's *REACH Initiative*, launched on March 2000, has jumpstarted the country's strategy of focusing on software and related ICT service industries.

That the vision of a country's national ICT strategy stems from the highest office of the land is a concrete depiction of the country's commitment to making a successful transition to the new economy. It reflects a leadership that is forward-looking and ready to steer the country into an accelerated path of development. The most visible national ICT strategies tend to have a key visionary, a chief architect. In Singapore, former Prime Minister and now Senior Minister Lee Kuan Yew played that role; in Malaysia, it was Prime Minister Mahathir Mohammed; and in Jordan, King Abdullah II. For a national ICT strategy to achieve international visibility and a competitive level of success, the strategy is indeed best initiated from no less than the office of the head of state.

Beyond a powerful articulation of a compelling vision, crafting a national ICT strategy entails an accurate and comprehensive assessment of a country's readiness to participate in the global networked economy. A careful and thorough analysis must be made of the country's strengths, and of target areas for policy intervention. The challenge is to enhance core competencies and maximize existing resources, all within the context of the country's development goals.

Crafting a national ICT strategy is a complex process that requires extraordinary policy coordination. A truly concerted national ICT strategy requires the cooperative efforts of several ministries, including education, finance, labor, communications, trade and industry, and information technology. The strategy entails the establishment of national priorities as reflected in policies and regulatory measures that create the conditions which will enable the country to reap more fully the rewards of the global networked economy.

Since information and communications technologies continue to evolve and revolutionary applications continue to be created in the process, the national ICT strategy must be sufficiently flexible to adapt appropriately. Flexibility entails that the national ICT strategy is not dependent on any particular technology, particularly in view of the odds against identifying winning technologies.

Along with flexibility, however, it is critical that the national ICT strategy has a clear focus. At its most basic, the strategy must be founded on two prerequisites: infrastructure and education. The strategy must then build upon this foundation by formulating an industrial policy designed to attract private investment in strategic segments of the ICT sector.

Indeed, vision, leadership commitment, and planning are all important in crafting a successful national ICT strategy. The presence of a clear vision provides guidance to the policy-making process, while the commitment of leadership encourages investment and ensures continuity in the deployment of various information infrastructure projects. Long-range planning is also important, particularly for large countries, as is evident by China and India's five-year plans. To ensure effective development of the country's information infrastructure, a distinct and dedicated Ministry or Department, as in the case of India's Ministry of Information Technology, or the United Kingdom's e-Envoy, would also be useful.

Human resources

To have a human resource base that is ready and capable of participating in and benefiting from the networked economy, the attention of policymakers and business leaders must be placed on two major areas: education and labor policies. In the area of education, the task is to create a set of structures and policies that provide and deliver relevant knowledge and skills to individuals. Meanwhile, in the area of labor, the task is to upgrade the knowledge and skills base of the workforce and to craft policies that attract and retain talent in the country.

Results of education and labor policies are partly reflected in selected indicators of the Market Environment subindex. One of the variables related to education policies, for example, is the survey question (in the Executive Opinion Survey)[3] asking if scientists and engineers are common in the country. Answers to this question reveal that many developing countries are among the top-ranked in this category. Such countries include Israel, India, Slovakia, and Romania, ranked 1st, 2nd, 3rd, and 5th, respectively. Among the developed countries, France ranked 4th, and Canada placed 6th.

In contrast, responses to the question asking if talented people leave the country show a different scenario. The United States ranked 1st in this regard, with Netherlands and Finland in 2nd and 3rd place, respectively, indicating that talented people tend to stay in these countries. Interestingly, of the four developing countries that scored among the top five places on the question of availability of scientists and engineers, only Israel remains among the top five countries that is able to successfully retain talented people in the country; Slovakia, India, and Romania are ranked 52nd, 54th and 80th, respectively, indicating that although these countries have a considerable pool of scientists and engineers, a considerable proportion of talented people leave the country.

Education

There are two sets of education policies that are required to develop the requisite skill base for the networked economy. The first set is infrastructure-related, and this entails computerization of schools and libraries and the networking of these computers. The second set is content-related, and involves the training of educators and the integration of ICT into the curriculum and pedagogy. A prerequisite for both sets of policies is the allocation to the education sector of sufficient resources from the government, supplemented by support from the private sector and nongovernmental organizations.

Canada and Estonia are among the countries with best practice in infrastructure-related education initiatives. The case of Canada, the first country in the world to connect its schools and public libraries to the Internet, demonstrates the importance of a government-led but collaborative initiative to meet the task of computerizing and networking the educational system. Canada achieved the latter through its Schoolnet initiative; and the former, through initiatives such as the Computer for Schools program that collects, refurbishes, and delivers surplus computers donated from the public and private sectors. Similarly, Estonia's Tiger Leap initiative has enabled the country to be one of the first developing countries to connect all its schools to the Internet.

A government-led approach to infrastructure-related education initiatives is only one of the many approaches to the task. In many countries, the private sector and nongovernmental organizations (NGOs) play a critical role. In the United States, a volunteer-driven initiative, Netday, has been instrumental in wiring more than 75,000 classrooms.[4] Another example comes from Brazil, which has an NGO-led initiative, launched by the Committee for Democracy in Information Technology, that provides free computer equipment and software—all of which have been collected in donation campaigns. Mexico has a similar project coordinated by a civic organization, the Union of Industrialists for Educational Technology, with participation from the state and federal governments. The aim of the project is to provide equipment for computer workshops in schools. In addition to providing computers and networking schools and libraries, it is also important for a country to have a network infrastructure that provides the necessary bandwidth at a very low cost (ideally free or subsidized for the education sector), so as to enable the sector to use ICT as solutions to many of the obstacles that typically face education systems in developing countries. Computer-aided instruction can facilitate distance learning, as well as the overcoming of teacher shortages and upgrading teacher skills. It also allows the creation of repositories of study materials that can be accessed at a very low cost. Mexico, for instance, has Educational Television of Satellital Net, in which more than 29,000 establishments participate and benefit from equipment installation, and which has ten channels to receive the Edusat signal. Edusat offers production services, programming, and transmission of educational material to institutions that require television in support of their education and training activities. The government of South Korea is also promoting distance education, offering ICT-related courses with the use of cable TV, satellite broadcasting, and the Internet.

For content-related initiatives, the training of educators and teachers is considered a must. While there is great variation in approach, the task is to incorporate ICT in the curriculum and the teaching process. Clearly, there are developing countries where the educational systems are barely able to provide basic education and literacy skills; for these countries, integrating ICT into the curriculum is, quite understandably, far from a priority. Yet there are also many examples of developing-country governments committed to promoting content-related initiatives. Costa Rica, for instance, has a program called Computers in Education, a public-private partnership spearheaded by Fundacion Omar Dengo and targeted at primary schools. Argentina and Chile have created respective education portals, educ.ar and educarchile, both equipped with an array of ICT-related learning resources for teachers and students.

Because they have fewer resource constraints, developed countries tend to have more advanced content-related initiatives. Canada has the GrassRoots Program, which has helped learners and educators become skilled users of ICT as well as creators of online collaborative classroom projects. Likewise, the United Kingdom has the National Grid for Learning, an Internet-based resource for education and lifelong learning that brings together an increasingly wide variety of institutions and content providers to provide access to high quality materials.

Indeed, a prerequisite for both infrastructure-related and content-related sets of policies is the allocation to the education sector of sufficient resources from the government. Given the funding constraints, government leaders often have to choose where to allocate most of the state's resources: should the focus be on higher education which is more specialized and may benefit only a few, or should it be on primary education, which is more general and would benefit a broader population? A similar funding dilemma is the choice between prioritizing formal graduate and postgraduate education, which is highly specialized but can also be availed by a few, or prioritizing more broad-based, though shorter-term, vocational training? While such policy choices are inevitable for developing countries, one of the ways to alleviate the constraint is to increase the pool of resources in the educational system by tapping the private sector and nongovernmental organizations. Another way for governments to increase education expenditures is by prioritizing it over expenditures for other sectors; in this regard, Costa Rica perhaps presents the most dramatic example of redirected priorities—the government has moved its defense funding to education. This commitment to education was further consolidated in Costa Rica by a 1998 constitutional reform, which mandated that 6 percent of the gross national product be invested in education.

Labor

The task for policymakers and business leaders is to ensure that there is a sufficient supply of skilled labor. Whereas the task for policymakers in the past was primarily to maximize employment, the networked economy requires more sophistication because of the faster-than-ever creation and destruction of jobs caused by advances in technology. Moreover, globalization has facilitated companies' relocation to areas that can satisfy their labor requirements, thereby rendering a skilled workforce to be one of the most, if not the most, important assets in a knowledge-based economy. A skilled labor force is crucial to encouraging new investment

and facilitating job creation; further, without a skilled labor force it would be very difficult to retain and sustain existing businesses.

To promote the upgrading of the workforce, initiatives can be pursued in two key areas: certification and skills development. In terms of certification, Finland is notable for its Computer Driving License, an ICT literacy examination that everyone takes, and that is designed to implement a nationwide ICT standard. A shared accreditation standard between countries is another area that needs to be pursued more vigorously. Japan has an information technology engineers' examination, for example, which other Association of Southeast Asian Nations (ASEAN) countries are interested in applying to facilitate mutual recognition of standards.

Skills development in the context of the networked economy entails preparing the workforce to meet the skill requirements of the labor market, and for this, a close coordination between academia and the business sector is required. Continuous learning is essential and takes various forms, including on-the-job training, distance learning, and other professional development opportunities. Many developed countries have launched various initiatives to promote skills development. Targeting increased participation of women in ICT skills development programs has been the thrust of initiatives in Belgium and Norway: Belgium has its Electronica project which aims to "demystify" ICT professions in the eyes of women; while Norway's Norwegian University of Science and Technology has introduced a special quota system for women in computer technology studies. Austria's tele.soft, a training program that introduces qualifications "on demand" for the ICT sector, targets the overall population. Similarly, the United Kingdom has Learndirect, and as many as 885 Learndirect centers offer more than 600 Learndirect courses, all aimed at adults—whether they are working, seeking work, considering returning to work, or retired. Canada is notable for addressing the issue of funding skills development by creating Registered Individual Learning Accounts; these accounts make it easier for Canadians to finance their learning and increase the loans available to part-time students.

Skills development initiatives in developing countries are particularly constrained by lack of government funding resources and the lack of know-how in the education system. In this regard, collaborating with the private sector is an effective way to address and overcome these constraints. The Philippines is particularly notable for tapping multinational information technology companies for training programs, among them Oracle (Oracle Academic Initiative), Cisco (Cisco Networking Academy Program), IBM (Advanced Career Education), Sun Microsystems, and Hewlett-Packard. These private-sector initiatives not only help to overcome resource constraints but, more important, ensure that the skills of the workforce are better matched to the requirements of the marketplace.

Skills matching is indeed critical and it is important that a country has job-matching tools and centers. Canada, for example, has SkillNet, an Industry Canada initiative that helps Canadian employers locate and recruit skilled workers. Without job-matching tools and centers, a skills gap may go undetected for a considerable period. In Europe, a skills gap became particularly apparent at the height of the technology boom, when there were an estimated one million information technology vacancies despite a fairly high youth unemployment rate in the region. While education and training action plans provide longer-term solutions to the skills gap, labor markets in countries facing this challenge must have sufficient flexibility in labor and immigration regulations as well as policies designed to attract skilled workers. The United States has also been successful in attracting highly skilled workers with policies that allow for the favorable tax treatment of income and stock options.

In addition to the task of accrediting, developing, and attracting a skilled labor force, one of the most critical challenges for policymakers is to retain talented people in the country. Brain drain is a challenging problem, particularly for developing countries. To prevent brain drain, two countries, Taiwan and South Korea, have launched programs specifically designed to reverse it: Taiwan has set up the National Youth Commission, an information clearing house for potential employers and for returning scholars seeking employment, while South Korea has focused on upgrading its research institutions, such as the Korea Institute for Science and Technology, as a way to attract returnees (UNDP 2001).

Capital

Capital is a key resource factor in the development of a networked economy. The availability of and access to low-cost capital at favorable terms is particularly critical for startup ventures. To foster an environment conducive to the development of innovative, high-growth technology companies, policies must be designed to ensure that capital markets have the requisite breadth and depth to allow for efficient financial intermediation and capital allocation towards activities and projects involving technological creation, diffusion, and innovation. To this end, policymakers can pursue initiatives at two levels: early-stage financing (especially government-funded venture capital), and later-stage financing (to facilitate access to equity and bond markets).

Early-stage financing

For a local ICT industry to emerge, capital, ranging from grants, government bank funding, or more typically, venture capital, must be available for startups. While the private sector provides most of the venture capital in the world, in some countries governments play a substantial role in providing early-stage financing. Australia, for instance, has the Innovation Investment Fund, which provides venture capital

to small, high-tech companies at the seed, startup, or early expansion stages; the country also has Build On IT Strengths, an incubator program. Likewise, Austria has implemented the Austrian Industrial Research Promotion Fund, a seed financing program that supports technology-oriented startups with capital and know-how. In Mexico, the National Bank for Foreign Trade has invested in different risk capital investment funds, which are directed at supporting small- and medium-sized Mexican enterprises. The government of Greece is the single shareholder of the New Economy Development Fund, which was created to co-finance the formation of venture capital funds. In Israel, the government has set up a venture capital company, Yozma, with an initial budget of US$100 million, designed to attract foreign capital for investment in local companies (UNDP 2001:84). In Singapore, the state agency, Economic Development Board, serves as, among other functions, a venture capital entity with US$7.7 billion in funds under its management; in addition, the Singaporean government has added a US$1 billion fund, the Technopreneurship Investment Fund. Meanwhile, in addition to providing about KRW 500 billion in early-stage financing and research and development (R&D), the Korean government also operates an IT Venture Investment Mart to match promising information and communications businesses and venture capital.

While government initiatives in this area are noteworthy, most venture capital comes from the private sector. The bulk of this type of capital is also concentrated in a handful of countries, with the United States serving as the base for most venture capital companies. In 2001 for instance, the United States had US$103 billion of venture capital invested, thirty-five times more than the United Kingdom, the country with the next largest amount of venture capital invested at US$2.9 billion (UNDP 2001:84). Indeed, of the eighty-two countries ranked in the *Global Competitiveness Report 2002–2003*, the United States ranks 1st in terms of ease of access to venture capital.

Later-stage financing

As ventures expand and mature, it becomes necessary to tap stock and bond markets for further financing. Policymakers seeking to facilitate access to stock markets may, for instance, encourage the creation of a secondary board that has less stringent listing requirements, such as shorter operating history requirements. Greece, for instance, has launched the New Stock Market for trading shares of innovative and dynamic "new economy" small- and medium-sized enterprises (SMEs).

In terms of access to funding, stock and bond markets provide, in addition to bank credit, the bulk of financing for technology-related investments. While developed countries have the benefit of mature stock and bond markets in addition to highly competitive banking sectors, developing countries are still in the process of building their banking and financial markets. In this regard, governments need to pursue banking-sector reforms, as well as capital-market reforms. Care must be taken to avoid undue taxation of transactions, because this could inhibit capital market and banking activities. Governments can also pave the way for local companies to tap international markets by seeking sovereign credit ratings and launching sovereign bonds in international markets.

Technology

Technology is the third resource factor that is critical to the creation of a foundation for Networked Readiness. To enable an economy to capture more fully the benefits of ICT, policies designed to promote technological transfer and diffusion, as well as technological innovation, are critical. The former involves trade liberalization and investment promotion, while the latter entails the creation of clusters, promotion of corporate R&D, and facilitation of patent registration.

Box 3. Special Technology Zones

If the prospect of laying out a nationwide network infrastructure is daunting for developing countries given resource constraints, special technology zones provide an option of focusing infrastructure efforts in a geographically prescribed area. Special technology zones, often referred to as technology parks, can range from a single building development to a several-thousand-hectare master-planned development.

To be successful, a technology park must be carefully designed in order to maximize fully the economic benefits and synergies of clustering. In addition to ensuring that state of the art infrastructure, such as power and high bandwidth communications twenty-four hours a day seven days a week, are in place, an ICT park must also be adjacent to centers of innovation and talent pools such as research and development centers and universities. Typical facilities of technology parks include: research and testing laboratories, intelligent buildings, on-site teleport earth station, technology incubator, wide area network, recreational facilities, shared business services, training and consultancy center, and exhibition areas. To be more attractive, other technology parks include housing developments for expatriate and other employees as well as schools, hospitals, and religious establishments.

However technology parks are designed, it is important to have highly competitive facilities and incentives. Formulating policy incentives for investing in a technology park is just as critical as deploying infrastructure. Incentives typically include income tax holidays, import duty and indirect tax exemptions, subsidies, foreign investment privileges, one-stop-shop investment and business registration processing, and simplified export and import procedures. United Arab Emirates is host to the leading examples in technology parks: Dubai Internet City, Dubai Ideas Oasis, and Dubai Media City. It is notable, for instance, that Dubai Internet City offers a whole host of benefits, including 100 percent foreign ownership and zero tax on sales, profits, and personal income. Dubai has also positioned itself as a leading leisure destination, with a wide variety of sporting and leisure facilities. Dubai offers world-class medical and education facilities, in addition to a modern housing infrastructure.

The importance of telecommunications infrastructure cannot be understated. Malaysia's Multimedia Super Corridor, for example, has a fiber-optic backbone with a 2.5 to 10 gigabits per second capacity, direct high-capacity fiber links to international centers, a 100 percent digital open multimedia network, as well as open standards, high-speed switching, and multiple protocols. Performance guarantees include installation of telephone services within twenty-four hours, ATM circuits within five days, and 99.9 percent service availability.

The role that governments play in the creation of technology parks can vary. From one end, it can be government-led and funded, as in the cases of Singapore, Malaysia, and the United Arab Emirates; on the opposite end, it can be purely private sector–driven. In many cases, however, it can be both, resulting in a private sector-initiated but government-supported technology park. With regards to the latter, Hong Kong's Cyberport is a case in point, whereby the government has contributed the land for the project but the financial risk and other requirements of the project have been borne by the private sector.

In terms of actual application, the phenomenal development of India's software industry is perhaps one of the best examples of a successful technology park strategy. In 1990, India's Department of Electronics established seven software technology parks, which granted export-oriented software firms a zero-tariff regime, competitive telecommunications facilities, and low taxes. Aware of the problems of infrastructure in the country, the government has designated certain geographic areas in which the necessary infrastructure, such as power and communications twenty-four hours a day seven days a week, are in place. In addition, an export promotion council was also created for electronics and computer software, with representatives from the Ministry of Commerce, Ministry of Finance, and Department of Electronics. Today, India has more than forty software technology parks, and the entire sector's exports exceed US$1.7 billion.

Technology diffusion

International trade and foreign direct investment are the two mechanisms by which countries can acquire, adopt, and adapt existing technologies. Policymakers must focus on both mechanisms to facilitate technology transfer. The transfer of technology is of particular benefit to emerging market countries seeking to harness global technologies for local use. Significantly, it is the absorption of advanced technologies and capital from core economies that has allowed certain non-core economies to achieve the highest economic growth rates in the world,[5] and enabling economies such as Taiwan, Ireland, Hong Kong, Singapore, and Korea—which were non-core economies in the 1980s—to become core innovators by the year 2000.

International trade is vital to Networked Readiness because it allows domestic producers and consumers to have access to a greater variety of ICT products and services at prices lower than they would otherwise. Equally essential is the role of international trade in facilitating technological diffusion. To create an environment conducive to technological diffusion, policymakers must liberalize trade by lowering tariff and nontariff barriers that are applied to ICT.

Foreign direct investment contributes to Networked Readiness through the facilitation of technology transfer. To acquire relevant technologies and gain employment and other positive spillovers, governments seek foreign direct investment. As competition for foreign direct investment has intensified, governments have become increasingly aggressive in investment promotion, offering fiscal and nonfiscal incentives, which, if availed, come at a cost, either in terms of taxpayer burden or foregone revenues for the government. More often than not, however, calculus of costs and benefits of incentives to promote foreign direct investment tend to be positive, leading policymakers to offer targeted incentives in selected strategic sectors.

The importance of trade and investment as mechanisms to facilitate technology transfer and diffusion is best illustrated by China's experience in liberalizing the telecommunications equipment sector. As early as 1978, China allowed direct importation of foreign telecommunications equipment. In addition to facilitating the importation of technologies, the government also encouraged the establishment of joint ventures with foreign companies that are leading the world in specific areas. Domestic producers now control at least 15 percent of China's telecommunications equipment market, excluding handsets and office equipment. In terms of phone sets, China now seeks export opportunities; it manufactures around 100 million home phone sets, exceeding domestic demand. In terms of wireless products, China has more than 100 telecommunications plants producing parts and equipment for mobile telephones. Most of these ventures are foreign-funded companies with names such as Tianjin

Motorola, Beijing Nokia, Beijing Ericsson, Beijing Matsushita, Wuhan NEC, Shanghai Siemens, and Shenzhen Philips (Paua et al 2001). More important, China's ability to produce telecommunications equipment at low prices has enabled the country to post the highest telecommunications diffusion rates in the world.

Technological innovation

Technological innovation, or the creation of new technologies, is a widely acknowledged engine of growth. A country that is seeking to promote Networked Readiness must create an environment that fosters innovation. To this end, policies can be directed towards encouraging research and development in academia or corporations, or through industry-academia collaborations.

Apart from state-owned research institutions, policymakers have four basic tools with which to promote R&D: grants, subsidies, tax concessions, and concession loans. Most developed countries have pursued a mixture of all four tools. Australia for instance, has an R&D tax concession program, R&D grants and loans program, as well as concession loans. Likewise, Canada has Technology Partnerships Canada (TPC), which has an annual base budget of CAD 300 million; TPC invests in high-risk, near-market development and demonstration projects across Canada. Indeed, Canada ranks 4th in direct R&D subsidies and tax credits to companies based on the Executive Opinion Survey. Other countries in the top five places are Israel at 1st place, Singapore at 2nd, Taiwan at 3rd, and Ireland at 5th.

Outside of Israel, Singapore, Taiwan, and Ireland, best practice cases studies of R&D promotion in developing countries tend to be rare. R&D initiatives are cost-intensive, risky, and have long-term time horizons; for many developing countries, many other resource priorities, such as education and health, take precedence over R&D. In this context, Mexico's initiatives to promote R&D are particularly noteworthy. Mexico has created the National Council of Science and Technology, which serves as the vehicle for the promotion and sponsoring of specific projects concerning research and the dissemination of scientific and technological information. Mexico also has the Integrated System for Information on Scientific and Technological Research, an information and registration system of activities and institutions involved in science and technology that also serves as a mechanism for R&D institutions to obtain support from the federal government. The country also has the Technological Services Information System, which seeks to foster a technological culture in small and medium enterprises by offering a database with information provided by more than 225 development research institutes and centers.

Another way to promote R&D is to encourage academia-business collaboration. Canada, for example, operates the

Industrial Research Assistance Program, which assists SMEs across Canada in R&D leading to new products and processes. Likewise, Austria's Kplus Competence Center Programs stimulate the long-term cooperation between innovative enterprises and top-quality research organizations. And in Australia, the government is funding twenty-eight projects involving university and industry partnerships over three years under its Science Lectureship Initiative. Significantly, academia-business collaboration also facilitates the exploitation of the commercial potential of research outputs.

For many countries, industry cluster strategies embody both policies directed toward encouraging R&D and policies designed to foster industry-academia collaboration. The notion of industry clustering, a variant of industrial policy theories that assert that competitive advantages can be created, seems paradoxical when taken in the context of the much-heralded "death of distance" ushered by ICT. Yet clustering as a strategy makes sense, as it lends positive network externalities generated by the density of interactions within areas where there is a concentration of technology companies, financing sources, and pool of talent from adjacent university centers.

Successful clusters contain, in close proximity to the businesses, sources of intellectual capital, usually a major university. Universities are sources of potential employees, but seedbeds of entrepreneurial ideas as well. Also present in every cluster are incubators and other sources of risk capital for funding of startups. The presence of major locators is also one of the strongest indicators of the success of a cluster.

The United States is home to the best known and perhaps the most successful industry cluster, Silicon Valley (California), which includes Stanford University and the University of California, and has among its major locators Hewlett-Packard, Sun Microsystems, and Cisco. Also in the United States is Route 128 (Massachusetts), anchored to Harvard University and Massachusetts Institute of Technology and that has, among its major locators, Lotus and EMC. Outside the United States, Finland has a Helsinki cluster with Nokia as an anchor company, and the Helsinki University of Technology; Ireland has the Dublin-National Digital Park with the University of Dublin and the major locators Dell and Intel; while Sweden's Stockholm-Kista cluster has Ericsson as an anchor locator together with the Royal Institute of Technology.

In addition to clusters, policymakers can promote innovation by facilitating the ease of patent registration. Two countries that have recent initiatives in this regard are Belgium and Mexico. The Belgian Office for Industrial Property has asked the European Patent Office to integrate the electronic filing of Belgian national applications into the epoline communication environment, the electronic filing of European patent applications. In Mexico, the Mexican Institute of Intellectual

Property has set up the National Bank of Patents, an Internet-based database that provides information about registered patents, utility models, industrial models, and patent applications.

Part II: Legal and Regulatory Framework

An environment conducive to promoting Networked Readiness requires clear and up-to-date legal frameworks. In addition, it also requires a regulatory regime marked by an independent regulator that is empowered and equipped to craft and implement regulatory policy, allocate scarce resources, adjudicate disputes, and balance goals of efficiency, equity and innovation.

Among the eighty-two countries covered in this *Report*, Singapore is number one with respect to the legal and regulatory environment. The other leading countries, in descending order, are: Israel at 2nd place, Finland at 3rd, the United States at 4th, and Canada at 5th.

Legal Framework

An effective legal framework for promoting Networked Readiness has three prerequisites: first, a clear legal framework; second, an up-to-date, ICT-relevant legislation with a degree of built-in flexibility; and third, relevant legislation must be harmonized with international law. In terms of the quality of the supporting legal framework for ICT, Singapore, the United States, and the United Kingdom achieved the highest ranks (in descending order); while Haiti and Argentina received the worst, and second-to-the-worst ranks, respectively.

First, a clear basic legal framework must be in place. The basic legal framework must include provisions for property rights (including intellectual property), and legal certainty of contracts—both of which are essential to encouraging long-term and large-scale investments.

Second, the legal framework must be up-to-date, reflecting corporate changes in technological developments. For many countries, existing legislation pertaining to telecommunications and communications are separate, and requires revision and updating in order to reflect the convergence of technologies. Moreover, most contract law is still paper-based in many countries; new legislation is required to recognize and accept electronic signatures. Care must be taken, however, that there is sufficient flexibility built into the legislation governing ICT given the dynamic nature of technological advances and the difficulty of crafting and passing legislation. For example, a standing law that was more than a hundred years old, the Indian Telegraph Act of 1885, had, until recently, handicapped India's telecommunications sector. At the opposite extreme, China had no direct legislation governing the telecommunications sector until after 1999, although the lack of legal framework appeared to allow for a degree of experimentation prior to legislation. Ideally, the legal framework must have the clarity to encourage investment but the flexibility to accommodate changes in technology without being quickly rendered outdated and irrelevant.

Third, to the extent possible, relevant legislation must be harmonized with international law. The borderless nature of e-commerce lends to cross-border, territorial jurisdiction disputes. In this regard, it is useful when crafting e-commerce legislation to use as a basis the Model Law on Electronic Commerce created by the United Nations Commission on International Trade Law and designed to offer national legislators a set of internationally acceptable rules on how a number of legal obstacles may be removed, and how a more secure legal environment may be created for e-commerce (Townsend 1999:55). Further, in 1997 the International Chamber of Commerce adopted the General Usage for International Digitally Ensure Commerce, which was based on existing law and practices in different legal systems, to facilitate and promote the emerging global electronic trading system.

Regulatory Framework

Attention to three aspects is most critical when establishing a regulatory framework that is most conducive to Networked Readiness: the first aspect is regulatory capacity; the second, degree of regulation; and third, the regulatory process. In analyses and discussions on regulation, it is best to remember that a regulatory regime appropriate to one country may not necessarily be suitable or enforceable in another. Regulatory regimes do not emerge from a vacuum; rather it emerges from, and is influenced by, a country's unique economic, political, social, and economic context.

Regulatory capacity

The rise of the ICT-sector specific regulatory agency is a recent phenomenon, and it arose from the need to eliminate conflicts of interest that emerge from state-owned monopolies holding the overlapping roles of regulator, operator, and administrator—a situation typical in many developing countries. In some countries, the regulator also has broad oversight; that is, there is a "super-regulator" or a "multisector regulator" with responsibilities straddling telecommunications, broadcast, and Internet regulation. Indeed, among the many questions countries have to decide when designing the regulatory framework is: what services or industry segments should come under which regulatory authority? Should there be a single-sector or multisector regulator? If it is the latter, should telecommunications be combined with other utilities or with other communications sectors such as broadcasting?

Whatever regulatory structure emerges, one requirement is indisputable: the regulator must be independent, ensuring a level playing field. "Independence" means being independent of any operator or service provider, of any government department that is a shareholder in an operator, and of political interference with regard to individual reforms. Because they are a recent phenomenon, regulatory agencies in many countries lack not only the independence, but also the capacity to perform their functions; they often lack staff with the necessary expertise, and the legal clarity of their powers to enforce dispute resolution and other regulatory decisions.

Singapore presents a best-practice case study in ICT regulation. In 1992, Singapore became one of the first countries worldwide to create a sector-specific telecommunications regulatory body, Telecommunications Authority of Singapore, which later merged with the National Computer Board to become the Info-Communications Development Authority of Singapore (IDA). IDA has established the Code of Practice for Competition in the Provision of Telecommunications Services, based on principles of technological neutrality and asymmetric regulation between dominant and nondominant licensees. A complementary regulatory body is the Singapore Broadcasting Authority, responsible for regulating content.

Degree of regulation

Distinctions must be made between the telecommunications sector, the Internet sector, and broadcasting sector when analyzing how much regulation is appropriate. Whereas self-regulation is the predominant regulatory regime for the Internet sector, and to a lesser extent, the broadcasting sector, the telecommunications sector tends to require, at the very least, a fair amount of regulation. The telecommunications sector is often misunderstood, and there are frequent calls for its "deregulation." As telecommunications sectors undergo reforms, such as liberalization, however, greater, rather than lesser, regulation is required. At least in the initial stages, regulation is needed for the licensing of new entrants, resolving interconnection issues, and choosing and implementing a pricing regime, among other concerns.

Although different countries are likely to have varying degrees of telecommunications regulation, one task remains the same for all countries: that of balancing the goals of efficiency, equity, and innovation. In choosing a pricing regime for instance, the regulator has to grapple with the competing objectives of ensuring just and reasonable rates for users, while recognizing investors' expectations regarding capital recovery and also ensuring that companies will have enough return on investment to encourage further innovation and the continued upgrading and maintenance of the network infrastructure. An overview of regulatory levers is depicted on the following page.

Figure 1. **Overview of Regulatory Levers**

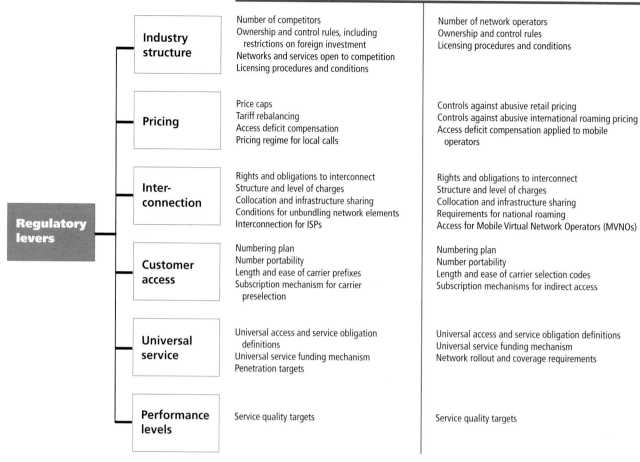

	Levers for fixed services	Levers for mobile services
Industry structure	Number of competitors Ownership and control rules, including restrictions on foreign investment Networks and services open to competition Licensing procedures and conditions	Number of network operators Ownership and control rules Licensing procedures and conditions
Pricing	Price caps Tariff rebalancing Access deficit compensation Pricing regime for local calls	Controls against abusive retail pricing Controls against abusive international roaming pricing Access deficit compensation applied to mobile operators
Inter-connection	Rights and obligations to interconnect Structure and level of charges Collocation and infrastructure sharing Conditions for unbundling network elements Interconnection for ISPs	Rights and obligations to interconnect Structure and level of charges Collocation and infrastructure sharing Requirements for national roaming Access for Mobile Virtual Network Operators (MVNOs)
Customer access	Numbering plan Number portability Length and ease of carrier prefixes Subscription mechanism for carrier preselection	Numbering plan Number portability Length and ease of carrier selection codes Subscription mechanisms for indirect access
Universal service	Universal access and service obligation definitions Universal service funding mechanism Penetration targets	Universal access and service obligation definitions Universal service funding mechanism Network rollout and coverage requirements
Performance levels	Service quality targets	Service quality targets

Source: Beardsley et al (McKinsey) in "The Elements of Successful Telecommunications Sector Reform" in *The Global Information Technology Report 2001–2002*

Regulatory process

Whatever form the final regulatory structure takes, it is important that attention also be placed on the process by which regulation is undertaken. Transparency in the regulatory process, as well as in consultations with stakeholders such as consumers and service providers, is advisable, particularly when deciding on major issues such as rate rebalancing.

Other regulatory functions, such as licensing or setting standards, also require due attention to process. The choice, for instance, on the mode of licensing has significant implications for the outcome. One mode of licensing is to conduct comparative evaluations, often referred to as "beauty contests," but this can be criticized for a lack of transparency and objectivity. The other mode of licensing is through auctions, which bear the hazard of raising bids so high that winners are put in a disadvantageous financial position, at the very least, in the near-to-medium term.

Regarding the allocation of finite resources such as spectrum, Finland provides a best-practice example of a "light licensing" policy, which is one that involves no license fees and no extra burdens for investors. The case of Singapore illustrates the importance of flexibility. Singapore had initially planned to hold an auction for four third-generation (3G) licenses, but with only three bidders for three licenses, the government decided to simply award the incumbents the licenses for the price of SGD 100 million each (*The Economist* 2002). Meanwhile, Germany and the United Kingdom demonstrate the perils of auctions; from their auction of 3G mobile licenses, these governments earned only US$46 billion and US$36 billion, respectively (Isern and Ríos 2002).

Post-licensing rules also need to be clear; otherwise, companies can become mired in litigation. In the area of spectrum allocation, litigation could mean that the resource is left unused until the dispute is resolved. Legal uncertainty regarding license awards may prevent industry consolidation, given the implications of merger and acquisition activities, as well as bankruptcy proceedings.

Other than licensing, regulatory process issues requiring attention include rights of way issues, the allocation of universal service funds, and standard setting. The importance of setting standards is often underappreciated, but there is considerable lingering debate regarding the process and the extent of government/regulatory intervention. In some countries, the task of setting standards is solely in the domain of the private sector; in others, it is purely government-led, and in the remaining countries, both government and private sector take on the task or whatever international standards are in place are adopted. Significantly, the U.S. experience in setting standards for the wireless sector, which has been industry-led, compares much less favorably with government-led initiatives in Europe or Japan. Whereas a single wireless standard was adopted in Europe and Japan, the United States has several, illustrating how conflicting interests in the private sector can prevent the choosing of a single standard, which has the benefit of reducing the cost and complexity of the diffusion of a technology.

Another area in which regulatory process matters is the resolution of disputes. The most common dispute for telecommunications regulators involves interconnection, which entails correcting for the imbalance of negotiating power between incumbents and new entrants. The entry of numerous service providers means that regulators must ensure that the different networks are interoperable. Where possible, open access to networks must be promoted as it is essential to guarantee consumer choice; however, consumer choice must be balanced with the need to support innovation and provide incentives to innovate. A suggested principle in the area of convergence is technological neutrality; that is, equal terms and conditions in legislation for competition among different delivery channels (e.g., the same policies in broadcasting and telecommunication networks such as broadcast, cable, wire, wireless, and satellite). Indeed, open access and negotiation of interconnection costs are among the most contentious issues in ICT regulation.

Part III: Infrastructure

Without network infrastructure, a country cannot avail itself of the benefits of ICT. Thus, the third component of the environment index addresses the question: what type of policies need to be in place to ensure that the network infrastructure is accessible and is of a quality that will enable individuals, businesses, and governments to participate and benefit more fully in the networked economy?

While there is considerable complexity in the range of policy options and considerations involved, there are essentially six infrastructure-relevant issues that policymakers need to address: market structure (extent of privatization and liberalization), pricing, universal service, content, network quality, and supporting infrastructure. These sets of policy issues bear the greatest impact on the availability, affordability, and quality of network infrastructure. Countries that have achieved the highest rankings in terms of infrastructure are Iceland, the United States, Luxembourg, Japan, and Sweden, in descending order. Meanwhile, countries with the most room for improvement in infrastructure are Nicaragua, Zimbabwe, Bangladesh, and Haiti, also in descending order.

Market structure

The issue of market structure has perhaps the most direct and greatest impact on the rate of infrastructure deployment. Infrastructure deployment is a capital-intensive activity and, as such, the issue of market structure essentially has two aspects: what is the role of the government vis-à-vis the private sector, and how much competition is optimal? The former determines the government's privatization strategy, if any, while the latter defines the government's liberalization strategy.

It is important to note that the issue of market structure applies differently to telecommunications services, broadcasting, Internet services depending on the sector's scale of network economies and technology specifications. Even within the telecommunications sector, the optimal market structure can vary depending on the service: basic wireline, wireless, national long distance, international long distance, and Internet services.

What is the appropriate role of government in the provision of network infrastructure and services? The answer to this question varies not only among, but also within, countries. In the United States, more than 200 state and local governments are operating telecommunications businesses of one form or another, with more than 100 providing cable television service and others offering everything from Internet access to local telephony (Fidelman 1999). In some states, however, such as Texas and Missouri, local governments are banned from providing telecommunications services.[6]

In the international arena, remarkably, privatization of telecommunications has been the prevailing norm in recent years. The benefits of privatization in expanding network access and coverage, improving service quality, and increasing government revenues have been extolled in many countries by the private sector, governments, and multilateral organizations alike. In this context it is thus remarkable that China, the country that had the world's fastest rate of infrastructure deployment in the 1986 to 1999 period, accomplished such a feat without privatization and with the state firmly in control of management and ownership. China was also closed to direct foreign participation during this period; except for the last seven years of this period, the Chinese government was a monopoly.

That China liberalized its telecommunications sector underscores the importance of competition, although as its experience demonstrates, competition does not have to come from the private sector. The important thing is timing, as well as the design and execution of the liberalization process. In fact, if the regulatory capacity is in place, the earlier a sector is liberalized, the better. Finland is a case in point. From as early as the late 1980s, Finland began liberalizing its telecommunications sector, and today the country has one of the most extensive network diffusion and penetration rates in the world, with a wide availability of high-quality services at affordable prices.

It is also important to note that while privatization involves relinquishing government shares to private investors, the change in ownership does not guarantee effective introduction of competition; it may even still perpetuate a monopoly. But is a monopoly, or the absence of competition, necessarily disadvantageous? The case of Costa Rica demonstrates that it can be advantageous. The country has a national regulated monopoly, and also has one of the highest telephone penetration rates in the world. Indeed, the telecommunication sector lends to significant economies of scale and network economies present barriers to entry; often for developing countries, the sizes of the markets are too small to encourage competition.

Pricing

The issue of pricing relates to the problem of affordability, which itself has several dimensions ranging from affordability of access devices such as computers, telecommunications, and Internet services to (a lesser degree) affordability of upkeep and maintenance.

In the area of affordability of access devices, which is a prevalent problem among developing countries, Brazil shows a promising way of dealing with the problem. In Brazil, the government taps international computer manufacturers to develop a prototype for low-cost personal computers (PCs)—priced at about US$200 to US$250 per PC—while providing loans to low-income households to purchase the computers.

In terms of affordability of telecommunications services, the issue is significantly more complicated. ICT-related services have two facets: domestic and international. In the international arena, pricing issues include accounting rates, treatment of Internet telephony, and international telephone service pricing. Internet affordability in developing countries is particularly affected by the cost of connecting to international gateways. The International Private Lease Circuit still comprises the bulk of ISP costs (up to 80 percent in some cases), and like the cost of routers and switching equipment, is denominated in U.S. dollars; this makes Internet affordability highly sensitive to fluctuations in exchange rates. It is also important to note that end-user prices for Internet access are also affected by the degree of competition. Embratel of Brazil for instance, is cited as charging up to nine times the U.S. price for leasing high-speed circuits to ISPs and other telecommunications service providers (Bastos 2002). It is notable that the high cost of Internet access and, in some countries, telecommunication services, has precipitated innovations such as pre-paid Internet cards and pre-paid telephone cards for wireline and wireless services.

In the domestic arena, policymakers face decisions regarding three issues: a pricing regulatory regime, metered or non-metered service, and subsidies. The choice of pricing regime is a decision usually undertaken by the regulatory agency when choosing between price-cap regulation or rate-of-return regulation, or a variant of either regime. Like other pricing decisions, the choice of pricing regimes has direct implications for user affordability and the propensity of the service provider to invest in infrastructure. With regard to infrastructure, governments have other measures in their toolkit, such as revising depreciation schedules and accounting treatment of property and other physical assets.

On the issue of the choice between metered and unmetered service, the empirical evidence is most helpful. An Organisation for Economic Co-operation and Development (OECD) report on local access pricing and e-commerce shows the difference in the penetration of Internet hosts between countries with unmetered local telecommunication charges for Internet access and those with metered service to be a multiple of 6:1; that is, in countries with unmetered Internet access, including all charges, the average price for 150 hours of use at peak rates is US$38.06, while the average price in countries with metered Internet access is US$235.67 (Bastos 2002).

The third domestic pricing issue is that of subsidies. The issue of subsidies arises because of market failure; market mechanisms alone are not sufficient to ensure widespread individual access, particularly in distant and sparsely-populated areas and in places with challenging geographic terrain. Historically, one of the ways policymakers have addressed this issue is through geographically-based cross-subsidies. More recently, many countries have sought to address this issue through universal access/service schemes.

Universal access/service

In light of the market's failure to provide services in certain areas and problems of affordability in certain segments of society, most governments have universal service or universal access goals either covering basic telecommunications only or basic Internet access as well. In other countries, universal service goals have even been extended to broadband diffusion.

While a universal scheme, in which each household has access to the service, may be appealing, it may not be the most feasible course of action (particularly for developing countries) given the large amount of funding required for such an undertaking. A universal access scheme, which relies on community access points instead of individual household access, may be more appropriate. Interesting universal access initiatives have been launched in Brazil, Mexico, Canada, and United Kingdom. In Brazil, the postal service has launched Porta Aberta, or Open Door, a project that gives the public free access to Internet kiosks, but only in selected post offices in Sao Paolo and Rio de Janeiro.

Similarly, Mexico has established TELECENTROS, which at present is comprised of sixty public service centers that provide informatic and communications services, such as Internet access in twenty-eight cities of the Mexican Republic. More important, the Mexican government is planning the Mexican Telecommunications Program, which will develop a network of 2,000 informatic and communication centers and integrate 1,400 telegraphic offices and 600 post offices in the next two years. Despite one of the highest household Internet penetration rates, Canada has the Community Access Program, a federal government initiative administered by Industry Canada with 8,800 public Internet access sites. Likewise, the United Kingdom has set up UK Online centers to enable anyone who wants it to have access to the Internet and e-mail near home. A UK Online center could be in an Internet café, a public library, college, community center, village hall—anywhere that is accessible to the public. The U.K. government has allocated GBP 252 million of over a three-year period to set up a network of UK Online centers.

For developing countries, funding options for universal access strategies are noteworthy, given resource constraints. In several Latin American countries such as Peru, Brazil, and Chile, the governments have set up specific funds for this purpose. Peru has a rural telecommunications fund, while Brazil requires telecommunications operators to contribute one percent of total revenues to a universalization fund. Chile is particularly remarkable—it has launched a program that provides one-time subsidies for the installation of public telephones. Subsidies are paid out from a Telecommunications Development Fund (Fondo de Desarollo de las Telecomunicaciones), which is funded from the Chilean national government budget. Private operators are selected through a competitive bidding process, and it is remarkable that in the 1995 to 1999 period, US$21 million subsidies were granted to 183 projects covering 5,916 localities and 2.2 million inhabitants (Intven 2000:6–31).

Instead of creating a pool of funds for universal access, Estonia and the Philippines used another mechanism, concession agreements. Estonia awarded a concession agreement to Estonian Telephone Company that ensured connectivity in rural and scarcely-populated areas in return for lucrative urban contracts. However, a similar scheme had disappointing results in the Philippines. The Philippines' service access scheme required recipients of licenses to install 300,000 to 400,000 lines in designated areas in exchange for obtaining their licenses. Several carriers failed to comply with the requirements for various reasons, including the peso devaluation and difficulty in securing right of way permits. Of greater concern, however, is the fact that many of the lines installed under the scheme had no subscribers; for the carrier, these lines represent nonrevenue generating investments. From the perspective of the entire economy, the service area scheme has resulted in an inefficient allocation of resources.

Several countries have extended the definition of service goals beyond the traditional universal service to include broadband; the amount of bandwidth required, the funding mechanism, and the role of government vary among these countries. In the United States, the 1996 Telecommunications Act established a benchmark of 200 kbps—both upstream and downstream—for broadband access, but it did not stipulate universal access; rather, in Section 706 it urged the Federal Communications Commission and the state public utility commissions to encourage the deployment of "advanced telecommunications capabilities." Canada went further than the United States when it announced the goal of ensuring that broadband access is available to all communities in Canada by 2004. Japan is also ahead, and has already set up a special financing system for the deployment of fiber-optic and broadband networks.

The three countries that are among the furthest ahead in broadband rollout are South Korea, Singapore, and Sweden. South Korea has the highest per capita broadband penetration in the world, with 9.2 million broadband connections, or nearly two out of three of the country's 14 million households (Williams 2002). This penetration was made possible by the fact that South Korea has one of the lowest price levels of broadband in the world—partly because of liberalization in the telecommunications sector, and partly because years ago the government allowed the electric utility company, Kepco, to lease its unutilized fiber optic cables for its own use.

In contrast to South Korea, Singapore and Sweden represent more active and interventionist approaches by their respective governments.[7] In Singapore, the Government has launched a national initiative to provide access to information and communications infrastructure to all its citizens. The definition of infrastructure includes not only broadband access but also the delivery of advanced applications and services. The initiative, Singapore ONE, involves private sector partners, but the government has pledged full commitment, partly manifested in its US$300 million investment in infrastructure, as well as in fiscal and financial programs for the initiative. While Singapore may have the world's first nationwide broadband network, increasing demand for, and usage of, broadband applications is a lingering issue.

In Sweden, the legislature has passed a bill to provide high-speed Internet access to every household. To implement the "broadband everywhere" legislation, the government has planned to invest about US$20 billion to create an infrastructure that will be open to everyone. While the funding pool is considerable, each municipality is responsible for creating an infrastructure plan for developing local solutions through a system of state tax incentives. Although the planned network may compete with the infrastructure of Telia and other telecommunications companies, the state's role in the provision of infrastructure is well defined; the provision of services is clearly left to market forces.

Box 4. Regional Initiatives

Regional initiatives, such as e-Europe and e-ASEAN, provide excellent opportunities for concerted efforts at an intergovernmental level to create an environment supportive of Networked Readiness. Regional initiatives can be particularly relevant for developing countries in the areas of infrastructure, coordinating research and development efforts and harmonization of legal frameworks. A case in point is the Southern African Development Community which has produced, in collaboration with the World Economic Forum, a consultation report on e-readiness. One of the areas where a regional effort would be beneficial is in physical infrastructure. The need for interoperability is a compelling rationale. Moreover, benefits from economies of scale can be derived from joint procurement of equipment and other products and services. Other activities that benefit from being done on a regional scale include the creation of a regional backbone as well as establishing hubs and peering arrangements.

Regional organizations like ASEAN are also excellent platforms for gaining leverage when negotiating and settling disputes with countries such as the United States. For instance, several telecommunications operators in the Asia-Pacific region have issued a statement urging U.S. operators and ISPs to share the cost of the international Internet backbone between the United States and the Asia-Pacific region. Unlike other networks, such as in telecommunications, where the cost is shared between two parties, ISPs in developing countries currently shoulder the full cost of leased lines to Internet backbones in the United States. In the past, such an arrangement may have been justified since most of the content flowing on the Internet originated from the United States. Presently however, and looking ahead, traffic flow will increasingly come from the developing countries to the United States, and as regional Internet infrastructures improve, the amount of transit routed through the United States will also decrease. Given that the cost of international leased lines accounts for the bulk of ISP costs in developing countries, no other measure that will improve affordability of Internet access other than the successful negotiation of this petition. Developing countries can avail themselves of regional organizations and multilateral settings to successfully negotiate a cost-sharing arrangement of international Internet circuits.

Outside of physical infrastructure, there are benefits from the harmonization of laws, regulations, and technical standards in regional settings. Given the increasing amount of intraregional trade that has been spurred by regional free-trade areas, harmonization of regulations would facilitate seamless e-commerce transactions and logistics between member states.

In addition, regional organizations allow developing countries to share policy experiences and research and development efforts. Currently, developing countries do not have enough expertise to guide policymakers in using new technologies to accelerate economic development. Since many countries are in a similar catch-up mode, there is great value in learning from other countries' strategies and experiences. Formalizing this learning process by conducting it in a regional setting also has cost advantages in terms of producing benchmark studies and readiness assessments. Equally important, developing countries should combine research and development efforts, rather than rely on developed countries. Developed countries, for example, cannot be expected to expend significant effort developing affordable access devices that are less powerful, since demand in their markets is oriented towards technical enhancements rather than cost reductions.

In delineating the optimal scope of regional initiatives in the digital arena, developing countries must be careful to avoid redundancies. Given the urgency of the task and scarcity of resources, it is not optimal for regional initiatives to supplant national initiatives or duplicate other activities that are taking place in a broader, multilateral setting. Neither should regional initiatives in the digital arena venture into the realm of the private sector. Commercial projects such as profit-seeking portals and industry exchanges are better left to the private sector barring a clear case of market failure.

Content

In terms of promoting the use of networks by businesses, Canada, Norway, and the United Kingdom have notable initiatives. Canada's Ministry of Industry has ebiz.enable, which is a comprehensive online resource for guiding commercial organizations through the issues and options encountered in implementing e-business strategies. Likewise, Norway has the BIT Program, which includes twenty-two sectors and about 200 pilot companies, particularly targeting SMEs and their use of general ICT solutions. In the United Kingdom, the government has launched UK Online for Business, a major program within UK Online to help businesses succeed in new ways of working online.

Of the various ways to encourage use, promoting local content is one of the most direct and effective. South Korea, Austria, Costa Rica, Italy, and Portugal are among the countries offering the most remarkable array of initiatives designed to promote Internet use by individuals. South

Korea, for example, has launched its Ten Million People Informatization Education Program, targeting the part of the population that has not yet tapped into ICT. Austria has Circus Internet, a mobile training unit for Internet and ICT access, which started touring in June 2001 and will continue touring Austria for two years. The project is sponsored by the Federal Ministry of Science, Research, and Culture as well as by private companies. Austria also has eContent Austria, a program that consists of promotional activities for the content industry. Likewise, Costa Rica has become the first country in the world to offer all of its citizens their own e-mail account through its national portal costaricense.com. In Italy, the government provides 50 percent co-financing of libraries and multimedia centers that provide access and training to the public and are open at times other than standard office hours, such as late evening and weekends. In Portugal, the Ministry of Science and Technology has set up Access Unite to encourage access to, and inclusion of, citizens with special needs (physical or learning) in the networked economy.

Content regulation is a sensitive issue because it includes censorship and has an adverse effect on usage and consumer interest. Singapore and China are among the countries that exercise content regulation. While banning certain content is a matter of principle for government, as in the case of Singapore's ban on pornography, effective enforcement of content regulation is questionable.

Taxation of electronic commerce is also an important factor in encouraging network use by businesses and individuals, particularly for electronic commerce. A "technology-neutral" approach to electronic commerce avoids levying taxes on Internet-based electronic transactions. Thus far, the World Trade Organization has imposed a moratorium on customs duties for e-commerce transactions. It is notable, however, that this moratorium has a negative effect for developing countries that derive considerable customs duties for products, such as software, music, and movies, that lend themselves to electronic delivery.

Privacy and consumer data protection are important issues in promoting trust in the system, and trust encourages use. The OECD has launched several initiatives in this area, and of the OECD countries, Canada is particularly notable for its Personal Information Protection and Electronic Documents Act, which sets the rules for the protection of personal information and consumer data; moreover, industry and consumer representatives have also jointly developed a set of principles and guidelines for the protection of consumers conducting transactions online.

Significantly, not only do privacy and consumer data protection standards vary among countries, so does the implementation of these standards. In the United States, for instance, the government relies on industry self-regulation in the area of consumer data protection. Indeed, variations in standards and implementation cause frictions in cross-border electronic commerce and give rise to the question of whether harmonization would result in a ratcheting up or ratcheting down of standards.

Network quality

Networked Readiness requires that the information infrastructure and associated services operate within certain quality standards to ensure the optimal functioning of the networks. Ensuring network quality requires network service and support, monitoring of quality standards, and ensuring network security.

With regard to network service and support, Australia is particularly notable for its Internet Assistance Program, a three-year joint venture between the government and Telstra. Under the program, residential users have access to a range of help services to solve Internet problems, and are provided with an Internet speed of at least 19.2 kbps per second no matter where they live. In the area of software, Australia also has a Software Engineering Quality Centers Program, which was established to improve the quality and reliability of software produced in Australia.

In terms of monitoring standards of service, Singapore offers an example of vigorous implementation. The Singapore regulatory agency requires operators to publish data each year indicating their track record in meeting standards such as speed in supplying an ordered service and in responding to repair requests and billing inquiries, and other indicators of service quality, such as the percentage of calls dropped or terminated abnormally and calls lost due to busy channels (ITU 2001:28).

In addition to promoting trust through privacy and consumer data protection policies, a country's network infrastructure must also be secure from threats such as terrorism or fraudulent activities. One of the ways to address security concerns is by using cryptography, but governments have to balance law enforcement with security of transactions. The United States is notable for its stringent cryptography policies; because of the threat of terrorism, network security for this country is, more than ever before, a top priority.

Supporting infrastructure

Without the necessary supporting infrastructure, countries will be unable to fully capture the benefits of participating in the networked economy. The need for policies in this area is particularly relevant for developing countries with a deficient infrastructure in any or all of the four areas: electricity, postal system, customs and transport logistics, and financial payment infrastructure.

Most ICT devices, particularly computers, require electricity. As such, an electricity supply is a basic requirement for a country to be ready for the networked economy. Electrification alone, however, is not enough. It is important to ensure a stable supply in order to prevent power fluctuations that may otherwise adversely affect the functioning of ICT devices. Moreover, electricity costs have to be low or affordable enough to encourage continued use of ICT devices.

Improvements in postal systems, as well as in customs and transport logistics, are also particularly important if countries are to reap the full benefits of electronic commerce. Any gains of electronic commerce in the form of speed of transaction or costs of transaction have the potential to be nullified if the delivery of the product is impeded by problems in the postal system, such as slow delivery, theft, and difficulties returning goods through international parcel delivery. Problems in transport logistics, due to poor road, railroad, airport, and container port infrastructure, are all partly manifest in delays in parcel delivery. In addition, customs offices in most developing countries are bogged down with delays and high transaction costs due to cumbersome procedures. In the Philippines for instance, the Tariffs and Customs Code requires the following paper-based documentation for imports: sixty-nine copies of eighteen documents (Lallana et al 1999).

The benefits of electronic commerce will likewise be negated if there are no means in countries to facilitate electronic payment. This problem is most apparent in developing countries, where transactions are still done mostly through cash and checks. Even if credit card, debit card, and other cashless transactions gain popularity, countries must still address the challenge of setting up a payment gateway that facilitates the automated processing of settlements, whereby as soon as the pertinent information is sent to the bank or other settlement institutions, the payment is made to the merchant. In most developing countries, online merchants have to establish relationship with each bank separately, because the various banks are not yet able to smoothly interact with each other for online processing of settlements. This is partly because of conflicting banking systems.

Another area of the financial infrastructure that policymakers need to address is the need for identification and authentication. Developed countries are much more advanced in this regard, but even in these countries the most basic issues are still debated; that is: should certification authorities be government or commercial entities? If the authorities are commercial, should they be licensed or accredited by the government? If they are licensed or accredited, based upon what criteria? It is also notable that even when developed countries have resolved these questions, they still face problems in implementation. Finland, for

instance, instituted the government's Population Register Center as the certification authority and established FINEID, an electronic identification card. But after a year, only 11,000 electronic identification cards were issued and the associated electronic services did not become popular.

Conclusion

In the context of a global economy that is increasingly integrated, technology-driven, and knowledge-based, policymakers must craft a national ICT strategy that ensures that a country has the requisite environment for promoting Networked Readiness. The task entails ensuring that the market conditions, regulatory framework, and network infrastructure are in place to enable individuals, businesses, and governments to participate and benefit more fully in the networked economy.

In terms of market conditions, areas of attention include human resource development, access to capital markets, and promoting technological diffusion and innovation. To create appropriate market conditions, the policy framework must incorporate coordinated education, labor, trade, investment, banking, capital markets, and industrial policies.

Similarly, the legal and regulatory framework requires that in addition to the basic legal provisions for property rights and contract law, existing legislation must be renewed and complemented with provisions that reflect changes in technology as well as institutional and economic contexts. Regulatory capacity must be enhanced and due attention given to regulatory processes and the strategic use of various regulatory levers.

In terms of network infrastructure, there is considerable complexity in the range of policy options and considerations involved. But most considerations can be distilled into six infrastructure-relevant issues that policymakers need to address: market structure (extent of privatization and liberalization), pricing, universal service, content, network quality, and supporting infrastructure. These sets of policy issues have the greatest impact on the availability, affordability, and quality of network infrastructure.

Crafting the "right" environment for Networked Readiness may appear daunting to policymakers, particularly in developing countries. However, with policy guidance, the task is attainable when combined with a well-defined vision, the political will to commit the necessary resources, and the initiative to collaborate with the private sector and other key stakeholders in the development process.

Endnotes

1. Unless otherwise indicated, examples of initiatives are drawn from the country profiles of the Organisation for Economic Co-operation and Development *OECD Information Technology Outlook 2002* (2002), the Digital Opportunity *Initiative's Creating a Development Dynamic* (July 2001), and the World Economic Forum's *Annual Report of the Global Digital Divide Initiative* (January 2002).

2. A detailed discussion of the subindex components, corresponding weights, and the strengths and limitations of the methodology, has been included in a previous chapter of this *Report*.

3. Refer to the *Global Information Technology Report: Readiness for the Networked World 2001–2003* chapter that explains the Executive Opinion Survey.

4. For more information, visit http://www.netday.org.

5. Sachs and McArthur (2001) note that catch-up growth has its inherent limits. A non-core economy's ability to narrow the income gap between it and technology leaders further diminishes with the size of the remaining divide. In order to close the income gap fully, the non-core country must become a technology innovator; in other words, it must become part of the group of core countries.

6. See Moura (1999). A good source for understanding the legal underpinnings of the dispute is an article by James Baller and Sean Stokes entitled, *The Public Sector's Authority to Engage in Telecommunications Activities*. Online. http://munitelecom.org/v1i1/Baller.html.

7. For a detailed overview of broadband infrastructure deployment in OECD countries, read Umino (2002).

References

Bastos, T., P. O'Connor, and D. O'Connor. 2002. *Policies and Institutions for e-Commerce Readiness: What Can Developing Countries Learn from the OECD Experience?* (CD-ROM). Paris: Organisation for Economic Co-operation and Development.

Beardsley, S., et al. 2002. "The Elements of Successful Telecommunications Sector Reform." In *Global Information Technology Report: Readiness for the Networked World 2001–2002.* New York: Oxford University Press for the World Economic Forum.

Beardsley, S. and L. Enriquez. 2002. "A Regulatory Remedy for European Broadband," *McKinsey Quarterly* 1. Online. http://mckinseyquarterly.com.

The Economist. 2002. "Hanging on a Line," *Economist Global Agenda.*

Digital Opportunity Initiative. 2001. *Creating a Development Dynamic.* United Nations Development Program and Accenture (Markle Foundation).

Fidelman, M. 1999. "Welcome to the Journal of Municipal Telecommunication," *Journal of Municipal Telecommunications* 1(1).

International Telecommunication Union (ITU). 2001. *The Info-Communications Development Authority (IDA): A Case Study on Singapore's "Converged" Regulatory Agency.* Geneva: International Telecommunication Union.

Intven, H., ed. 2000. *Telecommunications Regulatory Handbook* (infoDev Program). The World Bank.

Isern, J. J. and M. M. Isabel Ríos. 2002. "Facing Disconnection: Hard Choices for Europe's Telcos," *McKinsey Quarterly* 1:82–90. Online. http://mckinseyquarterly.com.

Koselka, R. 2002. "Weathering Telecoms Dark and Stormy Night," *McKinsey Quarterly* 4:118–128. Online. http://mckinseyquarterly.com.

Lallana, E. C., R. N. S. Quimbo, and L. C. Salazar. 1999. "Business@Philippines.com: Electronic Commerce Policy Issues in the Philippines." Monograph.

Lopez-Bassols, V. 2002. *ICT Skills and Employment* (DSTI/DOC 10). Organisation for Economic Co-operation and Development.

McArthur, J. and J. D. Sachs. 2002. "Growth Competitiveness Index: Measuring Technological Advancement and the Stages of Development." In *Global Competitiveness Report 2001–2002.* New York: Oxford University Press for the World Economic Forum.

Moura, B. 1999. "A Look at Municipal Telecommunications," *Journal of Municipal Telecommunications* 1(1). Online. http://munitelecom.org/v1i1Moura.html.

Organisation for Economic Co-operation and Development (OECD). 2002. *OECD Information Technology Outlook 2002.* Paris: Organisation for Economic Co-operation and Development.

Paua, F. et al. 2001. "Information Infrastructure Development in China and India: Comparative Analysis, 1986–2000." Unpublished manuscript.

Townsend, D. N. 1999. "Telecommunications Regulatory Issues for Electronic Commerce." Briefing Report. International Telecommunication Union, Eighth Regulatory Colloquium.

Umino, A. 2002. *Broadband Infrastructure Deployment: The Role of Government Assistance* OECD No. DSTI/DOC 15. Organisation for Economic Co-operation and Development.

United Nations Development Programme (UNDP). 2001. *Human Development Report 2001.* New York: Oxford University Press.

Williams, M. 2002. "South Korean Broadband Subscriptions Pass 9 Million," *InfoWorld* July 30.

World Economic Forum (WEF). 2002. *Annual Report of the Global Digital Divide Initiative.* Geneva: World Economic Forum.

Chapter 3

Ready for the Networked Future?

The Role of the Individual in the Networked Society

**Dirk Reiter, Helmut Meitner, and
Carsten H. Rossbach**

Roland Berger Strategy Consultants

The Information and Communication Technology Context

By supporting information exchange and communication between individuals, information and communication technology (ICT) enables the growth of a knowledge-based society, which is deemed to be a natural and desirable development step for nations. ICT is widely accepted as being a major driver of growth. ICT increases economic welfare or, to put it simply, it improves the standard of living. This improvement occurs in two ways.

First, the growth of ICT industries in itself contributes to overall welfare. Second, and more important, however, ICT—as a function—contributes to growth in all other industry segments. It has been "the catalyst of change in business, partly responsible for a major restructuring of firms, a change in work organization, and enabling the firms to reorganize transactions, reduce routine transaction costs and rationalize and restructure supply chains. Manufacturing has become more efficient, inventories and overheads have been reduced as coordination cost along supply chains have dropped, and ICT applications have been part of innovation in services" (OECD 2001a).

The extent to which a nation can profit from the potential of ICT is therefore crucial to the economic prospects of its citizens. The Global Information Technology Report 2002–2003 assesses countries' "Networked Readiness" by calculating a Networked Readiness Index (NRI). This index reflects the level of information and communication in a particular country via a hierarchical indicator model. Naturally, a major factor within the NRI model is the individual, and his or her motivation and ability to take advantage of ICT.

In order for ICT to function as a catalyst for growth, individuals must adopt certain skills and behaviors. However, individual behaviors and skills are also subject to certain framework conditions.

Accordingly, the goal of this article is to sketch a picture of ICT demand and usage by individuals, now and in the coming years, to determine what action items need to be on the agendas of stakeholders in governments and businesses in order to prepare for this networked future.

To determine what actions will be necessary, we first discuss ICT usage and readiness requirements in individual, real-life situations. This offers insights, but presents only partial implications; we proceed, therefore, by proposing a more general ICT framework model from the perspective of the individual. This allows us to identify the necessary enablers, motivations, and supply-side structures, and to analyze each in terms of current status and trends. In this way we determined the fields of action, summarized in our "action agenda for the networked future."

Some Scenarios of ICT Usage by Individuals

ICT providers propose a wealth of devices and applications that have one common element: the vision of a completely networked world. But what does this "networked world" look like? What does "ubiquitous information and communication" really mean? In order to gain a better understanding of these concepts, we will discuss some specific ICT usage scenarios.

To do so, we will focus on two environments:

1. Working space, and

2. Living space.

The boundaries between these two areas are naturally blurred. Furthermore, ICT itself is increasingly integrating living and working environments by, for example, enabling teleworking. However, we will use these focal points to differentiate between the relevant technology and its development.

Working space—knowledge workers

What is a knowledge worker? Presumably, we could call someone a knowledge worker if his or her primary means of production is information. Since this description is very general, it can apply to doctors, journalists, lawyers, teachers, researchers, and so on (Drucker 2001). Let's take a look at one of these professions and imagine how it can be further affected by ICT.

The Internet initiated many changes in the workplace. Journalists have always been the classic prototype of a knowledge worker. Their input is information. Journalists add value by evaluating, collating, and editing this information. In order to perform their tasks, they have to research and communicate.

Since information and communication are the core factors in any journalist's tasks, ICT offers massive potential for increasing productivity. Mobile access to databases for researching and submitting draft articles represents a major productivity gain. In addition, with the proliferation of mobile bandwidth, photographic and video content, in particular, will be submitted electronically directly from the scene. Videoconferencing will increase teamwork. Communication tools will support supraregional and even global collaboration of widely dispersed teams. Draft articles can be discussed interactively using groupware and collaborative tools. These applications can help journalists become more efficient in their daily tasks, if they have the training necessary to use such tools. However, the tools will not change the nature of the journalist's work.

Many of these examples, such as on-site research and editing via mobile Internet access as well as text processing, are already standard tasks for many journalists. However, ICT can help journalists become not only more efficient, but also more effective. How? Imagine a scenario in which intelligent software agents perform basic tasks such as research, filtering, and even editing. The journalist's value-added thus shifts from evaluating, collating, and editing information to approving pre-researched and pre-edited drafts and refining processing frameworks for software agents. Once configured, these software applications can scan various information sources and process the information they obtain. Over time, through processing and interacting with journalists via framework adjustments, these agents will develop recognition patterns that can perform increasingly evaluative, and even creative, work that previously had to be done by journalists.

In this way, ICT could eventually trigger even more disruptive shifts in journalists' tasks by changing the very nature of their work. Journalists might experience the same challenges they would have faced were they promoted from a professional to a managerial position. This would, of course, have an impact on training and qualification requirements. In contrast to efficiency gains through ICT support, the use of such intelligent agents requires a more holistic and management-oriented education. This leads us to the conclusion that the knowledge economy transforms not only industrial workers into knowledge workers—or knowledge technicians, according to Peter Drucker (2001)—but also "classic" knowledge workers into knowledge-leveraged workers; that is, information-based professionals whose tasks are fundamentally changed by ICT. A basic PC training class will not be sufficient for developing the guidance and approval skills that will comprise the journalists' core capabilities.

The ICT-driven evolution of working requirements also goes hand in hand with other developments in the working space. These are probably explained more adequately from a macroeconomic or sociological perspective than by ICT development. Take the example of rapid growth in the older population in developed countries. With medical development moving at a fast pace, it is expected that people will have to work much longer than they do today before reaching retirement. At the same time, the average duration of employment at a specific company or institution is decreasing. Working relations are becoming more flexible and project based. Again, this is strongly connected to the potential offered by communication and interaction, leveraged by technology that permits geographic decoupling of employer, client, and fulfillment location.

These issues show that ICT will not only accelerate a society's transformation from an industrial- and service-based into a knowledge-based one through efficiency gains, but that ICT will also change the nature of the knowledge work performed by humans. This, however, will require a shift in the way we develop skills and professions for individuals.

Living space—ICT teenagers

Let us discuss ICT exposure for teenagers in developed countries. From an ICT perspective, children's and teenagers' lives are extensively influenced by "natural" ICT exposure. Children are exposed to ICT from the very first days of their lives. They are growing up with these technologies, and perceive them as a natural part of the environment—in their cognizance of technology in their family surroundings, and in kindergarten, school, and leisure-time experiences. However, interest in ICT is not only a voluntary "pull" phenomenon, but also a "push" development triggered by group pressure and social requirements.

At home, ICT exposure has expanded from personal computers (PCs) and classic consumer electronics to a wide variety of devices and applications. Widespread access to broadband will change the PC from a working and gaming device to a communication/rich media device. Consumer electronics such as televisions, videocassette recorders, and stereos are converging. Digital music files in MP3 format have replaced a significant portion of the more traditional compact disc format. Digital video disc writers and players are bridging the gap between the PC and video/music worlds. Fixed network video telephony will also be fostered by the arrival of broadband access on the mass market. Though still struggling with mass-market penetration, digital and interactive television will slowly replace traditional analog broadcast technology. Home security and facility automation are each being connected to internal networks and becoming more intelligent. Wireless networks will be increasingly used for local area networks that connect facility/building components and home appliances. Electronic games are "cool" and subject to fashion cycles, be it the infamous "tamagotchi" wave or multi-user local area network (LAN) parties. However, there is one ICT device that has become a true cultural symbol: the mobile telephone.

Technology-driven innovations in ICT have often been associated with great expectations. Take European 3G/Universal Mobile Transmission Standard (UMTS) license auctioning, for example. Even as the new economy was already struggling, billions of dollars were spent on exploiting a new mobile telephone technology. Nobody could anticipate time-to-market or even the kind of mobile data services that would refinance investments in licenses and infrastructure. While today's applications and business case pricing focus on corporate high-yield users, a key mass-market segment is often overlooked: children and teenagers.

The mobile telephone penetrates our children's lives from as early on as elementary school. According to the Wireless World Forum (2002), at the beginning of 2002 there were more than 100 million mobile phone users aged five to twenty-four in North America, Western Europe, Japan, and China. Though originally designed as a voice-transmitting device, text messaging remains the most popular application by far in this segment. However, there is more to mobile teenagers than voice, data, and text messages. A strong "mobile culture" has established the mobile telephone "as an icon of the physical day-to-day world that exists in the youth's own world, whereas the Internet, in many cases, is still considered virtual" (Wireless World Forum 2002).

Nowhere is the symbolic significance of the mobile telephone for young people more clearly visible than in Japan. With the mobile Internet service I-mode and its successor FOMA, NTT DoCoMo has created an amazing youth culture that is expressed in mobile communications and entertainment applications, and in the richly decorated mobile telephone itself. There is not a Japanese teenager to be found who has not attached to his or her mobile telephone a "sutorappu," a gadget-adorned strap that symbolizes ideals, values, and idols, or that represents just another electronic gizmo.

This is a good example of the incentive aspect, as opposed to "natural" exposure. The behavior of children and teenagers is increasingly determined by incentives, pressure, and the persuasion of consumer goods advertising and corresponding brand positions. ICT devices and usage patterns are also becoming more and more important when it comes to group adherence and status. In fact, they are a fashion product, bought not to be used, but to achieve status within the peer group.

Of course, the use of ICT devices for status bears many risks as well. As a symbol of social status, ICT devices provoke conflict. Another risk is that the misuse of Internet and mobile devices can cause serious harm through interaction with the output of the device. For example, there is potential danger to a child's development through unsuitable content, such as violence and sexually-oriented offerings available via the Internet. Furthermore, unsuitable use of the Internet also creates security risks, since a child, if not supervised, might not be aware that he or she is opening confidential information or effecting significant financial transactions.

In the special case of the mobile telephone, there has been extensive discussion about kids generating excessive charges on their parents' mobile subscriber contract. Prepaid offerings provide an opportunity to control children's mobile telephone usage and mitigate the dangers described. Finally, there is one major area of concern for young, heavy-ICT users: the threat of isolation. While increased communication via the Internet can expand a person's horizon and network of peers, it can also isolate that person from real-world social interaction. It is the task of all relevant parts of society to act responsibly to manage the risks associated with ICT use.

ICT Environment for the Individual—Trends of Today and Tomorrow

As can be seen in both the living and working space examples, there are common factors that enable ICT usage and that serve as incentives to do so. Therefore, it is worthwhile to take a look at the underlying mechanisms that are necessary to facilitate universal access to and use of ICT by individuals. The examples above also provide an initial indication of how decision-making requirements for relevant stakeholders are changing due to the impact of ICT in terms of, for example, providing education and training.

So what are the more general trends and observations that affect these scenarios? To be more complete, we have to adopt a broader view of the ICT environment of the individual. To discuss this, we have proposed a model based on three core elements: enablers, incentives, and the value chain of ICT activity (see Figure 1).

Figure 1. **The ICT Environment of the Individual**

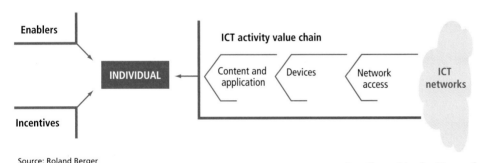

Source: Roland Berger

Typically, we would discuss the ICT environment from an economic supply and demand perspective, incorporating innovation and technological change. Alternatively, a more political, psychological, or sociological approach could be applied.

In discussions about the digital divide, authors often focus on creating access possibilities for women, minorities, and developing countries (Twist 2002). Therefore, access—which we consider part of an industry value chain—is typically treated as an "enabler" for bridging the digital divide. In contrast, we think it is worthwhile to consider not just access, but the complete ICT industry picture. Access and interconnection, even in the case of subsidized community telecenters, will always be provided through private services at some point in the network, not through government institutions or non-governmental organizations (NGOs).

Therefore, we think it is essential for governments to not only provide funding for specific minority access projects, but to also establish and secure a stable and prospering private industry in all parts of the ICT value chain. This will guarantee efficient and effective capitalization of ICT potential, while at the same time addressing the challenges of the digital divide.

We therefore propose a framework model that describes three core ICT areas from the perspective of the individual. First, there are "enablers," which we understand to be activities and framework conditions initiated by government or NGOs and supranational and other bodies, such as educational and training organizations. "Incentives" are intended to incorporate motivational and behavioral factors into our framework. Finally, "value chain components" describe a rough and simplified structure of the relevant industries. This model element comprises network access, devices, and content and applications. Let us take a look at each of these areas and discuss some of the current trends and future developments in this ICT framework.

Enablers: socioeconomic and educational aspects

When referring to the digital divide, a lot of research analyzes the context of information-haves and information-have nots in developed countries.[1] Less attention is paid to the international digital divide between developed and developing countries. Across the countries of the world, there are different framework conditions that enable individuals to use ICT. This is reflected in the Networked Readiness Index. Developing countries, in particular, face great challenges in their effort to not lose ground in ICT developments while struggling with very serious and basic problems in their societies. Peace, health, a decent standard of living, literacy, and civil rights; a stable political environment; and economic growth are far from omnipresent in all countries of the world. Of course, certain advancements in ICT cannot be compared directly with these goals. However, we strongly believe that ICT can help to achieve at least some of these conditions by, for instance, supporting freedom of speech through exchange of information and communication. In addition, economic growth, and thus the general standard of living, will be affected by ICT-related industry structures.

The starting positions of many countries are poor; ICT penetration in developing countries is still very low. How do nations escape the chicken-and-egg problem of fostering ICT usage? We see two aspects to the issue of creating ICT enablers. First, education and training are necessary. Second,

47

Chapter 3 Ready for the Networked Future? The Role of the Individual in the Networked Society

Figure 2. Characteristics of Developing Regions

Sociocultural context

Latin America and Caribbean–Western culture patterns, from religion to "life style" matters–Iberian heritage

Middle East and North Africa–Rich and complex cultural heritage, with some Western influences

South Asia–Rich and complex cultural heritage, with overall few Western influences

Sub-Saharan Africa–Many nature-oriented cultures with little Western influence on most of the population (varies from country to country)

GNI per capita (US$, 2000)

Latin America and Caribbean $7,030

Middle East and North Africa $5,240

South Asia $2,200

Sub-Saharan Africa $1,580

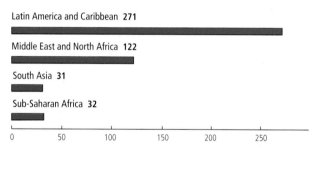

Fixed and mobile telephone lines per 1,000 people

Latin America and Caribbean 271

Middle East and North Africa 122

South Asia 31

Sub-Saharan Africa 32

PCs per 1,000 people (2000)

Latin America and Caribbean 44

Middle East and North Africa 31

South Asia 4

Sub-Saharan Africa 9

Youth illiteracy ages 15–24 (2000) ■ Female □ Male

Latin America and Caribbean F=6% M=6%

Middle East and North Africa F=24% M=12%

South Asia F=40% M=23%

Sub-Saharan Africa F=27% M=17%

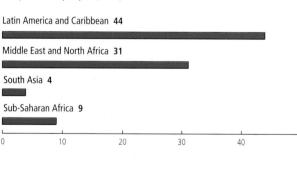

Source: World Bank, Roland Berger

the general population has to have access to ICT. In our model, the value chain represents a functioning ICT industry. Within this economic perspective, which is described below, we assume, of course, that there is enough demand-side buying power to support this industry. However, this is often not the case. The mobile telephone environment in Brazil, for example, shows that access coverage in many countries is restricted to only the wealthiest regions.

However, network access is a prerequisite and has to be treated as an enabler if the majority of individuals cannot afford it privately. If this is the case, ICT must be subsidized by both local government activities and the efforts of the international community. Since ICT is an information product, financial development aid will not suffice. In addition, international bodies will have to initiate training programs for local experts who can further develop local ICT infrastructures.

Consider sub-Saharan Africa. A good example of the latter approach is the United Nations Educational, Scientific, and Cultural Organization's publication of the Community Telecenter Cookbook for Africa (Jensen 2001), a guide for establishing local ICT access structures in rural areas.

Local initiatives are increasing, as well, at the government level (e.g., The African Information Society Initiative), in private industry (e.g., the AfricaOne broadband venture), and at the NGO level (e.g., SchoolNetAfrica). However, there is still a long way to go. As the Nobel laureate economist Amartya Sen pointed out, "no substantial famine has ever occurred in a democratic and independent country, no matter how poor." The same is true for the information famine (Akst and Jensen 2001).

Apart from sociodemographic, political, and economic aspects, there is one universal enabler that is a prerequisite for ICT usage by individuals in any country: education. As ICT enablers, education and training have two dimensions. First, by teaching individuals how to use ICT, education and training have a direct impact on understanding and employing ICT in both living and working spaces. Second, because ICT increasingly supports and replaces basic and even advanced professional activities, as seen in the journalist example, general and holistic adaptation of the education and training environment is urgently needed.

For most countries, this probably goes hand in hand with increasing expenditures for education. There are still a lot of differences, even between developed countries. For example, macroeconomic figures tell us that most European countries rank well behind the United States in expenditures on education as a percentage of gross domestic product.

Figure 3. **Mobile Coverage of Brazil Through Telefónica and Portugal Telecom**

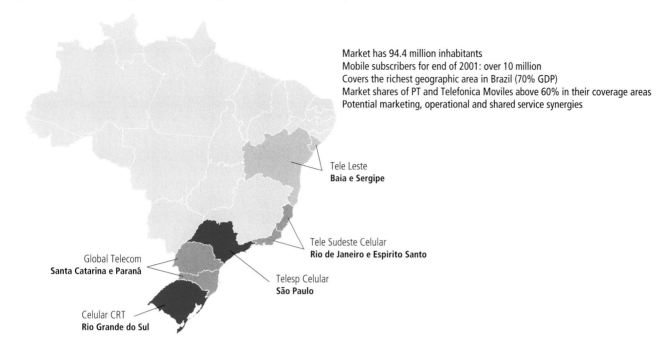

Market has 94.4 million inhabitants
Mobile subscribers for end of 2001: over 10 million
Covers the richest geographic area in Brazil (70% GDP)
Market shares of PT and Telefonica Moviles above 60% in their coverage areas
Potential marketing, operational and shared service synergies

Tele Leste
Baia e Sergipe

Tele Sudeste Celular
Rio de Janeiro e Espirito Santo

Global Telecom
Santa Catarina e Paraná

Telesp Celular
São Paulo

Celular CRT
Rio Grande do Sul

Source: Portugal Telecom report

Figure 4. **EU Education Expenditures**

Education expenditure (private)
2000 (percent of GDP)

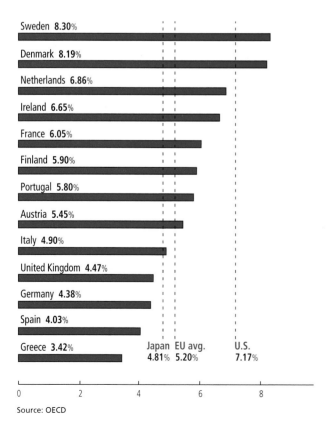

Sweden **8.30**%
Denmark **8.19**%
Netherlands **6.86**%
Ireland **6.65**%
France **6.05**%
Finland **5.90**%
Portugal **5.80**%
Austria **5.45**%
Italy **4.90**%
United Kingdom **4.47**%
Germany **4.38**%
Spain **4.03**%
Greece **3.42**%

Japan **4.81**% EU avg. **5.20**% U.S. **7.17**%

0   2   4   6   8

Source: OECD

Figure 5. **Education Expenditure per Capita and NRI Ranking**

Education expenditure
per capita 2000 (EUR)

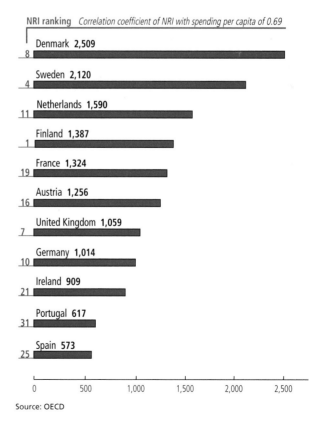

NRI ranking   *Correlation coefficient of NRI with spending per capita of 0.69*

Denmark **2,509**
8

Sweden **2,120**
4

Netherlands **1,590**
11

Finland **1,387**
1

France **1,324**
19

Austria **1,256**
16

United Kingdom **1,059**
7

Germany **1,014**
10

Ireland **909**
21

Portugal **617**
31

Spain **573**
25

0   500   1,000   1,500   2,000   2,500

Source: OECD

49

Chapter 3 Ready for the Networked Future? The Role of the Individual in the Networked Society

However, the essential relationship between ICT development, Networked Readiness, and education is also obvious. Looking at a European sample, a correlation coefficient of 0.69 shows there is a relatively high correlation between education spending per capita and NRI ranking.

ICT incentives: motivational and behavioral aspects

What incentives are there for the individual to use ICT? In order to discuss this question, it is important to keep in mind that individuals do not always voluntarily initiate their exposure to ICT. Voluntary "pull" usage of ICT—in addition to supporting professional tasks—is comprised of the following:

1. Fulfilling flexible communication needs;

2. Bridging time gaps;

3. Investing in one's own human capital;

4. Gaining social status; and

5. Leisure and entertainment.

However, there are also "push" forces, such as channel restrictions and peer pressure.

Of course, fulfilling communication needs is the most basic incentive for people to use ICT. We believe in the hypothesis that most actual ICT use is triggered by professional business requirements, be it the use of a PC or a mobile telephone.

However, in analyzing the perspective of the individual, we find that there are also other triggers apart from purely professional ones; it is not only the need to be informed or to communicate that stimulates ICT usage. Generally, human beings are dependent on social interaction. However, modern life situations, especially in large urban agglomerations, are threatening the individual with isolation. The mobile telephone fulfills the psychological function of a helpful companion; it is always there and it offers the individual a certain sense of security. Similarly, Internet access promises communication with peer groups, perhaps even anonymously. You can always get connected.

These devices not only offer insurance against isolation and emergency situations, but also act as the individual's "little helper" in bridging time. Here is a typical situation after stepping out of an airplane: people turn on their mobile telephones to immediately notify others that they have now landed and will arrive at their destination shortly. If the airplane was on time, the useful content of such calls often approaches zero. Instead of fulfilling the need to communicate, mobile telephone usage is triggered by randomly appearing waiting times. A

personal digital assistant (PDA) organizer often performs the same task. It offers the individual something to do other than light a cigarette. In the case of the mobile telephone, there is the additional benefit that the activity appears useful and important to others. The result is a sense of elevated social status.

There are also incentives that are based more on rational than on emotional grounds. ICT usage can be an investment by the individual in his or her own human capital, thereby raising the individual's market value. Command of ICT usage enables the individual to benefit from time, cost, and quality advantages for professional tasks. The hope of the individual is that this increase in efficiency will, in turn, be rewarded with (potential) employers. The result is a direct return on investment that is measurable in financial terms or career progress.

Usage for entertainment and leisure purposes is another incentive. The basic benefits of the Internet, such as bridging distance, fast communication, and the possibility of finding information and peers that are not readily available in the individual's physical environment, are just as applicable to leisure activities as they are to business activities.

On the "push" side, there are many situations where individuals have no choice other than to use ICT services.

In some cases, an electronic communication channel may be the only option an individual has to contact others. This is particularly true in the field of customer relationship management, where many corporations have streamlined their customer interaction channels by introducing ICT-based intelligent applications. Call centers are trying to increase efficiency by using voice technology and interactive voice response systems to handle routine customer calls. Web-based channels that automate most standard transactions are being established in the financial services sector. The rationale for companies is obvious, but older people, in particular, are not yet fully convinced that their inquiries are an 80:20-rule standard process that can be answered and processed by computers. Of course, traditional sales and service channels are still available most of the time, but customers have to help bear the higher transaction cost of these channels by paying higher fees.

Gaining social status via ICT possession and command is just one side of the coin, however. Group pressure arises, even among our young children, when it comes to flaunting the most innovative ICT gizmo in the schoolyard, be it a mobile telephone, PDA, or some other device. The individual fear of "falling behind" is further amplified by the peer pressure resulting from open and hidden symbols of exclusion of the late-adopter community.

Finally, one could even argue that the sum of incentives add so much value to the economic, psychological, and motivational well-being of the individual that, in some cases, typical symptoms of addiction can be found in ICT usage patterns. Returning to the example of stepping off an airplane: sometimes the mobile telephone even wins the priority battle against the first cigarette after a nonsmoking flight, even after leaving the airport premises.

ICT value chain: technological and economic aspects

A networked world supports a knowledge-based society in which information is the main resource. We are already seeing information and knowledge workers gaining an important share in the sectoral structures of developed economies.

Even a very general view of industry structure shows significant differences in the degree to which various industries are advancing into the knowledge- and service-based economy. There is, of course, a high correlation between the Networked Readiness Index and the share of private services in national gross national products. Among developed countries, Europe is clearly the slowest region in terms of migrating to a knowledge- and service-based economy. Comparing employment by sector in 2000, Europe, with just 55 percent of employment in the private services sector, is still far behind the United States (62 percent).

More specifically, investments in ICT are low in Europe compared to the United States and Japan. While average ICT expenditure per capita between 1995 and 2000 reached EUR 2,050 in the U.S. and EUR 1,578 in Japan, the EU average is just EUR 1,117. This is also reflected in specific ICT indicators, such as the number of Internet hosts per 1,000 inhabitants or the percentage of population online. But how can we increase these figures? Let us look at what is happening at each step in the ICT value chain.

Network access

Innovations in multiplexing technology make it possible to dramatically increase the capacity of existing fiber networks within network backbones. This is one of the main reasons for the currently ongoing consolidation among telecommunications carriers. This overcapacity could easily enable rich media for individuals. As we have seen, rich media is one of the basic requirements for advanced ICT applications. However, the bottleneck that has yet to be overcome is the limitations of local access networks.

According to the Organisation for Economic Co-operation and Development (OECD), in 2001, only one out of every 100 inhabitants of OECD countries subscribed to high speed Internet access; the leading OECD country surpassed ten subscribers per 100 inhabitants in 2001. The OECD

suggests that the challenge for all countries is to emulate and exceed that target as quickly as possible to break through current access bottlenecks (OECD 2001b). For video-on-demand to become available to the mainstream, it is necessary to operate the last mile at minimum speeds of around 256 kbps for downstream transmission. About half of the broadband services offered to residential customers in OECD countries in June 2001 were based on access via cable modems, and the other half via digital subscriber line technology. Other technologies, such as direct satellite services and fiber-to-home, were neglected, however—they could be much more economically efficient for most consumers through near-video-on-demand applications instead of full-fledged video streaming.

How can that minimum bandwidth speed be achieved in the last mile? Liberalization of local access was seen as the key enabler of mass-market broadband access. Most developed countries have taken initial steps to introduce a competitive environment. However, regarding opening the network elements, the results of unbundling the local loop and line sharing are not yet in line with expectations. The process of upgrading network hardware was found to be costly, and nobody has volunteered to take on the financial burden. If these problems are not circumvented, telecommunications incumbents will continue to have a dominant position in non–city-center access locations. This could result in the consolidation of Internet service providers if the regulators are not preventing these natural monopolies from taking over the internet service provision market. In that case, consumer pricing and individual usage of course would behave accordingly.

The mobile industry also faces challenges. As we have discussed, infrastructure investments, and in some cases licensing costs, have caused the stability of the mobile industry to deteriorate—this deterioration includes carriers, network equipment providers, handset manufacturers, and content providers. From a network operator point of view, we can see three major uncertainties within the mobile business system that have not yet been resolved.

First, which nonvoice services and applications will the customer demand? We will discuss this question later, in the section on content.

Second, alternatives to 3G technologies are appearing. Will wireless LAN (WLAN), bluetooth, or other technologies replace current GSM- or CDMA-based technology platforms? We believe WLAN will dominate in low-security applications, but that it will not be used in business models to replace entire 3G mobile plans. WLAN network technologies are unlikely to be economically feasible for the mass market in the medium-to-long term. Therefore, these technologies will be provided for free as part of larger service offerings (e.g., for

Figure 6. Global Presence of Major Mobile Operators (2001)

Source: Company reports, Roland Berger

hotels and airports) or will keep their "guerilla status" based on illegal flat-fee fixed-line subscriber activity that provides WLAN access to large urban agglomerations. Similarly, bluetooth seems to have found its niche applications, but will not endanger 3G mobile access.

Third, and most interesting, is the fact that industry structure is highly dynamic and creates uncertainty in the competitive environment. How will it consolidate? What kind of vertical structure will evolve? Which layer will coordinate content, and will the same players provide customer care and billing? Will we see a worldwide carrier oligopoly? Or will we perhaps see the appearance of budget and premium operators? Will liquidity problems drive even incumbent players back into the safe haven of government? Since these issues will determine the kind and quality of mobile service offerings for individuals, we want to analyze these developments in greater depth.

From our point of view, there will be no dominant customer ownership strategy across all carriers and regions. In the new economy, customer ownership suddenly became one of the most important criteria in determining the value of a firm. Transaction prices of mergers and acquisitions were measured in U.S. dollars per customer, especially in the Internet portal and mobile telecommunications industries. Customer ownership was regarded as the one sustainable competitive advantage a company could have. Existing customer relations were to be capitalized using various approaches that, of course, were not really tangible in most business models. Finally, these business models became

obsolete when it began to become clearer that capitalization of customer interfaces was not easy as it was supposed to be.

However, it is the legacy of this school of thought—among other reasons—that caused the first attempt at mobile Internet, the wireless application protocol, or WAP, to be a substantial flop, as the carriers kept the client interface vigorously within their reach. The result: unlike the classic fixed Internet, there was no decentralized development of applications by independent programmers in the mobile Internet. Mobile Internet applications were scarce and quality was poor. In the end, the market did not accept the offerings.

Despite this experience, scale, as measured by the number of customers and capitalization of the installed network infrastructure, is still the driving force in the mobile business. Through rigorous internationalization, a few players have been able to achieve critical scales (see Figure 6).

Of course, each region of the world has a different market environment for mobile carriers. This means that business models have to be adapted. For example, the voice markets in Europe and the United States are rather mature, with decreasing average revenue per user (ARPU) currently around EUR 20 to EUR 25. Carrier attention has shifted to data services that are taking an increasingly important share of ARPU. In contrast, in the Asia Pacific region, voice revenue still accounted for more than 95 percent of ARPU in 2000, and is expected to decrease to around 75 percent in 2005 (Gartner Group 2001).

So what might the mobile industry look like in five years? One scenario—which is not unlikely—could be a shift to Asia Pacific-centric industry structures, away from current European domination of the industry. Let us assume European 3G rollout is further delayed due to the heavy investment burdens under which European carriers suffer. Legal action by disappointed carriers who cannot capitalize on the 3G licenses auctioned in 2000 will stifle further moves by regulators to ease that burden. Additionally, Europe will suffer greatly from health-related concerns. Governments are being forced to stiffly regulate base station locations and emission levels. Carrier networks are consolidating; smaller players will pull back from 3G strategies. As in the airline industry, some will become low-cost mobile carriers that focus on pure voice offerings for mass-market customers.

In contrast, the mobile industry will grow in the Asia Pacific region; China will be the region's mobile growth engine. China Mobile has recently overtaken Vodafone as the world's number one carrier in terms of number of customers. Similar to the development in other industries, Asian corporations are currently building up core and radio networks and handset technology step by step, with the help of European and U.S. know-how. Industrial politics in Asian nations is focusing increasingly on mobile industries, and government backing excludes local players from the worldwide consolidation. Strong subsidy activity will attract further technology transfer from the jump-starting mass-market penetration of 3G technology in Asia.

What does this scenario mean from an individual perspective? Basically, countries like China have the opportunity to offer their citizens network access in a state-of-the-art environment, taking over traditional mobile industry centers. As an ICT enabler, mobile network access is leveraging even rural and distant populations, and simply skipping some steps in the development path taken by Western populations.

Devices

The strongly expected convergence of hardware devices has lost momentum during the past year, and the promised universal access device does not seem to have penetrated the mass market. Specialized devices for different applications such as organizers, transactions, gaming, and so on, seem to remain superior to universal devices. However, the fixed relationship between individual Internet access and a personal access device such as the firmly installed home PC is disappearing.

Instead, Internet accounts are being increasingly used on a call-by-call basis. Third parties are hosting corresponding communication services. Internet access is thus becoming increasingly device independent, enabling a rich variety of access devices to accommodate the individual's location and life-style. These include laptop and palmtop PCs, data-enabled mobile telephones, specialized e-mail devices, set-top boxes for televisions, and telematics devices for vehicles. In reality, many people already carry at least three digital devices when on vacation: a mobile telephone, a PDA, and a digital camera, each with its own set of basic data, such as addresses. One major task for the industries of this sector is, therefore, to align and standardize synchronization processes since, for the time being, the PC will remain the data hub of the device universe.

Undoubtedly, introducing vehicle telematics devices into private vehicles will be a major trend from the individual's perspective. Telematics devices are, in effect, introducing ICT into the vehicle. In 2000, each person in Germany spent 270 hours in a car. The potential of telematics devices include car-specific applications such as navigation, safety and emergency, and vehicle control and maintenance, as well as noncar specific services such as communication, mobile commerce, and information services. Which one of these services will decide the mass-market success of telematics devices?

The application the industry is looking for is the most basic one: safe, mobile, in-vehicle communication. Triggered by increased personal mobility, the definition of successful telematics offerings revolves around this need. However, the real question the industry has not answered so far is how much individuals are willing to pay for such services. Current original equipment manufacturer strategies in the automotive arena to connect telematics features as a standard component are not helping to find the answer to that question, since consumers are learning about the standard, commodity-like character of telematics devices at the same time they are learning about potential applications.

Then there is the interface challenge of telematics. Today, most features and applications of in-vehicle communication still suffer from inadequate man-machine interfaces. Telematics applications will not truly penetrate the individual's daily life until simple voice-controlled systems are introduced (Roland Berger Strategy Consultants 2001).

One major shift to be expected in the medium-to-long term is the introduction of personal fuel cells. All devices, of course, are dependent on their specific source of energy. All portable ICT devices, from mobile phones to digital cameras, include a (rechargeable) battery. Although battery power is continuously being extended, physical laws provide natural limitations in existing battery technology. A new approach using a hydrogen/oxygen mix creates rechargeable personal fuel cells, and this could be the next quantum leap in device design. These more powerful and longer-lasting energy sources could result in greater independence for individuals.

Application and content

Online business models went out of fashion with the collapse of the new economy. The much-hyped startups have disappeared, and many of those remaining are struggling. Even well-established old economy media companies are cutting back much of their online activity and are going back to their roots by focusing on core competencies and traditional virtues. In August 2002, this process reached its most recent climax with the resignation of Bertelsmann CEO and Internet visionary Thomas Middelhoff. Middelhoff's exit also symbolized the "back-to-the-roots" strategy of the entire industry.

Still, the networked world will provide fast and convenient exchange of information and transactions. Companies like Bertelsmann, the German media conglomerate, are not stopping their ventures in online media; they are merely aligning it with other strategic business units.

With more healthy growth, e-transactions are on the rise again, and e-commerce will see its revival, based on value-added transactions rather than on revolutionary fantasies. Since coming down from the hype, e-commerce has established itself as the dominant commerce channel for a variety of goods and applications. As in the early days of the "Internet revolution," online sales of books and music have achieved significant growth in market share. Entertainment is content that consumers finally seem willing to pay for, especially adult entertainment, games, and music. Online auctioning, particularly via eBay, is the killer application in terms of consumer content. Weekly free-advertising papers worldwide are struggling with this online competition.

Online auctioning capitalizes on one major Internet benefit that remains valid even after the new economy collapse: the Internet will always be the easiest and fastest way for all individuals to make contact with like-minded people within a community of interest. No matter what object might interest someone, he or she will very likely find a counterpart somewhere on the Internet. Thus, the Internet also fulfills the most simple and basic task that ICT has today: to get individuals together to exchange information; that is, to communicate.

But how do content and the demand for content evolve? Over time, the Internet has undoubtedly become a more dynamic and interactive environment—content is no longer static, but has become rich in multimedia features. The dynamic nature of the Internet allows for content that is also dynamically transferred through streaming (i.e., a continuous transfer of data that is processed by the user at the same time the content is viewed or heard). Consumers are beginning to pay for downloadable music. Even motion pictures are being transferred via the net in flat-fee environments.

Regardless of what content is comprised—music, movies, or other intellectual property assets—there is one important characteristic of these offerings that has also changed since the early days of the Internet: people are beginning to pay for content. Business models will finally shift from access provision to content provision.

An increasing amount of content will be kept secure from public Internet traffic in order to support online business models. Access barriers via passwords, proxy servers, or dedicated dial-in connections are increasingly dominating as the business and billing model. Print media with online activities are slowly introducing micropayments for parts of their offerings. And, among the first to master the challenges of Internet billing, the adult content industry is at the forefront of successfully managing restricted access to its websites.

Controlling content is critical. The same technology that can be used to protect young Internet users from pornography and violence can, of course, be used to restrict freedom of speech and, even at a national level, to stabilize totalitarian regimes. Careful deliberation is necessary, and every individual bears a little bit of the responsibility to defend the potential of the Internet while denouncing its misuse for totalitarian regimes, crime, and terrorism.

What other ICT applications will be noticeable to individuals in the years to come? We already mentioned vehicle telematics and home automation. The digitizing of radio and television is underway. Videoconferencing has so far established itself only in business environments but is now penetrating educational institutions. Photography has seen the successful introduction of digital cameras and camcorders, and now those devices are converging with mobile telephones. e-Tags are being discussed as a substitution for traditional barcode systems. IP (Internet Protocol) telephony is gaining ground in the corporate segment, and residential markets will soon follow. Security technology will be far more ICT-based than in the past, be it in connection with identity documents, biometric measuring for identification, or newly established identity services.

Directly connected to identity services is payment. Payment will continue to be massively influenced by ICT developments. However, the first wave of digital payments has failed. Similarly, early attempts to establish holistic mobile payment services have not materialized. Instead, all sorts of micropayments can already be performed with the help of the mobile phone or niche services on the Internet.

Revolutionary Internet payment methods, however, will not—in our opinion—be available anytime soon. However, we do not believe that the structural advantages of real-time billing capability via mobile networks are being fully utilized. We still expect to see a breakthrough in combining various payment methods with a mobile device, thereby creating a secure tool for all point-of-sale, e-payments, and mobile payments.

The last—but certainly not least—ICT application for the individual that we want to mention is voice technology. The term comprises different approaches such as speech recognition, text-to-speech, speech-to-text technology, or natural language processing. The use of next-generation voice portals, in particular, seems promising in terms of entering a variety of real-life situations involving individuals, in the form of customer service, enterprise service, and information portals. All sorts of customer interaction channels will employ this technology because it takes classic interactive voice response to a new level of application intelligence.

Action Agenda: Learning From Model Observations to Strengthen the Individual Within the ICT Environment

We have seen the various developments in our model structure for ICT from the perspective of the individual. Focusing on the three main elements of ICT development—ICT enablers, ICT incentives, and ICT value chain—we can establish an agenda that businesses and governments can use to facilitate the journey to a networked society.

This report proposes the Networked Readiness Index for benchmarking the use of ICT for the competitiveness and development of nations globally.

One could argue, of course, that a nation-state should not be the object of analysis and thus of comparison and ranking, since ICT readiness and usage patterns of individuals and institutions obviously transcend national borders. It should be safe to assume that, with growing Networked Readiness, individuals will increasingly associate themselves with groups that are defined more by socioeconomic, cultural, and lifestyle/environmental criteria rather than purely by country.

We believe in this assumption, but we also deem it valuable to understand the behavior and impact of ICT readiness and usage from a country perspective. Though the networked society transcends national borders, there are still many country-focused elements on the path to its achievement. Therefore, it is correct to initiate actions differentiated across countries. Consequently, most of our agenda items have to be initiated at the country level, and in a synchronized effort with the international community.

Let us thus summarize our discussions into seven action items for government and business leaders:

1. Initiate additional activities in training and education. Enable people 50 years and older, and allow overall training and education measures to be technology-neutral to avoid lock-in. Encourage life-long learning, and establish frameworks and offerings for doing so.

2. Eliminate subsidies in smokestack industries and agriculture. Invest the freed-up capital in general, not just ICT-related research, development, and education.

3. Set up programs to increase public access to ICT. Link schools, libraries, residential homes for the elderly, and other public institutions. Migrate public administration processes online and subsidize basic equipment for residential users.

4. Finalize and update legal frameworks for transactions and commerce. Define privacy and security standards to enable consumer protection. Develop passports with digital certificate/signature technology. Agree on payment rules and procedures.

5. Lower local access costs. Further liberalize the telecommunications sector. Increase broadband access to homes and small businesses. Allow for infrastructure competition, and create competition in network elements that are critical to dominant players.

6. Enable and stimulate investments in the ICT industry. Build industry clusters. Support venture capital financing. Set up special small- and medium-sized enterprises programs to stimulate ICT use.

7. Benchmark initiatives of other countries, organizations, and businesses. Plan your own activities carefully. Be consequent in implementation. Measure your success systematically. Adapt. And act.

Of course, these action items are very general and the specific decision-making environment must be accounted for. However, the items do show clear direction for activity; the aim is to not just achieve a knowledge-based society, but one that cares about the networked individual.

55

Chapter 3 Ready for the Networked Future? The Role of the Individual in the Networked Society

Endnote

1. Jarboe, K.P. 2002. *Extending the Information Revolution—A White Paper on Policies for Prosperity and Security.* Washington: Athena Alliance; or Kubicek, H. and S. Welling. 2001. *Öffentliche Internet-Zugangs- und Lernorte als Sprungbretter in die digitale Welt.* Bremen, Germany: University of Bremen.

References

Akst, D. and M. Jensen. 2001. *Africa Goes Online.* New York: Carnegie Corporation.

Drucker, P. 2001. "The Next Society. A Survey of the Near Future," The Economist Nov 3.

Gartner Group. 2001. *Asia Pacific and Japan Mobile Telephony Services Market Share and Forecast.* Stamford: Gartner Group.

Jensen, M. and A. Esterhuysen. 2001. *The Community Telecentre Cookbook for Africa: Recipes for Self-Sustainability.* Paris: United Nations Educational, Scientific and Cultural Organization.

OECD. 2001a. *Science, Technology and Industry Outlook* (Special Edition). Paris: Organisation for Economic Co-operation and Development.

OECD Working Party on Telecommunications and Information Services Policy. 2001b. *The Development of Broadband Access in OECD Countries.* Paris: Organisation for Economic Co-operation and Development.

Roland Berger Strategy Consultants. 2001. *Telematics: How to Hit a Moving Target.* Detroit, Stuttgart, Tokyo: Roland Berger Strategy Consultants.

Twist, K. 2002. *Addressing the Demand for an Information Age Workforce.* Online. http://www.digitaldividenetwork.org/content/stories/index.cfm?key=20.

Wireless World Forum w2f. 2002. *Mobile Youth Market Intelligence.* http://www.worldwideyouth.org.

Chapter 4

The Business Dimension

ICT: A Critical Enabler of Managerial Innovation

Scott Beardsley, Ingo Beyer von Morgenstern, Luis Enriquez, Stefan Mytilineos, and Jürgen Wunram

McKinsey & Co.

Executive Summary

This chapter outlines the impact of information and communication technology (ICT) on individual firms, industry sectors, and the economy. It draws implications for policymakers and business leaders, focusing especially on recommendations for leveraging ICT more effectively.

The chapter also builds on the findings of a study on productivity growth completed in 2001 by the McKinsey Global Institute (MGI). It is also supported by research that has followed the first MGI report and that extends the findings to the rest of the world. Finally, supporting case studies and insights are based on extensive McKinsey experience serving corporations to help leverage ICT to create value.

In summary, this chapter has five key messages:

1. *In the aggregate, ICT is not a "silver bullet" to increase productivity.* ICT cannot by itself promote economic growth. It is, however, an essential element of any holistic strategy to improve productivity at the economy, sector, or company level.

2. *The main driver of productivity growth is managerial innovation.* Structural changes in market regulation and competition act as triggers to stimulate innovation and facilitate the widespread adoption of new processes and products. Cyclical factors, such as short-term market pressure or demand fluctuation, also play a role.

3. *ICT has played a key role in facilitating managerial innovation.* Evidence from sectoral case studies suggests that ICT has enabled many of the most important process and product innovations of the last decade.

4. *Managing e-execution at a detailed level is critical.* Successful implementation of ICT at the company level remains one of the major challenges faced by CEOs. Even within the same industry some companies seem to do exceedingly well leveraging ICT while others fail to realize value, despite significant investment.

5. *ICT's enabling role means that ICT strategy must be subsumed within broader goals.* ICT is effectively a tool to achieve broader performance improvements, be it at the firm, industry, or economy level. Therefore, policymakers must pursue broader strategies to encourage structural reform and increase the likelihood that triggers will drive managerial innovation at the firm level. These strategies often include facilitating industrywide restructuring and increasing competition. At the firm level, successful ICT must support a business's strategic imperatives and be driven by senior management to support clear internal innovation to improve performance.

ICT can have a proportionally larger impact in third world countries, as it can become a catalyst for the transfer of best practice innovations from advanced economies. However, as is the case in advanced economies, ICT by itself will not deliver these benefits unless combined with structural reform.

Introduction

"[Y]ou can see the computer age everywhere except in the productivity statistics."

Robert Solow, 1987

Between 1973 and the late-1980s, productivity growth in the United States dropped below the historic average. This occurred despite major increases in ICT investments throughout the economy, with major waves of computer innovation and adoption taking place throughout the country's businesses. This apparent paradox led Robert Solow, a distinguished economist, to make his famous statement.

From 1995 to 2000, however, the U.S. experienced a reversal of fortunes. Measured labor productivity grew at 2.5 percent per year during that period. This was a dramatic improvement from the 1.4 percent rate achieved between 1972 and 1995. Labor productivity growth was accompanied by rapid economic growth, unemployment declines to 3.9 percent (the lowest levels in three decades), and inflation rates that hovered at around 2 percent. This acceleration in productivity was accompanied by a 20 percent annual surge in real business investment in ICT, almost double the rate from 1987 to 1995 (Figure 1).

Figure 1: **Growth in Labor Productivity and IT Investment**

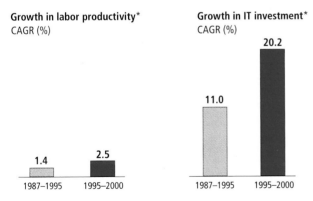

Growth in labor productivity* CAGR (%)

Growth in IT investment* CAGR (%)

*Excludes output from farms and government; labor productivity is defined here as output per hour worked

Source: Bureau of Labor Statistics (www.bls.gov)

Were these phenomena connected? Had investments in ICT raised the "speed limit"[1] of the U.S. economy? Four decades after General Electric first took delivery of a UNIVAC and less than a decade after Solow made his famous statement, it seemed that the computer age might finally have showed up in productivity statistics.

Although U.S. observations have prompted discussion around this "paradox," the wider question of the true impact of ICT on an economy is relevant across the world. Indeed, a study performed by the McKinsey Global Institute on the impact of ICT on productivity in Europe confirms that patterns similar to the U.S. are also found in Europe. Given the importance of allocating resources and government effort in developing countries, the "paradox" question is at least as pertinent to the developing world.

ICT: Not a Silver Bullet to Increase Productivity

In the aggregate, ICT is not a "silver bullet" to increase productivity. ICT cannot by itself promote economic growth. It is, however, an essential element of any holistic strategy to improve productivity at the economy, sector, or company level.

While Solow has since rescinded his famous statement,[3] at the aggregate level the relationship between ICT spending and productivity remains unclear. Just six "jumping" sectors can explain almost all of America's productivity growth from 1995 to 2000, and all six of them increased their ICT capital intensity growth rate over the period. However, many "paradox" sectors increased their pace of ICT expenditure but experienced stagnant or even slower productivity growth. Overall, the correlation between the acceleration in ICT investment growth and the acceleration in productivity growth was found to be statistically insignificant (Figure 2).

Similarly, research performed by the Japanese authorities indicates a similar level of complexity between ICT investment and productivity growth. Over the period 1997 to 2000, the average level of IT expenditure per enterprise as a ratio to total annual revenues rose from 0.99 percent to 1.16 percent.[4] However, the impact on the economy was hard to measure or not found to be significant.

This ambiguous relationship between ICT growth and productivity increases does not imply that ICT investment is not productive. On the contrary, ICT played a significant role in driving productivity increases in six leading industries. Of the six sectors, two were ICT producers (semiconductors and computer manufacturing), while the remainder (wholesale, retail, securities and brokerage, and telecommunications) had all experienced, to a greater or lesser degree, technology-enabled transformation. In the securities industry, for example, online securities trading delivered an order of magnitude labor productivity advantage over traditional channels. Similarly, in mobile communications, cellular equipment employing new digital standards made better use of the available spectrum, spurring rapid price declines and a surge in usage.

Figure 2. **Industry Level Relationship Between IT Intensity and Productivity Growth Acceleration**

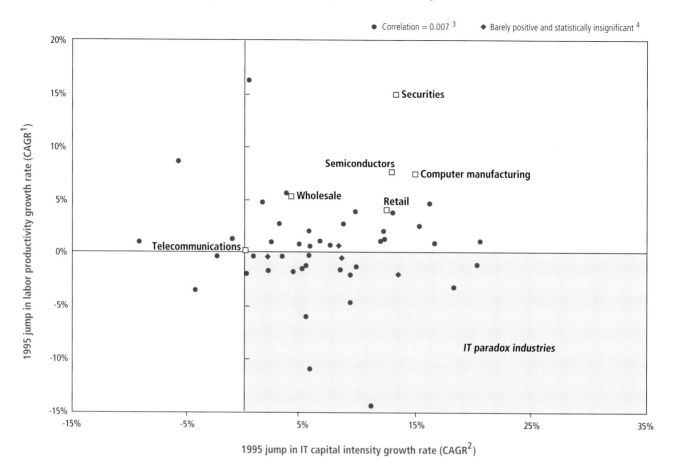

● Correlation = 0.007 [3]   ◆ Barely positive and statistically insignificant [4]

1995 jump in IT capital intensity growth rate (CAGR[2])

[1] Acceleration in real value added per People Employed in Production (PEP) growth rate between 1987–95 and 1995–99

[2] Acceleration in real IT capital stock per PEP growth rate between 1987–95 and 1995–99

[3] Excludes farms, coal mining, and metal mining industries due to low initial levels of IT capital stock and holding companies for measurement reasons

[4] Although weighting each sector by its share of employment yields a statistically significant correlation of 0.26, excluding the six "jumping" sectors yields statistically insignificant results

Source: Bureau of Economic Analysis; McKinsey analysis

Even in paradox sectors, ICT has clearly helped deliver baseline growth. For example, investments in credit scoring systems in retail banking dramatically reduced the amount of labor required to process loan applications. However, ICT's impact on productivity is complex and varies across industries.

That no unambiguous solution to Solow's paradox emerges from aggregate level analysis should perhaps be no surprise. Notwithstanding the weighty problems of term definitions and measurement, it is clear that the way in which ICT affects productivity is likely to vary substantially by industry, firm, and investment. Differences in industry structure, investment horizon, organizational capability, and demand, for example, all serve to complicate the relationship between the intensity[5] of ICT and productivity growth. Therefore, tracing the impact of ICT on business performance requires analysis at the sector or even firm level.

The case studies outlined in the following section describe the interaction between the impact of ICT investments on productivity growth and other factors that are industry specific. The case studies highlight the importance of understanding the specific environment and dynamics of each particular industry, as well as its business processes and key performance levers, to determine ICT's impact on industry performance.

The Main Driver of Productivity Growth: Managerial Innovation

The main driver of productivity growth is managerial innovation. Structural changes in market regulation and competition act as triggers to stimulate innovation and to facilitate the widespread adoption of new processes and products. Cyclical factors like short-term market pressure or demand fluctuation also play a role.

Increasing productivity requires either reducing input for a given output or increasing output for a given input. The first can be achieved by either reducing labor input by, for example, reducing headcount through automation or deploying labor more effectively, or by reducing the cost of materials and other nonlabor input . The latter can be achieved by either increasing utilization of resources (labor or asset) to increase the number of units of output produced or by increasing the value of the portfolio of output. This last fact implies that market conditions will have a significant impact on measured productivity improvement, as the ability to increase the value of goods sold will depend on two critical market factors. First, competitive intensity will determine how much a market price will increase when quality increases (in many industries, increases in quality are rapidly matched by competitors and prices do not increase). Second, the level of consumer demand growth will stabilize prices even though there may be rapid reductions in the cost and levels of inputs required to produce a given output.

Modern productivity measures are used to try and capture the impact of all of these levers. To capture increases in the value of goods that may not be reflected in the price—increases which may be due to a number of reasons—modern measures try to compensate by making adjustments to reflect the value to the consumer.

While cyclical factors, like changes in consumer demand, can impact productivity (by, for example, leading to an increase in the prices of outputs), the dominant driver of sustainable productivity growth is innovation. Through innovation, managers may adopt processes that make more effective use of labor, find creative ways to reduce costs or, indeed, introduce new features or new products or services.

Competition and market regulation: critical triggers to innovation

Competition is the impetus for managerial innovation and its consequent diffusion. When there are competitive pressures on a firm, managers will endeavor to innovate in order to build advantages over competitors. This competitive intensity essentially creates "triggers" that push management to seek improvements in their business models and products to either match competitors, or gain an advantage over them. Once an innovation has been implemented and is evidently successful, other industry participants will attempt to adopt comparable innovations in order to remain competitive.

An example of competitor action acting as a trigger can be found in the U.S. general merchandise retail industry. Wal-Mart's success in the early 1990s drove a number of its competitors to follow the lessons of Wal-Mart and launch their own transformational initiatives. Indeed, the vice chairman of Target, Gerald Storch, told the *Economist* that his company was the "world's premier student of Wal-Mart."[6] As

a result, competitors managed to increase their productivity by 28 percent from 1995 to 1999.

The same competitive forces encouraging innovation, however, may result in managerial innovations that do not deliver improved financial performance for an industry. Intense competition sometimes leads to such rapid diffusion of technology that any innovation is immediately copied, presenting no sustainable advantage to the innovator and passing on most of the value generated to the consumer.

An example of rapid diffusion of innovation can be found in the automotive industry. The industry is highly competitive, and is characterized by limited market growth combined with overcapacity and pricing pressures; automotive manufacturers have been introducing new models and product segments at increasing rates in an attempt to create competitive advantage. In so doing, they have had to dramatically shorten the product development period by extensive introduction of ICT-enabled applications and processes such as simulation technologies, to substitute virtual prototypes for hardware mockups. In the absence of competition, it is unlikely that we would have been witness to the almost 40 percent decrease in average product development times over the last fifteen years.

Thus, competitive intensity drives productivity growth by acting as a crucial catalyst encouraging firms to innovate and by speeding diffusion of each innovation across the sector. However, this increased productivity does not always translate into profits for firms, as all surplus may be captured by consumers.

The evolution of consumer demand can also drive productivity growth but its impact may be cyclical

Changes in consumer demand can also impact productivity growth measures. For example, productivity growth in the semiconductors industry in the late 1990s can in part be explained by the accelerated growth in the use of computers and upgrade activity by consumers, driven in some measure by the rapid penetration of e-mail and the World Wide Web.

However, consumer behavior may be cyclical, and future slowdowns in demand can cause subsequent slowdowns in productivity growth. The U.S. securities productivity growth jump in the late 1990s was in part attributable to the significant demand growth in equity trading associated with buoyant financial markets in the late 1990s. The surge in trading volume was not matched by commensurate increases in labor inputs (due to, for example, the automation of trade processing and also economies of scale). This had the effect of increasing measured productivity.

During this same period, almost 50 percent of the measured productivity jump in general merchandise retail was caused by an accelerated shift by consumers toward higher-value goods. This was brought on, according to retail experts, by growing confidence, increasing income, and increased wealth. The question is whether such exuberance is sustainable or simply cyclical.

Thus, while demand factors can influence productivity measures—and have definitely done so over the period 1995 to 2000—their effects may not be sustainable in the long term.

In our review, we found that triggers fall into four broad categories:

1. Performance challenges. These include competitor actions, as discussed above; a dramatic shift in consumer demand; or pressure from the financial markets to deliver short-term performance in an uncertain economy;

2. Feasibility demonstration. Players within or outside the industry demonstrating the viability and potential of a managerial innovation;

3. Regulatory. A regulatory change with significant implications; and

4. Governance changes. A change in the top management triggers wholesale change.

Other cyclical or structural factors that can trigger the creation or adoption of innovations play a somewhat lesser role. In summary, managerial innovation is the primary driver of sustainable productivity growth. Major structural as well as cyclical factors play a role in "triggering" initiatives to push through efforts to innovate. The next question is, what is the role of ICT in all this?

ICT: A Key Role in Facilitating Managerial Innovation

ICT has played a key role in facilitating managerial innovation. Evidence from sectoral case studies suggests that ICT has enabled many of the most important process and product innovations of the last decade.

ICT has enabled many of the most important product and process innovations of the last decade. MGI's detailed analysis of a number of industries indicated that ICT plays a crucial role in enabling innovation. Indeed, even in the so-called "paradox" industries such as retail banking, many innovations (e.g., using document imaging to improve workflow in loans processing or Internet banking) would not have been possible without ICT. The example above also highlights the multiple aspects of ICT's impact. The improved workflow through the use of document imaging is an example of ICT-enabled process innovation, leading

to lowered nonlabor document storage costs and reduced labor requirements. Internet banking is an example of using ICT to offer an enhanced product with a higher value to the consumer.

Process innovation

ICT enables managerial innovation in three critical ways:

1. Improving operations,

2. Enabling the reconfiguration of business systems, and

3. Creating new business opportunities.

Improving operations

Operational improvements impact productivity by reducing the quantity and cost of inputs required to produce a certain amount of output. When it comes to cost reduction, ICT may allow process automation and thereby substitute capital for labor (which would improve labor productivity but not necessarily total factor productivity) or permit efficiency gains in other sources of costs. A great example is the impact ICT can have on supply chain inventory levels, which account for a large part of the costs in the wholesale business. However, in all of these cases, a significant amount of process change needs to accompany the ICT investment.

The use of ICT applications to aid product development can also improve product quality. For example, heavy use of computer aided design (CAD) in the automotive industry has not only helped reduce product development times from fifty-one months in 1988 to thirty-six months in 2000, but with the introduction of high-powered simulation technologies, there has been a shift in the product creation process from hardware mock-ups towards digital prototypes using virtual technologies. This shift allows more product iterations to take place with more design options explored, leading to better products.

The financial impact of operational improvement initiatives will differ across industries because of differences in their fundamental cost structures. Thus, a different mix of ICT initiatives is required for each industry. For example, an ICT initiative focusing on inventory management will have a greater financial impact in those industries (such as consumer goods) where inventory levels constitute a considerable portion of the business and are often the result of high levels of supply/demand uncertainty.

Nevertheless, in discrete manufacturing, the functional areas thought to have the greatest potential for operational improvement resulting in actual/expected cost savings, are in the areas of supply chain management (SCM) and product development. Indeed, the largest portion of ICT investment is directed towards SCM (Figure 4).

Figure 3. **Hypothetical Impact of IT Initiatives on Industries**

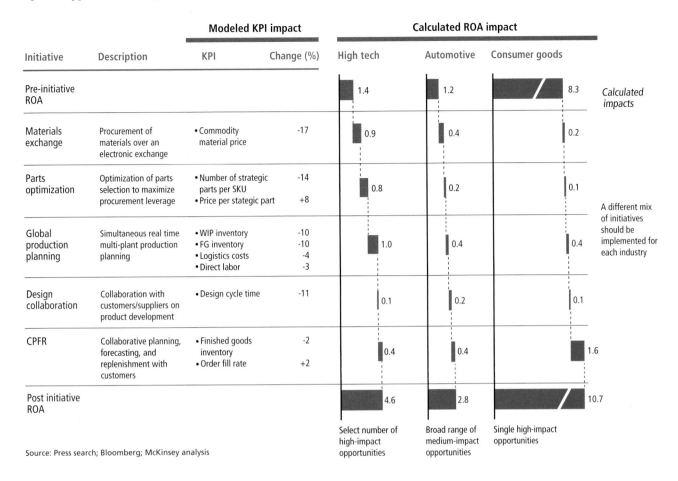

Initiative	Description	Modeled KPI impact		Calculated ROA impact			
		KPI	Change (%)	High tech	Automotive	Consumer goods	
Pre-initiative ROA				1.4	1.2	8.3	*Calculated impacts*
Materials exchange	Procurement of materials over an electronic exchange	• Commodity material price	-17	0.9	0.4	0.2	
Parts optimization	Optimization of parts selection to maximize procurement leverage	• Number of strategic parts per SKU • Price per stategic part	-14 +8	0.8	0.2	0.1	*A different mix of initiatives should be implemented for each industry*
Global production planning	Simultaneous real time multi-plant production planning	• WIP inventory • FG inventory • Logistics costs • Direct labor	-10 -10 -4 -3	1.0	0.4	0.4	
Design collaboration	Collaboration with customers/suppliers on product development	• Design cycle time	-11	0.1	0.2	0.1	
CPFR	Collaborative planning, forecasting, and replenishment with customers	• Finished goods inventory • Order fill rate	-2 +2	0.4	0.4	1.6	
Post initiative ROA				4.6	2.8	10.7	
				Select number of high-impact opportunities	Broad range of medium-impact opportunities	Single high-impact opportunities	

Source: Press search; Bloomberg; McKinsey analysis

Figure 4. **IT Investment and Functional Areas**

Funtional areas of actual/expected cost savings
(percent of observations)

- Supply chain management **88**%
- Product development **88**%
- Sourcing **50**%
- Human resources **38**%
- Marketing **25**%
- Finance **25**%

0   20   40   60   80

Source: McKinsey

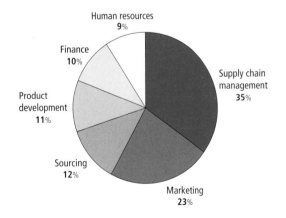

IT investment in funtional areas
(in percent)

- Human resources 9%
- Finance 10%
- Product development 11%
- Sourcing 12%
- Supply chain management 35%
- Marketing 23%

Enabling the reconfiguration of business systems

Business process outsourcing (BPO) refers to the transfer of operations delivery (and assets) to a third party with the aim of leveraging economies of scale and skill and/or factor costs. To the extent that BPO can reduce the cost structure of the industry value chain, measured productivity will increase.

ICT facilitates outsourcing by reducing the costs of interaction between parties. The dramatic drop in the cost of communication across continents has also opened up opportunities in offshoring, the process of migrating operations to a usually cheaper, sometimes higher-quality, overseas location. For example, HSBC and GE Capital found

Figure 5. **Motivation for Offshoring**

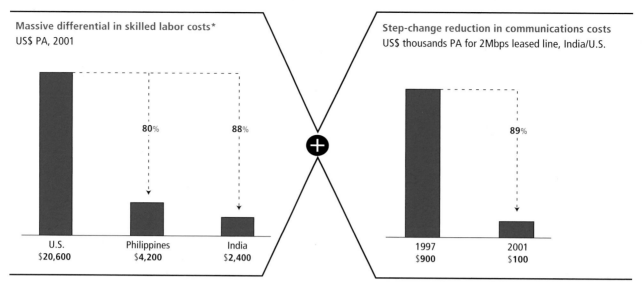

Massive differential in skilled labor costs*
US$ PA, 2001

| U.S. $20,600 | Philippines $4,200 | India $2,400 |

80% 88%

Step-change reduction in communications costs
US$ thousands PA for 2Mbps leased line, India/U.S.

| 1997 $900 | 2001 $100 |

89%

*Based on call center operators – direct wages only

Source:Joint McKinsey/NASSCOM Study, Telegeography, 2001

that while labor costs could be reduced by 88 percent by moving resources to India, the quality of service also actually improved (Figure 6).

Outsourcing is usually the step that follows the creation of internal shared services; sharing brings together a number of functions to operate under a central department. The concept of shared services is a significant source of value in itself because it eliminates duplication. Shared services would create further value through scale economies. Offshoring[7], in particular labor offshoring, would improve cost performance even further (although its impact on

measured productivity at a macro level would depend on national income accounting methodology).

One note of caution is that execution of outsourcing deals is complex and often fails to deliver the anticipated savings or performance improvements. Dun & Bradstreet has reported that 20 to 25 percent of all outsourcing relationships (manufacturing, finance, information technology, and so on) fail within two years, and that 50 percent fail within five. Frequent reasons given for failure include misunderstandings between the outsourcer and the outsourcing provider about roles and responsibilities, higher than expected costs, or poor service.

Figure 6. **Impact of Offshoring**

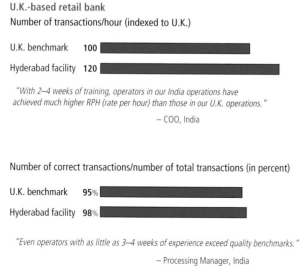

U.K.-based retail bank
Number of transactions/hour (indexed to U.K.)

| U.K. benchmark | 100 |
| Hyderabad facility | 120 |

"With 2–4 weeks of training, operators in our India operations have achieved much higher RPH (rate per hour) than those in our U.K. operations."
— COO, India

Number of correct transactions/number of total transactions (in percent)

| U.K. benchmark | 95% |
| Hyderabad facility | 98% |

"Even operators with as little as 3–4 weeks of experience exceed quality benchmarks."
— Processing Manager, India

U.S. financial service company
Average speed of answer (in seconds)

U.S. benchmark	20
Delhi facility (average talk time)	8
U.S. benchmark (seconds)	180
Delhi facility	100

Total satisfaction factor

| U.S. benchmark | 85 |
| Delhi facility (average talk time) | 92 |

"We follow our sigma quality methodology…our India operations have performed better than U.S. benchmarks on almost all parameters."
— Senior Executive, India

Source: Industry interviews

Creating new business opportunities

Infraservices (infrastructure management services such as call center management) is one example of new business arenas that have been enabled by ICT investment. It can be seen as the "other side of the outsourcing coin" but some countries may be net users and some net providers of infraservices. According to Dun & Bradstreet, third-party providers of infraservices generated more than US$1 trillion in revenues around the world in the year 2000. Furthermore, the market for these services doubled in size between 1997 and 2000.

The costs of interaction associated with the outsourcing of infrastructure activities have declined significantly, in large part due to ICT enabled factors. This has resulted in significant growth of this industry segment. Reduced costs have been achieved through the rapidly decreasing cost of communications, the widespread use of standardized interfaces such as World Wide Web browsers, and the increasing level of data automation within organizations.

For example, in the mid-1990s, the company Cincinnati Bell (now known as Broadwing) consolidated its call centers. In doing so, the company found that they had both the scale and skill capabilities to offer other businesses call-center and related services, such as managing billing. In 1998 this business was spun off to become the stand-alone company Convergys, and in 2001 Convergys generated over US$2 billion in revenues.

Product innovation

ICT can enable significant improvements in end-product quality. This area is often overlooked, as most ICT-related projects are focused either in operational improvements or in enabling outsourcing. However, ICT-enabled product innovation is critical in the long run. BMW's latest 7-Series car, for example, makes heavy use of telematics, a form of ICT, to differentiate its product from the competition.[8]

These innovations have a direct impact on productivity statistics even if the increased consumer benefit is not measured accurately at a macro level (that will depend on the specific methodology of national income accounting) or even if the firm is unable to capture additional value from improved quality or features (due to competitive pressures). Product innovation of the type used by BMW is critically linked to process innovations. Functionality improvements in the car would not have been possible without the process innovations in the supporting design and manufacturing processes that allowed the hardware manufacturer, software provider, wireless network manager, content provider and all other players involved in the generation of a telematics solution, to coordinate and exchange information to support new product features.

Confirmation That Innovation is Often Driven by Triggers: Sector Case Studies

Sector case studies confirm that ICT is a critical enabler of innovation. ICT has had the most impact on productivity in sectors that also experienced high levels of competition and growing demand. However, even with all the right industry conditions, execution remains critical.

MGI analyzed in detail a number of U.S. industries to determine the impact of ICT on sector performance. McKinsey's experience in serving these sectors in other regions of the world broadly confirmed the U.S.-based findings, and the company's firm- and sector-level experience highlighted the critical role of triggers in stimulating waves of managerial innovation.

The largest impact of ICT on productivity was either in the ICT-producing sectors, which are mostly in the U.S., or in "information intensive" sectors such as the securities industry. This latter sector displays similar characteristics around the world; however, regulation plays a crucial differentiating role, and hence the impact of ICT may vary by country.[9]

The U.S. results do not only apply to extraordinary or successful industries. Similar effects have been found in industries where ICT intensity increased without an accompanying acceleration in productivity; that is, in the paradox sectors. If industries displayed similar characteristics as paradox sectors in the U.S., then those industries also appeared to demonstrate a weak link between increased ICT intensity and the rate of productivity growth. Indeed, a study of retail banking in Europe leads to conclusions analogous to the U.S.

Interpreting these findings in the context of the developing world requires the additional consideration of a number of factors. In many cases, the underlying technological infrastructure must be in place if the full potential of ICT is to be realized. This is plainly not the case in many developing economies. Therefore, policymakers have a significant role to play not just in driving competition, but also in taking steps to directly encourage ICT through appropriate regulation.[10] When the appropriate conditions are in place, however, the incremental impact on productivity can be enormous compared to developed countries. This is because ICT acts not only as an enabler of new innovation, but also as the catalyst to transfer best practices across the board, bringing the productivity of entire sectors closer to best-in-class.

Industries can be segregated into three categories according to the degree by which ICT intensity has affected the rate of productivity growth:

1. Extraordinary cases show that radical innovations in product quality or process efficiency enabled by ICT, combined with favourable structural as well as cyclical conditions, promote exceptional improvements in productivity.

2. Success cases indicate that ICT can enable innovation even in sectors that would not be considered "high-tech" (e.g., retail) and accelerate productivity as long as industry dynamics are conducive.

3. Paradox cases highlight the importance not only of external conditions, but also of on-the-ground execution.

Extraordinary cases

Some industries have experienced radical productivity growth that was linked to technology. However, technological innovation was combined with other factors in order to produce the observed exceptional productivity improvements.

The semiconductor industry is a good example of an ICT-producing sector that experienced great productivity growth. The securities industry is a non-ICT sector that has benefited from the spill-over of technology improvements.

Semiconductors

During the late 1990s, the semiconductor industry experienced a considerable increase in the rate of labor productivity growth. In the U.S. this was reflected in a rise in the productivity growth rate from 43 percent (1987-1995) to 66 percent (1995–1999).

This change was partly driven by important technological improvements within the industry as well as within complementary industries. Specifically, technological advances in manufacturing equipment, simulation, and wafer inspection improved overall production quality, which is a major driver of economics in this industry.

On top of the improved quality of production, enormous growth in the demand for computers combined with increasing demands for more powerful processors, which in turn was driven by innovations in operating system software, produced a huge increase in the demand for larger numbers of more powerful microprocessors. Whether this growth in demand can be sustained beyond the "Internet boom" is a matter of debate, but nobody will dispute its impact in the period spanning 1995 to 2000.

Finally, the emergence of competition against the dominant producer of desktop microprocessors in the mid-1990s forced accelerated innovation in the industry. By 1999 AMD had reduced the 1995 time lag of more than 18 months between Intel's release of a new design and the release of AMD's competing chip to almost nothing. This prompted Intel to schedule more frequent releases, which moved the mix of chips purchased each year closer to the cutting edge.

In summary, while ICT enabled tremendous improvements in the semiconductor production process, productivity growth was also driven by a large increase in consumer demand experienced in the late-1990s, combined with an increase in competition that encouraged the diffusion of technological innovations while pushing the whole industry towards more frequent cycles of innovation.

Securities

The securities industry accounted for nearly one-fifth of the total U.S. private sector, nonfarm labor productivity growth increase in the period 1995 to 1999, making it the third largest contributor of any sector in the U.S. economy. The sector's labor productivity growth rate accelerated more than seven percentage points between the two periods (1987–1995 and 1995–1999).

The sector's strong productivity performance was due to the combination of buoyant financial markets, exploitation of ICT, and pro-competition regulations.

1. The extraordinary performance of the stock market between 1995 and 1999 contributed to productivity growth by triggering heightened equity trading activities in the late 1990s, and inflating both the value of portfolio assets under management and the transaction volumes of investment banking services.

2. An information-intensive industry, the securities sector has been an aggressive adopter of information technology to automate trading processes. ICT have replaced labor to create enormous trading capacity over the last 20 years. Online trading, the latest example of automation, contributed significantly to the productivity growth acceleration.

3. The SEC's 1997 Order Handling and 16th rule[11] promoted competition among market makers and lowered price floors, which resulted in lower equity trading costs and contributed to more trading volume by active traders.

Success stories

Despite not being in what one would call "high-tech" sector, a number of technology users had accelerated productivity. What was common across these sectors was the impact of managerial innovation, which was driven by commercial goals and enabled by technology. Competition encouraged the diffusion of these innovations, but other factors such as high barriers to entry, allowed company margins to be retained.

A great example of such a sector is retail trade.

Retail trade

Retail trade contributed nearly one-fourth of the U.S. economy-wide productivity growth jump from 1987 to 1995, and 1995 to 1999.

The McKinsey Global Institute focused its analysis on general merchandise retailing. In general merchandise (representing 16 percent of the total retail productivity growth acceleration), we found that the leading player, Wal-Mart, directly and indirectly caused the bulk of the productivity acceleration through ongoing managerial innovation that increased competitive intensity and drove the diffusion of best practice.

These innovations range from non-ICT-related managerial innovations like the "big-box" format and "everyday low prices," to technology-enabled ones like electronic data interchange links with suppliers, bar codes, and wireless scanning guns.

We also found that external demand factors contributed meaningfully to the productivity acceleration, as consumers spent an increasing portion of their incremental income on higher-value goods (e.g., deciding to purchase a more expensive shirt rather than a less expensive one).

In summary, the success of the retail trade sector in applying ICT lies in selective investment in ICT to support the most productive managerial innovations. A healthy competitive environment encouraged the diffusion of these innovations, while growing consumer demand added to the productivity gains.

Paradox cases

The so-called paradox industries experienced a lack of growth or even a drop in productivity growth rates despite significant acceleration in ICT investments.

Our case studies show that this can be attributed to poor planning and execution, exacerbated by industry factors that may have reduced pressure on management to take full advantage of their ICT capability and improve productivity.

Retail banking

Retail banking experienced a drop in labor productivity growth rates despite a substantial acceleration of ICT investment between 1995 and 1999.

Most post-1995 ICT capital investments were associated with banks' focus on increasing revenues. The largest portion of these investments was focused on customer information management and support, and on sales automation. This investment facilitated banks' shift from product-centric to customer-centric organizations. Industry consolidation, new channels, and increased product range also contributed to the massive growth in ICT capital in the late 1990s. Together, these strategies further raised systems' complexity and information transaction volume, increasing processing power requirements.

Most ICT investments failed to produce expected productivity gains due to a number of reasons.

1. Investments were focused on increasing revenue. This is inherently more difficult than reducing costs in a mature industry. Despite offering customers more products and greater customization potential, customer satisfaction levels dropped. A McKinsey survey found that consumers care more about reliability and trust than having a wide choice of product and service offerings.

2. Planning and execution was poor. For example, many of the revenue-generation investments required close cooperation between departments—banks are usually organized by product lines—in order to maximize value. However, lack of top-management commitment failed to create the incentive for the organization to focus on productivity improvements and cost reduction.

These findings should be examined within the context of the industry at the time that the investments were undertaken. During the mid- to late-1990s, the banking sector enjoyed a period of high profitability, driven mostly by favorable macroeconomic forces that impacted the whole industry. Buoyant financial markets in that period produced significant amounts of non-interest income. This not only skewed decisions away from cost cutting, but also failed to create the pressure required to force managers to maximize value from their ICT investments.

The example of retail banking highlights the importance of incentives and execution.

The Importance of Managing Execution in Detail

Successful implementation of ICT at the company level remains one of the major challenges faced by CEOs. Even within the same industry, some companies seem to do exceedingly well leveraging ICT while others fail to realize value despite significant investment.

It is critical to maintain close monitoring of the implementation detail of ICT projects. It is not uncommon to hear stories about ICT projects gone completely awry: budget overruns, costly delays, and investment black holes. The late 1990s were associated with a number of high-profile cases of enterprise resource planning (ERP) implementations experiencing difficulties. A major confectionery manufacturer implemented an integrated ERP solution at a cost of US$112 million and involving three different software and computer systems. The system went live during the fall of 1999. However, major disruptions resulted in shipments not being made for the Halloween season, with problems continuing through to Christmas and Valentine's Day. Similarly, a white goods manufacturer experienced difficulties in 1999 with the introduction of its new ERP system. Shipments of appliances to distributors and retailers had to be delayed by six to eight weeks, and a major customer had to temporarily stop ordering appliances from them.

Gartner, a market analysis firm, estimates that a 60 percent failure rate is associated with customer relationship management (CRM) solution implementations, despite worldwide spending increasing from US$2.1 billion in 1999 to US$3.7 billion in 2001. Further research by the Standish Group suggests a mere 10 percent of ERP implementations are completed on time, on budget, and with the originally proposed functionality. A further 35 percent of ERP implementation projects are cancelled. Of those experiencing overruns, the average cost overrun is 178 percent of expected cost and the average time overrun 230 percent, with a 59 percent reduction in functionality on average.

In contrast, however, a number of companies have actually been able to utilize ICT to generate value for their businesses. For example, Shell Chemical, a member of the Shell Group, introduced a supplier-managed inventory system, thereby creating transparency in the supply chain and breaking the vicious cycle of safety stocks, rush orders, and delays. Both Shell and its customers can view each other's supply, inventory, consumption, and forecast data. The system also automatically schedules the delivery of raw materials from Shell, removing the need by customers to place orders. The outcome was a reduction in customers' rush orders by 80 percent. Further, one consumer goods manufacturer was able to slash its safety stocks for one product by 60 percent, from 1,000 tons to only 400 tons. Through the automation of the accounting and billing process, transaction and overhead costs were similarly reduced. Revenue also increased, as satisfied customers made Shell their sole supplier. In all, Shell Chemical managers estimate that their investment in the system has already paid for itself tenfold.

This presents a residual problem for business leaders: ICT is a critical element of productivity-boosting innovation, yet simply spending on ICT guarantees no advantage. How, therefore, should firms ensure that ICT investments deliver value?

Companies that do manage to realize value from ICT-investments exhibit a number of traits:

1. A portfolio of initiatives uses all aspects of ICT's potential whose structure reflects the overall business strategy.

2. The CEO actively oversees and facilitates the selection and execution of ICT programs.

3. Implementation is systematically managed.

Portfolio of ICT initiatives

Companies employing ICT effectively invest in a portfolio of initiatives that leverage all aspects of ICT's potential. The portfolio in total reflects the overall business strategy. Three categories of initiatives capture the range of benefits that ICT delivers at the company level:

1. Efficiency through integration;

2. Efficiency and flexibility through process innovation; and

3. Differentiation through product innovation.

Efficiency through integration

Data inconsistency is frequently quoted as a major hurdle in the implementation of major ICT initiatives. Companies that manage to realize value from ICT-investments have typically first gone through a period of consolidation. This course of action entails integrating numerous data sources, systems, and processes into a stable and standardized foundation. Often this action results in dramatic streamlining and the size reduction of existing systems and infrastructure. For example, during such a consolidation phase, one automotive manufacturer reduced the number of its procurement systems from thirty to a single system. Another manufacturing company is planning to reduce the number of its legacy systems by 90 percent, from 400 to only 40.

While the investment required to integrate systems and processes is very large, particularly in many industries that have just undergone a period of consolidation, it is a prerequisite for reaping the full potential benefits of subsequent ICT-based initiatives. The good news is that most firms have already invested significant sums, and just need to make better use of their existing ICT capabilities. Indeed, our experience indicates that although most of the ICT budget of a typical corporation goes into maintaining the existing systems, little effort is made to explicitly restructure business processes and organization in order to capitalize on the available capabilities (Figure 7).

Efficiency and flexibility through process innovation

Process innovation can occur as new ICT-enabled projects using the capabilities of a new technology yet to be implemented, or by taking fuller advantage of the company's existing ICT capabilities.

Process innovation starts inside the company with streamlining and optimizing existing processes, and extends outside, releasing efficiencies across the whole supply chain. As discussed above, well-integrated systems are a prerequisite for successful wholesale internal process optimization.

Figure 7. **IT Spending**

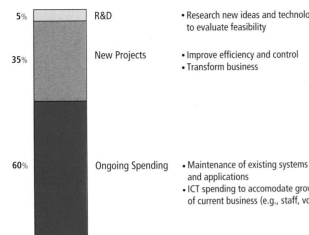

100% = Total Corporate IT Budget	Purpose of spending	Required business change to achieve full potential
5% — R&D	• Research new ideas and technology to evaluate feasibility	• Ability to step outside of day-to-day activities to assess business implications
35% — New Projects	• Improve efficiency and control • Transform business	• Redefinition of operational processes, organizational structure, etc.
60% — Ongoing Spending	• Maintenance of existing systems and applications • ICT spending to accomodate growth of current business (e.g., staff, volume)	• Adjustment of processes and organizations to capitalize on existing ICT infrastructure

Source: McKinsey analysis based on experience in corporate sector

However, short-term benefits can be realized by making full use of existing capabilities.

A well-implemented connection between the company's procurement system and that of the suppliers can radically reduce response times and misunderstandings in its own right. However, collaboration with suppliers in the areas of demand planning and forecasting can lead to better-managed inventory levels and flows. For example, Wal-Mart's Retail Link program was designed to capture sales data and give vendors real-time stock and flow information—a form of micromerchandizing to manage inventory levels more optimally and to minimize inventory stockouts.

When it comes to cross-company collaboration, the importance of integration—to make possible well-implemented direct connections with suppliers and customers—is only outdone by the importance of industrywide standards. Companies in a variety of industries are forming bodies to develop and promote the adoption of standards that allow companies to not only agree on methods for exchanging data, but eventually to be able to easily share processes.

In summary, process innovation is a powerful lever, particularly in mature industries where profit margins are created by reducing costs rather than enhancing revenues, or in times of economic uncertainty. Although well-integrated systems are a prerequisite for capturing the full potential of process innovation, the majority of today's corporations can simply make better use of their existing capabilities without further ICT investments. Capturing the full value of interindustry collaboration, however, requires the establishment of industrywide standards. Although

governments may play a role, many industries have chosen to form independent consortia to develop such standards.

Differentiation through product innovation

The BMW 7-Series example has already been discussed in this chapter. A driver of this car can control, from the steering wheel, the steptronic transmission and activate the voice control, which operates the audio, television, telephone, and navigation systems. These controls are displayed on an LCD screen, which also displays e-mail and news that are downloaded via mobile telephone. Behind the functionality lie numerous microprocessors, including behind the key-proximity sensor, which unlocks the car and allows the driver to start the ignition without taking the key out of his or her pocket. BMW was only able to achieve these advances by working with its partners. The video screen is from Sharp; the navigation system, from VDO; graphical user interface software, from CAA; computing hardware, from Becker; phone board, from Delphi; and the operating system, from Microsoft.

As is demonstrated by the BMW example, successful product development many times requires developing and fostering a "value network" of companies from other sectors. Value networks can be very powerful in creating innovation, not necessarily through the use of new technologies, but through novel ways of bringing previously disparate technologies together.

Value networks also come into play in the development of new standards. For example, the Bluetooth Special Interest Group includes a number of the most prominent players in the computing hardware and software industry, working together to develop and establish a new standard for short-range wireless communications.

Active CEO oversight and facilitation of the selection and execution of ICT programs

One of the most quoted implementation hurdles is internal resistance to change. Thus, top-level commitment is necessary in order to drive the organizational and cultural changes down and across the entire organization. Without top-level commitment, there is a high risk that the initiatives will either stall or become isolated within the organization.

For example, research has shown that a major hurdle in implementing product data management (PDM) systems are the organizational barriers caused by a functional instead of process orientation, and the fact that work flows were not adapted to the new technology. In fact, around 30 percent of PDM implementation projects reportedly face a lack of user acceptance according to McKinsey research.

In the case of Dow Chemical, a specialty and commodities chemical provider, it was four years after the Siebel CRM software licenses were initially purchased for US$50 million that the companywide CRM application was rolled out; the company worked on making the necessary organizational and process changes during the interim period (Banham 2002).

Box 1. An Automotive Industry Company

Context

In the automotive industry, there is a growing trend by large manufacturers to concentrate on their core competencies of brand and customer management. They are, therefore, increasingly outsourcing large portions of product development and manufacturing. Furthermore, module and system suppliers are increasing systems integration know-how so as to exploit specialized functional knowledge and cost advantages. Modules and systems are becoming more important, increasing as a percent of the value of supplied parts from 22 percent in 1993 to 43 percent in 2000. For example, suppliers such Magna, Johnson Controls, and Bosch are already developing and manufacturing increasingly complex and comprehensive modules and systems.

Business Strategy

The strategy of "Company A" is to transform itself from a Tier one automotive parts supplier into an integrated systems supplier. In order to achieve this, they need to build systems integration know-how, reengineer their processes, and build networks of suppliers. At the same time, they must also dramatically lower total product cost while significantly improving design quality. Moreover, they aim to increase revenues by 14 percent per year using the same capital and people base, and they aggressively divest all noncore and lower value-added activities. A privotal element of their change program is the transformation of the product development function.

Consolidation

As its first step in the transformation of their product development processes, the firm integrated all its systems to create a single bill of materials and parts library. They ensured that their system was compatible with suppliers' data, thereby achieving strategic flexibility in relation to its value network and consequent linkages.

Process Innovation

Through the consolidation of databases and systems alone, the company was able to reduce capital costs by reusing designs, tooling, and molds.

Their product life-cycle management (PLM) system was then integrated with suppliers' systems. This facilitated virtual procurement of components, as well as "virtual collaboration" with suppliers in product development, thereby freeing procurement staff and allowing them to do more value-added work.

Moreover, by also linking the PLM system to a database of consumer research, they were able to incorporate consumer preferences and other survey data into their product development process.

Top-level involvement

The ICT-implementation program had the open support of the CEO. Furthermore, a high-level manager was given full responsibility to oversee the transformation. The philosophy of change was well heralded throughout the organization, with the transformation successes being used in marketing material targeted at automobile manufacturers.

Execution

The company focused on the introduction of a global-standard product development process for improvement. In doing so, each new initiative reinforced and benefited from previous successfully implemented initiatives.

Furthermore, the company explicitly utilized an e-enabled program management with consistent metrics and milestone tracking to ensure that the organization understood the impact of the initiatives.

Outcome

In addition to the strategic long-term impact, the changes to the company's processes and ICT systems resulted in a 30 percent increase in product development productivity and a total annual savings of US$125 million through lower total system costs.

Implementation is systematically managed

It often takes years for many ICT investments to deliver their full potential. Some projects depend on long and challenging implementations, with long-term strategic goals. Although successful companies encourage using ICT for longer-term benefits, they manage their investments through tight setting of short-term deliverables. Multi-year transformation programs should follow a clear roadmap and release plan with strictly defined financial or other milestones.

On the other hand, our experience shows that, although most companies create business plans to manage the process, only around 30 percent actually measure the outcomes. Developing measures forces agreement within the organization as to what constitutes real value and creates a real implementation imperative.

ICT Strategy Subsumed Within Broader Goals

ICT is effectively a tool to achieve broader performance improvements, be it at a firm, industry, or economywide level. Therefore, policymakers must pursue broader strategies to encourage structural reform to increase the likelihood that triggers would drive managerial innovation at the firm level. These strategies often include facilitating industrywide restructuring and increasing competition. At the firm level, successful ICT must support a business's strategic imperatives, and must be driven by senior management to support clear internal innovation to improve performance.

ICT plays a supporting role that complements other economic forces

This chapter has highlighted several key findings from McKinsey's review of the role of ICT in supporting productivity growth.

1. ICT cannot by itself drive productivity improvements, which helps to partially explain the weak measured link between ICT investments and productivity growth.

2. ICT impacts productivity by supporting and enabling managerial innovations at the firm and industry level, but the triggers that spur managerial innovation are themselves driven by broader economic forces such as structural change, regulation, and competitive forces. (Whether the improvements are measurable in national accounts will depend on the methodology used and an industry's ability to capture the value created through innovation.)

3. Case studies show that ICT enables critical elements of managerial innovation at the firm level

4. Even where economic forces encourage innovation (and hence the use of ICT), the details of execution are critical to ensuring that ICT supports strategic goals.

Implications for policymakers

Productivity improvements are driven by economic factors (competition, regulation, structural change) that create triggers or incentives for industries and firms to pursue managerial innovation. ICT plays a supporting, but critical, role in this process. Therefore, policymaker objectives must focus on broader goals for the economy, and view ICT as a key supporting element of that strategy but not the primary goal by itself.

1. Policymakers need to take a holistic approach to ICT by linking the role of ICT to broader national goals. It is critical that policymakers consider how ICT will help them achieve economic, societal, or other goals, and not promote ICT for its own sake.

2. Ensuring that ICT successfully supports productivity growth requires a complementary set of policies focused on increasing the number of triggers for firms, in order to stimulate managerial innovation. Only through this complementary set of incentives can policymakers be assured that ICT-enabled capabilities will improve productivity.

3. Policymakers must, therefore, pursue a two-pronged approach to economic performance: broader macroeconomic policies that create incentives for and facilitate firm level innovation (e.g., policies that promote more intense competition, permit work force flexibility and restructuring, and improve human capital to facilitate adoption of innovation); and specific ICT-related constraints that hamper its role as an enabler (e.g., fostering standardization, education, supporting industry level applied research and development, and establishing the required underlying infrastructure)[10]

4. Successfully leveraging ICT will usually require a number of policymakers working together across government departments. Each department needs to assess the impact of ICT within their domain as well as the implications of department decisions on the overall ICT strategy.

Developing countries may actually find that ICT itself can act as a trigger to managerial innovation because of the impact that ICT training and capability building may have on a firm's workforce (as human capital levels in advanced countries are higher, this effect if probably less pronounced). In addition, the process of rolling-out ICT may catalyze best practice transfer by highlighting business processes that are significantly underperforming in a developing country firm.

Implications for business managers

ICT's enabling role means that it is a critical element in the pursuit of managerial innovation. ICT by itself, however, will not deliver performance improvement unless it is coupled with business change that is consistent with a firm's strategic goals.

1. ICT investment execution requires CEO or senior management attention. This is because the success of ICT implementation will depend on a firm's strategic goals (which are clearly the purview of senior management), and poor execution could severely damage a firm's competitive position.

2. Despite the possibility that most of the value creation from ICT-enabled innovation could be transferred to consumers, competitor investments mean that not investing in ICT is often not an option for the vast majority of firms.

3. Firms should invest in a portfolio of ICT initiatives that leverages all aspects of ICT potential. The balance of this portfolio of investments should reflect the firm's strategic priorities.

4. Firms are sitting on a large potential source of managerial improvements, as most have already undertaken substantial ICT investments. The absence of strategic triggers has often meant that those investments were undertaken without concurrent changes to business processes, limiting the performance impact of ICT. Because of this, firms can often tap existing ICT capabilities to drive a first wave of managerial innovation.

4. Large incremental ICT programs should focus on leveraging what is available first and on consolidating existing systems, data, and processes before seeking further efficiency through internal and external process optimization.

6. Successful product development often requires developing and fostering a "value network" of companies from other sectors. Value networks can be very powerful in creating innovation, not necessarily through the use of new technologies, but through novel ways of bringing previously disparate technologies together.

7. Execution is key, but management must focus new investments on: a) capturing short-term efficiency opportunities, and b) creating longer-term strategic advantages with strict "pay-as-you-go" milestones.

Conclusion

The relationship between economic performance and ICT is not straightforward. This is reflected in the difficulties of measuring correlations between ICT investments and productivity improvements at the national level. However, a relationship definitely exists.

This chapter has traced the link between ICT investment and productivity improvements, and concluded that ICT is a critical enabler of productivity. The key source of productivity improvement is managerial innovation, and the key stimuli of managerial innovation are broader economic forces such as competition, structural change for industries, and regulation.

These forces provide triggers that create incentives for firms to improve performance. ICT then enables the changes to the business model that are needed to improve performance. However, even in those cases where triggers were present, the complexity of ICT implementation meant that in many cases, ICT failed to deliver performance improvements.

While ICT's role in most modern innovations has been crucial, its function as an enabler means that it should not be the primary focus of policymakers' or CEOs' and senior managers' strategies to improve productivity. Instead, both stakeholders should approach ICT as a tool to support broader strategic goals, and look to complement ICT with actions and policies that promote managerial and firm innovation. Examples of these tools at the country level are policies that promote competition or structural change, and at the firm level, business process changes that support the firm's strategic priorities.

Endnotes

The authors would like to thank Gerlinde Gniewosz and Joshua Wine for their significant contributions.

1. An economy's "speed limit" is the maximum growth rate of real gross domestic product that an economy can sustain without running into capacity constraints; that is, without stoking inflation.

2. The UNIVAC was the first commercial computer that entered the American market in the early 1950s. The name stood for "Universal Automatic Computer", and it weighed approximately 16,000 pounds.

3. Solow subsequently declared, "You can see computers in the productivity statistics" (Uchitelle 2000).

4. In 1997 (2000) 3,170 (3,285) companies responded to METI's annual survey on Data Processing. [Statistics Bureau/ Statistical Research and Training Institute. 2001.]

5. Measured as real IT capital stock ÷ PEP (people employed in production)

6. The Economist. 2001.

7. The moving of outsourced functions to another country with a lower cost structure.

8. BMW website: www.bmw.com. September 2002.

9. For example, U.S. regulatory changes reduced the frictional cost of performing a trade; this stimulated an increase in trading volumes, capitalizing on the scale economies enabled by ICT.

10. See chapter on Network Readiness in the World Economic Forum. 2002. *Global Information Technology Report 2001–2002*. New York: Oxford University Press.

11. The 16th Rule refers to the SEC's 1997 mandate to quote securities prices in increments of 1/16th rather than 1/8th. The New York Stock Exchange and the Nasdaq started experimenting with decimalization even before the SEC's April 2001 deadline.

References

Banham, R. 2002. *CRM Rollouts: Mulligans Required. The Key to Successfully CRM Software? Often, Doing it Again*. August 1, 2002. CFO.com. Online http://www.cfo.com.

Bosworth, B.P. and Triplett, J.E. 2000. *What's new about the new economy? IT economic growth and productivity*. Rev. Dec 12, 2000. Washington D.C.: Brookings Economic Papers. http://www.brook.edu/scholars/bbosworth.htm

The Economist. 2001. *On Target*. May 5.

Gordon, R.J. 2001. *Technology and Economic Performance in the U.S. Economy* Rev. April 2001. NBER Working Paper No. w8771. http://faculty-web.at.northwestern.edu/economics/gordon/

Howarth, B. 2002. *The CRM Backlash*. Australia: Business Review Weekly. August 8.

McKinsey Global Institute (MGI).2001 *U.S. Productivity Growth 1995–2000*. Washington D.C.: McKinsey Global Institute.

Molineaux, P. 2002. *CRM—what went wrong?* London: Financial Services Distribution. July 1.

Statistics Bureau/Statistical Research and Training Institute. 2001 *IT Indicators in Japan, 2001*. Japan: Statistics Bureau & Statistics Center. http://www.stat.go.jp/english/data/it/index.htm,

Triplett, J.E. 1999. *The Solow productivity paradox. What do computers do to productivity?* Canadian Journal of Economics. Vol 32(2). April. pp. 309–334.

Uchitelle, L. 2000. *Economic View: Productivity Finally Shows the Impact of Computers* New York Times, March 12, section 3, p. 4.

Chapter 5

Leaders and Facilitators:

The New Roles of Governments in Digital Economies

Bruno Lanvin[1]

infoDev, The World Bank

Overview

In trying to identify the determinants of information and communication technology (ICT) development and competitiveness, the *Global Information Technology Report* uses a certain number of variables generally perceived as being in the hands of governments. The purpose of this chapter is to deepen and broaden the view provided by this exercise, by bringing the role of governments into perspective; in order to assess how governments can affect ICT development, it is vital to also understand how profoundly, over the last two decades, ICT have been affecting governments and governments' functioning and roles.

Fifteen years ago, Nobel Prize winner Robert Solow was lamenting that, "we see computers everywhere but in the productivity statistics."[2] Since then, productivity statistics have indeed shown how profound an impact the ICT revolution had had on practically every area of economic life.[3] This is yet another illustration of a simple truth about ICT and technological innovations in general: their effects are often overestimated in the short run, and underestimated in the longer run.

For governments, this situation creates a Cornelian dilemma: how can the fact that innovations in the ICT field will continue to spring from the private sector be combined with the expectation that governments will keep an eye on the "longer term" view and hence provide the necessary support, environment, and guidance for technologies and approaches that may not live long enough to impact the productivity statistics and network competitiveness of their respective countries?

Between the two extremes of "getting out of the way" and "controlling the information revolution," the recent period has generated a vast array of governmental practices and strategies, varying from the highly successful to the disastrous. Based on such experiences, this chapter will attempt to identify the ways in which ICT have changed the potential and actual roles and functioning of governments, as well as the ways in which governments have successfully contributed to the enhancement of national competitiveness.

How the Digital Economy Transforms Governments

The creation of modern governments in the nineteenth century was first guided by the political imperatives attached to the concept of nation states. Their roles were then largely of a regalian nature; that is, relating to royal prerogatives as in inheritances from centralized smaller kingdoms transposed to larger geographical entities. With the industrial revolution came fresh challenges, and governments took on new roles in those areas of the economy most affected by technological changes and in those where it was felt that markets would not suffice to bring social and economic stability; this was the time when central governments stepped in the area of antitrust and consumer protection laws, and established institutions and mechanisms to regulate stock exchanges, for example. It was also the time when an intergovernmental organization (the International Telecommunication Union [ITU]) was created to address issues of telecommunications at the international level.

Over the last twenty years or so, the world has seen a significant retreat by governments from many sectors of economic and social life. Market forces have become the main tool on which countries rely to ensure the optimal allocation of resources; many activities traditionally carried out by the public sector (including telecommunications) have been privatized on a large scale. By and large, this shift has generated significant benefits for consumers, and has helped to break some of the vicious circles in which many developing countries had been locked for a long time. On the other hand, the globalization of the world economy is raising new questions about governance, management, and accountability.

It has been argued[4] that recent changes in the field of global information and communications are now calling for a new shift in governments' roles—similar to, if not greater than, the one that followed the first industrial revolution. Of the main reasons this could be the case, the following characteristics of a global information-intensive economy are most often mentioned:

1. In an information-intensive economy, output is more and more composed of public goods.[5]

2. A global information economy generates an increasing amount of network externalities.[6]

3. A globally networked world economy is taking us much closer to a perfect market economy; that is, one in which information is instantaneously available to producers and consumers.[7]

4. The pace of changes in ICT related fields is too fast to allow governments to regulate appropriately.[8]

Of those four characteristics of a digital economy, the first and second (rising public goods and network externalities) seem to call for more (rather than less) government, while the third characteristic (fewer market imperfections) should lead to the opposite position. The last one (the ICT world moves too fast for governments) is more ambiguous, and could go either way.

In order to assess whether the current trend in the emerging global information economy is movement towards more or less government responsibilities, it is now useful to look at the other side of the coin: How can governments affect ICT development? What have they done so far in that area? And how successful have they been?

How Governments Can Affect ICT Development

The model used in the present report considers that governments play important roles in creating the proper environment for ICT development, and also have a significant role as users of these technologies. There is now widespread evidence that those countries that adopted strong competition policies in the area of telecommunications have generally achieved faster development of infrastructure and services, while registering steady decreases in consumer prices.

However, beyond the simple recipes of independent regulation, competition, and privatization, each national economy is a special case in which the identification of "best practices" combined with the exploitation of specific comparative advantages, is likely to lead to the differentiated strategies and approaches that are most likely to enhance its ICT competitiveness and Networked Readiness.

Governments' involvement in ICT: changes over time

In their traditional roles as hosts of large public monopolies for telecommunications and other ICT-intensive activities, governments used to adopt policies and take measures that had a direct impact on the supply and demand of technology. In many cases they would be both the main supplier and main buyer of ICT equipment and services.

Figure 1. **The Old Paradigm of Direct Government Intervention in ICT**

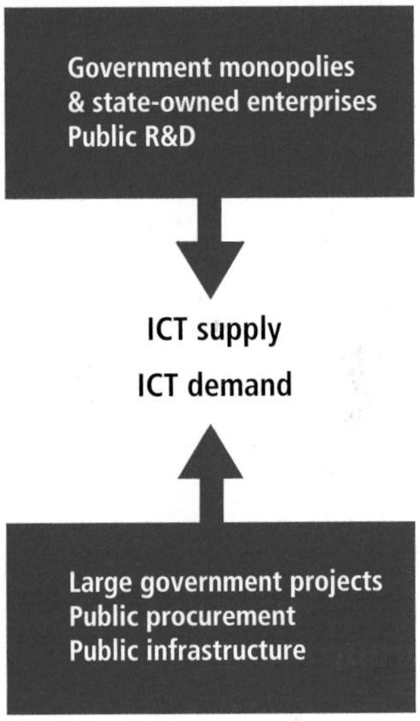

Government monopolies & state-owned enterprises Public R&D

ICT supply
ICT demand

Large government projects
Public procurement
Public infrastructure

Although this role of government is still prevalent in economies with a large public sector (e.g., China), it is rapidly diminishing. Governments are increasingly exerting a more indirect (but not less important) role as a promoter of ICT supply and ICT demand in their respective countries. On the supply side, the capacity of a country to innovate, and hence produce and adapt new technologies, is largely influenced by the ability of governments to mobilize and attract both financial and human resources. On the demand side, governments play strategic roles in the emergence of domestic markets for ICT, and in shaping international market conditions that will influence the flows of ICT and ICT-related knowledge across their national borders.

Figure 2. **The Modern Paradigm of Indirect Government Influence in ICT**

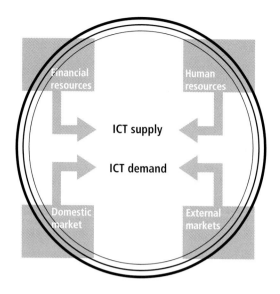

Governments' circles of influence

Around the world and in all types of economic systems, governments have all, by and large, tried to influence more or less directly the four determinants of ICT supply and

demand: human resources, financial resources, and domestic and international market conditions. They did it less and less from a producer (and buyer) point of view, and more and more as facilitators (creating the proper environment for innovation and growth in ICT, channeling and mobilizing financial and human resources to the ICT sector and related activities) and as leaders (establishing ICT as a national priority, providing a national vision for ICT and Networked Readiness, launching large ICT projects, and accelerating the adoption of ICT by government departments and the public sector by, for example, promoting e-government).

Figure 3 below outlines some of the main tools used by governments in these various functions (buyer, facilitator, leader) and contexts (environment, readiness, and usage).

On the grid below, governmental actions fall into five major groups.

G1. In the old styles of central governments, laying out fixed infrastructure has generally been the responsibility of national monopolies; these monopolies were frequently also producing terminals and various switching equipment for the telecommunication network. Research and development was often publicly subsidized, or carried

Figure 3. **How Governments Make and Influence ICT Decisions**

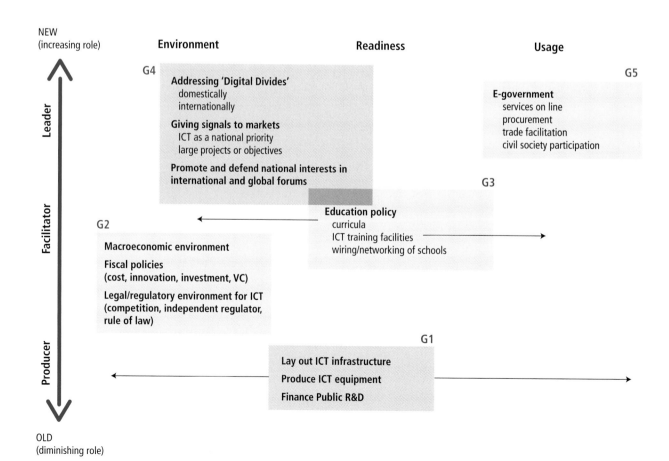

out through large public projects, civil or military.[9] In more recent times, public projects have remained important in countries like China, but also in Korea (broadband rollout), Malaysia (Multimedia Super Corridor), and Singapore (Singapore One), although those latter projects belong more to G4 (involving public-private partnerships). When such government initiatives have been undertaken as public projects, they have spanned the whole spectrum of possible impact zones, affecting the ICT environment, ICT readiness, and ICT usage.

G2. The responsibility of providing a proper macroeconomic, legal, and regulatory environment is part of the "traditional" responsibility of governments; in the digital age, however, these functions have implied new responsibilities, proper to the ICT field (e.g., in the area of spectrum management). G2 includes mostly "environmental" tasks, with significant spillover effects on readiness. Their effects on usage are not necessarily tangible in the absence of specific additional measures.

G3. Providing the right amount and quality of human resources for a network-ready economy is very much linked to the long-standing involvement of governments in the area of education. In this area, however, the emergence of a digital economy requires original approaches; for instance, changes in basic and advanced education curriculums require that schools be adequately equipped and connected. Another important element in the area of education is that constant changes in technologies and their applications require that life-long learning and vocational training capabilities be put in place; although most enterprises will consider G3 as environmental and readiness measures, this group has significant usage consequences and linkages with usage if, for instance, a national policy of equipping and connecting schools is set in motion.

G4. Large public initiatives in the area of ICT, as well as governments' ability to provide a society-wide vision of ICT development, have already been described above (as different from the more traditional public programs financed by governments under G1). In the area of ICT, the role of governments as "vision providers" cannot be underestimated; since it is in the nature of the budgetary allocations process to pit different ministries and departments against each other, it is important that ICT be established as a priority at the highest levels of the decision-making process (as opposed to the priority of an IT ministry).[10] G4 also overlaps some of the other traditional roles of governments, like ensuring social justice and equity through the pursuance of objectives such as universal services; when pursuing such objectives, governments have a mission to keep track of recent technological developments, as they may significantly affect the relative cost of the solutions selected.[11] Another of the new aspects of this group of governmental

responsibilities is the growing importance of the global debates that surround them. In an increasing number of areas, governments cannot address ICT issues without considering their global underpinnings; this is the case for intellectual property (where World Intellectual Property Organization [WIPO] and World Trade Organization [WTO] treaties and agreements apply), governance (Internet Corporation for Assigned Names and Numbers [ICANN]), and norms and standards (International Organization for Standardization [ISO], ITU, World Wide Web Consortium [W3C]). Last, but not least, over the last few years governments have been called to take a leading role in the formulation of international plans of action and strategies to bridge the digital divide and create digital opportunities for all,[12] and although such broad initiatives should not be expected to generate massive amounts of external financing in the immediate future, their importance should not be underestimated, as they often constitute the "think tanks" that could generate some of the guiding principles on which future actions and international agreements will be based.

G5. This last group of possible governmental responsibilities is clearly the one that is closest to "usage" objectives. By promoting the use of ICT in its own services, a government can acquire both experience and credibility, while leading through example. The new possibilities offered by ICT in the area of e-government are to be closely looked at in this context. By focusing initially on activities that can generate significant savings in the use of public resources, governments have been able to broaden their "legitimacy base" in the field of ICT and generate important externalities. For example, online procurement, trade facilitation, or customs automation can not only generate resources, but also enhance transparency in government operations, thus contributing to the fight against corruption, and this in turn may encourage foreign investors to partake in the Networked Readiness efforts of the country. Offering government services online with some degree of interactivity is also a way to engage individuals and civil society in public sector activities and reforms, and thus strengthen the democratic process.

Who is doing what? How governments address ICT issues

When one defines the involvement of governments along the lines described above (i.e., as leader and facilitator rather than as major producer and buyer of ICT and ICT-related products), one obtains a striking picture of governments' involvement in the ICT field in relation to income per capita. Contrary to what can be observed in many other sectors of the economy (e.g., the manufacturing sector, but also services such as health, education, or tourism), in ICT the roles played by governments increase with income.

Figure 4. "ICT Government" Leaders Can Be Found at All Levels of Income

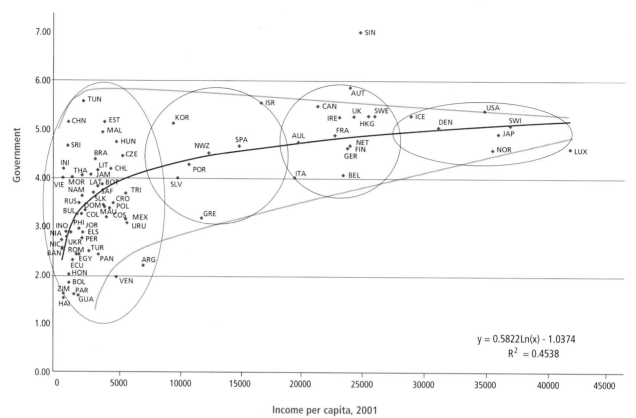

Source: Author's analysis of Networked Readiness Index results, 2002–2003

However, depending on relative income levels, there seems to be a certain number of thresholds that a country has to pass in order to be network-ready and ICT-competitive. Many of these thresholds are income-dependent, reflecting the fact that in poorer countries, for instance, governments are still faced with difficult choices between ICT-related objectives on one hand, and urgent and basic needs including food, health, and education on the other hand. Many middle-income countries still lack the regulatory and competition policy frameworks that would allow other ICT-related measures to gather momentum and generate measurable effects on readiness and usage.

Figure 4 shows, however, that each income group has its champions in terms of governmental involvement in achieving Networked Readiness and ICT competitiveness. For instance, among poor and middle-income countries,[13] countries such as Estonia, China, and Tunisia are clearly showing the way. Among the group of countries whose gross domestic product per capita is between US$7,000 and US$18,000, Korea and Israel are the leaders, whereas examples of leaders from among the next group of rich countries (between US$18,000 and US$28,000 per capita) include Singapore (the shining star of government leadership), but also Austria, Canada, Ireland, Hong Kong, and the United Kingdom; among the richest economies

(higher than US$28,000 per capita), the United States and Iceland show the highest degree of involvement from their respective governments.

The strong correlation between the list of "government champions" identified above and the overall Networked Readiness ranking provided in the present *Report* shows that, by and large, the involvement of governments has been successful when their role has been one of influence and facilitation rather than direct intervention.

How ICT Affects the Functioning and Roles of Governments

A fundamental difference exists between the functions and the roles of governments. Governments' functions (and functioning) correspond to what is delivered by and expected from governments once their roles have been defined and accepted. Governments' roles correspond to the missions with which a democratic process has entrusted them, or which they have given themselves or have been given by a higher authority. For example, promoting social justice is a role, whereas tax collection is a function.

The emergence of a digital economy has affected both the functions and the roles of governments. On one hand, ICT have been instrumental in changing the ways in

Figure 5. **Functions versus Roles of Governments**

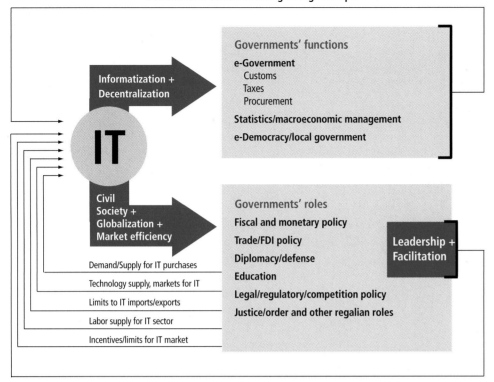

Demand for IT solutions/leading through example

Informatization + Decentralization

IT

Civil Society + Globalization + Market efficiency

Governments' functions

e-Government
Customs
Taxes
Procurement

Statistics/macroeconomic management
e-Democracy/local government

Governments' roles
Fiscal and monetary policy
Trade/FDI policy
Diplomacy/defense
Education
Legal/regulatory/competition policy
Justice/order and other regalian roles

Leadership + Facilitation

Demand/Supply for IT purchases
Technology supply, markets for IT
Limits to IT imports/exports
Labor supply for IT sector
Incentives/limits for IT market

e-Strategy, national ambition/social project pursued through IT

which governments and administrations operate; through informatization and decentralization, the advent of e-government has been one of the main manifestations of the impact of ICT on governments' functions. On the other hand, the information revolution has played a central role in encouraging and enabling governments to accept new roles. In addition to the traditional ("regalian") roles of central governments (in the areas of economic and social policies, education, diplomacy, defense, and justice, for example), new importance has been granted to the ability of governments to provide a vision, lead by example, and facilitate major socioeconomic changes. The main forces at work in this context are the rise of civil society as an organized player in local and global issues, globalization, and the emergence of new market efficiencies and inefficiencies. These elements are summarized in Figure 5.

Each of the mechanisms by which ICT affects governmental functions and roles has its own "feedback" effect. Such feedback effects generally consist of the actions and responsibilities taken by governments to influence the development of ICT and ICT-related activities at the environment, readiness, and usage levels. They therefore correspond to the groups of actions (G1 to G5) identified in the previous section.

The functional side: ICT and the delivery of government services

As users of ICT, governments can play a significant leading role by creating new modes of behavior in the public at large, educating their own personnel to the opportunities and challenges of ICT, improving the delivery of government services, strengthening the democratic process, and generating significant savings and revenues for the economy as a whole. Using the terminology adopted by the United Nations (UN),[14] one can identify three major levels at which governmental functions can significantly be affected (and generally improved) by ICT:

1. *e-Government*. This applies to interorganizational relationships, and includes:
    i. Policy coordination
    ii. Policy implementation
    iii. Public service delivery

2. *e-Administration*. This applies to intraorganizational relationships, and includes:
    i. Policy development
    ii. Organizational activities
    iii. Knowledge management

3. *e-Governance*. This applies to interaction between citizens, government organizations, and public and elected officials, and includes:

i. Democratic processes
ii. Open government
iii. Transparent decision-making

Of those three components, the first (e-government) is clearly the one on which a large number of countries (including many developing countries) have made the most measurable progress over the last few years. There is a stark difference between the "publishing" stage reached by many governments around the world (the UN estimates that some 169 out of 190 governments has some kind of website presence), the "interactive" elements that only a few dozen government sites provide, and the "transactional" e-government services available in seventeen countries.[15] The correlation between e-government achievements and overall network competitiveness indicators is strong, but not as strong as that between e-government performance and income per capita.[16] However, e-government is rapidly becoming a priority in developing countries in all regions.[17]

Governments' roles: from rulers/producers to leaders/facilitators

As the boundaries of their traditional areas of competence and power become increasingly unsettled, modern nation states are faced with difficult and unprecedented challenges. The field of ICT is probably one of the most revealing in that respect. Governments should have many reasons to tread carefully on, and even fear, ICT since it is an area in which (1) practice tends to precede legislation; (2) networks defy centralized structures; (3) externalities (and hence the risk of unintended consequences) are remarkably high; and (4) in spite of the burst of the 2001 techno-bubble, the ICT sector remains a high-growth area, which tends to increase business's pressure for a "hands-off" approach by governments. On the other hand, governments are expected to play a central role in shaping their respective countries' ICT policies and strategies, because (1) in a rapidly-changing technological environment, civil society expects a "vision" to guide public and private decisions; (2) some "regalian" functions of the state (taxation, legislation, regulation, social equity, education inter alia) become even more essential in this rapidly changing context; and (3) the "horizontal" nature of ICT is such that any ICT-centered decision is bound to affect a large array of sectors, thus requiring a higher level of arbitration when the respective interests of such sectors happen to conflict.

The diagram below (which does not change radically when other proxies are selected)[18] shows that the degree of

Figure 6. **Governments as Leaders and Facilitators**

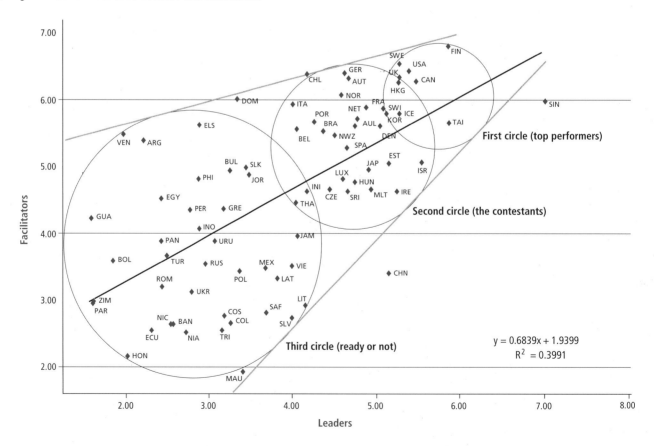

Note: The 'Government' variable of the NRI has been used as proxy for Government leadership (x), whereas 'Competition in telecoms' has been used as an indicator of the effectiveness of Governments as facilitators (y)

Source: Author's analysis of Networked Readiness Index results and data, 2002–2003

dispersion on facilitation indexes is higher at lower levels of government leadership. On the contrary, in those countries in which governments have fully endorsed a role as leader, performance on the facilitator scale is constantly high. This is illustrated by the cloud of points in the diagram converging towards the top-right corner of the chart; from these convergences one can hence identify three groups of countries:

1. The first circle—top performers of government's participation in the ICT revolution: Singapore is conspicuous in this group, in which one finds Finland, the United States, and Canada, but also Sweden, the United Kingdom, Taiwan, Hong Kong, Switzerland, Iceland, and Korea. Most of the top performers on the overall index of Networked Readiness can be found in this first circle.

2. The second circle—contestants: Some members of this group have too-small market sizes (Estonia, Ireland, Israel) to be part of the first circle,[19] but they clearly remain important sources of best practices in ICT development; other "contestants" include most of the European Union countries as well as Japan, Australia, and New Zealand, but also some emerging economies such as Brazil, Chile (which is especially strong on the facilitation axis), Hungary, the Czech Republic, India, Thailand, and Sri Lanka.

3. The third circle—ready or not: Some countries in this group are rather close to moving into the circle of contestants (Jordan, for example), whereas the laggards include some large economies (e.g., Russia) and most of the smaller economies of Central and South America.

By and large, the data available confirm that government leadership in offering a vision in the field of ICT on one hand, and the ability of governments to facilitate the adoption and dissemination of ICT, on the other, are increasingly correlated as one moves up the scale of Networked Readiness. This suggests that when those governments that have accepted and endorsed leadership responsibilities in the ICT field did not do so "the old fashioned way" (i.e., through direct involvement in ICT demand and supply), but by combining indirect influence (on financial and human resources available to ICT-related activities, and on domestic and external market conditions) with a strong facilitation role, encouraging competition and supporting market efficiency and transparency.

Conclusion: Theoretical and Practical Roles of Governments

The principle

To compete successfully in a network-based global economy, governments need to be both leaders and facilitators. The larger and the more "ICT mature" their domestic market base, the greater the emphasis they should put on their facilitation role. At earlier stages of ICT adoption and for smaller economies, providing a vision and setting a high level of priority for ICT development is a key responsibility that only governments can successfully endorse.

The reality

However, within these broad guiding principles, each national environment will remain a special case. The field of ICT is one in which both governments and the private sector have proven able to make mistakes. In the ICT field, the high degree of product and process innovation likely to prevail in the coming years will continue to necessitate brutal changes in production functions, market mechanisms, and public policies; business models will continue to be challenged on a daily basis, and well established laws, regulations, and disciplines will have to be adjusted domestically and internationally. In such an unsettled environment, much of the process of decision-making (public and private) will still rely on trial and error.[20]

Yet, to some extent, the concept of trial and error seems to be more acceptable for private individuals and entities than for governments. However, over the last few years, operating largely through trial-and-error approaches, many governments have made significant progress in their ability to handle the information revolution and foster their respective countries' Networked Readiness and competitiveness. In the process, they have learned to minimize the probability of failure and maximize expected outcome by (1) granting increasing importance to the experience of other governments (trying to identify best practices and not repeat other countries' mistakes); (2) promoting global norms and international rule-making in a number of ICT-related sectors; and (3) developing new working relationships and consultation mechanisms with the private sector and civil society in general.

The predicament

In exerting their dual role as leaders and facilitators of the network revolution, governments need to grant priority importance to the following elements, finding between them the mix best adapted to their respective national environments.

Leadership: Providing a vision and an example

1. Make ICT adoption and Networked Readiness a national priority; identify innovative projects (at home and abroad) that could "make a difference" in the country's Networked Readiness, and push their adoption

2. Use ICT to lead government reform projects by promoting e-government and a greater use of ICT in "regalian" fields such as health, education, justice, or tax administration. Public procurement and customs automation are generally good starting points because they generate revenues and savings; providing of data and statistics are also a ways to increase government transparency.

3. Generate broad and active support from civil society for a national "e-strategy" based on policies which will help the country to "bridge the digital divide" between it and other countries without increasing the divide at home; rural connectivity and low-cost access solutions should be preferred to high-visibility/urban-centered projects;[21] foster public-private partnership as often as possible

4. Promote the production of national content online and through electronic media

5. Grant high priority to the protection of individuals' rights, privacy, security, and to consumer protection; involve civil society as much as possible in related choices and decisions

6. Keep track of other governments' best practices and worst failures and consider ways to benefit from such knowledge.

Facilitation: Providing a supportive environment for early adoption of ICT

1. Provide the proper legal and regulatory environment for ICT-related activities (e.g., fixed line and mobile telecommunications, e-commerce, Internet services provision)

2. Provide the proper environment for innovation and risk-taking (e.g., through fiscal exemptions, availability of venture capital)

3. Provide the proper environment for investment, both domestic and foreign

4. Promote ICT training, education, and research

5. Negotiate and influence the adoption of proper international frameworks, norms, and standards by participating actively in the governance of the global information economy.

When pondering the relative value of all such possible actions, governments will of course be reminded by their respective business communities and civil societies that Networked Readiness can also been stimulated by governments who know when *not* to step in. The evidence described in this chapter, however, seems to show that governments should be as quick at giving up some of their traditional roles and developing new ones. The rulers and administrators of the industrial age have remarkably little time to become the leaders and facilitators of the digital age.

Endnotes

1. Bruno Lanvin is manager of the Information for Development Program (*info*Dev) at the World Bank. The views expressed here are the author's personal opinions, and they do not necessarily reflect those of the World Bank or *info*Dev. The author wishes to acknowledge the statistical and graphical support received from Rafael Hernandez Rios and Rajesh Vasudevan.

2. Solow R. 1987. "We'd Better Watch Out," *New York Times Book Review*, 12 July.

3. Joe Stiglitz et al. (2000) quoted the following figures for the United States: from 1991 to 1995, U.S. productivity increased by 1.6 percent; from 1996 to 1999, the increase was 2.7 percent. The striking difference between the two periods (1.1 percent) is explained on one hand by the impact of investment made in the ICT sector (plus 0.5 percent) and on the other hand by increased efficiency in the production of computers and semiconductors (plus 0.2 percent); the remainder of the productivity gains differential (plus 0.4 percent) is explained by other (i.e., non ICT-related) factors. In other words, ICT can be considered as responsible of two-thirds of the tremendous acceleration of productivity gains enjoyed by the U.S. economy from 1996 to 1999.

4. For example, by Joseph Stiglitz and others. See Stiglitz et al. (2000).

5. If one defines a public good as (1) displaying zero marginal cost and (2) having nonexcludability effects, one quickly realizes that an information-intensive economy is more prone to generate public goods than traditional industrial economies. For example, in a nonencrypted broadcasting network, an additional customer has a cost of zero and nobody can be excluded from it, since the only requirement is to be equipped with a receiver. The Internet has been the most recent example of the emergence of global public goods, raising unprecedented issues in the area of intellectual property rights (e.g., in the case of Napster and other peer-to-peer MP3 files-swapping fora).

6. The concept of network externalities is often summarized by the so-called "Metcalfe law of the telecosm" (George Gilder's expression), by which the potential value of a network connecting "n" machines or individuals increases with the square of n. Metcalfe's law suggests that partial private interests, which may lead to market segmentation, would prevent network externalities from being fully reaped; it also suggests that in the absence of public intervention, suboptimal choices might be made, for example, in the area of technical norms and interoperability of networks.

7. For instance, the existence of perfect (i.e., instantaneous, ubiquitous, and cost-free) information is one of the hypotheses on which modern trade theory (HOS) relies. Because it is never realized in practice, this hypothesis has been considered as a major indicator of market imperfections, thus justifying various types of government interventions and corrections.

8. The pace at which changes are taking place in the ICT sector and in related activities is clearly higher than in most other sectors of the economy. For governments in all countries and economic systems, this is more a challenge than an opportunity. This difference between tempos is well described by Jean-Francois Rischard: "Like two geysers, the two forces of population increase and the new world economy spew unprecedented complexity in economic, social, political and environmental matters. Human problems are becoming more pressing, more global, and more difficult to solve—technically and politically. A crisis of complexity is brewing. The rate of change produced by the two forces contrasts starkly with the slow evolution of human institutions. Whether they are nation-states, government departments, international institutions, or large outfits of any types, human institutions tend to evolve only slowly, in a linear way." (*High Noon*. New York: Basic Books, 2002:38).

9. As in the case of DARPA (a Ministry of Defense project) in the early days of the Internet in the United States.

10. The same diagnosis/prognosis applies to all levels of government, including local (e.g., regional, state, municipal), and also "supranational:" The success of the European Union in launching some of its technology programs (Eureka for example) has often been attributed to its ability to transcend some of these internal obstacles.

11. For example, mobile telephony and WiFi—802.11 wireless connections—have considerably enhanced the possibilities of connecting rural areas.

12. Among such initiatives, the more noteworthy include the G-8's Digital Opportunity Task Force (DOT Force), created by the Okinawa Summit of 2000, and the World Economic Forum's Digital Divide Initiative, initiated a few months earlier. Multilateral institutions have also contributed to this effort either through their regular work (ITU, United Nations Development Programme, the World Bank) or through special bodies such as the United Nations ICT Task Force, created in 2001.

13. Here defined arbitrarily as countries having an annual gross domestic product per capita lower than US$7,000 in 2001.

14. See UN and ASPA (2002).

15. The typology (publish, interact, transact) is the one used by *info*Dev and the Center for Democracy and Technology. See Center for Democracy and Technology (2002). The number of countries in each category is derived from UN and ASPA (2002).

16. According to the e-government index compiled by UN/ASPA, the ten "global e-government leaders" are: the United States (index 3.11), Australia (2.60), New Zealand (2.59), Singapore (2.58), Norway (2.55), Canada (2.52), the United Kingdom (2.52), the Netherlands (2.51), Denmark (2.47), and Germany (2.46).

17. Regional leaders include Brazil and Mexico in Latin America, Korea in Asia (after Singapore), the United Arab Emirates in the Middle East, and Egypt and South Africa in Africa.

18. Interesting "special cases" include Singapore and China. Singapore undoubtedly belongs to the first circle, of which many analysts of government action in the digital economy would easily consider it as the leader. If Singapore appears so neatly below the trend line of Figure 6, it is not only because it has taken responsibility for the launching and execution of large scale government programs (such as Singapore One), but also because the index chosen to measure the "facilitation role" of countries creates a distortion in favor of large markets, where competition is more easily sustained between a larger number of players. Taiwan, Malta, Israel, and to some extent Estonia and Ireland suffer from the same distortion. In the case of China, the explanation is of a political, not technical, nature: competition in the telecommunications field is still in its infancy (see the *Report*'s chapter on China for a more detailed analysis of possible consequences of China's WTO commitments on the degree of competition in telecommunications).

19. See previous endnote.

20. This may be a sign of the times, as indicated by George Gilder in a stunning comparison between nations and networks: "Nations and networks can win by shunning determinism and finding stability in a constant shuffle of collisions and contentions in ever-expanding arenas of liberty. Because of an acceptance of setbacks, capitalist markets are more robust than socialist systems that plan for perfection. In the same way, successful people and companies have more failures than failures do. The successes use their faults and collisions as sources of new knowledge. Companies that try to banish chance by relying on market research and focus groups do less well than companies that freely make mistakes and learn from them." George Gilder in "Metcalfe's Law and Legacy," first published in *Forbes ASAP* on September 13, 1993. This piece then became part of Gilder's bestseller *Telecosm* (New York: Simon and Schuster, 1996).

21. On the possibilities of adopting such "non-kuznetsian approaches to bridging the digital divide," see Lanvin (2001).

References

Center for Democracy and Technology. 2002. *The e-Government Handbook*. Online. http://www.infodev.org.

G-8 Digital Opportunities Task Force (G-8 DOT Force). 2001. "Digital Opportunities for All." Report presented at the G-8 Summit of Genoa, Italy, July 2001.

Gilder, G. 1993. "Metcalfe's law and legacy," *Forbes ASAP*.

Italian Presidency. 2002. "The Italian Initiative on e-Government for Development: The e-Model." Presented at the G-8 Summit of Kananaskis, Canada, June 2002. Mimeo.

Lanvin, B. 2001. "La fracture numérique n'est pas une fatalité," *Les Cahiers du Numérique*.

Rischard, J.F. 2002. *High Noon*. New York: Basic Books.

Stiglitz, J. 1988. *Economics of the Public Sector*. New York: W.W. Norton.

Stiglitz, J., P. Orszag, and J. Orszag. 2000. "The Role of Government in a Digital Age." Commissioned by the Computer and Communications Industry Association. Mimeo.

United Nations and American Society for Public Administration (UN and ASPA). 2002. *Benchmarking e-Government: A Global Perspective*. New York: United Nations Division for Public Economics and Public Administration.

World Bank Group. 2002. *Information and Communications Technologies—A World Bank Group Strategy*. Washington D.C.: The World Bank.

Part 2

Regional Analyses and Country Case Studies

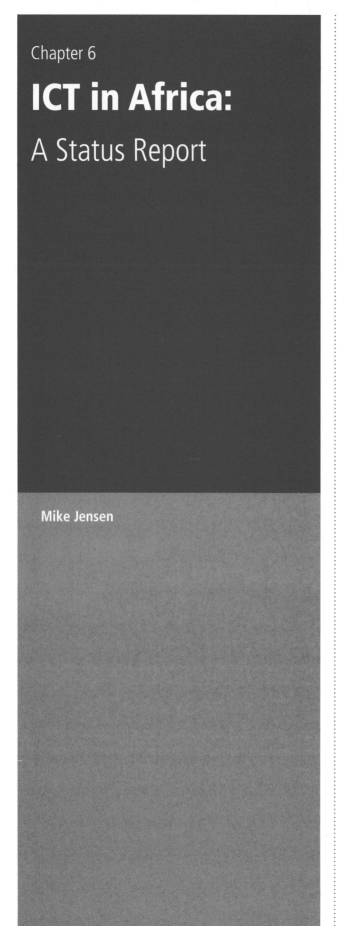

Chapter 6

ICT in Africa:

A Status Report

Mike Jensen

Environment and Readiness

The environment for networked readiness has improved relatively rapidly in most urban areas in Africa. Five years ago, only a handful of countries had local Internet access or mobile telephones; now, devices and access are available in virtually every major city. Hundreds of new radio stations and newspapers have been licensed over the last few years and digital satellite television has also become widely available. The "digital divide" however, is still at its most extreme in Africa. In absolute terms, networked readiness is still at a very early stage of development compared to other regions of the world. Of the approximately 816 million people in Africa in 2001, it is estimated[1] that only:

one in four have a radio (200 million);

one in 13 have a television (62 million);

one in 35 have a mobile telephone (24 million);

one in 39 have a fixed line (21 million);

one in 130 have a personal computer (PC) (5.9 million);

one in 160 use the Internet (5 million);

one in 400 have pay-television (2 million).

These figures do not take into consideration the widespread sharing of media that takes place in Africa (often ten people may read the same newspaper or share an Internet account, and a whole village may use a single telephone line or crowd around a television set at night); nevertheless, it appears that sub-Saharan Africa may be slipping behind when compared to south Asia, the other least developed region. As Table 1 shows, the two regions are at the bottom of the list in Internet usage surveys around the world, but south Asia has caught up considerably since 1998.

Table 1. **Internet Users as Percentage of Total Population**

Region	1998	2000
United States	26.30	54.3
High-income OECD (excluding the U.S.)	6.90	28.2
Latin America and the Caribbean	0.80	3.2
East Asia and the Pacific	0.50	2.3
Eastern Europe and CIS	0.80	3.9
Arab States	0.20	0.6
Sub-Saharan Africa	0.10	0.4
South Asia	0.04	0.4
World	2.40	6.7

Source: United Nations Development Program, *World Development Report 2001*.

Because the region is so diverse, it can be misleading to generalize about Africa. The averages given above obscure the great variation between countries, but it can be said that most of the continent's population are amongst the poorest in the world (Africa had US$766 in gross domestic product (GDP) per person in 2000), with the divide between urban and rural areas being particularly marked. Most services are concentrated in the towns, while the majority of Africans (70 to 80 percent) reside in smaller communities scattered across the vast rural areas. In some countries, more than 75 percent of the country's telephone lines are concentrated in the capital city. Irregular or nonexistent electricity supplies are also common in Africa, especially outside major towns.

Another systemic problem is that road, rail, and air transport networks are limited, costly to use, and often in poor condition, resulting in barriers to the increased movement of people and goods; increased mobility is needed to implement and support a pervasive network infrastructure and also for the increased economic and social activity that would occur with greater physical movement of people. Visa requirements and congested border posts add to these difficulties. Furthermore, many tax regimes still treat computers and cellular telephones as luxury items, which makes these imported items all the more expensive.

Another problem is that the brain drain and generally low levels of education and literacy have together resulted in a great scarcity of skills and expertise (at all levels, from policy making down to the end user). Rural areas in particular have limited human resources. Along with the very low pay scales in the African civil service, this is a chronic problem for governments that are continually losing their brightest and most experienced to the private sector. The fact that this situation is not unique to Africa or other developing countries, but is also being faced by the developed world, is simply exacerbating the situation in Africa, because experienced professionals are able to find much higher paying jobs in Europe and North America.

Finally, while a good business climate is acutely needed or the information and communications sector, the general investment climate in Africa often suffers from the well-known problems of small markets, nontransparent and time-consuming business procedures, limited opportunities (partly due to the historic pattern of state monopolies), scarce local capital, currency instability, exchange controls, and inflation.

Usage

Telecommunication

Overall, a substantial increase in the rate of expansion and modernization of fixed networks is currently taking place, along with an explosion of mobile networks. The number of main lines in Africa grew about 9 percent per year between 1995 and 2001, although the overall fixed line teledensity as of 2001 is still only about one in 40 inhabitants, and

one in 130 in sub-Saharan Africa (excluding South Africa). Taking into account population growth, the effective annual increase in lines is only 6 percent. Also, much of the existing telecommunications infrastructure is out of the reach of most people—50 percent of the available lines are in the capital cities, where only about 10 percent of the population lives. In more than fifteen countries in Africa, including Côte d'Ivoire, Ghana, and Uganda, more than 70 percent of the fixed lines are still located in the largest city (International Telecommunication Union [ITU] 2002).

Overall, the number of fixed lines increased from 12.5 million to 21 million across Africa between 1995 and 2001, a teledensity growth rate of 6.7 percent (i.e., taking into account population growth). North Africa had 11.4 million of these fixed lines and South Africa, 5 million lines; this means there were only 4.6 million lines in the rest of the continent. Therefore, while the sub-Sahara has about 10 percent of the world's population (626 million), it has only 0.2 percent of the world's 1 billion fixed telephone lines. Compared to all of the low-income countries (which house 50 percent of the world's population and 10 percent of the telephone lines), the penetration of telephone lines on the subcontinent is about three times worse than the "average" low-income country.

The situation is not quite as bad as it would appear, however, because of the penetration of mobile networks, where subscribers (now numbering 23.5 million) have surpassed fixed line users in most countries; this demonstrates that there is pent-up demand for basic voice services. Most of the subscribers use prepaid accounts, and because of the low cost and long range of the cellular base stations, many rural areas have also been covered. But the high cost of mobile usage (US$0.25 to US$0.50/minute) makes it too expensive for regular local calls or Internet access. A common response to this is the use of text messaging; in some countries, for example, Uganda, Kenya, and South Africa, text messaging now includes delivery of information services such as news, weather, and market prices.

Even if telecommunications infrastructure is beginning to spread, domestic use has, until recently, been largely confined to the small proportion of the population that can actually afford their own telephone—the cost of renting a connection averages almost 20 percent of GDP per capita, versus a world average of 9 percent and only 1 percent in high-income countries.[2] Despite these high charges relative to income levels, the number of public telephones is still much lower than elsewhere. According to the ITU (2001), there are approximately 350,000 public telephones in the whole continent of Africa—75,000 of which are in the sub-Sahara—or about one telephone for every 8,500 people, compared to a world average of one to 500 and a high-income average of one to 200.

However, an increasing number of operators in Africa are now passing the responsibility for maintaining public telephones to the private sector, and this has resulted in a rapid growth of public "phone shops" and "telecenters" in many countries; the most well-known case is that of Senegal, which now has more than 10,000 commercially-run public phone bureaus employing more than 15,000 people and generating more than 30 percent of the entire network's revenues. While most of these are in urban areas, a growing number are being established in more remote locations, and some networks also provide Internet access and other more advanced ICT services to the public.

Public telephone operators (PTOs) in some countries, such as Botswana and South Africa, are now launching prepaid fixed line services, or providing a "virtual telephone" alternative for those unable to obtain their own telephone. Subscribers are issued their own unique phone number and pay a small rental for a voice mailbox, from which they can retrieve their messages from any telephone. A pager can also be tied to the system to immediately inform the subscriber that a voice message is waiting.

Although there is substantial gray-market use of Voice over Internet Protocol (VoIP) services in Africa wherever international bandwidth allows, these are not officially permitted for the end user anywhere in the region except in Egypt and Nigeria. In Egypt, the national telecommunications operator provides a PC-to-phone service, and in Nigeria, the regulator has sanctioned all licensed cybercafes to provide VoIP. However, many telecommunications operators are now using or planning to use VoIP as a transport layer on their international and national links, and operators in countries such as Egypt, Gambia, Nigeria, Senegal, South Africa, and Zimbabwe have established joint ventures with international VoIP companies such as ITXC, GatewayIP, and Ibasis to implement these facilities.

Nevertheless, high telecommunications charges (often up to ten times greater than rates for equivalent services in Europe or North America) and limited service are still generally prevalent, largely because of the monopoly environment in which most national state-run providers operate. This is now slowly changing, with the first step usually being to seek an international strategic equity partner in a partial-privatization process. Generally, there have been two modes of partial privatization; selling less than (some countries are selling 30 to 33 percent) or more than 51 percent of shares. The largest international partners and their ownership levels are currently as follows: France Telecom (Côte d'Ivoire Telecom, 51 percent; SONATEL [Senegal], 33 percent; Mauritius Telecom, 40 percent); Malaysia Telecom (Telkom SA [South Africa], 30 percent; Ghana Telecom, 30 percent;

SOTELGUI [Guinea Conakry], 60 percent); Maroc Telecom (Mauritel [Mauritania], 54 percent); Vivendi Universal (Maroc Telecom, 35 percent).

While most African PTOs are, or will shortly be, partially privatized, there are still a few countries lagging behind in privatizations, notably Nigeria, Gambia, Democratic Republic of the Congo, the Comoros Islands, Sierra Leone, Liberia, Zimbabwe, and Libya. Of worldwide distribution of privatization in the year 2000 (by region, based on ninety-eight countries), the African continent represented 15 percent; Europe, 35 percent; the Americas, 24 percent; the Asia Pacific region, 20 percent; and the Arab states accounted for 6 percent. In terms of the percentage of privatized operators, in 2000 Africa had 35 percent; Europe, 63 percent; the Americas, 74 percent; Asia Pacific, 53 percent; and the Arab states, 29 percent.

The availability of specialist training in telecommunications is currently extremely limited on the continent. In Africa, there are only two major regional centers for training in telecommunications: ESMT in Senegal for francophone countries, and AFRALTI in Kenya for Anglophone countries. It is expected that these centers, with the support of an ITU program, will be transformed into Centers of Excellence in Telecommunications Administration (CETA). CETA is intended to provide senior-level, advanced training, and professional development in the areas of telecommunications policies, regulatory matters, and the management of telecommunications networks and services.

A number of telecommunication operators maintain their own training schools but these, similar to the operators, usually lack financial resources. Over the last twenty years, the German international technical training assistance agency, Carl Duisberg Gesellschaft, has sent a large number of telecommunications trainees from Africa to Germany; many other development agencies have similar, if smaller, programs. At a global level, one initiative that may have an impact in the future is the ITU's Global Telecommunications Academy. This will operate as a brokerage service for distance-learning courses. Once established, the Academy is to be self-financed through a fee payable by every course participant. The aim of the Academy is to create a cooperative network of partners by pooling existing resources in universities, training institutes, financing bodies, governments, regional organizations, and telecommunications operators.

Table 2. **Telecommunications Usage in Africa, 2001**

Country	Fixed Lines (000)	Fixed Line Penetration (% of Population)	Public Telephones (000)	Mobile Users (000)	Mobile Penetration (% of Population)
Algeria	1,880.0	6.04	5.00	100.0	0.32
Angola	80.0	0.59	0.27	86.5	0.64
Benin	59.3	0.92	0.51	125.0	1.94
Botswana	150.3	9.27	3.00	278.0	16.65
Burkina Faso	57.6	0.47	1.44	75.0	0.61
Burundi	20.0	0.29	0.08	20.0	0.29
Cameroon	101.4	0.67	6.55	310.0	2.04
Cape Verde	62.3	14.27	0.39	31.5	7.21
Central Africa	10.0	0.26	0.09	11.0	0.29
Chad	11.0	0.14	0.06	22.0	0.27
Comoros	8.9	1.22	0.17	—	—
Republic of Congo	22.0	0.71	—	150.0	4.82
Côte d'Ivoire	293.6	1.80	1.93	728.5	4.46
Djibouti	9.9	1.54	0.42	150.0	0.29
D. R. C.	20.0	0.04		3.0	0.47
Egypt	6,650.0	10.30	21.99	2,793.8	4.33
Equatorial Guinea	6.9	1.47	—	15.0	3.19
Eritrea	32.0	0.84	0.42	—	—
Ethiopia	310.0	0.48	1.56	27.5	0.04
Gabon	37.2	2.95	0.83	258.1	20.45
Gambia	35.0	2.62	0.68	43.0	3.22
Ghana	242.1	1.16	3.18	193.8	0.93
Guinea	25.5	0.32	0.85	55.7	0.69
Guinea Bissau	12.0	0.98	0.20	—	—
Kenya	313.1	1.00	9.03	500.0	1.60
Lesotho	22.2	1.03	0.37	33.0	1.53
Liberia	6.7	—	—	—	—
Libya	610.0	10.93	0.45	50.0	0.90
Madagascar	58.4	0.36	0.46	147.5	0.90
Malawi	54.1	0.47	0.54	55.7	0.48
Mali	49.9	0.43	2.37	45.3	0.39
Mauritania	19.0	0.72	0.89	—	—
Mauritius	306.8	25.56	2.92	300.0	25.00
Mayotte	10	6.98	—	—	—
Morocco	1,193.3	3.92	46.84	4,771.7	15.68
Mozambique	89.4	0.44	1.86	169.9	0.84
Namibia	117.4	6.57	5.30	100.0	5.59
Niger	21.7	0.19	0.06	1.8	0.02
Nigeria	500.0	0.43	1.60	330.0	0.28
Réunion	268.5	—	—	—	—
Rwanda	21.5	0.27	0.40	65.0	0.82
SaoTomé	5.4	3.63	0.08	—	—
Senegal	237.2	2.45	13.49	390.8	4.04
Seychelles	21.4	26.73	0.22	44.1	55.15
Sierra Leone	22.7	0.47	0.31	26.9	0.55
Somalia	15.0	—	—	—	—
South Africa	4,969.0	11.35	178.11	9,197.0	21.00
Sudan	453.0	1.42	5.25	105.0	0.33
Swaziland	32.0	3.14	0.83	66.0	6.47
Tanzania	148.5	0.41	0.72	427.0	1.19
Togo	48.1	1.03	0.16	95.0	2.04
Tunisia	1,056.2	10.89	19.31	389.2	4.01
Uganda	63.7	0.28	1.38	322.7	1.43
Zambia	85.4	0.8	0.87	98.3	0.92
Zimbabwe	253.7	1.86	3.23	328.7	2.41
Total	**21,210.3**	**3.52**	**346.67**	**23,545.2**	**2.95**

Source: International Telecommunication Union

Countries with Advanced Data Services

Botswana—ISDN, Frame Relay

Egypt—ISDN, Frame Relay, ATM, DSL

Kenya—ISDN, DSL

Ghana—Frame Relay

Mauritius—ISDN, Frame Relay, DSL, ATM

Morocco—ISDN, GPRS, Frame Relay

Senegal—ISDN

Seychelles —ISDN

South Africa—ISDN, GPRS, Frame Relay

Tunisia—ISDN

Uganda—ISDN, DLS

The Internet

The use of the Internet is a good indicator of the use of information and communication technologies, as such use requires the integration of many of individual components—electricity, telecommunications infrastructure, computers, and the skills to use them. As the Figure 1 shows, both the number of Internet users and the amount of international bandwidth is still growing strongly across the continent.

Figure 1. **Growth of Internet Use in Africa**

Subscribers/Kbps

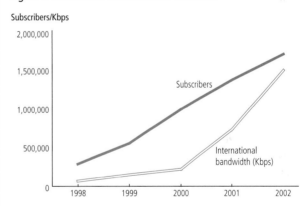

Source: Sangonet http://www3.sn.apc.org/africa

In Africa, the pattern of Internet diffusion has been similar to that of the mobile telephone networks. Although the Internet is not quite as widespread, it preceded the mobile telephone explosion; its greatest impact is at the top end of business and in wealthy families, primarily in major urban areas.

The rates of growth seen in the 1990s have slowed in most countries, because most users who can afford a computer and telephone have already obtained connections. However, although the total number of dial-up subscriber accounts is readily available, the large number of shared dial-up accounts, along with the relatively high use of public access services such as telecenters, and cybercafes, make it difficult to measure the total number of Internet users. Because the total number of dial-up accounts is only a partial gauge of the size of the Internet sector, the sector should be looked at along with other factors, such as the quantity of international traffic each country generates.

As measured by Network Wizards,[3] the total number of computers permanently connected to the Internet in Africa (excluding South Africa) exceeded 35,000 in 2001. However, such figures are becoming increasingly meaningless in Africa, with the widespread use of dot-com and dot-net domains along with the frequent re-use of Internet address space behind firewalls due to the difficulties of obtaining public Internet space. As a result, many African countries surveyed by Network Wizards show zero or only a handful of hosts, when in actual fact there might be hundreds, if not thousands, of machines connected to the Internet in each country.

As of mid-2002, the number of dial-up Internet subscribers was close to 1.7 million, which is 20 percent up from 2001, an increase mainly bolstered by growth in a few countries, such as Nigeria. North Africa and South Africa are responsible for about 1.2 million of these subscribers, leaving about 500,000 for the remaining forty-nine sub-Saharan African countries. If we assume that each computer with an Internet or e-mail connection supports a range of three to five users, this puts current estimates of the number of African Internet users at about 5 to 8 million. About 1.5 to 2.5 million of these users are outside North and South Africa; this suggests one user for every 250 to 400 people. The world average, in contrast, is one user for every fifteen people; the North American and European average is about one user in every two to three people. No studies have been made in Africa of the number of rural versus urban users, but it is safe to say that users in the cities and towns vastly outnumber rural users.

The use of public access facilities and corporate or academic networks is continuing to grow at greater rates than the number of dial-up users. Evidence of this pattern can be seen in the deployment of international Internet bandwidth, which is still expanding faster than the number of dial-up subscribers. International Internet bandwidth increased by more than 100 percent last year, from 700 Mbps of available outgoing bandwidth in 2001 to 1,500 Mbps in 2002. However, this is still slower growth than the rest of the world, which averaged 174 percent growth in 2001; further, some international links may only be as big as the circuit used by a small- or medium-sized business, or even a broadband home user, in a developed country—that is, about 128 Kbps. In most cases these circumstances are confined to very small and poor African countries, but there are many other regulatory, historic, and social factors that also influence slow growth.

Due to high international tariffs and lack of circuit capacity, obtaining sufficient international bandwidth is a major problem in most countries, and although conditions have improved recently, users generally still have to contend

Figure 2. **Countries with More Than 10,000 Internet Subscribers**

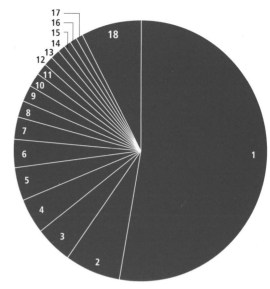

Dial-up subscriptions

1	South Africa	900,000
2	Egypt	120,000
3	Morocco	80,000
4	Algeria	75,000
5	Tunisia	7,0000
6	Nigeria	60,000
7	Reunion	47,000
8	Kenya	35,000
9	Mauritius	35,000
10	Tanzania	30,000
11	Zimbabwe	25,000
12	Botswana	20,000
13	Swaziland	20,000
14	Angola	16,000
15	Senegal	15,000
16	Ghana	15,000
17	Namibia	15,000
18	The rest	130,535

Source: Sangonet

with substantial congestion at peak times. This year, Egypt overtook South Africa as the country with the most international bandwidth (550 Mbps vs. 380 Mbps), following the launch of Nile-Online, a government-backed international connectivity provider. Today, twenty countries have links carrying 5 Mbps or more, and thirteen countries—Algeria, Botswana, Egypt, Kenya, Mauritius, Morocco, Nigeria, Senegal, South Africa, Sudan, Tanzania, Tunisia and Zimbabwe—have outgoing links of 10 Mbps or more. Also of note is that while the range in available international bandwidths continues to increase, eight countries in Africa (Liberia, Republic of Congo, Chad, Equatorial Guinea, Comoros, and São Tomé and Príncipe) are still on international links of 256 Kbps—less than that used by the average small- or medium-sized business user in Europe or North America.

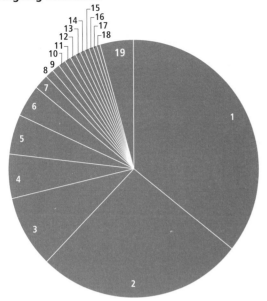

Figure 3. **Countries with More Than 5 Mbps International Outgoing Bandwidth**

Total outbound bandwidth in Kbps

1	Egypt	535,000
2	South Africa	398,512
3	Morocco	136,000
4	Algeria	83,000
5	Tunisia	75,000
6	Senegal	60,000
7	Kenya	28,000
8	Gabon	16,384
9	Nigeria	15,000
10	Botswana	14,000
11	Tanzania	12,000
12	Zimbabwe	11,000
13	Sudan	10,000
14	Uganda	9,250
15	Cameroon	9,000
16	Namibia	8,500
17	Angola	7,000
18	Cote D'Ivoire	6,500
19	The Rest	64,334

Source: http://www3.sn.apc.org/africa

Incoming bandwidth is about 50 percent greater, but is not as easy to monitor because much of it comes in via variable (uncommitted) bitrate satellite broadcast circuits. Use of this type of circuitry is a common response to the bandwidth problem; Internet service providers (ISPs) in Africa are now installing data broadcasting services. A basic satellite dish can be used to receive a stream of popular Web data for caching locally, as well as to receive encoded broadcasts of other user traffic. These can often provide far cheaper incoming bandwidth than that available via local operators.

Two-way satellite-based Internet services using very small aperture terminals (VSAT) to connect directly to the

United States or Europe have also been quickly adopted by ISPs wherever regulations allow—namely, in Democratic Republic of the Congo, Mozambique, Nigeria, Tanzania, and Zambia, which all have ISPs that are not dependent on the local telecommunications operator for their international bandwidth. Uganda used to allow public VSAT Internet services, but following the sale of the second operator license the issuing of new VSAT licenses has been suspended.

With the exception of some ISPs in Southern Africa, most of the international Internet circuits in Africa connect to the United States and Canada; other connections are to Belgium, Germany, the Netherlands, the United Kingdom, Italy, and France. Outgoing bandwidth totals approximately 1.5 Gbps, of which 1 Gbps lands in the United States, 375 Mbps in Europe, and 2 Mbps in Asia. Only 13 Mbps of bandwidth is intra-African. High intraregional telecommunications prices have limited the establishment of links between neighboring countries to just five—the Gambia-Senegal link, and South Africa's links to Namibia, Lesotho, Swaziland, and Botswana. (In South Africa, the telecommunications operator instituted low tariffs for international links to neighboring countries.) As a result of the high international tariffs charged by most telecommunications operators, private ISPs are discouraged from establishing multiple international links; increasing amounts of intra-African traffic are therefore transmitted through high-cost cross-continental links.

The high tariffs are also the reason behind the common practice amongst popular African Internet sites of being hosted on servers that are in Europe or the United States. This is especially necessary for the many countries, such as Tanzania and Nigeria, where ISPs operate their own independent international links without local interconnections (a practice called peering). Peering means that traffic between the subscribers of two ISPs in the same city must travel to the United States or Europe and back. Out-of-country routing makes it more efficient to host outside-country; also, Web hosting costs can be very high in Africa, whereas there are even a number of free hosting sites in the United States and Europe.

Local peering problems are now being addressed in some countries through the establishment of national Internet Exchange Points (IXPs), where all of the ISPs transfer local traffic. IXPs have already been set up by national ISP associations in Kenya, Mozambique, and South Africa, and plans are at an advanced stage to establish similar facilities in Ghana and Uganda. Although local traffic is only 15 to 25 percent of total traffic, the use of IXPs can still result in significant savings on international bandwidth and improves performance for the user.

The major international Internet suppliers are AT&T, BT, UUNET/AlterNet (with parent company WorldCom/MCI),

NSN, Teleglobe, Verio, Verestar, and OpenTransit (France Telecom/FCR). A number of other links are provided by Intelsat, PanamSat, New Skies and Inmarsat, direct-to-private and PTO groundstations in North America, Europe, and the Middle East, circumventing local PTO infrastructure.

International bandwidth is increasingly being used as a better measure of networked readiness than the total number of users, because it takes into account the range of use, "from those who write a few e-mails a week, to those who spend many hours a day on the net browsing, transacting, streaming, or downloading" (IDRC 2002). As most of the Internet traffic is international (75 to 90 percent), the size of a country's international bandwidth compared to population size provides a ready indication of the extent of its Internet activity (IDRC 2002).

An index of bits per capita (BPC) can be calculated by dividing the total international Internet bandwidth in a country by its total population (IDRC 2002). As is evident from the map in Figure 4, which charts to exact area scale the BPC per country, there is extremely large variation in the BPC index, ranging from 0.02 to greater than 40—a factor of more than 1,000. These figures reflect the wide range of wealth in different countries; however, GDP per capita only varies by a factor of about 30, which indicates that other variables affect the index. Bandwidth price is a major factor that varies considerably on the continent; high price heavily impacts demand. Price, in turn, is influenced by the regulatory environment—the presence of competition, availability of wireless and VSAT licences, as well as access to international fibre optic bandwidth.

The recent establishment of West African Submarine Cable (WASC), also shown below, has already resulted in plans by operators in Gabon, Côte d'Ivoire, Namibia, Nigeria, Senegal, and South Africa to establish large international Internet links. This should substantially increase the available Internet bandwidth and drive down prices. Senegal has already moved in this direction; last year the country enabled a 45 Mbps Internet circuit to France via the recently-installed Atlantis-2 cable, which it now shares with neighboring Gambia. Senegal is planning to become a regional hub, and will shortly be linking its Internet backbone to Mauritania and Mali, much like South Africa has done with its neighboring countries.

Most African capitals now have more than one ISP, and in mid-2002 there were about 560 public ISPs across the region (excluding South Africa, where the market has consolidated into three major players with 90 percent of the market and about 100 smaller players with the remainder of the market). In 2002, twenty countries had five or more ISPs, while seven countries (Egypt, Kenya, Morocco, Nigeria, South Africa,

Tanzania, and Togo) had ten or more active ISPs; seven countries, however, still had only one ISP. Although Ethiopia and Mauritius are the only countries where a monopoly ISP is still national policy (i.e., private companies are barred from reselling Internet services), monopolies are present in other countries, predominantly in the francophone and the Central African/Sahel subregions, where markets are small: Burkina Faso, Central African Republic, Republic of Congo, Djibouti, Ethiopia, Mauritius, and Niger.

Of the regional ISPs, African Lakes' AfricaOnline has been listed by the London Stock Exchange as the largest operation. The group now has services in Côte d'Ivoire, Egypt, Ghana, Kenya, Namibia, Swaziland, Tanzania, Uganda, and Zimbabwe. AfricaOnline is also engaged in a partnership with WorldCom/UUNET to provide AfricaOnline's infrastructure in Kenya and Zambia. UUNet South Africa also provides their own dial-up and leased line services in Namibia and Botswana. South Africa-based MediaPost is expanding its network, with operations currently in South Africa, Tanzania, Rwanda, Republic of Congo, Kenya, and Senegal and firm plans for Nigeria, Cameroon, Malawi, and Democratic Republic of the Congo. The next largest regional ISP is Swift Global, but after selling its Ugandan operation to AfricaOnline, it is now only present in Kenya and Tanzania, making South African ISP Mweb the other regional player, having purchased ISPs in Namibia, Uganda, and Zimbabwe.

Although many African countries now have Internet points of presence (POPs) in some of the secondary towns (totaling about 280, in different locations across the continent), most rural users still have to make a costly long distance call to connect to the Internet. However, some countries have now instituted local call charges for all calls to the Internet regardless of distance, which greatly reduces costs for those living in remote areas and increases the accessibility and viability of Internet services provided by rural public access facilities in these nations. So far, nineteen countries have adopted this strategy: Benin, Burkina Faso, Cape Verde, Chad, Ethiopia, Gabon, Malawi, Mali, Mauritius, Mauritania, Morocco, Namibia, Niger, Senegal, South Africa, Togo, Tunisia, Uganda, and Zimbabwe. Interestingly, the Seychelles has gone a step further to encourage use—tariffs for calls to the Internet are charged at a 50 percent lower rate than normal local voice calls.

Currently, the average total cost of using a local dial-up Internet account for twenty hours a month in Africa is about US$60 per month (price includes usage fees and local call telephone time included, but not telephone line rental). ISP subscription charges vary greatly (between US$10 and US$80 a month) and largely reflect the different levels of maturity of the markets, the varying tariff policies of the telecommunications operators, the different regulations on private wireless data services, and on access to international

Figure 4. **African Internet Bandwidth per Capita and Marine Fibre Cables**

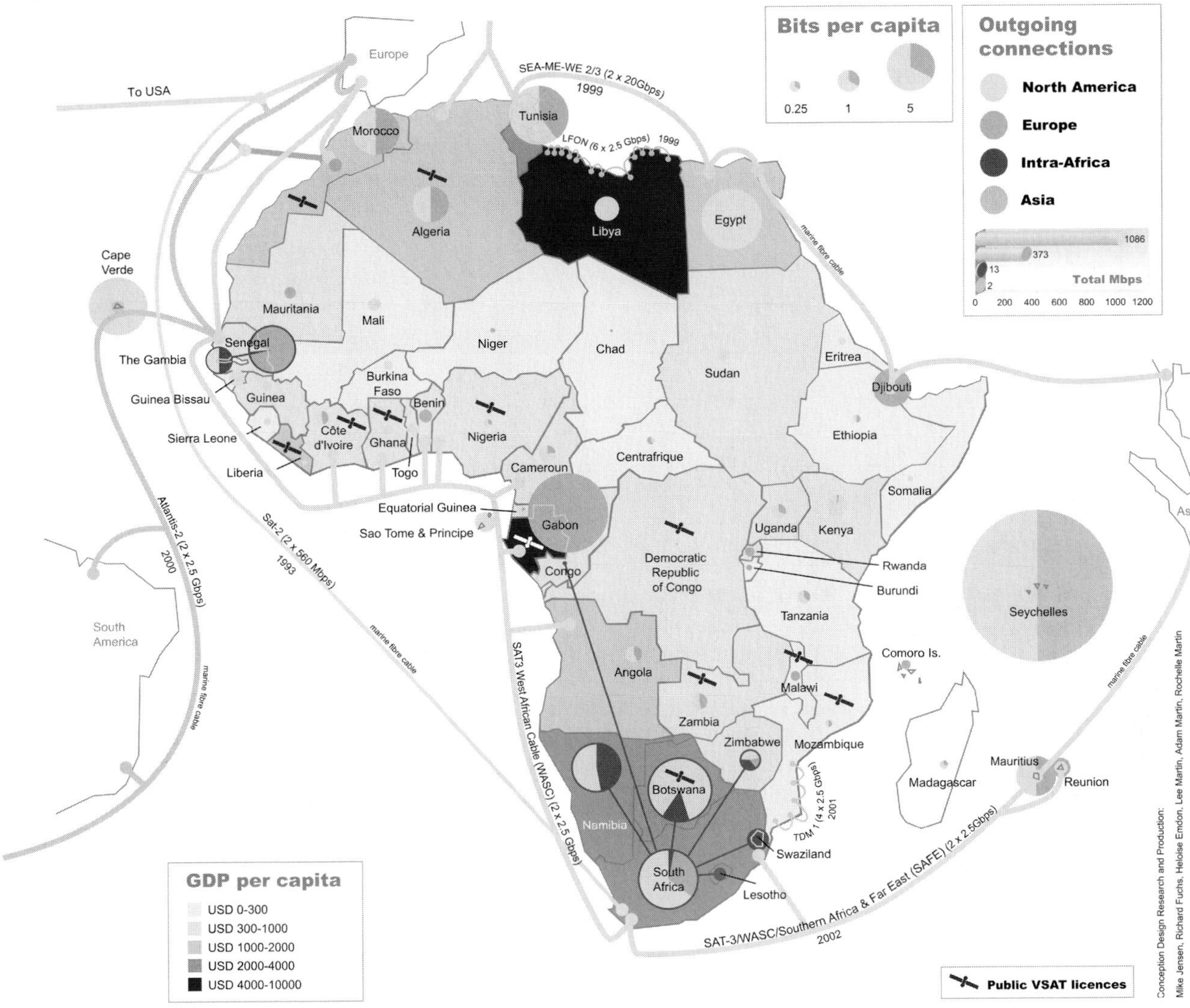

Source: International Development Research Center (2002)

telecommunications bandwidth. So far the "free-ISP" model has only been adopted in Egypt, where there are no monthly charges and revenues obtained from the local call tariffs are split between the telecommunications operator and the ISP.

According to the Organisation for Economic Cooperation and Development (OECD) (2000), twenty hours of Internet access in the United States costs US$22 per month (inclusive of telephone charges) in 2000. Although European costs were higher (US$33 in Germany, US$39 across the European Union), these countries have per capita incomes that are at least ten times greater than the African average. In fact, US$60 per month is higher than the average African monthly salary. Low income has limited individual use of the Internet and has, together with elements such as the low telephone and computer penetration, created the demand for public-access facilities (the cost of a single account being effectively shared amongst the customers who would not otherwise be able to afford access).

Public access services are already very much in evidence in most countries in Africa, particularly in those such as Nigeria and Senegal where telecommunications operators have relied on the private sector to provide public telephone services. Such services are also available in most other major urban areas across Africa, however, in rapidly-growing numbers of telecenters, kiosks, cybercafes, business centers as well as in other locations (e.g., in community phone-shops, schools, police stations, and clinics).

The concept has also received considerable support from members of the international community, as well as a number of national governments and public telecommunication operators as a means to establish access in rural areas. Public access to the Internet is being seen as one of the most important ways of realizing Universal Service Objectives in rural and remote locations. To achieve the objectives, many national government programs and more than twenty international pilot projects have been initiated

Table 3. African Internet Statistics 2002

Country	Dial-up Subscribers	International Band-width	Population (in Millions)	GDP/ Capita US$	Cities with POPs
		Outgoing Kbps	2000	1999	
Algeria	45,000	12,000	30.08	1,442	1
Angola	16,000	5,126	12.09	1,684	3
Benin	4,500	2,100	5.78	374	1
Botswana	20,000	14,000	1.57	3,252	11
Burkina Faso	4,700	256	11.31	199	1
Burundi	300	512	6.46	159	4
Cameroon	7,000	9,000	14.31	617	2
Cape Verde	2,456	1,024	0.41	876	1
Central Africa	700	64	3.48	276	1
Chad	900	64	7.27	149	2
Comoros	491	64	0.66	382	7
Republic of Congo	200	128	2.79	833	5
Côte d'Ivoire	13,000	6,000	16.20	767	13
D.R. C.	4,500	1,024	49.30	400	1
Djibouti	850	2,048	0.62	846	6
Egypt	100,000	535,000	65.98	1,195	1
Equatorial Guinea	200	64	0.43	668	1
Eritrea	2,500	512	3.58	161	1
Ethiopia	6,500	8,200	59.65	103	5
Gabon	5,000	16,384	1.17	5,121	7
Gambia	3,000	1,024	1.23	284	14
Ghana	15,000	4,096	19.16	372	3
Guinea	4,000	128	7.71	677	10
Guinea-Bissau	250	640	1.13	245	4
Kenya	35,000	28,000	29.01	347	2
Lesotho	750	784	2.06	547	2
Liberia	250	128	2.67	1,000	1
Libya	4,000	2,048	5.98	6,579	1
Madagascar	10,000	2,750	16.36	224	1
Malawi	3,500	2,300	10.75	242	2
Mali	6,000	4,096	10.69	230	1
Mauritania	960	384	2.53	455	1
Mauritius	35,000	4,096	1.15	3,661	1
Morocco	80,000	200,000	27.87	1,218	1
Mozambique	6,000	2,048	18.88	86	11
Namibia	15,000	6,144	1.66	2,051	100
Niger	2,000	384	10.08	161	1
Nigeria	60,000	15,000	113.50	551	2
Reunion	47,000	576	0.68	9,270	4
Rwanda	2,700	1,300	6.60	317	1
São Tomé	378	64	0.14	358	1
Senegal	15,000	48,000	10.00	518	4
Seychelles	3,000	4,098	0.08	6,995	3
Sierra Leone	1,000	512	4.57	209	1
Somalia	250	768	10.63	169	2
South Africa	750,000	342,000	44.31	2,979	2
Sudan	9,000	10,000	28.29	364	7
Swaziland	5,000	256	0.95	1,388	1
Tanzania	30,000	12,000	32.10	244	4
Togo	1,700	1,536	4.40	324	9
Tunisia	70,000	75,000	9.34	2,144	1
Uganda	10,000	9,250	20.55	317	5
Zambia	7,000	5,120	8.78	463	1
Zimbabwe	25,000	11,000	12.68	712	4
Africa	1,492,535	1,409,100	769.66	1,207.5	283

Source: Sangonet http://www3.sn.apc.org/africa

throughout Africa (mostly in Ghana, Mozambique, and Uganda, as well as in Benin, South Africa, Tanzania, Zambia, and Zimbabwe) to test different models, means of implementation, and mechanisms for sustainability. The demand for public phone shops and telecenters is also having spinoffs in the IT sector for small businesses, equipment providers, and franchisers.

However, the case for large, multibranch cybercafe chains is not yet proven, as regional ISP AfricaOnline learned when it rolled out hundreds of public access kiosks as part of its E-Touch franchise program in which local stores were provided with a PC to enable e-mail and Internet access. AfricaOnline had approximately 100,000 users spread across 740 outlets in Côte d'Ivoire, Kenya, Uganda, Tanzania, and Zimbabwe before it discovered these outlets were generating insufficient income to maintain them. The company has subsequently closed most of them, and is testing a new franchise strategy with fewer, better known, "I-cafes."

In the area of Internet-based content and applications, the African Web presence continues to increase, but there are generally few relevant applications for the general population. Almost all African countries now have some form of local or internationally-hosted Web server, unofficially or officially representing the country with varying degrees of comprehensiveness. French-speaking countries generally have a higher profile on the Web and greater institutional connectivity than the non-French speaking countries. This is largely due to the strong assistance provided by various francophone support agencies, as well as the Canadian and French governments, which are concerned about the dominance of English on the Internet. The two dominant francophone content developers are the Agence de Cooperation Culturelle et Technique (ACCT) (with the BIEF center), and AUPELF-UREF/REFER's Syfed Center; both centers are building websites of local information as well as providing access.

In response to the high cost of Internet services and the slow speed of Web access, and also because of the overriding importance of electronic mail, lower-cost e–mail-only services are continuing to attract subscribers. However, the relatively high cost of local e-mail services from African ISPs means that a large proportion of African e-mail users use the international, free Web-based services such as Hotmail, Yahoo, or Excite. These services are more costly and slower than using standard e-mail software because extra online time is needed to maintain the connection to the website. Unfortunately for the ISPs, these services can also use up scarce international bandwidth. In response to these issues and the growing use of shared accounts, some African ISPs, such as AfricaOnline and MailAfrica, have set up their own low-cost Web-based e-mail services.

Outside North and South Africa, there are generally few organizations using the Web to deliver significant quantities of information or to carry out transactions with their user base. Although large numbers of organizations now have a "brochure" website with basic descriptive and contact information, very few actually use the Internet for real business activities. This is mainly explained by the limited number of local people that have access to the Internet (and thus the limited importance of a Web presence to the institution), the lack of credit cards, the limited skills available for digitizing and coding pages, and the high costs of local Web-hosting services.

Similarly, although there are some notable official general government websites, such as those of Angola, Egypt, Gabon, Lesotho, Mauritius, Morocco, Mozambique, Senegal, South Africa, Togo, Tunisia, and Zambia, there is as yet little government use of the Internet for administrative purposes or for interacting with the public. Lack of timely information is known to be the largest constraint on the small-scale agricultural production and natural resource exploitation sector, which provide a livelihood for 70 to 80 percent of Africa's population. However, the potential for ICT to impact this sector has not yet received much attention, although some commodity markets in east Africa, such as coffee and tea, are now beginning to trade online.

Web presence is higher in sectors involved in tourism and foreign investment, because these sectors aim to develop an international market presence. Some administrations are also beginning to streamline their operations and improve internal efficiency by switching to a network environment within the organization. For example, the government of Lesotho recently declared that announcements for cabinet and committee meetings would be made only by e-mail. South Africa, Algeria, and Tunisia now provide immediate global access to tenders via the Web. Health and education departments in many countries are beginning to electronically transmit operational management information system statistics (e.g., disease occurrences and pupil registrations). The results of blood tests done in remote areas of South Africa are being transmitted to remote clinics that are off the telecommunications grid via mobile telephone text messages. As greater numbers of public officials gain low-cost access to the Web, the vast information resources available via Internet are becoming increasingly important tools in ensuring informed decision-making.

The "death of distance" introduced by the Internet has meant that the opportunities to be found in the much larger economies of the more developed countries can be exploited by some African companies. Examples of such initiatives include the following:

1. A local ISP in Morocco is digitizing the National Library of France's paper archives. They are scanned in France, sent to Morocco by satellite link, and are edited by keyboard operators in Rabat.

2. In Togo and Mauritius, call centers now provide telephone support services for international companies with customers in Europe and North America.

3. In Cape Verde "virtual security guards" have found jobs using the Internet to monitor webcams in office parks on the east coast of the United States. They notify local rapid response teams there if they see anything amiss.

4. Many African artists and craft makers are selling their wares on the World Wide Web.

In most major cities in Africa, various private companies provide Internet applications training. However, apart from a few universities, there are virtually no network engineering-level facilities. The United Nations Development Program (UNDP) and Cisco recently created a joint venture to assist in the establishment of nonprofit Cisco network training academies in all the less-developed countries. Many of these academies have opened in Africa, including in Democratic Republic of the Congo. The UNDP's Sustainable Development Networking Programme (SDNP) and the United States Agency for International Development's Leland initiative have also trained significant numbers of network technicians. Other initiatives include the following:

1. In Cameroon, United Nations Institute for Training and Research (UNITAR) and ORSTOM have collaborated in a joint project focusing on technical capacity-building in sub-Saharan francophone Africa. The first training center and courses have been established in Cameroon (CITI-CM) with support from the World Bank's infoDev fund and additional funds from from Orstom, ACCT, and others. A network engineering course is now being run regularly at CITI-CM. Funds are being sought for CITI-CI (Côte d'Ivoire), CITI-SN (Sénégal), CITI-BF (Burkina Faso), CITI-BE (Bénin), and CITI-ML (Mali).

2. An Internet training program for institutes, schools, and other agencies of higher learning in francophone and lusophone sub-Saharan African countries, called Internet pour les Ecoles Inter-Etat d'Afrique de l'Ouest et du Centre, has been established in a related effort to the UNITAR/ORSTOM project, under the Diderot Initiative.

3. COMNET-IT, established by the Commonwealth Secretariat (ComSec) in Malta to support ICT in Commonwealth developing countries, has initiated a number of ICT-support activities, such as the provision of scholarships for Commonwealth country students to obtain postgraduate degrees in computer science.

4. The African Virtual University (see website) is providing training in computer and Internet applications and programming languages to its twenty-nine university campuses in eighteen countries in Africa.

5. International volunteers are being seen as an increasingly important vehicle for training and technology transfer. This has been been boosted by the recently announced UNITeS program of the UN's UN Volunteers and other similar nongovernmental organization initiatives, such as the Global Netcorps (previously NetCorps Canada) and GeekCorps.

6. More general ICT applications and indeed "technology enhanced" teaching in other subjects is also now being tackled by the growing number of national school-based networking projects and foundations active on the continent, such as SchoolNet Africa (see SchoolNet website).

Hardware and Software

Most recent estimates (i.e., 2001 data) for the number of personal computers in Africa put the total at about 7.5 million—an average of about one per 100 people. These figures, however, are notoriously unreliable because of limited capacities for monitoring industry and the large numbers of machines brought in independently to avoid duties. Some studies, such as the 1995 ACCT survey, indicate that official figures are three to six times higher than actual figures, making the average closer to one PC per 500 people. Account should also be taken of the number of users sharing a single computer, which is much greater than in the more developed regions.

Underutilization of existing computer resources is also common. Often an office may have many machines but only one connected to the Internet, and there is a preponderance of stand-alone computers, indicating limited use of Local Area Networks. This usually means that there is competition for the Internet-connected machine and a shared e-mail account, which is not effective use of the Internet.

Few international companies operate offices in Africa, but some of the major companies such as Bull, HP, IBM, NCR, Oracle, and Microsoft have some form of local representation in most countries. Microsoft now has its own offices in Côte d'Ivoire, Kenya, Morocco, and South Africa. PC equipment is often clone equipment imported from Asia; but Dell, HP, IBM, and ICL also have significant shares of the market, and Dell South Africa is now selling via the Web.

Although there have been notable efforts in some countries to reduce import duties on computers, communications equipment and peripherals are still often charged at higher rates. The high cost of computer hardware in Africa has a major impact on the continent's ability to improve networked readiness, as this cost is often the largest component of network startup budgets. This situation is likely to become an even more critical bottleneck because low-cost bandwidth,

such as through Ku-Band VSAT and spread spectrum wireless (WiFi) links, is increasingly becoming available. As a result, the use of recycled PCs, thin clients, set-top boxes, or other low-cost Internet "appliances," as well as Open Source (free) software, is becoming more common.

Electronic Mass Media

Radio is still by far the most dominant electronic mass medium in Africa, with ownership of radio sets being far higher than for any other electronic device. The United Nations Educational, Scientific and Cultural Organization estimates that in 1997, radio ownership in Africa was close to 170 million with a 4 percent per annum growth rate. This puts current estimates for 2002 at more than 200 million radio sets, compared with only 62 million televisions. It is estimated that more than 60 percent of the population of the sub-continent are reached by existing radio transmitter networks, while national television coverage is largely confined to major towns. Some countries, even relatively well developed ones, still do not have their own national television broadcaster. For example, Botswana has only this year launched a national television broadcaster.

An increasing number of commercial stations are being established following liberalization of the sector in many countries. However, most of these stations concentrate on entertainment (music), and the news and information output is often limited to a re-broadcast either of news produced by the national (state-controlled) broadcaster, or of news produced by an international broadcaster or news agency. Local news and current affairs (especially that focusing on events outside of the capital) or educational programming is rarely broadcast, and local community stations have also been slow to take off.

In the last few years, there has been substantial growth of satellite-based broadcasting on the continent. In 1995, South African company M-Net launched the world's first digital direct-to-home subscriber satellite service (DSTV). Subscribers have access to more than thirty video channels and forty audio programs, and these are available to most of Africa through low-cost KU-band terminals. The US-based company, WorldSpace, launched a digital radio broadcasting satellite called AfriStar in late 1998. Radio broadcasters from many African countries, as well as from Europe and the United States, are using the service to broadcast their channels all over Africa and to most of Europe. WorldSpace ultimately aims to make a suite of more than eighty audio channels available to anyone who can afford the special digital radio (priced at US$50); the radio is also able to receive data services, including the transmission of Web pages and other information such as weather maps and crop disease images.

Outlook

As Figure 5 below shows, of all the major network components in Africa, the most impressive growth has been in the uptake of mobile telephones. This, combined with the not insignificant use of the Internet, has undoubtedly had a substantial impact on the ability of entrepreneurs to do business in urban areas, as well as for more wealthy individuals to stay in contact with friends and family.

Figure 5. **Growth in the Number of ICT Users in Africa**

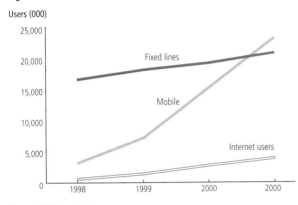

Users (000)

Source: ITU, Sangonet

Nevertheless, the vast majority of Africans remain unconnected. Efforts to promote broader use in Africa have been discussed among high-level policymakers since the early 1990s. Official recognition was given to the issue in 1996, when the Conference of African Ministers of Social and Economic Planning requested that the United Nations Economic Commission for Africa set up a "high-level working group" to help define a strategy for greater networked readiness in Africa. Subsequently, an expert group developed a framework document entitled the African Information Society Initiative (AISI). Since then, communications ministers from more than forty African countries have provided high-level endorsement for AISI, along with specific telecommunications development policies which they encapsulated in their common vision document, *African Connection*, published in 2001 (see African Connection website).

Among the proposals in AISI was a call for the formulation and development of a national information and communication infrastructure (NICI) plan that would be driven by national development priorities in every African country. AISI also proposed cooperation among African countries in order to share experiences. Most countries have begun the process of developing NICI plans, and seventeen countries have finalized their strategies—Benin, Burkina Faso, Cape Verde, Côte d'Ivoire, Egypt, Gambia, Mauritania, Mauritius, Morocco, Mozambique, Rwanda, Senegal, Seychelles, South Africa, Sudan, and Tunisia (see UNECA website). A high priority in many of these plans is improvement of public Internet access in rural areas

through the use of telecenters that exploit the convergence of technologies to provide cost-effective services in underserviced and remote locations.

As addressing the digital divide has become an even higher priority in the international community, the outlook for international support has also improved. This has culminated in the activities of the G8 Digital Opportunity Task Force (Dot Force), the United Nations ICT Task Force, and related efforts in 2002 that have resulted in developed countries creating a variety of new projects (such as Canada's Institute for Connectivity in Africa and Italy's e-Government Support Program in Mozambique, Nigeria, and Tunisia) to help developing countries achieve networked readiness.

Much of the impact of these efforts will depend on the extent of improvements to the telecommunication infrastructure on which the networks depend. The high costs of connectivity in remote areas will hopefully be addressed by the large number of low-cost, two-way Ku-band VSAT satellite-based data services that have been launched this year by companies such as Afsat and Web-Sat. These services will be a major boon to rural users, making use of the new high-powered satellite footprints now covering Africa, similar to services currently available in the United States and Europe. Costs are about US$1,500 to US$3,000 for the equipment and US$200 to US$400 per month for "better than dial-up" speeds (i.e., about 56 Kbps outgoing and 200 to 400 Kbps incoming). These are expected to see rapid uptake wherever regulations allow; unfortunately, most countries in Africa either charge excessively high license fees or do not allow these services at all, as they compete with the state-run telecommunications operator.

Liberalization of the telecommunication sector and the introduction of competition are increasingly seen as key factors needed to drive down prices and improve the quality of service, and although some countries have begun to open up their markets, there is a general sense that too little is being done. While a variety of efforts are underway to restructure national telecom operations and build better national and international infrastructures, many of these efforts lack a cohesive approach built on a clear understanding of the dynamics and impact of the blindingly fast-changing communications technologies. As a result, the pace of regulatory change is still generally seen by the Internet industry as too slow, conducted with insufficient transparency, and with not enough participation by the sector in developing policy. In general, strategies continue to favor an extension of the monopoly for the incumbent (usually for five to seven years) in return for a high share price sold to a foreign strategic investor, which is normally a multinational operator keen to shore up profits under threat from liberalization in their home markets.

The justification for continuing the exclusivity period of the national operator is usually to ensure that sufficient income is generated to roll out infrastructure without it being siphoned by competitors. Although this strategy may be logical, experience since the Federal Communications Commission (FCC) breakup of AT&T has shown that the only way of ensuring the efficiency of service delivery is to bring self-interest into play by opening the markets and using competition to do much of the regulating. This strategy also helps address the problem of limited resources that faces government policymakers and regulators worldwide (even the FCC); regulators do not have the capacity to keep up with the rapid technological change in order to fully enforce regulations.

Furthermore, the old model of an extensive regulatory apparatus supporting the slow entry of only one or two new operators is not as relevant in Africa as it is in developed countries, because developed countries are not burdened with huge state-owned operators holding 99.9 percent of the market, or encumbered with old technologies (used by the majority of the population) that need to be carefully moved into a competitive environment. In contrast to the massive incumbents in developed nations, emerging operators in Africa make use of much cheaper next-generation technologies that allow many smaller companies to enter the marketplace, and they are more self-regulated than operators in developed countries. African operators' self-regulation is even more evident when one takes into account their partial self-provisioning (as demonstrated by the rapid growth of the Internet, WiFi, and mobile telephony).

In practical terms, while competition in the ICT sector results in some overlap and duplication of resources by the different competitors, the overall operation of the sector is more efficient than that of a monopoly. Thus, the initial process of privatization and liberalization of the telecommunications sector in Africa should bypass the common first step of transforming a public monopoly into a private one; a private monopoly can be even more difficult to control, especially if it has a large foreign partner experienced in the use of litigation. Generally, the record of foreign participation in Africa indicates that even the strategy of a limited exclusivity period for basic services in urban areas is questionable, and it may ultimately be more efficient to transition directly from a public monopoly to a multiplayer-competitive environment, perhaps with small areas of exclusivity for rural locations.

Technology and design options for rural populations are becoming more readily apparent as technologies mature. Perhaps more important than decisions about technology, however, is a reassessment of the traditional view that rural communications services are unprofitable. The need for subsidized rural communications emerged decades ago in developed countries when telecommunication infrastructure costs were high, and where most of the population resided in densely populated urban areas that could be serviced at relatively low cost in conjunction with high-volume business users. In this environment, cross-subsidization and Universal Service Obligations were needed to cover the relatively greater costs of serving the small minority of mainly residential users living in sparsely populated rural areas.

These factors are not generally applicable in Africa and other developing countries today—most of the population is in rural areas, and network infrastructure roll-out and usage costs have already plummeted and will continue to do so for the foreseeable future. The growing availability of fibre, wireless, and satellite bandwidth services have the potential to make rural areas almost as easy to reach as urban ones, and technology convergence means that the same infrastructure can be used to provide many services, not just voice calls. Further, the use of the Internet for transaction purposes vastly increases the added value potential of the infrastructure, and thus the incentives to build it.

In addition to lowering usage and infrastructure costs, the overhead costs associated with centralized national network planning are no longer required. This is so because of the emergence of the Internet model of network development, which allows anyone to build a part of the network and be able to sell excess bandwidth to third parties in order to help cover their own costs or generate a profit. Examples of this model are already evident in the Universities of Zambia and Mozambique, which have become leading ISPs following the establishment of their own facilities for internal use. It is no coincidence that these service providers rely extensively on VSAT and wireless systems to access and deliver their services independent of the monopoly telecommunications operators in their countries.

In identifying appropriate strategies for broader network use, another important point to be made is that African models of infrastructure provision are likely to be quite different to those employed in developed countries, not only because of the generally low income levels in Africa, but also because, in Africa, informal business activity and rural populations are much more important.

Innovative models are necessary to address the low-income factor, and these models must focus on shared infrastructure, public access facilities, and the use of intermediaries to interact with the public (who may not be functionally literate, let alone computer literate). In other respects, strategies to improve network services are unlikely to be uniform across the continent because of the very large variations between countries. Aside from variations in annual per capita GDP levels, which range from US$200 to US$7,000, and market sizes that vary from 1 million to 100 million people, many other factors vary substantially, and may affect strategy. Some of the important issues that need to be taken into account include:

1. *The communications regulatory environment.* The national regulatory environment in Africa varies greatly, from relatively open competition in Internet service provision or even in mobile services and the local loop, to long-term monopolies in all of these areas. In particular, very few countries allow the use of VSAT or other wireless technologies that may bypass state-run operators, and if they do, they levy high bypass or license fees.

2. *The extent of existing fixed infrastructure and the cost of access,* for example fixed line penetration can vary from 20 percent to less than 1 percent, depending on the country.

3. *The existing usage of the radio spectrum.* Many countries do not have adequate resources to efficiently manage their radio spectrum allocation for use by either national or regional telecommunications and Internet operators. This has resulted in congestion in some wavebands, lack of a transparent licensing process, and difficulties in obtaining spectrum from the regulators.

4. *The resources that national governments and their international cooperating partners are allocating to national information and communication infrastructure building projects.* In some countries there is strong, if somewhat uncoordinated, support from both multilateral and bilateral development agencies in this area; other countries have yet to begin this process.

5. *The focus of national universal service goals.* Currently, the aim of most of these efforts is simply to improve the provision of public telephones within walking distance; however, some countries, such as South Africa and Uganda, have gone further, and have included the provision of more advanced network services and established universal service funds to redirect some of the profits made by telecommunications operators into the provision of network access in rural areas. Uganda has also developed an incoming termination fee, which is to be paid to telecenters for incoming calls.

Consolidating markets and building economies of scale will clearly require greater regional collaboration, both for deploying infrastructure and for creating content and applications. Encouraging efforts that warrant further support and adoption in other regions have been made at the regional level by South African Development Community (SADC) and Common Market for Eastern and Southern Africa (COMESA), which have both adopted a variety of measures to improve network use, most notably:

1. SADC's model telecommunication legislation, which has been adopted by most member states, and is therefore a legally-binding protocol

2. The formation of the Telecommunication Regulators Association of Southern Africa (TRASA); TRASA acts as a forum for regulators in the region to exchange information and experience

3. The ComTel project to develop the terrestrial telecommunication links between neighboring states in COMESA, and to harmonize and upgrade the cross-border information systems in transport, customs, import/export, and trade.

Obtaining startup financing for small businesses to establish public access services is an acute problem, because the level of investment usually required falls in the gap between traditional microcredit loans (US$50 to US$1,000); and financiers of venture capital or loan funds that are not generally interested in anything smaller than US$250,000 (mainly because of the overheads required to carry out due diligence). As a result, a public access startup project, which might only require between US$25,000 and US$100,000, has considerable difficulty in sourcing the necessary funds. Hopefully, this problem will in part be addressed through the newly created DOT Force Entrepreneurial Network (DFEN), which aims to provide financing and support to small- and medium-sized enterprises (SMEs) and entrepreneurs planning to use ICT in innovative and creative ways in the developing world. The initial focus of DFEN's activities will be Africa.

The African Union and their program, the New Partnership for African Development (NEPAD), which is supported by the international community, are addressing many of the more systemic issues. This many-faceted effort is aimed at accelerating Africa's development, and it should help to create an environment more conducive to networked readiness.

Endnotes

1. ITU; United Nations Educational, Scientific and Cultural Organization (UNESCO) statistics.

2. It should be noted, for example, that there is a large variation between countries in the charges for installation, line rental, and call tariffs. The average business connection in Africa costs more than US$100 to install, US$6 a month to rent, and US$0.11 per three minute local call. But installation charges are higher than US$200 in some countries (Egypt, Benin, Mauritania, Niger, and Togo), line rentals range from US$0.8 to US$20 a month, and call charges vary by a factor of 10—from US$0.60 an hour to more than US$5 an hour.

3. Network Wizards conducts a quarterly survey in which the number of hosts on the Internet is counted.

References

African Connection. Online. http://www.africanconnection.org.

African Internet Connectivity. 2002. *Continental Connectivity Indicators, July 2002*. Online. http://www3.sn.apc.org/africa/partial.html.

African Information Society Initiative (AISI) and Economic Commission for Africa Online. http://www.bellanet.org/partners/aisi/more/index.html.

African Virtual University. Online. http://www.avu.org.

Agence de Cooperation Culturelle et Technique (ACCT). 1995. *Survey of ICT Resources*. Online. http://inforoutes.cidif.org.

Computer Aid International. Online. http://www.computeraid.org.

GeekCorps. Online. http://www.geekcorps.org.

International Business Leaders Forum (IBLF) Digital Partnership. Online. http://www.digitalpartnership.org.

International Development Research Center (IDRC). 2002. *Mapping the Digital Divide in Africa*. Rev. Online. http://www.idrc.ca/acacia/divide/info/info.html.

International Development Research Center (IDRC). 2002. *The Internet: Out of Africa*. Rev. . Online. http://www.idrc.ca/acacia/divide.

International Telecommunication Union (ITU). *Rural Connectivity and Telecentres*. Rev. Online. http://www.itu.int/ITU-D-Rural.

International Telecommunication Union (ITU). 2002. *World Telecommunication Development Report 2002*.

Jensen, M. 1996. *Bridging the Gaps in Internet Development in Africa*. International Development Research Center. Online. http://www.idrc.ca/acacia/studies/ir-gaps.htm.

Jensen, M. and A. Esterhuysen. 2001. *The Telecentre Cookbook for Africa: Recipes for Self-Sustainability*. Paris: United Nations Educational, Scientific and Cultural Organization. Online. http://www.unesco.org/webworld/news/2001/010713_cookbook.shtml.

Netcorps. Canada International. Online. http://www.netcorps-cyberjeunes.org.

Network Wizards. Internet Domain Survey. Rev. Online. http://www.nw.com.

Partnership for Information and Communication Technologies in Africa (PICTA). Online. http://www.bellanet.org/partners/picta.

SchoolNet Africa. Online. http://www.schoolnetafrica.org.

The Information Society and Development: A Review. 2001. *European Commission* 1.

Digital Opportunity Task Force (DOT Force). *Digital Opportunities for All: Meeting the Challenge. Report of the Digital Opportunity Task Force.*

*Including a Proposal for a Genoa Plan of Action.*Online. http://www.dotforce.org/reports/DOT_Force_Report_V_5.0h.html.

United Nations Economic Commission for Africa. 2002. http://www.uneca.org/disd/_vti_bin/shtml.exe/nici_status.htm/map.

United Nations Development Program (UNDP). 2002. *Human Development Report 2001*. Rev. Online. http://www.undp.org.

United Nations Volunteers. Online. http://www.unv.org.

World Computer Exchange. Online. http://www.wordcomputerexchange.org.

Lionel C. Carrasco, Neoris

Rossana Fuentes-Berain, ITAM

Roberto Martínez Illescas, CECIC

Networked Readiness: A Matter of Survival

Latin America has missed the development train twice. When feudal agriculture was transformed into modern agribusinesses, landowners sat by and, at their own risk, decided not to change their feudal ways. During the industrial revolution, oligarchic forces clung to the comfortable zone of producing raw materials without transforming them. In both cases the common local inability to understand the sense and direction of change stressed the region's weaknesses, rather than its opportunities. The third major revolution started a decade ago with the advent of the Internet. This revolution is as pervasive as previous ones and, as the others did, will change not only production modes, but also all interaction between humans, institutions, and businesses. Such interaction will become faster—exponentially faster. Being networked ready on time is not optional; it is about survival.

The train is passing through the Latin American station this time with the additional cargo of globalization and democratization, trends that were not there in previous economic shifts and which now have to be considered as rightful ticket holders in need of care. A third new passenger, market capitalization, is capricious, and we need to watch out for its behavior.

Regardless of the Enron saga, companies worldwide will continue to be rewarded for their innovative leadership and ability to execute, and their reward will be reflected in market capitalization over profits. Latin American companies will not be treated differently. But the capricious element within the equation is capital; as former Spanish Prime Minister Felipe Gonzalez warns, capital "has no social sensibility," and left alone, it will continue to worsen the already blatant income disparity in the region.

Networked readiness, as other revolutions, entails risks and opportunities. This report (see Chapter 1) warns us of the generally mediocre performance in the region. Latin America, as a whole, performs below average. Latin Americans really need to jump on the train this time, or else bring to life the plot in Gabriel Garcia Marquez' famous story *Chronicle of a Death Foretold*, in which everybody knew that Jose, the main character, was going to die, but nobody acted to prevent it.

The Out-Of-The-Box Thinking Hypothesis

The formula, Fertility in the Environment + Level of Readiness x Usage = Readiness for the Networked Future, does apply to larger countries such as Mexico, Brazil, and Chile, as well as to other smaller, but comparable, high-income social strata scattered around the region.

In countries such as Nicaragua and Bolivia, or even in marginal urban populations within Rio de Janeiro, Santiago de Chile, or Mexico City, that formula still stands. Nevertheless, the self-fulfilling prophecy of "small markets equals high risk so why bother?" (a chicken-and-egg kind of dilemma) does not take into account unconventional and potentially profitable opportunities for enablers of networked readiness.

Therefore, the key is to identify within the economic and social environment of the region what unconventional factors need to be in place to enable individuals, governments, and businesses to participate in the benefits of the networked world.

Brazil has already identified these points—it fared well in the NRI rankings, and is a real success story. Argentina, the most aggressive Latin American country for Internet content production, has slowed—an obvious byproduct of its economic fall. Mexico and Chile have nothing to write home about; they are simply standing their ground while countries of smaller economic scale, such as Costa Rica, the Dominican Republic, and Trinidad and Tobago, are putting up a remarkable fight to achieve networked readiness by either leveraging a cluster approach, such as in the Intel case in Costa Rica, or betting on the financial industry strengths of the Caribbean nations and Panama.

So what is the lesson for Latin America in this year's *Global Information Technology Report*? Should we all learn to dance the samba? Is it that we need to follow the Brazilian government-led model? Is it feasible, desirable, or even possible to replicate it? Most likely, it is not.

Those who know Latin America, either for having made or lost money there, have learned that the region is extremely complex and diverse. Nevertheless, some common elements can be found. Those elements are the ones discussed in this article, although individual realities will force the design of specific national blueprints to expedite networked readiness.

For the bigger regional picture, such a blueprint calls for identifying the main stakeholders (government, individuals, and businesses) and the particular environment (market, political/regulatory, and infrastructure) in which it interacts in order to leverage and build a networked future.

The Networked Readiness Framework Cube represents the playground where individual governments and businesses interact, and that includes globalization, democratization, and market capitalization as part of a bigger set of variables to be considered.

Figure 1. **Networked Readiness Framework Cube**

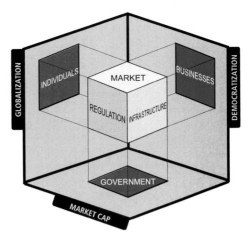

Source: Authors

Another useful tool to visualize the variables that stakeholders have to take into consideration is a SWOT chart analysis (strengths, weaknesses, opportunities, and threats).

Latin America's SWOT chart (Table 1) makes clear that information technology (IT) is a very important element of networked readiness, but it is just that—one element. Other factors in the table need to be assessed under a regional environment, which is primarily defined by three major forces: market, public policies, regulatory rules, and, yes, infrastructure.

In this chapter the region's market environment, composed of firms and individuals that interact within a country, is segmented into three different tiers: high-income markets, such as Brazil, Mexico, and Chile; emerging markets, such as Costa Rica, Colombia, and Uruguay; and developing, low-income markets such as Bolivia, Guatemala, and Haiti. This segmentation is based not only on gross domestic product (GDP) or other economic factors, but also on the maturity of the nations' political and legal systems as well as their social and cultural structures.

Corporate Latin America must also be divided into three groups: global competitive firms, large local firms that should be treated as such based on a local scale, and small- and medium-sized enterprises (SME).

Individuals within the market, for the purpose of this paper, do not include the low-income rural population that is not likely to have access to a Network Society in the medium term. Even without that sector, the Latin American urban population is large enough to constitute an interesting piece of the world pie.

Society in Latin America is an allegory of duality. Although high-end consumers are in the minority, their demographics

Table 1. **Latin America's Strengths, Weaknesses, Opportunities, and Threats (SWOT)**

Strengths	Weaknesses
Large, young Internet-avid population	Pervasive IT illiteracy
Common language and cultural identity	Acute imbalances of income distribution
Qualified intellectual capital at low cost	Deficiencies in the rule of law
Abundant potential consumers via the Internet	Corruption and political instability
Extended patterns of collective consumption of services and content	Inefficient legislative bodies
	Poor venture capital infrastructure
Government can jump-start Internet usage	SME and government bureaucracies slow adaptation to global economy
A handful of world-class companies with organizational leadership committed to IT	Political and economical instability
Adaptation of *maquila*[1] skills leveraging the Internet	Lack of coherent Internet readiness policies
Setting a tradition of providers of rich content that could increase Internet use in Spanish	Antiglobalization movements
U.S. Hispanic heritage as a hemispheric e-commerce detonator	Potential social disturbance due to deterioration of living conditions
Lucrative market of low-income consumers with pent-up demands	
Unfulfilled demand of communication services	
Enhanced civil participation through trust-building	
Opportunities	**Threats**

are more encouraging (they are younger and have larger families) than their peers in developed countries. Whereas moderately low-income and very low-income urban citizens, 88 percent of whom are literate, are poor by international standards, but they are also hungry for unconventional ways of becoming networked ready.

As for the political and regulatory environment, Latin America has been reservedly, but so far unmistakably, leaving behind its authoritarian heritage. Immature democracies nevertheless face a big challenge: they have to set in place a sound regulatory framework to give legal certainty to new activities; but more so, they simply have to make good on tenets for the rule of law that are badly needed to crystallize local and foreign investment.

Most Latin American governments are notorious for sitting at the train station watching as the Internet express passes by, because politicians in the region are focusing on urgent matters and leaving out of their agenda important ones, such as networked readiness, hoping to catch the train at the next (nonexistent) station.

Brazilians are the exception to the rule. Their performance in this year's NRI attests to the existence of a strategic public agenda based on a clear understanding of government's role as a triggering factor as well as consumer and regulator of networked readiness.

Last, but not least, a key element of the region's environment is the infrastructure required for the Internet. Measured in terms of availability and quality, acquiring infrastructure will clearly be an uphill battle. The Washington Consensus of the 1990s had as one of its core elements the privatization of the telecommunications sector. Although privatization started, it couldn't go far enough, entangled as it was in conventional capital behavior that didn't find the expected return on investment, and burdened by the twice-bursting of the bubble—first the Internet business itself, and then telecommunications.

Clearly, as the SWOT table points out, one of the weaknesses of Latin America is infrastructure; using the same analysis, however, that weakness can also be seen as an opportunity. The opportunity combines the need for government leadership in setting a proper set of incentives and enlightened regulation, as Costa Rica has done for Intel, and the search for unconventional business models in terms of content-driven usage and alternative access models by private companies, both international and local.

Enhanced usage based on a true-value proposition for businesses and government would be advisable, but it would be even more courageous to go out and look for individual customers who have pent-up demands and are willing to pay for services. Looking for customers could also be profitable. A case in point is the continuing boom in mobile telephony

Figure 2. **Networked Readiness Report Regional Data**

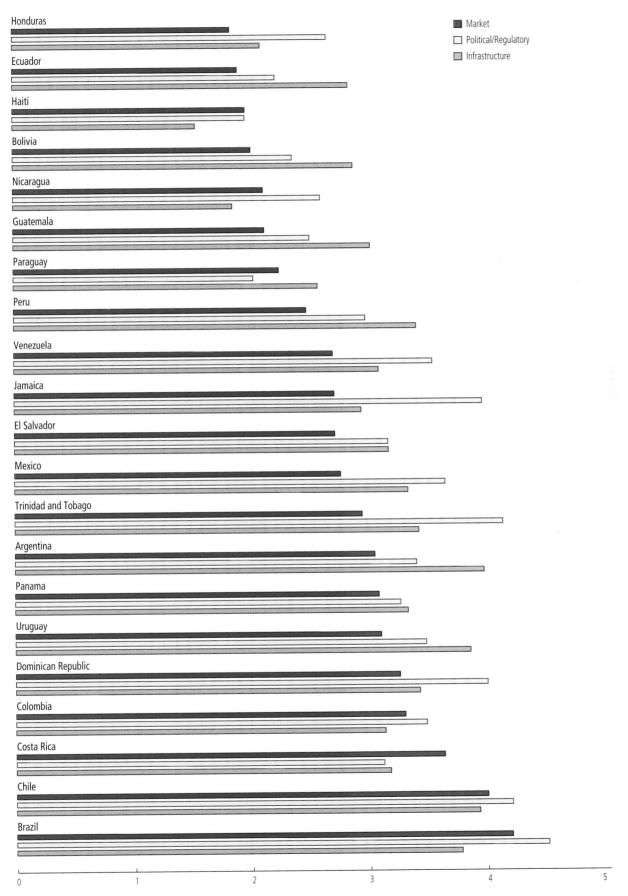

that has seen a 42.8 percent growth rate in the past five years, compared to land lines.

Having analyzed the market, political regulatory and infrastructure variables in order to rank the countries, and considering Latin America's SWOT analysis, the rest of this chapter will focus on identifying what possible actions, strategies, and models could be embraced by the three main stakeholders: governments, businesses, and individuals.

e-Nation: The Development of a Strategic Public Agenda in Latin America

Latin America has entered the twenty-first century facing pressing challenges and a myriad of elusive opportunities, foremost of which are the flourishing of the Internet, combined with other globalization effects and young local democratization processes as shown in the Networked Readiness Framework Cube. In this scenario, the region is presented with several challenges:

1. Catching up with other latitudes in the development of physical infrastructure for the digital era;

2. Resolving endemic budget constraints;

3. Fostering IT awareness and network culture in government agencies and legislative and judiciary branches;

4. Developing human capital as well as information, goods, services, and industries;

5. Preventing the developing digital era from aggravating social inequalities.

Latin America approaches the digital challenge from a public policy perspective along the lines of three distinct agendas, each with its own distinctive locus and issues. These are as follows:

1. *The e-government agenda.* This agenda has been developed along the "transaction systems" paradigm. Just as has happened elsewhere around the globe, here the locus was on efficiency through the transparency of government behavior. From this perspective, e-government policies can be traced along three main lines: government-to-government transactions (G2G), government-to-citizen transactions (G2C), and, finally, government-to-business transactions (G2B). The role of the government in adopting the network early in this model stresses its role as a trigger of network usage.

   Government can, and must, create traditional and transactional content to establish a critical mass of users through creative fiscal and other "soft" incentives. It can, and should, also use compulsory inducements such as nationwide digital identities and corporate and high-income digital tax payments.

2. *The e-nation agenda.* This is the most ambitious and complex agenda, as it implies the development of critical infrastructure for the digital era, where the locus is placed on achieving a balance between fostering competition in the provision of infrastructure and the delivery of digital public goods to counterbalance the widening of the digital gap. This puts a cap on market capitalization excesses.

   The government's role is critical in fostering infrastructure for the digital era that involves not only physical infrastructure, but also institutional infrastructure for innovation (universities, technology centers, public development agencies) and, finally, a growing stock of digital-enabled human/intellectual capital.

   A big task for government is creating the proper regulatory framework within a larger functional rule of law to promote and guarantee required local and foreign investments essential to building network infrastructure.

3. *The e-democracy agenda.* This agenda implies the enhancement of participatory/democratic governance, where the locus is citizen self-empowerment and public accountability.

   Democracy is a fragile object in Latin America. Anything that encourages democratic values in a region that has seen more than its share of military coups, public and private corruption, and lack of transparency, should be warmly embraced.

These three agendas have in some cases converged strategically, and in other cases have been adopted haphazardly in broad "statements of vision" without an appropriate strategy to turn them into "statecraft policies." A general overview of the achievements and shortcomings throughout the region will highlight the importance of developing a strategic public agenda for e-readiness, in which the state must play a proactive and catalyzing role. More detailed appraisals of the e-democracy agenda and aspects of the "nation online" agenda—the issue of e-business development and of the mechanism of social inclusion to fight the digital gap—will be treated in separate sections of this chapter.

Transaction Systems and the e-Government Agenda

G2G. Government-to-government interaction is desirable because it implies integration across a diverse array of platforms and management systems, which is a true challenge. Integration implies linking and synchronizing entire areas and divisions within and across agencies. Thus, it requires unifying systems, programs, and even standards within a common platform.

Moreover, information must flow seamlessly from one department to another and from agency to agency whenever any single issue arises, calling for timely and effective action or decision-making—more so when the issue at hand falls within policy areas such as public safety or even national security.

This kind of initiative is more than justified, because the increased efficiency of public services translates into cost reduction, the liberation of resources, and the creation of faster, better services vis-à-vis corporate and citizen customers.

G2C. Much has been said and written about the shortcomings of public services and bureaucratic corruption in Latin America, and about the great opportunities that will be created if IT is used to curtail abuses of power and empower citizen surveillance.

Online services could, and should, be linked to civil-society pressure for governments to deliver on their political commitments. It is important, nevertheless, to foster a strategic and proactive vision so as to ensure that high-income members of the public are not the only ones who can make their points of view visible, but that the public at large has ubiquitous access through public kiosks.

G2B. In the area of procurement, there has been a decisive push towards the establishment of robust online procurement systems. Mexico, Chile, and Brazil have made substantial progress. Key initiatives are those that reduce costs. For example, promoting integral purchasing systems that leverage the huge, but not currently coordinated, purchasing power of governments. Common public services for business such as licensing and issuing permits could also be made more efficient by adopting digital practices.

A very obvious by-product of network usage in G2B is transparency. Fighting corruption and bureaucratic discretional margins is as great a contribution as any.

Critical Infrastructure on the e-Nation Agenda

The development of telecommunications infrastructure was the outcome of a "deregulation and competition" wave that swept across the whole of Latin America through the second half of the 1990s, with mixed results. The most successful rapid deployment of telecommunications services through market liberalization occurred in Chile and, more pronounced, in Brazil. Mexico and Argentina embarked on a similar process of liberalization, yet their strategies had more pitfalls from an institutional perspective, insofar as their regulatory authorities were significantly weaker and had a less coherent package of policy instruments with which to enforce efficient competition and provide certainty

for private investors. This is easily seen in the varying rates of penetration of mobile services and in the rapid growth of online access services.

However, much less attention has been paid to two other aspects of critical infrastructure as part of the public agenda for digital readiness: institutional infrastructure for innovation and the stock of digital-enabled human capital. Compared to the more competitive group of emerging economies in Southeast Asia, Latin American governments channel far fewer resources to applied technology programs and cooperation between industry and public academic research institutions. Moreover, in this region, the private sector also invests much less in technology-intensive productive innovation. The pervasive Latin American trend is to neglect the strategic character of "innovating infrastructure"; the exception, to some extent, is Brazil, where there have been consistent policy steps to establish incentives for innovation in key sectors for technology transfer and domestic industrial competitiveness. It is no surprise then, that Brazil shows higher rates of foreign direct investment growth in areas such as software, telecommunications equipment, and biotechnology.

Similarly, lower relative importance is placed on developing a digital-enabled stock of human capital. This is not to say that there is no policy addressing this issue; rather, the policy initiatives dealing with the matter have not been purposefully linked to a "nation online" agenda that goes beyond universal access to online services. That is a pity, because a key area of opportunity in Latin America, according to the SWOT analysis, is establishing the conditions for clusters designed to foster IT intellectual *maquila*[1]. A case in point: the Costa Rica-Intel investment of 1998. This is certainly the most successful example of how attracting one firm and establishing the right conditions for an IT hub can jump-start networked readiness.

Whenever the issue of universal access to online services arises, the challenge for Latin American governments becomes that of delivering a new set of public goods; that is, goods and services that the free market by itself is incapable of generating efficiently. It is true that, given the presence of a critical mass of consumers, the market will generate goods and services that may help draw new segments of the population into the digital era. However, it is also true that this critical mass may never be reached without the catalytic action of a proactive government. This is particularly true in areas such as Web content and culture, but also in the support given to "public key" and other authentication- and certification-related policies behind the blossoming of e-commerce and e-government.

If human capital development in IT-related matters is important across the board, such development within all three branches of government activity and their interaction with the public (G2G, G2C, G2B) is essential. None of these goals will be achieved unless a higher understanding of the importance of networked readiness is embraced. Policy design, regulatory frameworks, and rule of law enforcement are essential to guarantee investment in network infrastructure.

The e-Democracy Agenda

Latin American countries have struggled for more than two decades to consolidate democratic rule. Great progress has been made, if only the peaceful transmission of power through democratic means is taken into account. However, there has also been growing disenchantment over the tangible benefits of democracy in the day-to-day lives of the population.

As the Chilean *Latinobarometro* statistics prove, levels of satisfaction with democracy in Latin America are very low. A staggering 60 percent of the population in Latin America thinks that the democratic system of values is unsatisfactory, 25 percent less than in European countries.

Only 29 percent of the population approves of government officials, 22 percent think positively of congress, and less than 15 percent trust political parties. In this context, direct tools of democracy such as the Internet, if wisely used, could offset the frustration of having to wait until elections to voice discontent and suggest alternative policies.

The Business Jungle

As a result of economic reforms implemented through the 1990s in almost all Latin American countries (i.e., open trading, privatization, liberalization of the financial markets, tax reforms), their enterprises faced a dramatic change in the competitive environment, going from a protectionist model limited to the local market, to an open market one that allowed foreign firms to come into the region. To survive in the new environment, Latin American enterprises had to implement structural reforms. Those fundamental changes contributed to the success of a handful of enterprises that stressed either making a high share of their sales exports or, if they did not have an ability to innovate, incorporating information technology as an integral part of their core business processes in order to help them achieve efficiency, reduce costs, increase productivity, and be competitive.

The business dimension of the Networked Readiness Framework Cube can be seen as an ecosystem that includes local/global companies, large local Fortune 500-equivalent companies, and small and medium enterprises.
The number of Latin American local/global companies that can swim confidently in the global 2000 sea is very small. But they are huge in terms of revenues, use of IT, and in the organizational leadership that permits them to innovate in their respective industry (e.g., Lorenzo Zambrano in CEMEX, the world's third-largest cement producer).

Large local enterprises are the ones that show sizeable revenues on a national, even regional in some cases, scale. They are linked to the international arena by their exports, although they have not yet established themselves as global players.

Most large local enterprises are latecomers to the networked readiness world. Conservative by nature, they waited too long to see if the whole IT thing was not simply a fad. Now they find themselves in a hostile environment because the economy has weakened, and they have learned that IT and being network-ready is not about buying expensive gadgets, but about making IT an integral part of business strategy.

Strained by the market contraction, large local firms surely do not have the resources to invest in IT, but they should rise to the occasion. Now that they need to streamline and reduce costs, they can do so by incorporating IT and network effects into their business landscape, not from the top down but from the bottom up. When this downward economic cycle ends, companies such as agro-industrial Bachoco in Mexico and food retailer CDB in Brazil could be in a better position to thrive in an intimidating and competitive environment.

When assessing SMEs, which comprise most of local business (around 80 percent of employment in the region is generated by SMEs), business analysts often divide them into medium and small. But for the purpose of Latin American networked readiness they should be lumped into a single category, because despite the differences of access and pricing models between the two business sizes, their IT needs are similar in terms of infrastructure.

The last thing on the priority list of an SME is networked readiness; SMEs simply have more urgent needs. That is why out-of-the-box thinking is essential for this business tier. To become network ready, they need an extremely pragmatic value proposition that is adapted to cultural particularities and investment capacity. The ultimate out-of-the-box thinking is required if they are to engage a huge amount of untapped network business: *los de abajo.*

It is important to note that our approach to Latin America business ecosystem does not account for two species: foreign multinationals that work with their homeland's corporate guidelines and that won't require incentives to hook into the network; and large state-owned enterprises that are under e-government because they are clearly public, rather than private, network catalyzers.

Box 1. An Example of Leadership: e-Readiness Policies in Brazil

Brazil shows an outstanding government readiness record. It ranks 32nd out of 82 countries, followed by Chile (34), Mexico (47), Colombia (56), and Argentina (75).

In terms of the Government Usage Index, Brazil's government ranks even higher at 10th out of 82 countries, even above developed competitors such as Hong Kong (11), Australia (12), the United Kingdom (13), Korea (14), and the Netherlands (15). Chile is ranked 21st for government usage, whereas Mexico ranks 35th and Argentina 46th. How is this remarkable Brazilian achievement to be explained? The answer lies in the effective translation of strategic vision into policy management, with the government acting as a catalyzing agent.

With less than two years remaining in his second four-year term, ex-President Fernando Henrique Cardoso set about reforming the Brazilian state and promoting the country's competitive insertion in the new international order. In this context, public management has definitely entered into the highest-level political agenda. Thus the president pledged to achieve three goals: paperless government, increased investment, and digital inclusion.

The Brazilian government already offers a wide range of services on the Internet. These services are completely integrated inside a government portal called Rede Governo. This portal offers more than 800 services and 4,800 categories of information. Some of the most important Internet services for citizens are:

1. Filing of income taxes—around 11 million people filed their income taxes electronically in 2000 and 13 million are forecast for 2002;

2. An e-procurement program, launched in January 2000;

3. Follow-up of judicial processes;

4. Information on retirement funds and other social security benefits (which registered 5.7 million transactions in the year 2000);

5. Distance learning programs;

6. E-mail services at public booths.

Brazil is 15th worldwide in information and communication technology (ICT) expenditures, and the federal government is the main consumer. The potential savings from lowering transaction costs, increasing productivity, and the injection of greater transparency are estimated to represent savings of nearly US$154 million a year. These savings are to be reinvested in public services.

Despite these remarkable advances, intercommunication among the various systems is still very limited. A further problem is the lack of a legal framework to ensure the authenticity of electronic documents, particularly electronic payments to the government. The federal government is responding to this problem by establishing standards for electronic certification and authentication as part of an information security policy.

The coordination of several concurrent projects is a major challenge. The most comprehensive of ongoing programs is the information society program, led by the Ministry of Science and Technology. This program carries out actions aimed at making the Brazilian economy more competitive and at extending access to IT benefits to the general public. The actions under this program involve government, business, and the scientific and technological communities in a diverse set of activities involving intensive use of ICT. However, most ongoing actions are brought together and coordinated in the electronic government program. An inter-ministerial committee overseen by the Presidency of the Republic supervises this program. The aim of the program is to develop public administration by enhancing public services delivery, improving access to information, reducing costs, and allowing social control over government actions.

Another important and ongoing Brazilian initiative is government transparency, which promotes legal and administrative action in order to encourage social control over the public sector. This is complementary to the advance in election automation in Brazil. In recent elections, more than 130 million people voted electronically, with the online system determining elected candidates in less than twenty-four hours.

Brazilian initiatives to achieve digital inclusion
In spite of the profound structural inequalities found across social groups and regions, the Brazilian government, as part of its responsibility in promoting effective policies to fight social exclusion, explicitly acknowledged that investment in IT is strategic and must constitute an instrument of social inclusion. e-Government must work as an instrument of social inclusion. Policies are, therefore, aimed at facilitating universal access to stimulate the creation and diffusion of services and opportunities so as to prevent IT from becoming another exclusionary factor.

With the privatization of the telecommunications sector, the Brazilian government had the strategic vision to make privatization conditional on the establishment of funding initiatives for the universalization of access to information technology. This ensured the creation of abundant financial resources to expand the telecommunication network in market segments that do not offer commercial viability, particularly those in remote communities. As a result, the federal government has been installing electronic points of presence to provide free access to the services delivered through the Internet. The main areas covered by access points are education, health, social security, labor, and public security. By 2002, even the smallest villages in the border areas and all the federal government field offices all over the country had at least one electronic point of presence.

By the end of 2002, the Brazilian government expects that 62,000 public schools will be connected to the Internet, and that by 2006 all 200,000 schools will be connected. In the health sector, 4,300 municipalities and 20,000 health units are being interconnected through a nationwide network. Further, personal magnetic cards are being used in the public health system, and the access points will be used as community telecenters opened to public. President Fernando Henrique Cardoso has achieved the challenging goal of offering all federal services through the Internet by the end of 2002.

Source: excerpts, Farias 2001

Box 2. **The Big Fish Swimming in the Networked Readiness Pond**

Sixty-four Latin American firms are considered globally competitive. The table below presents the fifteen largest ones (based on revenues). It is important to note that this study does not list the use of technology as a condition for being globally competitive, but if we take a close look at each enterprise, IT is clearly a fundamental part of its success.

	Enterprise	Country	Sector	Sales (US$ billion)	Foreign (% sales)
1.	Telmex	Mexico	Telecom	12.14	2.2
2.	Cemex	Mexico	Cement	6.94	61.9
3.	Grupo Bimbo	Mexico	Food	3.70	24.6
4.	Vitro	Mexico	Construction	3.08	26.5
5.	Embrear	Brazil	Airspace	2.58	88.3
6.	Gerdau	Brazil	Steel	2.54	8.7
7.	Grupo Imsa	Mexico	Steel	2.30	46.4
8.	Vale do Rio Doce	Brazil	Mining	2.24	32.7
9.	Grupo Televisa	Mexico	Media	2.15	13.8
10.	Codelco	Chile	Mining	1.78	82.9
11.	Grupo Elektra	Mexico	Retail	1.71	8.4
12.	Perez Companc (PECOM)	Argentina	Oil/Gas	1.64	25.5
13.	Sadia	Brazil	Food	1.57	25.6
14.	Lan Chile	Chile	Airline	1.42	4.3
15.	Arcor	Argentina	Food	1.10	19.7

Source: based on the list published by *América Economía* magazine

The world's third-largest bread maker is a Mexican firm called Grupo Bimbo. It has businesses in the United States and sixteen countries in Latin America and Europe and together they produce more than 750 products and ninety prestigious brands. According to the company's profile, Bimbo's commitment is "to be a highly productive and completely humane company, as well as to be innovative, competitive, and oriented to the full satisfaction of its customers and consumers."

To achieve its goals, in the 1990s Bimbo developed an effective client/server-based supply chain to manage its vast network of plants and distribution facilities. With the introduction of this system the company decentralized operations; and each of its units have information that tells them the needs of the market—especially useful because Bimbo's basic products are perishable. Recently, as part of its IT strategy, Bimbo invested more than US$50 million on IT projects to enhance supply/demand and operations processes.

The Argentinian Arcor Group is the number one producer of caramels worldwide. It is also the leading chocolate manufacturer in Latin America. Regardless of the current Argentinian crisis, Arcor is considered a top-notch company that could indeed help economic recovery in that country. According to its executives, a very important part of its strategy is to constantly reinvest in technology in an attempt to reach the highest world-class standards. It has launched a website (www.arcorsales.com) designed to encourage B2B transactions and marketing solutions, twenty-four hours a day, seven days a week. It offers a wide range of services and all the necessary elements to enhance operational efficiency.

The Brazilian company Embraer is the number three producer of airplanes in the world. As part of its IT strategy, Embraer has implemented the Transforming the Organization for Results (TOR) program, which includes entrepreneurship initiatives as well as the integration of business platforms and ERP systems. The company was also equipped with a Virtual Reality Center, a modern graphic computer enabling Embraer engineers to visualize, through electronic models, the aircraft's structure and systems during design and development phases, reducing the development time and allowing customers to follow the aircraft's development using the Internet as a collaborative tool. Embraer also relies on its Customer Integration System Internet portal-focus for improving customer satisfaction.

The International Institute for Management Development in Switzerland explained that, "The CEMEX Way was an information system and process standardization program [developed] to create an open corporate information infrastructure and [to ensure] that 60 percent of the company's business processes were managed in a Web-based environment by the end of 2001. The CEMEX Way impacted the business bottom line by saving US$150 million per year; [it] simplified business transactions, and enabled better customer service and increased loyalty." CEMEX is in good company—other Latin companies have understood how organizational leadership and innovation through IT can thrive regardless of a mediocre environment for networked readiness.

The agro-industrial sector in Mexico represents 22.5 percent of the GDP and employs 20 percent of the workforce. In 2005 the volume of transactions in this sector is expected to reach US$89.5 billion, and there is a margin of efficiency improvement for business processes estimated at between 25 and 30 percent.

One way to address this huge room for improvement is doing network-based out-of-the-box thinking, such as signing up small, medium, and large farms and cattle ranchers to the same Internet portal (see Agroenlinea.com website) so they can sell their products nationwide and export to the United States.

In the year 2000, Agroenlinea.com, a private company whose name translates to agro-online, launched an e-business initiative to provide an agricultural and food marketplace that could facilitate rapid and direct transactions between producers and buyers within the North American region. According to the company, by September 2002, approximately 1,200 Mexican agricultural businesses and producers were registered on Agroenlinea.com.

Also as of September 2002, Agroenlinea.com had signed partnership agreements with six state governments in Mexico. Five of the six state governments that have signed these partnerships, including those of Chiapas and Guerrero, are located in southern Mexico, where most of the country's poorest farmers are concentrated and where it is more difficult to gain access to the U.S. market.

Under the partnership agreements, local rural development agencies pay Agroenlinea.com a fee that allows local producers to use the company's portal at no cost. Thus, local farmers advertise their produce,

production and delivery capacity, and prices in the e-catalogue of Agroenlinea.com, and receive technical, logistical, and marketing services and advice from the company. Buyers can check the exact status and delivery time of their purchases, and also receive advice.

Rural development agencies play a critical role in helping small farms and individual producers form informal associations to increase their supply capacity and to homogenize quality standards. Such agencies also play a role in establishing communication between producers without access to the Internet or telephones and Agroenlinea.com, which in turn establishes communication between the producers and potential buyers.

To speed communications and the time needed for business transactions, Agroenlinea.com plans to provide Internet-ready computers to local producers. Installation of the computers inside the offices of governmental agencies in charge of rural development, whose facilities would in effect become rural kiosks, will reduce costs.

As part of the effort, Agroenlinea.com will also provide basic computer training to farmers and cattle ranchers. In the case of older farmers, who may find the use of new technologies difficult, Agroenlinea.com plans to train younger family members.

One of the main goals of Agroenlinea.com is to provide a cheaper option to producers and buyers, by eliminating expensive intermediary costs. Agroenlinea.com registers about 13,500 sessions per day. It has already opened new markets to poor, individual producers of pineapples in the state of Veracruz, women farmers in the state of Mexico, and coffee growers in Chiapas, among others.

Large global and local firms initiated business-to-business marketplaces with the aim of convincing smaller fish to invest in IT infrastructure so they (the smaller fish) could stay in the pond. The Latinexus initiative launched by Alfa, Bradesco, CEMEX, Botorantim, and Artikos, which was the business portal started by Banamex, did not work as expected partly because of the poor level of access to the internet of the targeted satellite companies, and also because of an immature IT culture and infrastructure.

Three years have gone by since the failed B2B portal. There have been some changes in the Networked Readiness Index— that is, in connectivity, usage, and availability—but more importantly there has been a cultural change that is reflected in, for example, the extended use of e-banking by companies in the first two tiers.

It is therefore advisable to revisit the idea of B2B marketplaces, leveraging the effect of the already existing industrial hubs not only to reduce costs and establish an efficient procurement for the big fish, but also to expedite networked readiness through incentives by government and large firms for those who wish to thrive in the pond.

The hub model, therefore, must provide clear value propositions for all players. This could be achieved by offering positive incentives such as faster payments, factoring options, and fiscal stimulus, especially for smaller firms.

Another area with substantial opportunity for businesses, both local and foreign, is the "intellectual *maquila*."

Backroom office services, like accounting, calling centers, and software services support, can be done either in English in the English-speaking Caribbean, or at selected areas that have invested in bilingual education for their citizenry; but it can also be done in Spanish everywhere in Latin America in order to serve the 35 million Hispanics recognized by the U.S. census as living in the United States.

Intellectual *maquila* could also mean using Latin American engineers and business professionals trained at top-notch international schools to assemble projects at significantly lower prices than what they would cost in North America, just as manual workers do in traditional *maquila*.

With Forrester Research predicting that B2B transactions for Latin America could reach US$84 billion by 2004, the game is not only about pushing for IT usage, but about making it an integral part of day-to-day operations and turning it into a big plus on the bottom line of every company. Doing so could very quickly heighten one of the main dimensions of the Networked Readiness Framework Cube.

A Society of Young, Poor, and Network-Hungry People

According to IDC, by 2006 only 6 percent of the Latin American population will be hooked up to the Internet, whereas they estimate that 70 percent of the U.S. population will have access.

Internet access through leased lines and shared devices in community centers—not just individual dial-up access—holds the key for growing the Internet as a mass medium in emerging economies, according to Red Científica Peruana, an organization promoting universal use in Peru.

A recent study financed by the Inter-American Development Bank about the use of telecenters (or Internet kiosks) in low-income neighborhoods in Peru (a country with significant experience in this area) concluded that community kiosks have benefited poor Peruvians and that these residents show potential to leave poverty behind. However, the study also showed that the direct impact of the telecenters had not been profound enough, particularly among Peruvians of lower educational and economic levels.

While access models are fundamental (they will be covered in some detail later in the text), there are two other key factors to promote network usage: content, understood as traditional and transactional, and network architecture and technology by themselves.

This section also stresses potential value propositions to get on board the network train most Latin American citizens in the urban areas: the young, poor, and network hungry.

Access models

Structural constraints like low income and high cost of Internet access services have limited the ability to replicate in Latin America access models based on mass-market and long-term profitability.

In order to overcome those barriers, efforts must be made at the community level to involve individuals and organizations in learning about electronic communications and in defining local access systems to meet their unique needs. Particular emphasis should be placed on establishing affordable and accessible community-driven systems; encouraging Internet service providers (ISPs) and community leaders to attract policymakers and community groups to the system; and on providing relevant content.

In many Latin American countries, including Brazil, new laws and regulations are necessary to allow citizens to pay flat rates to ISPs instead of paying for cost-per-minute connections. In the short term, this measure could potentially increase the number of narrowband dial-up subscribers in the regions, including many small businesses and students. According to a new Yankee Group forecast, the number of this type of subscriber could increase from 25 million in 2002 to 65 million in 2007. In Colombia, Internet traffic increased by 246 percent after a flat rate was imposed.

In the United States, pricing of Internet access not only is based on a flat rate, but for some ISPs this rate has dropped to as low as US$5 per month. Until such rates of access are established in the Spanish- and Portuguese-speaking part of the hemisphere, other models can serve as bridges.

People in the forty-plus age bracket who witnessed the previous communication splash in Latin America—that is, the introduction of television sets during the 1960s—know that sharing a television set was a common and widely-accepted practice. This "barrio" sharing is still prevalent for their sons, therefore building Network Access models based on propositions that leverage communal use is not only advisable, but is at hand and proven.

According to most statistics, there are 3.5 million users of the Internet in Mexico. Yet one mail service provider alone, Hotmail, registers 5 million active subscribers. This can only be explained by the sharing effect, as opposed to office usage, of the Internet.

A single computer school lab and professional staff can serve several schools in a poor community or neighborhood. There, students can obtain basic network literacy and skills, such as an understanding of how to search, browse, and retrieve desired materials, and how to manipulate information to add value in the process.

According to Harvard University professor Pippa Norris, "the development of human capital—meaning the investment in digital skills and capabilities and education, training, and lifetime learning—represents one of the most important factors that might facilitate Internet access." K-12 students throughout Latin America should be prepared with the skills necessary to survive in the information economy.

An economy whose largest, most dynamic engines are based on telecommunications (despite the current sector crisis), and which is thus far ruled by laws that describe the continuous price reduction of access while the capacity grows, has a natural upside for Latin America.

Fostering access is a must, but access to what? Transactional and traditional content in a language other than English is required to encourage greater network usage in Latin America.

Spanish Internet pages are 2.4 percent of all available content. English pages stand at 68.3 percent, but according to data retrieved in 2000 by the Tomas Rivera Policy Institute, the speakers-to-Web page ratio in each case is a correlation of 43:1 in Spanish and 1:5 in English.

Regarding transactional content, job kiosks, in addition to the government services, banking, and other services directed towards individuals already discussed, are an excellent example for urging usage to search for specific content.

Access and content notwithstanding, business propositions able to take advantage of the huge pool of low-income customers are what can truly generate a "viral" effect in network usage.

So far, network-based commerce is targeted at the high-income consumer who holds credit cards and has fixed home or office lines. The bottom end of the consumer barrel is too poor to even be considered—these people are scattered, many of them in unconnected rural communities. In between those extremes are basically urban populations that in countries such as Mexico have monthly family incomes that range from US$250 to US$750 per month.

Figure 3. **Mexico's Family Income (2002)**

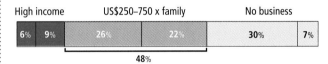

Creative businesses making their SWOT analysis of Latin American markets will spot this large chunk of consumers as the number-one opportunity.

Conclusions

There is no time for a "siesta." Networked readiness in Latin America could prove to be yet another missed opportunity if

---

Box 4. Banking on the Poor over the Internet

Latin American and Caribbean workers living in the United States are sending home more than US$15 billion every year. Common transfers of an average of US$200 each pay US$20 to US$30 in commissions, while the regular banking fee for a money transfer is US$10. The price difference is due to the fact that illegal workers cannot hold bank accounts without a social security number.

A Mexican Coalition of Foreign Residents in the United States discovered, nevertheless, that those illegal workers, issued with a tax and a consular identification, could, in fact, open bank accounts.

They tested the idea with ten different banks. It took a while to get them going, but now a myriad are offering the service, some as conservative in their practices as Citibank.

Many other companies are now targeting the same customers with services ranging from provision of long-distance services using voice over Internet protocol and health insurance paid by relatives living in the United States, to ordering gifts for Christmas and Mother's Day, all over the Internet.

In São Paulo, Brazil, Magazine Luisa (a domestic appliance store chain) opened several virtual stores in small low-income communities. The key to their service model is having an inventory near to zero. The small stores are empowered with a few large-screen PCs operated by store assistants who help customers not only order what they want at the e-store, but also sign them up with on-the-spot credit, because these kinds of customers are usually not cardholders.

Elektra in Mexico a company on the same retail sector has a similar business approach. With more than 1,000 networked branches scattered around low-income neighborhoods, Elektra recently got permission to start banking activities through Banco Azteca, which, according to company spokesmen, is targeting the very same low-income customers. At Elektra they are already able to collect 97 cents from every peso involved in their credit operations. Regardless of the fact that their highest interest rate can be as much as an astounding 40 percent, seven out of every ten are repeat customers.

Grupo Salinas, owner of Elektra, Banco Azteca, TV Azteca, Unefon, and Todito.com, is certainly going after the low-income market using all the tools of the Internet.

governments, businesses, and individuals do not seize the day. This year, Brazil, the number one Latin country in the Networked Readiness Index, has shown the benefits of using as a launching pad a presidential commitment to get the country going the e-way.

The State dutifully became the great digital content trigger, inviting both businesses and citizens to conduct business with it through the Internet. Legislation was put in place and incentives established to enhance the intellectual capital for networked readiness processes.

Brazil's best practices should be thoroughly studied and replicated where possible, but given this country's particular history, such practices will be hard to carbon copy.

In truth, using the *samba* or any other model and trying to fit everything into it is not going to work. As always, Latin America is far more complex than it appears from a viewpoint on Wall Street, or from Paris, Zurich, or Silicon Valley.

A country-by-country analysis is needed to set a specific agenda based on the combination of strengths, weaknesses, opportunities, and threats (SWOTs) that are to be found in individual countries in different combinations.

Granted, there are some characteristics that all Latin American countries share, such as, unfortunately, a large population of low-income citizens who are young and unserved in terms of communications.

How those consumers will be tackled should be an individual value proposition scheme, but it should be at the core of networked readiness advocacy.

Businesses or individuals that have the creativity, courage, and sensibility to work with "*los de abajo*," *los pobres*, show an interesting upside in the IT revolution. Despite complaints about a lack of or poor infrastructure, the "dirty little secret" is that infrastructure already in place (see Box 2) could be used, right now, by bold, bright entrepreneurs to offer the right pricing and to put forward the right access model.

Cultural tradition allows for shared access models that could be swiftly introduced as bridges to a more intense use of the Internet in urban populations with pent-up demands. But to what would these populations be gaining access? Less than 3 percent of Web pages are in Spanish. There is a desperate need for more content, both traditional and transactional, to enhance network usage in Latin America.

But nothing is more important than urging, within a general rule of law, the proper legislation that would allow stakeholders and agents of change to thrive in Latin America.

Figure 4. **Change Agents for Networked Readiness**

	STAKEHOLDERS	AGENDA	
Market	• Business • Individuals • Government	• Serve high- and low-income segments • Uncover unconventional opportunities • Meet pent-up demands • Government acting as e-business trigger	▶
Policy Regulation	• Executive branch • Legislators and parties • Business lobbies	• Rule of law enforcement • Regulatory framework release • Fiscal and other incentive programs • Education and innovation facilitation • Guarantee investment endurance	▶
Infrastructure	• Government agencies • Telcos and IT vendors • Content providers	• Regulate Internet-related investments • Ensure proper pricing per audience • Ascertain quality • Stimulate unconventional offering • Study new access methods	▶

	VEHICLES	CHANGE AGENTS
Business Fertility	• Internet-leveraging business clusters • Proper educational infrastructure • Expand Internet business value to low-income strata • Government to catalyze Internet business • Fulfill Internet-related services needs	• Embrace the business hub model to expedite SMEs' Internet adoption • Fostering B2B and G2B transactions • Blend maquila tradition with the Internet • Identify badly-attended services improvable by net • Government "enforced" digital transactions • Internet adoption incentives
e-Nation Agenda	• G2G to ensure the rule of law • Specialized SWAT expediting net regulation • G2C and G2B enhanced procurement of justice • Government incentives designed to embrace usage	• Transparency to empower civil participation • Presidential agenda sets a G2B, G2C, and G2G plan • Enhance educational infrastructure • Greater Internet literacy of civil servants
Value Proposition	• Compelling traditional and transactional content • Creative fair access models • Government incentives for investments and usage	• Guarantee flat access rates • Embrace shared access models as a bridge • Government digital services usage incentives • Incentives to connect migrant workers' families

Endnotes

The authors are part of Convergencia Digital, a not-for-profit organization involved in forwarding Network Readiness in Mexico. This paper could not have been written without the cooperation of Georgina Mendoza, Hugo Martinez—who contributed with additional research on access models—and Neoris, a global digital enabling company providing practical business solutions based on cutting edge technology.

1. A *maquila* is an assembly plant located in Mexico near the United States border to which materials are shipped; the finished product is shipped back across the border into the United States.

References

América Económica. Online. http://www.americaeconomica.com/

América Economía. "Tiempos Turbulentos," *América Economía* July 12–25:18. Online.

A Política de Governo Electrônico no Brasil, Brasilia, Agosto de 2001. República Federativa do Brasil, Ministerio do Planejamento, Orçamento e Gestao, Secretaria de Logística e Tecnología da Informaçao.

Bachoco. Online. http://www.bachoco.com.mx.

Ca'Zorzi, A. 2002. *Electronic Commerce and Development Implications for IDB Action.* Information Technology for Development Division, Inter-American Development Bank. Online. http://www.iadb.org/ict4dev/pdf/ITD%20 e-commerce%20paper%20Nov-00.pdf.

Commonwealth Network of Information Technology for Development (COMNET-IT) and United Nations Educational, Scientific and Cultural Organization (UNESCO). 2000. Estudio Mundial Sobre El Ejercicio Del Gobierno En Línea: Informe Final. UNESCO No. CII-2000/WS/09. Paris: United Nations Educational, Scientific and Cultural Organization.

de Ferranti, D., G. E. Perry, D. Lederman, and W. F. Maloney. 2001. *From Natural Resources to the Knowledge Economy: Trade and Job Quality.* Washington, DC: The World Bank.

Development Gateway and E. F. Ivanovic. 2002. *e-Gobierno en Chile, Entrevista Con el Ing. Enrique Fanta Ivanovic.* Online. http://www.developmentgateway.org/download/117925/ Entrevista_Fanta_OK.pdf.

Embraer. Online. http://www.embraer.com.

Eregion. Online. http://www.arcor.com.

Farias, P. 2001. "Electronic Government: The Brazilian Policy Document." Presented at Fostering Democracy and Development through e-Government, the Third Global Forum, Naples, Italy, March 12–15, 2001.

Goldstein, A. 2002. "Embrear: de Campeón Nacional a Jugador Global," *Revista de la Cepal* (77).

Grupo Bimbo. Online. http://www.gibsa.com.mx.

Iglesias, E. 2001. *MicroEnterprise Americas Magazine.*

Informes y formularios sobre el Gobierno Electrónico. Conferencia de Autoridades Iberoamericanas de Informática. Sesión Plenaria XIX de la CAIBI, Santo Domingo, Dominican Republic, September 27–28, 2001. Online. http://www.map.es/csi/caibi/ sesiones/xix/d19_008.htm.

Inter-American Development Bank (IADB), Sustainable Development Department. SME Observatory. Online. http://www.iadb.org/sds/sme/site_167_e.htm.

Latinobarometro. Online. http://www.latinobarometro.org.

Mason, O. 2001. "Institutional and Human Capacities for e-Government: Lessons from the Hemisphere." Presented at the Organization of American States Third Caribbean Ministerial Consultation and High Level Workshop, e-Government and ICT in Public Sector Management, Montego Bay, Jamaica, December 10, 2001.

Reforma Newspaper, August 22, 2002.

Rogelio, O. and F. Fernando Suarez. 2002. *Learning to Compete: How Firms Transform Themselves In The Face of Radical Environment Change.* Online. http://www.london.edu/otm/ Whos_Who/Fernando_Suarez/SO_CMR_12Feb2002.pdf.

Sun Microsystems. 1999. *Case Study: Grupo Bimbo's Winning Strategy for Latin American Prepared Foods Market.* Sun Microsystems.

The Americas Society. 2001 *Impact of the Internet and Information Technology in Latin America.* Online. http://www.americas-society.org/as/events/pdf.d/studygroupii.pdf.

The International Institute for Management Development, Lausanne Research, Switzerland, Copyright 2002 CEMEX case study

Chapter 8

ICT Challenges for the Arab World

Soumitra Dutta, INSEAD

Mazen E. Coury, Independent Consultant

Introduction

The purpose of this chapter is to discuss ongoing developments in the Arab world in the areas of information and communication technology (ICT) and to highlight the obstacles to and present recommendations for further development. We looked at the environment as well as individual, business, and government variables in assessing the current state of development and the impact of national and regional ICT strategies. Our recommendations are addressed to policymakers at the national and regional levels. The scope of this chapter encompasses thirteen countries, which we group according to geography. We define the "Gulf," the "Arabian Gulf," or "Gulf states" as comprising Kuwait, Saudi Arabia, Bahrain, Qatar, the United Arab Emirates, and Oman. Our definition of "Levant" includes Lebanon, Syria, Jordan, and Egypt. We classify Tunisia, Algeria, and Morocco as the "Maghreb states."

Overview of Progress in ICT in the Arab World

ICT strategic intent can be measured against published strategy documentation, actual progress in the implementation of ICT strategies, and the presence of technology-building initiatives and research and development (R&D) institutes. We reviewed the ICT-awareness of Arab governments by looking into their strategic plans and operational five-year plans, and observed that there are uneven levels of awareness of and importance given to ICT both in stated national strategies and demonstrated success in implementation.

Arab states are adapting their legal and regulatory frameworks for ICT

As Arab states join the World Trade Organization (WTO), they have been adapting their legal and regulatory systems to accommodate trademark, patent, and intellectual property rights (IPR) protection. Some states have been part of the early stages of IPR[1] protection; others have retroactively signed the agreements and sought membership of the World Intellectual Property Organization (WIPO) (see Figure 1). Nine of the countries in the scope of this study are members of the WTO, and eleven joined the Paris Convention for the Protection of Industrial Property,[2] on whose principles the WIPO was founded. Arab states' participation in interim treaties is uneven: only four have signed the Patent Cooperation Treaty[3] (PCT) and three the Patent Law Treaty (PLT). There has been improvement in the mid-to-late 1990s, when eight of them joined the Agreement on Trade-Related Aspects of Intellectual Property Rights (TRIPS). A joint WTO-WIPO framework, TRIPS revisits the entire IPR protection system, standardizing intellectual property definitions, affirming and enforcing national treatment and most favored nation principles through a series of procedures, and providing

Figure 1. **Status of Arab States on Intellectual Property Rights**

	WTO Member	WIPO Treaties									
		Paris Convention	WCT	PCT	Madrid Agreement	Hague Agreement	TLT	PLT	Nairobi Treaty	TRIPS
Gulf											
Kuwait	✓	✗	✓ (1998)	✗	✗	✗	✗	✗	✗	✓ (1995)
Saudi Arabia	✗	✗	✓ (1982)	✗	✗	✗	✗	✗	✗	✗
Bahrain	✓	✓ (1997)	✗	✗	✗	✗	✗	✗	✗	✓ (1995)
Qatar	✓	✓ (2000)	✓ (1976)	✗	✗	✗	✗	✗	✓ (1983)	✗
U.A.E.	✓	✓ (1996)	✓ (1974)	✓ (1999)	✗	✗	✗	✓ (1999)	✗	✓ (1996)
Oman	✓	✓ (1999)	✗	✓ (2001)	✗	✗	✗	✗	✓ (1986)	✓ (2000)
Levant											
Lebanon	✗	✓ (1924)	✓ (1986)	✗	✓ (1924)	✗	✗	✓ (2000)	✗	✗
Syrian AR	✗	✓ (1924)	✗	✗	✓ (1924)	✗	✗	✗	✓ (1984)	✗
Jordan	✓	✓ (1972)	✓ (1972)	✗	✗	✗	✗	✗	✗	✓ (2000)
Egypt	✓	✓ (1951)	✗	✗	✓ (1952)	✓ (1975)	✓ (1999)	✗	✓ (1982)	✓ (1995)
Maghreb											
Tunisia	✓	✓ (1984)	✗	✗	✓ (1982)	✓ (1930)	✗	✗	✓ (1983)	✓ (1995)
Algeria	✗	✓ (1966)	✓ (1975)	✓ (2000)	✓ (1972)	✗	✗	✓ (2000)	✓ (1984)	✗
Morocco	✓	✓ (1917)	✓ (1971)	✓ (1999)	✓ (1917)	✓ (1930)	✗	✗	✓ (1993)	✓ (1995)

Key: ✗, not signed or nonmember; ✓ (date) signed on date
WIPO: World Intellectual Property Organization; WCT: WIPO Copyright Treaties; PCT: Patent Cooperation Treaty;
TLT: Trademarks Low Treaty; PLT: Patent Law Treaty

for standard dispute treatment processes. At this stage, only Lebanon, Syria, Algeria, Saudi Arabia, and Qatar are yet to enact the agreement.

Arab states will increasingly become attractive investment targets as TRIPS regulations begin to be enforced. With a standardized IPR protection system and the fact that by January 2005 Arab states are required to extend product patent protection to types of products not previously patented, the region is due to witness further integration into global research and development. Arab states are also drafting new laws to foster ICT growth and investor confidence at the national levels. Figure 2 highlights Arab states' current efforts in adapting their IPR-related laws to the specific needs of technology and ICT. The legal framework upgrade has been uneven: the Levant area and the Maghreb have been, in general, more advanced in creating frameworks, thanks to their earlier exposure to the global legal culture. Latecomers include the Gulf states; their efforts pertaining to the upgrade of these laws have therefore been more recent.

Creation of a research-promoting environment

Arabs states display significant interest in technology initiatives. Materialized via technopoles[4] and/or technology incubators,[5] the benefits of these initiatives include

providing an environment for research and development in collaboration with private initiatives, developing technology diffusion, benefiting the social and economic fabric by creating new employment possibilities, building the ecosystem for business development, and enhancing technological transfers between the public and private sectors. In all cases, private-public partnerships and universities play central roles. The political and regulatory environment in the Arab world is being adapted in accordance with best practices from the United States and Europe.

Arab states have been prolific on both the technopole and incubator fronts: all countries discussed in this chapter have at least launched a national planning process for these technology-building initiatives, with varying degrees of success in implementation. Figure 3 highlights the readiness and operational facilities of Arab states. Technology-dedicated research facilities are operational components of Arab states' national strategies. In the Gulf, Kuwait, Saudi Arabia, and the United Arab Emirates stand out in terms of research facilities. Initially sector-oriented (mineral and petrochemical sectors), these facilities now encompass ICT and high technology. Levant and Maghreb states drafted plans for such facilities as early as the 1960s (for example, Lebanon drafted its National Council for Scientific Research in 1969 and a general framework to

Figure 2. **Selected IPR-related Laws Enacted per Country**

Country	Year:* Law/Decree/Act
Gulf	
Kuwait	2001: Patent Law 2001: Trademark Law 2000: Copyright Law
Saudi Arabia	1984: Trademark Law 1989: Patent Law 1989: Copyright Law
Bahrain	1977: Patent Law 1991: Trademark Law 1993: Copyright Decree
Qatar	1978: Trademark Law 1995: Copyright Law
U.A.E.	1992: Patent and Industrial Design Law 1992: Trademark Law
Oman	1987: Trademark Law 2000: Royal Decree on Patent Law 2000: Royal Decree and Law on Trademarks, Indications, and Secrets and Protection against Unfair Competition
Levant	
Lebanon	1946: Patent Law 1999: Copyright Law
Syrian AR	1949: Copyright Law 1980: Patent Legislative Decree
Jordan	1953: Patent and Industrial Design Act 1999: Trademark Law 1999: Copyright Law 2000: Layout Design of Integrated Circuits Law
Egypt	1949: Patent and Industrial Models Act 1969: Trademark Act 1992: Copyright Act
Maghreb	
Tunisia	1956: Patents decree 1936: Trademark decree 1994: Copyright decree
Algeria	1966: Decree 66–60 concerning patents and innovation certificates 1966: Ordonnance 66–57 relative aux marques de fabriques et de commerce 1966: Ordonnance 66–223 relative aux dessins et modèles industriels 1993: Décrêt legislative 93–17 relatif à la protection des inventions 1997: Ordonnance 97–10 relative aux droits d'auteurs 1998: Décrêt exécutif 98–366 portant statuts de l'Office National des Droits d'Auteurs et des Droits Voisins (ONDA)
Morocco	1916: Patents Dahir 1997: Industrial Property Law 2000: Copyright Law

*Dates indicate latest modifications and amendments

develop the country's scientific potential). Moroccan research and ICT involvement, led by the Centre National de la Recherche Scientifique et Technique, was inspired by leading French research institutes. Six countries operate technopoles dedicated to research and development in technology. Saudi Arabia's King Abdulaziz City for Science and Technology (KACST), for instance, has evolved from its petroleum focus to include atomic energy, astronomy and geophysics, computer and electronics, and aerospace. Other countries, such as Jordan, with its newly established ICT plan, have adopted a narrower focus. Technology incubators plans are ready, but we identified only three operational technology incubators of national magnitude across the area. As venture funding is still marginal in the area, most technology incubators have yet to flourish.

Deployment of ICT infrastructure improvement programs

There are several ongoing ICT-infrastructure development initiatives in the Arab world; they are strategically important because of the magnitude of investment, anticipated benefits, and fit with national ICT plans. Progress is measurable in network and teledensity achievements, regional and global connectivity, as well as in operational e-government facilities.

National network upgrades, teledensity improvements, enhanced national connectivity, and the gradual introduction of new Internet provider (IP) delivery technologies are creating a favorable environment for the uptake of ICT. However, much progress remains to be made. The International Telecommunication Union (ITU) has ranked states based upon national teledensities—Group A, the lowest rank, for countries with less than 1 percent fixed line penetration rates in 2001; and Group G, the highest rank, with teledensity rates higher than the 50 percent threshold in 2001 (ITU 2002). Of the thirteen countries under consideration in this chapter, six ranked in the C category (teledensity between the 5 percent and 10 percent); the D and E categories each had three countries, and the United Arab Emirates was on par with Spain and Portugal in the F category (35 percent to 50 percent). National teledensity improvement has to remain a priority in most Arab states.[6]

Geographical disparities between the Gulf states and the rest of the region have led to the adoption of diverging national fixed line development strategies. Most Gulf states are in the process of completing the digitalization of their public networks, whilst Maghreb states are working on densification and upgrading the existing telephone networks. With small populations but high investments in their national networks, Gulf states have matched or outperformed international standards in ICT infrastructure, whereas the densely populated Levant and Maghreb

Figure 3. Aspects of Political Leadership to Promote Use of ICT

	Aspects of Political Leadership to Promote Use of ICT							
	ICT Strategy Clearly Spelled Out*	ICT Implementation Plan Clearly Articulated**	Operational ICT-Dedicated Research Facilities	Plan of ICT-Dedicated Research Facilities	Operational Technopole Initiative	Plan of Technopole Initiative	Existence of Technology Incubator	Planned Technology Incubator
Gulf								
Kuwait	✓	✗	✓	✓	✗	✓	✗	✓
Saudi Arabia	✓	✓	✓	✓	✓	✓	✗	✓
Bahrain	✓	✓	✓	✗	✗	✓	✓	✓
Qatar	✓	✗	✗	✗	✗	✗	✗	✓
U.A.E.	✓	✓	✓	✓	✓	✓	✓	✓
Oman	✗	✗	✗	✓	✗	✗	✗	✓
Levant								
Lebanon	✓	✓	✓	✓	✗	✓	✗	✓
Syrian AR	✗	✗	✗	✓	✗		✗	✗
Jordan	✓	✓	✓	✓	✓	✓	✓	✓
Egypt	✗	✓	✓	✓	✓	✓	✓	✓
Maghreb								
Tunisia	✓	✓	✓	✓	✗	✓	✗	✓
Algeria	✗	✓	✓	✓		✓	✗	✓
Morocco	✓	✓	✓	✓	✓	✓	✓	✓

Key: ✓ = Yes, ✗ = No

* Our definition is that an ICT strategy is clear when individual countries publish a set of strategic objectives in the field, either through a national plan or some other medium, and mark measurable and quantifiable accomplishments unto a milestone path.

** Our definition is that an ICT plan is clear and operational when budgets have been dedicated to the ICT strategy, a task force, whatever the format, is operationally in place, and when clearly published implementation process is underway."

remain underserved. However, it is important to note that significant progress has been achieved over the last years, as budget allocation for national telephony has been (and continues to be) a priority for most states in the region.

Successful interregional connectivity initiatives are increasingly linking Arab states. ArabSat, an inter-Arab satellite communications and transmissions solution, is one of the best examples of the ability of Arab states to collaborate in creating a solid and resilient communications network. On the land connectivity front, the model has been replicated on a geographical area basis. The Gulf Cooperation Council (GCC) states have created the Fibre Optic Gulf[7] (FOG) network, a 1,300 km cable system jointly owned by the national telecommunications operators of Kuwait, Bahrain, Qatar, and the United Arab Emirates. Other examples of cooperation[8] include that between Syria, Lebanon, Egypt, and Cyprus.

Arab elite increasingly exposed to ICT

In many Arab states the speed of the introduction of Internet access devices is increasing rapidly. Individually, Arabian Gulf states display ICT and Internet penetration levels comparable to the West (see Figure 4). The United Arab Emirates penetration rate of almost 30 percent at the end of 2001 is higher than the European average. RIPE, the European IP

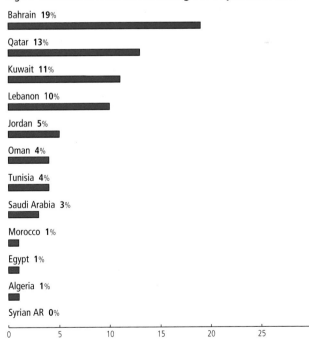

Figure 4. **Internet Users as Percentage of Population, 2001**

Bahrain **19**%
Qatar **13**%
Kuwait **11**%
Lebanon **10**%
Jordan **5**%
Oman **4**%
Tunisia **4**%
Saudi Arabia **3**%
Morocco **1**%
Egypt **1**%
Algeria **1**%
Syrian AR **0**%

Sources: World Markets Research Centre for Arab statistics, Harris Interactive for the U.S. statistics, and Jupiter for the U.K. statistics

association, ranked the United Arab Emirates 20th globally for Internet host penetration, with a population-to-host ratio of 37, placing it above Israel and six places below the United Kingdom (Finland was first with a ratio of six) (World Markets Research Centre 2002). In March 2001, computer chip manufacturer Intel stated that it expected the number of Internet users in the Arab region to reach 8 million by the end of 2002, and the demand for personal computers (PCs) to increase by 30 percent. Other sources predict that there would be 10 to 12 million Arab Internet users by the end of 2002. The expectation is that the Arab Internet market will double in size during 2002. We believe that national ICT plans will foster that growth through ubiquitous IP initiatives, PC subsidies, and government endorsement of ICT adoption. Lebanon, Jordan, and Egypt are good examples of government-endorsed Internet adoption strategies.

Poor technology awareness and a natural resistance against the English language-dominated medium are often given as underlying reasons for the poor spread of ICT in many parts of the Arab world. More generally, ICT and e-commerce only replicate on a wider scale the fragmentation of Arab society: educated elites versus a mostly illiterate population; thinly-populated high-income states in the Arabian Gulf versus highly populated low-income populations elsewhere; and the ensuing distortions in distribution of access facilities, payment tools, and technological literacy. The "digital divide," which we discuss later, is a strong indicator of Arab society's income inequalities. Internet access capabilities and individual online transactions remain the privilege of an elite. The gap in Internet connectivity devices between Arab states and the rest of the world is exceedingly large: in 2001, the ITU ranked the Arab region as having the third lowest Internet penetration (2.2 percent overall), ahead only of South Asia (0.3 percent) and sub-Saharan Africa (0.6 percent), and below the developing nations' average of 2.9 percent (Gray 2001). The United Arab Emirates and some Arabian Gulf states, with wealthy but relatively small populations, are statistical outliers in the overall Arab Internet access landscape.

ICT and e-commerce: benefits to Arab businesses

Corporate and multinational segments are responding favorably to ICT. By building transactional and e-commerce platforms, several Arab central banks are laying the ground for operational e-banking and online payments. Despite low levels of readiness in credit card penetration rates in the area, regulations are being designed for online payments. Good examples can be found in Saudi Arabia, the United Arab Emirates, Lebanon, and Jordan. More than one-fifth[9] of banks operating in the area now offer online services, from simple banking facilities to payment schemes. For example, by moving some documentary credit procedures online, Lebanese banks now offer escrow services to facilitate and guarantee e-commerce procedures. The United Arab Emirates Central Bank has introduced SSL (Secure Sockets Layer),

PKI (Public Key Infrastructure), and smart card technology to foster online banking, and payment gateways are being implemented by some of the large national players.

Entrepreneurial initiatives abound in the area of business e-commerce. Private business-to-business (B2B) marketplace ventures, both Arab and foreign, are entering the market and working with corporations. Commerce One and Aregon, to name a few, are building and offering value propositions covering the whole spectrum of supply chain, enterprise resource management, and procurement. The practice of moving business operations and transactions online is spreading within the corporate sector. Tejari,[10] one of the best examples, now has more than 1,000 members within the United Arab Emirates alone (see Box 1). The beneficial effects of these initiatives translate into large institutions changing their business habits and moving several of their functions online. The progress is uneven across sectors, with success mostly by large petrochemical groups, contractors, banks, and multinationals.

Traditional Arab businesses: largely unaffected by new technologies

To speak of a uniform Arab business community is a misnomer. Within large national corporations and multinationals, the Arab world's ability to effectively integrate and compete in e-commerce and ICT is largely proven. Digital marketplaces, exchanges and clearing house initiatives abound, with the large corporate players employing best practices in the field. Unfortunately, this is not true for the rest—in fact, for the vast majority of Arab businesses. Arab small- and medium-sized enterprises (SMEs) shy away from technology despite the anticipated benefits. Due to security concerns and linguistic barriers, most SMEs rely on personal interactions and have not moved their operations online. Banks, the traditional business facilitators in the area, are poor technological mentors, especially in Egypt and the Maghreb. Underprepared for the ICT revolution, few offer transaction platforms, security features, and credit facilities for SMEs to acquire access technology. Most Arab business websites remain informational, offering at best online cataloguing. With little training and poor levels of awareness, SMEs do not benefit from access to new markets and inter-Arab trade potential.

Progression of Arab e-government

The governments of Arab states are moving many of their operations online. From simple online availability of administrative forms to full online automation, several are migrating their procurement, customs, and citizen management capabilities onto electronic platforms. The rationale behind the move is multiple: better cost control, increased business efficiencies, greater global integration and in some cases, competition across states (especially in the Arabian Gulf area). Special mention has to be made of

Box 1. **Tejari**

Home to Tejari, Dubai is one of the few administrations globally to have moved its procurement and dealings with suppliers entirely online. Tejari.com is one tool that has helped to make this possible. Lubna Al-Qasimi, Tejari's CEO and managing director, states that, "the Dubai government is also investing in other developments in parallel to Tejari; but Tejari creates a pull which catalyzes many other sectors, such as education of the community and opportunities for youth in the high-tech sector." (Al-Qasimi 2002). Indeed, the benefits of Tejari.com are visibly spreading to the private sector, blurring the traditional geopolitical boundaries of the region. Tejari.com, inaugurated in 2000 by Sheikh Mohammed bin Rashid Al Maktoum, Dubai's Crown Prince and United Arab Emirates Defence Minister, was launched in a record-breaking eight weeks. Tejari.com (literally, "trade" in Arabic, Farsi, Turkish, Urdu, and Hindi) is an electronic online exchange, initially aimed at streamlining and generating efficiencies as part of the Dubai e-government initiative.

A public-private partnership, Tejari.com was originally planned as the vehicle through which government departments could procure goods and services online and benefit from time and cost efficiencies. "The decision on the strategy was to start with the Dubai government first, due to their large pool of suppliers and to create confidence, proof of concept, and critical mass," notes Al-Qasimi. Cooperation with the government was sealed through an agreement (Tejari 2001) with Dubai's Ruler Court (agency overseeing the twenty-four government departments of the Emirate of Dubai), where a three-month timeframe was imposed on Dubai government departments to migrate transactions online, and hence lure the private sector online if they were to continue transacting with the government. Sources agree that the early take-off of the e-marketplace can be attributed to leadership of the Dubai government "forcing" the participation of their constituencies (i.e., the administration and the upper crust of the corporate sector).

Operating an "open horizontal" business model, Tejari covers a wide range of commodities including oil and gas, construction, pharmaceuticals, automotive and spare parts, electronics, office equipment, stationery, fast-moving consumer goods, and food and services. Although Tejari is not the only regional e-marketplace, it is the only such government-owned project and, significantly, one of the few marketplaces with a guaranteed demand side. Tejari's vision today is to become the leading B2B exchange in the Middle East and to play an active role in the transformation of the regional online economy.

The policy of government participation proved successful, as within its first year of operation, Tejari boasted over 125 members within and outside the Emirates. Tejari now claims more than 1,040 members,

with an average of about 500 reverse auctions per month. Trade revenues are increasing, and plans are to triple or even quadruple trade through its network to US$400 million or more in 2002. Most interestingly, by removing geographical boundaries, Tejari operates beyond the borders of the Emirate of Dubai, through a series of partnerships between platforms, and by recruiting members in the GCC, including Saudi Arabia, and as far as Algeria. "Basically, it is a community of buyers and suppliers, many to many, independent of where the buyers and suppliers are at the end of the day," comments Al-Qasimi. Tejari does much to educate the market. According to Al-Qasimi, "training of local resources too has been done heavily, in partnership with the community…we have partnered with ITI Zayed University and the Higher Colleges of Technology to create a real pull for the technology."

Al-Qasimi emphasizes how Tejari.com has not only proven to be a local success but has also created an international best practice: "Tejari.com follows, and often leads, the technical best practices of global B2B marketplaces. The creation of Tejari.com is an example of high local technological and business strategy input. Tejari is all home-grown, and we are proud to say that we have been able to export some of what we have learned and developed; many exchanges in Europe and the United States [have] adopted some of our business guidelines. Some are, in fact, looking to us for such tools as e-learning and e-cataloguing, in terms of strategy."

Tejari breaks the rules of traditional Arab trade patterns, leveraging technology to change the procurement habits of an entire Arab state, whilst creating urgency in the private sector to join the e-commerce bandwagon. This is one of the first examples of digital liquidity and real market efficiency in the region, crossing over the natural geographical and mental commerce boundaries of the area. The Dubai government has used the Tejari platform to raise awareness and educate its national market on the benefits of e-commerce, via marketing campaigns, educational seminars, and financial incentives. The Dubai government is now showcasing Tejari as a model for other Arab states' e-government and e-procurement initiatives.

Tejari is a good example for other Arab states to follow to move their business online and ensure a critical mass of the private sector migrates to electronic platforms. e-Government procurement platforms also enable inter-Arab trade by creating new channels to otherwise inaccessible markets. Government support is critical in championing the move, educating the market, and improving economic efficiency. Ensuring technology transfers and arabization to the benefit of other Arab governments will be a critical success factor: Tejari plans on furthering the "arabization" of its platform, as the model moves into countries with less knowledge of the English language.

the United Arab Emirates, and of the Emirate of Dubai in particular. Three initiatives represent Dubai's governmental commitment to ICT: Dubai Internet City, the e-government initiative, and Tejari. The aim of these initiatives is to connect government offices and citizens, facilitate transactions, and provide convenient services (e-procurement) to citizens (e.g., online payment of utilities). The success of the e-government and e-procurement initiatives have "forced" businesses wishing to work with the government to adapt their processes, invest in technological platforms, raise technology awareness, and to seek training.

e-Government and e-procurement models are spreading across the area—Arab states are demonstrating responsiveness to the need to integrate digitally and migrate some of their administration online. All governments are not seeking to replicate Dubai's ambitious model. We identified at least three fully operational e-government platforms in the area, but it is important to note that more than eight (new or extensions of existing) e-government initiatives are planned, with varying levels of technological sophistication and scope of ambitions. There are many examples of implementation, such as in Jordan and Lebanon, where the two governments harmonized their customs data systems using the United Nations Conference on Trade and Development (UNCTAD) technological support (United Nations Economic and Social Commission for Western Asia [ESCWA] 2001). Others include Morocco's (see Hajji 2001) and Jordan's[11] e-government initiatives. As telecommunications continue to deregulate and ICT access tools become more available, e-government is expected to become more successful in the area.

Challenges for the Uptake of ICT

Obstacles relating to the environment

Most challenges in ICT adoption and usage lie in the political and regulatory environment. With uneven records in legal and regulatory issues, weak ICT strategies, chronic R&D shortages, excessive reliance on foreign technology, and ongoing weaknesses in ICT implementation, Arab states are frequently lagging in their readiness for the networked future.

High software piracy rates jeopardize confidence

With one of the highest software piracy rates in the world and displaying poor records on IPR protection, Arab states increasingly suffer bad press and a lack of credibility, with looming restrictions in technology transfers. The Business Software Alliance[12] estimated year 2000 software revenue lost to piracy at US$376 million in the Middle East and Africa, representing 3 percent of global losses, versus 26 percent and 25 percent of losses incurred, respectively, in Western Europe and North America (Figure 5). If negligible in absolute terms, losses incurred in Arab states are dismally high in percentage

levels, with Kuwait, Qatar, Bahrain, and especially Lebanon, ranking at or above the 80 percent threshold. The United Arab Emirates, Egypt, and Jordan have made considerable attempts at tackling the issue, enforcing stricter controls and enacting antipiracy laws. Arab software antipiracy measures remain one of the key elements of U.S. industrial policy in the region, far outweighing similar domestic policies or policies in Europe.

Regulatory framework ignores the Arab citizen

As they seek WTO membership, Arab states are taking action to harmonize their legal systems with TRIPS (see Figure 1). By 2005, Arab states, classified as developing countries, are

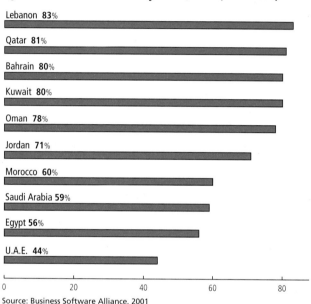

Figure 5. **Arab Software Piracy Rates, 2000 (in Percent)**

Lebanon **83**%
Qatar **81**%
Bahrain **80**%
Kuwait **80**%
Oman **78**%
Jordan **71**%
Morocco **60**%
Saudi Arabia **59**%
Egypt **56**%
U.A.E. **44**%

Source: Business Software Alliance, 2001

obliged to extend product patent protection on products not previously patented in these countries. Main provisions include standardized definitions of intellectual property, implementation of the "national treatment" and "most favored nation" principles, the establishment of antipiracy and protection enforcement procedures, and clauses for swift dispute treatment. While regulatory frameworks are being updated to ensure investor protection, personal liberty and consumer protection rights issues have not yet been fully addressed. Analysts question why Arab states maintain lax policies pertaining to encryption, while restricting and censoring the actual content available online. The fact that no Arab software company actually produces encryption technology or has such capabilities may be part of the explanation. With no national encryption technology at stake, Arab states do not have the same incentives as the United States in restricting encryption technology export or circulation. Conversely, moral and societal considerations seem to explain the tardiness of Internet introduction in the Arab world. Saudi Arabia, for example, has publicly stated[13] that it will seek to protect its citizens from immoral Internet content. Other states, for political reasons, monitor Internet connectivity at government agencies. Independent agencies such as the Human Rights Watch regularly question personal freedom on the Internet. However, while the Arab consumer is highly constrained, consumer protection is largely absent from the regulatory environment in the Arab states. Very few consumer protection laws have been enacted at this stage. We expect those requirements to be increasingly addressed, in line with WTO requirements.

No common plan: foregoing ICT efficiency opportunities

Arab states are forgoing ICT efficiency opportunities and incurring heavy costs by building incomplete and inconsistent national infrastructures. There is no common strategic Arab plan for ICT, and little cooperation on the matter. Although all Arab states have ICT and e-commerce on their agendas, their approaches are often competing and fragmented, replicating the divide between the Gulf and other states.

The Gulf countries have powerful funding capabilities, and ICT plans are prominently included in their national programs. Governments are taking an active role in promoting ICT and e-commerce, with variable success in implementation. Most have translated their ICT plans into research institutes, technopoles, and technology parks (Saudi Arabia's KACST and Dubai's Internet City are prime examples of successful planning and implementation). The development models often rely on national-foreign partnerships with, in some cases, skills being acquired from foreign corporations, and include little indigenous technological development. Few countries have a "visionary" approach to ICT as an integral part of a national, social, and economic strategy. Jordan's 2020 vision, with its clear ICT component (REACH 1.0, 2.0, and currently, 3.0; see Box 2) is one of the few countries to have actually measured ICT benefits with an ongoing implementation plan. The Levant and Maghreb states, highly populated and with limited funding, have recognized the importance of ICT in their national development. Some national plans (such as the Lebanese plan) date back to the 1960s, but most have been articulated over the last few years. Plans include the creation of research institutes, technopoles, and incubators. Research is relatively strong in these countries. The Maghreb and Lebanon rely on cooperation with France, and seek technology transfer to promote indigenous research using local talent. They aim to replicate more advanced research structures and have signed effective public-private partnerships with French universities and leading research institutions such as the Centre Nationale de la Recherche Scientifique. Other states were late in recognizing the importance of ICT. Oman amended its original 2001–2006 Sixth Development Plan (bin Said 2001) to include ICT; the U.A.E. ICT plan dates to the late 1990s.

Insufficient funding for ICT research and development

The absence of serious ICT R&D funding commitments translates into a virtual absence of national Arab ICT and software industries, intensifying reliance on foreign expertise and furthering the "brain drain." With a share of R&D in Arab gross domestic product at a record low of 0.5 percent and high reliance on foreign technology, Arab states are structurally net importers of technology and ICT. Arab reliance on foreign technology has been researched by several sources (United Nations Development Programme [UNDP] 2002; Zahlan 1999). With the exception of Tunisia, all states are net importers of technology. Science and technology research in the Arab world has not achieved significant progress in industrial applications. In 1999, Tunisia, the leading Arab exporter of "recent innovations in high and medium technology," ranked 51st (out of 72 countries) on the UNDP's global technology achievement index with technology exports that reached 19.7 percent of total exports. As a benchmark, technology exports represented between 50 percent and 80 percent of the total exports of world leaders Finland, the United States, and Japan (respectively 1st, 2nd, and 4th). Technology exports of most Arab states are below the 5 percent mark (Figure 6). The consequences of this poor performance in technology are to further the "brain drain" and to accentuate the loss of sovereignty in implementing national ICT strategies. Few Arab states (e.g., Algeria and Tunisia) retain some degree of technology independence. Reliance on foreign technology could be symptomatic of a certain lack of government and business leadership and understanding of the benefits of indigenous ICT research and autonomy.

Figure 6. **Diffusion of Recent Innovations, High and Medium Technology, 1999 (as Percent of Total Goods Exports)**

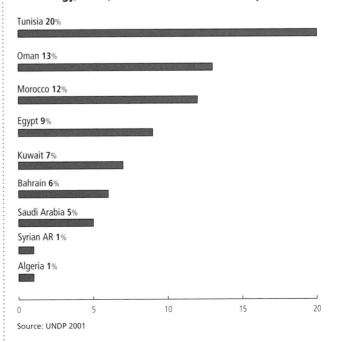

Tunisia 20%
Oman 13%
Morocco 12%
Egypt 9%
Kuwait 7%
Bahrain 6%
Saudi Arabia 5%
Syrian AR 1%
Algeria 1%

Source: UNDP 2001

Box 2. **REACH Case Study**

Some years ago, Jordan identified ICT as the industry with the most promising potential for generating foreign direct investment while leveraging local skills and creating sustainable employment opportunities. The REACH initiative was launched in 1999 as part of Jordan's 2020 development vision. REACH, which is an acronym for regulatory framework, estate and infrastructure, advancement programs, capital, and human resource development, stems directly from King Abdullah II's vision in building an export-oriented ICT sector in Jordan.

Championed by the Information Technology Association of Jordan (INTAJ), REACH was a collaborative and transparent model from its inception, incorporating key stakeholders of Jordan's digital future, including the Jordan Securities Commission, the Economic Consultative Council (ECC), and AMIR, a U.S. agency. Marwan Juma, INTAJ chairman, notes that: "from the beginning, the expectation was to educate government on the strategic priorities of ICT, its infrastructure and legal environment requirements, as well as the human resources and financial components to achieve sustainable results." REACH adopted an iterative development process where plans are formulated, quantified, and presented to the authorities; on a yearly basis, the plans are measured, revised, and adapted. According to Juma, "the model was compelling and successful in generating enthusiasm and commitment that the ECC adopted REACH as its model for other industries."

The initiative called on private and public sectors alike to assess Jordan's readiness in building an ICT industry, and to elaborate an action plan. From the onset, the objectives were impressive; the plan decided on quantified targets for 2004, including the creation of 30,000 IT-related jobs, generation of US$550 million in annual exports and US$150 million in cumulative foreign direct. Juma indicated that establishing the plan was not enough: "We had to explain that there was much more to building an ICT industry than taking the decision—the regulatory environment had to be adapted, the infrastructure upgraded and modernized, advocacy initiatives implemented, the financial system rendered more transparent and attractive, and most important, the human resources [had] to be prepared, not in terms of quantity but in quality."

Jordan amended several of its telecommunications regulations and revamped its administration to create the Ministry of Information and Communication Technology, elevating the sector's representation to the Cabinet level. To improve the investment climate, the regulatory body has been rendered more independent, modernizing more than thirty ICT and telecommunications-related laws and including the creation of an electronics transaction Act. The financial sector has also been tapped. By

focusing on capital markets and financing support requirements for building an industrial ICT plan, REACH is creating awareness in Jordan of the requirements for financial transparency, the need to offer exit strategies to investors, and the legal framework necessary to provide support. REACH is presently conducting its third series of workshops. Known as REACH 3.0, they aim to highlight the new challenges facing the development plan and what means will be taken to ensure the results are sustainable. An "e-readiness" assessment is expected to be published in September 2002. This assessment will cover such issues such as connectivity, e-leadership, information security, human capital, e-business climate, and public-private partnerships.

REACH is well on its way to accomplishing its 2004 objectives. According to INTAJ's chairman, 8,000 to 10,000 new jobs have been created because of the initiative; 45 percent of the foreign direct investment objectives have been achieved, and Jordanian annual ICT exports is estimated at between US$70 million and US$100 million. Specifically, ambitions focus on job creation by enabling the start of new companies, which become recipients of foreign investment, and by putting the emphasis on labor-intensive industries such as call centers and customer care. "Although our people are educated and [have] master[ed] the English language, we seek to increase the overall quality of [their] skills," says Juma. These developments are expected to showcase Jordan as an attractive ICT investment alternative in the region.

Foreign investment in the sector will be driven by deregulation and increased transparency on the financial front. Several acquisition moves by Arab and international investors into the Jordanian ICT arena[24] demonstrate that the country has become an attractive investment target. With further venture capital support and the creation of proper exit strategies on the Jordanian equity market, Jordan's appeal to foreign players is expected to increase.

By focusing on the development of local export-led IT businesses, Jordan expects to become a center of excellence in the Arab region: software creation, arabization, language localization, and consultancy services will enable Jordan to tap the developing but underserved markets of the Arabian Gulf and the Levant. REACH is a model that is transposable to other Arab states. The model is successful because it has managed to build consensus between the public and private sectors and because it has government endorsement at the highest level. The level of trust among stakeholders and the lack of complacency were critical factors in turning what was initially a sectoral plan into a national endeavor.

Telecommunications deregulation: slow and limited

The telecommunications sector, though not the central factor in explaining ICT development, is one of its founding components. Most Arab states are planning for telecommunications deregulation because of either pressures linked to imminent WTO membership or pursuits of privatization benefits. Deregulation has mostly applied to mobile telecommunications networks (GSM) and Internet Service Providers (ISP). With GSM, most Levant and Maghreb states present clear commitments to deregulation, with foreign entrants leading competitive offerings. Gulf states have been discussing deregulation and privatization possibilities over the last few years, but have not yet implemented GSM privatization. The ISP sector is thriving but is mostly limited to dial-up offerings; a few offer broadband connectivity and digital subscriber lines. However, land lines, fibre optic connectivity, and most broadband offerings remain government monopolies, with little deregulation and privatization. Consequently, unless steered in that direction by the state, national incumbents have few incentives to promote connectivity. Government monopolies leave little room for private infrastructure funding and pan-Arab connectivity initiatives. Also, connectivity charges remain high. Even for markets like Kuwait, analysts predict that dial-up connectivity will only become attractive under the US$20 per month mark (Figure 7). Speed of service remains a sensitive concern. With poor connectivity and high prices, the Internet has had little impact as far as changing business and working habits in the area. Arab entrepreneurs have little incentive to create communications ventures—although the ISP sector is privatized in most cases, high-value markets such as broadband remain off limits. Combined with the scarcity of seed money to create alternative communications champions, the slow pace of deregulation is stunting the development of competitive ICT offerings in the region.

"Digital poverty:" mediocre bandwidth and connectivity

The Arab world's mediocre performance on bandwidth and connectivity leaves some markets severely underserved. In 2000, the media announced staggering connectivity figures, equating the entire bandwidth availability for the Arab world to that of 500 U.S. cable modem subscribers. The image is more optimistic in 2002, but differences across states cause a "bandwidth divide." Basic infrastructure, in terms of national public switched telephone networks (PSTN) is uneven. Teledensity in the Gulf states exceeds international standards: the United Arab Emirates, Bahrain, Qatar, and Kuwait outperform most, and are rated by ITU in the F and D ranks, respectively, on par with Italy and Japan (F) and Eastern Europe (D) (ITU 2002). The densely populated Levant and Maghreb remain structurally underserved. Most (except for Syria and Lebanon) rank in the ITU's lowest categories, with teledensity under the

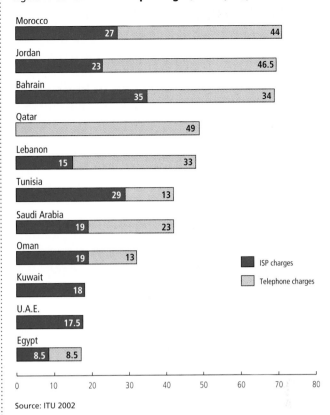

Figure 7. **Consumer Dial-up Charges, 2001 (US$)**

Source: ITU 2002

20 percent mark in 2002. IP connectivity follows the same pattern—there are bandwidth oases in Gulf countries that benefit from strong funding and rich client bases. In gulf countries the latest data transfer mediums and technologies are offered, from leased lines to ISDN (Integrated Services Digital Network)/DSL (Digital Subscriber Line) and WLL (Wireless Local Loop). In contrast, "bandwidth hunger" is rampant elsewhere, with poor dial-up connectivity rates and, of course, no broadband. Levant and Maghreb countries offer some broadband facilities, but those are usually reserved for corporate clients. As an alternative, Egypt and the Maghreb are relying on the multiplication of public access points to ensure that the population is connected to the Internet.

Poor interconnectivity of Arab IP systems

The various Arab IP systems do not interconnect, impeding interregional IP communications and inter-Arab trade and e-commerce. When a consumer in Cairo wants to access information on a Qatar-hosted website, his/her communication goes via the IP backbone into a New York gateway and is then redirected into Qatar! Figure 8 highlights the poor state of peering and interconnectivity between Arab states. With no Pan-Arab connectivity initiative, some Arab states rely on regional cooperation, linking their gateways to the global backbone. Fibre Optic Gulf, the leading GCC initiative, linking Kuwait, Qatar, Bahrain, and the United Arab Emirates, is a prime example of successful cooperation. Links between

Figure 8. **Connectivity Status of Arab States**

	National				Regional					International Direct Fibre Optic Connections		
	Tele dens. '02[2]	LL	ISDN	DSL	Satellite				Fibre Optic	SE-ME-WE	FLAG	Other
	%	Y/N	Y/N	Y/N	Arab Sat	Intel Sat	Eutel Sat	Inmar Sat	Name of Link			
Gulf												
Kuwait	20–35	✓	✓	✓	✓	✓	✗	✓	✓ FOG and link to KSA	✗	✗	✗
KSA	10–20	✓	✓	✓	✓	✓	✗	✓	✓ link to Kuwait	✓ (2 and 3)	✓ (Europe-Asia)	✗
Bahrain	20–35	✓	✓	✓	✓	✓	✗	✓	✓ FOG	✗	✗	✗
Qatar	20–35	✓	✓	✗	✓	✓	✗	✓	✓ FOG	✗	✗	✗
U.A.E.	35–50	✓	✓	✓	✓	✓	✗	✓	✓ FOG	✓ (3)	✓ (Link with New York)	✗
Oman	5–10	✓	✓	✗	✓	✓	✗	✓	✗	✓ (3)	✗	✗
Levant												
Lebanon	10–20	✓	✓	✗	✓	✓	✗	✗	✓ Berytar and Cyprus	✗	✗	✗
Syrian AR	10–20	?	?	?	✓	✗	✗	✓	✓ Berytar and Aletar	✗	✗	✗
Jordan	5–10	?	✓	✓	✓	✗	✗	✗	✗	✗	✓	✗
Egypt	5–10	✓	?	✓	✓ + NileSat	✗	✗	✓	✓ Aletar and links to Italy and Greece	✓ (1, 2, and 3)	✓	✗
Maghreb												
Tunisia	5–10	✓	✓	✓	✓	✗	✓	✓	✓ Links to Italy	✗	✓ (Europe-Asia)	✓ (Sprint)
Algeria	5–10	?	✗	?	✓	✓	✓	✗	✓ Links to France, Italy and Morocco	✓ (2)	✗	✗
Morocco	5–10	✓	✗	✓	✓	✓	✗	✗	✓ Links to Spain and Algeria	✓ (3)	✗	✓ (SAT 2)

Key: ✗, not signed or nonmember; ✓ (name) member of

LL: Local Loop; ISDN: Integrated Services Digital Network; DSL: Digital Subscriber Line; SE-ME-WE: South east Asia-Middle East-Western Europe

Levant states are underway. The consequences of infrastructure fragmentation are reflected in the Internet usage patterns of the area: slow service, minimal inter-Arab e-commerce, reliance on international private or semiprivate IP networks, and lack of competitiveness in connectivity alternatives. Few Arab states are privy to backbone connectivity initiatives at the global level. Saudi Arabia, one of the founding financers of FLAG[14] Europe-Asia, is linked via a 10 gbps gateway connection to the global backbone. It also partnered with France Cable Radio on the SE-ME-WE[15] project. The success of these initiatives in the early 1990s has not been met by expansion and upgrade plans. In subsequent developments, FLAG now offers its north east Asian loop a capacity of up to 3,800 gbps. Consequently, it is simpler for Arab end users to connect with European and U.S. IP destinations, rather than with IP destinations within Arab states.

Obstacles relating to individual capabilities and access to technology

Several of the obstacles faced by individual countries are deeply engrained. Such obstacles include societal rigidity, weaknesses in education, unfair income distribution, and uneven access to technology.

An increasing Arab "brain drain"

Arab states risk jeopardizing their efforts in building ICT and e-commerce industries—dissatisfaction with national economic reforms, and the deficits in work opportunities, research and education, are causing younger Arabs to seek expatriation. A cross-sectional poll of Arab youth conducted by the UNDP (2002) highlights a worrying trend: 45 percent of respondents expressed a desire to emigrate. The main concerns voiced in the poll were the lack of job opportunities (45 percent), education (23 percent), and distribution of income and wealth (8 percent). The term "educated elite" could be misleading: a two-tier educational system is emerging, where a wealthy minority enjoys expensive private education while the bulk of the population attends poorer-quality underfunded government universities. In the same report, the UNDP states that "the most worrying aspect of the crisis in education is its inability to provide the requirements for the development of Arabs, that is, [education is] losing its power as a conduit for social advancement." The budgets allocated to education are decreasing—in relative terms, per capita expenditure on education in Arab countries dropped from 20 percent of that in industrialized countries in 1980 to 10 percent in the mid-1990s. The "brain drain" is well researched: 1 million highly-qualified Arab scientists and professionals reside in the Organisation for Economic Co-operation and Development countries. Far from slowing, this trend has been intensifying over the last quarter of the last century. The brain drain is unevenly spread across the region. The Maghreb and Levant areas suffer higher rates than the Gulf because of difficult socioeconomic conditions, lack of social incentives, limited employment perspectives, shortages in research budgets, and chronic technology underinvestment.

The brain drain translates into slowing down the process and pace of creating indigenous ICT industries, furthering the technology gap between the Arab world and the rest of the world, and increasing the reliance of Arab states on foreign technology transfers and aid.

Digital divide remains

The digital divide is caused by a combination of the structural fragmentation of societies and the lack of leadership in many Arab states with regard to ICT policies and implementation. The divide is aggravated by the absence of cross-Arab initiatives, lack of financing, and poor education. There are three aspects to the digital divide in Arab states: (1) the divide between the Arab world as a whole and the rest of the world, (2) the divide across Arab states, and (3) the divide within Arab states. The digital divide with the rest of the world can be measured using variables such as teledensity, PC penetration, numbers of websites, and number of Internet users. Studies rank Arab states, as a whole, poorly as compared to other groups of nations (World Bank 2001). Although Arab states do not severely underperform when ranked by world standards in teledensity and PC penetration, they remain weak on number of websites and Internet users. Limited local content and the monopolistic nature of the telecommunications sector are key obstacles. The benefits of using the Internet as a source of knowledge creation, as opposed to accessing existing knowledge, is not sufficiently recognized in Arab societies.

The digital divide across Arab states reflects the income and population characteristics of the region. The UNDP contrasts the situation of the more advanced GCC states with countries in the rest of the region, which are largely characterized by poor infrastructure, an uncompetitive telecommunications industry, resistance to the introduction of new ICT services, limitations in banking facilities, and limited political and regulatory leadership. Others report little progress on the digital divide issue (Dewachi 2002). The same factors dividing Arab states seem to be at play on the national level, accentuated by the linguistic barrier (local educated elites accessing English language knowledge online vs. local-language literate and illiterate masses), cultural aspects (gender segregation), and weaknesses in the educational system.

Arab states have undertaken new initiatives[16] to reduce the digital divide. Although these initiatives create technology awareness, they highlight the inaccessibility of PC equipment for most of the population. We did not identify any large-scale public-private partnerships between policymakers and the banking sector to create credit facilities for computer purchases. Most are private initiatives, and do not address a national requirement or need for ICT penetration. Maintaining the digital divide negatively impacts the Arab market's uptake of ICT and e-commerce, as the equipment acquisition decision is endlessly postponed and e-commerce transactions remain unaffordable to the masses. Given the regional infrastructure deficiency, ESCWA estimates that an investment of around US$40 billion is required to bring ICT penetration rates up to the world average.

Obstacles in business and governmental sectors

The private sector, especially banks, is accentuating structural flaws by not actively promoting the necessary market uptake initiatives. Governmental initiatives remain limited, as they rely excessively on foreign policymakers in their procurement decisions and neglect the local language as a development tool.

Scarce Arab payment and transaction platforms

Few local banks offer operational transaction platforms, and credit card penetration is low amidst concerns of poor security and fraud. The lack of national financial development policies has a direct impact on private investment and business development in general, and on IT infrastructure in particular. The Arab retail banking market is excessively reliant on "brick and mortar"—from large multinational banking groups to regional players, and from generalists to specialized Islamic banking actors, transactional e-banking preparedness is low. In 2000, only 18 percent of banks offered online transactional facilities. Although there were some local players (in Lebanon and the Gulf), these were mostly foreign banks with regional presence. Thirty-nine percent of the banks in the region did not even maintain an informational website. Arab e-banking and e-transactions also suffer from the absence of clearing house alternatives to central banks, as most clearinghouses have yet to move their operations online. The absence of digital certification laws and the nonexistence of credible local third-party security enablers discourages Arab banks from moving online. Credit card penetration in Arab states is fragmented along income lines, which is caused by the same factors as those causing the digital divide. Gulf states rank above the 20 percent credit card penetration rate level, whilst most Levant states and the Maghreb are under the 5 percent threshold.

Weak local ICT capabilities

Statistics on Arab ICT procurement decisions show that nearly all equipment is imported. In the absence of local ICT production, Arab ICT, e-commerce, and related industries cannot be thought of as having a bright future unless local technological development plans are elaborated on and adopted, either by one champion nation, or through an inter-Arab decision. Weaknesses in local software development capabilities increase reliance on foreign technology, especially in terms of programming, language standards definition, and software development. Most servers belong to the UNIX system family, and almost all are in the public domain. There is also incompatibility between the Arabic provided on these platforms and the commercial Internet browsers that populate the overwhelming majority of Arab PCs. The proportion of software published and translated into Arabic is low, reflecting limited Arab software development demand. The conflict between proprietary and open standards[17] renders information available on servers only marginally displayable on proprietary platforms, and this deters Arab content developers.

Marginal local language content

The lack of local language content availability shuts out the Arab public from ICT and e-commerce. Most content available in the Arab world is informational (vs. transactional). Whereas there are 300 million Arabic speakers in the world, ranking the language as the 6th in terms of usage, websites in the Arabic language represented less than one percent of all websites in 2001[18]. Despite domain name registration progress in Arab states, the inability to offer reliable, up-to-date content in local languages is an obstacle. Because of the lack of capability to develop software and representation tools (e.g., Arabic HTML—HyperText Markup Language—tags), the absence of programming languages in Arabic (e.g., C++), and the absence of Arabic tools or protocols for data representation (e.g., HTML and XML—Extensible Markup Language), the limitations on content development are high, as technicians are required to master both English and Arabic. When added to the problem of standards, this human resource limitation severely restricts content development. Addressing this limitation calls for major policy decisions on standards enforcement and the buildup of local content skills capabilities. A single country cannot make these decisions; this highlights the need for inter-Arab cooperation.

Prescriptions

Based upon our research described in the previous sections, we outline below some policy prescriptions for business and government leaders in the Arab world.

Create a common Arab ICT strategy aligned with national ambitions

A Pan-Arab planning effort aiming to create a transnational ICT strategic plan[19] is recommended as a starting action item. Based upon a critical assessment of the region's capabilities, the plan would define the overall objectives of the various nations and translate objectives into measurable milestones. This common ICT strategy should be treated with a clear commitment for implementation. The strategic recommendations of a transnational Arab ICT-planning agency, independent of national contingencies, will nevertheless have to rely on Arab funding. Ensuring that the funding and commitment requirements will be met is key. That implies creating transnational teams devoted to the overall strategy and that are expected to lead the implementation of the initiative.

Arab ICT planning should not be reduced to infrastructure acquisition decisions, but should encompass all aspects of ICT, including software and content development. The importance of the plan being Arab, and building on Arab strengths and weaknesses, cannot be overstressed. The Arab ICT plan should, above all, seek to anchor the Arab world as a key player of the ICT revolution, not merely a participant at the buyer level. The plan should also include an assessment of how industrial and economic benefits can be generated, and seek to build regional centers of ICT excellence as a source of technology exports using local, not imported, skills. No ICT planning is conceivable without the freedom of movement of skills and capabilities across borders. The scarcity of local skills makes this condition essential. To reverse the brain drain effect, a special "technology passport" could be created as the symbol of inter-Arab policy.

Benefits should flow down to the regional and national levels, with appropriate implementation and funding support. The implications are threefold:

1. Creating an investment plan for inter-Arab technology development with allocation mechanisms across countries, aimed at financing the creation and growth of the critical components of an ICT industrial base.

2. Coordinating national funding plans with the overall Arab ICT funding program. An inter-Arab ICT strategy should build on the complementarities and competitive advantages of Arab nations. We expect this to generate substantial efficiencies compared to the overlaps caused by independent and parallel national approaches.

3. Engaging with the banking and financial community in building technology financing mechanisms with government support. This will be critical to developing a commercial credit policy that favors local companies that have the skill to compete and win contracts in both Arab and international markets.

Proceed towards technological sovereignty

Technological sovereignty means autonomy in choices, control of national destiny, and technological development. Technological sovereignty begins by "building not buying;" that is, by not reducing ICT-building initiatives to procurement decisions. Arab states should aim for the development of an indigenous ICT industry. Empowered with a national strategy in mind, Arab states should use joint-venture collaboration as sources of technology transfers, through local value-added requirements.[20] "Buying local" when the product and service are available and giving advantages to suppliers from fellow Arab countries, will enhance the overall inter-Arab ICT planning and implementation effort. ICT and e-commerce within the Arab states will require infrastructure decisions that encompass the entire area. A coordinated infrastructure plan across the region is critical. Secure and resilient, the Arab interconnectivity system will have to be technology independent and coupled with a human resources plan for installation, management, and maintenance. The inter-Arab connectivity plan will have to be institutionalized via a Pan-Arab structure, with official acceptance and funding. Such an endeavor should seek to leverage some of the national centers of excellence.

Increase the competitiveness of the telecommunications industry

Deregulation in the Arab world is often misunderstood, being perceived as a source of generating new money for budget deficits and as the government abandoning the sector. The competitive benefits of deregulation, such as better access to technology and enhanced creativity, are often misrepresented. Successful deregulation examples can be found in areas where local skills or local technological environments or a combination of both exist. We recommend ensuring that deregulation is a consistent part of the national strategic ICT plan to inject new technologies into the ICT sector and provide more competitive services to Arab citizens. Governments should continue the deregulation of the telecommunications industry, ensuring that results achieved are congruent with national plans, and intervene in a clearly defined legal framework to steer the industry when necessary. By promoting the spin-off of local centers of excellence, Arab states can deregulate certain sections of their national telecommunications industries to the benefit of national Arab players. Alternative connectivity providers and trade media, such as marketplaces, can extend the ISP deregulation footprint by generating economic activity, which would allow the emergence of Arab ICT champions. Deregulation can also be a tool to acquire technology transfers from foreign entities by including the stipulation that entry of foreign players requires technology transfer and investment in the training of local talent.

Recognize, attract, and build human capital

Researchers and technologists do not elicit the same level of respect in the Arab world as they do elsewhere. Arab states need to take measures to ensure that proper skills are developed and retained in the region. The skills lost in the brain drain cannot be attracted exclusively with financial incentives. Creating higher institutes of learning and R&D at the Pan-Arab level will garner respect, enthusiasm, and support from learning communities elsewhere. Such institutes could thrive in the region, were they to have a standardized knowledge base and be endowed with appropriate levels of funding. Committed to a national preference policy in research, the institutes would create incentives for educated elites to apply their talent locally. A good reference example is the investment made by the Indian government to create elite institutions of higher learning, such as the Indian Institutes of Technology and the Indian Institutes of Management. Graduates of these institutions play important roles in the development of the Indian ICT industry, and these institutions serve as magnets attracting expatriate Indian scientists home.

Reduce the digital divide

The Arab citizen should be at the center of efforts to develop ICT in the Arab world. Building the human base and reducing the digital divide are critical to these efforts. Reducing the digital divide and attenuating its effects offers benefits beyond ICT penetration, such as fostering social cohesion and producing a new generation of national leaders. While commending the initiatives underway, we highlight the importance of expanding these initiatives' magnitude, by

1. Multiplying ubiquitous IP initiatives to educate the market and generate enthusiasm to study and learn technology in schools and universities[21];

2. Encouraging the adoption of ICT access devices (such as PCs and personal digital assistants) as a national priority, with policies subsidizing ICT equipment purchases; and

3. Partnering with the banking sector to create policies and financial incentives for investments in ICT. The goal of such action should not be limited to ICT equipment acquisition, but should include the creation of the "ecosystem" necessary for a widespread adoption of ICT in Arab societies.

Stimulate Arabic content

The creation of Arabic content is central to the robust development of ICT in the Arab world. Enhanced ICT adoption and use allows for better communication and coordination across different stakeholders in the Arab world, such as individual citizens, businesses, and governments. Thus, it is natural that Arabic has to evolve as the language of choice. Standardization and the creation of a "language watchdog" are useful approaches. We recommend planning the evolution towards an institutionalized Arabic research watchdog and orientation team composed of industry leaders to collaboratively establish a research reference in the Arabic language and articulate current and future needs. Matching the Arab technological research and procurement mandates with local linguistic needs can be achieved by allocating research budgets for language localization initiatives in universities and the private sector, and signalling the critical role of "arabization." By favoring companies and universities that develop "arabization" using Arab human resources and researchers, member states will confirm their commitment to building a national ICT plan. This could entail buying only bilingual Arabic/foreign software adhering to the adopted standards, and making the usage of Arabic mandatory on government and administration systems.

Endnotes

1. The definition covers both industrial property, which includes inventions, patents, trademarks, and industrial designs, as well as copyrights, which include literary and artistic works, films, musical works, and architectural designs.

2. The Paris Convention provides for substantive rule on national treatment in each of the member countries, the right of priority, common rules in the field of substantive law, and the overall administrative framework.

3. The Patent Cooperation Treaty (PCT) provides for international patent application filing procedures, a single patent office, and other standardizing and centralizing measures.

4. "Technopoles" are defined as geographically delineated entities at which both industrial and research efforts are pursued with a view to fostering technology and expertise transfers. Various technopole "subflavors" include technology parks, innovation centers, and high-tech clusters, with varying degrees of scientific advancement.

5. "Technology incubators" are business incubators, with a clear emphasis on developing university research into industrial and commercial ventures, with selective financial output and measurement criteria.

6. U.S. Department of Commerce. *Overview of the Telecoms Sector*. Various reports. Office of Telecommunications Technologies in the International Trade Administration. Kuwait (1997), Saudi Arabia (1997), Qatar, Bahrain, Oman (1997), Syria (1997), Jordan (2002), Egypt (2000), Tunisia (2001), Algeria (2001), Morocco (2001). Online. http://www.ita.doc.gov/.

7. FOG offers a 5 gbps capacity and is capable of carrying 180,000 telephone calls or equivalent data circuits between the four countries to other parts of the world simultaneously. It cost more than US$83 million and was inaugurated in 1998. FOG also provides gateway access into Fibre Optic Link Around the Globe (FLAG; see endnote 14), with a landing site in the United Arab Emirates.

8. ALETAR link from Alexandria, Egypt to Tartous, Syria; and BERYTAR link, from Beirut, Lebanon to Tartous, Syria.

9. According to ESCWA, 18 percent of Arab banks offered online transaction facilities in 2000.

10. See Box 1 Tejari.com case study.

11. See Box 2 Reach 1.0, 2.0, 3.0 case study.

12. The BSA is an industrial alliance grouping the software and Internet industry, focussing on protecting software copyrights and cyber security.

13. Public statement of H.E. Saleh Abdulrahman Al-'Adhel, KACST president, February 1998.

14. FLAG is a global IP and telecommunications carrier. See http://www.flagtelecom.com.

15. SE-ME-WE is a global cable link between Southeast and East Asia, the Middle East, and Western Europe. See http://www.marine.francetelecom.fr.

16. Such initiatives include Tunisia's 1998 "Publinet" initiative, Algeria's "multiservice kiosks" 2000 initiative, and the recent Syrian Computer Society's "IT for everyone" campaign.

17. This conflict is due to the nonconformity of some corporations with internationally recognized language encoding standards such as the International Standards Organization's ISO 8859-X, and Unicode.

18. In 2001, Gartner, a consultancy firm, identified less than 1 percent of global websites in the Arabic language, with 43 percent in English and 32 percent in other European languages.

19. The institutions capable of carrying forward this mission statement already exist; they include the League of Arab States and ESCWA.

20. Following the Indian joint-venture law requiring majority local ownership and requiring technology transfers as a prerequisite to business operations.

21. They could be complemented with "electronic notebook" programs in schools as well as more pervasive approaches to create real "stickiness" of the technology.

22. For example, Microsoft acquired two local Internet portals and BATELCO, Bahrain's telecommunications operator, acquired local ISPs.

References

Al-Qasimi, S. L. and Marwan Juma. 2002. Personal interview. July 8, 2002.

bin Said, W. Q. 2001. Sixth Omani Development Plan (2001–2005). Online. http://www.moneoman.gov.om/ministry/fiveyearplan/plan_royal_decree.htm.

Dewachi, A. 2002. "Issues of Concern to the Telecom Sector in the ESCWA (Arab) Region." Presented at the International Telecommunication Union/Telecommunications Development Bureau Regional Forum on Telecommunications Policies and International Standards: Impacts and Implications, Cairo, Egypt, 19 - 21 May 2002.

Global Trading Web Association (GTWA). Online. http://www.gtwa.net.

Gray, V. and International Telecommunication Union (ITU). 2001. „Barriers to Internet Penetration in the Arab World." Presented at Arab States Internet and Telecom Summit, Muscat, Oman, May 28–30, 2001.

Hajji N. 2001. "Stratégie e-Maroc: Les 10 chantiers de la Stratégie e-Maroc 2001–2002." Presented at the Symposium e-Maroc, Casablanca, October 8, 2001.

International Telecommunication Union (ITU). 2002. *2002 Target Rates for Different Teledensity Groups*. Online. http://www.itu.int/itudoc/itu-t/com3/focus/80500.pdf.

Tejari. 2001. „Dubai Ruler's Court Inks Comprehensive Government Deal with Tejari.com." Press Release. Online. http://www.tejari.com/news1.htm.

United Nations Development Programme (UNDP). 2002. *Arab Human Development Report 2002: Creating Opportunities for future generations*. New York: United Nations Development Programme. Online. http://www.undp.org/rbas/ahdr/.

United Nations Economic and Social Commission for Western Asia (ESCWA). 2001. *Trade Facilitation and e-Commerce in the ESCWA Region. Promoting Effective Participation in Electronic Commerce: The Cases of Egypt, Jordan, Lebanon and the United Arab Emirates*. New York: United Nations Economic and Social Commission for Western Asia.

The World Bank. 2001. *Development Indicators: World Development Report*. Washington DC: The World Bank.

World Markets Research Centre. 2002. *The Expanding Universe: Internet Adoption in the Arab Region*. Online. http://www.worldmarketsanalysis.com/InFocus2002/articles/middleeast_internet.html

Zahlan, A.. 1999. *Arabs and the Challenges of Science and Technology: Progress Without Change*. Beirut: Centre for Arab Unity Studies (CAUS).

Chapter 9

ICT: Pockets of Leadership in East Asia

Arnoud De Meyer, INSEAD

Introduction

The group of countries discussed in this chapter is quite heterogeneous. It encompasses strongly-developed and quasi-developed industrial states such as Singapore, Korea, and Taiwan, and developing countries such as Indonesia and Vietnam. The region contains small city-states, such as Singapore and Hong Kong, with close to 4 and 6 million people respectively, as well as some of the most populous countries in the world, such as Indonesia, with more than 220 million inhabitants. Because of the region's diversity, one may wonder whether it makes sense to discuss them as a group. The countries do, however, have some characteristics in common which make it worthwhile to examine their efforts as a group in terms of IT deployment. Indeed, at least four reasons make this exercise relevant.

First, many of the countries included in the analysis belong to a common economic association: the Association of Southeast Asian Nations (ASEAN). This association is not yet as successful as some of the other economic groupings like the European Union or even the North American Free Trade Agreement. ASEAN is, however, a forum for discussion, collaboration, policy-building, and mutual learning. The initiatives taken by individual countries often find their translation quite rapidly in other member countries of ASEAN. Obviously Korea, Hong Kong, and Taiwan do not belong to ASEAN, but they each have close economic relationships with ASEAN. For example, Korea interacts with member nations in the context of ASEAN plus 3.

Second, all of the countries in the region have been confronted, in one way or another, with the challenge created by the recent industrial development of China and, to a lesser extent that of India. Korea and Taiwan have invested heavily in China, and see it as a major market for their high value-added products. Hong Kong is part of China, and has had to reposition itself vis-à-vis the development of cities like Shanghai. For many Southeast Asian countries, China has become a direct competitor, attracting foreign direct investment and exporting goods that benefit from low-cost labor production to Organisation for Economic Co-operation and Development (OECD) countries. Consequently, Southeast Asian countries see their traditional industrial policies of attracting Western or Japanese multinational corporations (MNCs) and exporting to the OECD countries (and in particular to the United States) undercut by a formidable competitor. Investing in IT developments has been identified by many of these countries as an important component of their new industrial policy. In many cases, this policy has been translated into plans to develop an information society or the intention to move from an economy based on low-cost labor to a knowledge society.

Third, in most of these countries, the industrial base is formed by the investments of large U.S. and Japanese MNCs. During the 1990s it was often argued that, exploitation of natural resources aside, up to 70 percent of the industrial production and wealth-creation in East Asia could be traced to Japanese companies. The lessening of Japan's economic influence and the emergence of China (and to some extent that of India) has created a serious long-term strategy problem for both industrialists and governments throughout the region.

Fourth, virtually all of the countries have a very strong commitment to education. Education is at the heart of the value systems in most East Asian societies. Governments are pursuing polices to provide quality education to the whole population, parents are willing to invest in the education of their children, and young people are willing to work hard—sometimes excessively—to obtain a relevant degree. Many countries have a predilection for education in IT, and an impressive cadre of engineers and IT-savvy users has been formed.

Common challenges, a set of common values, a framework in the form of ASEAN in which to exchange ideas and learn from each other, render it possible to draw some common conclusions about these countries while constantly keeping in mind that there is much variation.

In this chapter, we shall analyze some of the results of the research conducted to arrive at the Networked Readiness Index 2002–2003. This analysis will be followed up by some observations on the opportunities offered by the ICT development in Southeast Asia. These arguments will be built around four themes. First, Southeast Asia has developed into an effective partner in ICT developments through outsourcing. But that is not a satisfying situation for these countries. Southeast Asia should have the ambition to be a great inspiration for innovations that can leverage ICT. That will be our second argument. Third, the development of the region provides an interesting insight into some of the consequences of the "digital divide;" the linking of the major cities in South and East Asia through ICT offers the possibility of creating a different layer of cooperation between the countries of the region. The fourth and final observation will focus on the hurdles that these countries need to overcome in order to be successful: they need to create a regulatory framework that protects intellectual property-related software development in Asia, and there is a strong need to adapt educational systems.

The Position of East Asia

Data for the *Global Information Technology Report* are not available for all ASEAN countries. In our analysis we will focus on nine countries for which data were available: Hong Kong, Indonesia, Korea, Malaysia, Philippines, Singapore, Taiwan, Thailand, and Vietnam. One may want to compare the data for these countries with the data for Japan, China, India, Australia, and New Zealand. The reasons for this

should be clear: Japan remains a dominant economic player in the region; China and India are both posing an economic threat as well as an opportunity for the region; and Australia and New Zealand, while quite a world apart, have many economic interactions with Southeast Asia.

Let's first have a look at the Networked Readiness Index (NRI). One sees immediately that the region falls into three main groups. The first group is composed of leaders in networked readiness, even at a global level. This group is composed of Singapore, Taiwan, Korea, and Hong Kong, and they score even better than Japan or Australia. Singapore[1] and Taiwan stand out as leaders, and belong among the top ten worldwide. This group fully embraces the opportunities offered by information and communication technologies, offers high-speed access to the Internet, and is in the course of developing economies based on sophisticated services and knowledge. They are in direct competition with the best-performing economies in North America and Europe.

The second group consists of Malaysia and Thailand. In both countries, networked readiness seems similar to China and India; Malaysia and Thailand score somewhere in the middle of the total group of countries that are ranked in the *Report*. Malaysia and Thailand focus on providing high-quality services to their main cities, as well as to some high-tech parks. In Malaysia, the successful creation of the Multimedia Super Corridor close to Kuala Lumpur and the developments in Penang are examples of such developments. Because of these achievements, a certain dichotomy is developing between the well-developed concentrations of high-tech areas in major cities or industrial parks and the rest of the country. We will discuss this situation in more detail later in the chapter.

The third group, composed of the Philippines, Indonesia, and Vietnam, are among the developing countries. Their focus should continue to be on the further development of a skilled workforce and on basic infrastructure. ICT infrastructure is important in these countries, but it probably scores only as high in importance as the development of other basic services such as water supply, roads, and in some cases, electricity.

Table 1. **Networked Readiness Index**

Country	NRI Index	Ranking
Singapore	5.74	3
Taiwan	5.31	9
Korea	5.10	14
Australia	5.04	15
Hong Kong SAR	4.99	18
Japan	4.95	20
New Zealand	4.70	23
Malaysia	4.28	32
India	3.89	37
Thailand	3.80	41
China	3.70	43
Philippines	3.25	62
Indonesia	3.16	64
Vietnam	2.96	71

Table 2. **Ranking for the Three Components of Networked Readiness**

Usage		Readiness		Environment	
Singapore	5.58	Singapore	6.41	Singapore	5.22
Taiwan	5.22	Taiwan	5.82	Taiwan	4.88
Korea	5.22	Korea	5.60	Hong Kong SAR	4.71
Hong Kong SAR	4.80	Hong Kong SAR	5.46	Korea	4.50
Malaysia	3.64	Malaysia	4.95	Malaysia	4.24
Thailand	3.24	Thailand	4.49	Thailand	3.68
Philippines	2.99	Vietnam	3.90	Philippines	3.33
Indonesia	2.76	Indonesia	3.72	Indonesia	3.01
Vietnam	2.37	Philippines	3.43	Vietnam	2.61

Source: INSEAD

Figure 1. **Scores for Usage, Readiness and Environment**

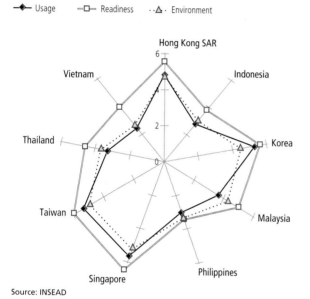

Source: INSEAD

Figure 2. **Scores for Environmental Fertility**

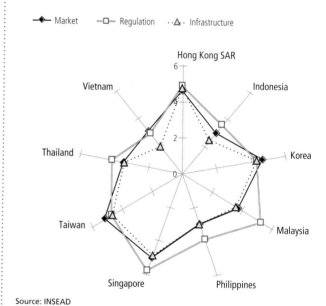

Source: INSEAD

Given this diversity, where does networked readiness come from?

We can derive some interesting perspectives from Figure 1. The three groups of countries that we just described can also be observed in the three components of networked readiness: usage, environmental fertility, and readiness. But the relative positions for each of these components may be slightly different. Singapore and Taiwan lead on all three components. Hong Kong beats Korea in terms of fertility of the environment, but is preceded by it in readiness and usage.

To what extent is the environment ready in the different countries? The data in Figure 2 suggest that, in general, the same pattern of scoring applies in terms of fertility of the environment. There is, however, an interesting difference between the extent to which the regulatory environment and policymakers have evolved compared to the physical infrastructure and market, in Malaysia, Thailand, the Philippines, and Indonesia. In these countries, the political leadership appears to be ahead of the country in its thinking.

Governments in these countries have made considerable efforts to position themselves as leading users of ICT. In Malaysia, for example, there has been a conscious effort to create an ICT-friendly environment with initiatives such as the Multimedia Super Corridor; legislation to guide and protect ICT developments; and investments in ICT-education, with a university specifically dedicated to information technology. However, the data also suggest that such efforts at creating an ICT-friendly environment can only pay off if there is real consistency between markets, the investment in infrastructure, and policymakers.

It is interesting to note that in Malaysia, the government seems (relatively speaking) to be the best prepared to leverage the potential of ICT (Figure 3). In Korea, Singapore, and Hong Kong, individuals seem to be better prepared. This is perhaps in line with the high penetration of asymmetric digital subscriber line (ADSL) in these countries, as we will see later. In countries like the Philippines, Indonesia, and Thailand, the governments seem to lag a bit compared to the citizens and companies.

Figure 3. Scores for Readiness of Individuals, Business and Government

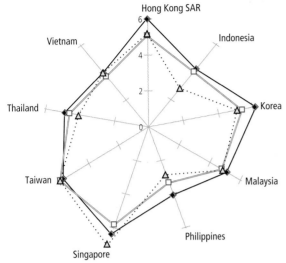

Source: INSEAD

Figure 4. Scores for Individual, Business and Government Usage of ICT

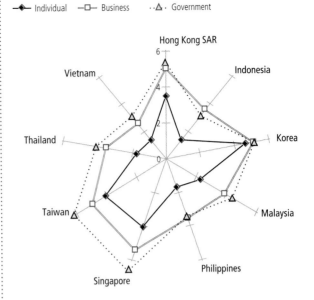

Source: INSEAD

What is perhaps striking for readers from other parts in the world is not simply the readiness, but the real usage and transaction activity displayed by governments in East Asia (Figure 4). With the exception of the Philippines and Indonesia, all other seven governments in our sample lead individual citizens and companies in the actual adoption of ICT applications.

In conclusion, one would reiterate two points. First, there is much diversity between the different countries. Second, most countries have made ICT-preparedness a priority. In doing so, some of the governments have actually provided leadership at a level that is beyond that of individuals and companies. Governments in Malaysia, Singapore, Taiwan, and Thailand are, relatively speaking, the most advanced users of ICT. This is perhaps not something that one would expect elsewhere in the world. But the example of Malaysia may also include a warning: if the government is too far ahead in it's thinking compared to the rest of the country, the country's overall networked readiness may not benefit the economy. One needs a more or less equal evolution among the different actors in the society. This is not an argument for governments to level down to the lowest performer, but rather, a plea to level up; that is, to invest in the rapid development of the slowest adopters of ICT applications.

Beyond the Numbers: East Asia as a Partner in ICT Development

Much has been said and written these days about outsourcing in ICT. It is a booming business, and the current pressure on

costs, engendered by the economic difficulties and challenges in the United States or Europe, can only speed up this evolution.

Currently, the country that is most successful in attracting outsourced jobs appears to be India. China is trying to follow India's example, but is still lagging seriously behind. Last year, India's software exports came to US$6.2 billion, while China's stood at a mere US$850 million; India has more than 520,000 IT professionals compared to China's 150,000. There is growth in China, however. Last year, software sales in China rose almost 40 percent to RMB 33 billion; by 2005, sales are projected to rise to RMB 250 billion (*Far Eastern Economic Review* 2002). Next to these two giants in software outsourcing, two countries in Southeast Asia are also very active as suppliers for the outsourcing market: the Philippines and Singapore. Both have positioned themselves very differently in the market. The Philippines competes at the low end, but is also getting reasonably good at obtaining quality certification for software development. Singapore positions itself at the high end of the market for complex developments and distant consulting and support. In fact, for some of the simpler modules or activities involving larger projects, Singapore-based companies will further subcontract to neighboring countries. The supply of software technicians and engineers is also growing. Commercial schools like Informatics or N.I.I.T. have built large subsidiaries in both Singapore and Malaysia. This means that Southeast Asia is developing itself into an alternative supplier of outsourcing services, next to the giant India and the rising ambitions of China. While these countries may not have the volume of output or the economies of scale one currently finds in India, there is perhaps another competitive advantage: cultural diversity and a reasonably good command of English. These two factors may be an advantage for East Asian countries, allowing them to offer such applications as international call centers or interface design that their monolythic competitors could not offer.

The Ambition to Become Leaders

Being excellent in providing outsourcing services for others may be a good business in the short run, but leads to a situation where one is always a follower. Followers are subject to the vagaries of the international markets. Followers rarely create big margins in the long run; followers in outsourcing often have to compete on price and are squeezed on their costs. In order to be successful in ICT, companies in Southeast Asia need to have the ambition to move up on the value added chain and develop their own unique selling positions in ICT.

In East Asia, there are pockets of outstanding performance in the exploitation of ICT; therefore, these countries do have applications that can lead to the development of a world-market application. The transformation that Korean companies have gone through since the financial crisis of 1997 is an example that is worth study by other countries' policymakers and company leaders; several Korean companies have become leaders in the design and the application of new business concepts. There are also some interesting evolutions in Malaysia, Hong Kong, and Singapore. These examples are worth study. If we can understand and document some of the reasons behind outstanding performance, we may be able to translate this knowledge into applications in the rest of the world. Let's look at four examples, which we have chosen somewhat randomly.

Broadband in Asia

The first example of this special performance is the use of broadband connections by individuals and companies. While the statistics change daily,[2] the pattern is clear: Korea and Singapore belong to the leading countries worldwide in terms of broadband access and usage, and Taiwan follows closely. By the end of 2001, more than 16 percent of Internet users in Korea were accessing it through a broadband connection. Further, Singapore's Infocomm Development Authority announced in March of 2002 that about one in three, or 950,000, Singapore residents, are now connected via broadband. This is a direct consequence of the deregulation of the telecommunications industry. In the case of Singapore, deregulation has led to a growth of broadband service providers from two providers to twelve over a two-year time frame; access costs have decreased in some cases by as much as five times over the period 2000 to 2002.

Deregulation and lower costs do not mean, however, that utilization of the Internet has changed dramatically. Consumers have more bandwidth at their disposal, but don't necessarily use it in a creative way. Most market studies converge on the observation that individuals in Asia still use the Internet mainly for e-mail and downloading of music, and to a lesser extent video clips and video games. The unexpected and creative killer applications not yet moneymakers; the situation in Korea is a vivid example of this.

At the start of 2002, more than seventy broadband service providers in Korea were permeating companies and households with new applications. Revenues from broadband applications services were worth US$3.5 billion in 2001, and both Korea Telecom and Hanaro Telecom seemed to have attained operational break-even in this sector. This is a substantial achievement—many operators, even in the United States and Europe, do not break even. The question is, what do Korean users do with this ample bandwidth?

The nine most important Internet access applications segments in the country are online gaming, Internet telephony, e-learning, movies-on-demand, online finance, online shopping, online broadcasting, online chatting community market and online music (*Internet News* March 2002). Most of these applications, however, do not realize high revenues. For example, e-learning and movies-on-demand are not expected to draw significant revenues over the next couple of years.

e-Learning does have real potential; this segment is expected to represent a compound annual growth rate of 138 percent over the period 2000 to 2004. Screening movies on the Internet before their launch in cinemas promises also to be a very successful strategy for service providers.

Where consumer applications such as online finance (which includes online trading, banking, and insurance) and Internet shopping are concerned, more than 65 percent of the total volume of stock exchange in the South Korean market is executed over the Internet. Insurance companies as well are rapidly developing channels for the Internet to enhance customer relationships. But once again, whether that leads to profitable business models remains unclear.

Frost & Sullivan, one of the leading consultants in the IT field, note that there is considerable demand for a variety of applications, as Koreans have become inculcated in the "broadband lifestyle" and spend an average of thirteen hours on the Internet each week.

Another example of broadband usage is evident in a March 2002 survey entitled, "Survey of Broadband Users in Singapore," commissioned by Infocomm Development Authority (IDA) and conducted by Precision Research Services. Results of the survey indicate that 92 percent of all broadband users went online at least two days a week (see IDA website). Amongst the home users of the Internet, 52 percent use broadband to get the latest news, 45 percent to download music, and about 33 percent played online games.

We are not yet living in a time where Asian consumers find creative and unexpected applications for interactive use of the Internet. However, the possibility is there. One of the more creative examples comes again out of Singapore, from the country's Supreme Court. In Singapore, there is multiparty web-based videoconferencing between the Supreme Court, Subordinate courts, the Attorney General's chambers, and legal firms; this is an example of how businesses can use broadband to be more productive. Lawyers should be able to conduct administrative or noncontentious hearings with the court from their offices. Savings in travelling and waiting time mean more productive billable time. It should reduce the waste of time for both clients and lawyers, and speed up handling of cases. If it works well, it is estimated that this system could save the legal industry US$16 million a year.

Pyramid Research Services projects that, after Korea and Singapore, Taiwan will be the next big market for broadband services. Currently, there are about 1.6 million broadband subscribers in Taiwan, representing approximately 20 percent household penetration. Pyramid Research forecasts that broadband Internet connections in Taiwan will reach 76 percent of households in 2006, with most new subscribers added between now and 2004.

It should be clear from these examples and the figures that East Asia has the potential to be a leader in the development of broadband applications. They have the infrastructure, and users are willing to subscribe. The question is whether they have the ambition and the leadership to translate infrastructure and user willingness into applications that will conquer the world.

Short Messaging Systems

The second area where Southeast Asia displays some leadership is in the use of Short Messaging Systems (SMS), an application that has recently gained major ground in Europe, and which is still an almost hidden treasure in the United States. An observer on the shopping streets of Singapore, Kuala Lumpur, Manila, or Hong Kong will wonder how much and how fast young and not-so-young cellular telephone users can type on their ever-smaller "handphones." This Asian-English word (for cellular telephone) has perhaps come closer to reality than was originally intended: the devices seem now to be used as often with the hands (for typing messages) as they are close to the ears!

The market data also indicate that SMS has become very popular among Asian cellular telephone users, with Singapore taking the lead and followed by the Philippines (see March 2002 data on AT Kearney and Asia Features websites). In Singapore, 52 percent of the cellular telephone users use SMS more than once a day, compared with 30 percent in

South Korea, 29 percent in Australia, and a global average of 23 percent. But only about 3 percent of Hong Kong cellular telephone users used the SMS more than once a day, and only 13 percent in Taiwan and 20 percent in China.

Most SMS applications are still extremely simple: downloading ringer tones and personalization of telephone screens, quick news updates, and the constant exchange of short "soundbites" (mostly between teenagers). Advertising is another area of interest for SMS providers. South Korea has the highest rate of SMS advertising, with 63 percent of the users receiving advertising messages. In Singapore, only 25 percent of customers received SMS advertisements; in Taiwan 43 percent receive advertising and in Hong Kong, 35 percent, while in the United States, only 8 percent receive advertising. The global average, including Europe, is 35 percent.

Innovations in SMS applications does not, and should not, come only from operators. In fact, most operators have been surprised by the rapid developments in the market for SMS. The real innovations often came from users, who have been exploiting the cheap and nonintrusive nature of short messages to develop a totally new communication style. A peculiar innovation, which was the consequence of the leveraging of SMS, is the management of mass movements. It has been argued that the toppling of President Estrada in the Philippines and the changeover from President Wahid to President Megawati in Indonesia were to a large extent "smoothed" (i.e., facilitated) by the widespread use of SMS. Through SMS, troop movements or news could be spread in a minimum amount of time to a very large group of demonstrators. Whether or not it is true that this use of SMS made a real difference probably requires further research, but it is an interesting (and hopefully not to be repeated) example of how users develop new applications not expected by either the engineers who designed the system or the marketers who launched the service.

Looking ahead, one can guess that improvements to SMS are expected in the form of enhanced message service and the addition of a multimedia messaging service, which will enable users to further personalize their messages with pictures, sounds, and animations. There are now cellular telephones with built-in cameras in Japan as well as Europe, and use of this technology is going to spread like wildfire through middle class Asia. The creativity this will unleash in Southeast Asia is probably limitless. But will Asian companies let European or American companies run away with the economic benefits of applications that had first been developed in Asia?

Top performance in applications

A third area where we can observe some interesting performance is in the area of applications (other than SMS). The world over, interesting applications appear in areas where companies are particularly successful and where markets are sufficiently free and developed and therefore able to sustain true innovation. Asia is no different in that respect. One interesting example of successful companies and markets is the health sector. The emergence of a middle class in East Asia has increased the demand for high-quality health care. Many hospitals are being developed, and the private sector often has a chance to experiment with new ideas. In fact, innovation is a necessity, because there is a dearth of high-quality and well-schooled medical personnel. Malaysia offers a good example of this lack. According to World Health Organization statistics, there are only 6.6 doctors and 11.3 nurses for every 10,000 people in Malaysia. In comparison, the United States has 27.9 doctors and 97.2 nurses per 10,000 people. Even in neighboring Philippines, where per capita income is just one-third that of Malaysia, there are almost twice as many doctors (12.3 per 10,000 people) and nearly four times as many nurses (41.8 per 10,000 people). No installed base, sufficient freedom for enterprise, limited human resources, and willing customers are usually a good breeding ground for innovation. One of the examples of an ICT-based innovation is a new hospital in Kuala Lumpur.[3]

Selayang Hospital in the suburbs of Kuala Lumpur is similar to most modern hospitals: sterile and filled with patients, doctors, and nurses. But deep inside its walls, a network of wires connects 1,200 computers, 300 printers, 150 bar code readers, 66 laptops and 77 servers throughout the building. In fact, the hospital has more computers than doctors and nurses, and more servers than specialists. It's one of the world's first paperless, filmless hospitals, and it works with wireless technology. Doctors at Selayang Hospital don't carry clipboards, because there are no paper files or X-ray films. Patients wear bar coded bracelets that can be scanned at any computer in the hospital to retrieve their vital information and medical history via a wireless local area network.

The Ministry of Health invested MYR 600 million (US$157 million) to build the hospital between 1997 and1998, at the height of Asia's financial crisis. The hope was that a high-tech hospital would ease the burden on Malaysia's stretched medical service. The hospital gradually became operational in August 1999; by 2003 its seven wings and 1,000-plus beds should be filled.

When nonemergency patients arrive, their experience is similar to checking in at a hotel. Nurses key their vital information into the central computer system and give them a bracelet bar coded with their file number. Everything that happens to the patient from then on is computerized. All doctors have laptops at their desks. When they scan the bracelet they can retrieve the patient's medical history, download test results, and record diagnoses.

Selayang keeps no paper files, storing everything from diagnoses to X-ray images and prescriptions in databases. Doctors at Selayang can order tests and scans with the click of a

mouse and see the results on their PCs within minutes. X-rays and magnetic-resonance-imaging scans, or MRIs, are rarely output on film. Instead, they are transmitted digitally through Selayang's intranet. Viewing these results on computer screens allows doctors to magnify images, get exact measurements and compare them quickly with previous results.

The hospital is one piece of a bigger e-health care plan. Inspired by Prime Minister Mahathir Mohamad's vision for a Multimedia Super Corridor, the US$3.7 billion high-tech zone in and around Kuala Lumpur, the ministry of health is now looking at the potential role of technology in public health. Pilot projects include a tele-medicine scheme, which would allow city-based doctors to offer care to the millions of Malaysians living in remote rural areas. Another is electronic, lifetime documentation of each citizen's health, accessible from any hospital in the country. Selayang's computerized patient records are the first step towards achieving that goal.

There are experiments with ICT-leveraged health care in other countries, but the speed with which these experiments can implemented in Southeast Asia is probably greater, and the knowledge that can be gained from these experiments, definitely important.

Another example of the sophisticated application of IT in a sector in which Asia is excelling is in port management. Both the Port Authority of Singapore and Hutchison Whampoa from Hong Kong are formidable companies with operations in many different ports all over the world. Their IT systems enable superior port management; their systems of handling transhipment activities are among the best and most efficient in the world. A whole series of smaller and very innovative companies have developed around these large port management companies, and they specialize in narrow competencies required by the big companies. Both Singapore and Hong Kong, and more recently Malaysia and China, have been developing innovative solutions in ship handling and integrated logistics, innovations which can be applied all over the world.

e-Government

A fourth area where Asia may well be one of the innovators is in e-government. Accenture's yearly ranking of leaders in e-government regularly place Singapore and Australia among the top in the world (see Accenture website). But as we can see from the data gathered for the *Global Information Technology Report*, other governments such as those of Malaysia and Hong Kong are, relatively speaking, leading users of ICT. Singapore's commitment to the deployment of ICT for innovative government applications is close to unlimited (International Telecommunication Union 2001)—from an almost unique prison management system to the transformation of the national library into a knowledge service provider (Hallowell et al. 2001) and local town council (e.g., Bishan Toa Payoh) rationalizing information and interaction via e-mail with citizens (see CIO Asia website)—Singaporean government is an advanced case study on state-of-the-art applications of IT in industry. The prison management system applies knowledge management to what is probably the most unpleasant type of institution in any country. But this particular example demonstrates process reengineering, change management, excellent project management in IT implementation, and so on (see CIO Asia website).

Learning from the best

Our reason for describing these four examples (broadband penetration, SMS exploitation, killer applications based on what Asian companies can be good at as well as the experiments with e-government) was to show that there is a rich pool of good ideas and experiments in Southeast Asia from which the world can learn. For non-Asians, this means that they may have to set up devices to listen to these experiments, screen the many ideas, and send the idea to their home base or to other parts of the world. Asia is not necessarily a follower in ICT deployment, and the region can be a source of information. Some companies have understood this, and, for example, have set up small application laboratories for SMS applications in Manila, experimented with health management companies in Bangkok, and followed the creativity of Korean kids in experimenting with broadband-based interactive games.

Using diversity as a base for experimentation

Learning from the best-in-class in Asia also implies that one needs to understand the diversity of Asia (and thus the necessity of setting up quasi-experiments). An interesting case study that shows how this diversity can be exploited is in the area of Internet banking. One might well expect that Singapore, with its high broadband coverage and high labor costs, would be a good place to implement Internet banking. This assumption was not correct. Even in Singapore, bank consumers who rarely go to a branch may still do no more than 1.8 consultations per month by Internet—not that much more than customers in far less well covered countries such as China (which averages 1.1 consultations per month; see IDC website). In fact, according to some observations, Malaysian consumers connected to the Internet are ahead of those (in this instance) in Singapore. According to a survey by McKinsey & Company, the numbers of online banking users could be higher were it not for the ready availability of ATMs and telephone banking in Singapore. That report also indicated that the conservative attitudes of Singaporeans towards new technologies also served as an obstacle. Despite the jump in numbers for online banking, activities are very much restricted to payment of bills, fund transfers, and balance enquiries. Transactions such as setting up fixed deposits and buying unit trusts have remained unpopular. This is an interesting example of how the diversity in use between Singapore, China, Malaysia, and other countries

can be exploited to study what the impact of ICT can be under different market conditions. Learning from the experiences of Asia involves not only learning about peak performance, but also about the influence of different factors in the environment. Being able to use the region's diversity to carry out experiments is one of the great advantages of studying Southeast Asia.

Diversity as a challenge for Asian companies

It would be unfortunate if only non-Asian companies benefited from the region's potential leadership in applications; the burgeoning creativity of users should also be captured by local companies. If appropriately managed, leadership in applications can give Asian companies an opportunity to conquer world markets. But in order to realize these benefits, Asian companies need to transform themselves. Key elements of this transformation are: 1) ambition; that is, the ambition to create brands and develop a global vision of markets; 2) a commitment to quality products and processes; and 3) a willingness to open up to cultural diversity in their management. Governments can help in this transformation by continuing to deregulate, and by supporting the further development of infrastructure. If these ingredients come together, there is a potential to "re-brand Asia," to change its image from a supplier of outsourcing services and subcontracting to a provider of innovative value propositions for the world. That this is possible is shown by the examples of companies like Samsung in Korea.

The Development of a New Layer of Economic Collaboration

As in many other areas in the world, Southeast Asia has to cope with a digital divide. But the one that we refer to here is not the divide between the "haves" and the "have nots" in terms of knowledge, but the literal divide between cities and the countryside. In many cases, the capital cities and a few large cities of East Asia are well equipped with good infrastructure, but the rest of the country remains underdeveloped.

Singapore is 100 percent wired, Kuala Lumpur's Multimedia Super Corridor has almost all the infrastructure in the country, Bangkok has good infrastructure, Manila has good coverage and able human resources, and one can find what one needs in terms of ICT in Jakarta. The countryside and smaller cities of these countries are however, far less well served. It is a real *physical* digital divide. This is perhaps not so different from the situation in India, or even in the United States or larger European countries such as France.

The notion of the Indonesian farmer or the Vietnamese trader in a small rural city benefiting from connectivity by gaining access to international markets and understanding international market prices is therefore misleading. A small minority may be able to short-circuit villainous middlemen, but the reality is that the villager or local trader still has too little information; they therefore still rely on middlemen for the value-adding services they provide. A story of a farmer from Flores or Mindanao coming from behind his buffalos and connecting onto the Internet is good for the Sunday issues of Western newspapers, but is far from reality. The communications infrastructure simply does not allow that level of connectivity.

In Southeast Asia, however, there is an interesting, and perhaps underestimated, side effect of this emerging digital divide. Currently, in many cases it is easier for a Southeast Asian citizen to communicate with friends, colleagues, or competitors in other capital cities of East Asian countries than with the same groups of people in the countryside in his or her own country. In many cases, such links between the different capital cities already existed through family or friendship ties between overseas Chinese and Indian communities in many ASEAN countries. But today, these ties of trust and friendship are strengthened by daily communications, swapping back and forth of data files, e-business links, and so on. Large conduits for data exchange link these cities together, and bring them closer every day. Links between top universities in the region, for example, National University of Singapore, Beijing University, or Tokyo University, have become very easy. This means that in addition to strong national structures, a new layer of networks is being developed, a new layer of interactions between the capital cities and major industrial cities of East Asia. In this case, economic integration is beginning to be preceded by information integration.

It is possible that this networking of cities will remain a low-key activity. But there is a strong "upside" potential. If the constant exchange of ideas and knowledge between the major cities of East Asia can be proactively stimulated, this belt of cities could well become an additional engine of growth for the region. That stimulation may come from the common organization of conferences, the stimulation of infrastructure links, or the creation of common research or commercial initiatives. ICT makes it possible to create a supranational economic structure based on the interaction of equal peers, and this would complement existing economic ties between the countries of Southeast Asia. With proactive stimulation of idea and knowledge exchange, one could probably stimulate intraregional commercial ties and reduce the dependence of the region on the United States and Europe. But most of all, such stimulation could lead to the development of a hotbed for innovation in the region. The potential is there; it only needs leadership to make it happen.

Tackling Some of the Hurdles

East Asia has many attributes that can enable it to become a serious player in the ICT world. But it also has some major shortcomings. "Showstoppers" to the realization of the full potential of the region could be the poor regulatory framework for intellectual property protection, and the rigidity in the educational system.

The creation of a regulatory framework for the protection of intellectual property

The most obvious hurdle that East Asia must overcome is the lack of serious commitment to the protection of intellectual property rights. Legislation may not be lacking; what is lacking is the willingness to make enforcement a priority.

Singapore may be an exception, but in most of the other countries, the amateur of pirated software will continue to be delighted. A short walk through the shopping centers of central Kuala Lumpur, Johor Bahru, Hong Kong, Taipei, the markets of Bangkok, or even some of the sleazier streets of Seoul, will leave the buyer of pirated software in a state of ecstasy. One sometimes hears the argument that this is a marginal issue, and that the companies in these countries do respect the value of knowledge. But these marginal sales shops are a symptom of a deeper sentiment that is rampant throughout East Asia; that is, that knowledge products should be free of cost. As long as countries in Southeast and East Asia do not develop the respect and willingness to enforce their intellectual property protection legislation, their position as a knowledge society is at risk. Governments may well be convinced of this need for enforcement, but a cultural change is needed. Respect for knowledge, for creativity in discovery, and for brand-building, needs to be instilled in the wider population. Otherwise, the enormous efforts to transform societies whose success was based on foreign direct investment in manufacturing into societies based on value-creation through knowledge production, is doomed to fail.

We do not argue that this change in value systems will be an easy process. Perhaps a serious discussion on what the coverage of intellectual property rights consists of, is needed. One can perhaps argue that in some cases, it is necessary to make software available cheaply in order to help educate a broad group in the population. But after such a discussion, there must be a serious commitment to intellectual property rights. This will require education; perhaps the development of guidelines for the auditing of how intellectual property rights is respected within companies, and some strong action by the governments.

Adapting the educational system

In the beginning of this chapter we argued that one of the common features of the region is the commitment to education. But the educational system can also be a hurdle to the achievement of successful exploitation of ICT. Throughout East Asian countries, the current educational system is still very much based on rote learning, respect for authority and elders, and a strong fear of losing face. While these principles have helped many generations to quickly catch up with the technological advantages of the West, the system has also reached its limits; it is good for catching up, not for stimulating independent thinking. If Asian societies want to succeed in the exploitation of ICT, they will need to invest in an educational system that stimulates creativity, leaves more room for making mistakes (and thus losing face), and allows established authority to be challenged. Leveraging ICT requires more than good technologists; such people are absolutely essential for success, but they need to be complemented by creative designers, entrepreneurs who can dream up new business models, charismatic marketers who can convince consumers to adopt innovations, and so on. Such people are bred in educational systems that emphasize creativity and individual initiative.

Changes in the educational system are underway. Several outstanding institutions in Asia have developed courses for technical entrepreneurs. The Asian Institute of Management in Manila is one of those farsighted institutions that has invested in graduate studies for entrepreneurs. Nanyang Technological University in Singapore and Waseda University in Tokyo have made similar investments. But many of these interesting experiments happen at the end of the curriculum, and in postgraduate education. What is also needed is an infusion of creativity and individual initiative at the primary and secondary level of the schooling system.

Conclusion

Where does this lead us? East Asia minus Japan and China is in fact a microcosm of the world. There are very sophisticated countries, such as Singapore, Korea, and Taiwan; middle-of-the-road countries, such as Malaysia and Thailand, with a strong commitment to moving up the ICT ladder; and there are laggards that are in the same category as other developing countries. At first sight, these three groups of countries do not seem to have much in common, but they share certain characteristics. All of them have a fear/love relationship with China, and to a lesser extent, with India. All of them are committed to ICT deployment. All of them are constantly interacting through trade and other forms of exchange, and they learn from each other and influence each other. All of them are heavily dependent on exports to the United States and Japan, and need to reduce that dependency.

These countries have a lot of potential for leveraging the possibilities offered by ICT. Their infrastructure is uneven, but when one limits oneself to the more sophisticated countries and the capital cities of the others, they seem to be as committed as can be to rapid deployment of broadband access and cellular technology (with wireless networks in the making). They have a commitment to education, an abundant and well-trained workforce, although they do not always have sufficient creative engineers. Above all, they have examples of excellence in applications, both in business and in government.

When one puts this all together, it appears that companies in these countries can be excellent partners for ICT companies in the OECD world. Perhaps they do not have the resources to collaborate across the board, but they may be a very viable alternative to companies in India and China. Southeast Asian companies can be more readily adapted, in some cases perhaps because of the cultural diversity and the higher standard of living. This brings them closer to understanding some of the needs of countries outside the region, for example, European countries. Also, Southeast Asian companies have leading applications that were developed for their own needs (or fashion trends) that may be transferred to other countries.

In order to realize this potential, however, these countries may need to overcome certain hurdles. A more creative educational system, greater emphasis on the protection of intellectual property rights, and the development of a more sophisticated marketing capability that puts them into contact with the needs of users in distant markets, may be three necessary conditions for success.

Endnotes

1. Singapore is a special case. Although it is an independent country, its small size gives it many characteristics of a city. (Measuring only about 600 sq km, it is perhaps more comparable to cities such as Los Angeles, London, or Munich rather than to a country with a large geographic surface area.) Investments in infrastructure such as cabling, or providing ADSL access or mobile telephone coverage, are easier to implement in a small area.

2. For more information on the broadband market, see Frost & Sullivan. Online. http://www.frost.com.

3. A full description of this hospital can be found in the Far Eastern Economic Review, March 30, 2002.

References

CIO Asia. 2002. e-Citizens. Rev. July 2002. Online. http://www.cio-asia.com.

CIO Asia. 2002. KM Goes to Jail. Rev. July 2002. Online. http://www.cio-asia.com.

Hallowell, R., C.-I. Knoop, and N. Boon Siong. 2001. "Transforming Singapore Public Libraries," HBS Case No. 9–802–009. Cambridge: Harvard Business School.

Infocomm Development Authority (IDA). 2002. Survey of Broadband Users in Singapore. Online. http://www.ida.gov.sg.

International Data Corporation (IDC) Asia/Pacific. Online. http://www.idc.com.sg.

International Telecommunication Union (ITU). 2001. The e-City: Singapore Internet Case Study. Online. http://www.itu.int.

Internet News. Online. http://internetnews.com.

Accenture. Online. http://www.accenture.com.

AT Kearney. Online. http://www.atkearney.com.

Asia Features. Online. http://www.asiafeatures.com.

Chapter 10

Driving the e-Economy

Contrasting Approaches in the United States, Europe, and Japan

**Mark Melford and
Constantijn van Oranje-Nassau,**
Booz Allen Hamilton

Soumitra Dutta, INSEAD

Introduction[1]

The e-economy: losing momentum?

The importance attached to the e-economy and matters of networked readiness by governments has decreased worldwide over the last two years, overtaken by the priorities of global security and economic stability. Nonetheless, the benefits of the e-economy, to citizens, businesses, and governments, remain real, and are only now beginning to be realized.

Booz Allen and INSEAD recently conducted one of the most detailed international comparisons ever undertaken of governments' progress in driving their e-agendas. The work was sponsored by the U.K. government's Office of the e-Envoy. In this article we examine the common challenges and widely contrasting approaches of governments in the United States, Europe, and Japan.

The approach: a comprehensive assessment of the e-economy at three levels

Our assessment of the "e-maturity" of countries, in line with the Networked Readiness Index (NRI), considers all levels of e-economy development; that is, environment, readiness, and uptake/use of information communication technologies (ICT). We also distinguish between the principal actors: individuals, business, and government.

> *e-Environment.* Environmental factors describe the fertility of the environment for e-commerce. This encompasses the level of political leadership, regulatory openness, innovation, capability, IT skills in the population, and the cost and availability of access.

> *e-Readiness.* Readiness describes the ability of a country's economic actors—individuals, businesses and governments—to capitalize on the opportunities that a strong environment brings. Readiness requires an appropriate access device, be it personal computer (PC), digital television (DTV) or even a mobile device, plus the skill and the willingness to use it for e-commerce.

> *e-Usage.* "Usage" expresses the uptake of online services, and the volume and sophistication of this use. For individuals, the sophistication of use ranges from surfing and e-mailing through transactions such as online banking and shopping, and publication of their own Web pages. For businesses and government, basic use is the publication of a website; more sophisticated use is characterized by transactional e-commerce applications and the integration of other business processes online, for example, Customer Relationship Management (CRM) or supply chain management.

When discussing Europe, the focus is on Sweden, Germany, the United Kingdom, France, and Italy, although developments in other Western, Central and Eastern European countries will be taken into account. When discussing the United States, some references will also be made to Canada, which has also shown an impressive performance in driving the e-agenda.

Regional Developments

The United States: building on environmental strength

The United States has been a leader in developing and using ICT in government and business, and at an individual level. The United States is pursuing an ambitious and wide-ranging e-government agenda, and is now refocusing its efforts to a more centralized cross-departmental approach in order to be able to provide seamlessly integrated services. The real driving force behind the e-economy, however, is U.S. business. Enthusiasm has been slightly tempered by the downturn in capital markets and concerns about security and consumer liability. Nevertheless, levels of e-commerce in business-to-business, business-to-consumer, government-to-business, and government-to-consumer are unrivalled anywhere in the world.

Two key challenges for the United States are to keep up the drive to increase the availability of broadband infrastructure and to bridge the significant digital divide between high- and low-income groups and between urban and rural areas. To narrow this divide, the federal government has taken several initiatives designed to increase access to the Internet. Examples include the Community Technology Centers program, which expands access to technology centers in low-income communities, and the "e-rate program," which subsidizes the cost of access for schools and libraries by between 20 and 90 percent.

Despite the early deregulation of the telecommunications industry, which began in 1996, the availability of broadband in the United States is somewhat less than expected, with only 59 percent of the population having access to either digital subscriber line (DSL) and/or a cable modem. DSL investment, made mostly by the incumbent telecommunications companies, has gone slowly; incumbents are struggling to raise capital because of tight capital markets and heavy debt resulting from investment in wireless infrastructure in the mid- and late-1990s. In addition, incumbent telecommunications companies feel limited incentives to invest in DSL because of Federal Communications Commission regulations concerning wholesale access and pricing.

Europe: energetic programs from some of the slow starters

Developments in Europe vary strongly between countries, depending on environmental factors and political drive. Leaders in Europe remain the Scandinavian countries, Finland and Sweden in particular, due to strong environmental factors and early adopter status. The Netherlands has also performed well on the citizen and business levels, but its e-government development has been lagging. The United Kingdom and Germany have made impressive progress in catching up, although the United Kingdom is hampered by limited broadband infrastructure. Italy and France, both coping with tough environmental challenges, have been slow to identify priorities in their e-policy approach. However, governments have realized the importance of the e-economy, and have put in place measures to make up for lost time. The energy of the programs in Germany and Italy is particularly impressive. Eastern Europe remains heavily disadvantaged in infrastructure, and faces other environmental barriers such as the limited purchasing power of citizens, lack of available financing, and an unsupportive business culture. Nevertheless, governments and citizens are embracing new technologies as a tool for rapid economic development, showing some impressive results in Estonia and the Czech Republic. These countries are already outperforming certain southern European Union (EU) member states on the NRI. New innovation centers, alignment to EU regulations and programs and the spread of mobile devices will allow certain Central European Countries to catch up in the medium-long term.

Key challenges for Europe are the rollout of broadband infrastructure, the development of e-government services, and the increase in business and citizen uptake and use of e-commerce. Most governments in Europe have policies to support the uptake of e-commerce by businesses and citizens, but this uptake remains very limited. The recent rise of alternate operators and Internet resellers has now almost fully receded; in most countries the incumbents are resuming their dominant positions, with the result that competition in broadband infrastructure continues to be weak. Because of the lack of capital, incumbents have been slow to unbundle the local loop and stalled investments in DSL rollouts.

Japan: a different culture, and consequently, a different response

Environmental factors and lagging political drive have slowed down Japan's ability to adjust and embrace the e-economy. Japanese businesses also see few advantages to going online. This is understandable given the strength of offline distribution channels in Japan, and the perceived lack of proven business models online. Nevertheless, the market environment in Japan is extremely conducive to the e-economy—it has a strong ICT infrastructure, a competitive broadband market, and an innovation-oriented business culture, which should allow Japan to adjust rapidly once the right policies are in place. The Japanese government has realized the challenge, and has set ambitious targets to catch up with the leaders in the e-economy.

But development of the Japanese e-economy is likely to follow a different model, reflecting the significant differences in culture between Japan and the West. Japanese citizens do not relish the use either of English nor indeed of computer keyboards, two of the Internet's key facets. The e-economy in Japan may be more mobile, using hand held devices more than PCs, more graphics-led, as opposed to the text-rich medium of the Web page, and more consumer-led than the business-dominated e-commerce of the West. Key challenges in Japan are the age divide, the limited spread of PCs in homes, and the development of an effective e-government program.

The Environment for e-Commerce

Different countries' environments have different levels of fertility for e-commerce. Some countries, such as Japan and Canada, have strong infrastructures, and others, such as Sweden, have a high propensity for new technologies. Governments have also chosen different approaches to developing the e-economy; from a hands-off approach in the United States to a more directive style in Europe. The environment for e-commerce is determined by three factors:

1. The *market environment*, which includes the propensity towards innovation, the level of ICT skills, and the cost and availability of Internet access;

2. The *political and regulatory environment*, which involves an assessment of political leadership, regulatory openness, and adequate regulation ;

3. The *infrastructure environment*, which describes the availability and quality of ICT infrastructure.

Market environment

The most fertile market environments are those with a strong brain pool and high levels of Internet penetration, such as exists in the United States, Finland, and Sweden. Two key policy themes emerge: ICT in education, and Internet access price regulation.

ICT in education

Only an ICT-skilled population will be able to exploit and develop the full potential of the e-economy. This is the population driving the supply of, as well as the demand for, new technologies and services. Therefore, ICT education and the integration of new online learning methods in the general curriculum are essential to a strong market environment. ICT investment in education is almost exclusively the domain of government policy, except in the United States, where private funding plays an important role, especially in higher education. All governments are concerned with the lack of

ICT user skills in the general population and the lack of specialist ICT skills. Furthermore, most see embedding ICT in education as a key lever for reducing the digital divide.

Typically, investment breaks down into three main areas: a) ICT equipment for schools, colleges, libraries, and so on; b) ICT training for teachers and librarians; c) putting educational content online. Most countries have put considerable resources behind these three factors, typically investing EUR 200 million to EUR 400 million annually in multiyear projects. Most ICT policies in education have been effective in the first two areas of equipping institutions and training teachers and librarians. In Europe the U.K.'s National Grid for Learning and Sweden's ITiS program have had the greatest impact, linking up close to 100 percent of all schools and significantly increasing the numbers of PCs per pupil.

Beyond these priorities, governments are only just discovering and developing the potential of new ICT-based education, or "e-learning." Though most countries have included computer science in the curriculum and provide ICT facilities in schools, courses are still largely determined by traditional teaching methods. The United States and Canada stand out in this area, as they have historically supported and integrated ICT in education. Here PCs have been used extensively in schools since the 1980s, which gives these countries a base of machines and skills on which to build. Nevertheless, educational ICT spending in the United States varies a great deal between states and even towns. The decentralized nature of the U.S. government and the important role of private funding reduce the influence of the federal and even state governments on ICT education.

Internet access prices

Low Internet access prices, in particular broadband, are a crucial prerequisite for widespread uptake of online technologies. The market power of the incumbent and their role as a monopoly provider of wholesale telephony (at least in most countries) has led almost to the failure of the market in this area. Regulators therefore, have been active in many countries reviewing wholesale rates and conditions under which access is provided to the local loop. However, the zeal with which they have pursued this has varied.

Competition at both the backbone and Internet service provider (ISP) level has driven down the cost of Internet access. At the time of writing, the United States and the United Kingdom are among the cheapest places for dial-up narrowband Internet access. At the backbone level, countries that deregulated earlier (e.g., the United Kingdom) have viable and cheaper alternatives to the incumbent (e.g., Energis in the United Kingdom), helping ISPs to lower their costs and pass these savings on to consumers. The introduction of "subscription-free ISPs" in countries that traditionally had metered local call charges, later followed by subscription ISPs with unmetered access, brought further competition and lowered prices. The United Kingdom in particular benefited from the early entry of Freeserve, the world's first subscription free ISP, which led to fierce competition. Those countries where local call charges are unmetered (e.g., the United States) have had cheaper dial-up access for some time.

Overall broadband access prices have fallen, driven down by a combination of increasing competition and regulatory pressure, with the balance of these factors varying by country. Japan's dramatic price cuts are competition driven, with strong players such as Yahoo moving aggressively to gouge market share from the incumbents. In France, by contrast, regulator ART has imposed deep wholesale price cuts on France Telecom. Prices in Germany, the United States, and Canada are not following the downward trend, and have been rising as of late. In the case of Germany, this reflects regulatory action on perceived predatory pricing. It is also notable that growth in broadband subscribers has tended to be triggered at a certain price point. Most countries seem to be converging on a sweet spot or "zone of take off" for broadband prices around this mark (US$35–US$50). The upward correction in prices in the United States and Germany will keep them in this zone, whereas Japan has overshot this mark.

Figure 1. **Residential DSL Lines Against DSL Prices (with Nine Month Lag)**

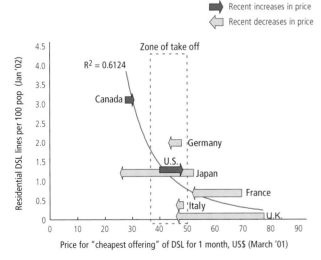

Source: PointTopic (March 2001, January 2002)

Political and regulatory environment

Political leadership is now strong in most European countries and the United States. The governments of Germany, the United States, Canada, and the United Kingdom are particularly active, and they have put in place strong political institutions and regulations to support e-commerce and drive the political momentum. Typically, slow starters like France and Italy, but also Germany and the

United Kingdom, are the most energetic in developing e-policies in an effort to make up for lost time.

Three different organizational models for effectively driving the e-agenda emerge as follows:

1. The U.K. approach, which is setting up a dedicated, cross-governmental organization, usually within the Cabinet Office or equivalent;

2. The U.S. method, which is establishing a dedicated organization (in case of the United States this organization's main focus is e-government) within the treasury / ministry of finance, and with, therefore, (some) budgetary influence;

3. The continental European set up, which is dividing responsibility across several departments, usually giving the e-commerce policy portfolio to the ministry for industry and the e-government portion to the ministry of the interior, although there are some variations on this theme.

Overall, countries that have set up dedicated and strong units or departments to drive the e-economy have shown the most impressive results. The exception is the United States. It has been a leader in the e-economy, even though the government has taken a hands-off approach, leaving the development of the e-economy largely to the market. Its strong central unit focuses on the development of e-government and the coordination of policies across departments.

Japan's e-economy organization resembles the U.K. approach, but on a much smaller scale. Japan has set up a small, dedicated Information Technology Policy Group (numbering twenty to thirty) that coordinates the e-agenda across government. Whilst it sits in the Cabinet Secretariat, it does not appear to have a clear leadership role, beyond coordinating across ministries. Until now it has focused on e-government and has been less effective in pushing the external policies of the e-Japan agenda.

In general, government leadership is especially effective in combination with a strong leadership by the corporate sector and involvement of industry in developing e-commerce policies. Canada provides one of the best examples of a private sector initiative—the e-Business Round Table. The Round Table was established in 1999 by a collection of industry leaders with a self-defined mandate of trying to grow the e-economy in Canada. The Round Table has provided input to the government regarding creating a supportive market environment for e-commerce. Effective policies include reducing the administrative and tax burden, ensuring competition in the telecommunications market (for broadband, in particular), helping to connect remote areas, and promoting a strategy for the spread of access devices.

e-Commerce regulation is fairly similar across the United States, Europe, and Japan, with the only significant difference being the U.S.'s unique position on sales tax. EU regulation on e-commerce is comprehensive, and ensures a relatively homogeneous regulatory landscape across the EU. The EU body of legislation also affects Central European countries, as they align themselves in view of future EU membership. Japanese regulation largely follows international standards set by organizations such as the World Trade Organization and the World Intellectual Property Organization.

Infrastructure environment

Broadband prices show an interesting correlation with the level of infrastructure and infrastructure competition in each nation. Broadly speaking, competition does demonstrably drive down prices. There are three levels of broadband competition, based on: competing technologies, different infrastructures, and reselling.

Figure 2. **Cost of Broadband (January 2002) versus Total Infrastructure Availability**

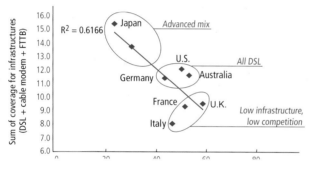

Source: Office of the e-Envoy/Analysys, PointTopic.com, BAH

Nations fall into three categories (see Figure 2):

1. "Advanced mix" or "competitive" nations, such as Japan and Canada, in which there is more than one infrastructure that is very available, real competition, as well as the lowest broadband prices

2. "All DSL" or "extensive" nations, such as Germany, in which telecommunications incumbents, with government encouragement, have rolled out DSL aggressively, and where cable infrastructure has yet to develop. Broadband availability in these countries is relatively high, but true infrastructure competition is lacking. Interestingly, broadband prices in these countries have not been dropping as quickly as elsewhere

3. Nations such as the United Kingdom and France, which have a more even balance of infrastructures—that is, low penetration of both. These nations have had the most stubbornly high broadband prices (although U.K. prices have at last fallen this year), and also some of the most aggressive price regulation.

By definition, reselling only provides limited competition, as the reseller is restricted in price by the wholesaler, and ultimately dependent on them. This is seen in the low market shares taken by resellers. In France, 90 percent of the 550,000 subscribers to France Telecom's asymmetric digital subscriber line (ADSL) network are with France Telecom's service provider, Wanadoo. In Germany, 87 percent of the 2.3 million subscribers are with T-Online, Deutsche Telekom's service provider. In the United Kingdom, resellers have gained a greater share of an admittedly small market. BT Openworld has secured just 50 percent of the 200,000 subscribers to BT's ADSL service. Moreover, BT has a smaller share than the cable companies in the overall broadband market, unlike resellers in France and Germany.

Local loop unbundling (LLU) is the process of forcing incumbents to open their exchanges for competitors to install their own kit, thereby enabling infrastructure-based competition. However, LLU has not lead to the expected level of competition. Whereas in the United States, Sweden, and Germany a significant number of exchanges have other operators' equipment installed, their market share remains very low—less than 3 percent in Germany (just 70,000 lines vs. 2.3 million for Deutsche Telekom). For this reason, many governments are now reviewing the effectiveness of their policies with regard to LLU. Only in Japan does LLU seem to have resulted in competition that has affected prices. There, the first entrant, Tokyo Metallic, beat the incumbent, Nippon Telegraph and Telephone Corporation (NTT), to offering DSL; intense competition ensued, and as a result NTT now has a relatively low market share for an incumbent (35 percent, vs. 94 percent in Germany) and prices in Japan are now the lowest worldwide.

Competing technologies provide the most solid basis for the development of a competitive broadband market. A number of countries are well-cabled for historical reasons, and therefore already have an existing second infrastructure that covers a significant portion of the population. For example, demand for U.S. programming led to the growth of cable television in Canada. Subsequently, in 1996, Canadian cable companies started to offer broadband, even before the incumbent telecommunications operators did. Thus, in Canada, 73 percent of the population are able to subscribe to DSL and 64 percent are able to subscribe to broadband cable, whereas in Germany 90 percent have DSL available but only 24 percent can subscribe to broadband cable services.

Best policies

All countries are concerned with how to extend and accelerate broadband rollout, whilst simultaneously creating a competitive market. Policymaking approaches vary, and include setting the competitive market framework to boost competition among private sector players, or leaning on a strong incumbent; investing public funds to provide infrastructure, as a necessary public good, or providing incentives for the private sector to lead.

The nations with the best infrastructure environment, in terms of availability and quality, are Japan and the United States. Availability of broadband and multiple infrastructures (cable, DSL, other) varies significantly between countries, primarily for environmental reasons. The United States is the only country with a high score on the quality and security of infrastructure, even though availability of DSL has been slightly disappointing.

Japan, Sweden, Italy, and Canada have taken best-practice measures to enhance the extent and quality of national infrastructure. Sweden has chosen to invest public funds to close the urban and rural divide. A comprehensive infrastructure program involving large investments by the national grid in backbone infrastructure, and tax incentives and grants for local infrastructure development, has been rolled out to connect rural communities. Canada and Japan have both enhanced the quality and availability of national networks by effectively creating a competitive market framework. In Canada, the prospect of increased competition drove cable and telecommunications companies to invest in upgrading their networks. In Japan, the regulator effectively forced the incumbent NTT to unbundle the local loop, and showed a willingness to act each time the incumbent presented an obstacle to DSL rollout. Finally, Italy acted to facilitate private sector leadership by reducing the cost of large-scale infrastructure development through special rate loans, grants, tax exemptions, and so on.

Individuals' Participation in the e-Economy

The extent to which individuals have embraced the e-economy differs widely. Finnish, American, and Swedish citizens are the most e-mature, while the citizens of Italy, France, Germany, and Japan have been more conservative in their behavior. The level of e-maturity is determined by two factors: readiness and usage.

> Individual *readiness* describes the skill and the willingness of a nation's citizens to participate in e-commerce, given that it is available to them; that is, to capitalize on the opportunities that the environment affords. Readiness is largely determined by the penetration of access devices, the perceptions of benefits, costs, and security of using the Internet, and the level of skill in using ICT.

> Individual *usage* describes the degree to which a nation's citizens are making purposeful use of Internet technologies.

Individual readiness

The most e-mature individuals combine a high level of adoption of access devices, such as PCs or mobile telephones, with a positive attitude to the Internet. U.S. citizens are the most ready, with high penetration of PCs and a favorable attitude toward the Internet. Despite a relatively low penetration of access devices, Italy follows the United States closely due to its citizens' overwhelmingly positive attitude toward the Internet. In contrast, Japanese citizens show greater reticence to embrace the Internet, for a variety of cultural and environmental reasons.

Access devices

Internet penetration and use is directly dependent on the availability of access devices. Consequently, those countries with a high penetration of access devices typically have a high level of readiness.

Figure 3. **Internet Usage versus Home PC Penetration**

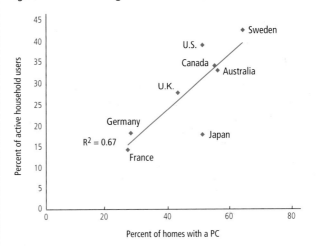

Source: Nielsen NetRatings (2002), Eurobarometer (2002) and BAH Analysis

The United States and Canada have a high penetration of ICT resulting from a combination of market forces and long-standing policies of the integration of ICT in education. In contrast, many European countries, such as the United Kingdom, France and Germany, have pursued initiatives designed specifically to increase penetration of access devices through the provision of Public Internet Access Points (PIAPs), or through PCs in the home. One particularly successful initiative for home PC penetration was the Swedish PC Tax Reform Initiative (see box The Swedish PC Tax Reform).

Many countries have also attempted to set up second hand computer schemes, without much success. In addition to requiring significant maintenance, old hardware does not support the latest software and is often too slow to deliver the kind of services that the Internet provides.

The Swedish PC Tax Reform
The scheme provides a tax incentive for purchasing PCs for the home and is available to all employees. It is managed by business, financed by the banks, and backed by a government guarantee. Not all such schemes have been successful. The two key success factors are that the scheme is open for all employees and that all involved parties benefit: the employees receive cheap PCs; the employers benefit from positive side effects such as IT literate staff and increased possibilities for teleworking; the banks see it as a low risk investment; and the government achieves its goals to increase PC penetration, connectivity, and ICT literacy.

Figure 4. **Increase in PC Penetration 1997–1999 (in Percent)**

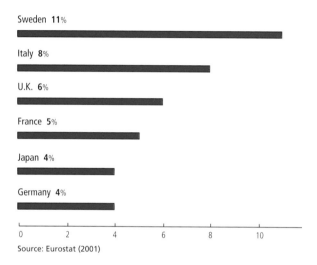

Sweden **11**%

Italy **8**%

U.K. **6**%

France **5**%

Japan **4**%

Germany **4**%

Source: Eurostat (2001)

Individual barriers to use

In addition to having access, individuals must also be *willing* to embrace the Internet. Many real and perceived hurdles must be overcome, including a lack of skills, a perceived lack of benefit, and prohibitive cost.

Many of the barriers related to skills and benefits are directly influenced by the length of time that ICT has been integrated into the education system and the degree to which it was integrated. In Europe, where ICT was integrated into education systems somewhat later than in North America, governments have provided adult education in computer skills in an effort to gain ground. Italy and France in particular have pursued significant initiatives designed to increase their population's familiarity with computers and the Internet. In Japan, computers have been prevalent in education for some time, although the use of the Internet in education has so far been very limited. Japan has taken a similar approach to Europe, using adult education to increase awareness and familiarity of the Internet.

Where citizens' perceptions of cost form a barrier, such as in Japan, Sweden, and Germany, the dominant form of access is usually expensive, metered narrowband. Many governments have attempted to address this issue through stimulating competition among telecommunication companies, an issue discussed in a following section on the Environment.

Environmental factors

Citizen readiness is also affected by a number of other factors, which are not easily influenced by government policy. For example, the fact that most Internet content is in English has proved a barrier in Japan as well as southern Europe. Moreover, a lack of familiarity with keyboards and the smaller size of many apartments also suppress the demand for PCs in Japan.

Individual usage

As might be expected, there is a strong correlation between high levels of readiness and high levels of use. In individual usage, the Americans and the Swedes are the most advanced, while those in France, Italy, and Japan exhibit more limited Internet use. High levels of usage are characterized by three primary factors:

1. *Basic Internet penetration* such as household narrowband Internet access, use of broadband and even diversification to non-PC channels;

2. *Equality of use* across a variety of demographic parameters such as gender, income, and age;

3. *Sophistication of use*; that is, use for transaction and interaction, including e-mail, banking, and online buying, and even publishing personal websites.

Basic Internet penetration

Basic Internet penetration is clearly a cornerstone of Internet usage; penetration is driven largely by the cost of both narrowband and broadband access. Though the relationship is not uniform, it is notable that the three expensive narrowband countries (Italy, France, and Japan) are among those with the lowest penetration rates. Similarly, countries with the highest penetration rates, such as the United States, have very cheap narrowband access. At the time of writing, significant price cuts have occurred in the United Kingdom and Japan; early indications are that these are spurring uptake. With regard to broadband uptake, a significant driver is the price *differential* between broadband and narrowband. As the chart (Figure 5) below shows, individuals are price sensitive when it comes to substituting broadband for narrowband, and will only "trade up" when the price premium they are effectively required to pay looks low relative to the increased utility, or benefit, the service brings.

Figure 5. Broadband-Narrowband Price Differential versus Increase in Broadband Uptake (2001)

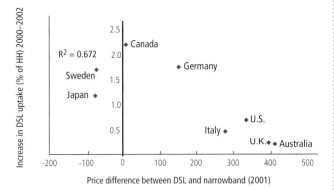

Source: ILO 2002, Forrester 2002

Germany's "Frauen ans Netz"

The Frauen ans Netz (Women to the Web) campaign provides a good example of a successful program to reduce the digital divide between genders. As part of a series of "Internet for All" initiatives, Frauen ans Netz provided training for women in using the Internet. Training was offered at more than 200 sites across the country on a subsidized basis—the fee was EUR 28. The initiative was supported by Brigitte magazine, a popular women's magazine. Key success factors have been the following:

1. Low cost. Women were willing to pay a little for training, enabling more to participate.

2. Public Private Partnership. By imaginatively leveraging the private sector through exposure in magazines, the scheme's impact was enhanced. Sponsorship from Deutsche Telekom also extended the scheme's reach.

3. Targeting. Each Internet for All initiative targeted specific user groups with lower rates of Internet uptake.

Though basic Internet penetration is usually achieved through the PC, other means of access are popular in various countries. In particular, 35 percent of Internet access in Japan is through a mobile device, suggesting mobile Internet use offers a genuine alternative. DTV, another access mode, shows promise in the United Kingdom, which is a leader in this technology. Almost 40 percent of households have a digital television, although it should be noted that use of DTV for Internet access is still in the nascent stage .

Equality of use

Equality of usage is important to ensure that all members of society are benefiting from the e-economy. Though the measure of equality of usage, known as the "digital divide," can have many dimensions, the three most salient are gender, age, and income.

For the gender divide, female labor force participation appears to be a strong driver. In the United States and Canada, female participation rates are greater than 65 percent; therefore the gender divide is small. In many European countries and in Japan, the gender divide is larger, although some countries are taking action to reduce it. The most successful campaign has been the German project "Women to the Web," in which Germany tackled the gender divide through action rather than incentives (see box Germany's "Frauen ans Netz").

The *age divide* is considerable in most countries, even with the "threshold" between young and old set at a relatively youthful 35. Sweden and the United States have the narrowest divide, while Japan and France have the broadest. The Japanese age divide is severe, with penetration among those younger than 35 around four times that of the 35 and older group. Similarly, labor force participation rates among older population segments correlates strongly with the age-based digital divide. This points again to the role of the Internet in the workplace in driving overall uptake. The significant exception is Japan, where the linguistic and cultural factors (e.g., unfamiliarity with a keyboard) appear to strongly influence behavior. This impact may become less important over time as most subsequent generations to leave work will do so with Internet experience.

For the age divide, the Swedes and Canadians appear to have been most active with policies such as SeniorNet and Generations CanConnect, respectively, achieving local success.

The *income divide* is typically the largest of the three dimensions. The income divide is largest in the United States, and smallest in Germany, Canada, and the United Kingdom.

The United Kingdom bucks the trend on the income divide, with considerably more Internet penetration among lower income groups than may be expected, given relatively high levels of income inequality. Mass marketing schemes, such as the television campaign for UK Online, may well have

Figure 6. Income Inequality Against Income Divide (2001)

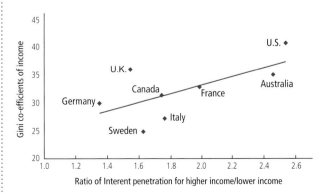

Source: ILO 2002, Forrester 2002

played a role in reaching these groups. The huge relative improvement in ICT penetration in schools may also have contributed. Another approach to closing the digital divide has been the development of a network of PIAPs. Most governments either directly provide access points or have implemented a system of accreditation.

Sophistication of use

To ensure a fully developed e-economy, it is important that individuals not just engage in basic use of the Internet, but also in more sophisticated use. Sophistication of use is defined primarily by activities such as online purchasing and online banking.

Fewer than half of all those who regularly use the Internet are willing to engage in online transactions, though there is considerable variation among users in each country. The citizens of the United States, Canada, and the United Kingdom are the most likely to buy online, with the United States far ahead in transaction volumes. Europeans, especially the Germans and Italians, are the most reluctant to buy online (U.K. Department for Trade and Industry International Benchmarking (DTIIB) Survey 2001).

Government policies to encourage online purchasing have been scare, with most governments choosing to leave it to the private sector. What initiatives there are have been confined to the area of building consumer confidence through promoting best practice in secure payment systems and protection of information. These policies appear to have worked, as the countries where individuals have a high propensity to transact online, such as the United States and the United Kingdom, are generally those where government has made conspicuous steps to create a framework for ensuring consumer confidence.

The United States's leading position in online purchasing is boosted by two other unique environmental factors: 1) the strong culture of and comfort with catalogue shopping, which has translated into comfort with ordering online; 2) a particular comfort with credit cards, which have been marketed as more secure than cash (the maximum downside for theft or fraud is always US$50).

Another form of sophisticated Internet use is online banking, which is prevalent in Canada, Germany, and Sweden. It is understandable that the uptake of online banking is different to online purchasing, as online banking does not require a high degree of comfort with credit cards. To date, no major government policies to stimulate online baking have been identified.

Policy summary

There are five broad themes in policymaking, with the similarities in approach being more noticeable than the contrasts.

- **Supporting the penetration of access devices,** either in the home, as with Sweden's PC Tax Reform, or in public places, as in France's program to develop 7,000 PIAPs by 2003. France also offers a variant of the Swedish tax incentive scheme, where firms can make tax-free gifts of PCs to staff for personal use. The United States also operates a scheme where employees can write off PC purchases against tax in certain circumstances.

- **Building the skills and confidence of target groups.** These target groups may be potentially excluded groups, as in the case of France's massive EUR 150 million campaign to train the unemployed, the elderly, and women; women were also targeted by German initiatives "Mission Internet" and "Frauen ans Netz." Alternatively, potential champions, such as teachers, are targeted, as by Japan's IT training programs.

- **Establishing "driving licences" or "passport" qualifications.** France, Italy, and the United Kingdom have somewhat comparable schemes aimed at granting simple IT qualifications, particularly in low-skilled groups such as the long-term unemployed. The Italians are supporting the European Computer Driving Licence (EDCL) as the "standard" of basic IT qualifications by providing fiscal incentives for businesses employing people with these skills.

- **Building trust, or allaying fears.** The best example of these approaches is the legislative approach of the United States, where the Child Online Protection Act of 1998 marked the start of actions by government to control content and promote schemes providing "kitemark"-type verification or certification of safe services. The United Kingdom and Sweden are also pursuing a legislative approach.

- **Direct marketing campaigns.** Only the United Kingdom, with its UK Online campaign, is directly marketing to citizens the benefits of the Internet in general.

Government activity to stimulate readiness

As a result of their ICT-in-education legacies, the United States and Canada enjoy a relatively high degree of individual readiness. Consequently, there have been relatively few government policies targeting this issue. By comparison, many European countries have felt the need to increase individual readiness, and have tackled the problems of access as well as attitude. The approach to access has varied from the Swedish PC Tax Reform, designed to get PCs in homes, to the provision of PIAPs by the United Kingdom, French, and German governments. In respect of attitude and skills, a common and successful approach has been to educate specific groups of people with low awareness of the Internet. The United Kingdom, France, Japan, and Italy have all implemented initiatives in this respect.

Government activity to stimulate usage

Government policy in the area of individual usage has focused primarily on closing the digital divide. Examples of these policies include the use of PIAPs in Canada and Europe to close the income divide. With respect to the age divide, Canada and Sweden have been active with programs such as Generations CanConnect and SeniorNet, respectively.

Government has not typically concerned itself with encouraging more sophisticated use of the Internet, such as online transactions. Among the exceptions is Canada, and to a lesser extent, the United States, both of which have begun to mark the boundaries of consumer protection for online transactions. In Canada, the government worked with businesses to develop "consumer protection for e-commerce," a suggested standards document for businesses selling online. In the United States, the government is currently enacting several bills guaranteeing consumer rights on the Internet. Furthermore, the Supreme Court has made clear its intention to protect consumer rights in the online sphere.

Best policies

Many European countries have focused on increasing skills and attitudes. Perhaps the most successful effort has been made in Italy, where familiarity with the Internet is typically low, yet citizen-focused policies to rollout the European Computer Driving Licence (EDCL) have been the most extensive. The Italian government have provided teachers, government employees, and students at 7,000 schools with an opportunity to gain the EDCL, and in so doing have given this qualification some currency. Coupled with significant increases in the use of IT, and especially the Internet, in schools, Italians are now among the most confident about their ability to use the Internet.

Though most successful policies have been targeted at increasing the awareness and skills of individuals, Sweden has enjoyed great success in increasing the penetration of access devices. As a result of the PC Tax Reform initiative, readiness in Sweden is amongst the highest in the world, and growth rates of PC sales in Sweden over the last few years have also been higher than anywhere else in Europe, or indeed, higher than in the United States and Japan.

Business Participation in the e-Economy

As with citizens, the degree to which businesses have embraced the e-economy varies widely, though there is consistency in the relative performance of nations. U.S.

businesses are the most e-mature overall, while Swedish, U.K., and German businesses also exhibit high e-maturity. Business e-maturity is determined by business readiness and business usage:

> Business *readiness* describes the readiness of a nation's businesses to participate in e-commerce, given that it is available to them.

> Business *usage* describes the degree to which a nation's businesses are making purposeful use of Internet technologies.

Business readiness

Business readiness requires, first, an access device such as a PC, but also software and other forms of hardware (e.g., servers). It also requires a positive attitude with regard to revenue and/or cost benefits and confidence in Internet skills. Broadly speaking, the United States and northern European countries, such as Germany, Sweden, and the United Kingdom, have the most "e-ready" businesses, while Italian, French, and Japanese businesses are more conservative.

Access device penetration

The availability of access devices is crucial to participation in the e-economy, though the question of what constitutes access is becoming more complex. PCs are now near ubiquitous (generally between 90 and 100 percent) penetration and differences between countries are only revealed by examining the wider investment picture. Greater divergence across nations is found when comparing the density of PCs within a business and the penetration of more advanced access tools such as hardware, software, and even services (indicated by percent of gross domestic product spent on IT).

Some governments, such as the U.K. and Italian, have taken action to support investment in ICT equipment through tax breaks, but overall penetration of ICT is determined by various environmental factors like investment climate, traditional strengths in ICT, and so on. Cost appears a weak driver of business access device penetration, although there is evidence that falling PC prices have driven business uptake of these access devices in the past (in real terms PC prices have declined by around 20 percent between 1995 and 2000, a period during which PC penetration increased by between 100 to 200 percent).

Barriers to use

In addition to having access, businesses must also be willing to use the Internet. Amongst the common obstacles to use are: lack of skills, perceived lack of benefit, and prohibitive cost.

Businesses, especially in Europe and Japan, are sceptical about the revenue growth opportunities of ICT. They have learned from the "dot-com crash" that the Internet's potential to boost top line performance is limited, but they remain confident about ICT's potential in cost reduction (U.K. DTI IBSurvey 2001). Moreover, a significant percentage of businesses— between 40 percent and 50 percent—believe that there are not enough online customers to make e-business a priority. Here, business attitudes mirror reality; businesses complain most about a lack of potential online value where Internet users have the least experience of buying online, such as in Japan.

The nations with the most enthusiastic businesses appear to be Italy and the United States— countries at opposite ends of the scale of experience. The U.S. boasts the largest market for e-commerce and the highest transaction volumes, and therefore has reason to be more positive. Italy came later to the dot-com boom, and hence may have been less burned in the crash.

Security is also a concern for businesses, and in the United States and Europe, well over 50 percent of businesses cite security as a barrier to their pursuit of e-business (U.K. DTI IBSurvey 2001). In Canada, where business concerns about security are greatest, the government has taken early steps to facilitate the development of industrywide standards for customer protection. However, across Europe and the United States where security still remains a key barrier to further development of e-commerce, government has been less active.

Business usage

Business usage is determined first by levels of basic Internet penetration by businesses, which includes connecting to the Internet via both narrowband and broadband, giving employees Internet access, and establishing a Web presence. Another element is equality of use; that is, Internet use by all sizes of business including small and medium enterprises. And, finally, sophistication of use, which includes information flows within the enterprise through an intranet and beyond the enterprise through an extranet, and buying and selling goods and services online. There is a strong correlation between readiness and use, with the highest usage being found in the United States, Sweden, and Germany, and the lowest usage being found in Italy, France, and Japan.

Basic Internet penetration: access and presence

As with access to hardware devices, Internet connectivity and presence is a clear prerequisite for businesses to benefit from the e-economy. The vast majority of employees in the United States, Europe (particularly in Scandinavia, Germany, Austria, Benelux, and the United Kingdom), and to a lesser degree, Japan, work for companies that have Internet access. However, typically only 20 to 40 percent of employees make regular use of the Internet or e-mail (U.K. DTI IBSurvey 2001). Generally, between 60 percent and 80 percent of people work for businesses that have websites. Although U.S. firms are overall not the most likely to have websites, it is clear that the majority of the world's businesses have their websites hosted in the United States, as measured by the number of hosts per

head. This "virtual trade" illustrates that businesses in any one country are not constrained by national markets and offerings when making decisions about whether or not to establish a Web presence.

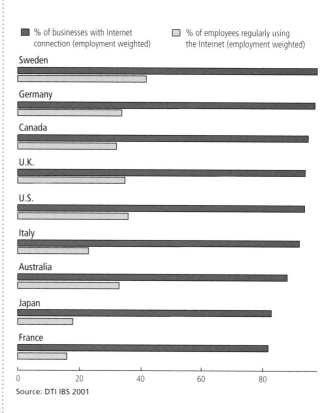

Figure 7. **Business Internet Penetration and Regular Employee Use (2001)**

■ % of businesses with Internet connection (employment weighted) □ % of employees regularly using the Internet (employment weighted)

Source: DTI IBS 2001

Business uptake of broadband is universally higher than residential uptake. This may partly be due to the longer time period broadband offerings have been available to businesses, but the strength of business demand for professional high-speed access seems a more likely explanation for the difference. Considerable variation exists between business uptake of broadband among the countries in Europe, the United States, and Japan, ranging from around 20 percent in Italy up to around 60 percent in the United States and Sweden (U.K. DTI IBSurvey 2001).

Although cost does not seem to drive business narrowband uptake, it has more of a role in the case of broadband. Many larger businesses that use broadband do so through leased lines, although use of leasing varies between countries. The cost of leasing these lines differs markedly between countries, and broadband penetration among businesses follows a similar pattern. Figure 8 seems to suggest that businesses are quite price sensitive to leased-line prices— perhaps this is where newer, super-high speed DSL and cable modem offerings have a role to play in driving further broadband penetration.

Figure 8. **Business Use of Broadband and Cost of Leased Lines (2001)**

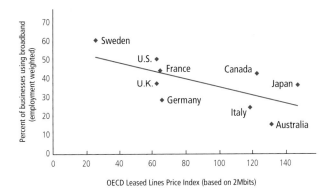

Source: OECD Comms Outlook 2001, DTI IBS 2001

Equality of use

In business, equality of usage typically refers to usage across large, medium, and small companies. Small- and medium-sized enterprises (SMEs) represent a large portion of the economy in each nation, and their participation in the e-economy is important.

In all countries, the smaller the business, the less likely they are to be online or selling online (taking orders or payment), although SME online activity varies significantly between countries. For example, SMEs in Sweden, Germany, and the United Kingdom make more use of the Internet than their counterparts in Canada, France, and Japan. Governments have been actively encouraging SMEs to go online, and some have made it a particular focus. Sweden has the NUTEK network, and also SVEA information and training system. Germany has a national network of SME e-commerce support centers, and beneath that are state-level and even city-level bodies providing an extensive, if heterogeneous, support network. The United Kingdom has seen SME uptake increase considerably since the launch of their extensive and multichannel "support network" UK Online for Business, with the government hitting their target of getting 1.5 million SMEs online by 2002. The French and Japanese, who have the lowest proportion of small businesses online, have also had the least targeted support. In both cases, and particularly Japan, support for SMEs going online is growing significantly, but from a limited current base. The French model, MINinfo, has been well received in trials—with 40,000 documents viewed online per month despite very limited exposure.

Sophistication of use

Interacting and transacting with customers is one of the primary benefits of the Internet for business, and it is important that companies reach this level of sophistication in use. Generally, more businesses buy online than sell online, and there is no evident link between the levels of online selling and buying. While businesses in the United States and Canada are the most *likely to buy* online, it is the businesses in Germany.

Figure 9a. **Small Business Internet Penetration and Online Selling (2001)**

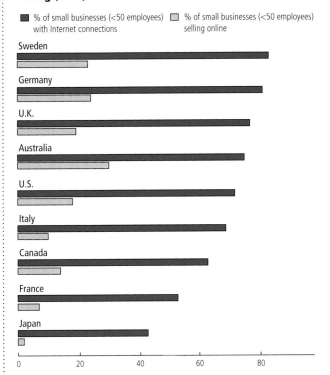

Figure 9b. **Business Buying and Selling Online (2001)**

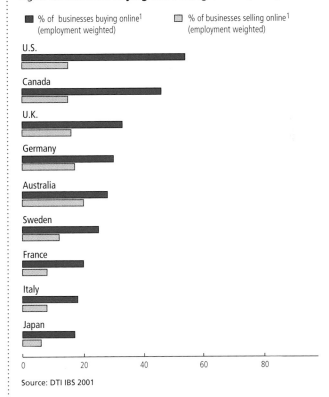

Source: DTI IBS 2001

that are more likely to *sell* online. The business sector in the United Kingdom seems to best "combine" online buying and selling. In spite of this paradox between the propensity to buy or sell, it is clear that the businesses in Japan and southern and eastern Europe are the least likely to buy or sell online.

The most direct drivers are the foregoing factors such as basic readiness and usage. It is noticeable that buying online correlates strongly with the overall NRI score. One notable exception is Sweden, whose level of online buying is low, given its high readiness score. Key drivers of e-commerce take up are environmental factors, such as language, and prevailing payment systems. Language seems to be a driver of business propensity to buy online, though not of the propensity to sell. Lack of familiarity with English may well cause potential purchasers to decide against purchases, especially in the context of business anxiety about the security of buying online. The top four of the top five online buyers are all native English speaking, with the bottom three having the lowest levels of English. There is no reason why selling should follow the same pattern, as the seller can determine the language of the trade. As stated earlier, payment systems, that is, plastic cards, are a plausible driver of online selling to consumers in most countries.

Four broad approaches to improving business readiness emerge:

Publicity/research. Much of business readiness is about attitudes, and almost all governments have made some effort to improve business attitudes towards the Internet in general, or to assuage particular concerns of the business community.

1. The U.K. approach has included straightforward marketing through television advertising for the UK Online for Business support network.

2. The ECOM network in Japan hosts exhibitions and symposia to spread experience of best practice.

3. In Italy, a national awareness campaign is being driven from 100 multimedia centers, which also provide training to 45,000 entrepreneurs.

4. A popular approach is to provide government information on e-business through a dedicated portal, such as Canada's BusinessGateway.ca, which provides a single access point for all government services and information needed to start, run, and grow a business.

5. Another common approach is to conduct primary research of business attitudes, either to "spread the gospel" among reticent businesses, or to identify problems that need to be prioritized.

Tax breaks for training. The government of the United States allows businesses to write off ICT training against tax through the Technology Education and Training Act of 2001. A tax credit of 100 percent applies to the first US$1500 of ICT training provided by a business on behalf of an employee. The Italian government has recently committed

EUR 4 billion to a policy of a much wider scope, that allows firms to write off tax on any investment over and above previous levels (five-year average). This includes investment in ICT training as well as equipment and software.

Access device tax breaks. Very few schemes use the tax system directly to encourage business investment in access devices. As mentioned, the Italian government is allowing tax write-offs on all incremental business investment—this explicitly includes ICT equipment. More directly, the Italians offer a national training scheme for entrepreneurs (currently 45,000 enrolled) that concludes with an exam; those who pass the exam receive an ICT set (e.g., PC, printer)

Filling the ICT skills "gap." All governments have made moves to increase the use of ICT in education to create a generally ICT-literate postschool population, and most governments have attempted to increase the numbers of highly ICT-skilled in the graduate population. A good example of the latter is the U.K. scheme, Skills for the Information Age, which brings business and universities together to ensure that the ICT skills being developed in graduates are those skills desired by business.

- The German government has gone furthest to fill the IT skills gap—perhaps understandable given that they have the largest shortfall in Europe (see box Best Policies).

- The U.S. government has also supported adult education in ICT as part of the Adult Education Program stemming from the Workforce Investment Act. The Department of Education provides grants to states, which then distribute funds via a competitive tender process among training service providers.

Policy summary

Government activity to stimulate readiness

Government policies to stimulate readiness have tended to focus on barriers to use, and in particular, barriers to uptake caused by skills deficiencies within the workforce. Typically, this action has focused on schools and universities in attempts to boost IT skills in the long term, but there are some examples, such as in Italy, of successful adult education schemes. Policies aimed at raising the awareness of the benefits of the Internet have been rather scarce, although the U.K. government has successfully generated brand recognition for its UK Online for Business initiative, a factor that may have driven the success of its advice network. Policies directly promoting access device penetration have been even less common, though some broader policies to encourage investment or even R&D are beginning to provide some tax relief on hardware spending.

Government activity to stimulate usage

Government activity around usage has been generally focused on ensuring smaller businesses are supported in establishing a Web presence, and in trading online. Information, advice, and training are the typical means of support, rather than financial incentives. Governments have also acted to lighten the regulatory burden, and to help firms find staff with the right skills.

Government Actions and the Emergence of e-Government

Governments have taken up the challenges of the networked world in different ways and at different times. The United States and Canada were clear frontrunners in the early and mid-1990s, and followers, like Japan, Italy, and France, launched their e-policy programs in the last two to three years. The level of e-maturity of governments is determined by the following:

1. *Readiness*, which is concerned with the existence of a clear e-government and e-economy vision, departmental strategy, and change programs for processes and staff

2. *Usage*, measured by the degree to which governments use e-commerce in a broad and sophisticated way. This requires that the Internet be embedded into the daily work routine of civil servants and public sector staff, and that departments establish and maintain an online presence, including of services. More sophisticated e-government offerings will include a full range of transactional services and be structured around user groups, rather than departments.

Government readiness

Governments with a high degree of readiness have articulated a clear *vision for the e-economy and e-government*, and put in place *delivery strategies* and *targets* with accountable government departments, including a change program for government processes and staff. This generally requires

---

Best Policies

The most successful policies in increasing business readiness and usage have been those targeted at increasing Internet awareness and skills.

In particular, the German Green Card scheme has clearly been a successful "emergency" approach to filling their ICT skills gap. The take-up of appropriately qualified specialists has been large, with more than half of the cards being taken before February 2002. A particularly interesting impact is the two to three jobs that are estimated to have been created around each Green Card; in effect, the ICT specialist creating jobs for less specialized support. The value of the policy, therefore, extends beyond simply filling ICT vacancies into job creation and potentially genuine skills transfer from the specialist. The scheme has, however, caused considerable political controversy in Germany.

The U.K. government's UK Online for Business has been successful in two regards. First, in terms of creating awareness of a support network for getting businesses online, the mass-marketing approach has been a useful fillip to more internationally common techniques. "Brand" awareness among SMEs now runs at 46 percent. Second, and more important, UK Online for Business is being used; by 2001 the scheme had helped over 160,000 businesses. Perhaps this owes something to its multichannel approach. The project provides the standard physical presence, although with more than 100 centers it is comparatively extensive, but these are supported by a telephone helpline, a website, and detailed advice from "virtual advisers." The United Kingdom has spent more on their version of the

business support scheme than most—GBP 67 million over three years.

The U.S. federal government has effectively supported the e-commerce development by reducing the regulatory burden for online trading. The Internet Tax Freedom Act of 2001 renewed a moratorium on states requiring businesses based in other states to collect sales tax from online purchases. The federal government recognised the burden that sales tax requirements—remitting tax to up to fifty authorities at different rates, and even identifying the location of the buyer—would impose on smaller companies considering trading online. The key success factor is Constitutional Prerogative; without the "interstate commerce" clause in the U.S. constitution, the federal government would not be able to control states' powers of taxation.

Of the few adult training schemes that aim to provide expert skills (as opposed to simple user skills), the Italian scheme has perhaps been the most successful. It is somewhat premature to judge ultimate success, but already 45,000 entrepreneurs are enrolled. A strong potential driver for this scheme is that at the conclusion the trainee is rewarded with an ICT set (e.g., PC, printer) Alternatively, the role of the Italian government in pushing qualifications as standards (including the ECDL) may encourage attendees of training in general. The government is pushing all public employees to take accredited courses, and making available other training resources for targeted sectors (e.g., the unemployed).

a dedicated (e-government) organization to drive and coordinate the e-government effort across all parts of government, and to set targets and track progress. The most ready governments will have seamless integration of departmental systems across all government levels and agencies, and a coherent, secure interface with citizens and businesses. This requires that plans for back office integration be implemented or already in place, and that interoperability frameworks have been adopted. The level of readiness of a government's ICT infrastructure and systems to support e-government is also key; a high number of networked PCs for staff, a sound ICT core infrastructure, and an effective and secure means of interacting with partners (e.g., Gateway, PKI—Public Key Infrastructure).

e-Government visions, strategies and targets

Most governments have articulated some kind of e-government strategy as a basis for comprehensive e-government programs. The United States is the exception to the rule; Firstgov, the U.S. portal, made significant strides in e-service delivery, even in the absence of an overarching strategy.

Although targets were announced some years ago (and often restated), e-government strategies only really appeared in 2000. In most countries, departments have published their own delivery strategies in line with the centrally established strategy framework. Generally, targets have been concerned with the number of government services online, and not with usage. There are sometimes also targets relating to e-procurement and e-tendering, although not all countries have set these out (at least not publicly). Typically, e-procurement targets involve moving a certain proportion of government spending online.

Local e-government

Most citizen and business interactions with government take place at the local government levels; therefore, local e-government requires specific attention. The most active have been countries with a federal structure, such as the United States, and countries with traditionally decentralized governments, such as Sweden. However, most initiatives remain ad hoc and lack the necessary coordination to provide scale and avoid the duplication of efforts. In more centrally-governed nations, governments typically have problems developing effective local programs. Therefore, in both cases it is important that local governments work together with central government in putting services online. There are two contrasting approaches, typified by the United Kingdom and Sweden.

The U.K. approach is centrally driven, and local government is mandated to meet targets set out by central government. Local authorities prepare their own plans for implementing e-government, in line with guidelines prepared by the

central government office of the e-Envoy. The United Kingdom has also launched twenty-five Pathfinder pilots, each a local government project that, if successful, can be rolled out across other local authorities. The aim is to stimulate competition across local authorities and encourage the transfer of best practice.

In Sweden, local authorities have a higher degree of tax-raising and policy autonomy. The central government cannot really mandate them to act in a certain way, but instead is developing tools for e-government that are made available for local governments use, but which are not compulsory. The intention is to provide incentives to local governments to act in a coordinated way by saving them money and eliminating duplications of effort.

Interoperability, standards, back-office integration and portals

To be able to provide online user-centered services across departments, governments need to integrate their back offices and set clear interoperability standards. Portals are at the front end of governments' efforts to coordinate e-government. Nearly all countries have set up a single, one-stop government portal, and most are moving towards a user-centered approach. The United States and Canada portals took the lead, and have extensive content focused on specific user groups. Most countries have laid out specific coordination standards that range from "common look and feel" for Web pages to plans for fully integrating back-office infrastructures across all government levels and agencies.

The approaches differ in level of ambition, but also in the level of authority granted to the relevant coordinating body and whether standards are made optional or mandatory. Until now, no country has managed to set in place a fully integrated back office system. The United States is the furthest along towards seamless back-office integration, with stretch targets, transparent and regular tracking against targets, and most important, strong leadership, empowered by the president, and backed up by budgetary power. European nations, such as France, Germany, and the United Kingdom, follow; they have mandatory interoperability frameworks in place (e.g., e-GIF in the United Kingdom, SAGA in Germany) and integration plans under development or partially deployed. In Japan, however, government integration remains limited to the publication of various standards, including one on the use of PKI within government and another on electronic registration forms.

Interaction with partners

For citizens and businesses to interact and transact with the government online, the services need to be effective, user-friendly and, above all, secure. All countries have, or plan to put in place, a channel for interfacing with external partners effectively (e.g., Gateway or PKI). A good example is the United Kingdom, with its Government Gateway, a centralized authentication engine that ascertains users' identities online and enables secure online transactions with any government department offering a service through it. A number of other countries like Sweden, the United States, and Italy are planning similar initiatives. In the remainder there are various PKI programs at various stages of readiness. The Italian government is rolling out a "smart-card" nationally, in the form of an electronic identification card. The digital signature contained on the card will constitute a single identity for all government interactions, ranging from tax payment to computer assisted voting.

Government usage

Countries strong in government usage are characterized by both a high proportion of services available online and by high usage rates of those services by citizens and businesses. Sophisticated e-government offerings will include a full range of transactional services and be structured around user groups, rather than built on department silos. Moreover, governments are moving from off-line to online e-procurement platforms in order to increase efficiency and transparency. Online technology is also widely used for the promotion of e-democracy, through e-voting, online consultations, and other forms of online citizen participation.

Services online

Initially, the Internet was used primarily to provide government information online; now all countries are making progress in developing online services. The German e-government policy, BundOnline, is among the most impressive. The program was launched only in November 2001, yet has managed to leapfrog its way to a leading position. This suggests that market followers have an advantage, in that they can learn lessons from the leaders. For example, countries that set up services early based around government silos now have the more complex task of moving towards user-centric services. The German program has a heavy focus on putting in place robust, scalable, back-office systems over which services can be delivered.

The main driver in getting services online appears to be the degree to which a government has prioritized e-government issues. The greatest improvements in e-government service offering are in Germany and Japan (Accenture 2002). Both countries were conscious of falling behind, and have put significant resources into e-government. The United Kingdom has also made good progress. For many, continued progress will depend on overcoming the challenge of restructuring back-office systems and processes in order to continue progressing, and to move towards user-centered services. Currently, these challenges are slowing their growth.

Governments have chosen different approaches to getting services online. Most countries have not prioritized by citizen demand, but instead put services online primarily in order of ease of implementation. Some, notably Canada, Italy, and Germany are putting services online according to priorities based on the use and popularity of the service. This has, to some extent, slowed progress as far as in getting high numbers of services online, but it has helped to foster stronger uptake of those services. Canada's uptake levels are world-leading, and Italy's are—for the modest number of services available—extremely encouraging. Interestingly, there is little evidence of governments offering incentives to users or businesses to go through the online learning curve. U.K. taxpayers were offered a GBP 10 reduction in their income tax if they filed over the Internet. The offer seems not to have produced a significant move to the online medium.

Italy's Prioritization Framework
Italy's prioritization framework is particularly impressive. A starting set of 800 services to be put online was pared down to just eighty, based on a four-stage framework:

- Likely frequency of use of the service by the end user
- Value added to the end user by using the service online
- Predisposition of the target group of the service to use the Internet
- Existence or nonexistence of better, alternative channels for the service (e.g., the telephone)

---

e-Procurement

e-Procurement offers the promise of a more transparent and efficient way for governments to purchase goods and to tender projects. All governments across Europe, as well as the governments of the United States and Japan, have expressed their intention to implement e-tendering and e-procurement programs, although they are all at varying stages. Most have set e-procurement targets, although few have met them and even fewer have made e-procurement mandatory. e-Procurement does not depend on the development of a single central system, though it is unlikely that economies of scale will be optimized without one. The United Kingdom, for

---

Consip, Italy's Procurement System
At the end of 2001, overall spending through Italy's procurement body was EUR 4.2 billion (15 percent of the total), with some 52,000 orders managed, 30 percent of them online. The average saving was as much as 31 percent on frame agreements and 35 percent on a series of pilot online auctions. There has also been a noticeable improvement in service levels, with lead times reduced by around five months. Procuring through Consip is mandatory for central public administrations and voluntary for local administrations.

example, has managed to shift roughly half the procurement of low-value goods and services to electronic channels without a central e-procurement system.

e-Democracy

Besides developing new online service offerings, governments are embracing ICT to achieve new forms of citizen participation in government and e-voting, often branded as e-democracy. This is particularly evident in countries with traditions in government transparency and citizen participation. Especially at the local level, governments are using the Internet as an interactive communication tool to give citizens an opportunity to influence decision-making and to gather information. In Sweden, towns like Kalix and Bollnas have set up virtual town halls that allow citizens to participate in council meetings, and in the United Kingdom, town councils in Newcastle and Newham now webcast meetings. Other countries have made consultations available online or have implemented online discussions of policy areas. The United States makes use of online "rule-making" to invite stakeholder input on potential legislation and regulation.

e-Voting is more difficult to implement due to issues of authentication and fraud. The United States was the first to try e-voting on a significant scale in selected states during the U.S. presidential elections in 2000, but has not pursued the matter since. However, it is planning to run e-voting pilots in the congressional elections of 2002. Currently, the United Kingdom is perceived to be leader in e-voting, having run the most extensive online voting pilots at their last local elections in May 2002.

Best policies

The most successful approaches to e-government are characterized by strong leadership and a dual focus on back-office integration and front-office service delivery.

The United States has been very effective in achieving a high degree of readiness. The government combines a clear, specific, comprehensive, and actionable strategy with a high degree of systems readiness, particularly the prevalence of networked PCs in government and the supporting ICT infrastructure. Strong leadership, with budgetary power that

> **The UK Government Gateway**
> The Gateway is a secure interface enabling any department to offer a service through it and to use it as an "authentication engine." A transactional authentication engine is vital for customer-centric service delivery. It was launched in January 2001 at a cost of GBP 16 million; five pilots were completed by December 2001. The key success factor is its operational quality. The Gateway is far ahead of similar schemes in other countries. However, take-up has been disappointing, and there are questions about its robustness.

allows the redistribution of department ICT budgets, pushes the program. Moreover, the United States has put in place a conspicuous and transparent tracking mechanism to measure progress—the Value Measurement Methodology (VMM).

The United Kingdom and Germany also have leading edge e-government strategies, balancing the need to set up robust back-office functions with the need for front-office service delivery. The United Kingdom has focused particularly on its portal and Gateway platforms, which are up and running, and which can be scaled up to accommodate the growing number of services online. It also was one of the first nations to publish an interoperability framework (eGIF), which other countries have since followed (e.g., SAGA in Germany). Germany, unveiling its e-government transformation program, BundOnline, slightly later, appears to have applied some lessons learned by early leaders, and put in place a particularly robust transformation process. BundOnline is a wholesale reform of federal administrative processes. As such it is costly relative to some less profound reform processes, but should result in a robust platform with a tangible impact on costs and efficiencies.

> **The BundOnline 2005 Program**
> The aim of the BundOnline program is to put all priority services of the federal government online by 2005. Project planning includes very definite linkages between development of back-office capability and front-end service delivery. Key success factors are its robustness and structure. Although services may take longer to get online, when delivered they will have robust back-office foundations, and will thus engender user confidence. A detailed implementation plan, with a clear timeline and prioritization of which services are transformed first, ensures accurate and timely implementation across departments.

Recommendations

Our research reveals that all countries have starkly different e-economy fingerprints. The 150 separate statistical indicators used by Booz Allen and INSEAD combine to create a revealing picture of the progress of each nation against the key elements of the e-economy described above. The most effective government policies are those that address an accurately pinpointed weakness in that country, and for this reason there are no generalizations for success.

Governments should bear in mind the hierarchy of the NRI framework, and seek first to address weaknesses in environment, as the environment underpins success in readiness and use. Weaknesses can be addressed by, for example, promoting the spread of access devices, the integration of ICT in education, the availability of broadband infrastructure, and by ensuring competition in the telecommunications market.

Broadband rollout and penetration will remain key priorities. Broadband will not take off by itself, as no "killer application" exists (yet), and the economics of wiring nonurban areas will remain unattractive. Governments may consider investing in infrastructure in order to stimulate competition and to allow link up in remote areas.

Businesses should focus on value capture and alignment to reap the benefits of large ICT investments. e-Business is unlikely to deliver significant benefits without a wholesale transformation of underlying business processes. Technology, processes, and capabilities should all be aligned to business strategy and supply chain architecture.

Beside costs and availability, security and trust issues are becoming the main barriers for uptake of e-commerce and e-enabled government services. Security concerns are genuine and in part culturally determined, often linked to the prevailing payment systems. It is proving very hard to increase trust through national publicity campaigns. Governments can, and should, do more to fight cyber crime, push for stricter industrywide security standards, and invest in the research and development of security systems.

Successful and sustained e-government efforts require a dedicated central coordinating unit, preferably with influence over funding, to ensure consistency, drive, and interoperability, especially as back-office integration, common-look-and-feel, and KPI become policy priorities.

To successfully develop e-government services, governments must resist the temptation to take a current set of

services and rush headlong to put them online. Citizens are demonstrably ignoring such approaches. Effective e-government services start with a deep understanding of what citizens want, and using the availability of the online medium to catalyze a more fundamental and innovative rethink of the way in which services are delivered. Implementation starts with installing the right technology, tested through pilot projects selected on the basis of user demand (instead of ease of implementation). From these experiences, interdepartmental processes and protocols should be drawn up—including security standards and performance measurement systems—to allow seamless service offerings.

The benefits of the e-economy, so long anticipated, and so long in coming, are just beginning to arrive. Governments who accurately gauge the conditions and unique constraints of their countries, and who apply the lessons learned by the leading nations, are already beginning to make impressive progress. The best is still yet to come.

Endnotes

1. Research for this report was undertaken as part of a twenty-week project during summer 2002. Quantitative data were gathered from the latest available robust sources that offered data comparable between nine sample countries. This data collection was complemented by an international program of interviews with key policymakers for either e-economy or e-government policy in each of the nine sample countries.

Assessment of countries' level of progress was conducted through compilation of a detailed composite index covering the facets of the e-economy discussed in this article. More than 130 independent statistical indicators were used in compiling the indexes. Sources include those listed in the references.

More than 100 interviews were conducted with key policymakers throughout national and local governments in nine countries. We would like to thank all of those who took part in the interview process. The following departments/agencies participated.

Australia
National Office for the Information Economy (NOIE)
Attorney General's Office
Department for Communications, Information Technology and the Arts (DCITA)

Canada
Industry Canada (e-Commerce Branch, ICT Branch, Telecoms Policy Branch, e-Business Roundtable, Spectrum Information Technologies and Telecoms Branch)
Treasury Board (Chief Information Office Branch)

France
Mission pour l'Economie Numérique (Digital Economy Taskforce)
Direction générale de l'Industrie, des Technologies de l'Information et des Postes, General Direction for the Industry, IT and Postal Services (DIGITIP)
COPERNIC project team

Germany
Federal Ministry of Economics
Federal Ministry of the Interior
State Government of Bavaria

Italy
Ministry of Innovation and Technology
Authority for IT in the Public Administration (AIPA)
Ministry of Culture
Ministry for Education, University and Research (MIUR)
Ministry for Productive Activities
Ministry for the Health System

Japan
Cabinet Secretariat
Ministry of Education, Culture, Sports, Science, and Technology (MEXT)
Ministry of Public Management, Home Affairs, Posts and Telecommunications (MPHPT)
Ministry of Economy, Trade, and Industry (METI)

Sweden
Ministry of Industry, Employment and Communications
Swedish Alliance for Electronic Commerce
Telecoms and Post Regulator (PTS)
Confederation of Swedish Enterprise
Svekom (Swedish Association of Local Authorities)
Statskontoret (Swedish Agency for Public Management)
Ministry of Education and Science
Ministry of Justice
Nutek (Swedish Business Development Agency)
The City of Malmö

United Kingdom
Office of the e-Envoy (Cabinet Office)
Department of Trade and Industry
Office of National Statistics
Information Age Partnership
Office for Government Commerce
HM Treasury
Office of the Telecommunications Regulator (Oftel)
Department for Education and Skills (DfES)

United States of America
Office of Management and Budget
Department of Commerce
Federal Communications Commission
Council for Excellence in Government
Information Technology Association of America

References

Accenture. 2000–2002. Accenture e-government survey.

Cap Gemini Ernst & Young and the European Commission. 2001. *Web-based Survey on Electronic Public Services.* Online. http://www.cgey.com/eu-eservices/index.shtml.

Colecchia, A. and P. Schreyer. 2002. "ICT Investment and Economic Growth in the 1990s: Is the United States a Unique Case? A Comparative Study of Nine OECD Countries," *Review of Economic Dynamics* 5(2):408–442.

Committee on the Global Financial System (CGFS) and Bank for International Settlements (BIS). 2002. *IT Innovations and Financing Patterns: Implications for the Financial System.* Online. http://www.bis.org/publ/cgfs19.htm.

Compaq. Online. Websites for Australia, Canada, France, Germany, Italy, Sweden, Japan, the United Kingdom, and the United States.

Department of Trade and Industry (DTI). 2000, 2001. *Business in the Information Age: International Benchmarking Study.*

Department for Trade and Industry [DTI] International Benchmarking Survey 2001.

Deiss, R. 2002. *e-Commerce in Europe.* Online. http://europa.eu.int/comm/eurostat/Public/datashop/print-catalogue/EN?catalogue=Eurostat.

Dell. Online. Websites for Australia, Canada, France, Germany, Italy, Sweden, Japan, the United Kingdom, and the United States.

Eurobarometer. 2002. European Commission. Online http://europa.eu.int/comm/public_opinion/.

European Competitive Telecommunications Association (ECTA). 2002. *ECTA Scorecard.* Online. http://www.ectaportal.com.

Eurostat. 2001. *Information Society Statistics Pocketbook.* Online. Online. http://europa.eu.int/comm/eurostat/Public/datashop/print-catalogue/EN?catalogue=Eurostat.

European Information Technology Observatory (EITO). 2002. "The ICT Market in Europe." In *European Information Technology Observatory 2002*, 10th Edition. Part 1. Online. http://www.eito.com/tables.html.

International Labour Organisation (ILO). 2002. *Key Indicators of the Labour Market.* Online. http://www.ilo.org/public/english/employment/strat/kilm/.

International Telecommunication Union (ITU). Online. http://www.itu.org.

Keynote. Online. http://www.keynote.com.

Laafia, I. 2001. *How Much Do Governments Budget for R&D Activities?* Online. http://europa.eu.int/comm/eurostat/Public/datashop/print-catalogue/EN?catalogue=Eurostat.

Mulligan, M. 2001. *European Consumer Commerce Forecasts 2000–2006.* Jupiter MMXI.

National Office for the Information Economy (NOIE). 2001, 2002. *The Current State of Play: Australia and the Information Economy.* Online. http://www.noie.gov.au/projects/framework/progress/csop.htm.

Nielsen/ Netratings, Nordicom 2001.

Netcraft. 2001. TLD statistics. Online. http://www.netcraft.co.uk/survey.

Nuechterlein. J. D. 2001. International Venture Capital: The Role of Start-Up Financing in the United States, Europe, and Asia. In P. DeSouza, ed., *Economic Strategy and National Security.* Boulder, CO: Westview Press. Online. http://www.gvia.org/gvia_vc_outlook.doc.

Office of the e-Envoy and Analysys Limited. 2001–2002. *International Broadband Market Comparisons*.

Office of Telecommunications (Oftel). 2001–2002. Broadband Briefings.

Online Point Topic. 2000–2002. *DSL Worldwide Directory*, 3rd, 4th, and 5th editions. Online. http://www.pointtopic.com.

Organisation for Economic Co-operation and Development (OECD). 2001. *Education at a Glance: OECD Indicators*. Paris: Organisation for Economic Co-operation and Development.

Organisation for Economic Co-operation and Development (OECD). 2000. *Measuring the ICT Sector*. Organisation for Economic Co-operation and Development.

Organisation for Economic Co-operation and Development (OECD). 2001. *OECD Communications Outlook*. Organisation for Economic Co-operation and Development.

Organisation for Economic Co-operation and Development (OECD). 2001. *STI Scoreboard*.

World Markets Research Centre and Brown University. 2001. *Global e-Government Survey*. Online. http://www.respondanet.com/english/financial_mgmt/reports/Globalegovsurvey.pdf.

Chapter 11

Born Global:

The Impact of the WTO Process on China's ICT Competitiveness

Bruno Lanvin, Pamela C. M. Mar,
Christine Zhen-Wei Qiang, and
Frank-Jürgen Richter[1]

Introduction

On December 11, 2001, after fifteen years of negotiations, China became the 143rd member of the World Trade Organization (WTO). China's entry into the WTO will undoubtedly accelerate previous trends and diminish obstacles on the country's road to integration in the global information economy. But its entry will also contribute to the emergence of new conflicts, both internal (among sectors and priorities) and external (regarding "philosophical" or cultural issues, in particular). It is also likely that the implementation of WTO commitments will be accompanied by a strengthening, rather than by a diminution, of governmental involvement in technology; this especially concerns flows of information, development and transfer of technological know-how, and investment.

China has already begun to carve a distinct and new way of complying with WTO obligations. This may in turn feed new ways of thinking and operating within the WTO universe. In this interactive process it is likely that, among developing countries and economies in transition, China will be increasingly regarded as the intellectual and political leader of a progressive trend to strengthen the development and supportive aspects of trade liberalization and globalization.

The coming years will accentuate the importance and urgency of fundamental economic and social issues. For example, will China be able to move away from labor cost-based competitiveness? And will the WTO implementation process provide enough fresh opportunities to offset the negative effects on employment and social cohesion in certain key sectors?

Of all the sectors, the information and communication technology (ICT) sector is perhaps the one that will be most visibly transformed by these trends, and thus it offers excellent ground for viewing China's accession to a more important role on the global economic stage.

A Global Player

Because of the size of its domestic market, labor-cost advantage, and deep labor markets, China has rapidly emerged as a global player in the ICT field. This is true on both the supply and demand side of the ICT equation.

China's rise in the global ICT supply chain

China has become one of the world's most competitive sites for manufacturing numerous ICT products, from simple electronics and personal computers (PCs), to high-end mobile telephones and semiconductors wafers. Its rise has been driven by the confluence of a number of global and domestic trends, including (1) the commoditization of technology products; (2) the creation of transferable manufacturing lines; and (3) China's own economic liberalization and opening, which enabled these trends to touch the mainland. As competition in those markets has increased, China's ability to compete on price, which is attributable to its deep labor markets, is lending it a clear advantage. High-tech products, which are manufactured mostly in and around coastal and southern cities in Jiangsu, Fujian, Shanghai, Guangdong, Tianjin, Qingdao and now, Beijing, comprise one of the fastest-growing sources of exports for China. Exports of high-tech products grew from US$7.6 billion in 1996, to more than US$37 billion in 2000 (United Nations Conference on Trade and Development [UNCTAD] 2002:161–162). At the same time, large cities of the hinterland, such as Chonqing, clearly the most dynamic city in the western provinces, have started to develop and implement ambitious ICT-related plans.[2]

In their search for lower-priced manufacturing sites, companies initially based in Japan or Taiwan helped to fuel the upscale and shift of Asia's technology and electronics supply chain to mainland China. In Dongguan city in Guangdong Province, more than 95 percent of computer parts are available locally and, with more than 2,800 companies focusing on computer and information technology (IT) products, including 800 from Taiwan investors, the city and its environs are currently the world's largest processing and export base for computer parts (ChinaOnline 2000a). Over the last five years, much of Taiwan's IT and electronics manufacturing has gradually shifted to mainland China, where more than 56 percent of Taiwan's motherboards, 88 percent of the its scanners, and 58 percent of its monitors are now manufactured (ChinaOnline 2000b). Another example is Toshiba, which has closed all of its television production lines in Japan and instead produces in China. Up to half of the US$1 trillion of manufacturing value in Japan has moved to mainland China in the past decade (Chan 2002).

An emerging global site for research and development

China has also slowly become a key global site for research and development (R&D) for global ICT companies. In 1997, only 13 percent of foreign-invested firms were applying their most advanced technology to their Chinese businesses; by 2001 this figure had increased to 41 percent (Lim 2002). Currently, about 100 centers for R&D have been established in China by global giants such as Motorola, General Electric, JVC, Microsoft, Oracle, Ericsson, Nokia, Panasonic, and Mitsubishi. Motorola, for example, has more than 650 research personnel and more than US$200 million invested in a research center in China. Microsoft has committed more than US$130 million to a research joint venture and to setting up one of its five global research centers in Shanghai (UNCTAD 2002:166). In 2002, Oracle unveiled a new

software research facility in Shenzhen. This phenomenon of establishing is accompanied by China's own investment in the ICT sector, the largest in the Asia-Pacific region as a percentage of gross domestic product (GDP).

A new pole of demand for ICT products and services

The sharp downturn in ICT product demand in the United States and Europe and sustained high levels of growth of ICT on the mainland have meant that much of the current foreign direct investment (FDI) has been for local consumption. China is already the world's largest market for both fixed line telephones and mobile telephones.[3] In mid-2002, there were between 45 and 55 million Internet users in China. Although different organizations have produced different estimates, China is widely acknowledged to house one of the world's largest Internet-user market in the world, second only to the United States. Impressive as this may appear, this represents a rate of connection of only 3.6 percent of a population of 1.3 billion people, which is one of the lowest rates in the world.

Considering the rates at which China has been able to adopt new technologies in the recent past (see Figure 1), one can reasonably assume that the number of users will grow rapidly. Indeed, some analysts point to the current growth rate of Internet penetration in China (4 to 5 percent per month), anticipating that 25 percent of the Chinese population could be connected by 2005.[4] This would mean more than 300 million people could be connected—more than twice the present Internet population worldwide.

Figure 1. **ICT Penetration in China, 1982–2002**

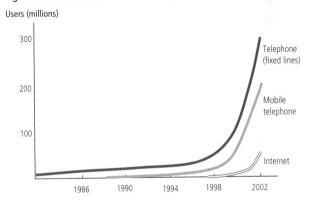

In 2002, Chinese consumers are expected to buy more than 10 million PCs, or one in thirteen Intel microprocessors (Sheff 2002). China is also a major importer of computer chips—domestic demand for semiconductors was forecast at US$270 million for 2002.[5]

Clearly, the trend that foresees China as perhaps the most significant emerging player in global ICT markets is unlikely to be reversed. However, leadership transition and the demands of the WTO implementation process will have a significant impact on the pace and nature of its growth.

Towards Full WTO Membership: Impact on ICT Competitiveness

The fifteen years of complex negotiations that eventually led to China's accession to the WTO have raised important policy issues, and many of the choices made to address these issues will have heavy implications for China's ICT competitiveness.

Milestones before WTO accession

Joining the WTO clearly provides China with an opportunity to further accelerate the changes needed to modernize its economy. First and foremost, the opening of numerous sectors across the economy will push forward reform in state enterprises and the rationalization of sectors in terms of capacity, production technologies, and delivery systems. Companies or sectors that have been reluctant to change, or found change politically difficult, will now have an iron deadline for reform. By the same token, there is widespread acknowledgement that although the WTO membership will bring long-term benefits, it will also require many short-term sacrifices from a number of social sectors. Government officials who would otherwise find their agenda jeopardized by the implied sacrifices of politically difficult or sensitive reforms could use the idea of WTO membership to justify these reforms.

In the ICT sector, WTO accession is being felt most significantly in the sector's regulatory framework. In the mid-1990s, even before the accession to the WTO was sealed, China had already begun the process of revising the regulatory regime and clarifying industry structures so as to be consistent with WTO commitments. More than 2,300 existing laws and regulations have been examined, and sometimes revised or invalidated, and additional statutes on foreign investment, intellectual property, and other on previously sparsely-regulated areas, have been implemented. Figure 2 illustrates a number of milestones in the ICT sector that the Chinese government has passed since 1997, on the road to WTO accession (1997 is the year of the WTO Basic Telecommunications Agreement [BTA]).

The following four elements prepared the ground for China's WTO accession as well as for its WTO commitments implementation:

1. The Ministry of Information Industry (MII)'s declared objective of dividing China Telecom into four separate operational entities; this was intended to create a competitive telecommunication services market. The restructuring of the telecommunications sector therefore reaches far beyond the dissolution of China Telecom.

2. China's Software Policy (adopted in June 2000), to ensure growth in its software and service industry. The policy, coupled with tax incentives and investment and funding policies, is strongly focused on setting up high-tech

Figure 2. **Timeline of Key ICT Policy Events Before China's WTO Accession**

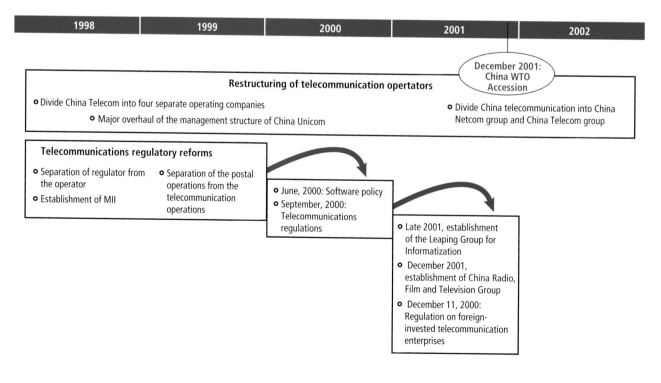

zones and on enhancing the competitiveness of domestic firms in software markets.

3. New Telecommunications Regulations.

4. The Regulation on Foreign-invested Enterprises, signed by Premier Zhu Rongji as chairman of the recently formed State Council Commission for Information Industries, which is a policymaking body set up to coordinate the development of the national information infrastructure.[6]

In the "pre-Doha" years, the government's "Golden projects" also played a major role in developing information networks. Initially (i.e., in 1993), these projects were comprised of three elements: Golden Bridge (National Public Information Communication Network), Golden Card (Electronic Payment Project), and Golden Gate (Foreign Trade Information Network). Since then, a series of other programs[7] have emerged. While the agenda of the initial projects was the rollout of information networks, these later projects have generally involved applications that use the information infrastructure (Qiang 2001).

In addition to these programs, local and national governments have provided assistance through preferential policies towards companies choosing to establish in high-tech and science parks. Beijing has been the most forthright in promoting itself as China's Silicon Valley through the development of Zhongguancun, which is close to top schools Peking University and Tsinghua University. A negligible presence three years ago, Beijing currently holds one-third of the national software industry production; this change in position is mostly because ten leading software companies are located in that city. Zhongguancun also houses a number of small and medium-sized software companies, which make up the vast majority of the 600 certified software companies in the city. Moreover, the city has committed to investing US$1.2 million to further promote itself in the international software community (ChinaOnline 2001). It has also established preferential conditions for overseas students to encourage them to return to the area and establish businesses.

Impact on China's ICT competitiveness

As Figure 3 shows, the impact of China's WTO accession on the country's ICT competitiveness is being felt through several key channels: the reform of the ICT-regulatory regime and operating environment, the creation of a framework to access capital, and the adoption of advanced technology in both the ICT sector and other areas of the economy.

Before China's accession to the WTO, the pressure from "entry requirements" played a direct and catalytic role in encouraging China's government to restructure the

country's ICT regulatory regime and industry.[8] The lengthy negotiations and the threat of foreign competition have thrown the country into a market mode, and paved the transition to a competitive ICT market. Sources of investment are changing, resource-planning management is undergoing radical changes as the industry restructures, and tariff policies have shifted away from transfer pricing and closer to cost-based pricing. As a result, the growth of China's ICT infrastructure has been more than three times faster than its growth in GDP. China is now the second largest fixed line and mobile telephone market in the world, just behind the United States, and it is the largest pager market in the world. Given current trends, China will soon become the largest telecommunications market in the world (at least for traditional voice services).

The establishment of the State Council Informatization Office clearly demonstrates that the Chinese government is now ready and eager to promote the development of ICT as a matter of strategic priority. Along with government-supported application projects, the internal operations of governments and the government's interface with the public can be strengthened.

The exact terms of the relevant WTO agreements (see Box 1) provide an external framework for sector reform and access to foreign capital markets, and they constitute a launching pad for a new wave of regulatory reforms that will underpin the next phase of the sector's competitive expansion. Improved market access and further tariff reductions will facilitate the import of advanced technology and equipment and help upgrade China's basic manufacturing capabilities and competitiveness. It will also provide an officially-sanctioned conduit for acquiring foreign technical expertise and management, an area in which China lags far behind its Asian peers. Equally important, the Chinese manufacturing sector can look forward to leveraging its low-cost base and manufacturing efficiencies in order to reach ICT global markets, particularly as the next generation of wireless and Internet product lines emerges. WTO entry will have an even greater impact in the adoption of technology into the services industries, which have, until now, been highly regulated, restricted, and fragmented, with little integration of technology. Boxes 2 and 3 provide more detail on two of those service industries: financial services and manufacturing supply chain integration.

Adhering To and Enforcing WTO Commitments: The Challenges Ahead

Although there is a consensus that China's WTO accession will have positive impacts on the importance of China's market and businesses at large, many have questioned China's compliance (see Table 1). China, like most other nations that signed the WTO agreement, expects obvious

Figure 3. Impact of the WTO Process on China's ICT Competitiveness

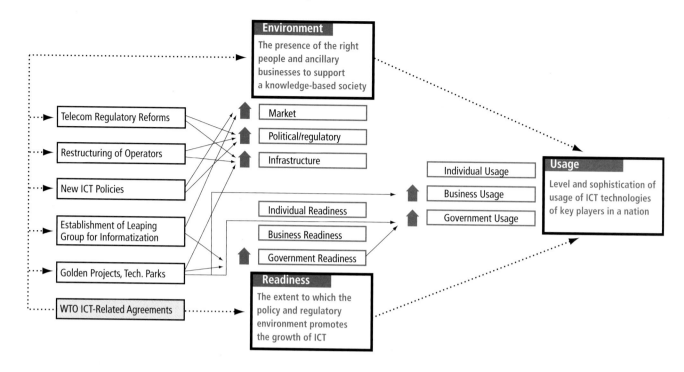

Box 1. China's ICT-related WTO Commitments

Telecommunications

1. China has conformed to the WTO's BTA and has agreed to adopt regulatory reforms in many areas. Reforms include the establishment of an independent regulatory authority and competitive safeguards, the introduction of cost-based pricing principles and technology-neutral scheduling,[9] and changes in the allocation and use of scarce resources and in rights of interconnection for different carriers.

2. Foreign equity and participation in the telecommunication sector[10]—foreign suppliers may use whatever technology they choose to provide telecommunication services.

3. China has agreed to remove quotas and other quantitative restrictions on the supply of telecommunications equipment. Quotas will be mostly phased out by 2002, and abolished by 2005.

Information Technology

4. China has agreed to participate in the Information Technology Agreement (ITA) and will eliminate all import tariffs on IT products (telecommunications equipment, computers, microprocessors, and Internet-related equipment). Starting from an average of 13.3 percent, reductions will be made in equal annual increments to reach 0 percent in 2005.

5. China's WTO agreements also entail the removal of restrictions on trading rights, such as the right of foreign companies to import, export, or distribute in China without going through middlemen or local partners. This measure will open up wholesale and retail businesses, and maintenance, repair, and other distribution activities related to direct foreign participation. Trading rights will be phased in over a three-year period.

6. Foreign companies will be able to compete in the provision of professional services in the computer and related service industries. China has also agreed to eliminate foreign exchange balancing requirements, local content obligations, and technology-transfer agreements in accordance with WTO agreements on the protection of intellectual property rights and trade-related investments.

In General

7. Fair competition—China will have to apply the same standards on taxes (such as value-added tax or tax deductions) to all firms, regardless of their origin (domestic or foreign).

8. Autonomous management strategy—China has pledged to respect the WTO rules in the area of Trade-related Investment Measures (TRIMs).

gains, such as increased efficiency, availability of a wider range of better-quality services, greater opportunities for the rapid introduction of new technologies and, most important, lower costs for consumers. These gains would translate into significant benefits for the Chinese economy as a whole; joining the WTO is seen as a catalyst, bringing such gains within reach in a shorter amount of time than would have been possible without accession.

In order to successfully advance their strategy to cultivate a "knowledge-based economy" that will fuel China's economic growth and trade, Chinese government officials will need to carefully consider the economic opportunity costs of and the policy challenges associated with developing the ICT sector. Likewise, the Chinese business community will also have its own series of trade-offs as it seeks to upgrade to face foreign competition, meet competing investment needs, satisfy various interest groups, and define core competitiveness. Overall, the question for China is how they can balance the need to strengthen ICT and industrial competitiveness while rigorously implementing WTO agreements.

Trade-offs

In adhering to its commitments as a WTO member, China will face difficult choices in at least five areas: foreign investment, content control, intellectual property, innovation, and competition. Analysis of these trade-offs grants an understanding both of the competing interests that government must balance in implementing WTO commitments and of the new competitive demands on business.

Ownership control versus foreign direct investment

In the area of FDI, the Chinese government is in a dilemma. On one hand, the government favors well-financed competitive telecommunications and IT markets; on the other hand, it intends to secure its control over the ICT sector. For centuries, China had a tradition of mistrust for and minimal contact with foreigners; then the country suffered a century and a half of mistreatment and subjugation by Western powers. The combination of these two periods could be expected to reinforce isolationist tendencies, yet modern China's growth is driven by foreign technology and investment, and its economic growth is highly dependent on exports. China routinely trades access to its market for foreign technology and investment while guarding its sovereignty and autonomy with a ferocious zeal. In strategic sectors such as ICT, the task of China's leadership is to simultaneously attract foreigners and hold them at bay.

There is also a worry in China that national security might be compromised by FDI. In some quarters it is thought that foreign ownership of telecommunications facilities

might enable state secrets to be leaked easily, and that telecommunications infrastructure might be out of national control during a state emergency, such as in a time of war (Wang 2001). The latest evidence of such concerns is the newly announced Regulation on Security Control over Computer System and Internet that forbids organizations from purchasing security-protection software from foreign vendors (Xu 2000).

China is now formally a member of the WTO. For the Chinese government, the challenge is no longer how to block FDI, but how to exploit the full benefits of FDI while maintaining a "forbidden zone" in which FDI is not allowed. WTO also provides Chinese operators with an opportunity to penetrate foreign markets. The state ownership of Chinese operators could place them in a vulnerable bargaining position, as was demonstrated by the merger negotiation between Singtel and Cable & Wireless HKT in 2000.[11]

Content control versus knowledge sharing (business opportunities)

The Chinese government is challenged by the conflicting goals of maintaining control over information entering and leaving China on one hand, and fostering the commercial potential of the Internet on the other hand (Perritt and Clarke 1998:407). It appears that the desire to foster greater technological development and expertise in China will be of such overriding priority that the government is willing to accept the challenges associated with regulating, and thus restricting, Internet access. Furthermore, the continued explosion of Internet access in China, combined with increased trade and electronic commerce[12] with foreign companies, will further challenge the ability of the Chinese government to control access to what it may consider objectionable content on the Internet.

Although Chinese individuals and businesses can access information on ChinaNet via the China World Web—a vehicle for electronic content meant to provide limited global Internet access and international business information to China—most Chinese people cannot access the global Internet due to regulations and firewalls imposed by the Ministry of Information Industry that block viewing of selected material and Internet sites. Currently, the Chinese government is using state control,[13] encryption,[14] Internet policing,[15] and news monitoring[16] to control much of the content that comes into the country and to decode and monitor Internet content and traffic. However, as the numbers of Internet users and websites continue to grow, the Chinese government will find it increasingly difficult (including financially and technologically) to censor material on the Internet.

Table 1. Foreign Businesses' Views About China's WTO Membership

	December 1998 Survey of US Businesses in China[17]	May 2000 Department of Commerce Survey[18]	2001 ACC Annual Membership Survey[19]	October 2001 Deloitte-Touche Tomatsu Survey[20]
Effects of China's WTO Membership	N/A	N/A	More than 75% expected China's WTO entry to have a positive impacts on their companies.	Importance of the Chinese market will increase (90%). Expect to expand existing business (65%).
Challenges of Doing Business in China	Problems with transparency (2/3); cost of doing business, customs procedures, foreign exchange volatility (more than 1/2).	Expected difficulties with corruption, transparency in practices, and in regulations (1/2).	Transparency, bureaucracy, weak enforcement of laws, business scope restrictions and protectionism (at least 2/3).	Increased competition from foreign competitors (2/3); fraud, piracy, political upheaval and foreign exchange volatility (1/3)
Potential Compliance Problems	N/A	Feared retaliation if they reported WTO compliance problems (1/2). Concerned about China's ability to develop a WTO-compliant legal framework and enforce the obligations consistently (70%).	Concerned about China's WTO agreement being ignored, new regulations to counter WTO commitments (75%).	Implementation of WTO commitments (90%), regulatory environment was the concern for most respondents.
Profitability	Already profitable (60%).	N/A	About 50% reported that their operating margins had improved while 25% had deteriorated from 2000 to 2001.	About 50% expected their investments to be profitable in less than three years while 33% in 3–4 years.
Familiarity with China's WTO Commitments	N/A	Reported they did not understand WTO obligations for their sector (66%).	N/A	Had great deal of familiarity (10%); had a certain amount of familiarity (64%).

Summarized by the authors from GAO (September 2002)

The Chinese government has to think in terms of being internationally competitive in business. Chinese businesspeople need to know as much as their foreign rivals in order to compete; therefore, they need the outside information, but this information may become almost inaccessible in China if the government bans too many outside sites.

The public good versus the intellectual property regime

Institutionally, China's entry into the WTO will also mean agreeing to be monitored and reviewed by the TRIPS (trade-related aspects of intellectual property rights) council and accepting the TRIPS dispute settlement mechanisms. The WTO gives developing countries a transition period of five years to enable them to adhere to all TRIPS requirements. China has been quite eager to embrace intellectual property regime (IPR) reforms in the last decade. Starting from a situation of near total absence, China has adopted laws covering patents, trademarks, integrated circuits, plant varieties, unfair competition, and copyrights. China has joined nearly all major international IPR conventions, and

is a member of international procedural treaties on the classification of patents and trademarks and the patenting of microorganisms. The country has also made considerable progress in establishing education and training programs in IPRs and in upgrading its administrative and legal enforcement systems in that area (Maskus 2000).

There are serious economic trade-offs involved in an IPR; these trade-offs arise from externalities and consequent market failures. Intellectual property is based on knowledge and information, and therefore has characteristics akin to those of public goods. Their efficient use requires wide access to all users at marginal social cost. At the same time, dynamic efficiency requires that innovation be encouraged over time, and this calls for intellectual property protection.

Many other problems remain, particularly from the point of view of outsiders who observe massive product counterfeiting and who doubt the effectiveness of enforcement mechanisms (LaCroix and Eby-Konan 1998). There seems to be a commercial reluctance in China to place monetary value on ideas and knowledge in its many forms, including software. It is understandable that placing value on intangibles, or services, is conceptually difficult to grasp in a society that has not previously worked in that mode, but until China develops substantially more domestic innovations that could make gains on global markets if they were patented and protected,[21] there will always be the temptation to pirate products. For this reason, the thorny problem of IPR is looming in China, and WTO membership is bound to exacerbate the potential for dispute.

Technology transfer versus innovation system

China's entry into the WTO can create a major opportunity for learning about technologies and for importing new technologies. The challenge is to learn quickly and develop domestic capability before costs become too high. Developing an interactive and sustainable innovation system with positive feedbacks will require the identification and development of strategic complementarities between capital expenditures, such as expenditures on R&D and human resources. Currently, the government estimates that more than 600,000 technicically skilled workers are needed annually, but it can only supply around 180,000 from all sources, including its own universities and technical institutes (ChinaOnline 2001). Therefore, upgrading education and training and rapidly developing ICT infrastructure have become urgent policy objectives for China.

Box 2. ICT and Financial Services in China

China's two leading state-owned banks, Bank of China (the most international) and ICBC (the largest in terms of assets) have accelerated technology integration internally and externally (through online banking for customers). In December 2001, the Industrial and Commercial Bank of China announced that trading on its electronic banking site had reached RMB 500 billion in the first eleven months of the year. This is minimal; as many as one-third of Internet users are still are not confident that online transactions will be secure.

A study by the People's Bank of China reveals that more than twenty banks offered Internet or telephone services to their customers. The level of uptake by customers of these services will only increase; this is one area of banking where Chinese banks can gain a lead over foreign competitors, who are thus far not allowed to compete in the online banking service market (Economist Intelligence Unit [EIU] 2002a). As it integrates technology into internal operations,[22] ICT is also enabling the Bank of China to increase its competitiveness. The effects of these moves on overall firm productivity remains to be seen, but if developed markets can be used as a guide, the impact will be significant.

Technology integration will also require a rational and innovative selection of those technologies (imported or developed indigenously) that best suit the local technological and economic context. The current lack of separation of R&D activities from production activities seriously hinders China's technological development. A critical element in China's efforts to build a sustainable innovation system will consist of the separation of pre-competitive support of innovation needs from the actual development and marketing of innovation-intensive products. In this area, clear guidelines and incentives for both state and nonstate enterprises will be necessary.

China is both a developing country and an economy in transition. Being a developing country means that, for some time, learning and imitation will be major sources of technological progress for China. The progression from an economy in transition with a command economy to that of an economy in transition with a market economy implies that the national innovation system is also being transformed. That is, the responsibility of carrying out technological learning process will shift from central research and design institutes to enterprises, and those very enterprises must adjust to a completely new environment.

The growing number of in-house R&D facilities run by overseas educated Chinese has helped to reverse China's brain drain so that now there is a brain "pull;" many of China's top students who studied abroad and stayed away to work are considering returning home.[23] Legend, early in its development, even took the unusual step of offering its employees stock options after listing a subsidiary in Hong Kong in 1994.

Another side of the problem of technology transfer lies in the tendency for attention to be focused on only the top tier of most competitive of domestic companies in considering the industry as a whole. For instance, in supporting indigenous technology development or facilitating the acquisition of foreign technology, the government may be tempted to focus on the larger companies which lead the market, while in fact most companies in the sector may be smaller companies. These smaller companies—which may be private or converted township and village enterprises— have foundered because their products do not match the quality of their urbanized or coastal cousins.[24]

Survival of the fittest versus social stability

China's accession to the WTO means not only more opportunities,[25] but also more competition. Now that the market is open, China's best enterprises have to compete with the best in the world, but China's enterprises can enhance their competitiveness and ensure their long-term survival through improved access to imported technology, materials, human resources, and services as well as by access to outside markets. The divide will not only be between Chinese and foreign companies, but also between companies that previously benefited from China's closed economy and those that suffered from it. The domestic level of awareness, acceptance and preparation is still low.

For smaller companies, an expanding market existing alongside new-found competition could be simultaneously beneficial and detrimental. Good products do not guarantee survival. Problems in accessing capital for growing technology companies are widespread. Foreigners come to China expecting to invest before making profits, and while large state-owned cousins have deeper pockets or access to state capital, many private or hybrid small- and medium-sized enterprises (SMEs) cannot secure bank loans because there is a bias against private companies. SMEs are thus neither able to expand their operation nor retain workers. In response to this funding problem, the government has pushed forward several programs specifically to ensure funding for growing ventures. While some have benefited from these programs, others—especially township and village enterprises—have foundered because their products do not match the quality of companies in urban or coastal areas. For many, survival depends on their relationships as subcontractors or service providers to multinationals or larger Chinese companies, on the high rate of China's economic expansion.

Undoubtedly there will be winners and losers. Technology has the potential to enable and catalyze the restructuring of China's old industrial enterprises, but in the short term, these dramatic changes will yield more jobless for local governments whose coffers cannot sustain the load. If social safety nets and re-skilling mechanisms are not in place, joblessness can in turn cause social instability and diminishing public confidence in the government, which could erode China's commitment to adhering to its trade obligations. Thus, mastering the art of transitioning unemployed laborers of the old economy into the age of technology will be a formidable challenge, which in scale alone will be unlike any attempted in other areas of the world.

Rule of law and enforcement of WTO commitments

A key concern about China's WTO accession has been the ability and willingness of the Chinese government to fully implement its WTO obligations. China's domestic problems—corruption, protectionism, unemployment, and inefficient state-owned enterprises and farms—could make it difficult for Beijing to comply with the WTO agreement. China's traditional legal system poses additional obstacles to the rule of law, especially problems of enforcement of civil court orders.

Starting around 1999, various bodies of the Chinese government have promulgated a series of laws and regulations on the Internet that appear hard to implement and are sometimes contradictory. There are several explanations for this situation. The separation between Internet control protocols, Internet service providers (ISPs), and e-commerce ventures is not always strict, making it difficult to ban only certain kinds of Internet activity. Moreover, the implementation of Internet regulations is often subject to competition between the MII, regulating ISPs, the State Bureau of Secrecy (which enforces the ban on transmitting "state secrets"), and the State Administration of Radio, Film and Television (which generally oversees content provision).[26] This reinforces the urgent need for Chinese authorities to jointly address and analyze Internet and telecommunications.

China's accession to the WTO requires that Chinese leadership accept greater transparency and accountability, as well as international norms that are essential to the proper implementation of the rule of law. Having accepted the legal structure and agreements endorsed by other WTO members, China now faces greater pressure to reform its own judicial and regulatory systems in order to make investors confident that they will receive fair and equal treatment in their business transactions with China. Among the international business community, some still fear that:

1. New invisible trade barriers could emerge to thwart market entrants;

2. There will be no indication anytime soon about what licenses or radio spectrum may be available for foreign-backed enterprises;

3. No date would be mentioned soon for the establishment of an independent regulatory authority and the implementation of the Telecommunications Law

4. Policy would remain unclear over the repatriation of proceeds by foreign investors;

5. Uncertainty over local employment regulations would linger;

6. Freshly detailed regulations could impose complex investment criteria;[27]

7. The influx of competition may create a price meltdown and thus diminish investor's anticipated margins, especially in the equipment sector.

For the business community, access to investment capital and the capital to acquire the most relevant technologies are critical to realizing the benefits of ICT—this applies to ICT companies and to companies in other sectors. The current capital-raising environment in China still presents many obstacles for the business community:

1. Stock listings take relatively long, and conditions for approval of listing are not always transparent;

2. Banks are under pressure to upgrade risk levels and may be wary of lending, especially to private or small and medium-sized firms;

3. Venture capital is still relatively underdeveloped because of the lack of exits, unclear shareholding rights, and the inability to gauge firm quality, among other reasons.[28]

The outside world is concerned that China will implement WTO protocols without having first established a clear set of regulations, procedures, and enforcement mechanisms. Against the prospect of a chaotic influx of foreign capital into dubious service ventures, heavy-handed intervention—which may have been acceptable in the past—will be open to scrutiny by the WTO courts. Any perceived increase in the level of uncertainty affecting China's regulatory environment would be likely to raise the level of investment risk and act as a brake on foreign capital inflows.

Multiple Roles of the Government and Building Blocks of Competitiveness for Businesses in the Post-Doha Era

In the field of ICT, as in many other areas, the Chinese government is expected to remain a central player for quite some time. WTO commitments should help combine this fact of life with imperatives that enhance enterprises' competitiveness.

Government roles, old and new

Now that China is a full member of the WTO, its decision makers will have to carefully try to seize opportunities while addressing significant challenges. In this complex game, the Chinese central government still holds many of the major cards of the post-Doha era. One of its main tasks will be to think and decide the extent and nature of its own role. Many major changes are currently called for in China, not only about ways of doing business, but also of thinking about business. This may prove to be a difficult, and even painful, process.

In China, the role of the state is bound to remain of central economic importance. However, the government's role can slowly be shifted from micromanagement to macrocontrol. By being vision provider, lawmaker and regulator, innovation promoter and coordinator, and an ICT leader (see Figure 4), the government can provide the predictable, accountable, and reliable environment that enterprises need to be able to make their own decisions and take their own risks.

Vision provider

Resource allocation. Matching the supply of resources to competing demands and estimating likely resource growth to fuel future development is a process of fundamental importance to the achievement of economic and social progress. The Chinese government needs to prioritize resource allocation for the country's information infrastructure. The development of ICT competes with other urgent needs on the government's budget agenda. Therefore, government officials should concentrate the country's limited resources into developing the basic facilities of the ICT industry.

Fighting digital divides. Growth by itself will alleviate some poverty; but for ICT to have a significant impact on the poor and low-income groups in China, policies will have to be developed for allowing these groups' access to ICT in such a way that their capabilities are rapidly enhanced. This is unlikely to happen simply as a by-product of joining the WTO. China remains committed to a national information infrastructure that includes among its goals access in the underserved central and western provinces[29] where most of the population reside. Therefore, a comprehensive approach that includes both growth and distributional objectives, in particular, policies for poverty alleviation that are also growth-promoting along with structural reform and technological modernization policies, seems to be the most reasonable course for the Chinese economy.

Education and training. The government needs to accelerate the education and training of qualified personnel for ICT development. China encourages educational universities to have R&D alliances with leading international companies and academia. In 2001 the top ten Chinese universities received more than US$200 million from the Ministry of Education for research projects.

Lawmaker/regulator

Establish rule of law. To solidify its membership in the WTO, China must first establish and promote the rule of law upon which all economic activities will depend; China must develop the required policies and regulations that fit its own political, economic, and cultural realities. Currently, there is no telecommunications law governing policy formulation, nor is there a consensus-based framework for guiding decisions. The lack of a codified law makes regulation often intractable, conflicted, complicated, and inconsistent. In addition, the absence creates a gray area; sometimes opportunities are increased, and sometimes risks. Without a sound institutional infrastructure, China cannot stimulate the formation of domestic companies and facilitate technology transfer and investment from foreign firms.

Figure 4. **Multiple Government Roles**

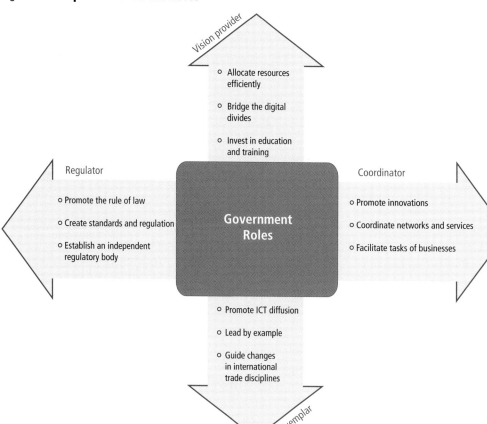

education. The long-term expectation is that China will have an innovation system in which enterprises play a critical role in close collaboration with universities, academic institutions, and nonprofit and government research institutions.

Coordinator. The government has a critical role to play in coordinating networks and information services and promoting healthy competition in order to increase efficiency and avoid waste. The poor performance of the former State Council's National Information Infrastructure Steering Committee between 1996 and 1998 cast

Modify legal framework. Entering the WTO provides China with a perfect opportunity and incentive to adjust its legal framework. China needs to change its traditional pattern of sporadic and ad hoc interventions into a transparent legal and regulatory framework. This could very well be the next revolution in China's economy. Clear signals about standards and regulations governing interconnection, commercial transactions, international technology transfer or adoption, and service benchmarks, as well as the creation of a truly independent regulatory body to oversee the ICT industries and convergence, would be welcomed by the international community. These steps are crucial for China to develop an environment of greater openness and transparency; such an environment would have a positive impact on investor and consumer confidence, and further stimulate economic development.

Innovation promoter and coordinator

Innovation promoter. A partnership between the state and the private sector is developing in China through financial, infrastructural, and other supporting relationships in the ICT sector. Both the government and the nonstate actors emphasize the fundamental importance of technological education. In the computer sector, many Chinese enterprises began with foreign-designed products and planned to ultimately produce their own designs; this type of strategy requires scientific knowledge and technical/higher

doubts on the effectiveness of this new group. To overcome these doubts, the new State Council Informatization Office will have to prove able to transcend competing individual interests among its members.

Facilitator. Government authorities (central and local) have a critical and leading role to play in facilitating enterprises' (Chinese and foreign) creation of wealth and jobs. Government leadership in providing fiscal incentives and the simplifying procedures is valuable in this area. Applying ICT to traditional public fields (e.g., through e-government) could enhance governmental efforts in that context.

Exemplar: ICT leader at home and internationally

The Chinese government has recognized IT as a potential thrust area, and plans to be a leading international player in this sector. In order for new technologies to be diffused in a society, however, they need to reach a critical mass. Some experts note that the critical mass is achieved when 10 percent to 20 percent of the population has adopted the innovation. In a society and economy dominated by government, as is China, the government can set the example for the country; it can promote the widespread diffusion of ICT applications, encourage ICT use at educational institutions, and improve information systems in government departments and industries. The government can demonstrate the benefits

Transport and logistics, as the key elements in supply chain integration, are undergoing drastic consolidation and technology upgrading because of increased competition from foreign entry (post-WTO accession). A difficult terrain, fragmented networks, and lack of competition have produced an inefficient industry that the government now recognizes is stunting the country's growth. WTO accession opens up the sector to limited foreign participation through joint ventures in logistics, distribution, and freight services, and to full competition by 2004.[30] Market growth will be 16 percent to 25 percent in the near term as manufacturers integrate their supply chains and hone their product distribution, largely through technology integration (EIU 2002b).

Currently, China spends 15 percent to 17 percent of GDP on logistics, compared to 10 percent for most developed markets (Atkinson 2002). Companies reportedly pay 40 percent to 50 percent more than they do in the United States to move basic manufactured products (Barling 2002). The role of technology in bringing China's logistics industry up to global standards is clear: customers are now demanding better tracking and a more integrated supply chain. Technology companies are anticipating the business to be had; Legend, for example, has already set up a joint venture with APL logistics (of the NOL group) to provide supply-chain services for the IT industry (Asia Pulse 2002).[31]

Clearly, the changing framework of the ICT industry has a major impact as a ripple effect throughout the economy as businesses gain access to capital and technology to upgrade productivity and efficiency. The government is aware of the huge impact that managing information effectively, reducing transaction costs, and upgrading productivity using technology, can have on performance and productivity; businesses and individuals have begun to grasp the scale of upgrading that is becoming possible.

The elements and examples discussed above show how the newly opened environment created by China's WTO membership is likely to allow ICT to radically transform key industries and services. In order for this process to take off, the country needs to build readiness and capacity among all stakeholders in the society to enable them to use, and benefit from, the new technologies. A key ingredient in this complex process will be the manner in which the Chinese authorities choose to implement their WTO obligations and address the challenges that will accompany such implementation.

---

of improving efficiency, reducing costs, and of transparency and openness, if its own operations are streamlined and technology-enabled. Public databases can be developed to further encourage the sharing of information between users. Efforts in e-government (e.g., in fiscal and customs matters) can have a strong exemplary value for businesses and individuals alike.

At the regional and international level, it is not unreasonable to think that China will have the potential to guide significant changes in how the international community evaluates international trade disciplines on one hand, and development on the other. The field of ICT could be a fertile ground for such progress, and China benefit from establishing itself as a political leader in that area.

Conclusion

After fifteen years of difficult negotiations to become a member of the WTO, China is now faced with the difficulties of implementing its WTO commitments. Opening the market and allowing deeper foreign participation in the economy will drastically increase competition across the economy and place new demands on Chinese corporations. WTO accession could provide the catalyst for China to become a center of innovation, content creation, and R&D, thereby enabling the country to progressively move away from purely labor cost-based competitiveness. Its success in the ICT field will be an essential element in the countries' ability to address other challenges, such as the predictable negative impact of WTO membership on sectors of low productivity such as agriculture, and the negative impact on public sector employment (especially in state-owned enterprises).

Moreover, the adoption of modern technologies in all sectors of the economy will be essential to enabling industries that are currently saddled with overcapacity, outdated technology, and low productivity (e.g., agriculture, the public sector, heavy industry) to upgrade and improve efficiency. The government will inevitably have a crucial role in ensuring that the ICT revolution and its dynamism are brought into "problem areas" and loss-making enterprises. Significant resources have already been committed to address the digital divide and to develop "ICT poles" in poorer and predominantly agricultural areas in the west and inland provinces.

The government will also continue to play a difficult but indispensable role in addressing the "trade-offs" of WTO full membership. For enterprises, both Chinese and foreign, this means that finding the areas in which business interests, competitiveness, and profitability can be developed in tandem with the Chinese governments longer-term objectives will be a key ingredient for survival and success on the Chinese market. Business will hence also have crucial roles to play and important responsibilities to exercise in contributing to the implementation of WTO commitments while nurturing the ICT competitiveness process. The "survival kit" proposed above (Box 4) could provide some guidance in that context.

> ### Box 4. A Survival Kit for Businesses
>
> Just as China's entry into the WTO has changed the regulatory and policy framework for ICT, it has also instigated a fundamental reshaping of industrial demand and of the factors of competitiveness for ICT companies. The new competitors and new market opportunities have created a new business environment, one with changing rules of competitiveness. To survive in a newly-opened market, companies, domestic and foreign, will need to redefine their core competencies while constantly assessing and responding to changing market circumstances, including the evolving regulatory framework. From an era where survival required size and a slight edge over domestic peers, competitiveness in today's and tomorrow's ICT markets is being redefined around the following key characteristics:
>
> 1. Awareness of WTO commitments and related laws and regulations
>
> 2. Access to capital and the most appropriate technologies
>
> 3. Adjustment to a management style that will lead and empower employees
>
> 4. Adaptation to consumer needs with innovation.

In many respects, the problems affecting China's ICT policies and strategies are not significantly different from those that the country is will encounter in other sectors. However, the rapid pace of technology development means that ICT issues are being addressed first or more urgently than problems in other sectors. Moreover, it is clear that the sector's development will be felt throughout the economy via the adoption of technology therefore, the government's decisions concerning ICT can also be seen as decisions on the course of the economy as a whole.

Thus far, it is clear that China's implementation of its WTO commitments is accelerating and increasing the importance of change, rather than slowing or de-accentuating it. If this trend continues in the ICT field, one may envision a situation in which China shapes global trade and the technology sector more than the world shapes China. On a broader level, this raises an even more fundamental question: will China change WTO and international trade more than WTO and international trade will change China?

Endnotes

1. Bruno Lanvin and Christine Qiang are respectively manager and economist in the World Bank's Department on Global Information and Telecommunications Technology (GICT); Pamela Mar and Frank-Jürgen Richter are respectively Senior Regional Manager for Asia and Director for Asia at the World Economic Forum. The views expressed here should be considered as the authors' personal opinions. They do not necessarily reflect those of the World Bank or the World Economic Forum. The authors gratefully acknowledge the contribution of Heini Shi, who provided useful comments on earlier drafts.

2. "In ten years, Chongqing will catch up to where Shanghai is today" (Vice-Mayor Huang Qifan, quoted in *Business Week* October 21, 2002). Chongqing is the centerpiece of China's "Go West" program, designed to boost development in the western provinces. Over the next ten years, the Chinese government is planning for investments of up to $200 billion in the Chongqing municipality. Investments in key industries (including IT) will be encouraged through a five-year tax exemption, followed by a permanent 15 percent permanent tax rate—this is less than half of the normal corporate tax rate of 33 percent. See Business Week (2002).

3. Tan and Ouyang (2002:9). There are more than 140 million mobile users and that number is forecast to increase to 210 million by 2004.

4. The composition of Internet users in China has evolved as rapidly as their number. In October 1997, only 500,000 Chinese individuals were Internet users; of these users, 80 percent were technicians or engineers and 88 percent were male. By mid-2002, of the 45 to 55 million Internet in China, the proportion of technicians and engineers has dropped below 20 percent, and women now constitute more than 40 percent of users.

5. Local supply capabilities were estimated at about 30 percent of that amount. See Yong (2002).

6. The Commission is served by the Office of Informatization, headed by Zeng Peiyan, head of the State Development Planning Commission, who is charged with implementing the policies of the Commission.

7. More than ten, such as Golden Sea (Leadership Information Network), Golden Tax (Computerized Tax Return and Invoice System Project), Golden Intelligence (China Education and Research Network), and Golden Health (National Health Information Network).

8. In an interesting paper that used a simple game theory model, Mueller and Lovelock (2000) analyzed the way four players (the Chinese government, MII/China Telecom, domestic rivals, and foreign strategic investors) interacted over access to foreign capital and technology. They concluded that China would not have opened up to foreign investment in telecommunications services without the need to bargain for WTO accession.

9. Technology-neutral scheduling precludes regulators from specifying which technologies operators should use to provide particular telecommunications services (contrary to what happened during the deliberations that held up the deployment of cdmaOne technology in China).

10. WTO Requirements and Timetable for Foreign Investment in China's Telecommunications Sector

Sector	Phase	Permitted percentage of foreign investment	Date	Geographic Scope
Value-added and paging services [a]	I	30	Upon accession	Beijing, Shanghai, Guangzhou
	II	49	One year after	Extended to 14 other cities
	III	50	After 3 years	Nationwide
Mobile voice and data services	I	25	One year after	Beijing, Shanghai, Guangzhou
	II	35	After 3 years	Extended to 14 other cities [b]
	III	49	After 5 years	Nationwide
Fixed service (including long-distance)	I	25	After 3 years	Beijing, Shanghai, Guangzhou
	II	35	After 5 years	Extended to 14 other cities
	III	49	After 6 years	Nationwide

a. This category includes electronic mail, voice mail, online information and database retrieval, electronic data interchange, enhanced value-added fax services, code and protocol conversion, data processing, and paging services.

b. The cities are: Chengdu, Chongqing, Dalian, Fuzhou, Hangzhou, Nanjing, Ningbo, Qingdao, Shenyang, Shenzhen, Xiamen, Xi'an, Taiyuan and Wuhan.

11. Singtel is the dominant telecommunications operator in Singapore, where the government indirectly holds 78 percent of its shares via its investment arm, Temasek Holdings. On January 25, 2000, Cable & Wireless announced that it was negotiating with Singtel about the possibility of merging into a single company. Hong Kong was alerted to this deal and the legislator, Chungkai Sin, pointed out that this merger might enable Singapore's government to intervene in Hong Kong's domestic telecommunications market and take over Hong Kong's position as information hub of Asia. Finally, a local Hong Kong company, Pacific Century CyberWorks, presented a counter-bid to take over Cable &. Wireless HKT. This case had not been without precedent. A few years earlier, when the mainly government-owned company Deutsche Telecom tried to take over Telecom Italia, it was a local company (Olivetti) that eventually succeeded in light of concerns that the national telecommunications system could be controlled by a foreign government. These experiences show that China may need to privatize its telecommunications system before it talks to foreign operators about mergers and alliances.

12. "Recent reports indicate that China's e-commerce transactions in 2000 totalled $9.33 billion which included $47.17 million in B2C transactions and $9.29 billion in B2B transactions" UNCTAD (2001:235).

13. In order to control the content coming in from outside the country, the Chinese government limits the number of organizations with access to the international gateways to only four state-controlled entities.

14. Last year, the Chinese government issued regulations by the newly formed State Encryption Management Commission that banned Chinese companies or individuals from using foreign encryption software. In doing so, the state is attempting to decode and monitor Internet traffic in China and thereby restrict transmissions that may be considered a threat to the government.

15. The State Secrecy Bureau promulgated regulations for computer systems on the Internet, which extended the ban on the publication of loosely-defined "state secrets" on the Internet, including e-mail, bulletin boards, chat rooms, and news groups.

16. New laws have been drafted in China to bar commercial websites from hiring their own reporters or from publishing "original" content. As a result, only news that has already been published by a state source (i.e., People's Daily, the official Communist mouthpiece, or Xinhua, the state news agency) is permitted.

17. Members of the Beijing American Chamber of Commerce (ACC) and U.S. companies identified by the U.S. and Foreign Commercial Service (FCS)

18. U.S. companies in China on the ACC and U.S.-China Business Council lists

19. Member companies of the Beijing ACC

20. Subscribers to CFO Asia, CFO US, and a China-specific newsletter; European executives surveyed in Europe.

21. Currently, product development (as opposed to basic research) is perhaps the weakest link in China's innovation system.

22. The Bank of China Hong Kong plans to invest around HKD 1.1 billion (US$141 million) into upgrading its IT infrastructure over the next two years (South China Morning Post 2002). The items to be upgraded include cooperation between departments, improving product processing, implementing a CRM function, and setting IT priorities for online services.

23. Over the past three years, Zhongguancun, China's "Silicon Valley," has attracted more than 3,500 returnees from abroad, and thus far more than 130,000 of approximately 400,000 overseas students have returned home (People's Daily Online 2002).

24. It is true that most township and village enterprises (TVEs) are engaged in low-end manufacturing, and even when uncompetitive, often have the protection of the local government to enable them to subsist until a buyer or solution can be found. However, as discussed below, among smaller companies in the IT field, good products do not guarantee survival. The days of rapid and bubble-like growth of China's manufacturing economy has produced an intricate, yet fragmented, network of competing and overlapping local concerns, which may be further overlaid by another web of ministerial departments, each vying for power and influence. Supported by provincial or regional-power networks, TVEs form the backbone of the economy outside the rich coastal areas. TVEs are ripe for restructuring and upgrading with ICT, yet face the most resistance from those who have vested interests. Enabling these TVEs to grasp technology will do much to upgrade their competitiveness and ensure their long-term survival and the survival of the rural economy.

25. In December 1999, the Development and Research Center of China State Council conducted a survey of Chinese IT-industry experts and officials on the impact of China's entry in the WTO on the country's IT industry. The results of the survey showed that 77 percent of industry experts and officials

canvassed believe that foreign investment is beneficial to the development of China's information industry in the long term.

26. Apparently irrelevant ministries often become involved in regulatory issues. For example, in March 2000, the Ministry of Culture issued the Notice Concerning Issues Related to Online Business Activities in Audio and Video Products, which barred foreign-invested enterprises that operate information networks from engaging in the online publication, rental, or sale of audio and video products. The same rules also banned all companies, Chinese or foreign-invested, from engaging in business involving the import of audio and video products or the downloading of any musical product from the Internet.

27. For example, there is no mention of management control in the newly published Provisions on the Administration of Foreign-Invested Telecommunications Enterprises. Online. http://www.tdctrade.com/report/reg/020603.htm.

28. Partnerships between domestic and foreign companies to obtain both capital and technology, has been one alternative. For example, TCL, which holds around 20 percent of China's television market share, has deepened its initial distribution partnership with Dutch company Philips, and is now considering an equity investment. Sumitomo and Toshiba have already become strategic investors in TCL, with a 2 percent share. Companies' ability to access, and adapt or enhance the latest technologies for domestic use is the key. As such, foreigners seeking local knowledge can meet their needs while satisfying a domestic company's need for capital.

29. Ongoing efforts to bring advanced telecommunications (including wireless, WiFi-type Internet connectivity) to the western provinces are evidence that this objective is a priority of both Chinese authorities and of multilateral institutions such as the World Bank.

30. Logistics is not part of the current (tenth) five-year plan, although distribution is a part of the plan. Numerous government officials have spoken out about the need to modernize and upgrade the logistics and distribution sector.

31. Legend has already signed with i2 Technologies to use their supply chain management software, and other state owned enterprises looking for the clearest way to boost efficiency in production are also seeking technology (Financial Times 2002).

References

Asia Pulse. 2002. "China's Legend to Set up JV with APL Logistics," Asia Pulse June 25, 2002.

Atkinson, H. 2002. "Opportunity Knocks: As China Develops in Logistics Sophistication, 3PLs Grow In Importance," Journal of Commerce January 7, 2002.

Barling, R. 2002. "Trade Firms Urge Faster Opening: New Industry Regulations Prompt Allegations of Added Bureaucracy in China Business," South China Morning Post April 23, 2002.

Business Week. 2002. "Wesward Ho ! Can Chongqing's $200 billion Upgrade Shift China's Center of Gravity?" Business Week October 21, 2002.

Chan, C. 2002. "Mainland Funds Inflow Biggest in Monthly Spurt," South China Morning Post September 14, 2002.

ChinaOnline. 2001. "Beijing Forms Software Alliance to Beef Up Industry," ChinaOnline December 21, 2001.

ChinaOnline. 2000a. "Southern China Becomes Global Manufacturing Centre for Computers," ChinaOnline Online. October 24, 2000.

ChinaOnline. 2000b. "Taiwan's IT Hardware Producers Rush to Mainland," ChinaOnline August 28, 2000.

Kanellos, M. 2002. A Legend in the Making. Online. http://news.com.com/2009–1001–948983.html.

Economist Intelligence Unit (EIU). 2002a. „Online Banking Begins, but Customers are Wary," Economist Intelligence Unit July 26, 2002.

Economist Intelligence Unit (EIU). 2002b. "Linking the Chain" EIU Viewswire August 23, 2002.

Financial Times. 2002. "IT: The Supply Chain. Formidable Hurdles Ahead," Financial Times July 19, 2002.

Jussawalla, M., and R. D. Taylor. 2000. "Is China Ready to Enter the WTO?" Presented at the International Telecommunications Society Thirteenth Biennial Conference, Buenos Aires, Argentina, July 2–5, 2000.

Khan, H. A. 2001. "China's Entry into the WTO: ICT Sectors, Innovation, Growth and Distribution." University of Denver/CIRJE, University of Tokyo. Working Paper No. CIRJE-F-157. Prepared for the Conference on China and the WTO, Vail, Co, May 25–27, 2001. Revised July 2002.

LaCroix, S. J. and D. Eby-Konan. 1998. Intellectual Property Rights in China: American Pressure and Chinese Resistance. University of Hawaii (mimeo, working paper).

Lim, V. "China Set to Strengthen Impressively in Technology Product Categories," New Straits Times (Malaysia) September 1, 2002.

Maskus, K. E. 2000. Intellectual Property Rights in the Global Economy. Washington DC: Institute for International Economics.

Mueller, M. and P. Lovelock. 2000. "The WTO and China's Ban on Foreign Investment in Telecommunication Services: A Game-theoretic Analysis," Telecommunications Policy 24(8–9):731–759.

National Association of Software and Service Companies (NASSCOM). 2002. "NASSCOM Reveals China IT Market Findings." Press release, April 17, 2002. National Association of Software and Service Companies.

People's Daily Online. 2002. "China Sees Tide of Returning Talents." People's Daily Online. Online. http://english.peopledaily.com.cn/200206/28/eng20020628_98732.shtml.

Perritt, H. H., Jr. and R. R. Clarke. 1998. "Chinese Economic Development, Rule of Law, and the Internet," Government Information Quarterly 15(4):393–418.

Qiang, C. Z. 2001. Building the Information Infrastructure. In C.J. Dahlman and J. E. Aubert, eds., China and the Knowledge Economy: Seizing the 21st Century. Washington, DC: World Bank.

Sheff, D. 2002. "Enter the Dragon," Wired August 2002.

South China Morning Post. 2002. "IT Needs Sharp Focus in Realm of Uncertainties," South China Morning Post July 25, 2002.

Tan, Z. T. and W. Ouyang. 2002. Global and National Factors Affecting e-Commerce Diffusion in China. Center for Research on Information Technology and Organizations (CRITO). University of California at Irvine. Online. http://www.crito.uci.edu/publications/pdf/GEC2_China.pdf.

United Nations Conference on Trade and Development (UNCTAD). 2001. e-Commerce and Development Report. Geneva: United Nations Conference on Trade and Development.

United Nations Conference on Trade and Development (UNCTAD). 2002. World Investment Report. Geneva: United Nations Conference on Trade and Development.

United States General Accounting Office (USGAO). 2002. „ WTO, Selected US Company Views about China's Membership." USGAO No. GAO-02-1056. Washington, DC: United States General Accounting Office.

Ure, J. "China's Telecommunications and IT: Planning and the WTO?" Working Paper. Online. http://www.trp.hku.hk/papers/2002/china_planning_wto.pdf.

Wang, H. 2001. Weak State, Strong Networks: the Institutional Dynamics of Foreign Direct Investment in China. New York: Oxford University Press.

Xu, Y. 2000. "Dancing with Wolves: Is Chinese Telecommunications Ready for the WTO?" Presented at the International Telecommunications Society Thirteenth Biennial Conference, Buenos Aires, Argentina, July 2–5, 2000.

Yong, Z. "Taiwan Firm to Build Chip Plant in Shanghai," Business Weekly (China Daily) September 3–9, 2002.

Zhang, B. 2000. "Promoting Liberalization and Regulatory Reforming: the Impacts of the WTO on China's Telecom Industry." Presented at the International Telecommunications Society Thirteenth Biennial Conference, Buenos Aires, Argentina, July 2–5, 2000.

Chapter 12

Influence of ICT on the Development of India's Competitiveness

Sukumar S.

Head, Corporate Planning, Infosys Technologies Ltd.

N.R. Narayana Murthy

Chairman of the Board and Chief Mentor,
Infosys Technologies Ltd.

Introduction

Information and communication technologies (ICT) have contributed tremendously to the progress of nations over the past couple of decades. Rapid technology evolution and innovative applications have contributed to the development of various sectors and subsectors in many countries. However, achievement of sustainable competitiveness for an economy as a whole depends on the reach of these technologies; the ability of ICT to bring large sections of the population onto the "network." This is especially relevant in the Indian context where unfulfilled basic development needs prevent a vast majority of the population from being a part of the knowledge society. Hence, the focus of this chapter will be not only on the technological progress achieved by specific sectors of the economy, but also on the extent to which the process of developing competitiveness has involved the population.

We start this chapter with a brief socioeconomic background of the country and then move on to discuss the current state of ICT readiness in terms of the existence of an enabling environment for its proliferation. The section that follows presents a sectoral analysis of ICT utilization that seeks to highlight the level of ICT usage and a few innovative applications in some of the specific sectors in the economy. Finally, we address the key challenges on the path of ICT expansion and possible ways to overcome these challenges.

The Broad Socioeconomic Context

Independent India (i.e., post-1947) adopted socialism as the dominant economic paradigm to guide its development. Government played a role in all major sectors of the economy, and stringent regulations made growth for the private sector cumbersome. Self-reliance[1] was the predominant theme of successive governments. The focus, therefore, was on import substitution rather than on developing global competitiveness. As a result of this, economic growth gradually slowed down to around 3 percent per annum by the 1960s, a rate hardly sufficient to sustain a population that was growing rapidly. With a bloated government sector, low per capita income and very little encouragement for entrepreneurship, priority development areas such as primary education, health care, and other basic services for citizens suffered significantly. It must, however, be mentioned that the foundation for a strong higher education system was put in place in the early years of independent India, and this system is now contributing to the economy's progress.

Since developing competitiveness was not a thrust area, trade deficit continued to creep up all the time. Gradually, export growth declined to a level where the foreign exchange earnings were not even sufficient to pay for essential imports.

This resulted in a serious balance of payments crisis in 1991 that required a bail-out package from the International Monetary Fund. This crisis was only a manifestation of the deep economic ills of the country that cried out for reform.

The year 1991 saw a new government coming to power under the leadership of P.V. Narasimha Rao. Having realized the grave need for deep structural reforms, he invited Dr. Manmohan Singh, a former chief of the Reserve Bank of India,[2] to take up far-reaching economic reforms as the finance minister of the country. Dr. Singh changed the economic philosophy drastically, from that of socialism to market economics. Over the following few years, the government took significant steps in terms of rationalizing and lowering tariff structures, reducing restrictions on private enterprise and competition, improving the velocity of decision-making in the government, ushering in current account convertibility, freeing-up capital markets, and privatizing public sector enterprises. The resultant impact on the growth of the economy is shown in Table 1.

Table 1. **Growth in GDP, 1950s to 1990s**

Decade	Real GDP Growth (Average per Annum in Percent)
1950s	3.7
1960s	3.1
1970s	3.9
1980s	5.5
1990s	6.7

Source: *India Development Report 2002*

An economy that was largely agrarian in the 1950s had, by the 1990s, moved gradually towards the industrial and the services sectors. The services sector, in particular, got a significant boost as a result of economic reforms, and the contribution of this sector to the economy has been growing rapidly since then.

Table 2. **Composition of the Economy (in Percent), 1971–2000**

Year	Agriculture	Manufacturing	Services	Other *
1971	44.5	16.1	28.4	11.0
1976	42.6	16.4	29.5	11.6
1981	38.3	17.8	31.0	13.0
1986	34.6	19.4	32.7	13.3
1991	30.9	21.1	33.8	14.1
1996	27.6	17.4	37.7	17.3
2000	25.2	17.1	40.5	17.2

* Other includes mining, construction, utilities, and transportation
Source: *India Development Report 2002*

Economic reforms have also had a positive effect on human development parameters such as literacy, health care, and poverty alleviation, as indicated in the Tables 3 and 4. However, even at these levels, there is clearly a substantial developmental need.

Table 3. **Movement of Select Human Development Indicators, 1961–2001**

Year	Literacy (in Percent)			Life expectancy (in Years)
	Males	Females	Total	
1961	40.4	15.4	28.3	
1971	46.0	22.0	34.5	45.6
1981	56.4	29.8	43.5	54.4
1991	64.1	39.3	52.2	55.9
2001	75.9	54.2	65.4	62.4

Source: *India Development Report 2002*

Table 4. **Poverty Levels (in Percent), 1973–1999**

Year	Poverty*		
	Rural	Urban	All India
1973	56.4	49.0	54.9
1978	53.1	45.2	51.3
1983	45.7	40.8	44.5
1988	39.1	38.2	38.9
1994	37.3	32.4	36.0
1999	27.1	23.6	26.1

Source: *Economic Survey 2000–2001*
* Poverty data is based on the government definition, which is the inability to purchase food to achieve a minimum consumption of 2,400 calories per day.

Around 70 percent of the country's population resides in rural areas. The means of livelihood for most of these people is related to agriculture in one way or another. Hence, even factors such as seasonality of crops have a significant impact on the living conditions of many of these people. In many of these areas, access to basic services, such as primary education and health care, is also poor.

While ICT can serve as a potential equalizer of the significant socioeconomic differences, until now it has only served to accentuate them. The main reasons for this are non-uniform access to ICT and differences in people's ability to derive benefits from ICT. Creation of an enabling environment for proliferation of ICT and its benefits is critical to resolving these issues. Significant steps are now being taken in this regard.

An Enabling Environment for ICT Expansion

Usage of ICT has been on the rise in recent years, especially in the urban centers of the country. Rural areas have not had the same exposure to these technologies, and hence, face the risk of being left behind. In order to enhance the reach of ICT to even rural areas, it is important to establish an enabling environment in the country. Critical factors of such an enabling environment include widespread availability of access devices such as telephones, personal computers (PCs), and mobile telephones, connectivity to the Internet through Internet service providers, ICT literacy among a significant portion of the population, and the availability of knowledge professionals in the economy.

Penetration of access devices and Internet connectivity

Access penetration has historically been quite low and non-uniform, although the situation is fast changing. The current state of ICT penetration is indicated in Table 5.

Table 5. **ICT Penetration Data**

PC Population	5.07 million
PC density (PCs per '000 population)	4.94
No. of Internet users	6.7 million
No. of Internet subscribers	1.1 million
No. of telephone lines	33.8 million
Teledensity (fixed lines per '000 population)	32
No. of mobile telephones	2 million

All figures are as of March 31, 2001
Source: National Association of Software and Service Companies (NASSCOM)[3] estimates

The reasons for this historically low penetration have been high cost of access devices and government regulation.

High hardware cost. Due to high tariff levels, the cost of PCs and other hardware in India is significantly higher than in the rest of the world. A PC in India costs around twenty-four months of average per capita income, as compared to China's four months and the United States' twelve days. Tariffs form about 30 to 40 percent of the basic cost of an assembled PC, thereby making it unaffordable to a significant portion of the population.

Regulation and centralization of communications development. The provision of basic telephone services, long distance telephony, and data communications services was the monopoly of government agencies until very recently. Private players were not allowed to provide these services, therefore the public sector enterprises had no incentive or imperative to extend the reach, enhance the quality, or reduce the cost of services delivered to customers.

History notwithstanding, the telecommunications sector is poised for a dramatic change. Most parts of the sector have already been deregulated, although some issues still remain to be resolved. Many domestic and international private players have started operations in the country, and in a brief period have demonstrated the difference to the consumer by providing higher quality services at drastically reduced prices.

The data communications sector, too, has experienced significant growth over the last three years with the bandwidth available tripling to reach 1.2 gbps (gigabits per second). This is, however, a far cry from international standards. Large projects are currently underway that would take the overall capacity to about 16 tbps (terrabits per second) by the end of 2003. This would bring the bandwidth capacity to international standards and lead to lower prices and higher quality of services.

The National Association of Software and Services Companies (NASSCOM) forecasts that by 2005, PC penetration will reach around fifteen per 1,000 people and the number of Internet subscribers will increase to 7.7 million (with a user base of around 50 million). While these estimates still seem quite low compared to international standards, lower Internet subscription and PC penetration rates may not affect access levels, given the development of a kiosk model in the country. While the telephone kiosk (Public Call Office) concept has gained popularity and penetrated deep into the rural areas, cyber cafes in urban centers and village information kiosks in rural areas are gradually enhancing the reach of ICT to a larger section of the population.

Although expansion of access penetration in terms of PCs and communication lines is expected to grow rapidly in the near future, high cost of ownership, alien language, and illiteracy may still prevent a large rural population from using ICT. It is in this context that inventions such as the Simputer and corDECT offer enormous potential to dramatically alter ICT usage. The concept and benefits offered by these innovative technologies are described in Box 1.

Availability of knowledge professionals

Availability of knowledge professionals is crucial for the development of ICT. Apart from enabling ICT penetration through the development of suitable adaptations of technology, it also acts as a critical ingredient for the development of the ICT industry itself. In India, especially, the IT industry has been a significant contributor to the nation's economy, and the demand for knowledge professionals from this industry has been substantial.

Box 1. **Innovative Technologies to Enhance ICT Penetration**

Simputer: The Simple Computer

Simputer was developed by scientists from the Indian Institute of Science in Bangalore and Encore, a software company. At US$200 each, Simputer offers computing facilities at a drastically lower cost compared to US$650 for a PC. Apart from the low cost, Simputer has many other advantages:

1. It is roughly the size of a hand-held electronic organizer, thereby making it really portable.

2. It can run on an AAA battery, thereby not relying on power connection, which, in rural India, is unreliable.

3. It uses IML (Information Mark-up Language) to convert English content (from the Internet) into many local languages.

4. It has a text-to-speech converter that reads out the content.

All these make the interface natural and easy to use, thereby ensuring that a first-time user is not intimidated by the technology but rather, is attracted to the exciting world of Internet. The most important aspect, however, is that illiteracy is no longer an impediment for the masses to derive benefits from ICT, given the Simputer's voice output.

Even at US$200, the price may be a little too high for rural folks. Hence, the simputer was made to be multi-user compatible. Smart cards help store personal information, thereby making the base equipment shareable with many people. Rural associations, village information kiosks, or schools can use this equipment to provide access to the people there.

The inventors say they would like to see this as a platform for further evolution to enhance coverage of the Internet to rural areas. In line with this philosophy, they are licensing the manufacture of these devices at a low fee and have also used open source software based on Linux to ensure further development of applications.

Simputer is currently going into commercial manufacture, and holds enormous promise to reduce the digital gap between the rich and the poor, the urban and the rural.

Voice and Internet Connectivity through corDECT

corDECT is an advanced, wireless access system developed by the TeNeT group of the Indian Institute of Technology Madras (IITM), Midas Communications (a company set up by the alumni of IITM) and Analog Devices Inc. in the United States. It provides a complete access solution with seamless integration of voice and Internet services. The investment in the equipment is as low as around US$45,000 and can serve about 1,000 customers in a radius of 10 to 25 km in rural areas.

This technology is now being used to provide low cost Internet access to village areas through support from the industry. One such instance of usage can be seen in the Nellikuppam village in Tamil Nadu, a southern state of the country. The access center located in this village is providing Internet connectivity to around fifty nearby villages. EID Parry, a southern Indian industrial conglomerate, is funding this program and has also created a portal that provides information to the farmers on farm practices, crop prices in and around the region, financing information, and personalized content such as the payment details of the company to the farmers.

corDECT is the only cost-effective WLL (Wireless in local loop) system in the world today that provides simultaneous high quality voice and 35 to 70 kbps Internet connectivity. As such, this technology offers enormous potential to help connect rural areas of the country at an affordable cost.

The country has one of the largest higher education systems in the world, with 237 universities, 58 deemed universities, and 12,600 colleges. Further, these numbers are continuously increasing with newer colleges emerging every year. The total output of engineers per year from the system is more than 200,000 (in various disciplines). A significant proportion of these engineers choose to take up ICT jobs (a large percentage of them in the software and service export sector). NASSCOM estimates that more than 520,000 people are currently employed in the Indian IT sector.

Even with such high volumes, it is estimated that the country could face a shortage of anywhere between 65,000 to 530,000 IT professionals by the year 2005, depending on market conditions. This shows the need for these institutions to grow even further to cater to the needs of the industry. Apart from the likely shortage, significant concerns in this sector are as follows:

1. *Enrollment.* It is estimated that enrollment in higher education is only around 6 percent. This indicates the potential for increase in the overall supply and quality of the talent pool entering the higher education sector.

One of the reasons for this low enrollment is the poor economic condition of students. Many families expect their sons and daughters to start contributing to the revenue of the family as soon as possible. Such a demand prevents these students from pursuing further studies. They also do not receive much support, from either the government or the university/college, in meeting their study expenses, and this also acts as a deterrent.

2. *Quality of education and research activities.* Poor remuneration and lack of infrastructure mean that most educational institutions are not able to attract or retain high-quality faculty members. This, in turn, has affected the quality of education delivered, the standing of the institutes, their ability to attract high-quality students, and industry interest.

3. *Funding.* Government spending on education is only 3.2 percent of the gross national product, and of this around 16 percent goes towards higher education. This level of spending is clearly not sufficient to enhance either the number of institutions or the quality of education offered. Further, private funding of higher education has slowed, leading to lack of quality infrastructure in most institutions.

Thus, while the number of engineers produced by the system is growing, there is significant scope for improvement in the quality of output. Notable exceptions to this have been some of the premiere institutions in the country, such as the Indian Institutes of Technology (IITs), Indian Institute of Science, and the Regional Engineering Colleges (RECs). The high quality of education delivered by these institutions has been recognized the world over, and the alumni of these institutions are shaping positive developments in various parts of the world today.

Given the extent of demand, IT companies have had to take graduates from many universities that are facing issues described earlier. Most of the large companies have developed their own training infrastructure in order to ensure that they continue to deliver high-quality services to their clients. Further, many private IT training institutes have also sprung up in recent years, offering IT-focused training for those desirous of enhancing their skills. Together, these have ensured that the quality of the knowledge professionals available in the country is among the best in the world.

ICT literacy

While availability of knowledge professionals ensures technology development, ICT literacy is critical to ensure that people can derive appropriate benefits from the technology revolution.

Availability of private ICT training institutes and peer pressure to develop these skills have led to the development of

ICT knowledge among many non-ICT professionals in urban areas. Further, most private schools in urban centers have their own ICT infrastructure and provide basic ICT literacy to their students. Some state governments have also initiated steps to link up various schools across the state in order to better transfer knowledge and improve the education of students. However, this effort is not uniform, and the levels of infrastructure and skilled trainers available vary vastly.

The situation in rural areas, on the other hand, is of significant concern. Many areas do not even have access to basic education, let alone ICT infrastructure. While many non-governmental organizations (NGOs) and private companies have been working in this sector to implement innovative methods of providing education, these efforts can at best supplement, and not be a substitute for, government efforts in ensuring total literacy. Inventions such as the Simputer and corDECT are expected to help raise awareness in rural areas, thereby creating a pull for developing ICT knowledge.

Sectoral Analysis of ICT Utilization

The Indian IT industry

The direct influence of ICT on the country's competitiveness can be seen in the success of the Indian IT industry. This sector has succeeded not only in achieving global competitiveness but also in raising awareness of the benefits of ICT within the country, thereby laying a platform for future growth.

As in the case of other industries, this sector too suffered from the restrictions of the pre-1991 regimes. In fact, there was a stage when the decisions of capacity and configuration of a computer to be installed by a company were decided by bureaucrats in Delhi, rather than by managers of the company.

Liberalization measures introduced from the year 1991 onwards, however, have allowed free access to capital, simplified import procedures, reduced duties and tariffs on hardware and software, allowed foreign investment in the sector, eased foreign exchange regulations and, most importantly, enabled easier availability of data communication facilities at reduced rates. Around the same time, the information technology revolution was fundamentally transforming the business landscape all around the world at a rapid pace, opening up the market potential for Indian IT companies.

Availability of high-quality, English-speaking, technically-trained personnel, as well as the low cost of operations, provided the sector with ingredients for success. Successive governments, too, recognized the potential of this industry and shaped policies to encourage its growth. With the factor conditions being positive and the government policies favorable, companies in this sector were free to innovate and leverage the market opportunity.

During the initial phase of the industry evolution, companies focused on providing only people with IT skills to their clients. This was called "body shopping." In such a paradigm, Indian IT companies would send people to the client's site and the responsibility for project management and for containing the associated project risks rested with the client's Information Systems department. The sole reason for clients to do business with Indian companies was the severe skills shortage in their own countries.

However, the economic reforms of 1991 provided easy and cost-effective access to computers, software, and data communication facilities. Thus, Indian IT companies had the opportunity to fundamentally transform their business model leveraging the power of India-based software development. By developing strong processes and methodologies to execute projects from India (offshore), they could offer a much better value proposition to their clients, leveraging the talent base and lower cost of operations in the country. The industry has thus been a demonstrator of true globalization of businesses—producing where it is most cost-effective to produce (in this case India) and selling where it is most profitable to sell (the developed world).

By developing high-quality processes, Indian IT companies were successful in allaying quality and reliability concerns of client organizations. The quality-focus of the Indian software companies can be seen in the fact that thirty-seven out of the fifty-plus companies in the world that have been accredited with CMM[4] Level 5 (highest level) certification are in India.

The industry has been continually evolving to meet the needs of the global market. Many companies have moved up the value chain and are now offering end-to-end solutions to clients, from high-end IT consulting services to maintenance and call center operations.

The Indian IT industry achieved revenues of over US$13.5 billion[5] for the year 2001–2002. The software and services exports sector, which constitutes the largest portion of this industry, has demonstrated a compounded annual growth rate (CAGR) of 48 percent over the past five years, to reach US$7.68 billion for the year 2001–2002. The Indian IT industry now contributes 2.87 percent of the country's GDP and more than 16 percent of its total exports. According to NASSCOM-McKinsey[6] projections, this industry is expected to grow at a CAGR of 38 percent, to reach US$77 billion by the year 2008. By that year it is also expected to employ more than 2 million people directly and create indirect employment for another 2 million. More importantly, the industry is expected to contribute around 20 percent of the country's anticipated GDP growth over the next six years.

Though the industry constitutes only a small portion of global IT spending, the trend towards offshoring[7] could, in the next few years, make it a dominant player in the global market. The recent economic turmoil has emphasized to companies world over that offshoring their IT requirements can help realize higher value for their IT dollars. Already, one in four global 1000 corporations outsource their IT requirements to India, and this number is expected to dramatically increase in the near future. A Merrill Lynch survey indicates that the proportion of IT spending outsourced to India could potentially increase from less than 5 percent to more than 15 percent in the next few years.

Buoyed by its success in the IT services sector, the industry is now gearing up to offer other IT-enabled services to its global clients. IT-enabled services covers a gamut of activities, from maintaining call centers at the lowest level to outsourcing the entire business process, as in claims processing, sales order processing, and accounting. The global demand for such services is expected to multiply in the next few years. The same advantages that helped the growth of India's IT industry are also expected to benefit the IT-enabled services sector. The NASSCOM–McKinsey study estimates that this sector will grow from the current estimate of US$1.5 billion to US$17 billion by 2008. The employment opportunities in this sector are expected to multiply tenfold, from the current 107,000 to more than 1.1 million in the next six years.

The success of the IT industry has also influenced the competitiveness of the country in other sectors as well, by

a. retaining talent within the country, which, otherwise, had been a serious concern;

b. providing a boost to the local economy by offering high-disposable-income jobs;

c. building confidence in the Indian industry, and thus encouraging businesses to aim for achieving global competitiveness;

d. enhancing the country's brand equity in the world; and

e. offering entrepreneurial opportunities on a global scale.

Non-IT sectors of the industry

The Indian industry has been going through a transition from a protected environment to a turbulent global market in the last decade. While global competition is eating into its margins, affecting capability to invest in IT, local conditions have made these investments even more difficult.

Total spending on IT in the Indian economy (including government spending) was 1.1 percent of GDP, compared to 5 percent in the United States. Reasons for this historically low level of spending have been the high level of regulation, lack of local applications, lack of economies of scale, and unfavorable economics (due to high tariffs).

1. *Regulation.* Studies have shown that the extent to which companies spend on ICT is inversely proportional to the extent of government regulation in the economy. This is mainly due to the fact that companies are exposed to more competition as regulation is reduced, which, in turn, forces them to spend on ICT to enhance competitiveness. As described earlier, until recently, the Indian industry was severely regulated, providing little incentive or imperative for companies to utilize ICT. As the Indian industry integrates with the world, the need for investing in ICT will be increasingly felt by companies and the level of spending is expected to increase in the years to come.

2. *Lack of local applications.* Given the global shortage of ICT skills, Indian IT services are in demand; companies in this sector are experiencing high price realizations for the services they offer. Most Indian IT companies have, therefore, concentrated on servicing the global market rather than the domestic market. Since these IT companies also attract the best talent, the availability of talent for developing local software applications is lower than desirable. As a result, the number and quality of local ICT applications have been inadequate. Thus, although the Indian industry has specific ICT needs, the lack of quality ICT applications has led to a reliance on global software products.

3. *Lack of economies of scale.* The Indian industry hasn't yet fully realized the power of economies of scale. Scale leads to higher efficiency, enables higher investment in ICT, and provides the flexibility to build global brand equity. A large proportion of Indian companies, however, are in the small- to medium-sized enterprise sector, preventing higher investment levels and competitiveness.

4. *Unfavorable economics.* The tariff structure in India results in high-priced hardware. Hence, the level of investment required to implement ICT effectively is much higher than in other countries. Further, Indian companies are forced to invest in global software products, which, while not satisfying their local needs completely, also cost much more than what a local product would have cost; these factors deter investments.

Recently, however, investments in ICT have been growing, especially in the services sector. For example, spending on ICT is rapidly growing in the banking and financial services sector, especially spending by private sector banks. Many ICT-enabled business models are also being used by some of the new companies in the services sector. As the domestic demand for IT products/services grows, firms focusing on the domestic market needs are likely to emerge thereby leading to a further development of this sector.

A case study of an innovative and effective use of ICT to enhance the competitiveness of the dairy industry and to provide benefits to the rural masses is briefly described in Box 2.

Box 2. Achieving Competitiveness Through Effective Use of IT in the Dairy Industry

The National Dairy Development Board, a government agency, started the milk cooperative movement in India to enhance India's milk production and market its produce more effectively. This movement has led to a tremendous increase in milk production and has, in fact, made India the largest producer of milk in the world.

Around 2,500 of these cooperatives, which impact more than half a million people, have an ICT-enabled milk collection center. These computerized milk collection centers provide an effective interface with the producers and also act as information kiosks providing other information services to its members.

Each member is provided with an electronic card for identification purposes. While visiting the kiosk, the member is expected to punch in the card, deposit the milk (which is then weighed and the fat content checked electronically) and collect the payment (automatically determined and displayed by the computer based on the weight and fat content). This process ensures transparency to the farmer and shorter processing times. The equipment used for checking the fat content of the milk is a local adaptation of a Danish product. The local adaptation is made more rugged and much cheaper (US$500 as against US$4,000 for the original Danish product).

A new software application has now been developed by the Indian Institute of Management Ahmedabad, which not only caters to local transactional needs, but also connects the local cooperative to a dairy portal. This helps collect critical aggregated information and provide decision support, such as forecasting of milk production.

Information on epidemics affecting cattle as well as vaccination schedules and the like, is also made available to the farmers through the dairy portal. Other services, such as placing orders for products, information about services delivered by the cooperative, information on agricultural tools and techniques, and best practices in cattle farming, are made available to the members.

Utilization of ICT has speeded up the process of milk collection, delivered a transparent mechanism of payments, and provided value-added information services. Above all, the key to enhanced production capacity has been the fact that these cooperatives have helped individual farmers effectively market their produce for a better return, thereby attracting other people to become members of the cooperative by producing milk.

e-Commerce

Regulatory issues and the lack of availability of payment gateways had significantly delayed the start of e-commerce activity in India. However, a significant number of sites have recently sprung up in business-to-business e-commerce, business-to-consumer e-commerce, and consumer-to-consumer e-commerce (typically through auction sites). While data on the total volume of activity are difficult to obtain, the trend is clearly towards growing volumes. A survey on online buying habits indicated that the percentage of people having purchased online had increased from 2 percent in 2001 to 4 percent in 2002. Some of the popular products sold online are branded clothes, music CDs/cassettes, and books, though many sites do offer online purchasing facilities for items from groceries to banking services.

The dot-com boom period saw a significant surge both in terms of the number of online players and consumer confidence in purchasing online. This led to a significant growth in the volume of transactions as well. However, with the dot-com bust and the ensuing slowdown, many players have had to close shop, leading to a reduction in growth rates.

Some of the key reasons for e-commerce not taking off in a big way in India are as follows.

1. Low Internet user base, which keeps the pool low. However, with the gradual development of the kiosk model, the user base is projected to increase thereby having a positive effect on transaction levels.

2. Failure of companies to convince users of online payment security.

3. Uncertainty about the quality of products available in the market. Having experienced problems in quality in their purchases, discerning consumers want to get a feel of the product/service before they decide to buy. Given that this cannot be achieved on the Internet, activity levels have lowered.

e-Governance

In a large developing country like India, there is a significant need for introducing transparency and efficiency in government functioning. This alone can lead to the creation of an environment conducive to free enterprise and enhanced productivity levels of individuals and corporations. Such a transformation in government functioning can have a multiplier effect on economic progress.

Large-scale implementation of e-governance initiatives offers an elegant and effective way of achieving this transformation. However, progress in this area has been rather slow and non-uniform across the country. Some of the more progressive states, especially those in the southern region such as Karnataka and Andhra Pradesh, have made significant strides in recent years, while many others lag behind substantially.

The few cases of e-governance implementations that have been completed have demonstrated significant benefits in terms of drastically enhanced speed of response, significantly reduced errors, and most importantly reduced corruption in services delivered to the citizens. A couple of case studies illustrating these benefits are presented in Box 3.

Such projects indicate that most of these initiatives can actually pay for themselves through the levying of nominal user charges. Given the enhanced quality of service and reduced corruption, people do not mind paying these charges.

There are, however, some key issues in e-governance implementations that need to be considered:

1. *Implementation champions.* Given that these initiatives can affect a potential revenue source for government employees (albeit illegal), the resistance for such implementations will be very high. In fact, many e-governance ideas in the country have failed due to the substantial resistance offered by government employees and politicians. Only a strong leader who can push these initiatives through will succeed. It has been observed that in all the successful initiatives, there was a visionary bureaucrat, or in some recent cases a political leader, who steered these initiatives to success in spite of stiff resistance. This dependence on individuals to drive e-governance implementations could bottleneck the growth of such applications. Training and awareness-building among government employees on the benefits of ICT can help to an extent in reducing the resistance.

2. *Uniformity of implementation.* Given the links between various government functions, implementing ICT-enabled processes in narrowly defined departmental silos can have only a limited impact on the quality of services delivered. This is also true for differential implementation of initiatives across states. For instance, in the check-post automation case, it has been found that some of the operators are now taking longer routes through adjoining states (where it is much easier to get away given the existence of manual systems) to avoid paying penalties.

It is, therefore, critical that integrated initiatives that cover multiple government departments are implemented to ensure maximum value to the citizens. Further, in order to gain higher coverage, efforts should be made to transfer e-governance best practices from those states that have implemented it to laggard states. The benefits of the new practices should be communicated to the larger population in these laggard states to pressure the administration to change.

3. *Back-end transformation.* While improvement in the interface with the citizens should be a key focus of e-governance initiatives, it should be accompanied by an even larger effort to transform back-end processes. It

Box 3. **Successful e-Governance Implementations**

BHOOMI: Online Delivery of Land Titles

Bhoomi is a project implemented by the state government of Karnataka, one of the country's favored ICT havens. The objective of the project was to computerize approximately 20 million village land records and provide an effective interface to around 6.7 million farmers. Farmers need these land records to buy and sell land, and even to obtain farm credits. The manual system that existed before was cumbersome and prone to error and delays, and provided opportunities for the officials to harass farmers and extort bribes. Bhoomi has introduced an ICT-enabled process in place of the manual system to provide an effective service to the farmers. Land record kiosks (also known as Bhoomi centers) have been installed in all the 177 *taluks*[8] of the state. These centers have been equipped with computers linked to a central database. Farmers can now obtain land records by paying a nominal fee of INR 15 (as compared to the few hundreds rumored to be paid as bribes earlier). While this transaction took several days under the manual set-up, it takes only a couple of minutes in the new system. Access to farm credit is also faster and easier now that there is online connectivity to the banks providing loans—the process now takes only around five days, compared to the twenty-five to thirty it had taken in the past. Similar drastic reductions in response times have been achieved in other services as well.

Given that transactions are now posted online to a database, administrators are able to get aggregated information and can generate reports based on soil type, land size, type of crops grown, number of mutation requests filed every day, and so on. The system also makes monitoring of government lands more effective. The estimated loss to the state on this account was INR 25 billion every year due to encroachments and tampering of land records by officials. A state-of-the-art biometrics-based log-on system ensures complete accountability, and prevents any possibility of tampering by the users of the system.

The government has also plans to provide other information-based services to farmers through these Bhoomi centers.

Apart from reducing transaction time and corruption, the concept of kiosks could also lead to helping rural folks benefit from the growth of Internet.

Computerized Interstate Check-posts

Gujarat, a western state adjoining Mumbai, is known for the entrepreneurial spirit of its people. An innovative use of ICT in this state has led to a significant improvement in government revenues and a reduction in corruption and in the harassment of people.

A significant amount of manufactured goods pass through the state by road. Vehicle owners often overload their vehicles to enhance their earnings. Overloaded trucks are not only a safety hazard, but also lead to revenue leakage since the government's excise duty levy is based on number of trucks (depending on the maximum allowed capacity of a truck). Check-posts located at interstate borders are responsible for monitoring this menace. However, because of the time needed to monitor each and every vehicle in the manual system, proper monitoring was impractical and led to traffic congestions. This gave officials at these check-posts an opportunity to collect bribes and harass vehicle drivers. Hence, while some vehicle owners could escape with heavily overloaded trucks, the genuine ones were being harassed.

The government then introduced a new ICT-enabled system in all the ten interstate check-posts to help reduce this menace. In the new system, a video camera scans the number plate of the vehicle as it approaches the check-post. This signal is converted into a digital form and transmitted to a central database for validation. The database would provide information in terms of the type of vehicle, capacity, validity of permit, availability of insurance, vehicle tax dues, and so on. As soon as the vehicle arrived on the weigh bridge, the system would compute the extent of overweight, correlating the actual weight with the permissible capacity. A ticket would automatically be issued for any dues or penalty to be paid by the driver. The vehicle owners were also issued smart cards to make dues and penalty payments at these counters immediate and easy.

The introduction of the new system not only led to the reduction in processing time per vehicle from thirty minutes to two minutes, but also helped to curb corruption and enhance government revenues. It is estimated that tax collections improved threefold in a short time, and helped pay back the investments made in hardware and software.

---

is very difficult to sustain people's interest in initiatives that tinker only with the front end of the process as fundamental transformation of services is feasible only through automation of the back-end processes. For instance, for ICT-enabled check-posts to be effective, it is necessary for millions of vehicle records to be computerized and maintained in a central database for easy access by the system.

4. *Support infrastructure.* Success of the new ICT-based systems greatly depend on the reliability of electric power and communication links. Currently, in many parts of the country, these services are not very reliable. Further, it could take several days for any power faults (which happen rather frequently) to be rectified. Appropriate back-up mechanisms to restore normal functioning quickly are critical for the success of the new systems.

5. *Maintenance and training*. Given the current lack of proficiency in handling these technologies, government personnel need substantial training in order to ensure their smooth functioning. Further, appropriate maintenance of hardware and software is also critical for continuous operations. If these aspects are not accorded due attention, the services delivered could be severely impacted, thereby, at least in the initial stages, affecting people's confidence in the new system. At the same time, however, given the lack of infrastructure in remote areas, such as proper accommodation and schools, getting ICT professionals to train personnel and maintain these systems is a significant challenge.

Other sectors

Use of ICT in the agricultural sector has been relatively low due to the high cost of access devices, and low level of literacy and awareness among the farmers in rural areas. However, India has been a leader in the use of remote sensing satellite information for locating irrigation projects. The Internet has also been effectively used in some villages to ensure effective dissemination of agricultural commodity price information.

Tele-medicine is another application that is increasingly finding use in many parts of the country. Using this application, expert medical advice is provided to remote areas where access to such expertise is not available. This application of ICT is especially beneficial in India, where rural areas do not have access to good health care facilities.

A case study of the efforts made by a super specialty hospital in this regard is presented in Box 4.

Challenges to the Rapid Adoption of Technology

Apart from the challenges in specific sectors that have been discussed earlier, there are a few generic issues that have impacted the pace of ICT penetration in the country. These challenges, discussed below, will have to be overcome effectively if the country is to transform itself into a knowledge society.

1. *The problem of priority*. In a country where around 300 million people live in abject poverty, and where many more do not even have access to basic health care facilities, the question that is often asked, and justifiably so, is: Can ICT-implementation be high-priority?

   Once basic social infrastructure, such as schools and primary health care centers, are in place, ICT can certainly play a significant part in ameliorating the living conditions of people. Given the lack of these basic facilities, significant effort and resources would have to be invested in creating this infrastructure. At the same time, however, not investing in developing ICT could affect the competitiveness of the economy and, hence, compromise future economic growth. Balancing these two priorities needs a clear vision at the highest level, significant resources, and innovative methods.

2. *The adversity of diversity*. India is a diverse nation. While there are plus points of this in terms of cultural diversity and the quality of the genetic pool, associated problems pose challenges for the growth of ICT in the country:

   i. India has the second largest English-speaking scientific talent pool after the United States. However, a large proportion of the population, especially in rural areas, do not understand English. There are eighteen official languages in the country, and many more derivatives of them, in use. If ICT is to reach this vast population,

Box 4. Tele-medicine

Narayana Hrudayalaya, a super specialty cardiac care hospital in Bangalore (the technology capital of the country), has been a pioneer in the use of tele-medicine to provide heart care to remote areas in the country.

Tele-medicine links health care centers in remote locations via satellite with super specialty hospitals at major towns and cities, connecting patients in remote areas with specialist doctors for medical consultations and treatment. The system consists of customized medical software integrated with computer hardware and diagnostic instruments connected to the VSAT (Very Small Aperture Terminal) at each location. The medical record and history of the patient is sent to specialist doctors through this system and they, in turn, provide diagnoses and treatments during videoconference sessions with patients.

Narayana Hrudayalaya has entered into a joint venture with the Indian Space Research Organization (ISRO) and six state governments besides the governments of Malaysia and Mauritius for tele-medicine consultancy in remotely located health care centers. In the short period that tele-medicine has been operating, more than 3,500 people in the country have received expert consultation from doctors in Narayana Hrudayalaya.

Around 300 children are born with heart diseases in India every day, and only a fraction of them have access to quality heart care. Tele-medicine is making a difference in the lives of thousands of such people needing heart care who otherwise would have no hope of accessing expert advice.

local-language applications and content will have to be developed. Given the sheer number of such operating languages, the task of making ICT suitable for local use is mammoth, to say the least.

ii. There are several hundred castes and subcastes in the country, and the division along caste lines runs deep in the psyche of people. This has led to social inequalities and, more importantly, has provided an opportunity for politicians to play on caste-based sentiments and avoid being assessed by demonstrated performance. For instance, successive governments have increased the caste-based reservation of government jobs and seats in educational institutions; so much so that currently, the level of such reservations is a very high 25 percent. Given the pressure to fill these seats, merit is often sacrificed. Such policies introduce tremendous inefficiencies into the system.

The above factors coupled with the rich-poor and urban-rural divide makes the task of providing ICT to a larger population difficult.

3. *The perversity of the political class.* While a few visionaries have come to the helm in recent years, a large majority of politicians lack the capability or the will to understand the implications of ICT despite the fact that they derive personal benefits from them. In fact, these very politicians can be seen talking on mobile telephones saying that they don't believe technology can help the country. As mentioned before, exploitation of caste differences and "vote banks" is enabling these politicians to get away with non-performance. Providing the benefits of ICT to places where such divisive forces are at play, is a significant challenge.

4. *An unwieldy government.* In India, central and state governments employ a massive number of people. The combined center and state government wage bill formed 6.8 percent of GDP in 1999–2000. The revenue deficit for that year was at a high of 6.2 percent of GDP, indicating that the government was not even able to meet its day-to-day expenses from revenues.

Further, a combination of low quality people and lack of incentives for performance has led to significant inefficiencies and corruption in government. The debatable policy of caste-based reservations has only contributed to a further deterioration of the system.

Thus, not only does the government find it difficult to invest in development due to the cost burden, but it also faces enormous resistance for change due to its corrupt and largely ICT-illiterate workforce.

5. *Low scope of economic activity.* The 1980s, especially the latter half, saw very high inflation rates (as much as 17 percent). This, coupled with the conservative nature of a large proportion of the population, led to depressed consumption levels. People consciously curbed their life styles in order to "save for a rainy day." This is indicated by the high rate of savings in the economy until the early 1990s.

Because consumption levels were low, there was no incentive for enterprise. This disincentive was compounded by the lack of venture capital funds; together these factors reduced the overall scope of economic activity. This reduced activity, in turn, affected growth and, hence, the ability of the economy, to invest in ICT. While the situation has changed quite significantly in the recent past, there is still substantial scope for enhancement in economic activity.

6. *An overpowering IT export sector.* It is ironic that a highly successful IT export sector is in some ways affecting the adoption of ICT applications in the country. Though the industry has positively influenced the acceptance of ICT in India, its very success has affected other sectors by sucking away a sizeable portion of the available talent. Many sectors have faced an exodus of people into the software exports industry (as the companies in this sector even hire non-IT engineers and train them to become software developers). Further, a significant proportion of bright young students today opt for a career in one of the software export companies or migrate to developed economies such as the United States. This has led to a situation where the other sectors of the industry, educational institutions and domestic market-focused IT companies, are starved of high-quality talent, and this negatively impacts their effectiveness.

The Way Forward

If the country is to achieve rapid penetration of ICT and resolve the internal digital gaps, the government, industry, academia, and NGOs, must each play their part.

Steps to be taken by the government

1. *Create a suitable environment for business and competition to flourish.* The government will have to carry the economic reforms agenda to its logical conclusion, and at a rapid pace; speed is crucial if the pangs of transition for the industry are to be minimized. Resolution of regulatory issues in the communications sector, and reduction and rationalization of tariff structures on hardware and software, can significantly boost ICT penetration.

In general, the aim should be to reduce government's role in non-essential sectors, thereby freeing private enterprise. By reducing their role, the government would also be able to focus its energies and resources on the urgent needs of development.

2. *Reform the government sector.* As discussed earlier, the massive government sector is a source of inefficiencies,

a bottleneck for progress, and a significant drain on the treasury. The leverage of reforming this sector can be very high for the economy. The focus of government reform should be on

i. introducing performance orientation measures;

ii. re-training and re-deploying personnel;

iii. abolishing caste-based reservations; and

iv. computerizing operations and introducing efficiency.

Specifically, e-governance initiatives should be a priority in areas of government-industry interface, such as tax collections and customs clearances. Until this interface improves, the overall supply chain for the industry will remain inefficient, thereby making it difficult for the industry to compete effectively in the global economy.

Implementing the above measures needs a strong political will and innovative thinking. With the introduction of computerization and efficiency, there are bound to be redundancies. The very prospect of this could lead to significant resistance for such an initiative. However, offering re-training and re-deployment, additional incentives based on performance, and voluntary retirement schemes, can help to reduce resistance to implementing the change.

3. *Focus on creating basic social infrastructure.* Basic development needs of the country, such as primary education and health care, should be given top priority and addressed quickly. Instead of a piece-meal approach, the government should draw up an integrated plan to enhance literacy and health care services in the next few years by allocating significant resources to these areas. Enhancing efficiency of resource utilization is also of paramount importance, especially when resources are scarce.

4. *Enhance the reliability and reach of communication and other support infrastructure.* Low demand-density and high investment-intensity being characteristics of the rural sector, development of support infrastructure, such as power and communication, perforce depends on government spending. Unless there is improvement in this area, all efforts at e-governance and ICT penetration will be less effective.

5. *Overhaul the higher education sector.* As discussed earlier, while the quantity of output is growing, the quality of education, especially in the newer institutions, is a matter of concern. The following initiatives can help develop a vibrant higher education sector in the country:

   i. Provide autonomy to private institutions so that they are able to operate freely in terms of deciding their own screening mechanism for incoming students, course fees, curriculum, and faculty.

   ii. Create a rating mechanism for these institutions based on a transparent set of parameters related to education delivered and infrastructure available. Such rating information should be freely available to any student desirous of obtaining it, thereby enabling him or her to choose the appropriate institution.

   iii. Reduce generic subsidies and introduce scholarships and aid schemes targeted towards helping meritorious and economically weaker students.

These steps will help to enhance enrollment and introduce a market mechanism that will improve the quality of education. It would also provide an impetus to research and development activities, as the educational institutions would realize the need for cooperation with industry to engage in mutually beneficial activities.

6. *Encourage localization of ICT.* As described earlier, the global market opportunity has created a talent shortage in the local ICT development sector. The government should step in by providing fiscal incentives to encourage companies developing ICT to solve local needs. For instance, giving tax benefits on revenues from the sale of local language software products and services.

The government could also encourage the development of innovative ideas for ICT penetration by providing research funds for the development of these initiatives and instituting a prestigious award for ICT innovations.

The role of industry, academia, and the NGOs

There are various ways in which the industry, academia, and the NGOs can contribute towards the proliferation of ICT. A few of such ways are provided below:

1. Private companies, especially large industrial houses, should invest in creating global capacities in their respective fields. As mentioned earlier, size offers flexibility for technology investments that is critical for achieving competitiveness.

2. Large companies should contribute to the development of social infrastructure by providing basic amenities, such as a well-equipped school or a health care center, in at least one rural area.

3. ICT companies should help reduce digital gaps by contributing to one or more areas mentioned below:

   i. Enhanced ICT literacy, especially in rural areas. The "Rural Reach Program" being conducted by Infosys, a leading ICT consulting and services company, is an example of such an effort. As part of this program, ICT professionals and educators visit rural schools and help students get familiar with technology. Other programs being conducted by the company, such as "Train the Trainer" (for bridging the knowledge gap between industry and educators in local colleges) and "Catch Them Young" (for providing basic knowledge of software development and the ICT industry to young students), also aim to enhance ICT literacy.

ii. Social and technological research for enhancing ICT penetration. The "Hole in the Wall" experiment conducted by a researcher from NIIT, an IT education and services company, is an instance of such research. By installing an unmanned PC in a local slum, he proved that children can learn the basics of ICT literacy even without the help of instructors, and thereby indicated the potential to enhance literacy by just installing Internet enabled PCs in these areas with occasional guidance from instructors. The development of Simputer (discussed earlier in the chapter) is another example of such research.

iii. Local language content and applications. For instance, in a bid to promote local-language computing in India, Microsoft has built support for Indian scripts in Windows 2000.

While examples of each one of the above exist, more programs like them have to be implemented in order to make a difference to ICT literacy and penetration at the national level.

4. Research/academic institutions, private companies, NGOs, and government agencies should partner with each other to develop locally-relevant ICT solutions.

5. Private companies and educational institutions should work jointly to enhance research and development activities in the country.

6. NGOs should work to enhance awareness and utilization of ICT at the grass-roots level.

Conclusion

India is a country with tremendous socioeconomic diversity; the ICT revolution has further accentuated some of these inequalities. While on the one hand, the Indian IT industry and the country's IT professionals have been on the bleeding edge of technological evolution, a vast majority of the people, on the other hand, have neither the access nor the awareness and education to derive benefits from advancing technology. However, in the recent past the country has made progress in terms of creating infrastructure, developing technological innovations, and altering the mindset of its people towards better technology absorption. Some of the socio-technical innovations created in the country hold promise, not only to influence conditions in India, but also to help reduce the digital gap in many other developing countries.

As such, the enabling conditions for an explosion in ICT penetration are being created in the country. The momentum

that has been generated in recent years, coupled with the potential of technology and capability of bright young minds to effectively transcend barriers, make us optimistic about India's future.

Endnotes

1. Self-reliance is an inward-looking philosophy, wherein a country/individual reduces dependence on other countries/ individuals.

2. Reserve Bank of India is India's central bank; it controls the country's monetary policy.

3. NASSCOM, National Association of Software and Services Companies, is the representative body of the Indian IT services industry

4. CMM stands for Capability Maturity Model, which is a software-specific quality model propounded by the Software Engineering Institute at Carnegie Mellon University in the United States.

5. The source for all the figures mentioned in this paragraph is the NASSCOM report on the Indian software industry.

6. A joint study undertaken by NASSCOM and McKinsey & Company on the strategies to achieve the Indian IT services industry's aspirations.

7. Offshoring, in this context, means client outsourcing of ICT requirements for execution by Indian companies.

8. A taluk is an aggregation of villages that is created for administrative purposes.

References

Bhatnagar, Subhash C. 2001. *e-Government Case Studies in India.* Online. Rev. 15th Sep. 2002 http://www1.worldbank.org/ publicsector/egov/

Keniston, Kenneth. 2002. *IT for the Common Man.* Second M. N. Srinivas Memorial Lecture, National Institute of Advanced Studies, Bangalore.

National Association of Software and Service Companies (NASSCOM). 2002. *NASSCOM-McKinsey Report 2002: Strategies to Achieve the Indian IT Industry's Aspiration.* National Association of Software and Service Companies and McKinsey & Company.

National Association of Software and Service Companies (NASSCOM). 2002. *The IT Industry in India: Strategic Review 2002.* National Association of Software and Service Companies.

Parikh, Kirit S. and R. Radhakrishna. 2002. *India Development Report 2002.* Delhi: Oxford University Press.

Singhal, Arvind and Everett M. Rogers. 2001. *India's Communication Revolution: From Bullock Carts to Cyber Marts.* New Delhi: Sage Publications.

Thapar, Romila. 2000. *India : Another Millennium?* Penguin Books India.

Part 3
Country Profiles

How To Read the Country Tables

The country tables section presents the rankings of the eighty-two countries considered in the Global Information Technology Report 2002–2003. It provides a quick picture of the level of ICT development of a country by grouping information under the following sections:

1. **Key macroeconomic indicators** relating to the nations economy, such as population, gross domestic product (GDP) per capita, illiteracy rate, and GDP per capita growth.

2. **Overall Networked Readiness Index (NRI)** ranking for 2002 to 2003, which gives immediate insight into overall ICT competitiveness; one can compare this rank to that of the NRI 2001–2002 if the country was ranked for that year.

3. **Component indexes**, which is divided into three sections that are the same as the component indexes: environment, readiness, and usage. Rankings for a country can be found for each of the component indexes and for the subindexes comprising the component indexes.

4. **Main listing**, where one can find a list of all the variables grouped under the respective component index. Detailed rankings for the country presented can be found for each of the variables listed, and taken into consideration for the current NRI study.

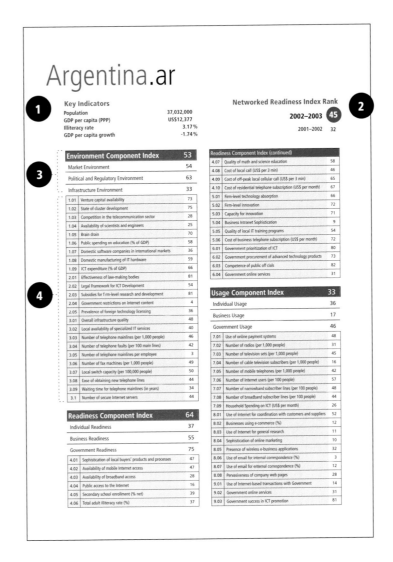

By looking at this information, and by identifying key areas of relative over- and underperformance, one can gain a rapid understanding of a country's ICT competitiveness. For example, one can aim to identify key parameters contributing to the country's performance in the environment component index by looking at the rankings of the variables contributing to it, such as venture capital availability or the state of cluster development.

The inferences that one makes from the ranking of a given country can be made more complete by having a closer look at the relative performance of other countries. All the variables are preceded by a variable number. For example, 1.01 and 2.03; these numbers provide a link to the Data Rankings section of the Report, where one can study the performance of all the eighty-two countries.

In this way, by looking at the performance of two countries that are similar, and at role models such as Finland, Singapore, and Korea, one can quickly assess the two countries' strengths and weaknesses, and key areas requiring development.

Argentina.ar

Key Indicators

Population	37,032,000
GDP per capita (PPP)	US$12,377
Illiteracy rate	3.17%
GDP per capita growth	-1.74%

Networked Readiness Index Rank

2002–2003	**45**
2001–2002	32

Environment Component Index	53
Market Environment	54
Political and Regulatory Environment	63
Infrastructure Environment	33

1.01	Venture capital availability	73
1.02	State of cluster development	75
1.03	Competition in the telecommunication sector	28
1.04	Availability of scientists and engineers	25
1.05	Brain drain	70
1.06	Public spending on education (% of GDP)	58
1.07	Domestic software companies in international markets	36
1.08	Domestic manufacturing of IT hardware	59
1.09	ICT expenditure (% of GDP)	66
2.01	Effectiveness of law-making bodies	81
2.02	Legal framework for ICT development	54
2.03	Subsidies for firm-level research and development	81
2.04	Government restrictions on Internet content	4
2.05	Prevalence of foreign technology licensing	36
3.01	Overall infrastructure quality	48
3.02	Local availability of specialized IT services	40
3.03	Number of telephone mainlines (per 1,000 people)	46
3.04	Number of telephone faults (per 100 main lines)	42
3.05	Number of telephone mainlines per employee	3
3.06	Number of fax machines (per 1,000 people)	49
3.07	Local switch capacity (per 100,000 people)	50
3.08	Ease of obtaining new telephone lines	44
3.09	Waiting time for telephone mainlines (in years)	34
3.1	Number of secure Internet servers	44

Readiness Component Index	64
Individual Readiness	37
Business Readiness	55
Government Readiness	75

4.01	Sophistication of local buyers' products and processes	47
4.02	Availability of mobile Internet access	47
4.03	Availability of broadband access	28
4.04	Public access to the Internet	16
4.05	Secondary school enrollment (% net)	39
4.06	Total adult illiteracy rate (%)	37

Readiness Component Index (continued)	
4.07	Quality of math and science education	58
4.08	Cost of local call (US$ per three min)	46
4.09	Cost of off-peak local cellular call (US$ per three min)	65
4.10	Cost of residential telephone subscription (US$ per month)	67
5.01	Firm-level technology absorption	66
5.02	Firm-level innovation	72
5.03	Capacity for innovation	71
5.04	Business Intranet sophistication	9
5.05	Quality of local IT training programs	54
5.06	Cost of business telephone subscription (US$ per month)	72
6.01	Government prioritization of ICT	80
6.02	Government procurement of advanced technology products	73
6.03	Competence of public officials	82
6.04	Government online services	31

Usage Component Index	33
Individual Usage	36
Business Usage	17
Government Usage	46

7.01	Use of online payment systems	48
7.02	Number of radios (per 1,000 people)	31
7.03	Number of television sets (per 1,000 people)	45
7.04	Number of cable television subscribers (per 1,000 people)	16
7.05	Number of mobile telephones (per 1,000 people)	42
7.06	Number of Internet users (per 100 people)	57
7.07	Number of narrowband subscriber lines (per 100 people)	48
7.08	Number of broadband subscriber lines (per 100 people)	44
7.09	Household spending on ICT (US$ per month)	26
8.01	Use of Internet for coordination with customers and suppliers	52
8.02	Businesses using e-commerce (%)	12
8.03	Use of Internet for general research	11
8.04	Sophistication of online marketing	10
8.05	Presence of wireless e-business applications	32
8.06	Use of email for internal correspondence (%)	3
8.07	Use of email for external correspondence (%)	12
8.08	Pervasiveness of company web pages	28
9.01	Use of Internet-based transactions with the government	14
9.02	Government online services	31
9.03	Government success in ICT promotion	81

Australia.au

Key Indicators

Population	19,182,000
GDP per capita (PPP)	US$25,693
Illiteracy rate	0.00%
GDP per capita growth	0.80%

Networked Readiness Index Rank

2002–2003 **15**

2001–2002　14

Environment Component Index — 14

Market Environment		24
Political and Regulatory Environment		13
Infrastructure Environment		8
1.01	Venture capital availability	22
1.02	State of cluster development	27
1.03	Competition in the telecommunication sector	22
1.04	Availability of scientists and engineers	16
1.05	Brain drain	28
1.06	Public spending on education (% of GDP)	35
1.07	Domestic software companies in international markets	29
1.08	Domestic manufacturing of IT hardware	41
1.09	ICT expenditure (% of GDP)	5
2.01	Effectiveness of law-making bodies	4
2.02	Legal framework for ICT development	8
2.03	Subsidies for firm-level research and development	14
2.04	Government restrictions on Internet content	77
2.05	Prevalence of foreign technology licensing	15
3.01	Overall infrastructure quality	11
3.02	Local availability of specialized IT services	6
3.03	Number of telephone mainlines (per 1,000 people)	18
3.04	Number of telephone faults (per 100 main lines)	2
3.05	Number of telephone mainlines per employee	38
3.06	Number of fax machines (per 1,000 people)	8
3.07	Local switch capacity (per 100,000 people)	20
3.08	Ease of obtaining new telephone lines	21
3.09	Waiting time for telephone mainlines (in years)	1
3.1	Number of secure Internet servers	3

Readiness Component Index — 19

Individual Readiness		8
Business Readiness		21
Government Readiness		23
4.01	Sophistication of local buyers' products and processes	6
4.02	Availability of mobile Internet access	14
4.03	Availability of broadband access	17
4.04	Public access to the Internet	12
4.05	Secondary school enrollment (% net)	18
4.06	Total adult illiteracy rate (%)	1

Readiness Component Index (continued)

4.07	Quality of math and science education	15
4.08	Cost of local call (US$ per three min)	34
4.09	Cost of off-peak local cellular call (US$ per three min)	41
4.10	Cost of residential telephone subscription (US$ per month)	13
5.01	Firm-level technology absorption	12
5.02	Firm-level innovation	44
5.03	Capacity for innovation	28
5.04	Business Intranet sophistication	25
5.05	Quality of local IT training programs	20
5.06	Cost of business telephone subscription (US$ per month)	23
6.01	Government prioritization of ICT	45
6.02	Government procurement of advanced technology products	33
6.03	Competence of public officials	13
6.04	Government online services	15

Usage Component Index — 14

Individual Usage		16
Business Usage		16
Government Usage		12
7.01	Use of online payment systems	9
7.02	Number of radios (per 1,000 people)	2
7.03	Number of television sets (per 1,000 people)	4
7.04	Number of cable television subscribers (per 1,000 people)	35
7.05	Number of mobile telephones (per 1,000 people)	27
7.06	Number of Internet users (per 100 people)	22
7.07	Number of narrowband subscriber lines (per 100 people)	19
7.08	Number of broadband subscriber lines (per 100 people)	31
7.09	Household spending on ICT (US$ per month)	15
8.01	Use of Internet for coordination with customers and suppliers	24
8.02	Businesses using e-commerce (%)	18
8.03	Use of Internet for general research	8
8.04	Sophistication of online marketing	25
8.05	Presence of wireless e-business applications	29
8.06	Use of email for internal correspondence (%)	10
8.07	Use of email for external correspondence (%)	22
8.08	Pervasiveness of company web pages	9
9.01	Use of Internet-based transactions with the government	11
9.02	Government online services	15
9.03	Government success in ICT promotion	29

Austria.at

Key Indicators

Population	8,110,240
GDP per capita (PPP)	US$26,765
Illiteracy rate	2.00%
GDP per capita growth	2.74%

Networked Readiness Index Rank

2002–2003	**16**
2001–2002	9

Environment Component Index	12
Market Environment	16
Political and Regulatory Environment	11
Infrastructure Environment	17

1.01	Venture capital availability	22
1.02	State of cluster development	17
1.03	Competition in the telecommunication sector	7
1.04	Availability of scientists and engineers	15
1.05	Brain drain	11
1.06	Public spending on education (% of GDP)	17
1.07	Domestic software companies in international markets	22
1.08	Domestic manufacturing of IT hardware	18
1.09	ICT expenditure (% of GDP)	31
2.01	Effectiveness of law-making bodies	12
2.02	Legal framework for ICT development	12
2.03	Subsidies for firm-level research and development	15
2.04	Government restrictions on Internet content	29
2.05	Prevalence of foreign technology licensing	22
3.01	Overall infrastructure quality	12
3.02	Local availability of specialized IT services	12
3.03	Number of telephone mainlines (per 1,000 people)	24
3.04	Number of telephone faults (per 100 main lines)	22
3.05	Number of telephone mainlines per employee	24
3.06	Number of fax machines (per 1,000 people)	15
3.07	Local switch capacity (per 100,000 people)	36
3.08	Ease of obtaining new telephone lines	16
3.09	Waiting time for telephone mainlines (in years)	1
3.1	Number of secure Internet servers	15

Readiness Component Index	18
Individual Readiness	13
Business Readiness	16
Government Readiness	24

4.01	Sophistication of local buyers' products and processes	22
4.02	Availability of mobile Internet access	7
4.03	Availability of broadband access	8
4.04	Public access to the Internet	20
4.05	Secondary school enrollment (% net)	20
4.06	Total adult illiteracy rate (%)	28

Readiness Component Index (continued)	
4.07	Quality of math and science education	3
4.08	Cost of local call (US$ per three min)	40
4.09	Cost of off-peak local cellular call (US$ per three min)	9
4.10	Cost of residential telephone subscription (US$ per month)	31
5.01	Firm-level technology absorption	30
5.02	Firm-level innovation	12
5.03	Capacity for innovation	10
5.04	Business Intranet sophistication	22
5.05	Quality of local IT training programs	16
5.06	Cost of business telephone subscription (US$ per month)	29
6.01	Government prioritization of ICT	38
6.02	Government procurement of advanced technology products	32
6.03	Competence of public officials	20
6.04	Government online services	18

Usage Component Index	18
Individual Usage	22
Business Usage	24
Government Usage	17

7.01	Use of online payment systems	23
7.02	Number of radios (per 1,000 people)	25
7.03	Number of television sets (per 1,000 people)	20
7.04	Number of cable television subscribers (per 1,000 people)	24
7.05	Number of mobile telephones (per 1,000 people)	3
7.06	Number of Internet users (per 100 people)	12
7.07	Number of narrowband subscriber lines (per 100 people)	34
7.08	Number of broadband subscriber lines (per 100 people)	10
7.09	Household spending on ICT (US$ per month)	36
8.01	Use of Internet for coordination with customers and suppliers	20
8.02	Businesses using e-commerce (%)	32
8.03	Use of Internet for general research	20
8.04	Sophistication of online marketing	16
8.05	Presence of wireless e-business applications	10
8.06	Use of email for internal correspondence (%)	32
8.07	Use of email for external correspondence (%)	61
8.08	Pervasiveness of company web pages	15
9.01	Use of Internet-based transactions with the government	21
9.02	Government online services	18
9.03	Government success in ICT promotion	26

Bangladesh.bd

Key Indicators

Population	131,050,000
GDP per capita (PPP)	US$1,602
Illiteracy rate	58.65%
GDP per capita growth	4.12%

Networked Readiness Index Rank

2002–2003 **77**

2001–2002 73

Environment Component Index — 77

Market Environment		75
Political and Regulatory Environment		65
Infrastructure Environment		81

1.01	Venture capital availability	64
1.02	State of cluster development	54
1.03	Competition in the telecommunication sector	76
1.04	Availability of scientists and engineers	59
1.05	Brain drain	79
1.06	Public spending on education (% of GDP)	76
1.07	Domestic software companies in international markets	79
1.08	Domestic manufacturing of IT hardware	81
1.09	ICT expenditure (% of GDP)	43
2.01	Effectiveness of law-making bodies	57
2.02	Legal framework for ICT development	71
2.03	Subsidies for firm-level research and development	71
2.04	Government restrictions on Internet content	21
2.05	Prevalence of foreign technology licensing	66
3.01	Overall infrastructure quality	77
3.02	Local availability of specialized IT services	82
3.03	Number of telephone mainlines (per 1,000 people)	82
3.04	Number of telephone faults (per 100 main lines)	81
3.05	Number of telephone mainlines per employee	80
3.06	Number of fax machines (per 1,000 people)	70
3.07	Local switch capacity (per 100,000 people)	79
3.08	Ease of obtaining new telephone lines	80
3.09	Waiting time for telephone mainlines (in years)	70
3.1	Number of secure Internet servers	79

Readiness Component Index — 77

Individual Readiness		81
Business Readiness		75
Government Readiness		69

4.01	Sophistication of local buyers' products and processes	68
4.02	Availability of mobile Internet access	81
4.03	Availability of broadband access	81
4.04	Public access to the Internet	82
4.05	Secondary school enrollment (% net)	74
4.06	Total adult illiteracy rate (%)	82

Readiness Component Index (continued)

4.07	Quality of math and science education	70
4.08	Cost of local call (US$ per three min)	75
4.09	Cost of off-peak local cellular call (US$ per three min)	70
4.10	Cost of residential telephone subscription (US$ per month)	74
5.01	Firm-level technology absorption	73
5.02	Firm-level innovation	66
5.03	Capacity for innovation	78
5.04	Business Intranet sophistication	58
5.05	Quality of local IT training programs	80
5.06	Cost of business telephone subscription (US$ per month)	62
6.01	Government prioritization of ICT	47
6.02	Government procurement of advanced technology products	75
6.03	Competence of public officials	47
6.04	Government online services	80

Usage Component Index — 74

Individual Usage		80
Business Usage		67
Government Usage		74

7.01	Use of online payment systems	80
7.02	Number of radios (per 1,000 people)	82
7.03	Number of television sets (per 1,000 people)	81
7.04	Number of cable television subscribers (per 1,000 people)	69
7.05	Number of mobile telephones (per 1,000 people)	81
7.06	Number of Internet users (per 100 people)	77
7.07	Number of narrowband subscriber lines (per 100 people)	72
7.08	Number of broadband subscriber lines (per 100 people)	44
7.09	Household spending on ICT (US$ per month)	44
8.01	Use of Internet for coordination with customers and suppliers	59
8.02	Businesses using e-commerce (%)	59
8.03	Use of Internet for general research	70
8.04	Sophistication of online marketing	46
8.05	Presence of wireless e-business applications	76
8.06	Use of email for internal correspondence (%)	63
8.07	Use of email for external correspondence (%)	11
8.08	Pervasiveness of company web pages	81
9.01	Use of Internet-based transactions with the government	43
9.02	Government online services	80
9.03	Government success in ICT promotion	71

Belgium.be

Key Indicators

Population	10,252,000
GDP per capita (PPP)	US$27,178
Illiteracy rate	2.00 %
GDP per capita growth	3.78 %

Networked Readiness Index Rank

2002–2003 (22)

2001–2002   18

Country Profiles | 198

Environment Component Index — 23

Market Environment	21
Political and Regulatory Environment	20
Infrastructure Environment	23

1.01	Venture capital availability	11
1.02	State of cluster development	25
1.03	Competition in the telecommunication sector	24
1.04	Availability of scientists and engineers	31
1.05	Brain drain	12
1.06	Public spending on education (% of GDP)	68
1.07	Domestic software companies in international markets	15
1.08	Domestic manufacturing of IT hardware	31
1.09	ICT expenditure (% of GDP)	20
2.01	Effectiveness of law-making bodies	35
2.02	Legal framework for ICT development	31
2.03	Subsidies for firm-level research and development	10
2.04	Government restrictions on Internet content	32
2.05	Prevalence of foreign technology licensing	12
3.01	Overall infrastructure quality	13
3.02	Local availability of specialized IT services	26
3.03	Number of telephone mainlines (per 1,000 people)	20
3.04	Number of telephone faults (per 100 main lines)	13
3.05	Number of telephone mainlines per employee	17
3.06	Number of fax machines (per 1,000 people)	24
3.07	Local switch capacity (per 100,000 people)	27
3.08	Ease of obtaining new telephone lines	24
3.09	Waiting time for telephone mainlines (in years)	24
3.1	Number of secure Internet servers	23

Readiness Component Index — 23

Individual Readiness	14
Business Readiness	17
Government Readiness	38

4.01	Sophistication of local buyers' products and processes	18
4.02	Availability of mobile Internet access	20
4.03	Availability of broadband access	7
4.04	Public access to the Internet	17
4.05	Secondary school enrollment (% net)	21
4.06	Total adult illiteracy rate (%)	28

Readiness Component Index (continued)

4.07	Quality of math and science education	4
4.08	Cost of local call (US$ per three min)	35
4.09	Cost of off-peak local cellular call (US$ per three min)	7
4.10	Cost of residential telephone subscription (US$ per month)	36
5.01	Firm-level technology absorption	35
5.02	Firm-level innovation	43
5.03	Capacity for innovation	11
5.04	Business Intranet sophistication	10
5.05	Quality of local IT training programs	22
5.06	Cost of business telephone subscription (US$ per month)	21
6.01	Government prioritization of ICT	39
6.02	Government procurement of advanced technology products	37
6.03	Competence of public officials	35
6.04	Government online services	36

Usage Component Index — 17

Individual Usage	13
Business Usage	22
Government Usage	29

7.01	Use of online payment systems	20
7.02	Number of radios (per 1,000 people)	23
7.03	Number of television sets (per 1,000 people)	18
7.04	Number of cable television subscribers (per 1,000 people)	2
7.05	Number of mobile telephones (per 1,000 people)	25
7.06	Number of Internet users (per 100 people)	18
7.07	Number of narrowband subscriber lines (per 100 people)	21
7.08	Number of broadband subscriber lines (per 100 people)	9
7.09	Household spending on ICT (US$ per month)	22
8.01	Use of Internet for coordination with customers and suppliers	22
8.02	Businesses using e-commerce (%)	27
8.03	Use of Internet for general research	24
8.04	Sophistication of online marketing	21
8.05	Presence of wireless e-business applications	23
8.06	Use of email for internal correspondence (%)	5
8.07	Use of email for external correspondence (%)	17
8.08	Pervasiveness of company web pages	23
9.01	Use of Internet-based transactions with the government	23
9.02	Government online services	36
9.03	Government success in ICT promotion	21

Bolivia.bo

Key Indicators

Population	8,328,700
GDP per capita (PPP)	US$2,424
Illiteracy rate	14.49%
GDP per capita growth	0.02%

Networked Readiness Index Rank

2002–2003 **78**

2001–2002   67

Environment Component Index	75
Market Environment	79
Political and Regulatory Environment	79
Infrastructure Environment	68

1.01	Venture capital availability	78
1.02	State of cluster development	73
1.03	Competition in the telecommunication sector	57
1.04	Availability of scientists and engineers	80
1.05	Brain drain	73
1.06	Public spending on education (% of GDP)	33
1.07	Domestic software companies in international markets	81
1.08	Domestic manufacturing of IT hardware	79
1.09	ICT expenditure (% of GDP)	64
2.01	Effectiveness of law-making bodies	73
2.02	Legal framework for ICT development	81
2.03	Subsidies for firm-level research and development	76
2.04	Government restrictions on Internet content	28
2.05	Prevalence of foreign technology licensing	81
3.01	Overall infrastructure quality	81
3.02	Local availability of specialized IT services	76
3.03	Number of telephone mainlines (per 1,000 people)	68
3.04	Number of telephone faults (per 100 main lines)	38
3.05	Number of telephone mainlines per employee	61
3.06	Number of fax machines (per 1,000 people)	72
3.07	Local switch capacity (per 100,000 people)	71
3.08	Ease of obtaining new telephone lines	65
3.09	Waiting time for telephone mainlines (in years)	36
3.1	Number of secure Internet servers	67

Readiness Component Index	79
Individual Readiness	74
Business Readiness	81
Government Readiness	78

4.01	Sophistication of local buyers' products and processes	82
4.02	Availability of mobile Internet access	60
4.03	Availability of broadband access	73
4.04	Public access to the Internet	24
4.05	Secondary school enrollment (% net)	60
4.06	Total adult illiteracy rate (%)	63

Readiness Component Index (continued)	
4.07	Quality of math and science education	72
4.08	Cost of local call (US$ per three min)	80
4.09	Cost of off-peak local cellular call (US$ per three min)	50
4.10	Cost of residential telephone subscription (US$ per month)	50
5.01	Firm-level technology absorption	82
5.02	Firm-level innovation	76
5.03	Capacity for innovation	77
5.04	Business Intranet sophistication	63
5.05	Quality of local IT training programs	78
5.06	Cost of business telephone subscription (US$ per month)	78
6.01	Government prioritization of ICT	75
6.02	Government procurement of advanced technology products	81
6.03	Competence of public officials	74
6.04	Government online services	73

Usage Component Index	76
Individual Usage	67
Business Usage	65
Government Usage	79

7.01	Use of online payment systems	79
7.02	Number of radios (per 1,000 people)	32
7.03	Number of television sets (per 1,000 people)	69
7.04	Number of cable television subscribers (per 1,000 people)	71
7.05	Number of mobile telephones (per 1,000 people)	59
7.06	Number of Internet users (per 100 people)	72
7.07	Number of narrowband subscriber lines (per 100 people)	73
7.08	Number of broadband subscriber lines (per 100 people)	44
7.09	Household spending on ICT (US$ per month)	42
8.01	Use of Internet for coordination with customers and suppliers	29
8.02	Businesses using e-commerce (%)	25
8.03	Use of Internet for general research	47
8.04	Sophistication of online marketing	76
8.05	Presence of wireless e-business applications	75
8.06	Use of email for internal correspondence (%)	66
8.07	Use of email for external correspondence (%)	45
8.08	Pervasiveness of company web pages	79
9.01	Use of Internet-based transactions with the government	78
9.02	Government online services	73
9.03	Government success in ICT promotion	76

Botswana.bw

Key Indicators

Population	1,602,000
GDP per capita (PPP)	US$7,184
Illiteracy rate	22.76 %
GDP per capita growth	2.53 %

Networked Readiness Index Rank

2002–2003	**44**
2001–2002	—

Environment Component Index — 42

Market Environment	43
Political and Regulatory Environment	36
Infrastructure Environment	54

1.01	Venture capital availability	42
1.02	State of cluster development	48
1.03	Competition in the telecommunication sector	64
1.04	Availability of scientists and engineers	74
1.05	Brain drain	35
1.06	Public spending on education (% of GDP)	2
1.07	Domestic software companies in international markets	47
1.08	Domestic manufacturing of IT hardware	57
1.09	ICT expenditure (% of GDP)	30
2.01	Effectiveness of law-making bodies	14
2.02	Legal framework for ICT development	37
2.03	Subsidies for firm-level research and development	49
2.04	Government restrictions on Internet content	52
2.05	Prevalence of foreign technology licensing	44
3.01	Overall infrastructure quality	34
3.02	Local availability of specialized IT services	41
3.03	Number of telephone mainlines (per 1,000 people)	62
3.04	Number of telephone faults (per 100 main lines)	64
3.05	Number of telephone mainlines per employee	71
3.06	Number of fax machines (per 1,000 people)	51
3.07	Local switch capacity (per 100,000 people)	15
3.08	Ease of obtaining new telephone lines	66
3.09	Waiting time for telephone mainlines (in years)	44
3.1	Number of secure Internet servers	80

Readiness Component Index — 46

Individual Readiness	53
Business Readiness	44
Government Readiness	44

4.01	Sophistication of local buyers' products and processes	65
4.02	Availability of mobile Internet access	44
4.03	Availability of broadband access	41
4.04	Public access to the Internet	40
4.05	Secondary school enrollment (% net)	55
4.06	Total adult illiteracy rate (%)	72

Readiness Component Index (continued)

4.07	Quality of math and science education	57
4.08	Cost of local call (US$ per three min)	16
4.09	Cost of off-peak local cellular call (US$ per three min)	77
4.10	Cost of residential telephone subscription (US$ per month)	23
5.01	Firm-level technology absorption	64
5.02	Firm-level innovation	21
5.03	Capacity for innovation	67
5.04	Business Intranet sophistication	45
5.05	Quality of local IT training programs	39
5.06	Cost of business telephone subscription (US$ per month)	15
6.01	Government prioritization of ICT	33
6.02	Government procurement of advanced technology products	45
6.03	Competence of public officials	33
6.04	Government online services	58

Usage Component Index — 48

Individual Usage	65
Business Usage	39
Government Usage	44

7.01	Use of online payment systems	56
7.02	Number of radios (per 1,000 people)	76
7.03	Number of television sets (per 1,000 people)	80
7.04	Number of cable television subscribers (per 1,000 people)	41
7.05	Number of mobile telephones (per 1,000 people)	51
7.06	Number of Internet users (per 100 people)	40
7.07	Number of narrowband subscriber lines (per 100 people)	59
7.08	Number of broadband subscriber lines (per 100 people)	37
7.09	Household spending on ICT (US$ per month)	54
8.01	Use of Internet for coordination with customers and suppliers	42
8.02	Businesses using e-commerce (%)	52
8.03	Use of Internet for general research	37
8.04	Sophistication of online marketing	50
8.05	Presence of wireless e-business applications	45
8.06	Use of email for internal correspondence (%)	42
8.07	Use of email for external correspondence (%)	31
8.08	Pervasiveness of company web pages	44
9.01	Use of Internet-based transactions with the government	41
9.02	Government online services	58
9.03	Government success in ICT promotion	33

Brazil.br

Key Indicators

Population	170,406,000
GDP per capita (PPP)	US$7,625
Illiteracy rate	14.76%
GDP per capita growth	3.16%

Networked Readiness Index Rank

2002–2003 **29**

2001–2002   38

Environment Component Index	**32**
Market Environment	25
Political and Regulatory Environment	32
Infrastructure Environment	37

1.01	Venture capital availability	46
1.02	State of cluster development	19
1.03	Competition in the telecommunication sector	25
1.04	Availability of scientists and engineers	44
1.05	Brain drain	21
1.06	Public spending on education (% of GDP)	41
1.07	Domestic software companies in international markets	37
1.08	Domestic manufacturing of IT hardware	16
1.09	ICT expenditure (% of GDP)	15
2.01	Effectiveness of law-making bodies	49
2.02	Legal framework for ICT development	30
2.03	Subsidies for firm-level research and development	36
2.04	Government restrictions on Internet content	23
2.05	Prevalence of foreign technology licensing	10
3.01	Overall infrastructure quality	47
3.02	Local availability of specialized IT services	19
3.03	Number of telephone mainlines (per 1,000 people)	50
3.04	Number of telephone faults (per 100 main lines)	10
3.05	Number of telephone mainlines per employee	45
3.06	Number of fax machines (per 1,000 people)	43
3.07	Local switch capacity (per 100,000 people)	49
3.08	Ease of obtaining new telephone lines	37
3.09	Waiting time for telephone mainlines (in years)	42
3.1	Number of secure Internet servers	46

Readiness Component Index	**33**
Individual Readiness	45
Business Readiness	24
Government Readiness	32

4.01	Sophistication of local buyers' products and processes	28
4.02	Availability of mobile Internet access	31
4.03	Availability of broadband access	35
4.04	Public access to the Internet	61
4.05	Secondary school enrollment (% net)	47
4.06	Total adult illiteracy rate (%)	65

Readiness Component Index (continued)		
4.07	Quality of math and science education	60
4.08	Cost of local call (US$ per three min)	32
4.09	Cost of off-peak local cellular call (US$ per three min)	30
4.10	Cost of residential telephone subscription (US$ per month)	66
5.01	Firm-level technology absorption	19
5.02	Firm-level innovation	18
5.03	Capacity for innovation	30
5.04	Business Intranet sophistication	11
5.05	Quality of local IT training programs	43
5.06	Cost of business telephone subscription (US$ per month)	60
6.01	Government prioritization of ICT	45
6.02	Government procurement of advanced technology products	36
6.03	Competence of public officials	50
6.04	Government online services	8

Usage Component Index	**26**
Individual Usage	44
Business Usage	19
Government Usage	10

7.01	Use of online payment systems	21
7.02	Number of radios (per 1,000 people)	44
7.03	Number of television sets (per 1,000 people)	41
7.04	Number of cable television subscribers (per 1,000 people)	62
7.05	Number of mobile telephones (per 1,000 people)	49
7.06	Number of Internet users (per 100 people)	51
7.07	Number of narrowband subscriber lines (per 100 people)	42
7.08	Number of broadband subscriber lines (per 100 people)	44
7.09	Household spending on ICT (US$ per month)	57
8.01	Use of Internet for coordination with customers and suppliers	46
8.02	Businesses using e-commerce (%)	37
8.03	Use of Internet for general research	10
8.04	Sophistication of online marketing	13
8.05	Presence of wireless e-business applications	17
8.06	Use of email for internal correspondence (%)	18
8.07	Use of email for external correspondence (%)	8
8.08	Pervasiveness of company web pages	21
9.01	Use of Internet-based transactions with the government	15
9.02	Government online services	8
9.03	Government success in ICT promotion	20

Bulgaria.bg

Key Indicators

Population	8,166,960
GDP per capita (PPP)	$5,710
Illiteracy rate	1.58%
GDP per capita growth	6.33%

Networked Readiness Index Rank

2002–2003	**68**
2001–2002	53

Environment Component Index — 69

Market Environment	70
Political and Regulatory Environment	75
Infrastructure Environment	59

1.01	Venture capital availability	62
1.02	State of cluster development	72
1.03	Competition in the telecommunication sector	75
1.04	Availability of scientists and engineers	39
1.05	Brain drain	78
1.06	Public spending on education (% of GDP)	63
1.07	Domestic software companies in international markets	41
1.08	Domestic manufacturing of IT hardware	51
1.09	ICT expenditure (% of GDP)	66
2.01	Effectiveness of law-making bodies	60
2.02	Legal framework for ICT development	72
2.03	Subsidies for firm-level research and development	66
2.04	Government restrictions on Internet content	70
2.05	Prevalence of foreign technology licensing	76
3.01	Overall infrastructure quality	61
3.02	Local availability of specialized IT services	60
3.03	Number of telephone mainlines (per 1,000 people)	34
3.04	Number of telephone faults (per 100 main lines)	15
3.05	Number of telephone mainlines per employee	58
3.06	Number of fax machines (per 1,000 people)	53
3.07	Local switch capacity (per 100,000 people)	43
3.08	Ease of obtaining new telephone lines	67
3.09	Waiting time for telephone mainlines (in years)	71
3.1	Number of secure Internet servers	49

Readiness Component Index — 57

Individual Readiness	43
Business Readiness	69
Government Readiness	55

4.01	Sophistication of local buyers' products and processes	71
4.02	Availability of mobile Internet access	71
4.03	Availability of broadband access	71
4.04	Public access to the Internet	37
4.05	Secondary school enrollment (% net)	32
4.06	Total adult illiteracy rate (%)	25

Readiness Component Index (continued)

4.07	Quality of math and science education	23
4.08	Cost of local call (US$ per three min)	5
4.09	Cost of off-peak local cellular call (US$ per three min)	56
4.10	Cost of residential telephone subscription (US$ per month)	15
5.01	Firm-level technology absorption	74
5.02	Firm-level innovation	80
5.03	Capacity for innovation	49
5.04	Business Intranet sophistication	69
5.05	Quality of local IT training programs	57
5.06	Cost of business telephone subscription (US$ per month)	39
6.01	Government prioritization of ICT	65
6.02	Government procurement of advanced technology products	54
6.03	Competence of public officials	36
6.04	Government online services	61

Usage Component Index — 75

Individual Usage	47
Business Usage	80
Government Usage	75

7.01	Use of online payment systems	74
7.02	Number of radios (per 1,000 people)	37
7.03	Number of television sets (per 1,000 people)	30
7.04	Number of cable television subscribers (per 1,000 people)	22
7.05	Number of mobile telephones (per 1,000 people)	55
7.06	Number of Internet users (per 100 people)	51
7.07	Number of narrowband subscriber lines (per 100 people)	27
7.08	Number of broadband subscriber lines (per 100 people)	44
7.09	Household spending on ICT (US$ per month)	80
8.01	Use of Internet for coordination with customers and suppliers	75
8.02	Businesses using e-commerce (%)	74
8.03	Use of Internet for general research	81
8.04	Sophistication of online marketing	79
8.05	Presence of wireless e-business applications	79
8.06	Use of email for internal correspondence (%)	75
8.07	Use of email for external correspondence (%)	78
8.08	Pervasiveness of company web pages	66
9.01	Use of Internet-based transactions with the government	80
9.02	Government online services	61
9.03	Government success in ICT promotion	70

Canada.ca

Key Indicators

Population	30,750,000
GDP per capita (PPP)	US$27,840
Illiteracy rate	3.00%
GDP per capita growth	3.63%

Networked Readiness Index Rank

2002–2003 **6**

2001–2002   12

Environment Component Index	4
Market Environment	9
Political and Regulatory Environment	5
Infrastructure Environment	7

1.01	Venture capital availability	12
1.02	State of cluster development	13
1.03	Competition in the telecommunication sector	8
1.04	Availability of scientists and engineers	6
1.05	Brain drain	30
1.06	Public spending on education (% of GDP)	23
1.07	Domestic software companies in international markets	11
1.08	Domestic manufacturing of IT hardware	12
1.09	ICT expenditure (% of GDP)	15
2.01	Effectiveness of law-making bodies	8
2.02	Legal framework for ICT development	7
2.03	Subsidies for firm-level research and development	4
2.04	Government restrictions on Internet content	42
2.05	Prevalence of foreign technology licensing	20
3.01	Overall infrastructure quality	8
3.02	Local availability of specialized IT services	17
3.03	Number of telephone mainlines (per 1,000 people)	7
3.04	Number of telephone faults (per 100 main lines)	16
3.05	Number of telephone mainlines per employee	14
3.06	Number of fax machines (per 1,000 people)	14
3.07	Local switch capacity (per 100,000 people)	26
3.08	Ease of obtaining new telephone lines	11
3.09	Waiting time for telephone mainlines (in years)	1
3.1	Number of secure Internet servers	4

Readiness Component Index	5
Individual Readiness	4
Business Readiness	12
Government Readiness	6

4.01	Sophistication of local buyers' products and processes	11
4.02	Availability of mobile Internet access	5
4.03	Availability of broadband access	2
4.04	Public access to the Internet	8
4.05	Secondary school enrollment (% net)	7
4.06	Total adult illiteracy rate (%)	35

Readiness Component Index (continued)	
4.07	Quality of math and science education	20
4.08	Cost of local call (US$ per three min)	31
4.09	Cost of off-peak local cellular call (US$ per three min)	3
4.10	Cost of residential telephone subscription (US$ per month)	28
5.01	Firm-level technology absorption	17
5.02	Firm-level innovation	9
5.03	Capacity for innovation	16
5.04	Business Intranet sophistication	4
5.05	Quality of local IT training programs	8
5.06	Cost of business telephone subscription (US$ per month)	44
6.01	Government prioritization of ICT	20
6.02	Government procurement of advanced technology products	15
6.03	Competence of public officials	6
6.04	Government online services	9

Usage Component Index	10
Individual Usage	11
Business Usage	14
Government Usage	7

7.01	Use of online payment systems	5
7.02	Number of radios (per 1,000 people)	8
7.03	Number of television sets (per 1,000 people)	6
7.04	Number of cable television subscribers (per 1,000 people)	6
7.05	Number of mobile telephones (per 1,000 people)	32
7.06	Number of Internet users (per 100 people)	13
7.07	Number of narrowband subscriber lines (per 100 people)	9
7.08	Number of broadband subscriber lines (per 100 people)	15
7.09	Household spending on ICT (US$ per month)	16
8.01	Use of Internet for coordination with customers and suppliers	7
8.02	Businesses using e-commerce (%)	48
8.03	Use of Internet for general research	22
8.04	Sophistication of online marketing	18
8.05	Presence of wireless e-business applications	6
8.06	Use of email for internal correspondence (%)	8
8.07	Use of email for external correspondence (%)	42
8.08	Pervasiveness of company web pages	5
9.01	Use of Internet-based transactions with the government	10
9.02	Government online services	9
9.03	Government success in ICT promotion	11

Chile.cl

Key Indicators

Population	15,211,300
GDP per capita (PPP)	US$9,417
Illiteracy rate	4.19%
GDP per capita growth	4.04%

Networked Readiness Index Rank

2002–2003 **35**

2001–2002   34

Environment Component Index	33
Market Environment	30
Political and Regulatory Environment	40
Infrastructure Environment	34

1.01	Venture capital availability	47
1.02	State of cluster development	46
1.03	Competition in the telecommunication sector	5
1.04	Availability of scientists and engineers	27
1.05	Brain drain	8
1.06	Public spending on education (% of GDP)	57
1.07	Domestic software companies in international markets	30
1.08	Domestic manufacturing of IT hardware	63
1.09	ICT expenditure (% of GDP)	23
2.01	Effectiveness of law-making bodies	38
2.02	Legal framework for ICT development	43
2.03	Subsidies for firm-level research and development	48
2.04	Government restrictions on Internet content	8
2.05	Prevalence of foreign technology licensing	50
3.01	Overall infrastructure quality	41
3.02	Local availability of specialized IT services	31
3.03	Number of telephone mainlines (per 1,000 people)	44
3.04	Number of telephone faults (per 100 main lines)	54
3.05	Number of telephone mainlines per employee	13
3.06	Number of fax machines (per 1,000 people)	47
3.07	Local switch capacity (per 100,000 people)	48
3.08	Ease of obtaining new telephone lines	15
3.09	Waiting time for telephone mainlines (in years)	26
3.1	Number of secure Internet servers	40

Readiness Component Index	34
Individual Readiness	44
Business Readiness	37
Government Readiness	34

4.01	Sophistication of local buyers' products and processes	38
4.02	Availability of mobile Internet access	39
4.03	Availability of broadband access	22
4.04	Public access to the Internet	46
4.05	Secondary school enrollment (% net)	41
4.06	Total adult illiteracy rate (%)	38

Readiness Component Index (continued)	
4.07	Quality of math and science education	59
4.08	Cost of local call (US$ per three min)	62
4.09	Cost of off-peak local cellular call (US$ per three min)	52
4.10	Cost of residential telephone subscription (US$ per month)	68
5.01	Firm-level technology absorption	38
5.02	Firm-level innovation	34
5.03	Capacity for innovation	53
5.04	Business Intranet sophistication	37
5.05	Quality of local IT training programs	31
5.06	Cost of business telephone subscription (US$ per month)	49
6.01	Government prioritization of ICT	31
6.02	Government procurement of advanced technology products	50
6.03	Competence of public officials	56
6.04	Government online services	14

Usage Component Index	32
Individual Usage	38
Business Usage	35
Government Usage	21

7.01	Use of online payment systems	37
7.02	Number of radios (per 1,000 people)	54
7.03	Number of television sets (per 1,000 people)	52
7.04	Number of cable television subscribers (per 1,000 people)	46
7.05	Number of mobile telephones (per 1,000 people)	35
7.06	Number of Internet users (per 100 people)	31
7.07	Number of narrowband subscriber lines (per 100 people)	38
7.08	Number of broadband subscriber lines (per 100 people)	26
7.09	Household spending on ICT (US$ per month)	29
8.01	Use of Internet for coordination with customers and suppliers	28
8.02	Businesses using e-commerce (%)	38
8.03	Use of Internet for general research	55
8.04	Sophistication of online marketing	40
8.05	Presence of wireless e-business applications	44
8.06	Use of email for internal correspondence (%)	34
8.07	Use of email for external correspondence (%)	39
8.08	Pervasiveness of company web pages	40
9.01	Use of Internet-based transactions with the government	27
9.02	Government online services	14
9.03	Government success in ICT promotion	34

China.cn

Key Indicators

Population	1,262,460,032
GDP per capita (PPP)	US$3,976
Illiteracy rate	15.88%
GDP per capita growth	7.19%

Networked Readiness Index Rank

2002–2003 **43**

2001–2002   64

Environment Component Index   51

Market Environment	50
Political and Regulatory Environment	52
Infrastructure Environment	53

1.01	Venture capital availability	50
1.02	State of cluster development	28
1.03	Competition in the telecommunication sector	63
1.04	Availability of scientists and engineers	66
1.05	Brain drain	41
1.06	Public spending on education (% of GDP)	77
1.07	Domestic software companies in international markets	34
1.08	Domestic manufacturing of IT hardware	24
1.09	ICT expenditure (% of GDP)	52
2.01	Effectiveness of law-making bodies	10
2.02	Legal framework for ICT development	50
2.03	Subsidies for firm-level research and development	21
2.04	Government restrictions on Internet content	81
2.05	Prevalence of foreign technology licensing	55
3.01	Overall infrastructure quality	54
3.02	Local availability of specialized IT services	59
3.03	Number of telephone mainlines (per 1,000 people)	56
3.04	Number of telephone faults (per 100 main lines)	50
3.05	Number of telephone mainlines per employee	43
3.06	Number of fax machines (per 1,000 people)	56
3.07	Local switch capacity (per 100,000 people)	58
3.08	Ease of obtaining new telephone lines	50
3.09	Waiting time for telephone mainlines (in years)	27
3.1	Number of secure Internet servers	74

Readiness Component Index   35

Individual Readiness	69
Business Readiness	41
Government Readiness	14

4.01	Sophistication of local buyers' products and processes	62
4.02	Availability of mobile Internet access	72
4.03	Availability of broadband access	72
4.04	Public access to the Internet	69
4.05	Secondary school enrollment (% net)	64
4.06	Total adult illiteracy rate (%)	68

Readiness Component Index (continued)

4.07	Quality of math and science education	54
4.08	Cost of local call (US$ per three min)	60
4.09	Cost of off-peak local cellular call (US$ per three min)	68
4.10	Cost of residential telephone subscription (US$ per month)	53
5.01	Firm-level technology absorption	49
5.02	Firm-level innovation	39
5.03	Capacity for innovation	22
5.04	Business Intranet sophistication	52
5.05	Quality of local IT training programs	69
5.06	Cost of business telephone subscription (US$ per month)	47
6.01	Government prioritization of ICT	18
6.02	Government procurement of advanced technology products	10
6.03	Competence of public officials	3
6.04	Government online services	42

Usage Component Index   51

Individual Usage	61
Business Usage	72
Government Usage	33

7.01	Use of online payment systems	57
7.02	Number of radios (per 1,000 people)	57
7.03	Number of television sets (per 1,000 people)	46
7.04	Number of cable television subscribers (per 1,000 people)	38
7.05	Number of mobile telephones (per 1,000 people)	60
7.06	Number of Internet users (per 100 people)	62
7.07	Number of narrowband subscriber lines (per 100 people)	61
7.08	Number of broadband subscriber lines (per 100 people)	33
7.09	Household spending on ICT (US$ per month)	77
8.01	Use of Internet for coordination with customers and suppliers	65
8.02	Businesses using e-commerce (%)	9
8.03	Use of Internet for general research	69
8.04	Sophistication of online marketing	41
8.05	Presence of wireless e-business applications	53
8.06	Use of email for internal correspondence (%)	74
8.07	Use of email for external correspondence (%)	79
8.08	Pervasiveness of company web pages	70
9.01	Use of Internet-based transactions with the government	47
9.02	Government online services	42
9.03	Government success in ICT promotion	13

Colombia.co

Key Indicators

Population	42,299,300
GDP per capita (PPP)	US$6,248
Illiteracy rate	8.30 %
GDP per capita growth	0.97 %

Networked Readiness Index Rank

2002–2003 59

2001–2002 57

Environment Component Index — 59

Market Environment		45
Political and Regulatory Environment		61
Infrastructure Environment		62
1.01	Venture capital availability	69
1.02	State of cluster development	56
1.03	Competition in the telecommunication sector	34
1.04	Availability of scientists and engineers	54
1.05	Brain drain	65
1.06	Public spending on education (% of GDP)	60
1.07	Domestic software companies in international markets	48
1.08	Domestic manufacturing of IT hardware	62
1.09	ICT expenditure (% of GDP)	2
2.01	Effectiveness of law-making bodies	69
2.02	Legal framework for ICT development	46
2.03	Subsidies for firm-level research and development	50
2.04	Government restrictions on Internet content	66
2.05	Prevalence of foreign technology licensing	63
3.01	Overall infrastructure quality	67
3.02	Local availability of specialized IT services	55
3.03	Number of telephone mainlines (per 1,000 people)	52
3.04	Number of telephone faults (per 100 main lines)	73
3.05	Number of telephone mainlines per employee	47
3.06	Number of fax machines (per 1,000 people)	37
3.07	Local switch capacity (per 100,000 people)	57
3.08	Ease of obtaining new telephone lines	51
3.09	Waiting time for telephone mainlines (in years)	66
3.1	Number of secure Internet servers	56

Readiness Component Index — 61

Individual Readiness		52
Business Readiness		65
Government Readiness		56
4.01	Sophistication of local buyers' products and processes	70
4.02	Availability of mobile Internet access	59
4.03	Availability of broadband access	48
4.04	Public access to the Internet	38
4.05	Secondary school enrollment (% net)	69
4.06	Total adult illiteracy rate (%)	52

Readiness Component Index (continued)

4.07	Quality of math and science education	61
4.08	Cost of local call (US$ per three min)	41
4.09	Cost of off-peak local cellular call (US$ per three min)	43
4.10	Cost of residential telephone subscription (US$ per month)	37
5.01	Firm-level technology absorption	70
5.02	Firm-level innovation	70
5.03	Capacity for innovation	51
5.04	Business Intranet sophistication	72
5.05	Quality of local IT training programs	68
5.06	Cost of business telephone subscription (US$ per month)	35
6.01	Government prioritization of ICT	55
6.02	Government procurement of advanced technology products	61
6.03	Competence of public officials	67
6.04	Government online services	38

Usage Component Index — 58

Individual Usage		55
Business Usage		62
Government Usage		51
7.01	Use of online payment systems	47
7.02	Number of radios (per 1,000 people)	36
7.03	Number of television sets (per 1,000 people)	50
7.04	Number of cable television subscribers (per 1,000 people)	63
7.05	Number of mobile telephones (per 1,000 people)	63
7.06	Number of Internet users (per 100 people)	51
7.07	Number of narrowband subscriber lines (per 100 people)	43
7.08	Number of broadband subscriber lines (per 100 people)	44
7.09	Household spending on ICT (US$ per month)	76
8.01	Use of Internet for coordination with customers and suppliers	73
8.02	Businesses using e-commerce (%)	17
8.03	Use of Internet for general research	71
8.04	Sophistication of online marketing	76
8.05	Presence of wireless e-business applications	41
8.06	Use of email for internal correspondence (%)	54
8.07	Use of email for external correspondence (%)	72
8.08	Pervasiveness of company web pages	57
9.01	Use of Internet-based transactions with the government	70
9.02	Government online services	38
9.03	Government success in ICT promotion	42

Costa Rica.cr

Key Indicators

Population	3,811,000
GDP per capita (PPP)	US$8,650
Illiteracy rate	4.41%
GDP per capita growth	-0.47%

Networked Readiness Index Rank

2002–2003 **49**

2001–2002　45

Environment Component Index — 58

Market Environment		36
Political and Regulatory Environment		68
Infrastructure Environment		60
1.01	Venture capital availability	68
1.02	State of cluster development	51
1.03	Competition in the telecommunication sector	73
1.04	Availability of scientists and engineers	42
1.05	Brain drain	25
1.06	Public spending on education (% of GDP)	19
1.07	Domestic software companies in international markets	14
1.08	Domestic manufacturing of IT hardware	25
1.09	ICT expenditure (% of GDP)	47
2.01	Effectiveness of law-making bodies	72
2.02	Legal framework for ICT development	56
2.03	Subsidies for firm-level research and development	55
2.04	Government restrictions on Internet content	79
2.05	Prevalence of foreign technology licensing	45
3.01	Overall infrastructure quality	72
3.02	Local availability of specialized IT services	33
3.03	Number of telephone mainlines (per 1,000 people)	41
3.04	Number of telephone faults (per 100 main lines)	74
3.05	Number of telephone mainlines per employee	19
3.06	Number of fax machines (per 1,000 people)	50
3.07	Local switch capacity (per 100,000 people)	47
3.08	Ease of obtaining new telephone lines	78
3.09	Waiting time for telephone mainlines (in years)	40
3.1	Number of secure Internet servers	30

Readiness Component Index — 43

Individual Readiness		46
Business Readiness		31
Government Readiness		57
4.01	Sophistication of local buyers' products and processes	41
4.02	Availability of mobile Internet access	76
4.03	Availability of broadband access	37
4.04	Public access to the Internet	23
4.05	Secondary school enrollment (% net)	73
4.06	Total adult illiteracy rate (%)	39

Readiness Component Index (continued)

4.07	Quality of math and science education	46
4.08	Cost of local call (US$ per three min)	12
4.09	Cost of off-peak local cellular call (US$ per three min)	29
4.10	Cost of residential telephone subscription (US$ per month)	22
5.01	Firm-level technology absorption	28
5.02	Firm-level innovation	48
5.03	Capacity for innovation	32
5.04	Business Intranet sophistication	46
5.05	Quality of local IT training programs	27
5.06	Cost of business telephone subscription (US$ per month)	33
6.01	Government prioritization of ICT	56
6.02	Government procurement of advanced technology products	58
6.03	Competence of public officials	65
6.04	Government online services	57

Usage Component Index — 49

Individual Usage		52
Business Usage		40
Government Usage		50
7.01	Use of online payment systems	53
7.02	Number of radios (per 1,000 people)	21
7.03	Number of television sets (per 1,000 people)	53
7.04	Number of cable television subscribers (per 1,000 people)	57
7.05	Number of mobile telephones (per 1,000 people)	64
7.06	Number of Internet users (per 100 people)	67
7.07	Number of narrowband subscriber lines (per 100 people)	41
7.08	Number of broadband subscriber lines (per 100 people)	44
7.09	Household spending on ICT (US$ per month)	64
8.01	Use of Internet for coordination with customers and suppliers	39
8.02	Businesses using e-commerce (%)	56
8.03	Use of Internet for general research	36
8.04	Sophistication of online marketing	57
8.05	Presence of wireless e-business applications	34
8.06	Use of email for internal correspondence (%)	39
8.07	Use of email for external correspondence (%)	32
8.08	Pervasiveness of company web pages	55
9.01	Use of Internet-based transactions with the government	60
9.02	Government online services	57
9.03	Government success in ICT promotion	38

Croatia.hr

Key Indicators

Population	4,380,000
GDP per capita (PPP)	US$8,091
Illiteracy rate	1.72%
GDP per capita growth	3.56%

Networked Readiness Index Rank

2002–2003 48

2001–2002 —

Environment Component Index		48
Market Environment		55
Political and Regulatory Environment		54
Infrastructure Environment		38
1.01	Venture capital availability	57
1.02	State of cluster development	65
1.03	Competition in the telecommunication sector	61
1.04	Availability of scientists and engineers	46
1.05	Brain drain	71
1.06	Public spending on education (% of GDP)	27
1.07	Domestic software companies in international markets	38
1.08	Domestic manufacturing of IT hardware	55
1.09	ICT expenditure (% of GDP)	40
2.01	Effectiveness of law-making bodies	56
2.02	Legal framework for ICT development	62
2.03	Subsidies for firm-level research and development	59
2.04	Government restrictions on Internet content	38
2.05	Prevalence of foreign technology licensing	33
3.01	Overall infrastructure quality	63
3.02	Local availability of specialized IT services	43
3.03	Number of telephone mainlines (per 1,000 people)	32
3.04	Number of telephone faults (per 100 main lines)	30
3.05	Number of telephone mainlines per employee	48
3.06	Number of fax machines (per 1,000 people)	28
3.07	Local switch capacity (per 100,000 people)	19
3.08	Ease of obtaining new telephone lines	31
3.09	Waiting time for telephone mainlines (in years)	52
3.1	Number of secure Internet servers	34

Readiness Component Index		48
Individual Readiness		33
Business Readiness		67
Government Readiness		50
4.01	Sophistication of local buyers' products and processes	54
4.02	Availability of mobile Internet access	51
4.03	Availability of broadband access	50
4.04	Public access to the Internet	47
4.05	Secondary school enrollment (% net)	34
4.06	Total adult illiteracy rate (%)	26

Readiness Component Index (continued)		
4.07	Quality of math and science education	30
4.08	Cost of local call (US$ per three min)	21
4.09	Cost of off-peak local cellular call (US$ per three min)	51
4.10	Cost of residential telephone subscription (US$ per month)	6
5.01	Firm-level technology absorption	46
5.02	Firm-level innovation	82
5.03	Capacity for innovation	42
5.04	Business Intranet sophistication	44
5.05	Quality of local IT training programs	63
5.06	Cost of business telephone subscription (US$ per month)	58
6.01	Government prioritization of ICT	50
6.02	Government procurement of advanced technology products	52
6.03	Competence of public officials	53
6.04	Government online services	41

Usage Component Index		44
Individual Usage		42
Business Usage		41
Government Usage		45
7.01	Use of online payment systems	44
7.02	Number of radios (per 1,000 people)	55
7.03	Number of television sets (per 1,000 people)	47
7.04	Number of cable television subscribers (per 1,000 people)	50
7.05	Number of mobile telephones (per 1,000 people)	34
7.06	Number of Internet users (per 100 people)	39
7.07	Number of narrowband subscriber lines (per 100 people)	32
7.08	Number of broadband subscriber lines (per 100 people)	26
7.09	Household spending on ICT (US$ per month)	47
8.01	Use of Internet for coordination with customers and suppliers	53
8.02	Businesses using e-commerce (%)	45
8.03	Use of Internet for general research	44
8.04	Sophistication of online marketing	47
8.05	Presence of wireless e-business applications	35
8.06	Use of email for internal correspondence (%)	40
8.07	Use of email for external correspondence (%)	40
8.08	Pervasiveness of company web pages	58
9.01	Use of Internet-based transactions with the government	46
9.02	Government online services	41
9.03	Government success in ICT promotion	58

Czech Republic.cz

Key Indicators

Population	10,273,300
GDP per capita (PPP)	US$13,991
Illiteracy rate	0.10%
GDP per capita growth	2.99%

Networked Readiness Index Rank

2002–2003 **28**

2001–2002   28

Environment Component Index	31
Market Environment	31
Political and Regulatory Environment	34
Infrastructure Environment	27

1.01	Venture capital availability	58
1.02	State of cluster development	67
1.03	Competition in the telecommunication sector	40
1.04	Availability of scientists and engineers	30
1.05	Brain drain	15
1.06	Public spending on education (% of GDP)	50
1.07	Domestic software companies in international markets	25
1.08	Domestic manufacturing of IT hardware	19
1.09	ICT expenditure (% of GDP)	8
2.01	Effectiveness of law-making bodies	50
2.02	Legal framework for ICT development	36
2.03	Subsidies for firm-level research and development	27
2.04	Government restrictions on Internet content	26
2.05	Prevalence of foreign technology licensing	16
3.01	Overall infrastructure quality	29
3.02	Local availability of specialized IT services	22
3.03	Number of telephone mainlines (per 1,000 people)	30
3.04	Number of telephone faults (per 100 main lines)	40
3.05	Number of telephone mainlines per employee	42
3.06	Number of fax machines (per 1,000 people)	31
3.07	Local switch capacity (per 100,000 people)	37
3.08	Ease of obtaining new telephone lines	28
3.09	Waiting time for telephone mainlines (in years)	33
3.1	Number of secure Internet servers	25

Readiness Component Index	25
Individual Readiness	23
Business Readiness	25
Government Readiness	31

4.01	Sophistication of local buyers' products and processes	24
4.02	Availability of mobile Internet access	13
4.03	Availability of broadband access	28
4.04	Public access to the Internet	27
4.05	Secondary school enrollment (% net)	33
4.06	Total adult illiteracy rate (%)	7

Readiness Component Index (continued)	
4.07	Quality of math and science education	2
4.08	Cost of local call (US$ per three min)	54
4.09	Cost of off-peak local cellular call (US$ per three min)	19
4.10	Cost of residential telephone subscription (US$ per month)	14
5.01	Firm-level technology absorption	36
5.02	Firm-level innovation	40
5.03	Capacity for innovation	27
5.04	Business Intranet sophistication	26
5.05	Quality of local IT training programs	28
5.06	Cost of business telephone subscription (US$ per month)	6
6.01	Government prioritization of ICT	30
6.02	Government procurement of advanced technology products	22
6.03	Competence of public officials	40
6.04	Government online services	26

Usage Component Index	29
Individual Usage	31
Business Usage	27
Government Usage	34

7.01	Use of online payment systems	39
7.02	Number of radios (per 1,000 people)	22
7.03	Number of television sets (per 1,000 people)	24
7.04	Number of cable television subscribers (per 1,000 people)	26
7.05	Number of mobile telephones (per 1,000 people)	28
7.06	Number of Internet users (per 100 people)	26
7.07	Number of narrowband subscriber lines (per 100 people)	35
7.08	Number of broadband subscriber lines (per 100 people)	26
7.09	Household spending on ICT (US$ per month)	62
8.01	Use of Internet for coordination with customers and suppliers	14
8.02	Businesses using e-commerce (%)	41
8.03	Use of Internet for general research	26
8.04	Sophistication of online marketing	29
8.05	Presence of wireless e-business applications	18
8.06	Use of email for internal correspondence (%)	26
8.07	Use of email for external correspondence (%)	20
8.08	Pervasiveness of company web pages	27
9.01	Use of Internet-based transactions with the government	40
9.02	Government online services	26
9.03	Government success in ICT promotion	45

Denmark.dk

Key Indicators

Population	5,336,000
GDP per capita (PPP)	US$27,627
Illiteracy rate	0.00%
GDP per capita growth	2.62%

Networked Readiness Index Rank

2002–2003 8

2001–2002 7

Environment Component Index — 11

Market Environment	15

Political and Regulatory Environment	12

Infrastructure Environment	9

1.01	Venture capital availability	10
1.02	State of cluster development	23
1.03	Competition in the telecommunication sector	23
1.04	Availability of scientists and engineers	36
1.05	Brain drain	19
1.06	Public spending on education (% of GDP)	3
1.07	Domestic software companies in international markets	12
1.08	Domestic manufacturing of IT hardware	34
1.09	ICT expenditure (% of GDP)	9
2.01	Effectiveness of law-making bodies	7
2.02	Legal framework for ICT development	16
2.03	Subsidies for firm-level research and development	27
2.04	Government restrictions on Internet content	6
2.05	Prevalence of foreign technology licensing	49
3.01	Overall infrastructure quality	6
3.02	Local availability of specialized IT services	9
3.03	Number of telephone mainlines (per 1,000 people)	3
3.04	Number of telephone faults (per 100 main lines)	35
3.05	Number of telephone mainlines per employee	31
3.06	Number of fax machines (per 1,000 people)	10
3.07	Local switch capacity (per 100,000 people)	8
3.08	Ease of obtaining new telephone lines	3
3.09	Waiting time for telephone mainlines (in years)	1
3.1	Number of secure Internet servers	16

Readiness Component Index — 11

Individual Readiness	10

Business Readiness	13

Government Readiness	17

4.01	Sophistication of local buyers' products and processes	15
4.02	Availability of mobile Internet access	9
4.03	Availability of broadband access	14
4.04	Public access to the Internet	3
4.05	Secondary school enrollment (% net)	16
4.06	Total adult illiteracy rate (%)	1

Readiness Component Index (continued)

4.07	Quality of math and science education	38
4.08	Cost of local call (US$ per three min)	22
4.09	Cost of off-peak local cellular call (US$ per three min)	8
4.10	Cost of residential telephone subscription (US$ per month)	33
5.01	Firm-level technology absorption	22
5.02	Firm-level innovation	20
5.03	Capacity for innovation	13
5.04	Business Intranet sophistication	8
5.05	Quality of local IT training programs	15
5.06	Cost of business telephone subscription (US$ per month)	19
6.01	Government prioritization of ICT	26
6.02	Government procurement of advanced technology products	28
6.03	Competence of public officials	12
6.04	Government online services	10

Usage Component Index — 6

Individual Usage	3

Business Usage	9

Government Usage	9

7.01	Use of online payment systems	13
7.02	Number of radios (per 1,000 people)	5
7.03	Number of television sets (per 1,000 people)	2
7.04	Number of cable television subscribers (per 1,000 people)	5
7.05	Number of mobile telephones (per 1,000 people)	16
7.06	Number of Internet users (per 100 people)	20
7.07	Number of narrowband subscriber lines (per 100 people)	4
7.08	Number of broadband subscriber lines (per 100 people)	12
7.09	Household spending on ICT (US$ per month)	12
8.01	Use of Internet for coordination with customers and suppliers	57
8.02	Businesses using e-commerce (%)	3
8.03	Use of Internet for general research	14
8.04	Sophistication of online marketing	5
8.05	Presence of wireless e-business applications	14
8.06	Use of email for internal correspondence (%)	6
8.07	Use of email for external correspondence (%)	23
8.08	Pervasiveness of company web pages	12
9.01	Use of Internet-based transactions with the government	3
9.02	Government online services	10
9.03	Government success in ICT promotion	32

Dominican Republic.do

Key Indicators

Population	8,373,000
GDP per capita (PPP)	US$6,033
Illiteracy rate	16.37%
GDP per capita growth	6.02%

Networked Readiness Index Rank

2002–2003 **57**

2001–2002　47

Environment Component Index		46
Market Environment		47
Political and Regulatory Environment		49
Infrastructure Environment		48
1.01	Venture capital availability	28
1.02	State of cluster development	37
1.03	Competition in the telecommunication sector	11
1.04	Availability of scientists and engineers	72
1.05	Brain drain	51
1.06	Public spending on education (% of GDP)	79
1.07	Domestic software companies in international markets	51
1.08	Domestic manufacturing of IT hardware	67
1.09	ICT expenditure (% of GDP)	26
2.01	Effectiveness of law-making bodies	61
2.02	Legal framework for ICT development	44
2.03	Subsidies for firm-level research and development	32
2.04	Government restrictions on Internet content	31
2.05	Prevalence of foreign technology licensing	39
3.01	Overall infrastructure quality	53
3.02	Local availability of specialized IT services	38
3.03	Number of telephone mainlines (per 1,000 people)	58
3.04	Number of telephone faults (per 100 main lines)	58
3.05	Number of telephone mainlines per employee	25
3.06	Number of fax machines (per 1,000 people)	68
3.07	Local switch capacity (per 100,000 people)	56
3.08	Ease of obtaining new telephone lines	49
3.09	Waiting time for telephone mainlines (in years)	61
3.1	Number of secure Internet servers	59

Readiness Component Index		56
Individual Readiness		57
Business Readiness		54
Government Readiness		54
4.01	Sophistication of local buyers' products and processes	37
4.02	Availability of mobile Internet access	53
4.03	Availability of broadband access	40
4.04	Public access to the Internet	67
4.05	Secondary school enrollment (% net)	61
4.06	Total adult illiteracy rate (%)	69

Readiness Component Index (continued)		
4.07	Quality of math and science education	71
4.08	Cost of local call (US$ per three min)	50
4.09	Cost of off-peak local cellular call (US$ per three min)	49
4.10	Cost of residential telephone subscription (US$ per month)	60
5.01	Firm-level technology absorption	23
5.02	Firm-level innovation	42
5.03	Capacity for innovation	34
5.04	Business Intranet sophistication	78
5.05	Quality of local IT training programs	53
5.06	Cost of business telephone subscription (US$ per month)	75
6.01	Government prioritization of ICT	61
6.02	Government procurement of advanced technology products	45
6.03	Competence of public officials	59
6.04	Government online services	47

Usage Component Index		63
Individual Usage		68
Business Usage		66
Government Usage		57
7.01	Use of online payment systems	60
7.02	Number of radios (per 1,000 people)	72
7.03	Number of television sets (per 1,000 people)	71
7.04	Number of cable television subscribers (per 1,000 people)	60
7.05	Number of mobile telephones (per 1,000 people)	58
7.06	Number of Internet users (per 100 people)	54
7.07	Number of narrowband subscriber lines (per 100 people)	57
7.08	Number of broadband subscriber lines (per 100 people)	44
7.09	Household spending on ICT (US$ per month)	58
8.01	Use of Internet for coordination with customers and suppliers	32
8.02	Businesses using e-commerce (%)	34
8.03	Use of Internet for general research	73
8.04	Sophistication of online marketing	65
8.05	Presence of wireless e-business applications	58
8.06	Use of email for internal correspondence (%)	73
8.07	Use of email for external correspondence (%)	65
8.08	Pervasiveness of company web pages	59
9.01	Use of Internet-based transactions with the government	76
9.02	Government online services	47
9.03	Government success in ICT promotion	44

Ecuador.ec

Key Indicators

Population	12,646,000
GDP per capita (PPP)	US$3,203
Illiteracy rate	8.39%
GDP per capita growth	0.44%

Networked Readiness Index Rank

2002–2003 75

2001–2002   71

Environment Component Index	78
Market Environment	81
Political and Regulatory Environment	80
Infrastructure Environment	71

1.01	Venture capital availability	82
1.02	State of cluster development	55
1.03	Competition in the telecommunication sector	79
1.04	Availability of scientists and engineers	73
1.05	Brain drain	77
1.06	Public spending on education (% of GDP)	65
1.07	Domestic software companies in international markets	72
1.08	Domestic manufacturing of IT hardware	70
1.09	ICT expenditure (% of GDP)	69
2.01	Effectiveness of law-making bodies	79
2.02	Legal framework for ICT development	77
2.03	Subsidies for firm-level research and development	75
2.04	Government restrictions on Internet content	78
2.05	Prevalence of foreign technology licensing	72
3.01	Overall infrastructure quality	75
3.02	Local availability of specialized IT services	63
3.03	Number of telephone mainlines (per 1,000 people)	59
3.04	Number of telephone faults (per 100 main lines)	68
3.05	Number of telephone mainlines per employee	30
3.06	Number of fax machines (per 1,000 people)	72
3.07	Local switch capacity (per 100,000 people)	64
3.08	Ease of obtaining new telephone lines	77
3.09	Waiting time for telephone mainlines (in years)	49
3.1	Number of secure Internet servers	65

Readiness Component Index	75
Individual Readiness	77
Business Readiness	77
Government Readiness	74

4.01	Sophistication of local buyers' products and processes	77
4.02	Availability of mobile Internet access	37
4.03	Availability of broadband access	55
4.04	Public access to the Internet	56
4.05	Secondary school enrollment (% net)	68
4.06	Total adult illiteracy rate (%)	54

Readiness Component Index (continued)	
4.07	Quality of math and science education	68
4.08	Cost of local call (US$ per three min)	79
4.09	Cost of off-peak local cellular call (US$ per three min)	82
4.10	Cost of residential telephone subscription (US$ per month)	76
5.01	Firm-level technology absorption	76
5.02	Firm-level innovation	49
5.03	Capacity for innovation	74
5.04	Business Intranet sophistication	68
5.05	Quality of local IT training programs	77
5.06	Cost of business telephone subscription (US$ per month)	76
6.01	Government prioritization of ICT	68
6.02	Government procurement of advanced technology products	76
6.03	Competence of public officials	78
6.04	Government online services	62

Usage Component Index	68
Individual Usage	72
Business Usage	55
Government Usage	73

7.01	Use of online payment systems	76
7.02	Number of radios (per 1,000 people)	46
7.03	Number of television sets (per 1,000 people)	55
7.04	Number of cable television subscribers (per 1,000 people)	52
7.05	Number of mobile telephones (per 1,000 people)	68
7.06	Number of Internet users (per 100 people)	64
7.07	Number of narrowband subscriber lines (per 100 people)	61
7.08	Number of broadband subscriber lines (per 100 people)	44
7.09	Household spending on ICT (US$ per month)	69
8.01	Use of Internet for coordination with customers and suppliers	54
8.02	Businesses using e-commerce (%)	70
8.03	Use of Internet for general research	53
8.04	Sophistication of online marketing	75
8.05	Presence of wireless e-business applications	52
8.06	Use of email for internal correspondence (%)	43
8.07	Use of email for external correspondence (%)	9
8.08	Pervasiveness of company web pages	71
9.01	Use of Internet-based transactions with the government	69
9.02	Government online services	62
9.03	Government success in ICT promotion	73

Egypt.eg

Key Indicators

Population	63,976,000
GDP per capita (PPP)	US$3,635
Illiteracy rate	44.68%
GDP per capita growth	3.14%

Networked Readiness Index Rank

2002–2003 ⬤65

2001–2002 60

Environment Component Index — 64

Market Environment		66
Political and Regulatory Environment		64
Infrastructure Environment		64

1.01	Venture capital availability	55
1.02	State of cluster development	63
1.03	Competition in the telecommunication sector	44
1.04	Availability of scientists and engineers	55
1.05	Brain drain	53
1.06	Public spending on education (% of GDP)	39
1.07	Domestic software companies in international markets	73
1.08	Domestic manufacturing of IT hardware	61
1.09	ICT expenditure (% of GDP)	79
2.01	Effectiveness of law-making bodies	65
2.02	Legal framework for ICT development	41
2.03	Subsidies for firm-level research and development	67
2.04	Government restrictions on Internet content	10
2.05	Prevalence of foreign technology licensing	73
3.01	Overall infrastructure quality	42
3.02	Local availability of specialized IT services	70
3.03	Number of telephone mainlines (per 1,000 people)	65
3.04	Number of telephone faults (per 100 main lines)	24
3.05	Number of telephone mainlines per employee	63
3.06	Number of fax machines (per 1,000 people)	63
3.07	Local switch capacity (per 100,000 people)	60
3.08	Ease of obtaining new telephone lines	72
3.09	Waiting time for telephone mainlines (in years)	65
3.1	Number of secure Internet servers	72

Readiness Component Index — 67

Individual Readiness		62
Business Readiness		46
Government Readiness		72

4.01	Sophistication of local buyers' products and processes	61
4.02	Availability of mobile Internet access	56
4.03	Availability of broadband access	64
4.04	Public access to the Internet	59
4.05	Secondary school enrollment (% net)	44
4.06	Total adult illiteracy rate (%)	79

Readiness Component Index (continued)

4.07	Quality of math and science education	52
4.08	Cost of local call (US$ per three min)	25
4.09	Cost of off-peak local cellular call (US$ per three min)	75
4.10	Cost of residential telephone subscription (US$ per month)	11
5.01	Firm-level technology absorption	60
5.02	Firm-level innovation	65
5.03	Capacity for innovation	55
5.04	Business Intranet sophistication	28
5.05	Quality of local IT training programs	56
5.06	Cost of business telephone subscription (US$ per month)	18
6.01	Government prioritization of ICT	67
6.02	Government procurement of advanced technology products	70
6.03	Competence of public officials	69
6.04	Government online services	69

Usage Component Index — 65

Individual Usage		71
Business Usage		61
Government Usage		59

7.01	Use of online payment systems	73
7.02	Number of radios (per 1,000 people)	56
7.03	Number of television sets (per 1,000 people)	60
7.04	Number of cable television subscribers (per 1,000 people)	37
7.05	Number of mobile telephones (per 1,000 people)	73
7.06	Number of Internet users (per 100 people)	78
7.07	Number of narrowband subscriber lines (per 100 people)	55
7.08	Number of broadband subscriber lines (per 100 people)	44
7.09	Household spending on ICT (US$ per month)	75
8.01	Use of Internet for coordination with customers and suppliers	66
8.02	Businesses using e-commerce (%)	77
8.03	Use of Internet for general research	29
8.04	Sophistication of online marketing	32
8.05	Presence of wireless e-business applications	67
8.06	Use of email for internal correspondence (%)	77
8.07	Use of email for external correspondence (%)	68
8.08	Pervasiveness of company web pages	54
9.01	Use of Internet-based transactions with the government	25
9.02	Government online services	69
9.03	Government success in ICT promotion	66

El Salvador.sv

Key Indicators

Population	6,276,000
GDP per capita (PPP)	US$4,497
Illiteracy rate	21.26%
GDP per capita growth	-0.02%

Networked Readiness Index Rank

2002–2003 **63**

2001–2002   55

Environment Component Index	66
Market Environment	65
Political and Regulatory Environment	67
Infrastructure Environment	61

1.01	Venture capital availability	48
1.02	State of cluster development	77
1.03	Competition in the telecommunication sector	21
1.04	Availability of scientists and engineers	65
1.05	Brain drain	44
1.06	Public spending on education (% of GDP)	75
1.07	Domestic software companies in international markets	80
1.08	Domestic manufacturing of IT hardware	71
1.09	ICT expenditure (% of GDP)	55
2.01	Effectiveness of law-making bodies	67
2.02	Legal framework for ICT development	60
2.03	Subsidies for firm-level research and development	77
2.04	Government restrictions on Internet content	22
2.05	Prevalence of foreign technology licensing	71
3.01	Overall infrastructure quality	58
3.02	Local availability of specialized IT services	57
3.03	Number of telephone mainlines (per 1,000 people)	60
3.04	Number of telephone faults (per 100 main lines)	34
3.05	Number of telephone mainlines per employee	49
3.06	Number of fax machines (per 1,000 people)	72
3.07	Local switch capacity (per 100,000 people)	66
3.08	Ease of obtaining new telephone lines	30
3.09	Waiting time for telephone mainlines (in years)	73
3.1	Number of secure Internet servers	55

Readiness Component Index	69
Individual Readiness	67
Business Readiness	66
Government Readiness	63

4.01	Sophistication of local buyers' products and processes	67
4.02	Availability of mobile Internet access	35
4.03	Availability of broadband access	24
4.04	Public access to the Internet	43
4.05	Secondary school enrollment (% net)	78
4.06	Total adult illiteracy rate (%)	71

Readiness Component Index (continued)	
4.07	Quality of math and science education	74
4.08	Cost of local call (US$ per three min)	63
4.09	Cost of off-peak local cellular call (US$ per three min)	60
4.10	Cost of residential telephone subscription (US$ per month)	71
5.01	Firm-level technology absorption	63
5.02	Firm-level innovation	46
5.03	Capacity for innovation	63
5.04	Business Intranet sophistication	65
5.05	Quality of local IT training programs	67
5.06	Cost of business telephone subscription (US$ per month)	70
6.01	Government prioritization of ICT	70
6.02	Government procurement of advanced technology products	71
6.03	Competence of public officials	46
6.04	Government online services	49

Usage Component Index	53
Individual Usage	54
Business Usage	46
Government Usage	60

7.01	Use of online payment systems	51
7.02	Number of radios (per 1,000 people)	43
7.03	Number of television sets (per 1,000 people)	56
7.04	Number of cable television subscribers (per 1,000 people)	43
7.05	Number of mobile telephones (per 1,000 people)	52
7.06	Number of Internet users (per 100 people)	82
7.07	Number of narrowband subscriber lines (per 100 people)	56
7.08	Number of broadband subscriber lines (per 100 people)	44
7.09	Household spending on ICT (US$ per month)	50
8.01	Use of Internet for coordination with customers and suppliers	36
8.02	Businesses using e-commerce (%)	61
8.03	Use of Internet for general research	52
8.04	Sophistication of online marketing	55
8.05	Presence of wireless e-business applications	36
8.06	Use of email for internal correspondence (%)	48
8.07	Use of email for external correspondence (%)	13
8.08	Pervasiveness of company web pages	72
9.01	Use of Internet-based transactions with the government	57
9.02	Government online services	49
9.03	Government success in ICT promotion	61

Estonia.ee

Key Indicators

Population	1,369,000
GDP per capita (PPP)	US$10,066
Illiteracy rate	0.00%
GDP per capita growth	7.81%

Networked Readiness Index Rank

2002–2003 **24**

2001–2002   23

Environment Component Index	28
Market Environment	27
Political and Regulatory Environment	30
Infrastructure Environment	28

1.01	Venture capital availability	24
1.02	State of cluster development	76
1.03	Competition in the telecommunication sector	31
1.04	Availability of scientists and engineers	41
1.05	Brain drain	33
1.06	Public spending on education (% of GDP)	13
1.07	Domestic software companies in international markets	26
1.08	Domestic manufacturing of IT hardware	15
1.09	ICT expenditure (% of GDP)	33
2.01	Effectiveness of law-making bodies	29
2.02	Legal framework for ICT development	13
2.03	Subsidies for firm-level research and development	56
2.04	Government restrictions on Internet content	12
2.05	Prevalence of foreign technology licensing	53
3.01	Overall infrastructure quality	38
3.02	Local availability of specialized IT services	24
3.03	Number of telephone mainlines (per 1,000 people)	33
3.04	Number of telephone faults (per 100 main lines)	45
3.05	Number of telephone mainlines per employee	35
3.06	Number of fax machines (per 1,000 people)	33
3.07	Local switch capacity (per 100,000 people)	9
3.08	Ease of obtaining new telephone lines	32
3.09	Waiting time for telephone mainlines (in years)	59
3.1	Number of secure Internet servers	18

Readiness Component Index	21
Individual Readiness	18
Business Readiness	28
Government Readiness	13

4.01	Sophistication of local buyers' products and processes	25
4.02	Availability of mobile Internet access	21
4.03	Availability of broadband access	16
4.04	Public access to the Internet	11
4.05	Secondary school enrollment (% net)	36
4.06	Total adult illiteracy rate (%)	1

Readiness Component Index (continued)	
4.07	Quality of math and science education	16
4.08	Cost of local call (US$ per three min)	49
4.09	Cost of off-peak local cellular call (US$ per three min)	38
4.10	Cost of residential telephone subscription (US$ per month)	25
5.01	Firm-level technology absorption	13
5.02	Firm-level innovation	61
5.03	Capacity for innovation	35
5.04	Business Intranet sophistication	40
5.05	Quality of local IT training programs	18
5.06	Cost of business telephone subscription (US$ per month)	31
6.01	Government prioritization of ICT	17
6.02	Government procurement of advanced technology products	27
6.03	Competence of public officials	20
6.04	Government online services	5

Usage Component Index	21
Individual Usage	28
Business Usage	31
Government Usage	8

7.01	Use of online payment systems	2
7.02	Number of radios (per 1,000 people)	6
7.03	Number of television sets (per 1,000 people)	13
7.04	Number of cable television subscribers (per 1,000 people)	29
7.05	Number of mobile telephones (per 1,000 people)	30
7.06	Number of Internet users (per 100 people)	41
7.07	Number of narrowband subscriber lines (per 100 people)	33
7.08	Number of broadband subscriber lines (per 100 people)	37
7.09	Household spending on ICT (US$ per month)	56
8.01	Use of Internet for coordination with customers and suppliers	8
8.02	Businesses using e-commerce (%)	52
8.03	Use of Internet for general research	28
8.04	Sophistication of online marketing	45
8.05	Presence of wireless e-business applications	65
8.06	Use of email for internal correspondence (%)	35
8.07	Use of email for external correspondence (%)	7
8.08	Pervasiveness of company web pages	31
9.01	Use of Internet-based transactions with the government	20
9.02	Government online services	5
9.03	Government success in ICT promotion	9

Finland.fi

Key Indicators

Population	5,177,000
GDP per capita (PPP)	US$24,996
Illiteracy rate	0.00%
GDP per capita growth	5.47%

Networked Readiness Index Rank

2002–2003 ①

2001–2002   3

Environment Component Index		2
Market Environment		2
Political and Regulatory Environment		3
Infrastructure Environment		11

1.01	Venture capital availability	3
1.02	State of cluster development	4
1.03	Competition in the telecommunication sector	1
1.04	Availability of scientists and engineers	9
1.05	Brain drain	2
1.06	Public spending on education (% of GDP)	10
1.07	Domestic software companies in international markets	3
1.08	Domestic manufacturing of IT hardware	5
1.09	ICT expenditure (% of GDP)	23
2.01	Effectiveness of law-making bodies	6
2.02	Legal framework for ICT development	1
2.03	Subsidies for firm-level research and development	9
2.04	Government restrictions on Internet content	3
2.05	Prevalence of foreign technology licensing	61
3.01	Overall infrastructure quality	2
3.02	Local availability of specialized IT services	2
3.03	Number of telephone mainlines (per 1,000 people)	15
3.04	Number of telephone faults (per 100 main lines)	26
3.05	Number of telephone mainlines per employee	55
3.06	Number of fax machines (per 1,000 people)	12
3.07	Local switch capacity (per 100,000 people)	6
3.08	Ease of obtaining new telephone lines	1
3.09	Waiting time for telephone mainlines (in years)	1
3.1	Number of secure Internet servers	10

Readiness Component Index		2
Individual Readiness		1
Business Readiness		2
Government Readiness		3

4.01	Sophistication of local buyers' products and processes	3
4.02	Availability of mobile Internet access	1
4.03	Availability of broadband access	1
4.04	Public access to the Internet	2
4.05	Secondary school enrollment (% net)	4
4.06	Total adult illiteracy rate (%)	1

Readiness Component Index (continued)		
4.07	Quality of math and science education	12
4.08	Cost of local call (US$ per three min)	33
4.09	Cost of off-peak local cellular call (US$ per three min)	20
4.10	Cost of residential telephone subscription (US$ per month)	18
5.01	Firm-level technology absorption	5
5.02	Firm-level innovation	17
5.03	Capacity for innovation	3
5.04	Business Intranet sophistication	12
5.05	Quality of local IT training programs	1
5.06	Cost of business telephone subscription (US$ per month)	9
6.01	Government prioritization of ICT	6
6.02	Government procurement of advanced technology products	9
6.03	Competence of public officials	8
6.04	Government online services	3

Usage Component Index		1
Individual Usage		2
Business Usage		4
Government Usage		1

7.01	Use of online payment systems	1
7.02	Number of radios (per 1,000 people)	3
7.03	Number of television sets (per 1,000 people)	7
7.04	Number of cable television subscribers (per 1,000 people)	13
7.05	Number of mobile telephones (per 1,000 people)	7
7.06	Number of Internet users (per 100 people)	14
7.07	Number of narrowband subscriber lines (per 100 people)	13
7.08	Number of broadband subscriber lines (per 100 people)	13
7.09	Household spending on ICT (US$ per month)	19
8.01	Use of Internet for coordination with customers and suppliers	1
8.02	Businesses using e-commerce (%)	29
8.03	Use of Internet for general research	4
8.04	Sophistication of online marketing	2
8.05	Presence of wireless e-business applications	13
8.06	Use of email for internal correspondence (%)	9
8.07	Use of email for external correspondence (%)	4
8.08	Pervasiveness of company web pages	1
9.01	Use of Internet-based transactions with the government	1
9.02	Government online services	3
9.03	Government success in ICT promotion	3

France.fr

Key Indicators

Population	58,892,000
GDP per capita (PPP)	US$24,223
Illiteracy rate	1.00%
GDP per capita growth	2.62%

Networked Readiness Index Rank

2002–2003 **19**

2001–2002   24

Environment Component Index   17

Market Environment	11
Political and Regulatory Environment	27
Infrastructure Environment	12

1.01	Venture capital availability	14
1.02	State of cluster development	22
1.03	Competition in the telecommunication sector	14
1.04	Availability of scientists and engineers	4
1.05	Brain drain	43
1.06	Public spending on education (% of GDP)	20
1.07	Domestic software companies in international markets	9
1.08	Domestic manufacturing of IT hardware	13
1.09	ICT expenditure (% of GDP)	12
2.01	Effectiveness of law-making bodies	40
2.02	Legal framework for ICT development	18
2.03	Subsidies for firm-level research and development	12
2.04	Government restrictions on Internet content	50
2.05	Prevalence of foreign technology licensing	51
3.01	Overall infrastructure quality	10
3.02	Local availability of specialized IT services	10
3.03	Number of telephone mainlines (per 1,000 people)	13
3.04	Number of telephone faults (per 100 main lines)	16
3.05	Number of telephone mainlines per employee	26
3.06	Number of fax machines (per 1,000 people)	9
3.07	Local switch capacity (per 100,000 people)	23
3.08	Ease of obtaining new telephone lines	18
3.09	Waiting time for telephone mainlines (in years)	1
3.1	Number of secure Internet servers	24

Readiness Component Index   16

Individual Readiness	19
Business Readiness	10
Government Readiness	20

4.01	Sophistication of local buyers' products and processes	16
4.02	Availability of mobile Internet access	26
4.03	Availability of broadband access	21
4.04	Public access to the Internet	33
4.05	Secondary school enrollment (% net)	5
4.06	Total adult illiteracy rate (%)	16

Readiness Component Index (continued)

4.07	Quality of math and science education	14
4.08	Cost of local call (US$ per three min)	28
4.09	Cost of off-peak local cellular call (US$ per three min)	33
4.10	Cost of residential telephone subscription (US$ per month)	29
5.01	Firm-level technology absorption	15
5.02	Firm-level innovation	54
5.03	Capacity for innovation	5
5.04	Business Intranet sophistication	7
5.05	Quality of local IT training programs	13
5.06	Cost of business telephone subscription (US$ per month)	25
6.01	Government prioritization of ICT	43
6.02	Government procurement of advanced technology products	8
6.03	Competence of public officials	22
6.04	Government online services	22

Usage Component Index   20

Individual Usage	25
Business Usage	13
Government Usage	24

7.01	Use of online payment systems	25
7.02	Number of radios (per 1,000 people)	15
7.03	Number of television sets (per 1,000 people)	11
7.04	Number of cable television subscribers (per 1,000 people)	45
7.05	Number of mobile telephones (per 1,000 people)	26
7.06	Number of Internet users (per 100 people)	30
7.07	Number of narrowband subscriber lines (per 100 people)	15
7.08	Number of broadband subscriber lines (per 100 people)	24
7.09	Household spending on ICT (US$ per month)	24
8.01	Use of Internet for coordination with customers and suppliers	10
8.02	Businesses using e-commerce (%)	40
8.03	Use of Internet for general research	12
8.04	Sophistication of online marketing	6
8.05	Presence of wireless e-business applications	24
8.06	Use of email for internal correspondence (%)	19
8.07	Use of email for external correspondence (%)	27
8.08	Pervasiveness of company web pages	17
9.01	Use of Internet-based transactions with the government	19
9.02	Government online services	22
9.03	Government success in ICT promotion	37

Germany.de

Key Indicators

Population	82,150,000
GDP per capita (PPP)	US$25,103
Illiteracy rate	1.00%
GDP per capita growth	2.87%

Networked Readiness Index Rank

2002–2003 **10**

2001–2002   17

Environment Component Index		9
Market Environment		6
Political and Regulatory Environment		14
Infrastructure Environment		6
1.01	Venture capital availability	17
1.02	State of cluster development	7
1.03	Competition in the telecommunication sector	4
1.04	Availability of scientists and engineers	21
1.05	Brain drain	16
1.06	Public spending on education (% of GDP)	40
1.07	Domestic software companies in international markets	8
1.08	Domestic manufacturing of IT hardware	7
1.09	ICT expenditure (% of GDP)	22
2.01	Effectiveness of law-making bodies	17
2.02	Legal framework for ICT development	20
2.03	Subsidies for firm-level research and development	7
2.04	Government restrictions on Internet content	57
2.05	Prevalence of foreign technology licensing	13
3.01	Overall infrastructure quality	3
3.02	Local availability of specialized IT services	5
3.03	Number of telephone mainlines (per 1,000 people)	9
3.04	Number of telephone faults (per 100 main lines)	16
3.05	Number of telephone mainlines per employee	22
3.06	Number of fax machines (per 1,000 people)	2
3.07	Local switch capacity (per 100,000 people)	17
3.08	Ease of obtaining new telephone lines	7
3.09	Waiting time for telephone mainlines (in years)	1
3.1	Number of secure Internet servers	17

Readiness Component Index		14
Individual Readiness		20
Business Readiness		5
Government Readiness		27
4.01	Sophistication of local buyers' products and processes	23
4.02	Availability of mobile Internet access	15
4.03	Availability of broadband access	9
4.04	Public access to the Internet	21
4.05	Secondary school enrollment (% net)	22
4.06	Total adult illiteracy rate (%)	16

Readiness Component Index (continued)		
4.07	Quality of math and science education	48
4.08	Cost of local call (US$ per three min)	23
4.09	Cost of off-peak local cellular call (US$ per three min)	26
4.10	Cost of residential telephone subscription (US$ per month)	21
5.01	Firm-level technology absorption	11
5.02	Firm-level innovation	10
5.03	Capacity for innovation	1
5.04	Business Intranet sophistication	1
5.05	Quality of local IT training programs	19
5.06	Cost of business telephone subscription (US$ per month)	12
6.01	Government prioritization of ICT	24
6.02	Government procurement of advanced technology products	11
6.03	Competence of public officials	41
6.04	Government online services	32

Usage Component Index		11
Individual Usage		17
Business Usage		1
Government Usage		20
7.01	Use of online payment systems	19
7.02	Number of radios (per 1,000 people)	16
7.03	Number of television sets (per 1,000 people)	15
7.04	Number of cable television subscribers (per 1,000 people)	8
7.05	Number of mobile telephones (per 1,000 people)	19
7.06	Number of Internet users (per 100 people)	28
7.07	Number of narrowband subscriber lines (per 100 people)	14
7.08	Number of broadband subscriber lines (per 100 people)	21
7.09	Household spending on ICT (US$ per month)	23
8.01	Use of Internet for coordination with customers and suppliers	3
8.02	Businesses using e-commerce (%)	4
8.03	Use of Internet for general research	1
8.04	Sophistication of online marketing	1
8.05	Presence of wireless e-business applications	1
8.06	Use of email for internal correspondence (%)	13
8.07	Use of email for external correspondence (%)	54
8.08	Pervasiveness of company web pages	10
9.01	Use of Internet-based transactions with the government	4
9.02	Government online services	32
9.03	Government success in ICT promotion	30

Greece.gr

Key Indicators

Population	10,560,000
GDP per capita (PPP)	US$16,501
Illiteracy rate	2.80%
GDP per capita growth	4.08%

Networked Readiness Index Rank

2002–2003 **42**

2001–2002 31

Environment Component Index	39
Market Environment	44
Political and Regulatory Environment	47
Infrastructure Environment	32

1.01	Venture capital availability	39
1.02	State of cluster development	69
1.03	Competition in the telecommunication sector	46
1.04	Availability of scientists and engineers	22
1.05	Brain drain	40
1.06	Public spending on education (% of GDP)	70
1.07	Domestic software companies in international markets	60
1.08	Domestic manufacturing of IT hardware	43
1.09	ICT expenditure (% of GDP)	48
2.01	Effectiveness of law-making bodies	47
2.02	Legal framework for ICT development	65
2.03	Subsidies for firm-level research and development	30
2.04	Government restrictions on Internet content	45
2.05	Prevalence of foreign technology licensing	32
3.01	Overall infrastructure quality	50
3.02	Local availability of specialized IT services	62
3.03	Number of telephone mainlines (per 1,000 people)	17
3.04	Number of telephone faults (per 100 main lines)	27
3.05	Number of telephone mainlines per employee	9
3.06	Number of fax machines (per 1,000 people)	39
3.07	Local switch capacity (per 100,000 people)	40
3.08	Ease of obtaining new telephone lines	38
3.09	Waiting time for telephone mainlines (in years)	35
3.1	Number of secure Internet servers	35

Readiness Component Index	47
Individual Readiness	40
Business Readiness	42
Government Readiness	58

4.01	Sophistication of local buyers' products and processes	53
4.02	Availability of mobile Internet access	42
4.03	Availability of broadband access	60
4.04	Public access to the Internet	73
4.05	Secondary school enrollment (% net)	24
4.06	Total adult illiteracy rate (%)	34

Readiness Component Index (continued)	
4.07	Quality of math and science education	43
4.08	Cost of local call (US$ per three min)	30
4.09	Cost of off-peak local cellular call (US$ per three min)	48
4.10	Cost of residential telephone subscription (US$ per month)	20
5.01	Firm-level technology absorption	69
5.02	Firm-level innovation	38
5.03	Capacity for innovation	59
5.04	Business Intranet sophistication	24
5.05	Quality of local IT training programs	45
5.06	Cost of business telephone subscription (US$ per month)	11
6.01	Government prioritization of ICT	57
6.02	Government procurement of advanced technology products	57
6.03	Competence of public officials	61
6.04	Government online services	59

Usage Component Index	42
Individual Usage	29
Business Usage	63
Government Usage	49

7.01	Use of online payment systems	65
7.02	Number of radios (per 1,000 people)	42
7.03	Number of television sets (per 1,000 people)	27
7.04	Number of cable television subscribers (per 1,000 people)	77
7.05	Number of mobile telephones (per 1,000 people)	23
7.06	Number of Internet users (per 100 people)	5
7.07	Number of narrowband subscriber lines (per 100 people)	18
7.08	Number of broadband subscriber lines (per 100 people)	16
7.09	Household spending on ICT (US$ per month)	31
8.01	Use of Internet for coordination with customers and suppliers	81
8.02	Businesses using e-commerce (%)	63
8.03	Use of Internet for general research	39
8.04	Sophistication of online marketing	43
8.05	Presence of wireless e-business applications	77
8.06	Use of email for internal correspondence (%)	52
8.07	Use of email for external correspondence (%)	63
8.08	Pervasiveness of company web pages	53
9.01	Use of Internet-based transactions with the government	49
9.02	Government online services	59
9.03	Government success in ICT promotion	53

Guatemala.gt

Key Indicators

Population	11,385,300
GDP per capita (PPP)	US$3,821
Illiteracy rate	31.36%
GDP per capita growth	0.63%

Networked Readiness Index Rank

2002–2003 **73**

2001–2002   68

Environment Component Index — 74

Market Environment		77
Political and Regulatory Environment		78
Infrastructure Environment		66
1.01	Venture capital availability	65
1.02	State of cluster development	70
1.03	Competition in the telecommunication sector	49
1.04	Availability of scientists and engineers	76
1.05	Brain drain	66
1.06	Public spending on education (% of GDP)	80
1.07	Domestic software companies in international markets	69
1.08	Domestic manufacturing of IT hardware	73
1.09	ICT expenditure (% of GDP)	75
2.01	Effectiveness of law-making bodies	78
2.02	Legal framework for ICT development	76
2.03	Subsidies for firm-level research and development	70
2.04	Government restrictions on Internet content	56
2.05	Prevalence of foreign technology licensing	79
3.01	Overall infrastructure quality	65
3.02	Local availability of specialized IT services	58
3.03	Number of telephone mainlines (per 1,000 people)	69
3.04	Number of telephone faults (per 100 main lines)	46
3.05	Number of telephone mainlines per employee	54
3.06	Number of fax machines (per 1,000 people)	72
3.07	Local switch capacity (per 100,000 people)	69
3.08	Ease of obtaining new telephone lines	63
3.09	Waiting time for telephone mainlines (in years)	62
3.1	Number of secure Internet servers	61

Readiness Component Index — 73

Individual Readiness		73
Business Readiness		71
Government Readiness		81
4.01	Sophistication of local buyers' products and processes	80
4.02	Availability of mobile Internet access	52
4.03	Availability of broadband access	38
4.04	Public access to the Internet	66
4.05	Secondary school enrollment (% net)	51
4.06	Total adult illiteracy rate (%)	75

Readiness Component Index (continued)

4.07	Quality of math and science education	81
4.08	Cost of local call (US$ per three min)	77
4.09	Cost of off-peak local cellular call (US$ per three min)	69
4.10	Cost of residential telephone subscription (US$ per month)	1
5.01	Firm-level technology absorption	75
5.02	Firm-level innovation	59
5.03	Capacity for innovation	62
5.04	Business Intranet sophistication	70
5.05	Quality of local IT training programs	73
5.06	Cost of business telephone subscription (US$ per month)	56
6.01	Government prioritization of ICT	82
6.02	Government procurement of advanced technology products	82
6.03	Competence of public officials	80
6.04	Government online services	60

Usage Component Index — 73

Individual Usage		69
Business Usage		69
Government Usage		76
7.01	Use of online payment systems	69
7.02	Number of radios (per 1,000 people)	80
7.03	Number of television sets (per 1,000 people)	77
7.04	Number of cable television subscribers (per 1,000 people)	51
7.05	Number of mobile telephones (per 1,000 people)	61
7.06	Number of Internet users (per 100 people)	59
7.07	Number of narrowband subscriber lines (per 100 people)	73
7.08	Number of broadband subscriber lines (per 100 people)	44
7.09	Household spending on ICT (US$ per month)	38
8.01	Use of Internet for coordination with customers and suppliers	69
8.02	Businesses using e-commerce (%)	76
8.03	Use of Internet for general research	59
8.04	Sophistication of online marketing	73
8.05	Presence of wireless e-business applications	54
8.06	Use of email for internal correspondence (%)	60
8.07	Use of email for external correspondence (%)	35
8.08	Pervasiveness of company web pages	69
9.01	Use of Internet-based transactions with the government	77
9.02	Government online services	60
9.03	Government success in ICT promotion	77

Haiti.ht

Key Indicators

Population	7,959,000
GDP per capita (PPP)	US$1,467
Illiteracy rate	50.18%
GDP per capita growth	-0.86%

Networked Readiness Index Rank

2002–2003 **82**

2001–2002 —

Environment Component Index — 82

Market Environment	80
Political and Regulatory Environment	82
Infrastructure Environment	82

1.01	Venture capital availability	75
1.02	State of cluster development	82
1.03	Competition in the telecommunication sector	71
1.04	Availability of scientists and engineers	82
1.05	Brain drain	82
1.06	Public spending on education (% of GDP)	26
1.07	Domestic software companies in international markets	27
1.08	Domestic manufacturing of IT hardware	78
1.09	ICT expenditure (% of GDP)	78
2.01	Effectiveness of law-making bodies	82
2.02	Legal framework for ICT development	79
2.03	Subsidies for firm-level research and development	80
2.04	Government restrictions on Internet content	51
2.05	Prevalence of foreign technology licensing	82
3.01	Overall infrastructure quality	82
3.02	Local availability of specialized IT services	54
3.03	Number of telephone mainlines (per 1,000 people)	80
3.04	Number of telephone faults (per 100 main lines)	77
3.05	Number of telephone mainlines per employee	81
3.06	Number of fax machines (per 1,000 people)	72
3.07	Local switch capacity (per 100,000 people)	52
3.08	Ease of obtaining new telephone lines	81
3.09	Waiting time for telephone mainlines (in years)	80
3.1	Number of secure Internet servers	75

Readiness Component Index — 82

Individual Readiness	80
Business Readiness	82
Government Readiness	82

4.01	Sophistication of local buyers' products and processes	78
4.02	Availability of mobile Internet access	64
4.03	Availability of broadband access	68
4.04	Public access to the Internet	58
4.05	Secondary school enrollment (% net)	76
4.06	Total adult illiteracy rate (%)	80

Readiness Component Index (continued)

4.07	Quality of math and science education	82
4.08	Cost of local call (US$ per three min)	73
4.09	Cost of off-peak local cellular call (US$ per three min)	79
4.10	Cost of residential telephone subscription (US$ per month)	78
5.01	Firm-level technology absorption	77
5.02	Firm-level innovation	79
5.03	Capacity for innovation	82
5.04	Business Intranet sophistication	50
5.05	Quality of local IT training programs	79
5.06	Cost of business telephone subscription (US$ per month)	80
6.01	Government prioritization of ICT	81
6.02	Government procurement of advanced technology products	79
6.03	Competence of public officials	64
6.04	Government online services	78

Usage Component Index — 80

Individual Usage	82
Business Usage	68
Government Usage	78

7.01	Use of online payment systems	77
7.02	Number of radios (per 1,000 people)	81
7.03	Number of television sets (per 1,000 people)	82
7.04	Number of cable television subscribers (per 1,000 people)	56
7.05	Number of mobile telephones (per 1,000 people)	80
7.06	Number of Internet users (per 100 people)	70
7.07	Number of narrowband subscriber lines (per 100 people)	70
7.08	Number of broadband subscriber lines (per 100 people)	44
7.09	Household spending on ICT (US$ per month)	74
8.01	Use of Internet for coordination with customers and suppliers	70
8.02	Businesses using e-commerce (%)	64
8.03	Use of Internet for general research	68
8.04	Sophistication of online marketing	52
8.05	Presence of wireless e-business applications	61
8.06	Use of email for internal correspondence (%)	47
8.07	Use of email for external correspondence (%)	59
8.08	Pervasiveness of company web pages	78
9.01	Use of Internet-based transactions with the government	51
9.02	Government online services	78
9.03	Government success in ICT promotion	82

Honduras.hn

Key Indicators

Population	6,417,000
GDP per capita (PPP)	US$2,453
Illiteracy rate	25.39%
GDP per capita growth	2.20%

Networked Readiness Index Rank

2002–2003 **81**

2001–2002 72

Environment Component Index — 80

Market Environment	82

Political and Regulatory Environment	76

Infrastructure Environment	77

1.01	Venture capital availability	80
1.02	State of cluster development	79
1.03	Competition in the telecommunication sector	81
1.04	Availability of scientists and engineers	78
1.05	Brain drain	60
1.06	Public spending on education (% of GDP)	55
1.07	Domestic software companies in international markets	82
1.08	Domestic manufacturing of IT hardware	76
1.09	ICT expenditure (% of GDP)	52
2.01	Effectiveness of law-making bodies	62
2.02	Legal framework for ICT development	74
2.03	Subsidies for firm-level research and development	72
2.04	Government restrictions on Internet content	73
2.05	Prevalence of foreign technology licensing	75
3.01	Overall infrastructure quality	71
3.02	Local availability of specialized IT services	69
3.03	Number of telephone mainlines (per 1,000 people)	72
3.04	Number of telephone faults (per 100 main lines)	51
3.05	Number of telephone mainlines per employee	77
3.06	Number of fax machines (per 1,000 people)	72
3.07	Local switch capacity (per 100,000 people)	74
3.08	Ease of obtaining new telephone lines	82
3.09	Waiting time for telephone mainlines (in years)	77
3.1	Number of secure Internet servers	66

Readiness Component Index — 78

Individual Readiness	78

Business Readiness	79

Government Readiness	76

4.01	Sophistication of local buyers' products and processes	81
4.02	Availability of mobile Internet access	70
4.03	Availability of broadband access	59
4.04	Public access to the Internet	79
4.05	Secondary school enrollment (% net)	65
4.06	Total adult illiteracy rate (%)	73

Readiness Component Index (continued)

4.07	Quality of math and science education	80
4.08	Cost of local call (US$ per three min)	78
4.09	Cost of off-peak local cellular call (US$ per three min)	80
4.10	Cost of residential telephone subscription (US$ per month)	56
5.01	Firm-level technology absorption	81
5.02	Firm-level innovation	56
5.03	Capacity for innovation	75
5.04	Business Intranet sophistication	74
5.05	Quality of local IT training programs	81
5.06	Cost of business telephone subscription (US$ per month)	65
6.01	Government prioritization of ICT	77
6.02	Government procurement of advanced technology products	78
6.03	Competence of public officials	62
6.04	Government online services	75

Usage Component Index — 79

Individual Usage	75

Business Usage	64

Government Usage	80

7.01	Use of online payment systems	78
7.02	Number of radios (per 1,000 people)	48
7.03	Number of television sets (per 1,000 people)	72
7.04	Number of cable television subscribers (per 1,000 people)	72
7.05	Number of mobile telephones (per 1,000 people)	69
7.06	Number of Internet users (per 100 people)	63
7.07	Number of narrowband subscriber lines (per 100 people)	77
7.08	Number of broadband subscriber lines (per 100 people)	44
7.09	Household spending on ICT (US$ per month)	45
8.01	Use of Internet for coordination with customers and suppliers	41
8.02	Businesses using e-commerce (%)	10
8.03	Use of Internet for general research	65
8.04	Sophistication of online marketing	69
8.05	Presence of wireless e-business applications	57
8.06	Use of email for internal correspondence (%)	69
8.07	Use of email for external correspondence (%)	67
8.08	Pervasiveness of company web pages	74
9.01	Use of Internet-based transactions with the government	81
9.02	Government online services	75
9.03	Government success in ICT promotion	79

Hong Kong SAR.hk

Key Indicators

Population	6,797,000
GDP per capita (PPP)	US$25,153
Illiteracy rate	6.45%
GDP per capita growth	9.23%

Networked Readiness Index Rank

2002–2003 **18**

2001–2002   13

Environment Component Index	21
Market Environment	23
Political and Regulatory Environment	18
Infrastructure Environment	18

1.01	Venture capital availability	8
1.02	State of cluster development	12
1.03	Competition in the telecommunication sector	6
1.04	Availability of scientists and engineers	50
1.05	Brain drain	20
1.06	Public spending on education (% of GDP)	72
1.07	Domestic software companies in international markets	28
1.08	Domestic manufacturing of IT hardware	50
1.09	ICT expenditure (% of GDP)	11
2.01	Effectiveness of law-making bodies	26
2.02	Legal framework for ICT development	11
2.03	Subsidies for firm-level research and development	46
2.04	Government restrictions on Internet content	7
2.05	Prevalence of foreign technology licensing	14
3.01	Overall infrastructure quality	14
3.02	Local availability of specialized IT services	32
3.03	Number of telephone mainlines (per 1,000 people)	12
3.04	Number of telephone faults (per 100 main lines)	11
3.05	Number of telephone mainlines per employee	62
3.06	Number of fax machines (per 1,000 people)	5
3.07	Local switch capacity (per 100,000 people)	16
3.08	Ease of obtaining new telephone lines	4
3.09	Waiting time for telephone mainlines (in years)	1
3.1	Number of secure Internet servers	14

Readiness Component Index	17
Individual Readiness	12
Business Readiness	23
Government Readiness	11

4.01	Sophistication of local buyers' products and processes	8
4.02	Availability of mobile Internet access	22
4.03	Availability of broadband access	10
4.04	Public access to the Internet	18
4.05	Secondary school enrollment (% net)	12
4.06	Total adult illiteracy rate (%)	45

Readiness Component Index (continued)	
4.07	Quality of math and science education	13
4.08	Cost of local call (US$ per three min)	1
4.09	Cost of off-peak local cellular call (US$ per three min)	21
4.10	Cost of residential telephone subscription (US$ per month)	27
5.01	Firm-level technology absorption	32
5.02	Firm-level innovation	26
5.03	Capacity for innovation	36
5.04	Business Intranet sophistication	17
5.05	Quality of local IT training programs	21
5.06	Cost of business telephone subscription (US$ per month)	22
6.01	Government prioritization of ICT	19
6.02	Government procurement of advanced technology products	30
6.03	Competence of public officials	9
6.04	Government online services	6

Usage Component Index	16
Individual Usage	23
Business Usage	15
Government Usage	11

7.01	Use of online payment systems	16
7.02	Number of radios (per 1,000 people)	30
7.03	Number of television sets (per 1,000 people)	26
7.04	Number of cable television subscribers (per 1,000 people)	31
7.05	Number of mobile telephones (per 1,000 people)	2
7.06	Number of Internet users (per 100 people)	16
7.07	Number of narrowband subscriber lines (per 100 people)	46
7.08	Number of broadband subscriber lines (per 100 people)	5
7.09	Household spending on ICT (US$ per month)	27
8.01	Use of Internet for coordination with customers and suppliers	11
8.02	Businesses using e-commerce (%)	31
8.03	Use of Internet for general research	23
8.04	Sophistication of online marketing	17
8.05	Presence of wireless e-business applications	16
8.06	Use of email for internal correspondence (%)	20
8.07	Use of email for external correspondence (%)	15
8.08	Pervasiveness of company web pages	14
9.01	Use of Internet-based transactions with the government	18
9.02	Government online services	6
9.03	Government success in ICT promotion	28

Hungary.hu

Key Indicators

Population	10,022,000
GDP per capita (PPP)	US$12,416
Illiteracy rate	0.68%
GDP per capita growth	5.63%

Networked Readiness Index Rank

2002–2003 ● **30**

2001–2002   30

Environment Component Index	30
Market Environment	29
Political and Regulatory Environment	31
Infrastructure Environment	31

1.01	Venture capital availability	41
1.02	State of cluster development	40
1.03	Competition in the telecommunication sector	38
1.04	Availability of scientists and engineers	12
1.05	Brain drain	39
1.06	Public spending on education (% of GDP)	43
1.07	Domestic software companies in international markets	18
1.08	Domestic manufacturing of IT hardware	27
1.09	ICT expenditure (% of GDP)	12
2.01	Effectiveness of law-making bodies	30
2.02	Legal framework for ICT development	49
2.03	Subsidies for firm-level research and development	20
2.04	Government restrictions on Internet content	17
2.05	Prevalence of foreign technology licensing	35
3.01	Overall infrastructure quality	40
3.02	Local availability of specialized IT services	30
3.03	Number of telephone mainlines (per 1,000 people)	31
3.04	Number of telephone faults (per 100 main lines)	39
3.05	Number of telephone mainlines per employee	29
3.06	Number of fax machines (per 1,000 people)	27
3.07	Local switch capacity (per 100,000 people)	38
3.08	Ease of obtaining new telephone lines	26
3.09	Waiting time for telephone mainlines (in years)	29
3.1	Number of secure Internet servers	36

Readiness Component Index	28
Individual Readiness	26
Business Readiness	32
Government Readiness	22

4.01	Sophistication of local buyers' products and processes	26
4.02	Availability of mobile Internet access	30
4.03	Availability of broadband access	33
4.04	Public access to the Internet	34
4.05	Secondary school enrollment (% net)	28
4.06	Total adult illiteracy rate (%)	15

Readiness Component Index (continued)	
4.07	Quality of math and science education	10
4.08	Cost of local call (US$ per three min)	48
4.09	Cost of off-peak local cellular call (US$ per three min)	34
4.10	Cost of residential telephone subscription (US$ per month)	48
5.01	Firm-level technology absorption	40
5.02	Firm-level innovation	58
5.03	Capacity for innovation	33
5.04	Business Intranet sophistication	34
5.05	Quality of local IT training programs	23
5.06	Cost of business telephone subscription (US$ per month)	40
6.01	Government prioritization of ICT	13
6.02	Government procurement of advanced technology products	24
6.03	Competence of public officials	28
6.04	Government online services	27

Usage Component Index	36
Individual Usage	34
Business Usage	54
Government Usage	28

7.01	Use of online payment systems	52
7.02	Number of radios (per 1,000 people)	29
7.03	Number of television sets (per 1,000 people)	31
7.04	Number of cable television subscribers (per 1,000 people)	19
7.05	Number of mobile telephones (per 1,000 people)	31
7.06	Number of Internet users (per 100 people)	45
7.07	Number of narrowband subscriber lines (per 100 people)	26
7.08	Number of broadband subscriber lines (per 100 people)	26
7.09	Household spending on ICT (US$ per month)	67
8.01	Use of Internet for coordination with customers and suppliers	68
8.02	Businesses using e-commerce (%)	41
8.03	Use of Internet for general research	51
8.04	Sophistication of online marketing	54
8.05	Presence of wireless e-business applications	56
8.06	Use of email for internal correspondence (%)	55
8.07	Use of email for external correspondence (%)	74
8.08	Pervasiveness of company web pages	33
9.01	Use of Internet-based transactions with the government	44
9.02	Government online services	27
9.03	Government success in ICT promotion	18

Iceland.is

Key Indicators

Population	281,000
GDP per capita (PPP)	US$29,581
Illiteracy rate	0.10%
GDP per capita growth	3.69%

Networked Readiness Index Rank

2002–2003 **5**

2001–2002 2

Environment Component Index		3
Market Environment		17
Political and Regulatory Environment		9
Infrastructure Environment		1
1.01	Venture capital availability	13
1.02	State of cluster development	18
1.03	Competition in the telecommunication sector	17
1.04	Availability of scientists and engineers	18
1.05	Brain drain	10
1.06	Public spending on education (% of GDP)	11
1.07	Domestic software companies in international markets	13
1.08	Domestic manufacturing of IT hardware	56
1.09	ICT expenditure (% of GDP)	23
2.01	Effectiveness of law-making bodies	5
2.02	Legal framework for ICT development	9
2.03	Subsidies for firm-level research and development	38
2.04	Government restrictions on Internet content	1
2.05	Prevalence of foreign technology licensing	41
3.01	Overall infrastructure quality	7
3.02	Local availability of specialized IT services	20
3.03	Number of telephone mainlines (per 1,000 people)	4
3.04	Number of telephone faults (per 100 main lines)	23
3.05	Number of telephone mainlines per employee	50
3.06	Number of fax machines (per 1,000 people)	11
3.07	Local switch capacity (per 100,000 people)	1
3.08	Ease of obtaining new telephone lines	2
3.09	Waiting time for telephone mainlines (in years)	1
3.1	Number of secure Internet servers	1

Readiness Component Index		6
Individual Readiness		3
Business Readiness		8
Government Readiness		9
4.01	Sophistication of local buyers' products and processes	1
4.02	Availability of mobile Internet access	8
4.03	Availability of broadband access	11
4.04	Public access to the Internet	1
4.05	Secondary school enrollment (% net)	25
4.06	Total adult illiteracy rate (%)	7

Readiness Component Index (continued)		
4.07	Quality of math and science education	17
4.08	Cost of local call (US$ per three min)	18
4.09	Cost of off-peak local cellular call (US$ per three min)	18
4.10	Cost of residential telephone subscription (US$ per month)	17
5.01	Firm-level technology absorption	4
5.02	Firm-level innovation	4
5.03	Capacity for innovation	18
5.04	Business Intranet sophistication	31
5.05	Quality of local IT training programs	6
5.06	Cost of business telephone subscription (US$ per month)	26
6.01	Government prioritization of ICT	21
6.02	Government procurement of advanced technology products	17
6.03	Competence of public officials	30
6.04	Government online services	2

Usage Component Index		5
Individual Usage		19
Business Usage		5
Government Usage		3
7.01	Use of online payment systems	4
7.02	Number of radios (per 1,000 people)	7
7.03	Number of television sets (per 1,000 people)	23
7.04	Number of cable television subscribers (per 1,000 people)	74
7.05	Number of mobile telephones (per 1,000 people)	20
7.06	Number of Internet users (per 100 people)	10
7.07	Number of narrowband subscriber lines (per 100 people)	5
7.08	Number of broadband subscriber lines (per 100 people)	44
7.09	Household spending on ICT (US$ per month)	11
8.01	Use of Internet for coordination with customers and suppliers	9
8.02	Businesses using e-commerce (%)	8
8.03	Use of Internet for general research	30
8.04	Sophistication of online marketing	23
8.05	Presence of wireless e-business applications	2
8.06	Use of email for internal correspondence (%)	25
8.07	Use of email for external correspondence (%)	2
8.08	Pervasiveness of company web pages	3
9.01	Use of Internet-based transactions with the government	1
9.02	Government online services	2
9.03	Government success in ICT promotion	10

India.in

Key Indicators

Population	1,015,923,008
GDP per capita (PPP)	US$2,358
Illiteracy rate	42.76 %
GDP per capita growth	2.04 %

Networked Readiness Index Rank

2002–2003	**37**
2001–2002	54

Environment Component Index — 34

Market Environment	28
Political and Regulatory Environment	16
Infrastructure Environment	70

1.01	Venture capital availability	30
1.02	State of cluster development	20
1.03	Competition in the telecommunication sector	42
1.04	Availability of scientists and engineers	2
1.05	Brain drain	54
1.06	Public spending on education (% of GDP)	71
1.07	Domestic software companies in international markets	2
1.08	Domestic manufacturing of IT hardware	21
1.09	ICT expenditure (% of GDP)	69
2.01	Effectiveness of law-making bodies	32
2.02	Legal framework for ICT development	27
2.03	Subsidies for firm-level research and development	18
2.04	Government restrictions on Internet content	64
2.05	Prevalence of foreign technology licensing	1
3.01	Overall infrastructure quality	64
3.02	Local availability of specialized IT services	11
3.03	Number of telephone mainlines (per 1,000 people)	75
3.04	Number of telephone faults (per 100 main lines)	80
3.05	Number of telephone mainlines per employee	75
3.06	Number of fax machines (per 1,000 people)	69
3.07	Local switch capacity (per 100,000 people)	78
3.08	Ease of obtaining new telephone lines	48
3.09	Waiting time for telephone mainlines (in years)	50
3.1	Number of secure Internet servers	76

Readiness Component Index — 40

Individual Readiness	70
Business Readiness	27
Government Readiness	33

4.01	Sophistication of local buyers' products and processes	30
4.02	Availability of mobile Internet access	62
4.03	Availability of broadband access	67
4.04	Public access to the Internet	29
4.05	Secondary school enrollment (% net)	77
4.06	Total adult illiteracy rate (%)	78

Readiness Component Index (continued)

4.07	Quality of math and science education	37
4.08	Cost of local call (US$ per three min)	45
4.09	Cost of off-peak local cellular call (US$ per three min)	76
4.10	Cost of residential telephone subscription (US$ per month)	77
5.01	Firm-level technology absorption	16
5.02	Firm-level innovation	13
5.03	Capacity for innovation	46
5.04	Business Intranet sophistication	36
5.05	Quality of local IT training programs	9
5.06	Cost of business telephone subscription (US$ per month)	67
6.01	Government prioritization of ICT	8
6.02	Government procurement of advanced technology products	56
6.03	Competence of public officials	37
6.04	Government online services	35

Usage Component Index — 43

Individual Usage	79
Business Usage	42
Government Usage	25

7.01	Use of online payment systems	59
7.02	Number of radios (per 1,000 people)	78
7.03	Number of television sets (per 1,000 people)	74
7.04	Number of cable television subscribers (per 1,000 people)	49
7.05	Number of mobile telephones (per 1,000 people)	79
7.06	Number of Internet users (per 100 people)	72
7.07	Number of narrowband subscriber lines (per 100 people)	79
7.08	Number of broadband subscriber lines (per 100 people)	44
7.09	Household spending on ICT (US$ per month)	79
8.01	Use of Internet for coordination with customers and suppliers	72
8.02	Businesses using e-commerce (%)	73
8.03	Use of Internet for general research	56
8.04	Sophistication of online marketing	34
8.05	Presence of wireless e-business applications	70
8.06	Use of email for internal correspondence (%)	27
8.07	Use of email for external correspondence (%)	34
8.08	Pervasiveness of company web pages	41
9.01	Use of Internet-based transactions with the government	39
9.02	Government online services	35
9.03	Government success in ICT promotion	8

Indonesia.id

Key Indicators

Population	210,420,992
GDP per capita (PPP)	US$3,043
Illiteracy rate	13.14%
GDP per capita growth	3.08%

Networked Readiness Index Rank

2002–2003	64
2001–2002	59

Environment Component Index — 65

Market Environment	61
Political and Regulatory Environment	55
Infrastructure Environment	75

1.01	Venture capital availability	67
1.02	State of cluster development	26
1.03	Competition in the telecommunication sector	51
1.04	Availability of scientists and engineers	69
1.05	Brain drain	38
1.06	Public spending on education (% of GDP)	81
1.07	Domestic software companies in international markets	39
1.08	Domestic manufacturing of IT hardware	36
1.09	ICT expenditure (% of GDP)	81
2.01	Effectiveness of law-making bodies	55
2.02	Legal framework for ICT development	73
2.03	Subsidies for firm-level research and development	69
2.04	Government restrictions on Internet content	10
2.05	Prevalence of foreign technology licensing	25
3.01	Overall infrastructure quality	66
3.02	Local availability of specialized IT services	71
3.03	Number of telephone mainlines (per 1,000 people)	77
3.04	Number of telephone faults (per 100 main lines)	36
3.05	Number of telephone mainlines per employee	32
3.06	Number of fax machines (per 1,000 people)	58
3.07	Local switch capacity (per 100,000 people)	80
3.08	Ease of obtaining new telephone lines	68
3.09	Waiting time for telephone mainlines (in years)	80
3.1	Number of secure Internet servers	71

Readiness Component Index — 62

Individual Readiness	60
Business Readiness	52
Government Readiness	62

4.01	Sophistication of local buyers' products and processes	59
4.02	Availability of mobile Internet access	61
4.03	Availability of broadband access	61
4.04	Public access to the Internet	50
4.05	Secondary school enrollment (% net)	71
4.06	Total adult illiteracy rate (%)	62

Readiness Component Index (continued)

4.07	Quality of math and science education	63
4.08	Cost of local call (US$ per three min)	43
4.09	Cost of off-peak local cellular call (US$ per three min)	44
4.10	Cost of residential telephone subscription (US$ per month)	58
5.01	Firm-level technology absorption	50
5.02	Firm-level innovation	57
5.03	Capacity for innovation	61
5.04	Business Intranet sophistication	39
5.05	Quality of local IT training programs	60
5.06	Cost of business telephone subscription (US$ per month)	59
6.01	Government prioritization of ICT	64
6.02	Government procurement of advanced technology products	41
6.03	Competence of public officials	68
6.04	Government online services	74

Usage Component Index — 64

Individual Usage	77
Business Usage	47
Government Usage	65

7.01	Use of online payment systems	66
7.02	Number of radios (per 1,000 people)	75
7.03	Number of television sets (per 1,000 people)	65
7.04	Number of cable television subscribers (per 1,000 people)	81
7.05	Number of mobile telephones (per 1,000 people)	75
7.06	Number of Internet users (per 100 people)	66
7.07	Number of narrowband subscriber lines (per 100 people)	81
7.08	Number of broadband subscriber lines (per 100 people)	44
7.09	Household spending on ICT (US$ per month)	71
8.01	Use of Internet for coordination with customers and suppliers	38
8.02	Businesses using e-commerce (%)	57
8.03	Use of Internet for general research	54
8.04	Sophistication of online marketing	28
8.05	Presence of wireless e-business applications	74
8.06	Use of email for internal correspondence (%)	44
8.07	Use of email for external correspondence (%)	44
8.08	Pervasiveness of company web pages	56
9.01	Use of Internet-based transactions with the government	36
9.02	Government online services	74
9.03	Government success in ICT promotion	62

Ireland.ie

Key Indicators

Population	3,794,000
GDP per capita (PPP)	US$29,866
Illiteracy rate	2.00%
GDP per capita growth	10.27%

Networked Readiness Index Rank

2002–2003 **21**

2001–2002   19

Environment Component Index — 16

Market Environment	12
Political and Regulatory Environment	8
Infrastructure Environment	26

1.01	Venture capital availability	6
1.02	State of cluster development	10
1.03	Competition in the telecommunication sector	41
1.04	Availability of scientists and engineers	32
1.05	Brain drain	18
1.06	Public spending on education (% of GDP)	46
1.07	Domestic software companies in international markets	7
1.08	Domestic manufacturing of IT hardware	3
1.09	ICT expenditure (% of GDP)	39
2.01	Effectiveness of law-making bodies	15
2.02	Legal framework for ICT development	14
2.03	Subsidies for firm-level research and development	5
2.04	Government restrictions on Internet content	37
2.05	Prevalence of foreign technology licensing	17
3.01	Overall infrastructure quality	55
3.02	Local availability of specialized IT services	13
3.03	Number of telephone mainlines (per 1,000 people)	28
3.04	Number of telephone faults (per 100 main lines)	16
3.05	Number of telephone mainlines per employee	67
3.06	Number of fax machines (per 1,000 people)	19
3.07	Local switch capacity (per 100,000 people)	4
3.08	Ease of obtaining new telephone lines	27
3.09	Waiting time for telephone mainlines (in years)	25
3.1	Number of secure Internet servers	11

Readiness Component Index — 20

Individual Readiness	29
Business Readiness	19
Government Readiness	12

4.01	Sophistication of local buyers' products and processes	19
4.02	Availability of mobile Internet access	24
4.03	Availability of broadband access	51
4.04	Public access to the Internet	31
4.05	Secondary school enrollment (% net)	37
4.06	Total adult illiteracy rate (%)	28

Readiness Component Index (continued)

4.07	Quality of math and science education	24
4.08	Cost of local call (US$ per three min)	39
4.09	Cost of off-peak local cellular call (US$ per three min)	28
4.10	Cost of residential telephone subscription (US$ per month)	41
5.01	Firm-level technology absorption	18
5.02	Firm-level innovation	47
5.03	Capacity for innovation	23
5.04	Business Intranet sophistication	32
5.05	Quality of local IT training programs	10
5.06	Cost of business telephone subscription (US$ per month)	27
6.01	Government prioritization of ICT	12
6.02	Government procurement of advanced technology products	16
6.03	Competence of public officials	11
6.04	Government online services	17

Usage Component Index — 23

Individual Usage	21
Business Usage	30
Government Usage	18

7.01	Use of online payment systems	22
7.02	Number of radios (per 1,000 people)	27
7.03	Number of television sets (per 1,000 people)	36
7.04	Number of cable television subscribers (per 1,000 people)	15
7.05	Number of mobile telephones (per 1,000 people)	14
7.06	Number of Internet users (per 100 people)	14
7.07	Number of narrowband subscriber lines (per 100 people)	28
7.08	Number of broadband subscriber lines (per 100 people)	14
7.09	Household spending on ICT (US$ per month)	19
8.01	Use of Internet for coordination with customers and suppliers	21
8.02	Businesses using e-commerce (%)	23
8.03	Use of Internet for general research	43
8.04	Sophistication of online marketing	36
8.05	Presence of wireless e-business applications	25
8.06	Use of email for internal correspondence (%)	24
8.07	Use of email for external correspondence (%)	55
8.08	Pervasiveness of company web pages	32
9.01	Use of Internet-based transactions with the government	42
9.02	Government online services	17
9.03	Government success in ICT promotion	14

Israel.il

Key Indicators

Population	6,233,210
GDP per capita (PPP)	US$20,131
Illiteracy rate	5.43%
GDP per capita growth	3.82%

Networked Readiness Index Rank

2002–2003 **12**

2001–2002 22

Environment Component Index — 5

Market Environment		5
Political and Regulatory Environment		2
Infrastructure Environment		22

1.01	Venture capital availability	4
1.02	State of cluster development	42
1.03	Competition in the telecommunication sector	30
1.04	Availability of scientists and engineers	1
1.05	Brain drain	4
1.06	Public spending on education (% of GDP)	7
1.07	Domestic software companies in international markets	4
1.08	Domestic manufacturing of IT hardware	6
1.09	ICT expenditure (% of GDP)	29
2.01	Effectiveness of law-making bodies	21
2.02	Legal framework for ICT development	21
2.03	Subsidies for firm-level research and development	1
2.04	Government restrictions on Internet content	17
2.05	Prevalence of foreign technology licensing	2
3.01	Overall infrastructure quality	28
3.02	Local availability of specialized IT services	3
3.03	Number of telephone mainlines (per 1,000 people)	22
3.04	Number of telephone faults (per 100 main lines)	5
3.05	Number of telephone mainlines per employee	12
3.06	Number of fax machines (per 1,000 people)	22
3.07	Local switch capacity (per 100,000 people)	25
3.08	Ease of obtaining new telephone lines	9
3.09	Waiting time for telephone mainlines (in years)	38
3.1	Number of secure Internet servers	80

Readiness Component Index — 8

Individual Readiness		24
Business Readiness		3
Government Readiness		5

4.01	Sophistication of local buyers' products and processes	14
4.02	Availability of mobile Internet access	38
4.03	Availability of broadband access	53
4.04	Public access to the Internet	32
4.05	Secondary school enrollment (% net)	29
4.06	Total adult illiteracy rate (%)	42

Readiness Component Index (continued)

4.07	Quality of math and science education	10
4.08	Cost of local call (US$ per three min)	6
4.09	Cost of off-peak local cellular call (US$ per three min)	16
4.10	Cost of residential telephone subscription (US$ per month)	26
5.01	Firm-level technology absorption	1
5.02	Firm-level innovation	14
5.03	Capacity for innovation	8
5.04	Business Intranet sophistication	16
5.05	Quality of local IT training programs	7
5.06	Cost of business telephone subscription (US$ per month)	16
6.01	Government prioritization of ICT	5
6.02	Government procurement of advanced technology products	2
6.03	Competence of public officials	7
6.04	Government online services	33

Usage Component Index — 19

Individual Usage		20
Business Usage		26
Government Usage		19

7.01	Use of online payment systems	30
7.02	Number of radios (per 1,000 people)	39
7.03	Number of television sets (per 1,000 people)	43
7.04	Number of cable television subscribers (per 1,000 people)	11
7.05	Number of mobile telephones (per 1,000 people)	10
7.06	Number of Internet users (per 100 people)	11
7.07	Number of narrowband subscriber lines (per 100 people)	10
7.08	Number of broadband subscriber lines (per 100 people)	42
7.09	Household spending on ICT (US$ per month)	6
8.01	Use of Internet for coordination with customers and suppliers	63
8.02	Businesses using e-commerce (%)	26
8.03	Use of Internet for general research	9
8.04	Sophistication of online marketing	30
8.05	Presence of wireless e-business applications	31
8.06	Use of email for internal correspondence (%)	29
8.07	Use of email for external correspondence (%)	5
8.08	Pervasiveness of company web pages	19
9.01	Use of Internet-based transactions with the government	38
9.02	Government online services	33
9.03	Government success in ICT promotion	4

Italy.it

Key Indicators

Population	57,690,000
GDP per capita (PPP)	$23,626
Illiteracy rate	1.57%
GDP per capita growth	2.84%

Networked Readiness Index Rank

2002–2003 **26**

2001–2002   25

Environment Component Index — 24

Market Environment		20
Political and Regulatory Environment		21
Infrastructure Environment		24
1.01	Venture capital availability	25
1.02	State of cluster development	1
1.03	Competition in the telecommunication sector	13
1.04	Availability of scientists and engineers	34
1.05	Brain drain	36
1.06	Public spending on education (% of GDP)	36
1.07	Domestic software companies in international markets	32
1.08	Domestic manufacturing of IT hardware	17
1.09	ICT expenditure (% of GDP)	51
2.01	Effectiveness of law-making bodies	31
2.02	Legal framework for ICT development	28
2.03	Subsidies for firm-level research and development	25
2.04	Government restrictions on Internet content	34
2.05	Prevalence of foreign technology licensing	9
3.01	Overall infrastructure quality	36
3.02	Local availability of specialized IT services	34
3.03	Number of telephone mainlines (per 1,000 people)	23
3.04	Number of telephone faults (per 100 main lines)	37
3.05	Number of telephone mainlines per employee	5
3.06	Number of fax machines (per 1,000 people)	17
3.07	Local switch capacity (per 100,000 people)	31
3.08	Ease of obtaining new telephone lines	43
3.09	Waiting time for telephone mainlines (in years)	1
3.1	Number of secure Internet servers	27

Readiness Component Index — 31

Individual Readiness		28
Business Readiness		30
Government Readiness		41
4.01	Sophistication of local buyers' products and processes	35
4.02	Availability of mobile Internet access	18
4.03	Availability of broadband access	30
4.04	Public access to the Internet	49
4.05	Secondary school enrollment (% net)	19
4.06	Total adult illiteracy rate (%)	24

Readiness Component Index (continued)

4.07	Quality of math and science education	33
4.08	Cost of local call (US$ per three min)	37
4.09	Cost of off-peak local cellular call (US$ per three min)	11
4.10	Cost of residential telephone subscription (US$ per month)	30
5.01	Firm-level technology absorption	44
5.02	Firm-level innovation	55
5.03	Capacity for innovation	19
5.04	Business Intranet sophistication	20
5.05	Quality of local IT training programs	33
5.06	Cost of business telephone subscription (US$ per month)	34
6.01	Government prioritization of ICT	52
6.02	Government procurement of advanced technology products	34
6.03	Competence of public officials	48
6.04	Government online services	25

Usage Component Index — 24

Individual Usage		27
Business Usage		21
Government Usage		31
7.01	Use of online payment systems	31
7.02	Number of radios (per 1,000 people)	20
7.03	Number of television sets (per 1,000 people)	25
7.04	Number of cable television subscribers (per 1,000 people)	78
7.05	Number of mobile telephones (per 1,000 people)	5
7.06	Number of Internet users (per 100 people)	25
7.07	Number of narrowband subscriber lines (per 100 people)	23
7.08	Number of broadband subscriber lines (per 100 people)	32
7.09	Household spending on ICT (US$ per month)	25
8.01	Use of Internet for coordination with customers and suppliers	27
8.02	Businesses using e-commerce (%)	16
8.03	Use of Internet for general research	12
8.04	Sophistication of online marketing	22
8.05	Presence of wireless e-business applications	12
8.06	Use of email for internal correspondence (%)	15
8.07	Use of email for external correspondence (%)	46
8.08	Pervasiveness of company web pages	24
9.01	Use of Internet-based transactions with the government	22
9.02	Government online services	25
9.03	Government success in ICT promotion	50

Jamaica.jm

Key Indicators

Population	2,633,000
GDP per capita (PPP)	US$3,639
Illiteracy rate	13.13%
GDP per capita growth	-0.86%

Networked Readiness Index Rank

2002–2003 **60**

2001–2002 56

Environment Component Index	62
Market Environment	67
Political and Regulatory Environment	51
Infrastructure Environment	67

1.01	Venture capital availability	70
1.02	State of cluster development	71
1.03	Competition in the telecommunication sector	52
1.04	Availability of scientists and engineers	68
1.05	Brain drain	69
1.06	Public spending on education (% of GDP)	15
1.07	Domestic software companies in international markets	70
1.08	Domestic manufacturing of IT hardware	68
1.09	ICT expenditure (% of GDP)	38
2.01	Effectiveness of law-making bodies	37
2.02	Legal framework for ICT development	45
2.03	Subsidies for firm-level research and development	68
2.04	Government restrictions on Internet content	17
2.05	Prevalence of foreign technology licensing	56
3.01	Overall infrastructure quality	56
3.02	Local availability of specialized IT services	64
3.03	Number of telephone mainlines (per 1,000 people)	49
3.04	Number of telephone faults (per 100 main lines)	68
3.05	Number of telephone mainlines per employee	33
3.06	Number of fax machines (per 1,000 people)	72
3.07	Local switch capacity (per 100,000 people)	30
3.08	Ease of obtaining new telephone lines	64
3.09	Waiting time for telephone mainlines (in years)	76
3.1	Number of secure Internet servers	51

Readiness Component Index	50
Individual Readiness	66
Business Readiness	58
Government Readiness	37

4.01	Sophistication of local buyers' products and processes	43
4.02	Availability of mobile Internet access	79
4.03	Availability of broadband access	79
4.04	Public access to the Internet	74
4.05	Secondary school enrollment (% net)	35
4.06	Total adult illiteracy rate (%)	61

Readiness Component Index (continued)	
4.07	Quality of math and science education	65
4.08	Cost of local call (US$ per three min)	68
4.09	Cost of off-peak local cellular call (US$ per three min)	42
4.10	Cost of residential telephone subscription (US$ per month)	69
5.01	Firm-level technology absorption	51
5.02	Firm-level innovation	31
5.03	Capacity for innovation	64
5.04	Business Intranet sophistication	75
5.05	Quality of local IT training programs	44
5.06	Cost of business telephone subscription (US$ per month)	61
6.01	Government prioritization of ICT	10
6.02	Government procurement of advanced technology products	47
6.03	Competence of public officials	42
6.04	Government online services	51

Usage Component Index	66
Individual Usage	48
Business Usage	76
Government Usage	63

7.01	Use of online payment systems	68
7.02	Number of radios (per 1,000 people)	24
7.03	Number of television sets (per 1,000 people)	58
7.04	Number of cable television subscribers (per 1,000 people)	25
7.05	Number of mobile telephones (per 1,000 people)	46
7.06	Number of Internet users (per 100 people)	47
7.07	Number of narrowband subscriber lines (per 100 people)	47
7.08	Number of broadband subscriber lines (per 100 people)	43
7.09	Household spending on ICT (US$ per month)	53
8.01	Use of Internet for coordination with customers and suppliers	43
8.02	Businesses using e-commerce (%)	52
8.03	Use of Internet for general research	63
8.04	Sophistication of online marketing	82
8.05	Presence of wireless e-business applications	80
8.06	Use of email for internal correspondence (%)	70
8.07	Use of email for external correspondence (%)	75
8.08	Pervasiveness of company web pages	63
9.01	Use of Internet-based transactions with the government	71
9.02	Government online services	51
9.03	Government success in ICT promotion	57

Japan.jp

Key Indicators

Population	126,870,000
GDP per capita (PPP)	US$26,755
Illiteracy rate	1.00%
GDP per capita growth	2.22%

Networked Readiness Index Rank

2002–2003 **20**

2001–2002 21

Environment Component Index — 19

Market Environment		18
Political and Regulatory Environment		37
Infrastructure Environment		4
1.01	Venture capital availability	45
1.02	State of cluster development	14
1.03	Competition in the telecommunication sector	33
1.04	Availability of scientists and engineers	7
1.05	Brain drain	7
1.06	Public spending on education (% of GDP)	61
1.07	Domestic software companies in international markets	42
1.08	Domestic manufacturing of IT hardware	2
1.09	ICT expenditure (% of GDP)	18
2.01	Effectiveness of law-making bodies	43
2.02	Legal framework for ICT development	52
2.03	Subsidies for firm-level research and development	19
2.04	Government restrictions on Internet content	60
2.05	Prevalence of foreign technology licensing	24
3.01	Overall infrastructure quality	21
3.02	Local availability of specialized IT services	15
3.03	Number of telephone mainlines (per 1,000 people)	11
3.04	Number of telephone faults (per 100 main lines)	31
3.05	Number of telephone mainlines per employee	1
3.06	Number of fax machines (per 1,000 people)	1
3.07	Local switch capacity (per 100,000 people)	33
3.08	Ease of obtaining new telephone lines	14
3.09	Waiting time for telephone mainlines (in years)	1
3.1	Number of secure Internet servers	22

Readiness Component Index — 13

Individual Readiness		21
Business Readiness		7
Government Readiness		19
4.01	Sophistication of local buyers' products and processes	5
4.02	Availability of mobile Internet access	2
4.03	Availability of broadband access	65
4.04	Public access to the Internet	26
4.05	Secondary school enrollment (% net)	27
4.06	Total adult illiteracy rate (%)	16

Readiness Component Index (continued)

4.07	Quality of math and science education	27
4.08	Cost of local call (US$ per three min)	15
4.09	Cost of off-peak local cellular call (US$ per three min)	17
4.10	Cost of residential telephone subscription (US$ per month)	44
5.01	Firm-level technology absorption	3
5.02	Firm-level innovation	1
5.03	Capacity for innovation	4
5.04	Business Intranet sophistication	21
5.05	Quality of local IT training programs	35
5.06	Cost of business telephone subscription (US$ per month)	42
6.01	Government prioritization of ICT	9
6.02	Government procurement of advanced technology products	18
6.03	Competence of public officials	5
6.04	Government online services	54

Usage Component Index — 22

Individual Usage		6
Business Usage		23
Government Usage		41
7.01	Use of online payment systems	33
7.02	Number of radios (per 1,000 people)	14
7.03	Number of television sets (per 1,000 people)	5
7.04	Number of cable television subscribers (per 1,000 people)	20
7.05	Number of mobile telephones (per 1,000 people)	24
7.06	Number of Internet users (per 100 people)	6
7.07	Number of narrowband subscriber lines (per 100 people)	1
7.08	Number of broadband subscriber lines (per 100 people)	3
7.09	Household spending on ICT (US$ per month)	4
8.01	Use of Internet for coordination with customers and suppliers	16
8.02	Businesses using e-commerce (%)	15
8.03	Use of Internet for general research	31
8.04	Sophistication of online marketing	19
8.05	Presence of wireless e-business applications	20
8.06	Use of email for internal correspondence (%)	30
8.07	Use of email for external correspondence (%)	43
8.08	Pervasiveness of company web pages	16
9.01	Use of Internet-based transactions with the government	30
9.02	Government online services	54
9.03	Government success in ICT promotion	47

Jordan .jo

Key Indicators

Population	4,886,810
GDP per capita (PPP)	US$3,966
Illiteracy rate	10.33%
GDP per capita growth	0.76%

Networked Readiness Index Rank

2002–2003 **51**

2001–2002 49

Environment Component Index	43

Market Environment	48

Political and Regulatory Environment	43

Infrastructure Environment	43

1.01	Venture capital availability	54
1.02	State of cluster development	52
1.03	Competition in the telecommunication sector	35
1.04	Availability of scientists and engineers	23
1.05	Brain drain	63
1.06	Public spending on education (% of GDP)	16
1.07	Domestic software companies in international markets	54
1.08	Domestic manufacturing of IT hardware	65
1.09	ICT expenditure (% of GDP)	63
2.01	Effectiveness of law-making bodies	45
2.02	Legal framework for ICT development	33
2.03	Subsidies for firm-level research and development	53
2.04	Government restrictions on Internet content	15
2.05	Prevalence of foreign technology licensing	60
3.01	Overall infrastructure quality	32
3.02	Local availability of specialized IT services	50
3.03	Number of telephone mainlines (per 1,000 people)	61
3.04	Number of telephone faults (per 100 main lines)	43
3.05	Number of telephone mainlines per employee	60
3.06	Number of fax machines (per 1,000 people)	34
3.07	Local switch capacity (per 100,000 people)	39
3.08	Ease of obtaining new telephone lines	41
3.09	Waiting time for telephone mainlines (in years)	39
3.1	Number of secure Internet servers	69

Readiness Component Index	53

Individual Readiness	51

Business Readiness	56

Government Readiness	49

4.01	Sophistication of local buyers' products and processes	66
4.02	Availability of mobile Internet access	57
4.03	Availability of broadband access	57
4.04	Public access to the Internet	44
4.05	Secondary school enrollment (% net)	52
4.06	Total adult illiteracy rate (%)	57

Readiness Component Index (continued)	
4.07	Quality of math and science education	35
4.08	Cost of local call (US$ per three min)	57
4.09	Cost of off-peak local cellular call (US$ per three min)	62
4.10	Cost of residential telephone subscription (US$ per month)	65
5.01	Firm-level technology absorption	48
5.02	Firm-level innovation	74
5.03	Capacity for innovation	58
5.04	Business Intranet sophistication	48
5.05	Quality of local IT training programs	40
5.06	Cost of business telephone subscription (US$ per month)	68
6.01	Government prioritization of ICT	14
6.02	Government procurement of advanced technology products	63
6.03	Competence of public officials	51
6.04	Government online services	64

Usage Component Index	59

Individual Usage	74

Business Usage	51

Government Usage	48

7.01	Use of online payment systems	71
7.02	Number of radios (per 1,000 people)	52
7.03	Number of television sets (per 1,000 people)	73
7.04	Number of cable television subscribers (per 1,000 people)	80
7.05	Number of mobile telephones (per 1,000 people)	62
7.06	Number of Internet users (per 100 people)	60
7.07	Number of narrowband subscriber lines (per 100 people)	58
7.08	Number of broadband subscriber lines (per 100 people)	44
7.09	Household spending on ICT (US$ per month)	68
8.01	Use of Internet for coordination with customers and suppliers	50
8.02	Businesses using e-commerce (%)	68
8.03	Use of Internet for general research	27
8.04	Sophistication of online marketing	38
8.05	Presence of wireless e-business applications	51
8.06	Use of email for internal correspondence (%)	72
8.07	Use of email for external correspondence (%)	56
8.08	Pervasiveness of company web pages	52
9.01	Use of Internet-based transactions with the government	67
9.02	Government online services	64
9.03	Government success in ICT promotion	17

Korea.kr

Key Indicators

Population	47,275,000
GDP per capita (PPP)	US$17,380
Illiteracy rate	2.24%
GDP per capita growth	7.85%

Networked Readiness Index Rank

2002–2003 14

2001–2002 20

Environment Component Index — 26

Market Environment	19
Political and Regulatory Environment	33
Infrastructure Environment	25

1.01	Venture capital availability	19
1.02	State of cluster development	8
1.03	Competition in the telecommunication sector	16
1.04	Availability of scientists and engineers	26
1.05	Brain drain	27
1.06	Public spending on education (% of GDP)	53
1.07	Domestic software companies in international markets	24
1.08	Domestic manufacturing of IT hardware	11
1.09	ICT expenditure (% of GDP)	41
2.01	Effectiveness of law-making bodies	54
2.02	Legal framework for ICT development	24
2.03	Subsidies for firm-level research and development	13
2.04	Government restrictions on Internet content	76
2.05	Prevalence of foreign technology licensing	8
3.01	Overall infrastructure quality	22
3.02	Local availability of specialized IT services	46
3.03	Number of telephone mainlines (per 1,000 people)	25
3.04	Number of telephone faults (per 100 main lines)	4
3.05	Number of telephone mainlines per employee	8
3.06	Number of fax machines (per 1,000 people)	32
3.07	Local switch capacity (per 100,000 people)	28
3.08	Ease of obtaining new telephone lines	25
3.09	Waiting time for telephone mainlines (in years)	1
3.1	Number of secure Internet servers	41

Readiness Component Index — 12

Individual Readiness	6
Business Readiness	18
Government Readiness	15

4.01	Sophistication of local buyers' products and processes	13
4.02	Availability of mobile Internet access	10
4.03	Availability of broadband access	3
4.04	Public access to the Internet	7
4.05	Secondary school enrollment (% net)	2
4.06	Total adult illiteracy rate (%)	31

Readiness Component Index (continued)

4.07	Quality of math and science education	26
4.08	Cost of local call (US$ per three min)	11
4.09	Cost of off-peak local cellular call (US$ per three min)	13
4.10	Cost of residential telephone subscription (US$ per month)	3
5.01	Firm-level technology absorption	10
5.02	Firm-level innovation	37
5.03	Capacity for innovation	15
5.04	Business Intranet sophistication	30
5.05	Quality of local IT training programs	29
5.06	Cost of business telephone subscription (US$ per month)	1
6.01	Government prioritization of ICT	16
6.02	Government procurement of advanced technology products	6
6.03	Competence of public officials	25
6.04	Government online services	24

Usage Component Index — 8

Individual Usage	1
Business Usage	12
Government Usage	14

7.01	Use of online payment systems	10
7.02	Number of radios (per 1,000 people)	9
7.03	Number of television sets (per 1,000 people)	40
7.04	Number of cable television subscribers (per 1,000 people)	14
7.05	Number of mobile telephones (per 1,000 people)	21
7.06	Number of Internet users (per 100 people)	2
7.07	Number of narrowband subscriber lines (per 100 people)	7
7.08	Number of broadband subscriber lines (per 100 people)	1
7.09	Household spending on ICT (US$ per month)	2
8.01	Use of Internet for coordination with customers and suppliers	6
8.02	Businesses using e-commerce (%)	5
8.03	Use of Internet for general research	33
8.04	Sophistication of online marketing	26
8.05	Presence of wireless e-business applications	22
8.06	Use of email for internal correspondence (%)	23
8.07	Use of email for external correspondence (%)	6
8.08	Pervasiveness of company web pages	18
9.01	Use of Internet-based transactions with the government	26
9.02	Government online services	24
9.03	Government success in ICT promotion	7

Latvia.lv

Key Indicators

Population	2,372,000
GDP per capita (PPP)	US$7,045
Illiteracy rate	0.20%
GDP per capita growth	8.29%

Networked Readiness Index Rank

2002–2003 **38**

2001–2002   39

Environment Component Index	41
Market Environment	41
Political and Regulatory Environment	48
Infrastructure Environment	41

1.01	Venture capital availability	40
1.02	State of cluster development	57
1.03	Competition in the telecommunication sector	65
1.04	Availability of scientists and engineers	56
1.05	Brain drain	55
1.06	Public spending on education (% of GDP)	12
1.07	Domestic software companies in international markets	39
1.08	Domestic manufacturing of IT hardware	35
1.09	ICT expenditure (% of GDP)	36
2.01	Effectiveness of law-making bodies	46
2.02	Legal framework for ICT development	57
2.03	Subsidies for firm-level research and development	51
2.04	Government restrictions on Internet content	27
2.05	Prevalence of foreign technology licensing	21
3.01	Overall infrastructure quality	52
3.02	Local availability of specialized IT services	35
3.03	Number of telephone mainlines (per 1,000 people)	37
3.04	Number of telephone faults (per 100 main lines)	57
3.05	Number of telephone mainlines per employee	36
3.06	Number of fax machines (per 1,000 people)	67
3.07	Local switch capacity (per 100,000 people)	18
3.08	Ease of obtaining new telephone lines	46
3.09	Waiting time for telephone mainlines (in years)	69
3.1	Number of secure Internet servers	28

Readiness Component Index	38
Individual Readiness	34
Business Readiness	40
Government Readiness	45

4.01	Sophistication of local buyers' products and processes	48
4.02	Availability of mobile Internet access	40
4.03	Availability of broadband access	32
4.04	Public access to the Internet	54
4.05	Secondary school enrollment (% net)	30
4.06	Total adult illiteracy rate (%)	9

Readiness Component Index (continued)	
4.07	Quality of math and science education	25
4.08	Cost of local call (US$ per three min)	67
4.09	Cost of off-peak local cellular call (US$ per three min)	47
4.10	Cost of residential telephone subscription (US$ per month)	51
5.01	Firm-level technology absorption	40
5.02	Firm-level innovation	27
5.03	Capacity for innovation	40
5.04	Business Intranet sophistication	52
5.05	Quality of local IT training programs	42
5.06	Cost of business telephone subscription (US$ per month)	55
6.01	Government prioritization of ICT	35
6.02	Government procurement of advanced technology products	53
6.03	Competence of public officials	27
6.04	Government online services	52

Usage Component Index	39
Individual Usage	32
Business Usage	50
Government Usage	40

7.01	Use of online payment systems	27
7.02	Number of radios (per 1,000 people)	28
7.03	Number of television sets (per 1,000 people)	3
7.04	Number of cable television subscribers (per 1,000 people)	33
7.05	Number of mobile telephones (per 1,000 people)	41
7.06	Number of Internet users (per 100 people)	33
7.07	Number of narrowband subscriber lines (per 100 people)	40
7.08	Number of broadband subscriber lines (per 100 people)	37
7.09	Household spending on ICT (US$ per month)	48
8.01	Use of Internet for coordination with customers and suppliers	55
8.02	Businesses using e-commerce (%)	49
8.03	Use of Internet for general research	57
8.04	Sophistication of online marketing	37
8.05	Presence of wireless e-business applications	62
8.06	Use of email for internal correspondence (%)	56
8.07	Use of email for external correspondence (%)	57
8.08	Pervasiveness of company web pages	49
9.01	Use of Internet-based transactions with the government	34
9.02	Government online services	52
9.03	Government success in ICT promotion	46

Lithuania.lt

Key Indicators

Population	3,695,000
GDP per capita (PPP)	US$7,106
Illiteracy rate	0.44%
GDP per capita growth	4.00%

Networked Readiness Index Rank

2002–2003 **46**

2001–2002 42

Environment Component Index — 45

Market Environment		39
Political and Regulatory Environment		59
Infrastructure Environment		39

1.01	Venture capital availability	27
1.02	State of cluster development	35
1.03	Competition in the telecommunication sector	70
1.04	Availability of scientists and engineers	37
1.05	Brain drain	64
1.06	Public spending on education (% of GDP)	14
1.07	Domestic software companies in international markets	56
1.08	Domestic manufacturing of IT hardware	37
1.09	ICT expenditure (% of GDP)	36
2.01	Effectiveness of law-making bodies	51
2.02	Legal framework for ICT development	67
2.03	Subsidies for firm-level research and development	52
2.04	Government restrictions on Internet content	58
2.05	Prevalence of foreign technology licensing	59
3.01	Overall infrastructure quality	45
3.02	Local availability of specialized IT services	48
3.03	Number of telephone mainlines (per 1,000 people)	35
3.04	Number of telephone faults (per 100 main lines)	48
3.05	Number of telephone mainlines per employee	27
3.06	Number of fax machines (per 1,000 people)	55
3.07	Local switch capacity (per 100,000 people)	32
3.08	Ease of obtaining new telephone lines	47
3.09	Waiting time for telephone mainlines (in years)	53
3.1	Number of secure Internet servers	33

Readiness Component Index — 41

Individual Readiness		41
Business Readiness		53
Government Readiness		35

4.01	Sophistication of local buyers' products and processes	51
4.02	Availability of mobile Internet access	66
4.03	Availability of broadband access	66
4.04	Public access to the Internet	57
4.05	Secondary school enrollment (% net)	26
4.06	Total adult illiteracy rate (%)	13

Readiness Component Index (continued)

4.07	Quality of math and science education	21
4.08	Cost of local call (US$ per three min)	52
4.09	Cost of off-peak local cellular call (US$ per three min)	57
4.10	Cost of residential telephone subscription (US$ per month)	43
5.01	Firm-level technology absorption	34
5.02	Firm-level innovation	60
5.03	Capacity for innovation	38
5.04	Business Intranet sophistication	73
5.05	Quality of local IT training programs	66
5.06	Cost of business telephone subscription (US$ per month)	51
6.01	Government prioritization of ICT	40
6.02	Government procurement of advanced technology products	48
6.03	Competence of public officials	34
6.04	Government online services	23

Usage Component Index — 52

Individual Usage		39
Business Usage		78
Government Usage		43

7.01	Use of online payment systems	61
7.02	Number of radios (per 1,000 people)	41
7.03	Number of television sets (per 1,000 people)	32
7.04	Number of cable television subscribers (per 1,000 people)	30
7.05	Number of mobile telephones (per 1,000 people)	48
7.06	Number of Internet users (per 100 people)	33
7.07	Number of narrowband subscriber lines (per 100 people)	39
7.08	Number of broadband subscriber lines (per 100 people)	37
7.09	Household spending on ICT (US$ per month)	48
8.01	Use of Internet for coordination with customers and suppliers	71
8.02	Businesses using e-commerce (%)	49
8.03	Use of Internet for general research	77
8.04	Sophistication of online marketing	74
8.05	Presence of wireless e-business applications	81
8.06	Use of email for internal correspondence (%)	76
8.07	Use of email for external correspondence (%)	70
8.08	Pervasiveness of company web pages	61
9.01	Use of Internet-based transactions with the government	56
9.02	Government online services	23
9.03	Government success in ICT promotion	55

Luxembourg.lu

Key Indicators

Population	438,400
GDP per capita (PPP)	US$50,061
Illiteracy rate	0.00%
GDP per capita growth	6.95%

Networked Readiness Index Rank

2002–2003 **27**

2001–2002 —

Environment Component Index		18
Market Environment		33
Political and Regulatory Environment		15
Infrastructure Environment		3
1.01	Venture capital availability	31
1.02	State of cluster development	11
1.03	Competition in the telecommunication sector	36
1.04	Availability of scientists and engineers	11
1.05	Brain drain	31
1.06	Public spending on education (% of GDP)	56
1.07	Domestic software companies in international markets	58
1.08	Domestic manufacturing of IT hardware	82
1.09	ICT expenditure (% of GDP)	15
2.01	Effectiveness of law-making bodies	16
2.02	Legal framework for ICT development	5
2.03	Subsidies for firm-level research and development	22
2.04	Government restrictions on Internet content	55
2.05	Prevalence of foreign technology licensing	40
3.01	Overall infrastructure quality	17
3.02	Local availability of specialized IT services	35
3.03	Number of telephone mainlines (per 1,000 people)	1
3.04	Number of telephone faults (per 100 main lines)	25
3.05	Number of telephone mainlines per employee	4
3.06	Number of fax machines (per 1,000 people)	4
3.07	Local switch capacity (per 100,000 people)	2
3.08	Ease of obtaining new telephone lines	10
3.09	Waiting time for telephone mainlines (in years)	1
3.1	Number of secure Internet servers	7

Readiness Component Index		30
Individual Readiness		32
Business Readiness		22
Government Readiness		28
4.01	Sophistication of local buyers' products and processes	33
4.02	Availability of mobile Internet access	68
4.03	Availability of broadband access	27
4.04	Public access to the Internet	68
4.05	Secondary school enrollment (% net)	43
4.06	Total adult illiteracy rate (%)	1

Readiness Component Index (continued)		
4.07	Quality of math and science education	28
4.08	Cost of local call (US$ per three min)	10
4.09	Cost of off-peak local cellular call (US$ per three min)	2
4.10	Cost of residential telephone subscription (US$ per month)	8
5.01	Firm-level technology absorption	33
5.02	Firm-level innovation	5
5.03	Capacity for innovation	26
5.04	Business Intranet sophistication	22
5.05	Quality of local IT training programs	48
5.06	Cost of business telephone subscription (US$ per month)	2
6.01	Government prioritization of ICT	23
6.02	Government procurement of advanced technology products	14
6.03	Competence of public officials	17
6.04	Government online services	48

Usage Component Index		31
Individual Usage		8
Business Usage		49
Government Usage		52
7.01	Use of online payment systems	18
7.02	Number of radios (per 1,000 people)	50
7.03	Number of television sets (per 1,000 people)	14
7.04	Number of cable television subscribers (per 1,000 people)	4
7.05	Number of mobile telephones (per 1,000 people)	1
7.06	Number of Internet users (per 100 people)	23
7.07	Number of narrowband subscriber lines (per 100 people)	3
7.08	Number of broadband subscriber lines (per 100 people)	17
7.09	Household spending on ICT (US$ per month)	8
8.01	Use of Internet for coordination with customers and suppliers	82
8.02	Businesses using e-commerce (%)	6
8.03	Use of Internet for general research	75
8.04	Sophistication of online marketing	6
8.05	Presence of wireless e-business applications	40
8.06	Use of email for internal correspondence (%)	53
8.07	Use of email for external correspondence (%)	80
8.08	Pervasiveness of company web pages	13
9.01	Use of Internet-based transactions with the government	74
9.02	Government online services	47
9.03	Government success in ICT promotion	31

Malaysia.my

Key Indicators

Population	23,270,000
GDP per capita (PPP)	US$9,068
Illiteracy rate	12.55%
GDP per capita growth	5.69%

Networked Readiness Index Rank

2002–2003 **32**

2001–2002 36

Environment Component Index — 29

Market Environment		35
Political and Regulatory Environment		7
Infrastructure Environment		40
1.01	Venture capital availability	38
1.02	State of cluster development	28
1.03	Competition in the telecommunication sector	39
1.04	Availability of scientists and engineers	53
1.05	Brain drain	29
1.06	Public spending on education (% of GDP)	42
1.07	Domestic software companies in international markets	71
1.08	Domestic manufacturing of IT hardware	22
1.09	ICT expenditure (% of GDP)	35
2.01	Effectiveness of law-making bodies	9
2.02	Legal framework for ICT development	17
2.03	Subsidies for firm-level research and development	8
2.04	Government restrictions on Internet content	65
2.05	Prevalence of foreign technology licensing	5
3.01	Overall infrastructure quality	16
3.02	Local availability of specialized IT services	74
3.03	Number of telephone mainlines (per 1,000 people)	47
3.04	Number of telephone faults (per 100 main lines)	65
3.05	Number of telephone mainlines per employee	28
3.06	Number of fax machines (per 1,000 people)	35
3.07	Local switch capacity (per 100,000 people)	53
3.08	Ease of obtaining new telephone lines	40
3.09	Waiting time for telephone mainlines (in years)	48
3.1	Number of secure Internet servers	45

Readiness Component Index — 29

Individual Readiness		31
Business Readiness		33
Government Readiness		18
4.01	Sophistication of local buyers' products and processes	29
4.02	Availability of mobile Internet access	48
4.03	Availability of broadband access	62
4.04	Public access to the Internet	45
4.05	Secondary school enrollment (% net)	8
4.06	Total adult illiteracy rate (%)	60

Readiness Component Index (continued)

4.07	Quality of math and science education	36
4.08	Cost of local call (US$ per three min)	13
4.09	Cost of off-peak local cellular call (US$ per three min)	25
4.10	Cost of residential telephone subscription (US$ per month)	40
5.01	Firm-level technology absorption	25
5.02	Firm-level innovation	16
5.03	Capacity for innovation	37
5.04	Business Intranet sophistication	41
5.05	Quality of local IT training programs	41
5.06	Cost of business telephone subscription (US$ per month)	46
6.01	Government prioritization of ICT	4
6.02	Government procurement of advanced technology products	7
6.03	Competence of public officials	24
6.04	Government online services	53

Usage Component Index — 38

Individual Usage		43
Business Usage		36
Government Usage		32
7.01	Use of online payment systems	46
7.02	Number of radios (per 1,000 people)	45
7.03	Number of television sets (per 1,000 people)	63
7.04	Number of cable television subscribers (per 1,000 people)	73
7.05	Number of mobile telephones (per 1,000 people)	37
7.06	Number of Internet users (per 100 people)	17
7.07	Number of narrowband subscriber lines (per 100 people)	36
7.08	Number of broadband subscriber lines (per 100 people)	35
7.09	Household spending on ICT (US$ per month)	52
8.01	Use of Internet for coordination with customers and suppliers	47
8.02	Businesses using e-commerce (%)	44
8.03	Use of Internet for general research	35
8.04	Sophistication of online marketing	51
8.05	Presence of wireless e-business applications	73
8.06	Use of email for internal correspondence (%)	16
8.07	Use of email for external correspondence (%)	19
8.08	Pervasiveness of company web pages	48
9.01	Use of Internet-based transactions with the government	52
9.02	Government online services	53
9.03	Government success in ICT promotion	6

Mauritius.mu

Key Indicators

Population	1,186,140
GDP per capita (PPP)	US$10,017
Illiteracy rate	15.47%
GDP per capita growth	6.95%

Networked Readiness Index Rank

2002–2003 **56**

2001–2002 51

Environment Component Index	54

Market Environment	71

Political and Regulatory Environment	42

Infrastructure Environment	44

1.01	Venture capital availability	49
1.02	State of cluster development	50
1.03	Competition in the telecommunication sector	82
1.04	Availability of scientists and engineers	61
1.05	Brain drain	46
1.06	Public spending on education (% of GDP)	54
1.07	Domestic software companies in international markets	64
1.08	Domestic manufacturing of IT hardware	75
1.09	ICT expenditure (% of GDP)	42
2.01	Effectiveness of law-making bodies	25
2.02	Legal framework for ICT development	47
2.03	Subsidies for firm-level research and development	57
2.04	Government restrictions on Internet content	40
2.05	Prevalence of foreign technology licensing	38
3.01	Overall infrastructure quality	35
3.02	Local availability of specialized IT services	78
3.03	Number of telephone mainlines (per 1,000 people)	42
3.04	Number of telephone faults (per 100 main lines)	72
3.05	Number of telephone mainlines per employee	46
3.06	Number of fax machines (per 1,000 people)	20
3.07	Local switch capacity (per 100,000 people)	7
3.08	Ease of obtaining new telephone lines	55
3.09	Waiting time for telephone mainlines (in years)	55
3.1	Number of secure Internet servers	38

Readiness Component Index	54

Individual Readiness	59

Business Readiness	50

Government Readiness	52

4.01	Sophistication of local buyers' products and processes	52
4.02	Availability of mobile Internet access	75
4.03	Availability of broadband access	82
4.04	Public access to the Internet	65
4.05	Secondary school enrollment (% net)	49
4.06	Total adult illiteracy rate (%)	67

Readiness Component Index (continued)	
4.07	Quality of math and science education	55
4.08	Cost of local call (US$ per three min)	20
4.09	Cost of off-peak local cellular call (US$ per three min)	14
4.10	Cost of residential telephone subscription (US$ per month)	5
5.01	Firm-level technology absorption	55
5.02	Firm-level innovation	25
5.03	Capacity for innovation	57
5.04	Business Intranet sophistication	55
5.05	Quality of local IT training programs	70
5.06	Cost of business telephone subscription (US$ per month)	8
6.01	Government prioritization of ICT	7
6.02	Government procurement of advanced technology products	64
6.03	Competence of public officials	49
6.04	Government online services	71

Usage Component Index	55

Individual Usage	51

Business Usage	70

Government Usage	47

7.01	Use of online payment systems	64
7.02	Number of radios (per 1,000 people)	51
7.03	Number of television sets (per 1,000 people)	51
7.04	Number of cable television subscribers (per 1,000 people)	44
7.05	Number of mobile telephones (per 1,000 people)	43
7.06	Number of Internet users (per 100 people)	42
7.07	Number of narrowband subscriber lines (per 100 people)	44
7.08	Number of broadband subscriber lines (per 100 people)	37
7.09	Household spending on ICT (US$ per month)	51
8.01	Use of Internet for coordination with customers and suppliers	78
8.02	Businesses using e-commerce (%)	49
8.03	Use of Internet for general research	45
8.04	Sophistication of online marketing	61
8.05	Presence of wireless e-business applications	60
8.06	Use of email for internal correspondence (%)	57
8.07	Use of email for external correspondence (%)	51
8.08	Pervasiveness of company web pages	80
9.01	Use of Internet-based transactions with the government	48
9.02	Government online services	71
9.03	Government success in ICT promotion	23

Mexico.mx

Key Indicators

Population	97,966,000
GDP per capita (PPP)	US$9,023
Illiteracy rate	8.59%
GDP per capita growth	5.33%

Networked Readiness Index Rank

2002–2003 **47**

2001–2002 44

Environment Component Index	60
Market Environment	62
Political and Regulatory Environment	57
Infrastructure Environment	55

1.01	Venture capital availability	74
1.02	State of cluster development	32
1.03	Competition in the telecommunication sector	60
1.04	Availability of scientists and engineers	77
1.05	Brain drain	50
1.06	Public spending on education (% of GDP)	52
1.07	Domestic software companies in international markets	45
1.08	Domestic manufacturing of IT hardware	28
1.09	ICT expenditure (% of GDP)	76
2.01	Effectiveness of law-making bodies	70
2.02	Legal framework for ICT development	68
2.03	Subsidies for firm-level research and development	37
2.04	Government restrictions on Internet content	14
2.05	Prevalence of foreign technology licensing	58
3.01	Overall infrastructure quality	60
3.02	Local availability of specialized IT services	52
3.03	Number of telephone mainlines (per 1,000 people)	54
3.04	Number of telephone faults (per 100 main lines)	7
3.05	Number of telephone mainlines per employee	52
3.06	Number of fax machines (per 1,000 people)	45
3.07	Local switch capacity (per 100,000 people)	63
3.08	Ease of obtaining new telephone lines	60
3.09	Waiting time for telephone mainlines (in years)	31
3.1	Number of secure Internet servers	50

Readiness Component Index	52
Individual Readiness	61
Business Readiness	49
Government Readiness	47

4.01	Sophistication of local buyers' products and processes	56
4.02	Availability of mobile Internet access	49
4.03	Availability of broadband access	34
4.04	Public access to the Internet	64
4.05	Secondary school enrollment (% net)	56
4.06	Total adult illiteracy rate (%)	55

Readiness Component Index (continued)	
4.07	Quality of math and science education	77
4.08	Cost of local call (US$ per three min)	66
4.09	Cost of off-peak local cellular call (US$ per three min)	64
4.10	Cost of residential telephone subscription (US$ per month)	72
5.01	Firm-level technology absorption	67
5.02	Firm-level innovation	36
5.03	Capacity for innovation	52
5.04	Business Intranet sophistication	18
5.05	Quality of local IT training programs	64
5.06	Cost of business telephone subscription (US$ per month)	66
6.01	Government prioritization of ICT	41
6.02	Government procurement of advanced technology products	59
6.03	Competence of public officials	43
6.04	Government online services	34

Usage Component Index	37
Individual Usage	45
Business Usage	32
Government Usage	35

7.01	Use of online payment systems	45
7.02	Number of radios (per 1,000 people)	61
7.03	Number of television sets (per 1,000 people)	49
7.04	Number of cable television subscribers (per 1,000 people)	55
7.05	Number of mobile telephones (per 1,000 people)	47
7.06	Number of Internet users (per 100 people)	48
7.07	Number of narrowband subscriber lines (per 100 people)	53
7.08	Number of broadband subscriber lines (per 100 people)	44
7.09	Household spending on ICT (US$ per month)	21
8.01	Use of Internet for coordination with customers and suppliers	37
8.02	Businesses using e-commerce (%)	30
8.03	Use of Internet for general research	41
8.04	Sophistication of online marketing	35
8.05	Presence of wireless e-business applications	29
8.06	Use of email for internal correspondence (%)	21
8.07	Use of email for external correspondence (%)	16
8.08	Pervasiveness of company web pages	45
9.01	Use of Internet-based transactions with the government	24
9.02	Government online services	34
9.03	Government success in ICT promotion	54

Morocco.ma

Key Indicators

Population	28,705,000
GDP per capita (PPP)	US$3,546
Illiteracy rate	51.13%
GDP per capita growth	-0.77%

Networked Readiness Index Rank

2002–2003 **52**

2001–2002 —

Environment Component Index		49
Market Environment		49
Political and Regulatory Environment		45
Infrastructure Environment		57
1.01	Venture capital availability	34
1.02	State of cluster development	34
1.03	Competition in the telecommunication sector	48
1.04	Availability of scientists and engineers	38
1.05	Brain drain	56
1.06	Public spending on education (% of GDP)	32
1.07	Domestic software companies in international markets	67
1.08	Domestic manufacturing of IT hardware	46
1.09	ICT expenditure (% of GDP)	69
2.01	Effectiveness of law-making bodies	48
2.02	Legal framework for ICT development	51
2.03	Subsidies for firm-level research and development	34
2.04	Government restrictions on Internet content	59
2.05	Prevalence of foreign technology licensing	23
3.01	Overall infrastructure quality	57
3.02	Local availability of specialized IT services	65
3.03	Number of telephone mainlines (per 1,000 people)	70
3.04	Number of telephone faults (per 100 main lines)	53
3.05	Number of telephone mainlines per employee	65
3.06	Number of fax machines (per 1,000 people)	61
3.07	Local switch capacity (per 100,000 people)	75
3.08	Ease of obtaining new telephone lines	35
3.09	Waiting time for telephone mainlines (in years)	30
3.1	Number of secure Internet servers	73

Readiness Component Index		49
Individual Readiness		72
Business Readiness		48
Government Readiness		40
4.01	Sophistication of local buyers' products and processes	42
4.02	Availability of mobile Internet access	50
4.03	Availability of broadband access	63
4.04	Public access to the Internet	48
4.05	Secondary school enrollment (% net)	62
4.06	Total adult illiteracy rate (%)	81

Readiness Component Index (continued)		
4.07	Quality of math and science education	44
4.08	Cost of local call (US$ per three min)	76
4.09	Cost of off-peak local cellular call (US$ per three min)	59
4.10	Cost of residential telephone subscription (US$ per month)	73
5.01	Firm-level technology absorption	14
5.02	Firm-level innovation	32
5.03	Capacity for innovation	56
5.04	Business Intranet sophistication	61
5.05	Quality of local IT training programs	52
5.06	Cost of business telephone subscription (US$ per month)	69
6.01	Government prioritization of ICT	36
6.02	Government procurement of advanced technology products	23
6.03	Competence of public officials	32
6.04	Government online services	63

Usage Component Index		57
Individual Usage		63
Business Usage		52
Government Usage		53
7.01	Use of online payment systems	63
7.02	Number of radios (per 1,000 people)	67
7.03	Number of television sets (per 1,000 people)	64
7.04	Number of cable television subscribers (per 1,000 people)	59
7.05	Number of mobile telephones (per 1,000 people)	57
7.06	Number of Internet users (per 100 people)	65
7.07	Number of narrowband subscriber lines (per 100 people)	75
7.08	Number of broadband subscriber lines (per 100 people)	44
7.09	Household spending on ICT (US$ per month)	34
8.01	Use of Internet for coordination with customers and suppliers	49
8.02	Businesses using e-commerce (%)	70
8.03	Use of Internet for general research	46
8.04	Sophistication of online marketing	70
8.05	Presence of wireless e-business applications	55
8.06	Use of email for internal correspondence (%)	51
8.07	Use of email for external correspondence (%)	33
8.08	Pervasiveness of company web pages	51
9.01	Use of Internet-based transactions with the government	65
9.02	Government online services	63
9.03	Government success in ICT promotion	25

Namibia.na

Key Indicators

Population	1,757,000
GDP per capita (PPP)	US$6,431
Illiteracy rate	18.02%
GDP per capita growth	1.59%

Networked Readiness Index Rank

2002–2003 53

2001–2002 —

Environment Component Index — 44

Market Environment	56

Political and Regulatory Environment	38

Infrastructure Environment	42

1.01	Venture capital availability	52
1.02	State of cluster development	64
1.03	Competition in the telecommunication sector	50
1.04	Availability of scientists and engineers	81
1.05	Brain drain	45
1.06	Public spending on education (% of GDP)	4
1.07	Domestic software companies in international markets	65
1.08	Domestic manufacturing of IT hardware	53
1.09	ICT expenditure (% of GDP)	55
2.01	Effectiveness of law-making bodies	28
2.02	Legal framework for ICT development	34
2.03	Subsidies for firm-level research and development	41
2.04	Government restrictions on Internet content	53
2.05	Prevalence of foreign technology licensing	48
3.01	Overall infrastructure quality	23
3.02	Local availability of specialized IT services	14
3.03	Number of telephone mainlines (per 1,000 people)	67
3.04	Number of telephone faults (per 100 main lines)	59
3.05	Number of telephone mainlines per employee	72
3.06	Number of fax machines (per 1,000 people)	46
3.07	Local switch capacity (per 100,000 people)	22
3.08	Ease of obtaining new telephone lines	57
3.09	Waiting time for telephone mainlines (in years)	47
3.1	Number of secure Internet servers	57

Readiness Component Index — 51

Individual Readiness	64

Business Readiness	45

Government Readiness	48

4.01	Sophistication of local buyers' products and processes	64
4.02	Availability of mobile Internet access	58
4.03	Availability of broadband access	49
4.04	Public access to the Internet	53
4.05	Secondary school enrollment (% net)	81
4.06	Total adult illiteracy rate (%)	70

Readiness Component Index (continued)

4.07	Quality of math and science education	67
4.08	Cost of local call (US$ per three min)	44
4.09	Cost of off-peak local cellular call (US$ per three min)	40
4.10	Cost of residential telephone subscription (US$ per month)	63
5.01	Firm-level technology absorption	53
5.02	Firm-level innovation	15
5.03	Capacity for innovation	60
5.04	Business Intranet sophistication	67
5.05	Quality of local IT training programs	30
5.06	Cost of business telephone subscription (US$ per month)	48
6.01	Government prioritization of ICT	49
6.02	Government procurement of advanced technology products	31
6.03	Competence of public officials	57
6.04	Government online services	50

Usage Component Index — 61

Individual Usage	73

Business Usage	58

Government Usage	54

7.01	Use of online payment systems	49
7.02	Number of radios (per 1,000 people)	77
7.03	Number of television sets (per 1,000 people)	78
7.04	Number of cable television subscribers (per 1,000 people)	48
7.05	Number of mobile telephones (per 1,000 people)	67
7.06	Number of Internet users (per 100 people)	58
7.07	Number of narrowband subscriber lines (per 100 people)	64
7.08	Number of broadband subscriber lines (per 100 people)	44
7.09	Household spending on ICT (US$ per month)	63
8.01	Use of Internet for coordination with customers and suppliers	58
8.02	Businesses using e-commerce (%)	61
8.03	Use of Internet for general research	64
8.04	Sophistication of online marketing	60
8.05	Presence of wireless e-business applications	59
8.06	Use of email for internal correspondence (%)	64
8.07	Use of email for external correspondence (%)	69
8.08	Pervasiveness of company web pages	36
9.01	Use of Internet-based transactions with the government	68
9.02	Government online services	50
9.03	Government success in ICT promotion	35

Netherlands.nl

Key Indicators

Population	15,919,000
GDP per capita (PPP)	US$25,657
Illiteracy rate	1.00 %
GDP per capita growth	2.76 %

Networked Readiness Index Rank

2002–2003 **11**

2001–2002   6

Environment Component Index — 10

Market Environment	8

Political and Regulatory Environment	6

Infrastructure Environment	16

1.01	Venture capital availability	7
1.02	State of cluster development	15
1.03	Competition in the telecommunication sector	18
1.04	Availability of scientists and engineers	40
1.05	Brain drain	3
1.06	Public spending on education (% of GDP)	31
1.07	Domestic software companies in international markets	10
1.08	Domestic manufacturing of IT hardware	9
1.09	ICT expenditure (% of GDP)	7
2.01	Effectiveness of law-making bodies	24
2.02	Legal framework for ICT development	6
2.03	Subsidies for firm-level research and development	16
2.04	Government restrictions on Internet content	2
2.05	Prevalence of foreign technology licensing	19
3.01	Overall infrastructure quality	15
3.02	Local availability of specialized IT services	18
3.03	Number of telephone mainlines (per 1,000 people)	8
3.04	Number of telephone faults (per 100 main lines)	3
3.05	Number of telephone mainlines per employee	39
3.06	Number of fax machines (per 1,000 people)	13
3.07	Local switch capacity (per 100,000 people)	14
3.08	Ease of obtaining new telephone lines	17
3.09	Waiting time for telephone mainlines (in years)	1
3.1	Number of secure Internet servers	20

Readiness Component Index — 15

Individual Readiness	11

Business Readiness	15

Government Readiness	21

4.01	Sophistication of local buyers' products and processes	17
4.02	Availability of mobile Internet access	11
4.03	Availability of broadband access	13
4.04	Public access to the Internet	9
4.05	Secondary school enrollment (% net)	9
4.06	Total adult illiteracy rate (%)	16

Readiness Component Index (continued)		
4.07	Quality of math and science education	19
4.08	Cost of local call (US$ per three min)	36
4.09	Cost of off-peak local cellular call (US$ per three min)	12
4.10	Cost of residential telephone subscription (US$ per month)	49
5.01	Firm-level technology absorption	45
5.02	Firm-level innovation	71
5.03	Capacity for innovation	11
5.04	Business Intranet sophistication	5
5.05	Quality of local IT training programs	2
5.06	Cost of business telephone subscription (US$ per month)	30
6.01	Government prioritization of ICT	37
6.02	Government procurement of advanced technology products	26
6.03	Competence of public officials	16
6.04	Government online services	16

Usage Component Index — 9

Individual Usage	4

Business Usage	6

Government Usage	15

7.01	Use of online payment systems	8
7.02	Number of radios (per 1,000 people)	12
7.03	Number of television sets (per 1,000 people)	19
7.04	Number of cable television subscribers (per 1,000 people)	1
7.05	Number of mobile telephones (per 1,000 people)	12
7.06	Number of Internet users (per 100 people)	7
7.07	Number of narrowband subscriber lines (per 100 people)	11
7.08	Number of broadband subscriber lines (per 100 people)	8
7.09	Household spending on ICT (US$ per month)	13
8.01	Use of Internet for coordination with customers and suppliers	12
8.02	Businesses using e-commerce (%)	7
8.03	Use of Internet for general research	3
8.04	Sophistication of online marketing	12
8.05	Presence of wireless e-business applications	11
8.06	Use of email for internal correspondence (%)	17
8.07	Use of email for external correspondence (%)	29
8.08	Pervasiveness of company web pages	8
9.01	Use of Internet-based transactions with the government	11
9.02	Government online services	16
9.03	Government success in ICT promotion	36

New Zealand.nz

Key Indicators

Population	3,830,800
GDP per capita (PPP)	US$20,070
Illiteracy rate	1.00%
GDP per capita growth	1.96%

Networked Readiness Index Rank

2002–2003 23

2001–2002 11

Environment Component Index — 22

Market Environment		22
Political and Regulatory Environment		28
Infrastructure Environment		15
1.01	Venture capital availability	18
1.02	State of cluster development	38
1.03	Competition in the telecommunication sector	27
1.04	Availability of scientists and engineers	51
1.05	Brain drain	57
1.06	Public spending on education (% of GDP)	9
1.07	Domestic software companies in international markets	21
1.08	Domestic manufacturing of IT hardware	40
1.09	ICT expenditure (% of GDP)	1
2.01	Effectiveness of law-making bodies	13
2.02	Legal framework for ICT development	15
2.03	Subsidies for firm-level research and development	61
2.04	Government restrictions on Internet content	43
2.05	Prevalence of foreign technology licensing	27
3.01	Overall infrastructure quality	18
3.02	Local availability of specialized IT services	29
3.03	Number of telephone mainlines (per 1,000 people)	19
3.04	Number of telephone faults (per 100 main lines)	60
3.05	Number of telephone mainlines per employee	6
3.06	Number of fax machines (per 1,000 people)	25
3.07	Local switch capacity (per 100,000 people)	34
3.08	Ease of obtaining new telephone lines	12
3.09	Waiting time for telephone mainlines (in years)	1
3.1	Number of secure Internet servers	5

Readiness Component Index — 24

Individual Readiness		16
Business Readiness		29
Government Readiness		30
4.01	Sophistication of local buyers' products and processes	10
4.02	Availability of mobile Internet access	19
4.03	Availability of broadband access	19
4.04	Public access to the Internet	14
4.05	Secondary school enrollment (% net)	13
4.06	Total adult illiteracy rate (%)	16

Readiness Component Index (continued)

4.07	Quality of math and science education	34
4.08	Cost of local call (US$ per three min)	1
4.09	Cost of off-peak local cellular call (US$ per three min)	15
4.10	Cost of residential telephone subscription (US$ per month)	55
5.01	Firm-level technology absorption	27
5.02	Firm-level innovation	64
5.03	Capacity for innovation	20
5.04	Business Intranet sophistication	33
5.05	Quality of local IT training programs	26
5.06	Cost of business telephone subscription (US$ per month)	57
6.01	Government prioritization of ICT	53
6.02	Government procurement of advanced technology products	39
6.03	Competence of public officials	15
6.04	Government online services	20

Usage Component Index — 27

Individual Usage		24
Business Usage		29
Government Usage		30
7.01	Use of online payment systems	11
7.02	Number of radios (per 1,000 people)	11
7.03	Number of television sets (per 1,000 people)	22
7.04	Number of cable television subscribers (per 1,000 people)	75
7.05	Number of mobile telephones (per 1,000 people)	22
7.06	Number of Internet users (per 100 people)	8
7.07	Number of narrowband subscriber lines (per 100 people)	22
7.08	Number of broadband subscriber lines (per 100 people)	19
7.09	Household spending on ICT (US$ per month)	33
8.01	Use of Internet for coordination with customers and suppliers	26
8.02	Businesses using e-commerce (%)	33
8.03	Use of Internet for general research	48
8.04	Sophistication of online marketing	44
8.05	Presence of wireless e-business applications	26
8.06	Use of email for internal correspondence (%)	11
8.07	Use of email for external correspondence (%)	24
8.08	Pervasiveness of company web pages	20
9.01	Use of Internet-based transactions with the government	33
9.02	Government online services	20
9.03	Government success in ICT promotion	49

Nicaragua.ni

Key Indicators

Population	5,071,000
GDP per capita (PPP)	US$2,366
Illiteracy rate	33.47%
GDP per capita growth	1.61%

Networked Readiness Index Rank

2002–2003 **79**

2001–2002   69

Environment Component Index — 81

Market Environment	78
Political and Regulatory Environment	77
Infrastructure Environment	79

1.01	Venture capital availability	71
1.02	State of cluster development	49
1.03	Competition in the telecommunication sector	77
1.04	Availability of scientists and engineers	75
1.05	Brain drain	72
1.06	Public spending on education (% of GDP)	51
1.07	Domestic software companies in international markets	78
1.08	Domestic manufacturing of IT hardware	74
1.09	ICT expenditure (% of GDP)	58
2.01	Effectiveness of law-making bodies	75
2.02	Legal framework for ICT development	75
2.03	Subsidies for firm-level research and development	64
2.04	Government restrictions on Internet content	74
2.05	Prevalence of foreign technology licensing	74
3.01	Overall infrastructure quality	80
3.02	Local availability of specialized IT services	73
3.03	Number of telephone mainlines (per 1,000 people)	78
3.04	Number of telephone faults (per 100 main lines)	76
3.05	Number of telephone mainlines per employee	73
3.06	Number of fax machines (per 1,000 people)	72
3.07	Local switch capacity (per 100,000 people)	81
3.08	Ease of obtaining new telephone lines	79
3.09	Waiting time for telephone mainlines (in years)	79
3.1	Number of secure Internet servers	62

Readiness Component Index — 80

Individual Readiness	79
Business Readiness	80
Government Readiness	68

4.01	Sophistication of local buyers' products and processes	79
4.02	Availability of mobile Internet access	73
4.03	Availability of broadband access	42
4.04	Public access to the Internet	72
4.05	Secondary school enrollment (% net)	79
4.06	Total adult illiteracy rate (%)	76

Readiness Component Index (continued)

4.07	Quality of math and science education	69
4.08	Cost of local call (US$ per three min)	81
4.09	Cost of off-peak local cellular call (US$ per three min)	72
4.10	Cost of residential telephone subscription (US$ per month)	80
5.01	Firm-level technology absorption	80
5.02	Firm-level innovation	69
5.03	Capacity for innovation	65
5.04	Business Intranet sophistication	62
5.05	Quality of local IT training programs	74
5.06	Cost of business telephone subscription (US$ per month)	81
6.01	Government prioritization of ICT	72
6.02	Government procurement of advanced technology products	68
6.03	Competence of public officials	45
6.04	Government online services	67

Usage Component Index — 71

Individual Usage	66
Business Usage	59
Government Usage	77

7.01	Use of online payment systems	58
7.02	Number of radios (per 1,000 people)	66
7.03	Number of television sets (per 1,000 people)	75
7.04	Number of cable television subscribers (per 1,000 people)	70
7.05	Number of mobile telephones (per 1,000 people)	74
7.06	Number of Internet users (per 100 people)	74
7.07	Number of narrowband subscriber lines (per 100 people)	80
7.08	Number of broadband subscriber lines (per 100 people)	44
7.09	Household spending on ICT (US$ per month)	14
8.01	Use of Internet for coordination with customers and suppliers	56
8.02	Businesses using e-commerce (%)	65
8.03	Use of Internet for general research	40
8.04	Sophistication of online marketing	61
8.05	Presence of wireless e-business applications	42
8.06	Use of email for internal correspondence (%)	61
8.07	Use of email for external correspondence (%)	48
8.08	Pervasiveness of company web pages	76
9.01	Use of Internet-based transactions with the government	73
9.02	Government online services	67
9.03	Government success in ICT promotion	75

Country Profiles | **245**

Nigeria.ng

Key Indicators

Population	126,910,000
GDP per capita (PPP)	US$896
Illiteracy rate	36.08%
GDP per capita growth	1.31%

Networked Readiness Index Rank

2002–2003 **74**

2001–2002   75

Environment Component Index	72
Market Environment	76
Political and Regulatory Environment	56
Infrastructure Environment	76

1.01	Venture capital availability	51
1.02	State of cluster development	39
1.03	Competition in the telecommunication sector	80
1.04	Availability of scientists and engineers	62
1.05	Brain drain	76
1.06	Public spending on education (% of GDP)	82
1.07	Domestic software companies in international markets	77
1.08	Domestic manufacturing of IT hardware	69
1.09	ICT expenditure (% of GDP)	58
2.01	Effectiveness of law-making bodies	63
2.02	Legal framework for ICT development	55
2.03	Subsidies for firm-level research and development	58
2.04	Government restrictions on Internet content	44
2.05	Prevalence of foreign technology licensing	34
3.01	Overall infrastructure quality	79
3.02	Local availability of specialized IT services	61
3.03	Number of telephone mainlines (per 1,000 people)	81
3.04	Number of telephone faults (per 100 main lines)	78
3.05	Number of telephone mainlines per employee	79
3.06	Number of fax machines (per 1,000 people)	72
3.07	Local switch capacity (per 100,000 people)	82
3.08	Ease of obtaining new telephone lines	75
3.09	Waiting time for telephone mainlines (in years)	60
3.1	Number of secure Internet servers	78

Readiness Component Index	81
Individual Readiness	82
Business Readiness	78
Government Readiness	67

4.01	Sophistication of local buyers' products and processes	55
4.02	Availability of mobile Internet access	78
4.03	Availability of broadband access	69
4.04	Public access to the Internet	81
4.05	Secondary school enrollment (% net)	80
4.06	Total adult illiteracy rate (%)	77

Readiness Component Index (continued)	
4.07	Quality of math and science education	66
4.08	Cost of local call (US$ per three min)	82
4.09	Cost of off-peak local cellular call (US$ per three min)	81
4.10	Cost of residential telephone subscription (US$ per month)	82
5.01	Firm-level technology absorption	56
5.02	Firm-level innovation	6
5.03	Capacity for innovation	81
5.04	Business Intranet sophistication	51
5.05	Quality of local IT training programs	75
5.06	Cost of business telephone subscription (US$ per month)	82
6.01	Government prioritization of ICT	71
6.02	Government procurement of advanced technology products	48
6.03	Competence of public officials	66
6.04	Government online services	68

Usage Component Index	70
Individual Usage	78
Business Usage	60
Government Usage	67

7.01	Use of online payment systems	75
7.02	Number of radios (per 1,000 people)	70
7.03	Number of television sets (per 1,000 people)	76
7.04	Number of cable television subscribers (per 1,000 people)	53
7.05	Number of mobile telephones (per 1,000 people)	82
7.06	Number of Internet users (per 100 people)	75
7.07	Number of narrowband subscriber lines (per 100 people)	71
7.08	Number of broadband subscriber lines (per 100 people)	44
7.09	Household spending on ICT (US$ per month)	66
8.01	Use of Internet for coordination with customers and suppliers	67
8.02	Businesses using e-commerce (%)	65
8.03	Use of Internet for general research	49
8.04	Sophistication of online marketing	39
8.05	Presence of wireless e-business applications	48
8.06	Use of email for internal correspondence (%)	65
8.07	Use of email for external correspondence (%)	64
8.08	Pervasiveness of company web pages	68
9.01	Use of Internet-based transactions with the government	54
9.02	Government online services	68
9.03	Government success in ICT promotion	62

Norway.no

Key Indicators

Population	4,491,000
GDP per capita (PPP)	US$29,918
Illiteracy rate	0.00%
GDP per capita growth	1.57%

Networked Readiness Index Rank

2002–2003 ⓱

2001–2002 5

Environment Component Index 20

Market Environment	14
Political and Regulatory Environment	26
Infrastructure Environment	20

1.01	Venture capital availability	9
1.02	State of cluster development	16
1.03	Competition in the telecommunication sector	10
1.04	Availability of scientists and engineers	28
1.05	Brain drain	6
1.06	Public spending on education (% of GDP)	6
1.07	Domestic software companies in international markets	19
1.08	Domestic manufacturing of IT hardware	29
1.09	ICT expenditure (% of GDP)	34
2.01	Effectiveness of law-making bodies	22
2.02	Legal framework for ICT development	22
2.03	Subsidies for firm-level research and development	26
2.04	Government restrictions on Internet content	13
2.05	Prevalence of foreign technology licensing	57
3.01	Overall infrastructure quality	20
3.02	Local availability of specialized IT services	27
3.03	Number of telephone mainlines (per 1,000 people)	16
3.04	Number of telephone faults (per 100 main lines)	33
3.05	Number of telephone mainlines per employee	59
3.06	Number of fax machines (per 1,000 people)	7
3.07	Local switch capacity (per 100,000 people)	3
3.08	Ease of obtaining new telephone lines	20
3.09	Waiting time for telephone mainlines (in years)	1
3.1	Number of secure Internet servers	13

Readiness Component Index 22

Individual Readiness	15
Business Readiness	20
Government Readiness	29

4.01	Sophistication of local buyers' products and processes	20
4.02	Availability of mobile Internet access	3
4.03	Availability of broadband access	26
4.04	Public access to the Internet	4
4.05	Secondary school enrollment (% net)	3
4.06	Total adult illiteracy rate (%)	1

Readiness Component Index (continued)

4.07	Quality of math and science education	49
4.08	Cost of local call (US$ per three min)	29
4.09	Cost of off-peak local cellular call (US$ per three min)	10
4.10	Cost of residential telephone subscription (US$ per month)	38
5.01	Firm-level technology absorption	20
5.02	Firm-level innovation	23
5.03	Capacity for innovation	17
5.04	Business Intranet sophistication	38
5.05	Quality of local IT training programs	17
5.06	Cost of business telephone subscription (US$ per month)	24
6.01	Government prioritization of ICT	51
6.02	Government procurement of advanced technology products	40
6.03	Competence of public officials	29
6.04	Government online services	4

Usage Component Index 13

Individual Usage	12
Business Usage	11
Government Usage	16

7.01	Use of online payment systems	6
7.02	Number of radios (per 1,000 people)	18
7.03	Number of television sets (per 1,000 people)	8
7.04	Number of cable television subscribers (per 1,000 people)	12
7.05	Number of mobile telephones (per 1,000 people)	4
7.06	Number of Internet users (per 100 people)	23
7.07	Number of narrowband subscriber lines (per 100 people)	17
7.08	Number of broadband subscriber lines (per 100 people)	18
7.09	Household spending on ICT (US$ per month)	8
8.01	Use of Internet for coordination with customers and suppliers	34
8.02	Businesses using e-commerce (%)	2
8.03	Use of Internet for general research	25
8.04	Sophistication of online marketing	27
8.05	Presence of wireless e-business applications	19
8.06	Use of email for internal correspondence (%)	31
8.07	Use of email for external correspondence (%)	21
8.08	Pervasiveness of company web pages	11
9.01	Use of Internet-based transactions with the government	16
9.02	Government online services	4
9.03	Government success in ICT promotion	52

Panama.pa

Key Indicators

Population	2,856,000
GDP per capita (PPP)	US$6,000
Illiteracy rate	8.11%
GDP per capita growth	1.03%

Environment Component Index — 61

Market Environment		53
Political and Regulatory Environment		66
Infrastructure Environment		56
1.01	Venture capital availability	35
1.02	State of cluster development	58
1.03	Competition in the telecommunication sector	54
1.04	Availability of scientists and engineers	63
1.05	Brain drain	24
1.06	Public spending on education (% of GDP)	29
1.07	Domestic software companies in international markets	43
1.08	Domestic manufacturing of IT hardware	64
1.09	ICT expenditure (% of GDP)	77
2.01	Effectiveness of law-making bodies	74
2.02	Legal framework for ICT development	53
2.03	Subsidies for firm-level research and development	65
2.04	Government restrictions on Internet content	72
2.05	Prevalence of foreign technology licensing	42
3.01	Overall infrastructure quality	43
3.02	Local availability of specialized IT services	42
3.03	Number of telephone mainlines (per 1,000 people)	53
3.04	Number of telephone faults (per 100 main lines)	68
3.05	Number of telephone mainlines per employee	69
3.06	Number of fax machines (per 1,000 people)	52
3.07	Local switch capacity (per 100,000 people)	59
3.08	Ease of obtaining new telephone lines	45
3.09	Waiting time for telephone mainlines (in years)	58
3.1	Number of secure Internet servers	39

Readiness Component Index — 63

Individual Readiness		38
Business Readiness		59
Government Readiness		73
4.01	Sophistication of local buyers' products and processes	44
4.02	Availability of mobile Internet access	27
4.03	Availability of broadband access	15
4.04	Public access to the Internet	41
4.05	Secondary school enrollment (% net)	42
4.06	Total adult illiteracy rate (%)	51

Readiness Component Index (continued)

4.07	Quality of math and science education	64
4.08	Cost of local call (US$ per three min)	56
4.09	Cost of off-peak local cellular call (US$ per three min)	58
4.10	Cost of residential telephone subscription (US$ per month)	32
5.01	Firm-level technology absorption	42
5.02	Firm-level innovation	51
5.03	Capacity for innovation	70
5.04	Business Intranet sophistication	66
5.05	Quality of local IT training programs	61
5.06	Cost of business telephone subscription (US$ per month)	63
6.01	Government prioritization of ICT	73
6.02	Government procurement of advanced technology products	74
6.03	Competence of public officials	77
6.04	Government online services	44

Usage Component Index — 56

Individual Usage		50
Business Usage		53
Government Usage		62
7.01	Use of online payment systems	41
7.02	Number of radios (per 1,000 people)	63
7.03	Number of television sets (per 1,000 people)	59
7.04	Number of cable television subscribers (per 1,000 people)	68
7.05	Number of mobile telephones (per 1,000 people)	45
7.06	Number of Internet users (per 100 people)	56
7.07	Number of narrowband subscriber lines (per 100 people)	50
7.08	Number of broadband subscriber lines (per 100 people)	44
7.09	Household spending on ICT (US$ per month)	32
8.01	Use of Internet for coordination with customers and suppliers	18
8.02	Businesses using e-commerce (%)	52
8.03	Use of Internet for general research	60
8.04	Sophistication of online marketing	67
8.05	Presence of wireless e-business applications	63
8.06	Use of email for internal correspondence (%)	59
8.07	Use of email for external correspondence (%)	50
8.08	Pervasiveness of company web pages	50
9.01	Use of Internet-based transactions with the government	59
9.02	Government online services	44
9.03	Government success in ICT promotion	67

Paraguay.py

Key Indicators

Population	5,496,000
GDP per capita (PPP)	US$4,426
Illiteracy rate	6.72%
GDP per capita growth	-2.79%

Networked Readiness Index Rank

2002–2003 76

2001–2002 63

Environment Component Index — 79

Market Environment		74
Political and Regulatory Environment		81
Infrastructure Environment		73
1.01	Venture capital availability	79
1.02	State of cluster development	81
1.03	Competition in the telecommunication sector	69
1.04	Availability of scientists and engineers	79
1.05	Brain drain	59
1.06	Public spending on education (% of GDP)	45
1.07	Domestic software companies in international markets	75
1.08	Domestic manufacturing of IT hardware	48
1.09	ICT expenditure (% of GDP)	49
2.01	Effectiveness of law-making bodies	77
2.02	Legal framework for ICT development	80
2.03	Subsidies for firm-level research and development	82
2.04	Government restrictions on Internet content	75
2.05	Prevalence of foreign technology licensing	80
3.01	Overall infrastructure quality	78
3.02	Local availability of specialized IT services	77
3.03	Number of telephone mainlines (per 1,000 people)	71
3.04	Number of telephone faults (per 100 main lines)	52
3.05	Number of telephone mainlines per employee	78
3.06	Number of fax machines (per 1,000 people)	72
3.07	Local switch capacity (per 100,000 people)	73
3.08	Ease of obtaining new telephone lines	74
3.09	Waiting time for telephone mainlines (in years)	45
3.1	Number of secure Internet servers	60

Readiness Component Index — 76

Individual Readiness		75
Business Readiness		74
Government Readiness		80
4.01	Sophistication of local buyers' products and processes	75
4.02	Availability of mobile Internet access	74
4.03	Availability of broadband access	78
4.04	Public access to the Internet	39
4.05	Secondary school enrollment (% net)	72
4.06	Total adult illiteracy rate (%)	47

Readiness Component Index (continued)

4.07	Quality of math and science education	79
4.08	Cost of local call (US$ per three min)	64
4.09	Cost of off-peak local cellular call (US$ per three min)	67
4.10	Cost of residential telephone subscription (US$ per month)	64
5.01	Firm-level technology absorption	79
5.02	Firm-level innovation	8
5.03	Capacity for innovation	80
5.04	Business Intranet sophistication	79
5.05	Quality of local IT training programs	71
5.06	Cost of business telephone subscription (US$ per month)	53
6.01	Government prioritization of ICT	78
6.02	Government procurement of advanced technology products	80
6.03	Competence of public officials	79
6.04	Government online services	72

Usage Component Index — 72

Individual Usage		59
Business Usage		74
Government Usage		72
7.01	Use of online payment systems	70
7.02	Number of radios (per 1,000 people)	71
7.03	Number of television sets (per 1,000 people)	54
7.04	Number of cable television subscribers (per 1,000 people)	58
7.05	Number of mobile telephones (per 1,000 people)	44
7.06	Number of Internet users (per 100 people)	81
7.07	Number of narrowband subscriber lines (per 100 people)	82
7.08	Number of broadband subscriber lines (per 100 people)	44
7.09	Household spending on ICT (US$ per month)	30
8.01	Use of Internet for coordination with customers and suppliers	74
8.02	Businesses using e-commerce (%)	79
8.03	Use of Internet for general research	67
8.04	Sophistication of online marketing	49
8.05	Presence of wireless e-business applications	64
8.06	Use of email for internal correspondence (%)	68
8.07	Use of email for external correspondence (%)	60
8.08	Pervasiveness of company web pages	77
9.01	Use of Internet-based transactions with the government	37
9.02	Government online services	72
9.03	Government success in ICT promotion	80

Peru.pe

Key Indicators

Population	25,661,000
GDP per capita (PPP)	US$4,799
Illiteracy rate	10.11%
GDP per capita growth	1.40%

Networked Readiness Index Rank

2002–2003 **67**

2001–2002   52

Environment Component Index — 67

Market Environment	73

Political and Regulatory Environment	71

Infrastructure Environment	51

1.01	Venture capital availability	77
1.02	State of cluster development	68
1.03	Competition in the telecommunication sector	47
1.04	Availability of scientists and engineers	64
1.05	Brain drain	68
1.06	Public spending on education (% of GDP)	67
1.07	Domestic software companies in international markets	59
1.08	Domestic manufacturing of IT hardware	66
1.09	ICT expenditure (% of GDP)	64
2.01	Effectiveness of law-making bodies	66
2.02	Legal framework for ICT development	57
2.03	Subsidies for firm-level research and development	79
2.04	Government restrictions on Internet content	69
2.05	Prevalence of foreign technology licensing	70
3.01	Overall infrastructure quality	69
3.02	Local availability of specialized IT services	44
3.03	Number of telephone mainlines (per 1,000 people)	66
3.04	Number of telephone faults (per 100 main lines)	41
3.05	Number of telephone mainlines per employee	10
3.06	Number of fax machines (per 1,000 people)	62
3.07	Local switch capacity (per 100,000 people)	70
3.08	Ease of obtaining new telephone lines	42
3.09	Waiting time for telephone mainlines (in years)	57
3.1	Number of secure Internet servers	58

Readiness Component Index — 68

Individual Readiness	65

Business Readiness	61

Government Readiness	66

4.01	Sophistication of local buyers' products and processes	74
4.02	Availability of mobile Internet access	65
4.03	Availability of broadband access	42
4.04	Public access to the Internet	13
4.05	Secondary school enrollment (% net)	50
4.06	Total adult illiteracy rate (%)	56

Readiness Component Index (continued)

4.07	Quality of math and science education	78
4.08	Cost of local call (US$ per three min)	65
4.09	Cost of off-peak local cellular call (US$ per three min)	73
4.10	Cost of residential telephone subscription (US$ per month)	79
5.01	Firm-level technology absorption	62
5.02	Firm-level innovation	35
5.03	Capacity for innovation	66
5.04	Business Intranet sophistication	56
5.05	Quality of local IT training programs	62
5.06	Cost of business telephone subscription (US$ per month)	73
6.01	Government prioritization of ICT	69
6.02	Government procurement of advanced technology products	72
6.03	Competence of public officials	72
6.04	Government online services	40

Usage Component Index — 60

Individual Usage	56

Business Usage	57

Government Usage	64

7.01	Use of online payment systems	36
7.02	Number of radios (per 1,000 people)	65
7.03	Number of television sets (per 1,000 people)	66
7.04	Number of cable television subscribers (per 1,000 people)	64
7.05	Number of mobile telephones (per 1,000 people)	66
7.06	Number of Internet users (per 100 people)	61
7.07	Number of narrowband subscriber lines (per 100 people)	68
7.08	Number of broadband subscriber lines (per 100 people)	44
7.09	Household spending on ICT (US$ per month)	35
8.01	Use of Internet for coordination with customers and suppliers	40
8.02	Businesses using e-commerce (%)	47
8.03	Use of Internet for general research	66
8.04	Sophistication of online marketing	78
8.05	Presence of wireless e-business applications	43
8.06	Use of email for internal correspondence (%)	45
8.07	Use of email for external correspondence (%)	41
8.08	Pervasiveness of company web pages	67
9.01	Use of Internet-based transactions with the government	63
9.02	Government online services	40
9.03	Government success in ICT promotion	68

Philippines.ph

Key Indicators

Population	75,580,000
GDP per capita (PPP)	US$3,971
Illiteracy rate	4.71%
GDP per capita growth	2.10%

Networked Readiness Index Rank

2002–2003 **62**

2001–2002 58

Environment Component Index		57
Market Environment		60
Political and Regulatory Environment		46
Infrastructure Environment		65
1.01	Venture capital availability	66
1.02	State of cluster development	44
1.03	Competition in the telecommunication sector	37
1.04	Availability of scientists and engineers	70
1.05	Brain drain	75
1.06	Public spending on education (% of GDP)	66
1.07	Domestic software companies in international markets	35
1.08	Domestic manufacturing of IT hardware	33
1.09	ICT expenditure (% of GDP)	69
2.01	Effectiveness of law-making bodies	59
2.02	Legal framework for ICT development	35
2.03	Subsidies for firm-level research and development	62
2.04	Government restrictions on Internet content	30
2.05	Prevalence of foreign technology licensing	18
3.01	Overall infrastructure quality	76
3.02	Local availability of specialized IT services	47
3.03	Number of telephone mainlines (per 1,000 people)	74
3.04	Number of telephone faults (per 100 main lines)	20
3.05	Number of telephone mainlines per employee	16
3.06	Number of fax machines (per 1,000 people)	60
3.07	Local switch capacity (per 100,000 people)	77
3.08	Ease of obtaining new telephone lines	71
3.09	Waiting time for telephone mainlines (in years)	68
3.1	Number of secure Internet servers	63

Readiness Component Index		70
Individual Readiness		63
Business Readiness		73
Government Readiness		64
4.01	Sophistication of local buyers' products and processes	57
4.02	Availability of mobile Internet access	46
4.03	Availability of broadband access	56
4.04	Public access to the Internet	70
4.05	Secondary school enrollment (% net)	53
4.06	Total adult illiteracy rate (%)	41

Readiness Component Index (continued)		
4.07	Quality of math and science education	76
4.08	Cost of local call (US$ per three min)	1
4.09	Cost of off-peak local cellular call (US$ per three min)	54
4.10	Cost of residential telephone subscription (US$ per month)	81
5.01	Firm-level technology absorption	65
5.02	Firm-level innovation	52
5.03	Capacity for innovation	72
5.04	Business Intranet sophistication	54
5.05	Quality of local IT training programs	34
5.06	Cost of business telephone subscription (US$ per month)	79
6.01	Government prioritization of ICT	42
6.02	Government procurement of advanced technology products	65
6.03	Competence of public officials	70
6.04	Government online services	66

Usage Component Index		54
Individual Usage		57
Business Usage		48
Government Usage		56
7.01	Use of online payment systems	34
7.02	Number of radios (per 1,000 people)	73
7.03	Number of television sets (per 1,000 people)	67
7.04	Number of cable television subscribers (per 1,000 people)	66
7.05	Number of mobile telephones (per 1,000 people)	56
7.06	Number of Internet users (per 100 people)	44
7.07	Number of narrowband subscriber lines (per 100 people)	78
7.08	Number of broadband subscriber lines (per 100 people)	44
7.09	Household spending on ICT (US$ per month)	41
8.01	Use of Internet for coordination with customers and suppliers	62
8.02	Businesses using e-commerce (%)	70
8.03	Use of Internet for general research	38
8.04	Sophistication of online marketing	61
8.05	Presence of wireless e-business applications	39
8.06	Use of email for internal correspondence (%)	37
8.07	Use of email for external correspondence (%)	66
8.08	Pervasiveness of company web pages	47
9.01	Use of Internet-based transactions with the government	50
9.02	Government online services	66
9.03	Government success in ICT promotion	41

Poland.pl

Key Indicators

Population	38,650,000
GDP per capita (PPP)	US$9,051
Illiteracy rate	0.27%
GDP per capita growth	4.01%

Networked Readiness Index Rank

2002–2003 **39**

2001–2002   35

Environment Component Index	47
Market Environment	38
Political and Regulatory Environment	58
Infrastructure Environment	47

1.01	Venture capital availability	36
1.02	State of cluster development	43
1.03	Competition in the telecommunication sector	62
1.04	Availability of scientists and engineers	35
1.05	Brain drain	37
1.06	Public spending on education (% of GDP)	25
1.07	Domestic software companies in international markets	53
1.08	Domestic manufacturing of IT hardware	23
1.09	ICT expenditure (% of GDP)	50
2.01	Effectiveness of law-making bodies	53
2.02	Legal framework for ICT development	70
2.03	Subsidies for firm-level research and development	43
2.04	Government restrictions on Internet content	61
2.05	Prevalence of foreign technology licensing	43
3.01	Overall infrastructure quality	62
3.02	Local availability of specialized IT services	37
3.03	Number of telephone mainlines (per 1,000 people)	38
3.04	Number of telephone faults (per 100 main lines)	55
3.05	Number of telephone mainlines per employee	44
3.06	Number of fax machines (per 1,000 people)	57
3.07	Local switch capacity (per 100,000 people)	46
3.08	Ease of obtaining new telephone lines	58
3.09	Waiting time for telephone mainlines (in years)	51
3.1	Number of secure Internet servers	42

Readiness Component Index	45
Individual Readiness	36
Business Readiness	43
Government Readiness	53

4.01	Sophistication of local buyers' products and processes	50
4.02	Availability of mobile Internet access	23
4.03	Availability of broadband access	47
4.04	Public access to the Internet	61
4.05	Secondary school enrollment (% net)	45
4.06	Total adult illiteracy rate (%)	10

Readiness Component Index (continued)	
4.07	Quality of math and science education	31
4.08	Cost of local call (US$ per three min)	51
4.09	Cost of off-peak local cellular call (US$ per three min)	53
4.10	Cost of residential telephone subscription (US$ per month)	54
5.01	Firm-level technology absorption	59
5.02	Firm-level innovation	67
5.03	Capacity for innovation	43
5.04	Business Intranet sophistication	29
5.05	Quality of local IT training programs	50
5.06	Cost of business telephone subscription (US$ per month)	36
6.01	Government prioritization of ICT	66
6.02	Government procurement of advanced technology products	55
6.03	Competence of public officials	55
6.04	Government online services	30

Usage Component Index	34
Individual Usage	41
Business Usage	25
Government Usage	38

7.01	Use of online payment systems	50
7.02	Number of radios (per 1,000 people)	40
7.03	Number of television sets (per 1,000 people)	35
7.04	Number of cable television subscribers (per 1,000 people)	27
7.05	Number of mobile telephones (per 1,000 people)	40
7.06	Number of Internet users (per 100 people)	45
7.07	Number of narrowband subscriber lines (per 100 people)	37
7.08	Number of broadband subscriber lines (per 100 people)	44
7.09	Household spending on ICT (US$ per month)	60
8.01	Use of Internet for coordination with customers and suppliers	33
8.02	Businesses using e-commerce (%)	41
8.03	Use of Internet for general research	18
8.04	Sophistication of online marketing	6
8.05	Presence of wireless e-business applications	8
8.06	Use of email for internal correspondence (%)	36
8.07	Use of email for external correspondence (%)	26
8.08	Pervasiveness of company web pages	37
9.01	Use of Internet-based transactions with the government	31
9.02	Government online services	30
9.03	Government success in ICT promotion	60

Portugal.pt

Key Indicators

Population	10,008,000
GDP per capita (PPP)	US$17,290
Illiteracy rate	7.78%
GDP per capita growth	3.12%

Networked Readiness Index Rank

2002–2003 **31**

2001–2002 27

Environment Component Index	27
Market Environment	32
Political and Regulatory Environment	25
Infrastructure Environment	30

1.01	Venture capital availability	37
1.02	State of cluster development	33
1.03	Competition in the telecommunication sector	19
1.04	Availability of scientists and engineers	47
1.05	Brain drain	23
1.06	Public spending on education (% of GDP)	22
1.07	Domestic software companies in international markets	52
1.08	Domestic manufacturing of IT hardware	38
1.09	ICT expenditure (% of GDP)	32
2.01	Effectiveness of law-making bodies	35
2.02	Legal framework for ICT development	29
2.03	Subsidies for firm-level research and development	24
2.04	Government restrictions on Internet content	16
2.05	Prevalence of foreign technology licensing	11
3.01	Overall infrastructure quality	33
3.02	Local availability of specialized IT services	45
3.03	Number of telephone mainlines (per 1,000 people)	26
3.04	Number of telephone faults (per 100 main lines)	28
3.05	Number of telephone mainlines per employee	15
3.06	Number of fax machines (per 1,000 people)	36
3.07	Local switch capacity (per 100,000 people)	41
3.08	Ease of obtaining new telephone lines	33
3.09	Waiting time for telephone mainlines (in years)	37
3.1	Number of secure Internet servers	29

Readiness Component Index	37
Individual Readiness	35
Business Readiness	51
Government Readiness	36

4.01	Sophistication of local buyers' products and processes	46
4.02	Availability of mobile Internet access	29
4.03	Availability of broadband access	45
4.04	Public access to the Internet	28
4.05	Secondary school enrollment (% net)	23
4.06	Total adult illiteracy rate (%)	50

Readiness Component Index (continued)	
4.07	Quality of math and science education	62
4.08	Cost of local call (US$ per three min)	42
4.09	Cost of off-peak local cellular call (US$ per three min)	39
4.10	Cost of residential telephone subscription (US$ per month)	42
5.01	Firm-level technology absorption	72
5.02	Firm-level innovation	77
5.03	Capacity for innovation	41
5.04	Business Intranet sophistication	42
5.05	Quality of local IT training programs	37
5.06	Cost of business telephone subscription (US$ per month)	28
6.01	Government prioritization of ICT	32
6.02	Government procurement of advanced technology products	43
6.03	Competence of public officials	52
6.04	Government online services	21

Usage Component Index	28
Individual Usage	26
Business Usage	34
Government Usage	26

7.01	Use of online payment systems	32
7.02	Number of radios (per 1,000 people)	62
7.03	Number of television sets (per 1,000 people)	10
7.04	Number of cable television subscribers (per 1,000 people)	28
7.05	Number of mobile telephones (per 1,000 people)	13
7.06	Number of Internet users (per 100 people)	29
7.07	Number of narrowband subscriber lines (per 100 people)	25
7.08	Number of broadband subscriber lines (per 100 people)	23
7.09	Household spending on ICT (US$ per month)	10
8.01	Use of Internet for coordination with customers and suppliers	60
8.02	Businesses using e-commerce (%)	24
8.03	Use of Internet for general research	21
8.04	Sophistication of online marketing	20
8.05	Presence of wireless e-business applications	46
8.06	Use of email for internal correspondence (%)	46
8.07	Use of email for external correspondence (%)	71
8.08	Pervasiveness of company web pages	42
9.01	Use of Internet-based transactions with the government	53
9.02	Government online services	21
9.03	Government success in ICT promotion	16

Romania.ro

Key Indicators

Population	22,435,000
GDP per capita (PPP)	US$6,423
Illiteracy rate	1.88%
GDP per capita growth	1.74%

Networked Readiness Index Rank

2002–2003	**72**
2001–2002	65

Environment Component Index — 71

Market Environment		72
Political and Regulatory Environment		70
Infrastructure Environment		72

1.01	Venture capital availability	63
1.02	State of cluster development	45
1.03	Competition in the telecommunication sector	66
1.04	Availability of scientists and engineers	5
1.05	Brain drain	80
1.06	Public spending on education (% of GDP)	48
1.07	Domestic software companies in international markets	66
1.08	Domestic manufacturing of IT hardware	80
1.09	ICT expenditure (% of GDP)	80
2.01	Effectiveness of law-making bodies	68
2.02	Legal framework for ICT development	82
2.03	Subsidies for firm-level research and development	63
2.04	Government restrictions on Internet content	47
2.05	Prevalence of foreign technology licensing	65
3.01	Overall infrastructure quality	74
3.02	Local availability of specialized IT services	81
3.03	Number of telephone mainlines (per 1,000 people)	51
3.04	Number of telephone faults (per 100 main lines)	63
3.05	Number of telephone mainlines per employee	66
3.06	Number of fax machines (per 1,000 people)	59
3.07	Local switch capacity (per 100,000 people)	55
3.08	Ease of obtaining new telephone lines	70
3.09	Waiting time for telephone mainlines (in years)	72
3.1	Number of secure Internet servers	52

Readiness Component Index — 71

Individual Readiness		49
Business Readiness		76
Government Readiness		71

4.01	Sophistication of local buyers' products and processes	73
4.02	Availability of mobile Internet access	80
4.03	Availability of broadband access	25
4.04	Public access to the Internet	78
4.05	Secondary school enrollment (% net)	38
4.06	Total adult illiteracy rate (%)	27

Readiness Component Index (continued)

4.07	Quality of math and science education	9
4.08	Cost of local call (US$ per three min)	71
4.09	Cost of off-peak local cellular call (US$ per three min)	61
4.10	Cost of residential telephone subscription (US$ per month)	57
5.01	Firm-level technology absorption	68
5.02	Firm-level innovation	53
5.03	Capacity for innovation	54
5.04	Business Intranet sophistication	82
5.05	Quality of local IT training programs	82
5.06	Cost of business telephone subscription (US$ per month)	41
6.01	Government prioritization of ICT	59
6.02	Government procurement of advanced technology products	62
6.03	Competence of public officials	71
6.04	Government online services	81

Usage Component Index — 82

Individual Usage		62
Business Usage		82
Government Usage		81

7.01	Use of online payment systems	82
7.02	Number of radios (per 1,000 people)	59
7.03	Number of television sets (per 1,000 people)	38
7.04	Number of cable television subscribers (per 1,000 people)	18
7.05	Number of mobile telephones (per 1,000 people)	53
7.06	Number of Internet users (per 100 people)	67
7.07	Number of narrowband subscriber lines (per 100 people)	48
7.08	Number of broadband subscriber lines (per 100 people)	44
7.09	Household spending on ICT (US$ per month)	81
8.01	Use of Internet for coordination with customers and suppliers	48
8.02	Businesses using e-commerce (%)	77
8.03	Use of Internet for general research	79
8.04	Sophistication of online marketing	66
8.05	Presence of wireless e-business applications	82
8.06	Use of email for internal correspondence (%)	79
8.07	Use of email for external correspondence (%)	82
8.08	Pervasiveness of company web pages	82
9.01	Use of Internet-based transactions with the government	82
9.02	Government online services	81
9.03	Government success in ICT promotion	51

Russian Federation.ru

Key Indicators

Population	145,555,008
GDP per capita (PPP)	US$8,377
Illiteracy rate	0.45%
GDP per capita growth	8.86%

Networked Readiness Index Rank

2002–2003 **29**

2001–2002   28

Environment Component Index	68
Market Environment	58
Political and Regulatory Environment	74
Infrastructure Environment	69

1.01	Venture capital availability	60
1.02	State of cluster development	41
1.03	Competition in the telecommunication sector	58
1.04	Availability of scientists and engineers	29
1.05	Brain drain	49
1.06	Public spending on education (% of GDP)	59
1.07	Domestic software companies in international markets	68
1.08	Domestic manufacturing of IT hardware	45
1.09	ICT expenditure (% of GDP)	73
2.01	Effectiveness of law-making bodies	52
2.02	Legal framework for ICT development	78
2.03	Subsidies for firm-level research and development	47
2.04	Government restrictions on Internet content	71
2.05	Prevalence of foreign technology licensing	77
3.01	Overall infrastructure quality	59
3.02	Local availability of specialized IT services	56
3.03	Number of telephone mainlines (per 1,000 people)	45
3.04	Number of telephone faults (per 100 main lines)	62
3.05	Number of telephone mainlines per employee	70
3.06	Number of fax machines (per 1,000 people)	66
3.07	Local switch capacity (per 100,000 people)	54
3.08	Ease of obtaining new telephone lines	69
3.09	Waiting time for telephone mainlines (in years)	74
3.1	Number of secure Internet servers	54

Readiness Component Index	60
Individual Readiness	48
Business Readiness	64
Government Readiness	61

4.01	Sophistication of local buyers' products and processes	58
4.02	Availability of mobile Internet access	69
4.03	Availability of broadband access	75
4.04	Public access to the Internet	77
4.05	Secondary school enrollment (% net)	47
4.06	Total adult illiteracy rate (%)	14

Readiness Component Index (continued)	
4.07	Quality of math and science education	22
4.08	Cost of local call (US$ per three min)	9
4.09	Cost of off-peak local cellular call (US$ per three min)	1
4.10	Cost of residential telephone subscription (US$ per month)	7
5.01	Firm-level technology absorption	57
5.02	Firm-level innovation	78
5.03	Capacity for innovation	31
5.04	Business Intranet sophistication	76
5.05	Quality of local IT training programs	72
5.06	Cost of business telephone subscription (US$ per month)	38
6.01	Government prioritization of ICT	63
6.02	Government procurement of advanced technology products	51
6.03	Competence of public officials	63
6.04	Government online services	65

Usage Component Index	78
Individual Usage	58
Business Usage	81
Government Usage	71

7.01	Use of online payment systems	72
7.02	Number of radios (per 1,000 people)	47
7.03	Number of television sets (per 1,000 people)	33
7.04	Number of cable television subscribers (per 1,000 people)	32
7.05	Number of mobile telephones (per 1,000 people)	72
7.06	Number of Internet users (per 100 people)	71
7.07	Number of narrowband subscriber lines (per 100 people)	51
7.08	Number of broadband subscriber lines (per 100 people)	44
7.09	Household spending on ICT (US$ per month)	81
8.01	Use of Internet for coordination with customers and suppliers	79
8.02	Businesses using e-commerce (%)	82
8.03	Use of Internet for general research	72
8.04	Sophistication of online marketing	53
8.05	Presence of wireless e-business applications	66
8.06	Use of email for internal correspondence (%)	82
8.07	Use of email for external correspondence (%)	81
8.08	Pervasiveness of company web pages	64
9.01	Use of Internet-based transactions with the government	64
9.02	Government online services	65
9.03	Government success in ICT promotion	69

Singapore.sg

Key Indicators

Population	4,018,000
GDP per capita (PPP)	US$23,356
Illiteracy rate	7.68%
GDP per capita growth	8.09%

Networked Readiness Index Rank

2002–2003 3

2001–2002 8

Environment Component Index	8
Market Environment	10
Political and Regulatory Environment	1
Infrastructure Environment	13

1.01	Venture capital availability	15
1.02	State of cluster development	6
1.03	Competition in the telecommunication sector	12
1.04	Availability of scientists and engineers	20
1.05	Brain drain	17
1.06	Public spending on education (% of GDP)	69
1.07	Domestic software companies in international markets	17
1.08	Domestic manufacturing of IT hardware	14
1.09	ICT expenditure (% of GDP)	5
2.01	Effectiveness of law-making bodies	1
2.02	Legal framework for ICT development	2
2.03	Subsidies for firm-level research and development	2
2.04	Government restrictions on Internet content	80
2.05	Prevalence of foreign technology licensing	4
3.01	Overall infrastructure quality	4
3.02	Local availability of specialized IT services	28
3.03	Number of telephone mainlines (per 1,000 people)	21
3.04	Number of telephone faults (per 100 main lines)	1
3.05	Number of telephone mainlines per employee	18
3.06	Number of fax machines (per 1,000 people)	20
3.07	Local switch capacity (per 100,000 people)	29
3.08	Ease of obtaining new telephone lines	6
3.09	Waiting time for telephone mainlines (in years)	1
3.1	Number of secure Internet servers	6

Readiness Component Index	1
Individual Readiness	2
Business Readiness	11
Government Readiness	1

4.01	Sophistication of local buyers' products and processes	12
4.02	Availability of mobile Internet access	12
4.03	Availability of broadband access	4
4.04	Public access to the Internet	6
4.05	Secondary school enrollment (% net)	11
4.06	Total adult illiteracy rate (%)	49

Readiness Component Index (continued)	
4.07	Quality of math and science education	1
4.08	Cost of local call (US$ per three min)	7
4.09	Cost of off-peak local cellular call (US$ per three min)	4
4.10	Cost of residential telephone subscription (US$ per month)	4
5.01	Firm-level technology absorption	9
5.02	Firm-level innovation	7
5.03	Capacity for innovation	25
5.04	Business Intranet sophistication	14
5.05	Quality of local IT training programs	5
5.06	Cost of business telephone subscription (US$ per month)	5
6.01	Government prioritization of ICT	1
6.02	Government procurement of advanced technology products	1
6.03	Competence of public officials	1
6.04	Government online services	1

Usage Component Index	2
Individual Usage	9
Business Usage	7
Government Usage	2

7.01	Use of online payment systems	12
7.02	Number of radios (per 1,000 people)	33
7.03	Number of television sets (per 1,000 people)	44
7.04	Number of cable television subscribers (per 1,000 people)	36
7.05	Number of mobile telephones (per 1,000 people)	11
7.06	Number of Internet users (per 100 people)	1
7.07	Number of narrowband subscriber lines (per 100 people)	6
7.08	Number of broadband subscriber lines (per 100 people)	6
7.09	Household spending on ICT (US$ per month)	3
8.01	Use of Internet for coordination with customers and suppliers	5
8.02	Businesses using e-commerce (%)	20
8.03	Use of Internet for general research	17
8.04	Sophistication of online marketing	11
8.05	Presence of wireless e-business applications	21
8.06	Use of email for internal correspondence (%)	2
8.07	Use of email for external correspondence (%)	1
8.08	Pervasiveness of company web pages	22
9.01	Use of Internet-based transactions with the government	9
9.02	Government online services	1
9.03	Government success in ICT promotion	1

Slovak Republic.sk

Key Indicators

Population	5,401,790
GDP per capita (PPP)	US$11,243
Illiteracy rate	0.00%
GDP per capita growth	2.07%

Networked Readiness Index Rank

2002–2003 **40**

2001–2002   33

Environment Component Index	37
Market Environment	37
Political and Regulatory Environment	41
Infrastructure Environment	36

1.01	Venture capital availability	56
1.02	State of cluster development	62
1.03	Competition in the telecommunication sector	32
1.04	Availability of scientists and engineers	3
1.05	Brain drain	52
1.06	Public spending on education (% of GDP)	49
1.07	Domestic software companies in international markets	50
1.08	Domestic manufacturing of IT hardware	42
1.09	ICT expenditure (% of GDP)	28
2.01	Effectiveness of law-making bodies	64
2.02	Legal framework for ICT development	23
2.03	Subsidies for firm-level research and development	39
2.04	Government restrictions on Internet content	35
2.05	Prevalence of foreign technology licensing	30
3.01	Overall infrastructure quality	48
3.02	Local availability of specialized IT services	21
3.03	Number of telephone mainlines (per 1,000 people)	36
3.04	Number of telephone faults (per 100 main lines)	56
3.05	Number of telephone mainlines per employee	57
3.06	Number of fax machines (per 1,000 people)	30
3.07	Local switch capacity (per 100,000 people)	42
3.08	Ease of obtaining new telephone lines	38
3.09	Waiting time for telephone mainlines (in years)	46
3.1	Number of secure Internet servers	32

Readiness Component Index	39
Individual Readiness	30
Business Readiness	39
Government Readiness	51

4.01	Sophistication of local buyers' products and processes	45
4.02	Availability of mobile Internet access	25
4.03	Availability of broadband access	20
4.04	Public access to the Internet	52
4.05	Secondary school enrollment (% net)	54
4.06	Total adult illiteracy rate (%)	59

Readiness Component Index (continued)	
4.07	Quality of math and science education	5
4.08	Cost of local call (US$ per three min)	53
4.09	Cost of off-peak local cellular call (US$ per three min)	31
4.10	Cost of residential telephone subscription (US$ per month)	12
5.01	Firm-level technology absorption	26
5.02	Firm-level innovation	29
5.03	Capacity for innovation	39
5.04	Business Intranet sophistication	57
5.05	Quality of local IT training programs	48
5.06	Cost of business telephone subscription (US$ per month)	4
6.01	Government prioritization of ICT	60
6.02	Government procurement of advanced technology products	44
6.03	Competence of public officials	54
6.04	Government online services	46

Usage Component Index	45
Individual Usage	35
Business Usage	44
Government Usage	55

7.01	Use of online payment systems	42
7.02	Number of radios (per 1,000 people)	13
7.03	Number of television sets (per 1,000 people)	34
7.04	Number of cable television subscribers (per 1,000 people)	21
7.05	Number of mobile telephones (per 1,000 people)	38
7.06	Number of Internet users (per 100 people)	38
7.07	Number of narrowband subscriber lines (per 100 people)	31
7.08	Number of broadband subscriber lines (per 100 people)	44
7.09	Household spending on ICT (US$ per month)	72
8.01	Use of Internet for coordination with customers and suppliers	44
8.02	Businesses using e-commerce (%)	81
8.03	Use of Internet for general research	76
8.04	Sophistication of online marketing	61
8.05	Presence of wireless e-business applications	28
8.06	Use of email for internal correspondence (%)	50
8.07	Use of email for external correspondence (%)	13
8.08	Pervasiveness of company web pages	34
9.01	Use of Internet-based transactions with the government	55
9.02	Government online services	46
9.03	Government success in ICT promotion	64

Slovenia.si

Key Indicators

Population	1,988,000
GDP per capita (PPP)	US$17,367
Illiteracy rate	0.36%
GDP per capita growth	4.47%

Networked Readiness Index Rank

2002–2003 33

2001–2002 29

Environment Component Index	36
Market Environment	46
Political and Regulatory Environment	35
Infrastructure Environment	29

1.01	Venture capital availability	33
1.02	State of cluster development	59
1.03	Competition in the telecommunication sector	59
1.04	Availability of scientists and engineers	58
1.05	Brain drain	32
1.06	Public spending on education (% of GDP)	21
1.07	Domestic software companies in international markets	49
1.08	Domestic manufacturing of IT hardware	47
1.09	ICT expenditure (% of GDP)	57
2.01	Effectiveness of law-making bodies	41
2.02	Legal framework for ICT development	42
2.03	Subsidies for firm-level research and development	29
2.04	Government restrictions on Internet content	24
2.05	Prevalence of foreign technology licensing	47
3.01	Overall infrastructure quality	37
3.02	Local availability of specialized IT services	49
3.03	Number of telephone mainlines (per 1,000 people)	29
3.04	Number of telephone faults (per 100 main lines)	49
3.05	Number of telephone mainlines per employee	23
3.06	Number of fax machines (per 1,000 people)	29
3.07	Local switch capacity (per 100,000 people)	10
3.08	Ease of obtaining new telephone lines	34
3.09	Waiting time for telephone mainlines (in years)	28
3.1	Number of secure Internet servers	19

Readiness Component Index	32
Individual Readiness	25
Business Readiness	34
Government Readiness	42

4.01	Sophistication of local buyers' products and processes	32
4.02	Availability of mobile Internet access	34
4.03	Availability of broadband access	46
4.04	Public access to the Internet	36
4.05	Secondary school enrollment (% net)	15
4.06	Total adult illiteracy rate (%)	11

Readiness Component Index (continued)	
4.07	Quality of math and science education	18
4.08	Cost of local call (US$ per three min)	14
4.09	Cost of off-peak local cellular call (US$ per three min)	32
4.10	Cost of residential telephone subscription (US$ per month)	10
5.01	Firm-level technology absorption	47
5.02	Firm-level innovation	63
5.03	Capacity for innovation	24
5.04	Business Intranet sophistication	43
5.05	Quality of local IT training programs	32
5.06	Cost of business telephone subscription (US$ per month)	3
6.01	Government prioritization of ICT	48
6.02	Government procurement of advanced technology products	38
6.03	Competence of public officials	30
6.04	Government online services	37

Usage Component Index	30
Individual Usage	18
Business Usage	37
Government Usage	39

7.01	Use of online payment systems	24
7.02	Number of radios (per 1,000 people)	49
7.03	Number of television sets (per 1,000 people)	39
7.04	Number of cable television subscribers (per 1,000 people)	17
7.05	Number of mobile telephones (per 1,000 people)	17
7.06	Number of Internet users (per 100 people)	4
7.07	Number of narrowband subscriber lines (per 100 people)	30
7.08	Number of broadband subscriber lines (per 100 people)	2
7.09	Household spending on ICT (US$ per month)	7
8.01	Use of Internet for coordination with customers and suppliers	30
8.02	Businesses using e-commerce (%)	75
8.03	Use of Internet for general research	34
8.04	Sophistication of online marketing	33
8.05	Presence of wireless e-business applications	33
8.06	Use of email for internal correspondence (%)	49
8.07	Use of email for external correspondence (%)	49
8.08	Pervasiveness of company web pages	38
9.01	Use of Internet-based transactions with the government	45
9.02	Government online services	37
9.03	Government success in ICT promotion	40

South Africa.za

Key Indicators

Population	42,800,992
GDP per capita (PPP)	US$9,401
Illiteracy rate	14.74%
GDP per capita growth	1.41%

Environment Component Index — 38

Market Environment	40
Political and Regulatory Environment	29
Infrastructure Environment	46

1.01	Venture capital availability	26
1.02	State of cluster development	36
1.03	Competition in the telecommunication sector	72
1.04	Availability of scientists and engineers	67
1.05	Brain drain	62
1.06	Public spending on education (% of GDP)	18
1.07	Domestic software companies in international markets	23
1.08	Domestic manufacturing of IT hardware	44
1.09	ICT expenditure (% of GDP)	14
2.01	Effectiveness of law-making bodies	27
2.02	Legal framework for ICT development	32
2.03	Subsidies for firm-level research and development	45
2.04	Government restrictions on Internet content	36
2.05	Prevalence of foreign technology licensing	6
3.01	Overall infrastructure quality	25
3.02	Local availability of specialized IT services	23
3.03	Number of telephone mainlines (per 1,000 people)	55
3.04	Number of telephone faults (per 100 main lines)	66
3.05	Number of telephone mainlines per employee	56
3.06	Number of fax machines (per 1,000 people)	40
3.07	Local switch capacity (per 100,000 people)	62
3.08	Ease of obtaining new telephone lines	59
3.09	Waiting time for telephone mainlines (in years)	56
3.1	Number of secure Internet servers	31

Readiness Component Index — 44

Individual Readiness	54
Business Readiness	35
Government Readiness	46

4.01	Sophistication of local buyers' products and processes	49
4.02	Availability of mobile Internet access	32
4.03	Availability of broadband access	54
4.04	Public access to the Internet	63
4.05	Secondary school enrollment (% net)	57
4.06	Total adult illiteracy rate (%)	64

Readiness Component Index (continued)

4.07	Quality of math and science education	73
4.08	Cost of local call (US$ per three min)	55
4.09	Cost of off-peak local cellular call (US$ per three min)	36
4.10	Cost of residential telephone subscription (US$ per month)	62
5.01	Firm-level technology absorption	29
5.02	Firm-level innovation	33
5.03	Capacity for innovation	44
5.04	Business Intranet sophistication	19
5.05	Quality of local IT training programs	47
5.06	Cost of business telephone subscription (US$ per month)	52
6.01	Government prioritization of ICT	44
6.02	Government procurement of advanced technology products	42
6.03	Competence of public officials	58
6.04	Government online services	39

Usage Component Index — 35

Individual Usage	49
Business Usage	28
Government Usage	37

7.01	Use of online payment systems	26
7.02	Number of radios (per 1,000 people)	58
7.03	Number of television sets (per 1,000 people)	68
7.04	Number of cable television subscribers (per 1,000 people)	42
7.05	Number of mobile telephones (per 1,000 people)	39
7.06	Number of Internet users (per 100 people)	43
7.07	Number of narrowband subscriber lines (per 100 people)	65
7.08	Number of broadband subscriber lines (per 100 people)	44
7.09	Household spending on ICT (US$ per month)	40
8.01	Use of Internet for coordination with customers and suppliers	17
8.02	Businesses using e-commerce (%)	28
8.03	Use of Internet for general research	15
8.04	Sophistication of online marketing	31
8.05	Presence of wireless e-business applications	27
8.06	Use of email for internal correspondence (%)	28
8.07	Use of email for external correspondence (%)	36
8.08	Pervasiveness of company web pages	26
9.01	Use of Internet-based transactions with the government	31
9.02	Government online services	39
9.03	Government success in ICT promotion	43

Spain.es

Key Indicators

Population	39,465,000
GDP per capita (PPP)	US$19,472
Illiteracy rate	2.36%
GDP per capita growth	3.94%

Networked Readiness Index Rank

2002–2003 **25**

2001–2002　26

Environment Component Index — 25

Market Environment	26

Political and Regulatory Environment	19

Infrastructure Environment	21

1.01	Venture capital availability	20
1.02	State of cluster development	31
1.03	Competition in the telecommunication sector	29
1.04	Availability of scientists and engineers	33
1.05	Brain drain	13
1.06	Public spending on education (% of GDP)	44
1.07	Domestic software companies in international markets	33
1.08	Domestic manufacturing of IT hardware	20
1.09	ICT expenditure (% of GDP)	61
2.01	Effectiveness of law-making bodies	18
2.02	Legal framework for ICT development	25
2.03	Subsidies for firm-level research and development	23
2.04	Government restrictions on Internet content	17
2.05	Prevalence of foreign technology licensing	28
3.01	Overall infrastructure quality	26
3.02	Local availability of specialized IT services	16
3.03	Number of telephone mainlines (per 1,000 people)	27
3.04	Number of telephone faults (per 100 main lines)	5
3.05	Number of telephone mainlines per employee	2
3.06	Number of fax machines (per 1,000 people)	26
3.07	Local switch capacity (per 100,000 people)	35
3.08	Ease of obtaining new telephone lines	36
3.09	Waiting time for telephone mainlines (in years)	23
3.1	Number of secure Internet servers	26

Readiness Component Index — 26

Individual Readiness	27

Business Readiness	26

Government Readiness	26

4.01	Sophistication of local buyers' products and processes	31
4.02	Availability of mobile Internet access	33
4.03	Availability of broadband access	23
4.04	Public access to the Internet	25
4.05	Secondary school enrollment (% net)	10
4.06	Total adult illiteracy rate (%)	33

Readiness Component Index (continued)

4.07	Quality of math and science education	41
4.08	Cost of local call (US$ per three min)	19
4.09	Cost of off-peak local cellular call (US$ per three min)	46
4.10	Cost of residential telephone subscription (US$ per month)	24
5.01	Firm-level technology absorption	52
5.02	Firm-level innovation	28
5.03	Capacity for innovation	21
5.04	Business Intranet sophistication	35
5.05	Quality of local IT training programs	24
5.06	Cost of business telephone subscription (US$ per month)	14
6.01	Government prioritization of ICT	27
6.02	Government procurement of advanced technology products	21
6.03	Competence of public officials	39
6.04	Government online services	19

Usage Component Index — 25

Individual Usage	30

Business Usage	20

Government Usage	27

7.01	Use of online payment systems	37
7.02	Number of radios (per 1,000 people)	60
7.03	Number of television sets (per 1,000 people)	12
7.04	Number of cable television subscribers (per 1,000 people)	67
7.05	Number of mobile telephones (per 1,000 people)	18
7.06	Number of Internet users (per 100 people)	21
7.07	Number of narrowband subscriber lines (per 100 people)	16
7.08	Number of broadband subscriber lines (per 100 people)	25
7.09	Household spending on ICT (US$ per month)	37
8.01	Use of Internet for coordination with customers and suppliers	13
8.02	Businesses using e-commerce (%)	13
8.03	Use of Internet for general research	32
8.04	Sophistication of online marketing	24
8.05	Presence of wireless e-business applications	4
8.06	Use of email for internal correspondence (%)	22
8.07	Use of email for external correspondence (%)	30
8.08	Pervasiveness of company web pages	25
9.01	Use of Internet-based transactions with the government	28
9.02	Government online services	19
9.03	Government success in ICT promotion	48

Sri Lanka.lk

Key Indicators

Population	19,359,000
GDP per capita (PPP)	US$3,530
Illiteracy rate	8.36%
GDP per capita growth	4.27%

Environment Component Index — 55

Market Environment	51

Political and Regulatory Environment	53

Infrastructure Environment	58

1.01	Venture capital availability	44
1.02	State of cluster development	47
1.03	Competition in the telecommunication sector	43
1.04	Availability of scientists and engineers	49
1.05	Brain drain	67
1.06	Public spending on education (% of GDP)	62
1.07	Domestic software companies in international markets	44
1.08	Domestic manufacturing of IT hardware	58
1.09	ICT expenditure (% of GDP)	52
2.01	Effectiveness of law-making bodies	19
2.02	Legal framework for ICT development	69
2.03	Subsidies for firm-level research and development	40
2.04	Government restrictions on Internet content	54
2.05	Prevalence of foreign technology licensing	67
3.01	Overall infrastructure quality	27
3.02	Local availability of specialized IT services	68
3.03	Number of telephone mainlines (per 1,000 people)	73
3.04	Number of telephone faults (per 100 main lines)	29
3.05	Number of telephone mainlines per employee	74
3.06	Number of fax machines (per 1,000 people)	72
3.07	Local switch capacity (per 100,000 people)	61
3.08	Ease of obtaining new telephone lines	53
3.09	Waiting time for telephone mainlines (in years)	64
3.1	Number of secure Internet servers	70

Readiness Component Index — 42

Individual Readiness	55

Business Readiness	57

Government Readiness	25

4.01	Sophistication of local buyers' products and processes	60
4.02	Availability of mobile Internet access	45
4.03	Availability of broadband access	70
4.04	Public access to the Internet	71
4.05	Secondary school enrollment (% net)	65
4.06	Total adult illiteracy rate (%)	53

Readiness Component Index (continued)

4.07	Quality of math and science education	50
4.08	Cost of local call (US$ per three min)	59
4.09	Cost of off-peak local cellular call (US$ per three min)	27
4.10	Cost of residential telephone subscription (US$ per month)	52
5.01	Firm-level technology absorption	58
5.02	Firm-level innovation	68
5.03	Capacity for innovation	45
5.04	Business Intranet sophistication	64
5.05	Quality of local IT training programs	51
5.06	Cost of business telephone subscription (US$ per month)	54
6.01	Government prioritization of ICT	28
6.02	Government procurement of advanced technology products	13
6.03	Competence of public officials	2
6.04	Government online services	77

Usage Component Index — 67

Individual Usage	70

Business Usage	71

Government Usage	61

7.01	Use of online payment systems	35
7.02	Number of radios (per 1,000 people)	69
7.03	Number of television sets (per 1,000 people)	70
7.04	Number of cable television subscribers (per 1,000 people)	79
7.05	Number of mobile telephones (per 1,000 people)	71
7.06	Number of Internet users (per 100 people)	69
7.07	Number of narrowband subscriber lines (per 100 people)	67
7.08	Number of broadband subscriber lines (per 100 people)	33
7.09	Household spending on ICT (US$ per month)	61
8.01	Use of Internet for coordination with customers and suppliers	51
8.02	Businesses using e-commerce (%)	10
8.03	Use of Internet for general research	74
8.04	Sophistication of online marketing	72
8.05	Presence of wireless e-business applications	78
8.06	Use of email for internal correspondence (%)	80
8.07	Use of email for external correspondence (%)	28
8.08	Pervasiveness of company web pages	65
9.01	Use of Internet-based transactions with the government	62
9.02	Government online services	77
9.03	Government success in ICT promotion	24

Sweden.se

Key Indicators

Population	8,869,000
GDP per capita (PPP)	US$24,277
Illiteracy rate	1.00%
GDP per capita growth	3.41%

Networked Readiness Index Rank

2002–2003 ● **4**

2001–2002   4

Environment Component Index   6

Market Environment	4
Political and Regulatory Environment	17
Infrastructure Environment	5

1.01	Venture capital availability	5
1.02	State of cluster development	9
1.03	Competition in the telecommunication sector	2
1.04	Availability of scientists and engineers	17
1.05	Brain drain	22
1.06	Public spending on education (% of GDP)	5
1.07	Domestic software companies in international markets	5
1.08	Domestic manufacturing of IT hardware	10
1.09	ICT expenditure (% of GDP)	3
2.01	Effectiveness of law-making bodies	20
2.02	Legal framework for ICT development	4
2.03	Subsidies for firm-level research and development	35
2.04	Government restrictions on Internet content	9
2.05	Prevalence of foreign technology licensing	52
3.01	Overall infrastructure quality	9
3.02	Local availability of specialized IT services	4
3.03	Number of telephone mainlines (per 1,000 people)	6
3.04	Number of telephone faults (per 100 main lines)	11
3.05	Number of telephone mainlines per employee	21
3.06	Number of fax machines (per 1,000 people)	6
3.07	Local switch capacity (per 100,000 people)	11
3.08	Ease of obtaining new telephone lines	13
3.09	Waiting time for telephone mainlines (in years)	1
3.1	Number of secure Internet servers	8

Readiness Component Index   4

Individual Readiness	5
Business Readiness	4
Government Readiness	10

4.01	Sophistication of local buyers' products and processes	7
4.02	Availability of mobile Internet access	4
4.03	Availability of broadband access	6
4.04	Public access to the Internet	5
4.05	Secondary school enrollment (% net)	1
4.06	Total adult illiteracy rate (%)	16

Readiness Component Index (continued)

4.07	Quality of math and science education	32
4.08	Cost of local call (US$ per three min)	38
4.09	Cost of off-peak local cellular call (US$ per three min)	22
4.10	Cost of residential telephone subscription (US$ per month)	39
5.01	Firm-level technology absorption	7
5.02	Firm-level innovation	30
5.03	Capacity for innovation	2
5.04	Business Intranet sophistication	6
5.05	Quality of local IT training programs	4
5.06	Cost of business telephone subscription (US$ per month)	37
6.01	Government prioritization of ICT	11
6.02	Government procurement of advanced technology products	20
6.03	Competence of public officials	23
6.04	Government online services	7

Usage Component Index   3

Individual Usage	5
Business Usage	2
Government Usage	5

7.01	Use of online payment systems	3
7.02	Number of radios (per 1,000 people)	17
7.03	Number of television sets (per 1,000 people)	16
7.04	Number of cable television subscribers (per 1,000 people)	10
7.05	Number of mobile telephones (per 1,000 people)	8
7.06	Number of Internet users (per 100 people)	9
7.07	Number of narrowband subscriber lines (per 100 people)	8
7.08	Number of broadband subscriber lines (per 100 people)	11
7.09	Household spending on ICT (US$ per month)	18
8.01	Use of Internet for coordination with customers and suppliers	22
8.02	Businesses using e-commerce (%)	1
8.03	Use of Internet for general research	16
8.04	Sophistication of online marketing	14
8.05	Presence of wireless e-business applications	3
8.06	Use of email for internal correspondence (%)	1
8.07	Use of email for external correspondence (%)	18
8.08	Pervasiveness of company web pages	4
9.01	Use of Internet-based transactions with the government	8
9.02	Government online services	7
9.03	Government success in ICT promotion	12

Switzerland.ch

Key Indicators

Population	7,180,000
GDP per capita (PPP)	US$28,769
Illiteracy rate	1.00%
GDP per capita growth	2.43%

Environment Component Index — 13

Market Environment	13
Political and Regulatory Environment	22
Infrastructure Environment	10

1.01	Venture capital availability	21
1.02	State of cluster development	21
1.03	Competition in the telecommunication sector	15
1.04	Availability of scientists and engineers	8
1.05	Brain drain	9
1.06	Public spending on education (% of GDP)	24
1.07	Domestic software companies in international markets	20
1.08	Domestic manufacturing of IT hardware	32
1.09	ICT expenditure (% of GDP)	4
2.01	Effectiveness of law-making bodies	11
2.02	Legal framework for ICT development	19
2.03	Subsidies for firm-level research and development	33
2.04	Government restrictions on Internet content	46
2.05	Prevalence of foreign technology licensing	25
3.01	Overall infrastructure quality	1
3.02	Local availability of specialized IT services	8
3.03	Number of telephone mainlines (per 1,000 people)	2
3.04	Number of telephone faults (per 100 main lines)	44
3.05	Number of telephone mainlines per employee	20
3.06	Number of fax machines (per 1,000 people)	18
3.07	Local switch capacity (per 100,000 people)	21
3.08	Ease of obtaining new telephone lines	5
3.09	Waiting time for telephone mainlines (in years)	1
3.1	Number of secure Internet servers	12

Readiness Component Index — 9

Individual Readiness	17
Business Readiness	6
Government Readiness	16

4.01	Sophistication of local buyers' products and processes	27
4.02	Availability of mobile Internet access	16
4.03	Availability of broadband access	18
4.04	Public access to the Internet	19
4.05	Secondary school enrollment (% net)	31
4.06	Total adult illiteracy rate (%)	16

Readiness Component Index (continued)

4.07	Quality of math and science education	8
4.08	Cost of local call (US$ per three min)	27
4.09	Cost of off-peak local cellular call (US$ per three min)	24
4.10	Cost of residential telephone subscription (US$ per month)	35
5.01	Firm-level technology absorption	8
5.02	Firm-level innovation	3
5.03	Capacity for innovation	7
5.04	Business Intranet sophistication	3
5.05	Quality of local IT training programs	14
5.06	Cost of business telephone subscription (US$ per month)	20
6.01	Government prioritization of ICT	25
6.02	Government procurement of advanced technology products	12
6.03	Competence of public officials	10
6.04	Government online services	28

Usage Component Index — 15

Individual Usage	15
Business Usage	10
Government Usage	22

7.01	Use of online payment systems	17
7.02	Number of radios (per 1,000 people)	10
7.03	Number of television sets (per 1,000 people)	17
7.04	Number of cable television subscribers (per 1,000 people)	3
7.05	Number of mobile telephones (per 1,000 people)	15
7.06	Number of Internet users (per 100 people)	27
7.07	Number of narrowband subscriber lines (per 100 people)	20
7.08	Number of broadband subscriber lines (per 100 people)	22
7.09	Household spending on ICT (US$ per month)	39
8.01	Use of Internet for coordination with customers and suppliers	25
8.02	Businesses using e-commerce (%)	19
8.03	Use of Internet for general research	5
8.04	Sophistication of online marketing	4
8.05	Presence of wireless e-business applications	5
8.06	Use of email for internal correspondence (%)	12
8.07	Use of email for external correspondence (%)	58
8.08	Pervasiveness of company web pages	7
9.01	Use of Internet-based transactions with the government	17
9.02	Government online services	28
9.03	Government success in ICT promotion	19

Taiwan.tw

Key Indicators

Population	22,276,672
GDP per capita (PPP)	US$17,400
Illiteracy rate	6.00%
GDP per capita growth	5.86%

Networked Readiness Index Rank

2002–2003 **9**

2001–2002   15

Environment Component Index — 15

	Market Environment	7
	Political and Regulatory Environment	23
	Infrastructure Environment	19

1.01	Venture capital availability	16
1.02	State of cluster development	2
1.03	Competition in the telecommunication sector	20
1.04	Availability of scientists and engineers	13
1.05	Brain drain	14
1.06	Public spending on education (% of GDP)	30
1.07	Domestic software companies in international markets	31
1.08	Domestic manufacturing of IT hardware	4
1.09	ICT expenditure (% of GDP)	21
2.01	Effectiveness of law-making bodies	34
2.02	Legal framework for ICT development	39
2.03	Subsidies for firm-level research and development	3
2.04	Government restrictions on Internet content	61
2.05	Prevalence of foreign technology licensing	7
3.01	Overall infrastructure quality	24
3.02	Local availability of specialized IT services	25
3.03	Number of telephone mainlines (per 1,000 people)	14
3.04	Number of telephone faults (per 100 main lines)	9
3.05	Number of telephone mainlines per employee	7
3.06	Number of fax machines (per 1,000 people)	23
3.07	Local switch capacity (per 100,000 people)	24
3.08	Ease of obtaining new telephone lines	22
3.09	Waiting time for telephone mainlines (in years)	32
3.1	Number of secure Internet servers	21

Readiness Component Index — 7

	Individual Readiness	22
	Business Readiness	9
	Government Readiness	2

4.01	Sophistication of local buyers' products and processes	9
4.02	Availability of mobile Internet access	55
4.03	Availability of broadband access	39
4.04	Public access to the Internet	22
4.05	Secondary school enrollment (% net)	17
4.06	Total adult illiteracy rate (%)	43

Readiness Component Index (continued)

4.07	Quality of math and science education	7
4.08	Cost of local call (US$ per three min)	17
4.09	Cost of off-peak local cellular call (US$ per three min)	23
4.10	Cost of residential telephone subscription (US$ per month)	2
5.01	Firm-level technology absorption	6
5.02	Firm-level innovation	11
5.03	Capacity for innovation	14
5.04	Business Intranet sophistication	13
5.05	Quality of local IT training programs	11
5.06	Cost of business telephone subscription (US$ per month)	32
6.01	Government prioritization of ICT	3
6.02	Government procurement of advanced technology products	3
6.03	Competence of public officials	19
6.04	Government online services	13

Usage Component Index — 7

	Individual Usage	14
	Business Usage	18
	Government Usage	4

7.01	Use of online payment systems	40
7.02	Number of radios (per 1,000 people)	26
7.03	Number of television sets (per 1,000 people)	37
7.04	Number of cable television subscribers (per 1,000 people)	9
7.05	Number of mobile telephones (per 1,000 people)	9
7.06	Number of Internet users (per 100 people)	3
7.07	Number of narrowband subscriber lines (per 100 people)	2
7.08	Number of broadband subscriber lines (per 100 people)	7
7.09	Household spending on ICT (US$ per month)	46
8.01	Use of Internet for coordination with customers and suppliers	4
8.02	Businesses using e-commerce (%)	21
8.03	Use of Internet for general research	19
8.04	Sophistication of online marketing	9
8.05	Presence of wireless e-business applications	9
8.06	Use of email for internal correspondence (%)	38
8.07	Use of email for external correspondence (%)	36
8.08	Pervasiveness of company web pages	28
9.01	Use of Internet-based transactions with the government	6
9.02	Government online services	13
9.03	Government success in ICT promotion	5

Thailand.th

Key Indicators

Population	60,728,000
GDP per capita (PPP)	US$6,402
Illiteracy rate	4.50%
GDP per capita growth	3.48%

Networked Readiness Index Rank

2002–2003 **41**

2001–2002   43

Environment Component Index		40
Market Environment		42
Political and Regulatory Environment		39
Infrastructure Environment		49
1.01	Venture capital availability	43
1.02	State of cluster development	24
1.03	Competition in the telecommunication sector	45
1.04	Availability of scientists and engineers	57
1.05	Brain drain	26
1.06	Public spending on education (% of GDP)	38
1.07	Domestic software companies in international markets	76
1.08	Domestic manufacturing of IT hardware	26
1.09	ICT expenditure (% of GDP)	74
2.01	Effectiveness of law-making bodies	33
2.02	Legal framework for ICT development	66
2.03	Subsidies for firm-level research and development	31
2.04	Government restrictions on Internet content	68
2.05	Prevalence of foreign technology licensing	3
3.01	Overall infrastructure quality	30
3.02	Local availability of specialized IT services	75
3.03	Number of telephone mainlines (per 1,000 people)	63
3.04	Number of telephone faults (per 100 main lines)	47
3.05	Number of telephone mainlines per employee	40
3.06	Number of fax machines (per 1,000 people)	48
3.07	Local switch capacity (per 100,000 people)	68
3.08	Ease of obtaining new telephone lines	29
3.09	Waiting time for telephone mainlines (in years)	63
3.1	Number of secure Internet servers	53

Readiness Component Index		36
Individual Readiness		39
Business Readiness		38
Government Readiness		39
4.01	Sophistication of local buyers' products and processes	21
4.02	Availability of mobile Internet access	43
4.03	Availability of broadband access	52
4.04	Public access to the Internet	51
4.05	Secondary school enrollment (% net)	58
4.06	Total adult illiteracy rate (%)	40

Readiness Component Index (continued)		
4.07	Quality of math and science education	42
4.08	Cost of local call (US$ per three min)	58
4.09	Cost of off-peak local cellular call (US$ per three min)	37
4.10	Cost of residential telephone subscription (US$ per month)	19
5.01	Firm-level technology absorption	31
5.02	Firm-level innovation	22
5.03	Capacity for innovation	50
5.04	Business Intranet sophistication	49
5.05	Quality of local IT training programs	38
5.06	Cost of business telephone subscription (US$ per month)	10
6.01	Government prioritization of ICT	22
6.02	Government procurement of advanced technology products	35
6.03	Competence of public officials	38
6.04	Government online services	56

Usage Component Index		47
Individual Usage		64
Business Usage		45
Government Usage		36
7.01	Use of online payment systems	55
7.02	Number of radios (per 1,000 people)	68
7.03	Number of television sets (per 1,000 people)	48
7.04	Number of cable television subscribers (per 1,000 people)	76
7.05	Number of mobile telephones (per 1,000 people)	65
7.06	Number of Internet users (per 100 people)	37
7.07	Number of narrowband subscriber lines (per 100 people)	66
7.08	Number of broadband subscriber lines (per 100 people)	44
7.09	Household spending on ICT (US$ per month)	65
8.01	Use of Internet for coordination with customers and suppliers	35
8.02	Businesses using e-commerce (%)	69
8.03	Use of Internet for general research	62
8.04	Sophistication of online marketing	42
8.05	Presence of wireless e-business applications	69
8.06	Use of email for internal correspondence (%)	41
8.07	Use of email for external correspondence (%)	47
8.08	Pervasiveness of company web pages	46
9.01	Use of Internet-based transactions with the government	29
9.02	Government online services	56
9.03	Government success in ICT promotion	27

Trinidad and Tobago.tt

Key Indicators

Population	1,301,000
GDP per capita (PPP)	US$8,964
Illiteracy rate	6.23%
GDP per capita growth	4.11%

Networked Readiness Index Rank

2002–2003 **58**

2001–2002 46

Environment Component Index		50
Market Environment		57
Political and Regulatory Environment		44
Infrastructure Environment		50
1.01	Venture capital availability	32
1.02	State of cluster development	53
1.03	Competition in the telecommunication sector	78
1.04	Availability of scientists and engineers	48
1.05	Brain drain	42
1.06	Public spending on education (% of GDP)	64
1.07	Domestic software companies in international markets	61
1.08	Domestic manufacturing of IT hardware	60
1.09	ICT expenditure (% of GDP)	45
2.01	Effectiveness of law-making bodies	44
2.02	Legal framework for ICT development	38
2.03	Subsidies for firm-level research and development	43
2.04	Government restrictions on Internet content	33
2.05	Prevalence of foreign technology licensing	46
3.01	Overall infrastructure quality	39
3.02	Local availability of specialized IT services	51
3.03	Number of telephone mainlines (per 1,000 people)	43
3.04	Number of telephone faults (per 100 main lines)	75
3.05	Number of telephone mainlines per employee	64
3.06	Number of fax machines (per 1,000 people)	38
3.07	Local switch capacity (per 100,000 people)	5
3.08	Ease of obtaining new telephone lines	62
3.09	Waiting time for telephone mainlines (in years)	43
3.1	Number of secure Internet servers	43

Readiness Component Index		58
Individual Readiness		50
Business Readiness		60
Government Readiness		59
4.01	Sophistication of local buyers' products and processes	39
4.02	Availability of mobile Internet access	82
4.03	Availability of broadband access	80
4.04	Public access to the Internet	55
4.05	Secondary school enrollment (% net)	40
4.06	Total adult illiteracy rate (%)	44

Readiness Component Index (continued)		
4.07	Quality of math and science education	40
4.08	Cost of local call (US$ per three min)	26
4.09	Cost of off-peak local cellular call (US$ per three min)	45
4.10	Cost of residential telephone subscription (US$ per month)	34
5.01	Firm-level technology absorption	39
5.02	Firm-level innovation	41
5.03	Capacity for innovation	69
5.04	Business Intranet sophistication	71
5.05	Quality of local IT training programs	46
5.06	Cost of business telephone subscription (US$ per month)	74
6.01	Government prioritization of ICT	58
6.02	Government procurement of advanced technology products	29
6.03	Competence of public officials	44
6.04	Government online services	79

Usage Component Index		62
Individual Usage		40
Business Usage		73
Government Usage		69
7.01	Use of online payment systems	28
7.02	Number of radios (per 1,000 people)	38
7.03	Number of television sets (per 1,000 people)	42
7.04	Number of cable television subscribers (per 1,000 people)	34
7.05	Number of mobile telephones (per 1,000 people)	54
7.06	Number of Internet users (per 100 people)	36
7.07	Number of narrowband subscriber lines (per 100 people)	45
7.08	Number of broadband subscriber lines (per 100 people)	26
7.09	Household spending on ICT (US$ per month)	43
8.01	Use of Internet for coordination with customers and suppliers	76
8.02	Businesses using e-commerce (%)	39
8.03	Use of Internet for general research	58
8.04	Sophistication of online marketing	59
8.05	Presence of wireless e-business applications	38
8.06	Use of email for internal correspondence (%)	78
8.07	Use of email for external correspondence (%)	77
8.08	Pervasiveness of company web pages	60
9.01	Use of Internet-based transactions with the government	66
9.02	Government online services	79
9.03	Government success in ICT promotion	39

Tunisia.tn

Key Indicators

Population	9,563,500
GDP per capita (PPP)	US$6,363
Illiteracy rate	28.98%
GDP per capita growth	3.54%

Networked Readiness Index Rank

2002–2003 **34**

2001–2002 —

Environment Component Index	35
Market Environment	34
Political and Regulatory Environment	24
Infrastructure Environment	52

1.01	Venture capital availability	29
1.02	State of cluster development	66
1.03	Competition in the telecommunication sector	55
1.04	Availability of scientists and engineers	14
1.05	Brain drain	34
1.06	Public spending on education (% of GDP)	8
1.07	Domestic software companies in international markets	63
1.08	Domestic manufacturing of IT hardware	39
1.09	ICT expenditure (% of GDP)	26
2.01	Effectiveness of law-making bodies	23
2.02	Legal framework for ICT development	26
2.03	Subsidies for firm-level research and development	11
2.04	Government restrictions on Internet content	48
2.05	Prevalence of foreign technology licensing	53
3.01	Overall infrastructure quality	31
3.02	Local availability of specialized IT services	53
3.03	Number of telephone mainlines (per 1,000 people)	64
3.04	Number of telephone faults (per 100 main lines)	67
3.05	Number of telephone mainlines per employee	53
3.06	Number of fax machines (per 1,000 people)	42
3.07	Local switch capacity (per 100,000 people)	51
3.08	Ease of obtaining new telephone lines	52
3.09	Waiting time for telephone mainlines (in years)	54
3.1	Number of secure Internet servers	68

Readiness Component Index	27
Individual Readiness	42
Business Readiness	36
Government Readiness	4

4.01	Sophistication of local buyers' products and processes	36
4.02	Availability of mobile Internet access	54
4.03	Availability of broadband access	44
4.04	Public access to the Internet	35
4.05	Secondary school enrollment (% net)	59
4.06	Total adult illiteracy rate (%)	74

Readiness Component Index (continued)	
4.07	Quality of math and science education	6
4.08	Cost of local call (US$ per three min)	24
4.09	Cost of off-peak local cellular call (US$ per three min)	55
4.10	Cost of residential telephone subscription (US$ per month)	16
5.01	Firm-level technology absorption	20
5.02	Firm-level innovation	24
5.03	Capacity for innovation	48
5.04	Business Intranet sophistication	60
5.05	Quality of local IT training programs	25
5.06	Cost of business telephone subscription (US$ per month)	7
6.01	Government prioritization of ICT	2
6.02	Government procurement of advanced technology products	4
6.03	Competence of public officials	18
6.04	Government online services	29

Usage Component Index	41
Individual Usage	60
Business Usage	43
Government Usage	23

7.01	Use of online payment systems	29
7.02	Number of radios (per 1,000 people)	74
7.03	Number of television sets (per 1,000 people)	57
7.04	Number of cable television subscribers (per 1,000 people)	61
7.05	Number of mobile telephones (per 1,000 people)	78
7.06	Number of Internet users (per 100 people)	54
7.07	Number of narrowband subscriber lines (per 100 people)	60
7.08	Number of broadband subscriber lines (per 100 people)	44
7.09	Household spending on ICT (US$ per month)	58
8.01	Use of Internet for coordination with customers and suppliers	45
8.02	Businesses using e-commerce (%)	34
8.03	Use of Internet for general research	61
8.04	Sophistication of online marketing	58
8.05	Presence of wireless e-business applications	49
8.06	Use of email for internal correspondence (%)	58
8.07	Use of email for external correspondence (%)	52
8.08	Pervasiveness of company web pages	30
9.01	Use of Internet-based transactions with the government	61
9.02	Government online services	29
9.03	Government success in ICT promotion	2

Country Profiles | **267**

Turkey.tr

Key Indicators

Population	652,93,000
GDP per capita (PPP)	US$6,974
Illiteracy rate	14.93%
GDP per capita growth	5.65%

Networked Readiness Index Rank

2002–2003 (50)

2001–2002 41

Environment Component Index — 56

Market Environment		69
Political and Regulatory Environment		50
Infrastructure Environment		45

1.01	Venture capital availability	81
1.02	State of cluster development	28
1.03	Competition in the telecommunication sector	56
1.04	Availability of scientists and engineers	52
1.05	Brain drain	48
1.06	Public spending on education (% of GDP)	78
1.07	Domestic software companies in international markets	74
1.08	Domestic manufacturing of IT hardware	52
1.09	ICT expenditure (% of GDP)	62
2.01	Effectiveness of law-making bodies	39
2.02	Legal framework for ICT development	47
2.03	Subsidies for firm-level research and development	60
2.04	Government restrictions on Internet content	49
2.05	Prevalence of foreign technology licensing	37
3.01	Overall infrastructure quality	51
3.02	Local availability of specialized IT services	67
3.03	Number of telephone mainlines (per 1,000 people)	39
3.04	Number of telephone faults (per 100 main lines)	71
3.05	Number of telephone mainlines per employee	11
3.06	Number of fax machines (per 1,000 people)	54
3.07	Local switch capacity (per 100,000 people)	44
3.08	Ease of obtaining new telephone lines	56
3.09	Waiting time for telephone mainlines (in years)	41
3.1	Number of secure Internet servers	48

Readiness Component Index — 59

Individual Readiness		47
Business Readiness		47
Government Readiness		70

4.01	Sophistication of local buyers' products and processes	34
4.02	Availability of mobile Internet access	28
4.03	Availability of broadband access	36
4.04	Public access to the Internet	30
4.05	Secondary school enrollment (% net)	63
4.06	Total adult illiteracy rate (%)	66

Readiness Component Index (continued)

4.07	Quality of math and science education	47
4.08	Cost of local call (US$ per three min)	69
4.09	Cost of off-peak local cellular call (US$ per three min)	63
4.10	Cost of residential telephone subscription (US$ per month)	46
5.01	Firm-level technology absorption	43
5.02	Firm-level innovation	73
5.03	Capacity for innovation	68
5.04	Business Intranet sophistication	27
5.05	Quality of local IT training programs	59
5.06	Cost of business telephone subscription (US$ per month)	17
6.01	Government prioritization of ICT	62
6.02	Government procurement of advanced technology products	77
6.03	Competence of public officials	73
6.04	Government online services	55

Usage Component Index — 40

Individual Usage		37
Business Usage		38
Government Usage		42

7.01	Use of online payment systems	14
7.02	Number of radios (per 1,000 people)	35
7.03	Number of television sets (per 1,000 people)	29
7.04	Number of cable television subscribers (per 1,000 people)	65
7.05	Number of mobile telephones (per 1,000 people)	33
7.06	Number of Internet users (per 100 people)	50
7.07	Number of narrowband subscriber lines (per 100 people)	24
7.08	Number of broadband subscriber lines (per 100 people)	36
7.09	Household spending on ICT (US$ per month)	73
8.01	Use of Internet for coordination with customers and suppliers	77
8.02	Businesses using e-commerce (%)	80
8.03	Use of Internet for general research	6
8.04	Sophistication of online marketing	48
8.05	Presence of wireless e-business applications	50
8.06	Use of email for internal correspondence (%)	33
8.07	Use of email for external correspondence (%)	36
8.08	Pervasiveness of company web pages	39
9.01	Use of Internet-based transactions with the government	13
9.02	Government online services	55
9.03	Government success in ICT promotion	65

Ukraine.ua

Key Indicators

Population	49,501,000
GDP per capita (PPP)	US$3,816
Illiteracy rate	0.39%
GDP per capita growth	6.67%

Environment Component Index — 70

Market Environment		63
Political and Regulatory Environment		69
Infrastructure Environment		74
1.01	Venture capital availability	59
1.02	State of cluster development	60
1.03	Competition in the telecommunication sector	67
1.04	Availability of scientists and engineers	45
1.05	Brain drain	74
1.06	Public spending on education (% of GDP)	47
1.07	Domestic software companies in international markets	55
1.08	Domestic manufacturing of IT hardware	30
1.09	ICT expenditure (% of GDP)	81
2.01	Effectiveness of law-making bodies	71
2.02	Legal framework for ICT development	63
2.03	Subsidies for firm-level research and development	54
2.04	Government restrictions on Internet content	41
2.05	Prevalence of foreign technology licensing	78
3.01	Overall infrastructure quality	68
3.02	Local availability of specialized IT services	66
3.03	Number of telephone mainlines (per 1,000 people)	48
3.04	Number of telephone faults (per 100 main lines)	61
3.05	Number of telephone mainlines per employee	68
3.06	Number of fax machines (per 1,000 people)	71
3.07	Local switch capacity (per 100,000 people)	72
3.08	Ease of obtaining new telephone lines	73
3.09	Waiting time for telephone mainlines (in years)	78
3.1	Number of secure Internet servers	64

Readiness Component Index — 66

Individual Readiness		58
Business Readiness		62
Government Readiness		65
4.01	Sophistication of local buyers' products and processes	72
4.02	Availability of mobile Internet access	63
4.03	Availability of broadband access	58
4.04	Public access to the Internet	75
4.05	Secondary school enrollment (% net)	70
4.06	Total adult illiteracy rate (%)	12

Readiness Component Index (continued)

4.07	Quality of math and science education	45
4.08	Cost of local call (US$ per three min)	8
4.09	Cost of off-peak local cellular call (US$ per three min)	78
4.10	Cost of residential telephone subscription (US$ per month)	9
5.01	Firm-level technology absorption	54
5.02	Firm-level innovation	81
5.03	Capacity for innovation	29
5.04	Business Intranet sophistication	80
5.05	Quality of local IT training programs	65
5.06	Cost of business telephone subscription (US$ per month)	13
6.01	Government prioritization of ICT	74
6.02	Government procurement of advanced technology products	66
6.03	Competence of public officials	60
6.04	Government online services	43

Usage Component Index — 69

Individual Usage		53
Business Usage		75
Government Usage		70
7.01	Use of online payment systems	62
7.02	Number of radios (per 1,000 people)	19
7.03	Number of television sets (per 1,000 people)	28
7.04	Number of cable television subscribers (per 1,000 people)	40
7.05	Number of mobile telephones (per 1,000 people)	76
7.06	Number of Internet users (per 100 people)	79
7.07	Number of narrowband subscriber lines (per 100 people)	54
7.08	Number of broadband subscriber lines (per 100 people)	44
7.09	Household spending on ICT (US$ per month)	78
8.01	Use of Internet for coordination with customers and suppliers	19
8.02	Businesses using e-commerce (%)	57
8.03	Use of Internet for general research	78
8.04	Sophistication of online marketing	71
8.05	Presence of wireless e-business applications	47
8.06	Use of email for internal correspondence (%)	81
8.07	Use of email for external correspondence (%)	76
8.08	Pervasiveness of company web pages	62
9.01	Use of Internet-based transactions with the government	74
9.02	Government online services	43
9.03	Government success in ICT promotion	74

United Kingdom.uk

Key Indicators

Population	59,738,900
GDP per capita (PPP)	US$23,509
Illiteracy rate	1.00%
GDP per capita growth	2.66%

Networked Readiness Index Rank

2002–2003 **7**

2001–2002   10

Environment Component Index   7

Market Environment	3
Political and Regulatory Environment	**10**
Infrastructure Environment	**14**

1.01	Venture capital availability	2
1.02	State of cluster development	5
1.03	Competition in the telecommunication sector	9
1.04	Availability of scientists and engineers	19
1.05	Brain drain	5
1.06	Public spending on education (% of GDP)	37
1.07	Domestic software companies in international markets	6
1.08	Domestic manufacturing of IT hardware	8
1.09	ICT expenditure (% of GDP)	10
2.01	Effectiveness of law-making bodies	3
2.02	Legal framework for ICT development	10
2.03	Subsidies for firm-level research and development	17
2.04	Government restrictions on Internet content	61
2.05	Prevalence of foreign technology licensing	31
3.01	Overall infrastructure quality	19
3.02	Local availability of specialized IT services	7
3.03	Number of telephone mainlines (per 1,000 people)	10
3.04	Number of telephone faults (per 100 main lines)	14
3.05	Number of telephone mainlines per employee	37
3.06	Number of fax machines (per 1,000 people)	16
3.07	Local switch capacity (per 100,000 people)	12
3.08	Ease of obtaining new telephone lines	19
3.09	Waiting time for telephone mainlines (in years)	1
3.1	Number of secure Internet servers	9

Readiness Component Index   10

Individual Readiness	9
Business Readiness	14
Government Readiness	8

4.01	Sophistication of local buyers' products and processes	4
4.02	Availability of mobile Internet access	6
4.03	Availability of broadband access	12
4.04	Public access to the Internet	15
4.05	Secondary school enrollment (% net)	6
4.06	Total adult illiteracy rate (%)	16

Readiness Component Index (continued)

4.07	Quality of math and science education	29
4.08	Cost of local call (US$ per three min)	47
4.09	Cost of off-peak local cellular call (US$ per three min)	6
4.10	Cost of residential telephone subscription (US$ per month)	47
5.01	Firm-level technology absorption	24
5.02	Firm-level innovation	19
5.03	Capacity for innovation	9
5.04	Business Intranet sophistication	15
5.05	Quality of local IT training programs	12
5.06	Cost of business telephone subscription (US$ per month)	45
6.01	Government prioritization of ICT	29
6.02	Government procurement of advanced technology products	19
6.03	Competence of public officials	4
6.04	Government online services	11

Usage Component Index   12

Individual Usage	10
Business Usage	8
Government Usage	13

7.01	Use of online payment systems	15
7.02	Number of radios (per 1,000 people)	4
7.03	Number of television sets (per 1,000 people)	9
7.04	Number of cable television subscribers (per 1,000 people)	39
7.05	Number of mobile telephones (per 1,000 people)	6
7.06	Number of Internet users (per 100 people)	19
7.07	Number of narrowband subscriber lines (per 100 people)	12
7.08	Number of broadband subscriber lines (per 100 people)	4
7.09	Household spending on ICT (US$ per month)	5
8.01	Use of Internet for coordination with customers and suppliers	15
8.02	Businesses using e-commerce (%)	14
8.03	Use of Internet for general research	7
8.04	Sophistication of online marketing	15
8.05	Presence of wireless e-business applications	15
8.06	Use of email for internal correspondence (%)	7
8.07	Use of email for external correspondence (%)	25
8.08	Pervasiveness of company web pages	6
9.01	Use of Internet-based transactions with the government	7
9.02	Government online services	11
9.03	Government success in ICT promotion	56

United States.us

Key Indicators

Population	281,550,016
GDP per capita (PPP)	US$34,142
Illiteracy rate	3.00%
GDP per capita growth	2.97%

Networked Readiness Index Rank

2002–2003 **2**

2001–2002 1

Environment Component Index	1
Market Environment	1
Political and Regulatory Environment	4
Infrastructure Environment	2

1.01	Venture capital availability	1
1.02	State of cluster development	3
1.03	Competition in the telecommunication sector	3
1.04	Availability of scientists and engineers	10
1.05	Brain drain	1
1.06	Public spending on education (% of GDP)	28
1.07	Domestic software companies in international markets	1
1.08	Domestic manufacturing of IT hardware	1
1.09	ICT expenditure (% of GDP)	19
2.01	Effectiveness of law-making bodies	2
2.02	Legal framework for ICT development	3
2.03	Subsidies for firm-level research and development	6
2.04	Government restrictions on Internet content	25
2.05	Prevalence of foreign technology licensing	64
3.01	Overall infrastructure quality	5
3.02	Local availability of specialized IT services	1
3.03	Number of telephone mainlines (per 1,000 people)	5
3.04	Number of telephone faults (per 100 main lines)	32
3.05	Number of telephone mainlines per employee	34
3.06	Number of fax machines (per 1,000 people)	3
3.07	Local switch capacity (per 100,000 people)	13
3.08	Ease of obtaining new telephone lines	8
3.09	Waiting time for telephone mainlines (in years)	1
3.1	Number of secure Internet servers	2

Readiness Component Index	3
Individual Readiness	7
Business Readiness	1
Government Readiness	7

4.01	Sophistication of local buyers' products and processes	2
4.02	Availability of mobile Internet access	17
4.03	Availability of broadband access	5
4.04	Public access to the Internet	10
4.05	Secondary school enrollment (% net)	14
4.06	Total adult illiteracy rate (%)	35

Readiness Component Index (continued)	
4.07	Quality of math and science education	39
4.08	Cost of local call (US$ per three min)	1
4.09	Cost of off-peak local cellular call (US$ per three min)	5
4.10	Cost of residential telephone subscription (US$ per month)	45
5.01	Firm-level technology absorption	2
5.02	Firm-level innovation	2
5.03	Capacity for innovation	6
5.04	Business Intranet sophistication	2
5.05	Quality of local IT training programs	3
5.06	Cost of business telephone subscription (US$ per month)	50
6.01	Government prioritization of ICT	15
6.02	Government procurement of advanced technology products	5
6.03	Competence of public officials	26
6.04	Government online services	12

Usage Component Index	4
Individual Usage	7
Business Usage	3
Government Usage	6

7.01	Use of online payment systems	7
7.02	Number of radios (per 1,000 people)	1
7.03	Number of television sets (per 1,000 people)	1
7.04	Number of cable television subscribers (per 1,000 people)	7
7.05	Number of mobile telephones (per 1,000 people)	29
7.06	Number of Internet users (per 100 people)	32
7.07	Number of narrowband subscriber lines (per 100 people)	51
7.08	Number of broadband subscriber lines (per 100 people)	20
7.09	Household spending on ICT (US$ per month)	1
8.01	Use of Internet for coordination with customers and suppliers	2
8.02	Businesses using e-commerce (%)	22
8.03	Use of Internet for general research	2
8.04	Sophistication of online marketing	3
8.05	Presence of wireless e-business applications	7
8.06	Use of email for internal correspondence (%)	4
8.07	Use of email for external correspondence (%)	10
8.08	Pervasiveness of company web pages	2
9.01	Use of Internet-based transactions with the government	5
9.02	Government online services	12
9.03	Government success in ICT promotion	15

Uruguay.uy

Key Indicators

Population	3,337,000
GDP per capita (PPP)	US$9,035
Illiteracy rate	2.26%
GDP per capita growth	-1.98%

Networked Readiness Index Rank

2002–2003 **55**

2001–2002   37

Environment Component Index	52
Market Environment	52
Political and Regulatory Environment	62
Infrastructure Environment	35

1.01	Venture capital availability	72
1.02	State of cluster development	80
1.03	Competition in the telecommunication sector	53
1.04	Availability of scientists and engineers	24
1.05	Brain drain	58
1.06	Public spending on education (% of GDP)	74
1.07	Domestic software companies in international markets	16
1.08	Domestic manufacturing of IT hardware	49
1.09	ICT expenditure (% of GDP)	46
2.01	Effectiveness of law-making bodies	58
2.02	Legal framework for ICT development	40
2.03	Subsidies for firm-level research and development	74
2.04	Government restrictions on Internet content	39
2.05	Prevalence of foreign technology licensing	68
3.01	Overall infrastructure quality	46
3.02	Local availability of specialized IT services	39
3.03	Number of telephone mainlines (per 1,000 people)	40
3.04	Number of telephone faults (per 100 main lines)	21
3.05	Number of telephone mainlines per employee	41
3.06	Number of fax machines (per 1,000 people)	41
3.07	Local switch capacity (per 100,000 people)	45
3.08	Ease of obtaining new telephone lines	23
3.09	Waiting time for telephone mainlines (in years)	1
3.1	Number of secure Internet servers	37

Readiness Component Index	65
Individual Readiness	56
Business Readiness	70
Government Readiness	60

4.01	Sophistication of local buyers' products and processes	76
4.02	Availability of mobile Internet access	41
4.03	Availability of broadband access	77
4.04	Public access to the Internet	42
4.05	Secondary school enrollment (% net)	46
4.06	Total adult illiteracy rate (%)	32

Readiness Component Index (continued)	
4.07	Quality of math and science education	53
4.08	Cost of local call (US$ per three min)	74
4.09	Cost of off-peak local cellular call (US$ per three min)	35
4.10	Cost of residential telephone subscription (US$ per month)	59
5.01	Firm-level technology absorption	78
5.02	Firm-level innovation	75
5.03	Capacity for innovation	73
5.04	Business Intranet sophistication	59
5.05	Quality of local IT training programs	36
5.06	Cost of business telephone subscription (US$ per month)	64
6.01	Government prioritization of ICT	54
6.02	Government procurement of advanced technology products	60
6.03	Competence of public officials	75
6.04	Government online services	45

Usage Component Index	46
Individual Usage	33
Business Usage	56
Government Usage	58

7.01	Use of online payment systems	54
7.02	Number of radios (per 1,000 people)	34
7.03	Number of television sets (per 1,000 people)	21
7.04	Number of cable television subscribers (per 1,000 people)	23
7.05	Number of mobile telephones (per 1,000 people)	50
7.06	Number of Internet users (per 100 people)	35
7.07	Number of narrowband subscriber lines (per 100 people)	29
7.08	Number of broadband subscriber lines (per 100 people)	44
7.09	Household spending on ICT (US$ per month)	28
8.01	Use of Internet for coordination with customers and suppliers	61
8.02	Businesses using e-commerce (%)	36
8.03	Use of Internet for general research	50
8.04	Sophistication of online marketing	56
8.05	Presence of wireless e-business applications	71
8.06	Use of email for internal correspondence (%)	62
8.07	Use of email for external correspondence (%)	62
8.08	Pervasiveness of company web pages	43
9.01	Use of Internet-based transactions with the government	58
9.02	Government online services	45
9.03	Government success in ICT promotion	59

Venezuela.ve

Key Indicators

Population	24,170,000
GDP per capita (PPP)	US$5,794
Illiteracy rate	7.42%
GDP per capita growth	1.24%

Environment Component Index — 63

Market Environment	68
Political and Regulatory Environment	60
Infrastructure Environment	63

1.01	Venture capital availability	76
1.02	State of cluster development	78
1.03	Competition in the telecommunication sector	26
1.04	Availability of scientists and engineers	60
1.05	Brain drain	61
1.06	Public spending on education (% of GDP)	34
1.07	Domestic software companies in international markets	57
1.08	Domestic manufacturing of IT hardware	72
1.09	ICT expenditure (% of GDP)	68
2.01	Effectiveness of law-making bodies	80
2.02	Legal framework for ICT development	61
2.03	Subsidies for firm-level research and development	73
2.04	Government restrictions on Internet content	5
2.05	Prevalence of foreign technology licensing	29
3.01	Overall infrastructure quality	70
3.02	Local availability of specialized IT services	72
3.03	Number of telephone mainlines (per 1,000 people)	57
3.04	Number of telephone faults (per 100 main lines)	8
3.05	Number of telephone mainlines per employee	51
3.06	Number of fax machines (per 1,000 people)	44
3.07	Local switch capacity (per 100,000 people)	67
3.08	Ease of obtaining new telephone lines	54
3.09	Waiting time for telephone mainlines (in years)	67
3.1	Number of secure Internet servers	47

Readiness Component Index — 72

Individual Readiness	71
Business Readiness	68
Government Readiness	77

4.01	Sophistication of local buyers' products and processes	63
4.02	Availability of mobile Internet access	36
4.03	Availability of broadband access	31
4.04	Public access to the Internet	60
4.05	Secondary school enrollment (% net)	82
4.06	Total adult illiteracy rate (%)	48

Readiness Component Index (continued)

4.07	Quality of math and science education	75
4.08	Cost of local call (US$ per three min)	72
4.09	Cost of off-peak local cellular call (US$ per three min)	66
4.10	Cost of residential telephone subscription (US$ per month)	75
5.01	Firm-level technology absorption	71
5.02	Firm-level innovation	45
5.03	Capacity for innovation	79
5.04	Business Intranet sophistication	47
5.05	Quality of local IT training programs	58
5.06	Cost of business telephone subscription (US$ per month)	77
6.01	Government prioritization of ICT	76
6.02	Government procurement of advanced technology products	69
6.03	Competence of public officials	81
6.04	Government online services	76

Usage Component Index — 50

Individual Usage	46
Business Usage	33
Government Usage	68

7.01	Use of online payment systems	43
7.02	Number of radios (per 1,000 people)	64
7.03	Number of television sets (per 1,000 people)	61
7.04	Number of cable television subscribers (per 1,000 people)	47
7.05	Number of mobile telephones (per 1,000 people)	36
7.06	Number of Internet users (per 100 people)	49
7.07	Number of narrowband subscriber lines (per 100 people)	61
7.08	Number of broadband subscriber lines (per 100 people)	44
7.09	Household spending on ICT (US$ per month)	17
8.01	Use of Internet for coordination with customers and suppliers	64
8.02	Businesses using e-commerce (%)	46
8.03	Use of Internet for general research	42
8.04	Sophistication of online marketing	68
8.05	Presence of wireless e-business applications	67
8.06	Use of email for internal correspondence (%)	13
8.07	Use of email for external correspondence (%)	3
8.08	Pervasiveness of company web pages	35
9.01	Use of Internet-based transactions with the government	35
9.02	Government online services	76
9.03	Government success in ICT promotion	72

Vietnam.vn

Key Indicators

Population	78,522,704
GDP per capita (PPP)	US$1,996
Illiteracy rate	6.61%
GDP per capita growth	4.15%

Networked Readiness Index Rank

2002–2003 **71**

2001–2002   74

Environment Component Index		73
Market Environment		59
Political and Regulatory Environment		72
Infrastructure Environment		78
1.01	Venture capital availability	61
1.02	State of cluster development	61
1.03	Competition in the telecommunication sector	74
1.04	Availability of scientists and engineers	43
1.05	Brain drain	47
1.06	Public spending on education (% of GDP)	73
1.07	Domestic software companies in international markets	46
1.08	Domestic manufacturing of IT hardware	54
1.09	ICT expenditure (% of GDP)	43
2.01	Effectiveness of law-making bodies	42
2.02	Legal framework for ICT development	64
2.03	Subsidies for firm-level research and development	42
2.04	Government restrictions on Internet content	82
2.05	Prevalence of foreign technology licensing	62
3.01	Overall infrastructure quality	73
3.02	Local availability of specialized IT services	80
3.03	Number of telephone mainlines (per 1,000 people)	76
3.04	Number of telephone faults (per 100 main lines)	79
3.05	Number of telephone mainlines per employee	82
3.06	Number of fax machines (per 1,000 people)	64
3.07	Local switch capacity (per 100,000 people)	76
3.08	Ease of obtaining new telephone lines	61
3.09	Waiting time for telephone mainlines (in years)	75
3.1	Number of secure Internet servers	77

Readiness Component Index		55
Individual Readiness		68
Business Readiness		63
Government Readiness		43
4.01	Sophistication of local buyers' products and processes	40
4.02	Availability of mobile Internet access	77
4.03	Availability of broadband access	76
4.04	Public access to the Internet	76
4.05	Secondary school enrollment (% net)	67
4.06	Total adult illiteracy rate (%)	46

Readiness Component Index (continued)		
4.07	Quality of math and science education	51
4.08	Cost of local call (US$ per three min)	61
4.09	Cost of off-peak local cellular call (US$ per three min)	71
4.10	Cost of residential telephone subscription (US$ per month)	61
5.01	Firm-level technology absorption	37
5.02	Firm-level innovation	50
5.03	Capacity for innovation	47
5.04	Business Intranet sophistication	81
5.05	Quality of local IT training programs	76
5.06	Cost of business telephone subscription (US$ per month)	43
6.01	Government prioritization of ICT	34
6.02	Government procurement of advanced technology products	25
6.03	Competence of public officials	14
6.04	Government online services	70

Usage Component Index		77
Individual Usage		81
Business Usage		77
Government Usage		66
7.01	Use of online payment systems	81
7.02	Number of radios (per 1,000 people)	79
7.03	Number of television sets (per 1,000 people)	62
7.04	Number of cable television subscribers (per 1,000 people)	53
7.05	Number of mobile telephones (per 1,000 people)	77
7.06	Number of Internet users (per 100 people)	79
7.07	Number of narrowband subscriber lines (per 100 people)	76
7.08	Number of broadband subscriber lines (per 100 people)	44
7.09	Household spending on ICT (US$ per month)	70
8.01	Use of Internet for coordination with customers and suppliers	31
8.02	Businesses using e-commerce (%)	59
8.03	Use of Internet for general research	82
8.04	Sophistication of online marketing	80
8.05	Presence of wireless e-business applications	72
8.06	Use of email for internal correspondence (%)	71
8.07	Use of email for external correspondence (%)	53
8.08	Pervasiveness of company web pages	73
9.01	Use of Internet-based transactions with the government	79
9.02	Government online services	70
9.03	Government success in ICT promotion	22

Zimbabwe.zw

Key Indicators

Population	12,627,000
GDP per capita (PPP)	US$2,635
Illiteracy rate	11.32 %
GDP per capita growth	-6.68 %

Networked Readiness Index Rank

2002–2003 **80**

2001–2002   70

Environment Component Index	76
Market Environment	64
Political and Regulatory Environment	73
Infrastructure Environment	80

1.01	Venture capital availability	53
1.02	State of cluster development	74
1.03	Competition in the telecommunication sector	68
1.04	Availability of scientists and engineers	71
1.05	Brain drain	81
1.06	Public spending on education (% of GDP)	1
1.07	Domestic software companies in international markets	62
1.08	Domestic manufacturing of IT hardware	77
1.09	ICT expenditure (% of GDP)	58
2.01	Effectiveness of law-making bodies	76
2.02	Legal framework for ICT development	57
2.03	Subsidies for firm-level research and development	78
2.04	Government restrictions on Internet content	67
2.05	Prevalence of foreign technology licensing	69
3.01	Overall infrastructure quality	44
3.02	Local availability of specialized IT services	79
3.03	Number of telephone mainlines (per 1,000 people)	79
3.04	Number of telephone faults (per 100 main lines)	82
3.05	Number of telephone mainlines per employee	76
3.06	Number of fax machines (per 1,000 people)	65
3.07	Local switch capacity (per 100,000 people)	65
3.08	Ease of obtaining new telephone lines	76
3.09	Waiting time for telephone mainlines (in years)	80
3.1	Number of secure Internet servers	80

Readiness Component Index	74
Individual Readiness	76
Business Readiness	72
Government Readiness	79

4.01	Sophistication of local buyers' products and processes	69
4.02	Availability of mobile Internet access	67
4.03	Availability of broadband access	74
4.04	Public access to the Internet	80
4.05	Secondary school enrollment (% net)	75
4.06	Total adult illiteracy rate (%)	58

Readiness Component Index (continued)		
4.07	Quality of math and science education	56
4.08	Cost of local call (US$ per three min)	70
4.09	Cost of off-peak local cellular call (US$ per three min)	74
4.10	Cost of residential telephone subscription (US$ per month)	70
5.01	Firm-level technology absorption	61
5.02	Firm-level innovation	62
5.03	Capacity for innovation	76
5.04	Business Intranet sophistication	77
5.05	Quality of local IT training programs	55
5.06	Cost of business telephone subscription (US$ per month)	71
6.01	Government prioritization of ICT	79
6.02	Government procurement of advanced technology products	67
6.03	Competence of public officials	76
6.04	Government online services	82

Usage Component Index	81
Individual Usage	76
Business Usage	79
Government Usage	82

7.01	Use of online payment systems	67
7.02	Number of radios (per 1,000 people)	53
7.03	Number of television sets (per 1,000 people)	79
7.04	Number of cable television subscribers (per 1,000 people)	82
7.05	Number of mobile telephones (per 1,000 people)	70
7.06	Number of Internet users (per 100 people)	75
7.07	Number of narrowband subscriber lines (per 100 people)	69
7.08	Number of broadband subscriber lines (per 100 people)	44
7.09	Household spending on ICT (US$ per month)	55
8.01	Use of Internet for coordination with customers and suppliers	80
8.02	Businesses using e-commerce (%)	65
8.03	Use of Internet for general research	80
8.04	Sophistication of online marketing	81
8.05	Presence of wireless e-business applications	37
8.06	Use of email for internal correspondence (%)	67
8.07	Use of email for external correspondence (%)	73
8.08	Pervasiveness of company web pages	75
9.01	Use of Internet-based transactions with the government	72
9.02	Government online services	82
9.03	Government success in ICT promotion	78

Part 4
Data Rankings

The Networked Readiness Index: Methodology

Michele Hibon and Gauri Goel

INSEAD

The Networked Readiness Index 2002–2003 is defined as "the degree of preparation of a nation or community to participate in and benefit from ICT developments." By looking at the overall index of a country, one can get an idea of how a country compares relative to other countries; specifically, countries facing similar global and ICT challenges. While calculating the Networked Readiness Index (NRI), the overriding aim was to provide the most scientific and credible interpretation of reality. The process included selecting qualitatively relevant variables, estimating missing data, and finally, calculating the index by averaging the normalized data. The main steps are shown in Figure 1 and are explained in greater detail in the following text.

Choosing Variables

The first step in our study was collecting the most complete and high-quality set of data possible relating to information and communication technology (ICT). At the onset, 130 variables were chosen, based on their qualitative relevance to the Networked Readiness Framework. These variables were then divided into three component indexes: environment, readiness, and usage. The next step was to differentiate the variables within each component index into different subindexes (e.g., within environment there are three subindexes: market, political/regulatory and infrastucture).

The variables that were short-listed were of two types: soft variables and hard variables. In the study, the subjective data gathered from survey questionnaires are termed "soft" data, and the data driven by statistics collected by independent agencies are termed "hard" data. The soft data used for the study is extracted from the Global Competitiveness Report (GCR; also referred to as the Executive Opinion Survey) for years 2001 and 2002. The hard data are extracted from five different sources: World Development Indicators (WDI), the World Information Technology and Service Alliance (WITSA), International Telecommunication Union (ITU), Pyramid, and the Central Intelligence Agency (CIA). While soft data are critical in determining the opinion of the decision makers and influencers who are intimately familiar with an economy, the hard data captures fundamental elements related to the development of infrastructure, human capital, and e-commerce.

Selecting the countries

The main criterion used in selecting countries was the extent of data availability for that country for the chosen variables. Limitations in the availability of reliable data led us to consider only eighty-two countries for our study—seventy-five countries from last year's Global Information Technology Report and seven additional countries. Of these additional seven countries, six had been included in this year's GCR: Croatia, Tunisia, Botswana, Morocco, Haiti, and Namibia. The seventh country is Luxembourg, which is not covered

Figure 1. **Steps in NRI Calculation**

in the current GCR but was covered in last year's GCR. We limited ourselves to the GCR countries because GCR data are extensively used to calculate the NRI.

A few of the eighty-two countries considered in the study are not covered by some of the data collection agencies in their research. For example, Taiwan is not covered by WDI, Egypt and Luxembourg are not covered by GCR 2002, and Croatia, Tunisia, Botswana, Morocco, Haiti, and Namibia are not covered by GCR 2001. This meant that for these countries, these data elements had to be estimated using an appropriate technique. For this report, eighteen variables are from the GCR 2002 and twenty-two other variables are from the GCR 2001. Thus, to get the complete set of soft data, 168 (2x18 + 6x22) observations had to be estimated.

Dropping Variables

After extracting the data from the different data sources, the variables with less than 50 observations were dropped. Next, the highly correlated variables in each block were dropped. For variable pairs that had a correlation coefficient greater than 0.8, we dropped the one that was qualitatively less relevant and had fewer observations. We dropped approximately 10 variables because each had fewer than 50 observations, and a further 34 variables because they were highly correlated to some other variable.

Data Transformation
Step 1: Making the variables comparable

In order to start the analysis, we needed to make the data comparable. There were a number of variables that could not be used in their absolute form for calculating the NRI. They had to be weighed against an external variable to make them comparable across different countries. The soft data such as those used in GCR 2001 and GCR 2002 did not need to be weighed. Some of the hard data did not require a change in the denominator, as by definition the variable was comparable (it was either mentioned as a percentage or had a common denominator). For example, mobile telephones per 1,000 people and illiteracy rate (percent of population older than fifteen years).

The rest of the data had to be transformed by dividing by an external variable. Two external variables chosen to weigh the data were GDP per capita (PPP) and population. They

were used to weigh different kinds of variables. For example, telecommunications revenue and residential monthly telephone subscription were weighed against GDP per capita, whereas local switch capacity was weighed against the population.

A list of variables transformed can be found in Table 1.

Table 1. **Transforming Variables to Make Them Comparable**

Variable Numbers	Variable Name	Variable Explanation	Denominator
3.07	Switch capacity	Local switch capacity	Population
3.10	Secure servers	Secure internet servers	Population
4.08	Cost local call	Telephone average cost of local call (US$ per three minutes)	GDP per capita
4.09	Cellular	Cellular telephone, cost of a 3-minute local call (off-peak, US$)	GDP per capita
4.10	Subscription	Residential telephone monthly subscription (US$)	GDP per capita
5.06	Subscription	Business telephone monthly subscription (US$)	GDP per capita

Estimating Data
Step 1: Regression method

After dropping some of the variables, the missing values had to be estimated. A decision was made to estimate the missing data rather than leave it blank because missing values would have led to a bias in calculating the index and would limit us in making comparisons across countries. The missing data were estimated using two approaches.

In the first approach the missing values were estimated using regression analysis. The process involved picking a variable (X) that was highly correlated with the variable that was missing values (Y), and then using X as the independent variable to estimate the dependent variable (Y) in the linear regression Y=a + bX. A more detailed description of this process is listed below.

Initially, a bi-variate correlation for 120 short-listed variables[1] and three external variables was done. The three external variables chosen were gross domestic product (GDP) per capita (PPP), GDP, and population. In case

Table 2. **Estimating Data**

Variable Number	Title of Variable Missing data	Description of Variable Missing Data	Description of Estimated by Variable
2.02	Legal	The extent to which the legal framework supports the development of online businesses and IT	IP protection is common
5.05	IT training	The level of IT related training programs	IP protection is common
8.08	Web pages B	The level of pervasiveness of Web pages for businesses	IP protection is common
1.03	Telecommunications competition	The level of competition amongst the telecommunication sector in a country	Sufficient competition in ISPs
3.01	General infrastructure	A general impression of the quality and availability of general infrastructure	Lease line and dial-up access
6.04	e-Services	The availability of online government services	Internet access in schools
7.01	e-Payments	The availability of online payment systems	Internet access in schools
9.02	Services	The number of online government services available	Internet access in schools
1.01	Ease of VC	Ease of obtaining venture capital funding for new and innovative but risky businesses and projects	Country's position in technology
1.05	Talented people	A measure to determine the general tendency of talented people to stay or leave their native country	Country's position in technology
4.01	Proactive buyers	Whether or not the buyers in a country are generally proactive in adoption of new products and processes	Country's position in technology
5.01	Company new IT	The eagerness of companies to adopt new technology for their businesses	Country's position in technology
5.03	Source of technology	Whether companies obtain new technologies by licensing or evolve through internal research and development activities	Country's position in technology
1.08	Manufacturing	The extent of manufacturing of IT hardware locally	Collaboration with local universities

there was more than one highly-correlated variable, then the variable with all 82 observations and the highest coefficient of correlation was chosen. In the event that there was no highly-correlated variable[2] that had all 82 observations, then we used a highly-correlated variable that had data for any country for which data in the other variable were missing. For example, GCR 2001 data could be estimated using GCR 2002 data because the two data sets did not have data missing for the same countries.

If the variable used in the regression analysis was not an external variable, but one of the 120 variables, it was dropped in the final calculation of the NRI. A list of the variables for which data were estimated using this approach is in Table 2. This method was not sufficient to estimate all the missing values; thus, a second approach was used at a later stage in the study to estimate the rest of the missing data.

Estimating Data
Step 2: Clustering

The variables that could not be estimated using the regression method were estimated using a clustering technique. The countries were clustered or grouped according to their gross national product (GNP) per capita. This method was chosen after trying different clustering approaches.

A more rigorous and obvious approach that could be considered for clustering countries is grouping them on the basis of geography and income. Bearing in mind that the study was being done for just eighty-two countries, a combination of geography and income was not feasible. Using both geography and income, we found that there were not enough countries in the resulting clusters to do a statistically significant estimation. Some of the clusters had only a single country, making estimation for a country in such a group practically impossible. For example, Sri Lanka was the only country in the Lower Middle Income: South Asia cluster.

As a result of this, clustering was based on income only, taking an average of the data of the countries that had a GNP per capita similar to the country for which the data were missing. It was decided that GNP per capita +/-20 percent would provide a large enough sample size to estimate the missing data.

Special care was taken not to estimate data using other estimated data.

Data Transformation
Step 2: Making the variables consistent

The next step in calculating the NRI required further transformation of variables to make them consistent. While a high score on most of the variables would lead to a higher Index, a few variables had a reverse effect on the Index. These variables were negatively correlated to the Index, and it was necessary to transform them to make them consistent with the other variables. The data of these variables were multiplied by a factor of -1. The soft data, once again, did not require modification, as the questions were all worded in the same way, and this made the data consistent. Some hard data, for example, illiteracy rate, residential monthly telephone subscription, cost of three-minute cellular call, and so on (Table 3 presents a complete list), required transformation.

Table 3. **Variables Needing Transformation**

Variable Number	Title of the Variable	Description of the Variable
3.04	Faults	Telephone faults per 100 main lines
3.09	Telephone wait	Telephone mainlines, waiting time
4.06	Illiteracy	Illiteracy rate, adult total (% of people aged 15 and older)
4.08	Cost local call	Average cost of a 3-minute local telephone call (US$)
4.09	Cellular	Cellular telephone, cost of a 3-minute local call (off-peak, US$)
4.10	Subscription	Residential monthly telephone subscription (US$)
5.06	Subscription	Business monthly telephone subscription (US$)

Data Reduction

To explore whether there might be a way of reducing the number of variables in calculating the NRI, two frequently used statistical techniques were applied: factor analysis, and Cronbachs alpha. A combination of these techniques led to a further reduction in the number of variables to 64.

Cronbachs alpha may be defined as "a coefficient that describes how well a group of items focuses on a single idea or construct."[3] The NRI framework was structured in nine different blocks; the analysis was done for each block. The variables were initially divided into nine blocks according to their qualitative relevance to the framework; the Cronbachs alpha technique ensured that the variables were also quantitatively of one dimension.

A threshold level of 0.65 was used for Cronbachs alpha. The alpha was measured using different combinations of variables, and the variable was dropped when the alpha was less than 0.65. Factor analysis was used to ensure that the right combination of variables was used while testing for the Cronbachs alpha.

Standardization of variables

Once the final list of variables was determined, the data were converted on a scale of one to seven, using linear transformation. The formula used to standardize the data was

6 x ((country value - sample min) / (sample max - sample min)) + 1

Calculation of the Index

The final step was the calculation of the NRI. First, each subindex was calculated by taking an average of all the variables in each block. Then, the average of the three subindexes was taken to calculate the three component indexes, namely, environment, readiness, and usage. Finally, the average of the three component indexes was used to arrive at the NRI.

Endnotes

1. The 130 variables at the start, minus the variables that had fewer that 50 observations

2. Correlation coefficient >0.8

3. http://www.u.arizona.edu/ic/forms/Help/alpha_rh.htm

How to Read the Data Tables

The data ranking section provides a list of all the variables with detailed data for all eighty-two countries included in the study.

The data are divided into nine sections, according to the Networked Readiness Framework.

   i. Environment-Market

   ii. Environment-Policy and Regulation

   iii. Environment-Infrastructure

   iv. Readiness-Individual

   v. Readiness-Business

   vi. Readiness-Government

   vii. Usage-Individual

   viii. Usage-Business

   ix. Usage-Government

As mentioned in the methodology section, two types of variables are used in our analysis; namely, hard variables and soft variables. For each variable, the short name and a description are listed in the beginning of each table.

Soft variables. For each soft variable, the original question is included in the description of the variable. The values for these variables in the majority of cases range from one to seven, where a response of one corresponds to a lower relative performance, and a response of seven corresponds to the highest level of relative performance. The values are responses to questionnaires and represent the average score of different respondents in a country. Variable 9.1, for example, corresponds to a question about the respondent's position in Internet-based interactions with the government versus international competitors; here, a low score means that the Internet is not actively used, while a high score shows high interaction on the level of the most advanced countries with respect to Internet interactions.

Hard variables. Some hard variables had to be "transformed" to ensure that they were comparable across countries; the hard data presented in the tables are transformed data. For more details on how the data were modified, please see the preceding section, NRI Index: Methodology.

Missing Data. The missing data were estimated to complete the data set. This was done primarily because the missing values would have led to a bias in calculating the Index, and would limit us in making comparisons across countries. The enclosed tables indicate the estimated data with an asterisk (*) superscript. For more details, please refer to the preceding section, NRI Index: Methodology' in the book.

Ranking. The countries have been ranked using the complete data set for each variable. The country responses shown in the tables are rounded off to two decimal places. Two countries with the same listed variable value can have different rankings. The differences in the rankings exist because exact figures, not rounded numbers, were used to rank the countries. In the case of variable 2.03, for example, Costa Rica's average score was 2.705, and the Ukraine's was 2.708. These countries are therefore ranked 55th and 54th, respectively, even though they are both listed with the same rounded score of 2.71.

If two countries have exactly the same value then they will have the same rank, and the rank that follows is not assigned, thereby ensuring that the last rank is 82. In the case of variable 9.01, for example, Finland's average score was 3 and Iceland's was also 3. Both these countries are therefore ranked 1st and the next country, Denmark, with a score of 2.89, is ranked 3rd.

1.01 Venture capital availability

Entrepreneurs with innovative but risky projects can generally find VC in your country:

1 = not true, 7 = true

MEAN 3.33

Rank	Country	Value
1	United States	5.75
2	United Kingdom	5.54
3	Finland	5.21
4	Israel	5.10
5	Sweden	4.93
6	Ireland	4.81
7	Netherlands	4.66
8	Hong Kong SAR	4.63
9	Norway	4.56
10	Denmark	4.45
11	Belgium	4.44
12	Canada	4.42
13	Iceland	4.39
14	France	4.34
15	Singapore	4.31
16	Taiwan	4.27
17	Germany	4.24
18	New Zealand	4.20
19	Korea	4.11
20	Spain	4.08
21	Switzerland	4.04
22	Australia	4.00
22	Austria	4.00
24	Estonia	3.79
25	Italy	3.78
26	South Africa	3.74
27	Lithuania	3.72
28	Dominican Republic	3.70
29	Tunisia	3.69
30	India	3.67
31	Luxembourg	3.65*
32	Trinidad and Tobago	3.50
33	Slovenia	3.47
34	Morocco	3.46
35	Panama	3.45
36	Poland	3.42
37	Portugal	3.41
38	Malaysia	3.40
39	Greece	3.33
40	Latvia	3.32
41	Hungary	3.26
42	Botswana	3.23
43	Thailand	3.19
44	Sri Lanka	3.17
45	Japan	3.14
46	Brazil	3.10
47	Chile	3.07
48	El Salvador	2.98
49	Mauritius	2.97
50	China	2.96
51	Nigeria	2.93
52	Namibia	2.91
53	Zimbabwe	2.89
54	Jordan	2.88
55	Egypt	2.76*
56	Slovakia	2.75
57	Croatia	2.67
58	Czech Republic	2.66
59	Ukraine	2.60
60	Russia	2.58
61	Vietnam	2.55
62	Bulgaria	2.51
63	Romania	2.47
64	Bangladesh	2.42
65	Guatemala	2.41
66	Philippines	2.39
67	Indonesia	2.38
68	Costa Rica	2.36
69	Colombia	2.35
70	Jamaica	2.34
71	Nicaragua	2.32
72	Uruguay	2.26
73	Argentina	2.25
74	Mexico	2.24
75	Haiti	2.16
76	Venezuela	2.15
77	Peru	2.12
78	Bolivia	2.10
79	Paraguay	2.00
80	Honduras	1.90
81	Turkey	1.71
82	Ecuador	1.66

Market Environment

1.01 Venture capital availability

Entrepreneurs with innovative but risky projects can generally find VC in your country:

1 = not true, 7 = true

Rank	Country	Value
1	United States	5.75
2	United Kingdom	5.54
3	Finland	5.21
4	Israel	5.10
5	Sweden	4.93
6	Ireland	4.81
7	Netherlands	4.66
8	Hong Kong SAR	4.63
9	Norway	4.56
10	Denmark	4.45
11	Belgium	4.44
12	Canada	4.42
13	Iceland	4.39
14	France	4.34
15	Singapore	4.31
16	Taiwan	4.27
17	Germany	4.24
18	New Zealand	4.20
19	Korea	4.11
20	Spain	4.08
21	Switzerland	4.04
22	Australia	4.00
22	Austria	4.00
24	Estonia	3.79
25	Italy	3.78
26	South Africa	3.74
27	Lithuania	3.72
28	Dominican Republic	3.70
29	Tunisia	3.69
30	India	3.67
31	Luxembourg	3.65*
32	Trinidad and Tobago	3.50
33	Slovenia	3.47
34	Morocco	3.46
35	Panama	3.45
36	Poland	3.42
37	Portugal	3.41
38	Malaysia	3.40
39	Greece	3.33
40	Latvia	3.32
41	Hungary	3.26
42	Botswana	3.23
43	Thailand	3.19
44	Sri Lanka	3.17
45	Japan	3.14
46	Brazil	3.10
47	Chile	3.07
48	El Salvador	2.98
49	Mauritius	2.97
50	China	2.96
51	Nigeria	2.93
52	Namibia	2.91
53	Zimbabwe	2.89
54	Jordan	2.88
55	Egypt	2.76*
56	Slovak Republic	2.75
57	Croatia	2.67
58	Czech Republic	2.66
59	Ukraine	2.60
60	Russian Federation	2.58
61	Vietnam	2.55
62	Bulgaria	2.51
63	Romania	2.47
64	Bangladesh	2.42
65	Guatemala	2.41
66	Philippines	2.39
67	Indonesia	2.38
68	Costa Rica	2.36
69	Colombia	2.35
70	Jamaica	2.34
71	Nicaragua	2.32
72	Uruguay	2.26
73	Argentina	2.25
74	Mexico	2.24
75	Haiti	2.16
76	Venezuela	2.15
77	Peru	2.12
78	Bolivia	2.10
79	Paraguay	2.00
80	Honduras	1.90
81	Turkey	1.71
82	Ecuador	1.66

MEAN 3.33

1.02 State of cluster development

How common are clusters in your country?

1 = limited and shallow, 7 = common and deep

Rank	Country	Value
1	Italy	5.73
2	Taiwan	5.54
3	United States	5.38
4	Finland	5.31
5	United Kingdom	4.92
6	Singapore	4.82
7	Germany	4.68
8	Korea	4.59
9	Sweden	4.36
10	Ireland	4.33
11	Luxembourg	4.33*
12	Hong Kong SAR	4.32
13	Canada	4.29
14	Japan	4.19
15	Netherlands	4.14
16	Norway	3.97
17	Austria	3.94
18	Iceland	3.90
19	Brazil	3.87
20	India	3.83
21	Switzerland	3.77
22	France	3.73
23	Denmark	3.70
24	Thailand	3.68
25	Belgium	3.59
26	Indonesia	3.59
27	Australia	3.54
28	China	3.50
28	Malaysia	3.50
28	Turkey	3.50
31	Spain	3.48
32	Mexico	3.45
33	Portugal	3.36
34	Morocco	3.33
35	Lithuania	3.32
36	South Africa	3.24
37	Dominican Republic	3.23
38	New Zealand	3.22
39	Nigeria	3.20
40	Hungary	3.19
41	Russian Federation	3.18
42	Israel	3.13
43	Poland	3.10
44	Philippines	3.03
45	Romania	3.01
46	Chile	2.99
47	Sri Lanka	2.97
48	Botswana	2.93
49	Nicaragua	2.92
50	Mauritius	2.92
51	Costa Rica	2.91
52	Jordan	2.90
53	Trinidad and Tobago	2.89
54	Bangladesh	2.88
55	Ecuador	2.85
56	Colombia	2.85
57	Latvia	2.82
58	Panama	2.76
59	Slovenia	2.74
60	Ukraine	2.74
61	Vietnam	2.74
62	Slovak Republic	2.73
63	Egypt	2.71*
64	Namibia	2.71
65	Croatia	2.67
66	Tunisia	2.67
67	Czech Republic	2.65
68	Peru	2.60
69	Greece	2.56
70	Guatemala	2.56
71	Jamaica	2.55
72	Bulgaria	2.55
73	Bolivia	2.54
74	Zimbabwe	2.50
75	Argentina	2.49
76	Estonia	2.46
77	El Salvador	2.44
78	Venezuela	2.38
79	Honduras	2.33
80	Uruguay	2.17
81	Paraguay	1.95
82	Haiti	1.93

MEAN 3.33

1.03 Competition in the telecommunication sector

Is there sufficient competition in the telecommunication sector in your country to ensure high quality, infrequent interruptions, and low prices?

1 = no, 7 = yes, equal to the best in the world

Rank	Country	Value	MEAN 4.53
1	Finland	6.82	
2	Sweden	6.56	
3	United States	6.45	
4	Germany	6.42	
5	Chile	6.39	
6	Hong Kong SAR	6.35	
7	Austria	6.33	
8	Canada	6.29	
9	United Kingdom	6.27	
10	Norway	6.10	
11	Dominican Republic	6.02	
12	Singapore	6.00	
13	Italy	5.95	
14	France	5.91	
15	Switzerland	5.89	
16	Korea	5.82	
17	Iceland	5.81	
18	Netherlands	5.73	
19	Portugal	5.68	
20	Taiwan	5.67	
21	El Salvador	5.64	
22	Australia	5.63	
23	Denmark	5.63	
24	Belgium	5.57	
25	Brazil	5.54	
26	Venezuela	5.50	
27	New Zealand	5.48	
28	Argentina	5.40	
29	Spain	5.29	
30	Israel	5.08	
31	Estonia	5.07	
32	Slovak Republic	5.00	
33	Japan	4.97	
34	Colombia	4.96	
35	Jordan	4.89	
36	Luxembourg	4.83	
37	Philippines	4.83	
38	Hungary	4.79	
39	Malaysia	4.68	
40	Czech Republic	4.68	
41	Ireland	4.65	
42	India	4.65	
43	Sri Lanka	4.64	
44	Egypt	4.54	
44	Thailand	4.47	
46	Greece	4.38	
47	Peru	4.37	
48	Morocco	4.33*	
49	Guatemala	4.24	
50	Namibia	4.16*	
51	Indonesia	4.08	
52	Jamaica	3.98	
53	Uruguay	3.90	
54	Panama	3.90	
55	Tunisia	3.73*	
56	Turkey	3.69	
57	Bolivia	3.61	
58	Russian Federation	3.56	
59	Slovenia	3.52	
60	Mexico	3.49	
61	Croatia	3.47*	
62	Poland	3.44	
63	China	3.41	
64	Botswana	3.40*	
65	Latvia	3.34	
66	Romania	3.22	
67	Ukraine	3.14	
68	Zimbabwe	3.00	
69	Paraguay	2.96	
70	Lithuania	2.94	
71	Haiti	2.85*	
72	South Africa	2.83	
73	Costa Rica	2.79	
74	Vietnam	2.74	
75	Bulgaria	2.67	
76	Bangladesh	2.66	
77	Nicaragua	2.66	
78	Trinidad and Tobago	2.56	
79	Ecuador	2.56	
80	Nigeria	2.53	
81	Honduras	2.17	
82	Mauritius	1.94	

1.04 Availability of scientists and engineers

Scientists and engineers in your country are:

1 = nonexistent or rare, 7 = widely available

Rank	Country	Value	MEAN 4.88
1	Israel	6.56	
2	India	6.21	
3	Slovak Republic	6.17	
4	France	6.14	
5	Romania	6.13	
6	Canada	6.09	
7	Japan	6.07	
8	Switzerland	6.01	
9	Finland	6.00	
10	United States	5.97	
11	Luxembourg	5.85*	
12	Hungary	5.73	
13	Taiwan	5.72	
14	Tunisia	5.66	
15	Austria	5.65	
16	Australia	5.64	
17	Sweden	5.57	
18	Iceland	5.57	
19	United Kingdom	5.50	
20	Singapore	5.47	
21	Germany	5.46	
22	Greece	5.46	
23	Jordan	5.45	
24	Uruguay	5.43	
25	Argentina	5.39	
26	Korea	5.37	
27	Chile	5.34	
28	Norway	5.33	
29	Russian Federation	5.32	
30	Czech Republic	5.28	
31	Belgium	5.28	
32	Ireland	5.26	
33	Spain	5.25	
34	Italy	5.24	
35	Poland	5.24	
36	Denmark	5.22	
37	Lithuania	5.22	
38	Morocco	5.21	
39	Bulgaria	5.19	
40	Netherlands	5.17	
41	Estonia	5.14	
42	Costa Rica	5.09	
43	Vietnam	5.04	
44	Brazil	5.03	
45	Ukraine	5.01	
46	Croatia	5.01	
47	Portugal	4.91	
48	Trinidad and Tobago	4.88	
49	Sri Lanka	4.81	
50	Hong Kong SAR	4.74	
51	New Zealand	4.71	
52	Turkey	4.71	
53	Malaysia	4.67	
54	Colombia	4.62	
55	Egypt	4.59*	
56	Latvia	4.55	
57	Thailand	4.43	
58	Slovenia	4.32	
59	Bangladesh	4.29	
60	Venezuela	4.24	
61	Mauritius	4.23	
62	Nigeria	4.20	
63	Panama	4.13	
64	Peru	4.13	
65	El Salvador	4.11	
66	China	4.10	
67	South Africa	4.07	
68	Jamaica	4.03	
69	Indonesia	4.00	
70	Philippines	3.97	
71	Zimbabwe	3.89	
72	Dominican Republic	3.74	
73	Ecuador	3.48	
74	Botswana	3.36	
75	Nicaragua	3.36	
76	Guatemala	3.30	
77	Mexico	3.26	
78	Honduras	3.26	
79	Paraguay	3.23	
80	Bolivia	3.23	
81	Namibia	3.16	
82	Haiti	2.91	

1.05 Brain drain

Your country's talented people:

1 = normally leave to pursue opportunities in other countries,
7 = almost always remain in the country

MEAN 3.76

Rank	Country	Value
1	United States	6.48
2	Finland	5.67
3	Netherlands	5.66
4	Israel	5.60
5	United Kingdom	5.54
6	Norway	5.42
7	Japan	5.35
8	Chile	5.35
9	Switzerland	5.34
10	Iceland	5.17
11	Austria	5.03
12	Belgium	5.00
13	Spain	4.97
14	Taiwan	4.96
15	Czech Republic	4.91
16	Germany	4.90
17	Singapore	4.88
18	Ireland	4.85
19	Denmark	4.85
20	Hong Kong SAR	4.68
21	Brazil	4.65
22	Sweden	4.64
23	Portugal	4.64
24	Panama	4.58
25	Costa Rica	4.55
26	Thailand	4.51
27	Korea	4.32
28	Australia	4.18
29	Malaysia	4.18
30	Canada	4.16
31	Luxembourg	4.14*
32	Slovenia	4.10
33	Estonia	4.09
34	Tunisia	4.06
35	Botswana	4.00
36	Italy	3.97
37	Poland	3.97
38	Indonesia	3.88
39	Hungary	3.80
40	Greece	3.79
41	China	3.65
42	Trinidad and Tobago	3.65
43	France	3.61
44	El Salvador	3.59
45	Namibia	3.47
46	Mauritius	3.46
47	Vietnam	3.44
48	Turkey	3.29
49	Russian Federation	3.24
50	Mexico	3.23
51	Dominican Republic	3.23
52	Slovak Republic	3.19
53	Egypt	3.15*
54	India	3.13
55	Latvia	3.09
56	Morocco	3.05
57	New Zealand	2.98
58	Uruguay	2.96
59	Paraguay	2.96
60	Honduras	2.95
61	Venezuela	2.92
62	South Africa	2.88
63	Jordan	2.78
64	Lithuania	2.75
65	Colombia	2.74
66	Guatemala	2.74
67	Sri Lanka	2.71
68	Peru	2.68
69	Jamaica	2.63
70	Argentina	2.63
71	Croatia	2.49
72	Nicaragua	2.48
73	Bolivia	2.40
74	Ukraine	2.39
75	Philippines	2.28
76	Nigeria	2.27
77	Ecuador	2.23
78	Bulgaria	2.21
79	Bangladesh	2.08
80	Romania	1.95
81	Zimbabwe	1.83
82	Haiti	1.70

1.06 Public spending on education (% of GDP)

Public spending on education as a percentage of GDP

MEAN 4.74

Rank	Country	Value
1	Zimbabwe	10.84
2	Botswana	9.13
3	Denmark	8.22
4	Namibia	8.10
5	Sweden	7.98
6	Norway	7.68
7	Israel	7.66
8	Tunisia	7.55
9	New Zealand	7.17
10	Finland	7.11
11	Iceland	7.09
12	Latvia	6.84
13	Estonia	6.79
14	Lithuania	6.38
15	Jamaica	6.34
16	Jordan	6.30
17	Austria	6.28
18	South Africa	6.09
19	Costa Rica	6.05
20	France	5.89
21	Slovenia	5.78
22	Portugal	5.66
23	Canada	5.61
24	Switzerland	5.49
25	Poland	5.42
26	Haiti	5.07*
27	Croatia	5.05
28	United States	5.01
29	Panama	4.96
30	Taiwan	4.91*
31	Netherlands	4.89
32	Morocco	4.88
33	Bolivia	4.83
34	Venezuela	4.78*
35	Australia	4.77
36	Italy	4.73
37	United Kingdom	4.71
38	Thailand	4.70
39	Egypt	4.67
40	Germany	4.65
41	Brazil	4.63
42	Malaysia	4.62
43	Hungary	4.56
44	Spain	4.54
44	Paraguay	4.52
46	Ireland	4.48
47	Ukraine	4.45
48	Romania	4.41
49	Slovak Republic	4.28
50	Czech Republic	4.20
51	Nicaragua	4.17
52	Mexico	4.11*
53	Korea	4.07
54	Mauritius	4.03
55	Honduras	4.02
56	Luxembourg	3.99
57	Chile	3.74
58	Argentina	3.73
59	Russian Federation	3.58
60	Colombia	3.51
61	Japan	3.48
62	Sri Lanka	3.39
63	Bulgaria	3.36
64	Trinidad and Tobago	3.25
65	Ecuador	3.22
66	Philippines	3.20
67	Peru	3.20
68	Belgium	3.14
69	Singapore	3.07
70	Greece	3.07
71	India	2.95
72	Hong Kong SAR	2.92
73	Vietnam	2.78
74	Uruguay	2.55
75	El Salvador	2.51
76	Bangladesh	2.35
77	China	2.29
78	Turkey	2.25
79	Dominican Republic	2.22
80	Guatemala	1.98
81	Indonesia	1.43
82	Nigeria	0.65

Source: World Bank, World Development Indicators 2002

1.07 Domestic software companies in international markets

Software and software services companies in your country compete internationally:

1 = strongly disagree, 7 = strongly agree

Rank	Country	Value
1	United States	6.51
2	India	6.47
3	Finland	6.33
4	Israel	6.23
5	Sweden	6.16
6	United Kingdom	6.13
7	Ireland	6.09
8	Germany	6.07
9	France	5.90
10	Netherlands	5.73
11	Canada	5.62
12	Denmark	5.47
13	Iceland	5.43
14	Costa Rica	5.41
15	Belgium	5.31
16	Uruguay	5.29
17	Singapore	5.22
18	Hungary	5.14
19	Norway	5.13
20	Switzerland	5.11
21	New Zealand	5.08
22	Austria	5.02
23	South Africa	4.97
24	Korea	4.95
25	Czech Republic	4.82
26	Estonia	4.78
27	Haiti	4.75*
28	Hong Kong SAR	4.69
29	Australia	4.68
30	Chile	4.67
31	Taiwan	4.63
32	Italy	4.61
33	Spain	4.60
34	China	4.60
35	Philippines	4.47
36	Argentina	4.39
37	Brazil	4.28
38	Croatia	4.27*
39	Indonesia	4.25
40	Latvia	4.25
41	Bulgaria	4.25
42	Japan	4.25
43	Panama	4.22
44	Sri Lanka	4.21
44	Mexico	4.16
46	Vietnam	4.15
47	Botswana	4.14*
48	Colombia	4.08
49	Slovenia	4.03
50	Slovak Republic	4.00
51	Dominican Republic	3.91
52	Portugal	3.89
53	Poland	3.88
54	Jordan	3.83
55	Ukraine	3.82
56	Lithuania	3.81
57	Venezuela	3.62
58	Luxembourg	3.60
59	Peru	3.55
60	Greece	3.55
61	Trinidad and Tobago	3.53
62	Zimbabwe	3.53
63	Tunisia	3.49*
64	Mauritius	3.47
65	Namibia	3.45*
66	Romania	3.42
67	Morocco	3.38*
68	Russian Federation	3.34
69	Guatemala	3.33
70	Jamaica	3.32
71	Malaysia	3.26
72	Ecuador	3.26
73	Egypt	3.17
74	Turkey	3.13
75	Paraguay	3.09
76	Thailand	2.98
77	Nigeria	2.92
78	Nicaragua	2.90
79	Bangladesh	2.88
80	El Salvador	2.58
81	Bolivia	2.40
82	Honduras	2.40

MEAN 4.34

1.08 Domestic manufacturing of IT hardware

Manufacturing of Information Technology hardware in your country is:

1 = nonexistent, 7 = as extensive as in the world's most advanced economies

Rank	Country	Value
1	United States	6.66
2	Japan	6.51
3	Ireland	6.28
4	Taiwan	6.16
5	Finland	5.94
6	Israel	5.86
7	Germany	5.66
8	United Kingdom	5.59
9	Netherlands	5.45
10	Sweden	5.36
11	Korea	5.24
12	Canada	5.18
13	France	5.18
14	Singapore	5.12
15	Estonia	4.92
16	Brazil	4.64
17	Italy	4.53
18	Austria	4.52
19	Czech Republic	4.44
20	Spain	4.36
21	India	4.35
22	Malaysia	4.35
23	Poland	4.33
24	China	4.31
25	Costa Rica	4.18
26	Thailand	4.13
27	Hungary	4.08
28	Mexico	3.98
29	Norway	3.94
30	Ukraine	3.93
31	Belgium	3.92
32	Switzerland	3.89
33	Philippines	3.88
34	Denmark	3.77
35	Latvia	3.71
36	Indonesia	3.71
37	Lithuania	3.67
38	Portugal	3.50
39	Tunisia	3.47*
40	New Zealand	3.45
41	Australia	3.44
42	Slovak Republic	3.40
43	Greece	3.33
44	South Africa	3.18
44	Russian Federation	3.18
46	Morocco	3.16*
47	Slovenia	3.16
48	Paraguay	3.13
49	Uruguay	3.08
50	Hong Kong SAR	3.08
51	Bulgaria	3.00
52	Turkey	2.94
53	Namibia	2.91*
54	Vietnam	2.87
55	Croatia	2.81*
56	Iceland	2.71
57	Botswana	2.66*
58	Sri Lanka	2.62
59	Argentina	2.57
60	Trinidad and Tobago	2.50
61	Egypt	2.33
62	Colombia	2.29
63	Chile	2.29
64	Panama	2.24
65	Jordan	2.15
66	Peru	2.08
67	Dominican Republic	2.06
68	Jamaica	2.00
69	Nigeria	1.97
70	Ecuador	1.95
71	El Salvador	1.93
72	Venezuela	1.84
73	Guatemala	1.83
74	Nicaragua	1.82
75	Mauritius	1.80
76	Honduras	1.77
77	Zimbabwe	1.76
78	Haiti	1.68*
79	Bolivia	1.65
80	Romania	1.64
81	Bangladesh	1.56
82	Luxembourg	1.33

MEAN 3.51

1.09 ICT expenditure (% of GDP)

Expenditure on ICT as a percentage of GDP

Rank	Country	Value
1	New Zealand	13.60
2	Colombia	12.00
3	Sweden	10.40
4	Switzerland	10.30
5	Australia	9.70
5	Singapore	9.70
7	Netherlands	9.40
8	Czech Republic	9.30
9	Denmark	9.20
10	United Kingdom	9.10
11	Hong Kong SAR	8.80
12	France	8.70
12	Hungary	8.70
14	South Africa	8.60
15	Luxembourg	8.40*
15	Brazil	8.40
15	Canada	8.40
18	Japan	8.30
19	United States	8.10
20	Belgium	8.00
21	Taiwan	7.98*
22	Germany	7.90
23	Chile	7.80
23	Finland	7.80
23	Iceland	7.80
26	Dominican Republic	7.80*
27	Tunisia	7.80*
28	Slovak Republic	7.50
29	Israel	7.36
30	Botswana	7.22*
31	Austria	7.20
32	Portugal	7.10
33	Estonia	7.00*
34	Norway	6.90
35	Malaysia	6.80
36	Latvia	6.73*
36	Lithuania	6.73*
38	Jamaica	6.70*
39	Ireland	6.70
40	Croatia	6.61*
41	Korea	6.60
42	Mauritius	6.56*
43	Bangladesh	6.50*
43	Vietnam	6.50
45	Trinidad and Tobago	6.47*
46	Uruguay	6.25*
47	Costa Rica	6.22*
48	Greece	6.10
49	Paraguay	5.97*
50	Poland	5.90
51	Italy	5.70
52	China	5.40
52	Honduras	5.40*
52	Sri Lanka	5.40*
55	El Salvador	5.40*
55	Namibia	5.40*
57	Slovenia	5.20
58	Nicaragua	5.15*
58	Nigeria	5.15*
58	Zimbabwe	5.15*
61	Spain	5.10
62	Turkey	4.80
63	Jordan	4.68*
64	Bolivia	4.60*
64	Peru	4.60*
66	Argentina	4.10
66	Bulgaria	4.10
68	Venezuela	3.90
69	Ecuador	3.80*
69	India	3.80
69	Morocco	3.80*
69	Philippines	3.80
73	Russian Federation	3.70
74	Thailand	3.60
75	Guatemala	3.22*
76	Mexico	3.20
77	Panama	3.13*
78	Haiti	3.00*
79	Egypt	2.40
80	Romania	2.30
81	Indonesia	2.20
81	Ukraine	2.20*

MEAN 6.45   14%

Source: World Bank, World Development Indicators 2002

Political and Regulatory Environment

2.01 Effectiveness of law-making bodies

How effective is your national parliament/congress as a lawmaking and oversight institution?

1 = very ineffective, 7 = very effective, the best in the world

MEAN 3.39

Rank	Country	Value
1	Singapore	6.00
2	United States	5.35
3	United Kingdom	5.31
4	Australia	5.25
5	Iceland	5.14
6	Finland	5.09
7	Denmark	5.05
8	Canada	5.03
9	Malaysia	4.93
10	China	4.81
11	Switzerland	4.61
12	Austria	4.61
13	New Zealand	4.54
14	Botswana	4.51
15	Ireland	4.41
16	Luxembourg	4.39*
17	Germany	4.34
18	Spain	4.34
19	Sri Lanka	4.31
20	Sweden	4.31
21	Israel	4.20
22	Norway	4.19
23	Tunisia	4.11
24	Netherlands	4.10
25	Mauritius	4.08
26	Hong Kong SAR	4.05
27	South Africa	3.98
28	Namibia	3.97
29	Estonia	3.91
30	Hungary	3.87
31	Italy	3.86
32	India	3.75
33	Thailand	3.68
34	Taiwan	3.66
35	Belgium	3.61
35	Portugal	3.61
37	Jamaica	3.61
38	Chile	3.57
39	Turkey	3.53
40	France	3.53
41	Slovenia	3.51
42	Vietnam	3.47
43	Japan	3.42
44	Trinidad and Tobago	3.39
45	Jordan	3.33
46	Latvia	3.23
47	Greece	3.22
48	Morocco	3.18
49	Brazil	3.15
50	Czech Republic	3.07
51	Lithuania	2.99
52	Russian Federation	2.93
53	Poland	2.90
54	Korea	2.90
55	Indonesia	2.88
56	Croatia	2.84
57	Bangladesh	2.77
58	Uruguay	2.65
59	Philippines	2.61
60	Bulgaria	2.53
61	Dominican Republic	2.51
62	Honduras	2.47
63	Nigeria	2.47
64	Slovak Republic	2.39
65	Egypt	2.27*
66	Peru	2.26
67	El Salvador	2.25
68	Romania	2.24
69	Colombia	2.18
70	Mexico	2.16
71	Ukraine	2.12
72	Costa Rica	2.03
73	Bolivia	2.02
74	Panama	1.96
75	Nicaragua	1.95
76	Zimbabwe	1.80
77	Paraguay	1.71
78	Guatemala	1.63
79	Ecuador	1.53
80	Venezuela	1.52
81	Argentina	1.35
82	Haiti	1.19

2.02 Legal framework for ICT development

The legal framework in your country supports the development of online businesses and informational technology businesses (including Internet service providers):

1 = no, strongly impede, 7 = yes, significantly promotes

MEAN 4.48

Rank	Country	Value
1	Finland	6.24
2	Singapore	6.18
3	United States	6.15
4	Sweden	5.72
5	Luxembourg	5.67
6	Netherlands	5.64
7	Canada	5.61
8	Australia	5.54
9	Iceland	5.52
10	United Kingdom	5.52
11	Hong Kong SAR	5.43
12	Austria	5.35
13	Estonia	5.35
14	Ireland	5.35
15	New Zealand	5.27
16	Denmark	5.26
17	Malaysia	5.25
18	France	5.14
19	Switzerland	5.13
20	Germany	5.11
21	Israel	5.04
22	Norway	5.03
23	Slovak Republic	5.00
24	Korea	4.96
25	Spain	4.94
26	Tunisia	4.91*
27	India	4.90
28	Italy	4.84
29	Portugal	4.74
30	Brazil	4.74
31	Belgium	4.69
32	South Africa	4.69
33	Jordan	4.68
34	Namibia	4.65*
35	Philippines	4.54
36	Czech Republic	4.44
37	Botswana	4.42*
38	Trinidad and Tobago	4.38
39	Taiwan	4.36
40	Uruguay	4.35
41	Egypt	4.33
42	Slovenia	4.32
43	Chile	4.31
44	Dominican Republic	4.31
44	Jamaica	4.29
46	Colombia	4.26
47	Mauritius	4.25
48	Turkey	4.25
49	Hungary	4.24
50	China	4.19
51	Morocco	4.17*
52	Japan	4.15
53	Panama	4.15
54	Argentina	4.13
55	Nigeria	4.12
56	Costa Rica	4.03
57	Latvia	4.00
58	Peru	4.00
59	Zimbabwe	4.00
60	El Salvador	3.98
61	Venezuela	3.96
62	Croatia	3.93*
63	Ukraine	3.92
64	Vietnam	3.90
65	Greece	3.88
66	Thailand	3.83
67	Lithuania	3.83
68	Mexico	3.81
69	Sri Lanka	3.72
70	Poland	3.70
71	Bangladesh	3.69
72	Bulgaria	3.63
73	Indonesia	3.63
74	Honduras	3.54
75	Nicaragua	3.38
76	Guatemala	3.37
77	Ecuador	3.34
78	Russian Federation	3.33
79	Haiti	3.20*
80	Paraguay	3.20
81	Bolivia	3.08
82	Romania	3.06

2.03 Subsidies for firm-level research and development

For firms conducting research and development (R&D) in your country, direct government subsidies to individual companies or R&D tax credits:

1 = never occur, 7 = are widespread and large

MEAN 3.28

Rank	Country	Value
1	Israel	6.33
2	Singapore	5.36
3	Taiwan	5.19
4	Canada	5.17
5	Ireland	5.00
6	United States	4.83
7	Germany	4.77
8	Malaysia	4.69
9	Finland	4.67
10	Belgium	4.65
11	Tunisia	4.65
12	France	4.58
13	Korea	4.58
14	Australia	4.57
15	Austria	4.39
16	Netherlands	4.36
17	United Kingdom	4.32
18	India	4.29
19	Japan	4.09
20	Hungary	4.07
21	China	4.04
22	Luxembourg	4.02*
23	Spain	3.98
24	Portugal	3.86
25	Italy	3.82
26	Norway	3.81
27	Czech Republic	3.67
27	Denmark	3.67
29	Slovenia	3.59
30	Greece	3.56
31	Thailand	3.43
32	Dominican Republic	3.38
33	Switzerland	3.37
34	Morocco	3.36
35	Sweden	3.31
36	Brazil	3.23
37	Mexico	3.20
38	Iceland	3.14
39	Slovak Republic	3.14
40	Sri Lanka	3.12
41	Namibia	3.03
42	Vietnam	3.02
43	Poland	3.00
43	Trinidad and Tobago	3.00
45	South Africa	2.97
46	Hong Kong SAR	2.89
47	Russian Federation	2.88
48	Chile	2.86
49	Botswana	2.85
50	Colombia	2.84
51	Latvia	2.81
52	Lithuania	2.81
53	Jordan	2.73
54	Ukraine	2.71
55	Costa Rica	2.71
56	Estonia	2.70
57	Mauritius	2.67
58	Nigeria	2.67
59	Croatia	2.66
60	Turkey	2.65
61	New Zealand	2.64
62	Philippines	2.63
63	Romania	2.61
64	Nicaragua	2.42
65	Panama	2.34
66	Bulgaria	2.34
67	Egypt	2.33*
68	Jamaica	2.26
69	Indonesia	2.25
70	Guatemala	2.19
71	Bangladesh	2.19
72	Honduras	2.17
73	Venezuela	2.14
74	Uruguay	2.08
75	Ecuador	2.01
76	Bolivia	2.00
77	El Salvador	1.95
78	Zimbabwe	1.88
79	Peru	1.88
80	Haiti	1.79
81	Argentina	1.68
82	Paraguay	1.53

2.04 Government restrictions on Internet content

Government restrictions to Internet content in your country are:

1 = rigid and strictly enforced by government agencies, 7 = nonexistent

MEAN 5.57

Rank	Country	Value
1	Iceland	6.71
2	Netherlands	6.45
3	Finland	6.44
4	Argentina	6.43
5	Venezuela	6.42
6	Denmark	6.41
7	Hong Kong SAR	6.35
8	Chile	6.24
9	Sweden	6.12
10	Egypt	6.08
11	Indonesia	6.08
12	Estonia	6.07
13	Norway	6.06
14	Mexico	6.06
15	Jordan	6.05
16	Portugal	6.02
17	Hungary	6.00
18	Israel	6.00
19	Jamaica	6.00
20	Spain	6.00
21	Bangladesh	5.97
22	El Salvador	5.96
23	Brazil	5.95
24	Slovenia	5.93
25	United States	5.91
26	Czech Republic	5.91
27	Latvia	5.89
28	Bolivia	5.89
29	Austria	5.89
30	Philippines	5.88
31	Dominican Republic	5.86
32	Belgium	5.86
33	Trinidad and Tobago	5.85
34	Italy	5.84
35	Slovak Republic	5.80
36	South Africa	5.78
37	Ireland	5.78
38	Croatia	5.76*
39	Uruguay	5.76
40	Mauritius	5.75
41	Ukraine	5.71
42	Canada	5.68
43	New Zealand	5.67
44	Nigeria	5.66
44	Greece	5.64
46	Switzerland	5.63
47	Romania	5.60
48	Tunisia	5.60*
49	Turkey	5.56
50	France	5.55
51	Haiti	5.54*
52	Botswana	5.52*
53	Namibia	5.51*
54	Sri Lanka	5.51
55	Luxembourg	5.50
56	Guatemala	5.44
57	Germany	5.43
58	Lithuania	5.41
59	Morocco	5.35*
60	Japan	5.34
61	Poland	5.33
62	Taiwan	5.33
63	United Kingdom	5.33
64	India	5.29
65	Malaysia	5.28
66	Colombia	5.28
67	Zimbabwe	5.24
68	Thailand	5.23
69	Peru	5.20
70	Bulgaria	4.96
71	Russian Federation	4.94
72	Panama	4.94
73	Honduras	4.88
74	Nicaragua	4.84
75	Paraguay	4.71
76	Korea	4.68
77	Australia	4.46
78	Ecuador	4.28
79	Costa Rica	4.26
80	Singapore	4.09
81	China	3.42
82	Vietnam	2.68

2.05 Prevalence of foreign technology licensing

In your country, licensing of foreign technology is:

1 = uncommon, 7 = a common means of acquiring new technology

Rank	Country	Value
1	India	5.92
2	Israel	5.78
3	Thailand	5.65
4	Singapore	5.64
5	Malaysia	5.60
6	South Africa	5.38
7	Taiwan	5.37
8	Korea	5.35
9	Italy	5.35
10	Brazil	5.34
11	Portugal	5.32
12	Belgium	5.24
13	Germany	5.24
14	Hong Kong SAR	5.18
15	Australia	5.18
16	Czech Republic	5.16
17	Ireland	5.11
18	Philippines	5.08
19	Netherlands	5.08
20	Canada	5.06
21	Latvia	5.03
22	Austria	5.03
23	Morocco	5.02
24	Japan	5.01
25	Indonesia	5.00
25	Switzerland	5.00
27	New Zealand	4.96
28	Spain	4.93
29	Venezuela	4.92
30	Slovak Republic	4.89
31	United Kingdom	4.88
32	Greece	4.87
33	Croatia	4.87
34	Nigeria	4.80
35	Hungary	4.79
36	Argentina	4.77
37	Turkey	4.76
38	Mauritius	4.76
39	Dominican Republic	4.74
40	Luxembourg	4.74*
41	Iceland	4.74
42	Panama	4.72
43	Poland	4.72
44	Botswana	4.72
45	Costa Rica	4.70
46	Trinidad and Tobago	4.70
47	Slovenia	4.69
48	Namibia	4.65
49	Denmark	4.65
50	Chile	4.64
51	France	4.63
52	Sweden	4.62
53	Estonia	4.59
53	Tunisia	4.59
55	China	4.57
56	Jamaica	4.55
57	Norway	4.52
58	Mexico	4.48
59	Lithuania	4.46
60	Jordan	4.46
61	Finland	4.45
62	Vietnam	4.44
63	Colombia	4.44
64	United States	4.43
65	Romania	4.38
66	Bangladesh	4.15
67	Sri Lanka	4.15
68	Uruguay	4.13
69	Zimbabwe	4.03
70	Peru	3.95
71	El Salvador	3.83
72	Ecuador	3.72
73	Egypt	3.71*
74	Nicaragua	3.70
75	Honduras	3.46
76	Bulgaria	3.45
77	Russian Federation	3.43
78	Ukraine	3.38
79	Guatemala	3.32
80	Paraguay	3.19
81	Bolivia	2.70
82	Haiti	2.49

MEAN 4.64

Infrastructure Environment

3.01 Overall infrastructure quality

General infrastructure in your country is:

1 = poorly developed and inefficient, 7 = is among the best in the world

Rank	Country	Value
1	Switzerland	6.73
2	Finland	6.67
3	Germany	6.63
4	Singapore	6.62
5	United States	6.60
6	Denmark	6.50
7	Iceland	6.43
8	Canada	6.36
9	Sweden	6.36
10	France	6.34
11	Australia	6.32
12	Austria	6.24
13	Belgium	6.06
14	Hong Kong SAR	5.95
15	Netherlands	5.83
16	Malaysia	5.76
17	Luxembourg	5.54*
18	New Zealand	5.50
19	United Kingdom	5.46
20	Norway	5.42
21	Japan	5.39
22	Korea	5.31
23	Namibia	5.04
24	Taiwan	5.02
25	South Africa	4.95
26	Spain	4.92
27	Sri Lanka	4.89
28	Israel	4.89
29	Czech Republic	4.83
30	Thailand	4.77
31	Tunisia	4.73
32	Jordan	4.71
33	Portugal	4.59
34	Botswana	4.59
35	Mauritius	4.41
36	Italy	4.38
37	Slovenia	4.35
38	Estonia	4.35
39	Trinidad and Tobago	4.34
40	Hungary	4.27
41	Chile	4.17
42	Egypt	4.04*
43	Panama	4.01
44	Zimbabwe	3.97
45	Lithuania	3.85
46	Uruguay	3.83
47	Brazil	3.80
48	Argentina	3.75
48	Slovak Republic	3.75
50	Greece	3.74
51	Turkey	3.71
52	Latvia	3.66
53	Dominican Republic	3.56
54	China	3.41
55	Ireland	3.37
56	Jamaica	3.32
57	Morocco	3.23
58	El Salvador	3.16
59	Russian Federation	3.12
60	Mexico	3.06
61	Bulgaria	3.01
62	Poland	2.89
63	Croatia	2.84
64	India	2.83
65	Guatemala	2.77
66	Indonesia	2.75
67	Colombia	2.72
68	Ukraine	2.67
69	Peru	2.64
70	Venezuela	2.62
71	Honduras	2.56
72	Costa Rica	2.56
73	Vietnam	2.51
74	Romania	2.47
75	Ecuador	2.44
76	Philippines	2.28
77	Bangladesh	2.26
78	Paraguay	2.00
79	Nigeria	1.87
80	Nicaragua	1.84
81	Bolivia	1.83
82	Haiti	1.30

MEAN 4.20

3.02 Local availability of specialized IT services

In your country, specialized information technology services are:

1 = not available in the country, 7 = available from world-class local institutions

Rank	Country	Value
1	United States	6.55
2	Finland	6.44
3	Israel	6.18
4	Sweden	6.08
5	Germany	6.07
6	Australia	6.04
7	United Kingdom	6.00
8	Switzerland	5.98
9	Denmark	5.90
10	France	5.90
11	India	5.83
12	Austria	5.74
13	Ireland	5.73
14	Namibia	5.71*
15	Japan	5.69
16	Spain	5.66
17	Canada	5.65
18	Netherlands	5.64
19	Brazil	5.63
20	Iceland	5.53
21	Slovak Republic	5.50
22	Czech Republic	5.48
23	South Africa	5.43
24	Estonia	5.40
25	Taiwan	5.32
26	Belgium	5.31
27	Norway	5.29
28	Singapore	5.23
29	New Zealand	5.19
30	Hungary	5.12
31	Chile	5.10
32	Hong Kong SAR	5.08
33	Costa Rica	5.07
34	Italy	5.06
35	Latvia	5.00
35	Luxembourg	5.00
37	Poland	4.96
38	Dominican Republic	4.95
39	Uruguay	4.93
40	Argentina	4.89
41	Botswana	4.84*
42	Panama	4.80
43	Croatia	4.79*
44	Peru	4.72
45	Portugal	4.72
46	Korea	4.72
47	Philippines	4.63
48	Lithuania	4.58
49	Slovenia	4.53
50	Jordan	4.53
51	Trinidad and Tobago	4.50
52	Mexico	4.49
53	Tunisia	4.47*
54	Haiti	4.47*
55	Colombia	4.39
56	Russian Federation	4.35
57	El Salvador	4.35
58	Guatemala	4.34
59	China	4.34
60	Bulgaria	4.29
61	Nigeria	4.25
62	Greece	4.24
63	Ecuador	4.23
64	Jamaica	4.23
65	Morocco	4.22*
66	Ukraine	4.20
67	Turkey	4.19
68	Sri Lanka	4.18
69	Honduras	4.13
70	Egypt	4.08
71	Indonesia	4.04
72	Venezuela	4.04
73	Nicaragua	3.99
74	Malaysia	3.92
75	Thailand	3.87
76	Bolivia	3.79
77	Paraguay	3.68
78	Mauritius	3.67
79	Zimbabwe	3.53
80	Vietnam	3.41
81	Romania	2.92
82	Bangladesh	2.84

MEAN 4.85

3.03 Number of telephone mainlines (per 1,000 people)

Telephone mainlines per 1,000 people

Rank	Country	Value	MEAN 297	800
1	Luxembourg	750.00		
2	Switzerland	726.60		
3	Denmark	719.50		
4	Iceland	701.00		
5	United States	699.70		
6	Sweden	682.00		
7	Canada	676.50		
8	Netherlands	617.90		
9	Germany	610.50		
10	United Kingdom	588.50		
11	Japan	585.70		
12	Hong Kong SAR	583.10		
13	France	579.20		
14	Taiwan	573.38 *		
15	Finland	550.20		
16	Norway	532.00		
17	Greece	531.60		
18	Australia	524.60		
19	New Zealand	499.80		
20	Belgium	498.00		
21	Singapore	484.40		
22	Israel	481.80		
23	Italy	473.80		
24	Austria	466.80		
25	Korea	463.60		
26	Portugal	430.30		
27	Spain	421.20		
28	Ireland	419.80		
29	Slovenia	386.30		
30	Czech Republic	377.90		
31	Hungary	372.40		
32	Croatia	364.80		
33	Estonia	363.20		
34	Bulgaria	350.30		
35	Lithuania	321.10		
36	Slovak Republic	314.10		
37	Latvia	303.00		
38	Poland	282.30		
39	Turkey	279.90		
40	Uruguay	278.40		
41	Costa Rica	249.40		
42	Mauritius	235.30		
43	Trinidad and Tobago	231.00		
44	Chile	221.30		
45	Russian Federation	218.20		
46	Argentina	213.10		
47	Malaysia	199.10		
48	Ukraine	198.80		
49	Jamaica	198.60		
50	Brazil	181.70		
51	Romania	174.60		
52	Colombia	169.10		
53	Panama	151.10		
54	Mexico	124.70		
55	South Africa	113.50		
56	China	111.80		
57	Venezuela	107.80		
58	Dominican Republic	104.50		
59	Ecuador	100.00		
60	El Salvador	99.70		
61	Jordan	92.90		
62	Botswana	92.60		
63	Thailand	92.20		
64	Tunisia	89.80		
65	Egypt	86.30		
66	Peru	63.70		
67	Namibia	62.70		
68	Bolivia	60.50		
69	Guatemala	57.00		
70	Morocco	50.20		
71	Paraguay	50.00		
72	Honduras	46.00		
73	Sri Lanka	40.50		
74	Philippines	40.00		
75	India	32.00		
76	Vietnam	31.80		
77	Indonesia	31.40		
78	Nicaragua	31.20		
79	Zimbabwe	18.40		
80	Haiti	8.90		
81	Nigeria	4.30		
82	Bangladesh	3.50		

Source: World Bank, World Development Indicators 2002

3.04 Number of telephone faults (per 100 main lines)

Telephone faults per 100 mainlines

Rank	Country	Value	MEAN 32.15	250
1	Singapore	0.02		
2	Australia	0.11		
3	Netherlands	0.50		
4	Korea	1.05		
5	Israel	1.50*		
5	Spain	1.50		
7	Mexico	1.90		
8	Venezuela	2.00		
9	Taiwan	2.06		
10	Brazil	2.81		
11	Hong Kong SAR	3.88*		
11	Sweden	3.88*		
13	Belgium	4.00		
14	United Kingdom	4.10		
15	Bulgaria	4.80		
16	Canada	4.95*		
16	France	4.95*		
16	Germany	4.95*		
16	Ireland	4.95*		
20	Philippines	5.20		
21	Uruguay	5.60		
22	Austria	6.27		
23	Iceland	6.34*		
24	Egypt	6.87		
25	Luxembourg	7.00		
26	Finland	8.40		
27	Greece	10.00		
28	Portugal	10.50		
29	Sri Lanka	11.00		
30	Croatia	12.90		
31	Japan	13.22*		
32	United States	13.43		
33	Norway	14.00		
34	El Salvador	14.50		
35	Denmark	15.30*		
36	Indonesia	15.96		
37	Italy	16.20		
38	Bolivia	16.25*		
39	Hungary	16.80		
40	Czech Republic	16.99		
41	Peru	17.11		
42	Argentina	17.29		
43	Jordan	18.19		
44	Switzerland	18.47		
45	Estonia	19.24		
46	Guatemala	19.26*		
47	Thailand	19.56		
48	Lithuania	19.80		
49	Slovenia	20.50		
50	China	23.16*		
51	Honduras	24.00		
52	Paraguay	24.80*		
53	Morocco	24.80		
54	Chile	25.00		
55	Poland	26.00		
56	Slovak Republic	27.04		
57	Latvia	28.70		
58	Dominican Republic	28.71*		
59	Namibia	30.40*		
60	New Zealand	30.70		
61	Ukraine	34.47		
62	Russian Federation	35.21		
63	Romania	35.70		
64	Botswana	37.20		
65	Malaysia	40.00		
66	South Africa	40.90		
67	Tunisia	43.00		
68	Ecuador	48.00		
68	Jamaica	48.00		
68	Panama	48.00		
71	Turkey	55.37		
72	Mauritius	56.42		
73	Colombia	59.90		
74	Costa Rica	65.10		
75	Trinidad and Tobago	75.00		
76	Nicaragua	79.30		
77	Haiti	141.65*		
78	Nigeria	143.45*		
79	Vietnam	173.98*		
80	India	186.00		
81	Bangladesh	207.60		
82	Zimbabwe	223.00		

Source: International Telecommunications Union Database, 2002

3.05 Number of telephone mainlines per employee
Telephone mainlines per employee

Rank	Country	Value	
			MEAN 168.58 / 500
1	Japan	461.72	
2	Spain	415.14	
3	Argentina	405.50	
4	Luxembourg	372.72	
5	Italy	358.13	
6	New Zealand	357.67	
7	Taiwan	323.97*	
8	Korea	315.67	
9	Greece	288.66	
10	Peru	258.24	
11	Turkey	253.96	
12	Israel	252.99	
13	Chile	242.80	
14	Canada	239.02	
15	Portugal	234.40	
16	Philippines	230.33	
17	Belgium	222.56	
18	Singapore	222.10	
19	Costa Rica	213.25	
20	Switzerland	211.07	
21	Sweden	210.87	
22	Germany	210.12	
23	Slovenia	207.29	
24	Austria	206.51	
25	Dominican Republic	202.36	
26	France	200.00	
27	Lithuania	196.56	
28	Malaysia	186.90	
29	Hungary	182.15	
30	Ecuador	181.15	
31	Denmark	179.79	
32	Indonesia	176.63	
33	Jamaica	174.61	
34	United States	172.16	
35	Estonia	171.55	
36	Latvia	169.94	
37	United Kingdom	169.91	
38	Australia	169.66	
39	Netherlands	168.86	
40	Thailand	168.82	
41	Uruguay	168.79	
42	Czech Republic	164.31	
43	China	158.68	
44	Poland	158.57	
45	Brazil	157.22	
46	Mauritius	152.80	
47	Colombia	151.09	
48	Croatia	150.64	
49	El Salvador	147.75	
50	Iceland	142.84	
51	Venezuela	136.61	
52	Mexico	133.39	
53	Tunisia	129.35	
54	Guatemala	127.63	
55	Finland	117.73	
56	South Africa	113.31	
57	Slovak Republic	112.35	
58	Bulgaria	111.51	
59	Norway	103.75	
60	Jordan	103.28	
61	Bolivia	102.88	
62	Hong Kong SAR	101.63	
63	Egypt	99.74	
64	Trinidad and Tobago	98.32	
65	Morocco	98.08	
66	Romania	92.15	
67	Ireland	91.10	
68	Ukraine	79.74	
69	Panama	78.00	
70	Russian Federation	74.96	
71	Botswana	70.54	
72	Namibia	66.07	
73	Nicaragua	64.77	
74	Sri Lanka	64.49	
75	India	62.77	
76	Zimbabwe	53.83	
77	Honduras	49.72	
78	Paraguay	45.54	
79	Nigeria	35.52	
80	Bangladesh	29.88	
81	Haiti	19.87	
82	Vietnam	16.73	

Source: World Bank, World Development Indicators 2002

3.06 Number of fax machines (per 1,000 people)
Fax machines per 1,000 people

Rank	Country	Value	
			MEAN 15.77 / 150
1	Japan	126.87	
2	Germany	79.11	
3	United States	78.39	
4	Luxembourg	68.85	
5	Hong Kong SAR	58.51	
6	Sweden	50.88	
7	Norway	49.80	
8	Australia	48.59	
9	France	48.10	
10	Denmark	47.93	
11	Iceland	47.55*	
12	Finland	38.47	
13	Netherlands	38.33	
14	Canada	35.71	
15	Austria	35.42	
16	United Kingdom	33.84	
17	Italy	31.38	
18	Switzerland	29.23	
19	Ireland	27.32	
20	Singapore	25.87	
20	Mauritius	25.87	
22	Israel	24.92	
23	Taiwan	24.08*	
24	Belgium	18.70	
25	New Zealand	17.90	
26	Spain	17.83	
27	Hungary	17.66	
28	Croatia	11.19	
29	Slovenia	10.44	
30	Slovak Republic	10.01	
31	Czech Republic	9.94	
32	Korea	8.87	
33	Estonia	8.76	
34	Jordan	8.42	
35	Malaysia	8.05	
36	Portugal	7.03	
37	Colombia	4.32	
38	Trinidad and Tobago	3.91	
39	Greece	3.82	
40	South Africa	3.64	
41	Uruguay	3.45	
42	Tunisia	3.36	
43	Brazil	3.13	
44	Venezuela	3.05	
45	Mexico	2.99	
46	Namibia	2.94*	
47	Chile	2.74	
48	Thailand	2.55	
49	Argentina	2.41	
50	Costa Rica	2.35	
51	Botswana	2.33	
52	Panama	2.11*	
53	Bulgaria	1.78	
54	Turkey	1.72	
55	Lithuania	1.67	
56	China	1.60	
57	Poland	1.43	
58	Indonesia	0.92	
59	Romania	0.91	
60	Philippines	0.73	
61	Morocco	0.65	
62	Peru	0.64	
63	Egypt	0.55	
64	Vietnam	0.39	
65	Zimbabwe	0.38	
66	Russian Federation	0.36	
67	Latvia	0.35	
68	Dominican Republic	0.29	
69	India	0.16	
70	Bangladesh	0.03	
71	Ukraine	0.00	
72	Bolivia	0.00*	
72	Ecuador	0.00*	
72	El Salvador	0.00*	
72	Guatemala	0.00*	
72	Haiti	0.00*	
72	Honduras	0.00*	
72	Jamaica	0.00*	
72	Nicaragua	0.00*	
72	Nigeria	0.00*	
72	Paraguay	0.00*	
72	Sri Lanka	0.00*	

Source: International Telecommunications Union Database, 2002

3.07 Local switch capacity (per 100,000 people)

Local switch capacity per 100,000 people

Rank	Country	Value	MEAN 49.79	400
1	Iceland	398.88*		
2	Luxembourg	235.89*		
3	Norway	125.43*		
4	Ireland	118.06*		
5	Trinidad and Tobago	115.30*		
6	Finland	113.60*		
7	Mauritius	103.58*		
8	Denmark	99.07*		
9	Estonia	96.77*		
10	Slovenia	85.89*		
11	Sweden	76.94*		
12	United Kingdom	76.81		
13	United States	76.63		
14	Netherlands	76.31		
15	Botswana	75.80*		
16	Hong Kong SAR	73.22		
17	Germany	72.44		
18	Latvia	71.25*		
19	Croatia	70.88*		
20	Australia	68.66*		
21	Switzerland	68.44		
22	Namibia	68.28*		
23	France	64.91		
24	Taiwan	64.52		
25	Israel	64.03		
26	Canada	62.30*		
27	Belgium	60.96		
28	Korea	56.27		
29	Singapore	55.44		
30	Jamaica	55.41*		
31	Italy	53.25		
32	Lithuania	52.84*		
33	Japan	52.72		
34	New Zealand	52.65*		
35	Spain	50.02		
36	Austria	49.76		
37	Czech Republic	48.55		
38	Hungary	48.51		
39	Jordan	44.75*		
40	Greece	44.57*		
41	Portugal	42.96		
42	Slovak Republic	40.30		
43	Bulgaria	39.92		
44	Turkey	39.87		
45	Uruguay	35.01		
46	Poland	34.68		
47	Costa Rica	27.50		
48	Chile	27.12		
49	Brazil	25.31		
50	Argentina	25.15		
51	Tunisia	24.98*		
52	Haiti	22.43*		
53	Malaysia	22.38		
54	Russian Federation	22.25		
55	Romania	20.28		
56	Dominican Republic	19.61*		
57	Colombia	19.52		
58	China	18.02		
59	Panama	17.78		
60	Egypt	17.29		
61	Sri Lanka	16.78*		
62	South Africa	16.18		
63	Mexico	15.90		
64	Ecuador	13.58		
65	Zimbabwe	13.40*		
66	El Salvador	12.69		
67	Venezuela	12.20		
68	Thailand	10.93		
69	Guatemala	9.99		
70	Peru	8.32		
71	Bolivia	8.23		
72	Ukraine	7.66		
73	Paraguay	6.26		
74	Honduras	5.57		
75	Morocco	5.42		
76	Vietnam	5.21		
77	Philippines	4.64		
78	India	3.83		
79	Bangladesh	3.79*		
80	Indonesia	3.75		
81	Nicaragua	3.75		
82	Nigeria	2.53*		

Source: Pyramid

3.08 Ease of obtaining new telephone lines

New telephone lines for your business are:

1 = scarce and difficult to obtain, 7 = widely available and highly reliable

Rank	Country	Value	1	MEAN 5.49	7
1	Finland	6.97			
2	Iceland	6.96			
3	Denmark	6.90			
4	Hong Kong SAR	6.89			
5	Switzerland	6.88			
6	Singapore	6.81			
7	Germany	6.78			
8	United States	6.76			
9	Israel	6.75			
10	Luxembourg	6.74*			
11	Canada	6.73			
12	New Zealand	6.72			
13	Sweden	6.71			
14	Japan	6.69			
15	Chile	6.69			
16	Austria	6.68			
17	Netherlands	6.66			
18	France	6.66			
19	United Kingdom	6.65			
20	Norway	6.64			
21	Australia	6.57			
22	Taiwan	6.45			
23	Uruguay	6.44			
24	Belgium	6.44			
25	Korea	6.43			
26	Hungary	6.37			
27	Ireland	6.26			
28	Czech Republic	6.24			
29	Thailand	6.23			
30	El Salvador	6.22			
31	Croatia	6.21			
32	Estonia	6.19			
33	Portugal	6.18			
34	Slovenia	6.18			
35	Morocco	6.12			
36	Spain	6.03			
37	Brazil	6.03			
38	Greece	6.00			
38	Slovak Republic	6.00			
40	Malaysia	5.96			
41	Jordan	5.93			
42	Peru	5.90			
43	Italy	5.86			
44	Argentina	5.84			
45	Panama	5.73			
46	Latvia	5.72			
47	Lithuania	5.72			
48	India	5.58			
49	Dominican Republic	5.54			
50	China	5.53			
51	Colombia	5.48			
52	Tunisia	5.48			
53	Sri Lanka	5.42			
54	Venezuela	5.31			
55	Mauritius	5.24			
56	Turkey	5.18			
57	Namibia	5.13			
58	Poland	5.11			
59	South Africa	5.07			
60	Mexico	5.02			
61	Vietnam	4.76			
62	Trinidad and Tobago	4.75			
63	Guatemala	4.74			
64	Jamaica	4.73			
65	Bolivia	4.65			
66	Botswana	4.63			
67	Bulgaria	4.53			
68	Indonesia	4.50			
69	Russian Federation	4.46			
70	Romania	4.44			
71	Philippines	4.39			
72	Egypt	4.30*			
73	Ukraine	3.72			
74	Paraguay	3.17			
75	Nigeria	3.07			
76	Zimbabwe	2.86			
77	Ecuador	2.82			
78	Costa Rica	2.70			
79	Nicaragua	2.30			
80	Bangladesh	1.83			
81	Haiti	1.80			
82	Honduras	1.57			

3.09 Waiting time for telephone mainlines (in years)

Telephone mainline waiting time in years

Rank	Country	Value	
			MEAN 1.54 · · · · · · · · · · · 10
1	Australia	0.00	
1	Austria	0.00	
1	Canada	0.00	
1	Denmark	0.00	
1	Finland	0.00	
1	France	0.00	
1	Germany	0.00	
1	Hong Kong SAR	0.00	
1	Iceland	0.00	
1	Italy	0.00	
1	Japan	0.00	
1	Korea	0.00	
1	Luxembourg	0.00	
1	Netherlands	0.00	
1	New Zealand	0.00	
1	Norway	0.00	
1	Singapore	0.00	
1	Sweden	0.00	
1	Switzerland	0.00	
1	United Kingdom	0.00	
1	United States	0.00	
1	Uruguay	0.00	
23	Spain	0.01	
24	Belgium	0.02	
25	Ireland	0.02*	
26	Chile	0.04	
27	China	0.05	
28	Slovenia	0.08	
29	Hungary	0.12	
30	Morocco	0.12	
31	Mexico	0.13	
32	Taiwan	0.15*	
33	Czech Republic	0.16	
34	Argentina	0.17	
35	Greece	0.19	
36	Bolivia	0.19	
37	Portugal	0.25	
38	Israel	0.25	
39	Jordan	0.25	
40	Costa Rica	0.33	
41	Turkey	0.47	
42	Brazil	0.52	
43	Trinidad and Tobago	0.54	
44	Botswana	0.55	
45	Paraguay	0.66	
46	Slovak Republic	0.68	
47	Namibia	0.70	
48	Malaysia	0.73	
49	Ecuador	0.75	
50	India	0.75	
51	Poland	0.81	
52	Croatia	0.88	
53	Lithuania	0.94	
54	Tunisia	0.95	
55	Mauritius	0.98	
56	South Africa	1.10	
57	Peru	1.25	
58	Panama	1.35	
59	Estonia	1.36	
60	Nigeria	1.37	
61	Dominican Republic	1.53*	
62	Guatemala	1.62	
63	Thailand	1.63	
64	Sri Lanka	1.90	
65	Egypt	1.92	
66	Colombia	1.96	
67	Venezuela	2.50	
68	Philippines	2.79	
69	Latvia	3.25	
70	Bangladesh	3.29	
71	Bulgaria	3.62	
72	Romania	3.83	
73	El Salvador	3.95	
74	Russian Federation	5.13	
75	Vietnam	5.78*	
76	Jamaica	6.53	
77	Honduras	7.82	
78	Ukraine	7.91	
79	Nicaragua	9.10	
80	Haiti	10.00	
80	Indonesia	10.00*	
80	Zimbabwe	10.00	

Source: World Bank, World Development Indicators 2002

3.10 Number of secure Internet servers

Secure Internet servers per 1,000,000 people

Rank	Country	Value	
			MEAN 30.69 · · · · · · · · · 300
1	Iceland	274.02	
2	United States	260.65	
3	Australia	167.19	
4	Canada	147.32	
5	New Zealand	140.70	
6	Singapore	120.21	
7	Luxembourg	118.61	
8	Sweden	105.31	
9	United Kingdom	89.96	
10	Finland	79.97	
11	Ireland	76.44	
12	Switzerland	74.33*	
13	Norway	70.81	
14	Hong Kong SAR	69.88	
15	Austria	68.31	
16	Denmark	62.22	
17	Germany	54.06	
18	Estonia	51.13	
19	Slovenia	49.30	
20	Netherlands	43.66	
21	Taiwan	39.69*	
22	Japan	32.62	
23	Belgium	30.24	
24	France	24.55	
25	Czech Republic	22.58	
26	Spain	21.72	
27	Italy	16.29	
28	Latvia	13.91	
29	Portugal	13.09	
30	Costa Rica	12.60	
31	South Africa	10.98	
32	Slovak Republic	10.92	
33	Lithuania	10.55	
34	Croatia	10.05	
35	Greece	10.04	
36	Hungary	9.98	
37	Uruguay	9.59	
38	Mauritius	9.27	
39	Panama	8.75	
40	Chile	7.36	
41	Korea	6.62	
42	Poland	6.49	
43	Trinidad and Tobago	6.15	
44	Argentina	5.91	
45	Malaysia	5.50	
46	Brazil	5.42	
47	Venezuela	3.56	
48	Turkey	2.62	
49	Bulgaria	2.33	
50	Mexico	2.23	
51	Jamaica	1.90	
52	Romania	1.78	
53	Thailand	1.70	
54	Russian Federation	1.66	
55	El Salvador	1.43	
56	Colombia	1.28	
57	Namibia	1.14	
58	Peru	1.01	
59	Dominican Republic	0.96	
60	Paraguay	0.91	
61	Guatemala	0.88	
62	Nicaragua	0.79	
63	Philippines	0.78	
64	Ukraine	0.75	
65	Ecuador	0.71	
66	Honduras	0.62	
67	Bolivia	0.60	
68	Tunisia	0.42	
69	Jordan	0.41	
70	Sri Lanka	0.26	
71	Indonesia	0.26	
72	Egypt	0.19	
73	Morocco	0.14	
74	China	0.14	
75	Haiti	0.13	
76	India	0.08	
77	Vietnam	0.05	
78	Nigeria	0.01	
79	Bangladesh	0.01	
80	Botswana	0.00*	
80	Israel	0.00*	
80	Zimbabwe	0.00*	

Source: World Bank, World Development Indicators 2002

Individual Readiness

4.01 Sophistication of local buyers' products and processes

Buyers in your country are:

1 = slow to adopt new products and processes,
7 = actively seeking the latest products, technologies, and processes

Rank	Country	Value
1	Iceland	6.22
2	United States	6.11
3	Finland	6.00
4	United Kingdom	6.00
5	Japan	5.96
6	Australia	5.85
7	Sweden	5.79
8	Hong Kong SAR	5.78
9	Taiwan	5.76
10	New Zealand	5.65
11	Canada	5.64
12	Singapore	5.62
13	Korea	5.52
14	Israel	5.44
15	Denmark	5.42
16	France	5.36
17	Netherlands	5.34
18	Belgium	5.29
19	Ireland	5.26
20	Norway	5.25
21	Thailand	5.21
22	Austria	5.18
23	Germany	5.18
24	Czech Republic	5.16
25	Estonia	5.12
26	Hungary	5.07
27	Switzerland	5.03
28	Brazil	5.03
29	Malaysia	5.02
30	India	4.96
31	Spain	4.94
32	Slovenia	4.93
33	Luxembourg	4.88*
34	Turkey	4.88
35	Italy	4.81
36	Tunisia	4.74
37	Dominican Republic	4.67
38	Chile	4.67
39	Trinidad and Tobago	4.67
40	Vietnam	4.58
41	Costa Rica	4.57
42	Morocco	4.53
43	Jamaica	4.53
44	Panama	4.52
45	Slovak Republic	4.46
46	Portugal	4.45
47	Argentina	4.42
48	Latvia	4.42
49	South Africa	4.33
50	Poland	4.31
51	Lithuania	4.20
52	Mauritius	4.16
53	Greece	4.15
54	Croatia	4.15
55	Nigeria	4.13
56	Mexico	4.11
57	Philippines	4.09
58	Russian Federation	4.07
59	Indonesia	4.06
60	Sri Lanka	4.03
61	Egypt	4.03*
62	China	4.01
63	Venezuela	3.96
64	Namibia	3.93
65	Botswana	3.91
66	Jordan	3.78
67	El Salvador	3.72
68	Bangladesh	3.64
69	Zimbabwe	3.61
70	Colombia	3.60
71	Bulgaria	3.60
72	Ukraine	3.55
73	Romania	3.47
74	Peru	3.41
75	Paraguay	3.31
76	Uruguay	3.30
77	Ecuador	2.93
78	Haiti	2.91
79	Nicaragua	2.84
80	Guatemala	2.82
81	Honduras	2.80
82	Bolivia	2.60

MEAN 4.55

4.02 Availability of mobile Internet access

Mobile Internet access:

1 = is not available, 7 = is widely used

Rank	Country	Value
1	Finland	5.94
2	Japan	5.71
3	Norway	5.70
4	Sweden	5.54
5	Canada	5.22
6	United Kingdom	5.06
7	Austria	4.85
8	Iceland	4.85
9	Denmark	4.81
10	Korea	4.78
11	Netherlands	4.73
12	Singapore	4.72
13	Czech Republic	4.67
14	Australia	4.65
15	Germany	4.52
16	Switzerland	4.50
17	United States	4.47
18	Italy	4.42
19	New Zealand	4.42
20	Belgium	4.42
21	Estonia	4.34
22	Hong Kong SAR	4.31
23	Poland	4.22
24	Ireland	4.21
25	Slovak Republic	4.20
26	France	4.19
27	Panama	4.18
28	Turkey	4.13
29	Portugal	4.00
30	Hungary	3.89
31	Brazil	3.86
32	South Africa	3.86
33	Spain	3.84
34	Slovenia	3.82
35	El Salvador	3.80
36	Venezuela	3.69
37	Ecuador	3.67
38	Israel	3.65
39	Chile	3.59
40	Latvia	3.57
41	Uruguay	3.53
42	Greece	3.53
43	Thailand	3.52
44	Botswana	3.50*
45	Sri Lanka	3.46
46	Philippines	3.46
47	Argentina	3.45
48	Malaysia	3.43
49	Mexico	3.43
50	Morocco	3.38*
51	Croatia	3.32*
52	Guatemala	3.29
53	Dominican Republic	3.29
54	Tunisia	3.25*
55	Taiwan	3.21
56	Egypt	3.17
57	Jordan	3.08
58	Namibia	3.04*
59	Colombia	3.03
60	Bolivia	3.00
61	Indonesia	2.96
62	India	2.92
63	Ukraine	2.91
64	Haiti	2.88*
65	Peru	2.80
66	Lithuania	2.79
67	Zimbabwe	2.76
68	Luxembourg	2.67
69	Russian Federation	2.62
70	Honduras	2.56
71	Bulgaria	2.54
72	China	2.50
73	Nicaragua	2.48
74	Paraguay	2.27
75	Mauritius	2.07
76	Costa Rica	2.04
77	Vietnam	2.03
78	Nigeria	1.93
79	Jamaica	1.90
80	Romania	1.88
81	Bangladesh	1.77
82	Trinidad and Tobago	1.41

MEAN 3.61

4.03 Availability of broadband access

Broadband Internet in your country (e.g., through DSL or cable modem):

1 = is not available, 7 = is widely used

Rank	Country	Value		MEAN 4.07	
1	Finland	6.35			
2	Canada	5.97			
3	Korea	5.93			
4	Singapore	5.83			
5	United States	5.72			
6	Sweden	5.56			
7	Belgium	5.46			
8	Austria	5.39			
9	Germany	5.38			
10	Hong Kong SAR	5.31			
11	Iceland	5.30			
12	United Kingdom	5.28			
13	Netherlands	5.27			
14	Denmark	5.23			
15	Panama	5.12			
16	Estonia	4.98			
17	Australia	4.96			
18	Switzerland	4.95			
19	New Zealand	4.90			
20	Slovak Republic	4.80			
21	France	4.76			
22	Chile	4.52			
23	Spain	4.52			
24	El Salvador	4.49			
25	Romania	4.39			
26	Norway	4.34			
27	Luxembourg	4.33			
28	Argentina	4.32			
28	Czech Republic	4.32			
30	Italy	4.32			
31	Venezuela	4.31			
32	Latvia	4.25			
33	Hungary	4.21			
34	Mexico	4.16			
35	Brazil	4.14			
36	Turkey	4.13			
37	Costa Rica	4.11			
38	Guatemala	4.10			
39	Taiwan	4.03			
40	Dominican Republic	4.02			
41	Botswana	4.00*			
42	Nicaragua	4.00			
42	Peru	4.00			
44	Tunisia	3.99*			
45	Portugal	3.98			
46	Slovenia	3.97			
47	Poland	3.96			
48	Colombia	3.94			
49	Namibia	3.90*			
50	Croatia	3.89*			
51	Ireland	3.88			
52	Thailand	3.86			
53	Israel	3.77			
54	South Africa	3.65			
55	Ecuador	3.64			
56	Philippines	3.63			
57	Jordan	3.61			
58	Ukraine	3.56			
59	Honduras	3.51			
60	Greece	3.49			
61	Indonesia	3.43			
62	Malaysia	3.42			
63	Morocco	3.39*			
64	Egypt	3.30			
65	Japan	3.29			
66	Lithuania	3.22			
67	India	3.17			
68	Haiti	3.16*			
69	Nigeria	3.12			
70	Sri Lanka	2.96			
71	Bulgaria	2.93			
72	China	2.92			
73	Bolivia	2.90			
74	Zimbabwe	2.88			
75	Russian Federation	2.73			
76	Vietnam	2.71			
77	Uruguay	2.68			
78	Paraguay	2.53			
79	Jamaica	2.53			
80	Trinidad and Tobago	2.31			
81	Bangladesh	2.22			
82	Mauritius	2.20			

4.04 Public access to the Internet

Public access to the Internet (through telecenters, libraries, post offices, etc.) is:

1 = very limited, 7 = pervasive, most people have frequent Internet access

Rank	Country	Value		MEAN 3.82	
1	Iceland	6.38			
2	Finland	6.33			
3	Denmark	5.97			
4	Norway	5.83			
5	Sweden	5.77			
6	Singapore	5.68			
7	Korea	5.52			
8	Canada	5.43			
9	Netherlands	5.36			
10	United States	5.36			
11	Estonia	5.30			
12	Australia	5.27			
13	Peru	5.24			
14	New Zealand	5.23			
15	United Kingdom	5.00			
16	Argentina	4.87			
17	Belgium	4.79			
18	Hong Kong SAR	4.76			
19	Switzerland	4.73			
20	Austria	4.71			
21	Germany	4.67			
22	Taiwan	4.36			
23	Costa Rica	4.25			
24	Bolivia	4.20			
25	Spain	4.14			
26	Japan	4.08			
27	Czech Republic	4.03			
28	Portugal	3.98			
29	India	3.96			
30	Turkey	3.94			
31	Ireland	3.93			
32	Israel	3.91			
33	France	3.91			
34	Hungary	3.74			
35	Tunisia	3.70*			
36	Slovenia	3.70			
37	Bulgaria	3.67			
38	Colombia	3.63			
39	Paraguay	3.60			
40	Botswana	3.60*			
41	Panama	3.55			
42	Uruguay	3.55			
43	El Salvador	3.53			
44	Jordan	3.47			
45	Malaysia	3.44			
46	Chile	3.44			
47	Croatia	3.43*			
48	Morocco	3.42*			
49	Italy	3.42			
50	Indonesia	3.42			
51	Thailand	3.41			
52	Slovak Republic	3.40			
53	Namibia	3.35*			
54	Latvia	3.32			
55	Trinidad and Tobago	3.30			
56	Ecuador	3.27			
57	Lithuania	3.25			
58	Haiti	3.20*			
59	Egypt	3.17			
60	Venezuela	3.12			
61	Brazil	3.11			
61	Poland	3.11			
63	South Africa	3.09			
64	Mexico	3.00			
65	Mauritius	2.94			
66	Guatemala	2.93			
67	Dominican Republic	2.91			
68	Luxembourg	2.83			
69	China	2.83			
70	Philippines	2.80			
71	Sri Lanka	2.80			
72	Nicaragua	2.78			
73	Greece	2.71			
74	Jamaica	2.69			
75	Ukraine	2.60			
76	Vietnam	2.59			
77	Russian Federation	2.56			
78	Romania	2.44			
79	Honduras	2.32			
80	Zimbabwe	2.24			
81	Nigeria	2.18			
82	Bangladesh	1.80			

4.05 Secondary school enrollment (% net)

Net enrollment ratio is the ratio of the number of children of official school age who are enrolled in school to the population of the corresponding official school age

MEAN 68.80 | 100

Rank	Country	Value
1	Sweden	99.54
2	Korea	96.94
3	Norway	96.39
4	Finland	94.85
5	France	94.22
6	United Kingdom	93.71
7	Canada	93.67
8	Malaysia	92.89
9	Netherlands	92.61
10	Spain	91.56
11	Singapore	90.56*
12	Hong Kong SAR	90.45*
13	New Zealand	90.28
14	United States	90.20
15	Slovenia	89.48
16	Denmark	89.48
17	Taiwan	88.97*
18	Australia	88.86
19	Italy	88.29
20	Austria	88.18
21	Belgium	87.95
22	Germany	87.83
23	Portugal	87.65
24	Greece	86.39
25	Iceland	85.41
26	Lithuania	85.38
27	Japan	85.36*
28	Hungary	84.83
29	Israel	84.59
30	Latvia	83.19
31	Switzerland	83.09
32	Bulgaria	80.79
33	Czech Republic	79.19
34	Croatia	79.03
35	Jamaica	78.95
36	Estonia	77.45
37	Ireland	77.00
38	Romania	75.53
39	Argentina	73.66
40	Trinidad and Tobago	72.47
41	Chile	70.30
42	Panama	68.56*
43	Luxembourg	67.59
44	Egypt	67.45
45	Poland	67.01*
46	Uruguay	65.57
47	Brazil	65.07*
47	Russian Federation	65.07*
49	Mauritius	62.87
50	Peru	61.49
51	Guatemala	59.72*
52	Jordan	59.52
53	Philippines	58.84
54	Slovak Republic	57.55*
55	Botswana	56.72
56	Mexico	56.06
57	South Africa	55.90
58	Thailand	55.23
59	Tunisia	54.81
60	Bolivia	54.55*
61	Dominican Republic	52.75
62	Morocco	52.39*
63	Turkey	51.30
64	China	50.27
65	Honduras	50.27*
65	Sri Lanka	50.27*
67	Vietnam	48.82
68	Ecuador	45.94
69	Colombia	45.63
70	Ukraine	45.14*
71	Indonesia	43.82*
72	Paraguay	42.05
73	Costa Rica	40.97
74	Bangladesh	40.73*
75	Zimbabwe	40.10*
76	Haiti	38.82*
77	India	38.82
78	El Salvador	37.48
79	Nicaragua	32.65
80	Nigeria	32.65*
81	Namibia	31.42
82	Venezuela	22.31

Source: World Bank, World Development Indicators 2002

4.06 Total adult illiteracy rate (%)

Illiteracy rate as a percentage of people ages 15 and older

MEAN 9.95 | 60

Rank	Country	Value
1	Australia	0.00
1	Denmark	0.00
1	Estonia	0.00
1	Finland	0.00
1	Luxembourg	0.00
1	Norway	0.00
7	Czech Republic	0.10
7	Iceland	0.10
9	Latvia	0.20
10	Poland	0.27
11	Slovenia	0.36
12	Ukraine	0.39
13	Lithuania	0.44
14	Russian Federation	0.45
15	Hungary	0.68
16	France	1.00
16	Germany	1.00
16	Japan	1.00
16	Netherlands	1.00
16	New Zealand	1.00
16	Sweden	1.00
16	Switzerland	1.00
16	United Kingdom	1.00
24	Italy	1.57
25	Bulgaria	1.58
26	Croatia	1.72
27	Romania	1.88
28	Austria	2.00
28	Belgium	2.00
28	Ireland	2.00
31	Korea	2.24
32	Uruguay	2.26
33	Spain	2.36
34	Greece	2.80
35	Canada	3.00
35	United States	3.00
37	Argentina	3.17
38	Chile	4.19
39	Costa Rica	4.41
40	Thailand	4.50
41	Philippines	4.71
42	Israel	5.43
43	Taiwan	6.00
44	Trinidad and Tobago	6.23
45	Hong Kong SAR	6.45
46	Vietnam	6.61
47	Paraguay	6.72
48	Venezuela	7.42
49	Singapore	7.68
50	Portugal	7.78
51	Panama	8.11
52	Colombia	8.30
53	Sri Lanka	8.36
54	Ecuador	8.39
55	Mexico	8.59
56	Peru	10.11
57	Jordan	10.33
58	Zimbabwe	11.32
59	Slovak Republic	11.54*
60	Malaysia	12.55
61	Jamaica	13.13
62	Indonesia	13.14
63	Bolivia	14.49
64	South Africa	14.74
65	Brazil	14.76
66	Turkey	14.93
67	Mauritius	15.47
68	China	15.88
69	Dominican Republic	16.37
70	Namibia	18.02
71	El Salvador	21.26
72	Botswana	22.76
73	Honduras	25.39
74	Tunisia	28.98
75	Guatemala	31.36
76	Nicaragua	33.47
77	Nigeria	36.08
78	India	42.76
79	Egypt	44.68
80	Haiti	50.18
81	Morocco	51.13
82	Bangladesh	58.65

Source: World Bank, World Development Indicators 2002

4.07 Quality of math and science education

Math and science education in your country's schools:

1 = lag far behind most other countries, 7 = are among the best in the world

Rank	Country	Value
1	Singapore	6.38
2	Czech Republic	6.00
3	Austria	5.94
4	Belgium	5.94
5	Slovak Republic	5.92
6	Tunisia	5.87
7	Taiwan	5.86
8	Switzerland	5.84
9	Romania	5.81
10	Hungary	5.80
10	Israel	5.80
12	Finland	5.79
13	Hong Kong SAR	5.63
14	France	5.61
15	Australia	5.61
16	Estonia	5.58
17	Iceland	5.57
18	Slovenia	5.56
19	Netherlands	5.48
20	Canada	5.47
21	Lithuania	5.15
22	Russian Federation	5.13
23	Bulgaria	5.11
24	Ireland	5.11
25	Latvia	5.11
26	Korea	5.11
27	Japan	5.07
28	Luxembourg	4.97*
29	United Kingdom	4.92
30	Croatia	4.91
31	Poland	4.87
32	Sweden	4.79
33	Italy	4.78
34	New Zealand	4.78
35	Jordan	4.77
36	Malaysia	4.76
37	India	4.75
38	Denmark	4.68
39	United States	4.67
40	Trinidad and Tobago	4.62
41	Spain	4.61
42	Thailand	4.55
43	Greece	4.55
44	Morocco	4.55
45	Ukraine	4.49
46	Costa Rica	4.41
47	Turkey	4.35
48	Germany	4.34
49	Norway	4.30
50	Sri Lanka	4.29
51	Vietnam	4.12
52	Egypt	4.12*
53	Uruguay	4.11
54	China	4.10
55	Mauritius	4.08
56	Zimbabwe	3.89
57	Botswana	3.85
58	Argentina	3.78
59	Chile	3.71
60	Brazil	3.59
61	Colombia	3.57
62	Portugal	3.50
63	Indonesia	3.47
64	Panama	3.40
65	Jamaica	3.37
66	Nigeria	3.33
67	Namibia	3.28
68	Ecuador	3.17
69	Nicaragua	3.13
70	Bangladesh	3.00
71	Dominican Republic	2.98
72	Bolivia	2.94
73	South Africa	2.93
74	El Salvador	2.89
75	Venezuela	2.88
76	Philippines	2.86
77	Mexico	2.84
78	Peru	2.83
79	Paraguay	2.46
80	Honduras	2.41
81	Guatemala	2.39
82	Haiti	2.21

MEAN 4.43

4.08 Cost of local call (US$ per 3 min)

Cost of three minute local call weighted against GDP

Rank	Country	Value
1	Hong Kong SAR	0.00
1	New Zealand	0.00
1	Philippines	0.00
1	United States	0.00
5	Bulgaria	0.38
6	Israel	0.85
7	Singapore	1.05
8	Ukraine	1.27
9	Russian Federation	1.94
10	Luxembourg	2.27
11	Korea	2.29
12	Costa Rica	2.44
13	Malaysia	2.61
14	Slovenia	2.68
15	Japan	2.95
16	Botswana	3.00
17	Taiwan	3.11
18	Iceland	3.31
19	Spain	3.68
20	Mauritius	3.80
21	Croatia	3.89
22	Denmark	3.90
23	Germany	3.93
24	Tunisia	3.96
25	Egypt	3.96
26	Trinidad and Tobago	4.07
27	Switzerland	4.13
28	France	4.27
29	Norway	4.37
30	Greece	4.48
31	Canada	4.50*
32	Brazil	4.73
33	Finland	4.88
34	Australia	4.98
35	Belgium	5.02
36	Netherlands	5.27
37	Italy	5.30
38	Sweden	5.40
39	Ireland	5.72
40	Austria	5.79
41	Colombia	6.08
42	Portugal	6.35
43	Indonesia	6.67
44	Namibia	6.72
45	India	7.55
46	Argentina	7.58
47	United Kingdom	7.64
48	Hungary	7.71
49	Estonia	8.08
50	Dominican Republic	8.40*
51	Poland	8.89
52	Lithuania	9.50
53	Slovak Republic	9.58
54	Czech Republic	9.63
55	South Africa	9.66
56	Panama	10.00
57	Jordan	10.65
58	Thailand	11.68
59	Sri Lanka	12.14
60	China	12.31*
61	Vietnam	12.73
62	Chile	12.77
63	El Salvador	13.71
64	Paraguay	14.39
65	Peru	14.51
66	Mexico	16.28
67	Latvia	16.29
68	Jamaica	16.49
69	Turkey	17.06
70	Zimbabwe	17.09
71	Romania	17.36
72	Venezuela	17.75
73	Haiti	18.89*
74	Uruguay	18.93
75	Bangladesh	20.35
76	Morocco	21.22
77	Guatemala	22.26
78	Honduras	24.72
79	Ecuador	26.23
80	Bolivia	36.05
81	Nicaragua	37.04
82	Nigeria	48.68*

MEAN 9.36 $50

Source: International Telecommunications Union Database, 2002

4.09 Cost of off-peak local cellular call (US$ per 3 min)

Cost of three minute local cellular call weighted against GDP

Rank	Country	Value	MEAN .68	$5.00
1	Russian Federation	0.03		
2	Luxembourg	0.07		
3	Canada	0.07		
4	Singapore	0.07		
5	United States	0.09		
6	United Kingdom	0.10		
7	Belgium	0.10		
8	Denmark	0.12		
9	Austria	0.12		
10	Norway	0.12		
11	Italy	0.12		
12	Netherlands	0.12		
13	Korea	0.13		
14	Mauritius	0.13		
15	New Zealand	0.14		
16	Israel	0.14		
17	Japan	0.14		
18	Iceland	0.14		
19	Czech Republic	0.14		
20	Finland	0.15		
21	Hong Kong SAR	0.15		
22	Sweden	0.16*		
23	Taiwan	0.16		
24	Switzerland	0.19		
25	Malaysia	0.20		
26	Germany	0.22		
27	Sri Lanka	0.22		
28	Ireland	0.22		
29	Costa Rica	0.23		
30	Brazil	0.23		
31	Slovak Republic	0.23		
32	Slovenia	0.23		
33	France	0.24		
34	Hungary	0.25		
35	Uruguay	0.30		
36	South Africa	0.34		
37	Thailand	0.35		
38	Estonia	0.39		
39	Portugal	0.41		
40	Namibia	0.44		
41	Australia	0.45		
42	Jamaica	0.45		
43	Colombia	0.46		
44	Indonesia	0.48		
45	Trinidad and Tobago	0.50		
46	Spain	0.53		
47	Latvia	0.56		
48	Greece	0.61		
49	Dominican Republic	0.62		
50	Bolivia	0.62		
51	Croatia	0.63		
52	Chile	0.63		
53	Poland	0.63		
54	Philippines	0.68		
55	Tunisia	0.70		
56	Bulgaria	0.70*		
57	Lithuania	0.74		
58	Panama	0.75		
59	Morocco	0.80		
60	El Salvador	0.81		
61	Romania	0.84*		
62	Jordan	0.85		
63	Turkey	0.85		
64	Mexico	0.90		
65	Argentina	0.99		
66	Venezuela	1.04		
67	Paraguay	1.06		
68	China	1.09*		
69	Guatemala	1.14		
70	Bangladesh	1.20		
71	Vietnam	1.21		
72	Nicaragua	1.31*		
73	Peru	1.50		
74	Zimbabwe	1.54		
75	Egypt	1.66		
76	India	1.71		
77	Botswana	1.81		
78	Ukraine	2.07		
79	Haiti	2.17*		
80	Honduras	2.88		
81	Nigeria	3.12*		
82	Ecuador	4.68		

Source: International Telecommunications Union Database, 2002

4.10 Cost of residential telephone subscription (US$ per month)

Residential monthly telephone subscription charge weighed against GDP

Rank	Country	Value	MEAN 8.60	$50
1	Guatemala	0.00		
2	Taiwan	0.82		
3	Korea	2.03		
4	Singapore	2.07		
5	Mauritius	2.28		
6	Croatia	2.39		
7	Russian Federation	2.42		
8	Luxembourg	2.51		
9	Ukraine	2.59		
10	Slovenia	2.62		
11	Egypt	2.97		
12	Slovak Republic	3.07		
13	Australia	3.13		
14	Czech Republic	3.24		
15	Bulgaria	3.30		
16	Tunisia	3.52		
17	Iceland	3.53		
18	Finland	3.83		
19	Thailand	3.89		
20	Greece	3.98		
21	Germany	4.00		
22	Costa Rica	4.13		
23	Botswana	4.18		
24	Spain	4.36		
25	Estonia	4.39		
26	Israel	4.57		
27	Hong Kong SAR	4.59		
28	Canada	4.68*		
29	France	4.75		
30	Italy	4.98		
31	Austria	4.98		
32	Panama	5.00		
33	Denmark	5.08		
34	Trinidad and Tobago	5.14		
35	Switzerland	5.19		
36	Belgium	5.46		
37	Colombia	5.62		
38	Norway	5.66		
39	Sweden	5.66		
40	Malaysia	5.80		
41	Ireland	5.91		
42	Portugal	5.93		
43	Lithuania	5.98		
44	Japan	6.07*		
45	United States	6.09		
46	Turkey	6.31		
47	United Kingdom	6.44		
48	Hungary	6.47*		
49	Netherlands	6.51		
50	Bolivia	6.68		
51	Latvia	6.98		
52	Sri Lanka	7.36		
53	China	7.59		
54	Poland	7.75		
55	New Zealand	8.23		
56	Honduras	8.24		
57	Romania	8.89		
58	Indonesia	8.94		
59	Uruguay	9.05		
60	Dominican Republic	9.26*		
61	Vietnam	9.55		
62	South Africa	9.61		
63	Namibia	9.62		
64	Paraguay	9.72		
65	Jordan	9.94		
66	Brazil	10.11		
67	Argentina	10.68		
68	Chile	11.47		
69	Jamaica	13.65*		
70	Zimbabwe	13.67		
71	El Salvador	15.85		
72	Mexico	17.22		
73	Morocco	17.24		
74	Bangladesh	17.96		
75	Venezuela	19.12		
76	Ecuador	19.36		
77	India	23.59		
78	Haiti	27.00*		
79	Peru	28.31		
80	Nicaragua	30.87		
81	Philippines	34.72		
82	Nigeria	49.24*		

Source: International Telecommunications Union Database, 2002

Business Readiness

5.01 Firm-level technology absorption

Companies in your country are:

1 = not interested in absorbing new technology,
7 = aggressive in absorbing new technologies

Rank	Country	Value	1	MEAN 4.92	7
1	Israel	6.56			
2	United States	6.55			
3	Japan	6.32			
4	Iceland	6.30			
5	Finland	6.24			
6	Taiwan	6.04			
7	Sweden	5.93			
8	Switzerland	5.92			
9	Singapore	5.86			
10	Korea	5.82			
11	Germany	5.76			
12	Australia	5.64			
13	Estonia	5.63			
14	Morocco	5.59			
15	France	5.47			
16	India	5.46			
17	Canada	5.45			
18	Ireland	5.44			
19	Brazil	5.35			
20	Norway	5.33			
20	Tunisia	5.33			
22	Denmark	5.32			
23	Dominican Republic	5.32			
24	United Kingdom	5.31			
25	Malaysia	5.29			
26	Slovak Republic	5.29			
27	New Zealand	5.26			
28	Costa Rica	5.21			
29	South Africa	5.21			
30	Austria	5.21			
31	Thailand	5.17			
32	Hong Kong SAR	5.16			
33	Luxembourg	5.16*			
34	Lithuania	5.09			
35	Belgium	5.06			
36	Czech Republic	5.04			
37	Vietnam	5.04			
38	Chile	5.04			
39	Trinidad and Tobago	5.01			
40	Hungary	5.00			
40	Latvia	5.00			
42	Panama	4.97			
43	Turkey	4.88			
44	Italy	4.84			
45	Netherlands	4.83			
46	Croatia	4.82			
47	Slovenia	4.82			
48	Jordan	4.78			
49	China	4.74			
50	Indonesia	4.69			
51	Jamaica	4.68			
52	Spain	4.68			
53	Namibia	4.63			
54	Ukraine	4.61			
55	Mauritius	4.61			
56	Nigeria	4.60			
57	Russian Federation	4.58			
58	Sri Lanka	4.57			
59	Poland	4.56			
60	Egypt	4.49*			
61	Zimbabwe	4.46			
62	Peru	4.43			
63	El Salvador	4.42			
64	Botswana	4.41			
65	Philippines	4.39			
66	Argentina	4.34			
67	Mexico	4.33			
68	Romania	4.28			
69	Greece	4.25			
70	Colombia	4.24			
71	Venezuela	4.19			
72	Portugal	4.09			
73	Bangladesh	4.08			
74	Bulgaria	4.05			
75	Guatemala	3.95			
76	Ecuador	3.88			
77	Haiti	3.83			
78	Uruguay	3.69			
79	Paraguay	3.54			
80	Nicaragua	3.47			
81	Honduras	3.40			
82	Bolivia	3.28			

5.02 Firm-level innovation

In your business, continuous innovation plays a major role in generating revenue:

1 = not true, 7 = true

Rank	Country	Value	1	MEAN 5.30	7
1	Japan	6.45			
2	United States	6.26			
3	Switzerland	6.16			
4	Iceland	6.13			
5	Luxembourg	6.09*			
6	Nigeria	6.00			
7	Singapore	5.98			
8	Paraguay	5.96			
9	Canada	5.94			
10	Germany	5.90			
11	Taiwan	5.88			
12	Austria	5.88			
13	India	5.88			
14	Israel	5.80			
15	Namibia	5.78			
16	Malaysia	5.78			
17	Finland	5.66			
18	Brazil	5.63			
19	United Kingdom	5.58			
20	Denmark	5.50			
21	Botswana	5.49			
22	Thailand	5.49			
23	Norway	5.48			
24	Tunisia	5.47			
25	Mauritius	5.47			
26	Hong Kong SAR	5.47			
27	Latvia	5.44			
28	Spain	5.44			
29	Slovak Republic	5.43			
30	Sweden	5.43			
31	Jamaica	5.42			
32	Morocco	5.42			
33	South Africa	5.40			
34	Chile	5.40			
35	Peru	5.40			
36	Mexico	5.39			
37	Korea	5.39			
38	Greece	5.38			
39	China	5.35			
40	Czech Republic	5.35			
41	Trinidad and Tobago	5.35			
42	Dominican Republic	5.34			
43	Belgium	5.33			
44	Australia	5.32			
45	Venezuela	5.31			
46	El Salvador	5.30			
47	Ireland	5.30			
48	Costa Rica	5.30			
49	Ecuador	5.28			
50	Vietnam	5.26			
51	Panama	5.25			
52	Philippines	5.25			
53	Romania	5.23			
54	France	5.22			
55	Italy	5.19			
56	Honduras	5.16			
57	Indonesia	5.13			
58	Hungary	5.10			
59	Guatemala	5.09			
60	Lithuania	5.08			
61	Estonia	5.07			
62	Zimbabwe	5.06			
63	Slovenia	5.03			
64	New Zealand	5.00			
65	Egypt	4.99*			
66	Bangladesh	4.99			
67	Poland	4.97			
68	Sri Lanka	4.93			
69	Nicaragua	4.91			
70	Colombia	4.91			
71	Netherlands	4.90			
72	Argentina	4.77			
73	Turkey	4.76			
74	Jordan	4.76			
75	Uruguay	4.75			
76	Bolivia	4.70			
77	Portugal	4.50			
78	Russian Federation	4.47			
79	Haiti	4.21			
80	Bulgaria	4.13			
81	Ukraine	4.05			
82	Croatia	2.89			

5.03 Capacity for innovation

Companies obtain technologies:

1 = exclusively from licensing or imitating foreign companies,
7 = by conducting formal research and pioneering their own new products and processes

Rank	Country	Value
1	Germany	6.03
2	Sweden	6.00
3	Finland	5.94
4	Japan	5.80
5	France	5.77
6	United States	5.70
7	Switzerland	5.68
8	Israel	5.63
9	United Kingdom	5.58
10	Austria	5.27
11	Belgium	5.24
11	Netherlands	5.24
13	Denmark	5.21
14	Taiwan	4.74
15	Korea	4.69
16	Canada	4.61
17	Norway	4.52
18	Iceland	4.43
19	Italy	4.41
20	New Zealand	4.41
21	Spain	4.37
22	China	4.28
23	Ireland	4.23
24	Slovenia	4.20
25	Singapore	4.07
26	Luxembourg	4.02*
27	Czech Republic	3.93
28	Australia	3.93
29	Ukraine	3.84
30	Brazil	3.83
31	Russian Federation	3.75
32	Costa Rica	3.67
33	Hungary	3.57
34	Dominican Republic	3.56
35	Estonia	3.50
36	Hong Kong SAR	3.44
37	Malaysia	3.44
38	Lithuania	3.41
39	Slovak Republic	3.40
40	Latvia	3.31
41	Portugal	3.30
42	Croatia	3.28
43	Poland	3.21
44	South Africa	3.19
45	Sri Lanka	3.17
46	India	3.17
47	Vietnam	3.15
48	Tunisia	3.07
49	Bulgaria	3.06
50	Thailand	2.98
51	Colombia	2.97
52	Mexico	2.97
53	Chile	2.96
54	Romania	2.94
55	Egypt	2.93*
56	Morocco	2.91
57	Mauritius	2.89
58	Jordan	2.88
59	Greece	2.87
60	Namibia	2.86
61	Indonesia	2.75
62	Guatemala	2.73
63	El Salvador	2.72
64	Jamaica	2.71
65	Nicaragua	2.68
66	Peru	2.67
67	Botswana	2.65
68	Turkey	2.59
69	Trinidad and Tobago	2.52
70	Panama	2.52
71	Argentina	2.49
72	Philippines	2.44
73	Uruguay	2.35
74	Ecuador	2.29
75	Honduras	2.25
76	Zimbabwe	2.23
77	Bolivia	2.21
78	Bangladesh	2.21
79	Venezuela	2.16
80	Paraguay	2.07
81	Nigeria	1.87
82	Haiti	1.86

MEAN 3.59

5.04 Business Intranet sophistication

Please rate your company's position in intranet sophistication versus international competitors in its largest business:

1 = behind other local companies, 7 = equal to the best in the world

Rank	Country	Value
1	Germany	4.03
2	United States	3.83
3	Switzerland	3.74
4	Canada	3.74
5	Netherlands	3.73
6	Sweden	3.73
7	France	3.70
8	Denmark	3.68
9	Argentina	3.61
10	Belgium	3.60
11	Brazil	3.58
12	Finland	3.56
13	Taiwan	3.48
14	Singapore	3.38
15	United Kingdom	3.38
16	Israel	3.36
17	Hong Kong SAR	3.36
18	Mexico	3.31
19	South Africa	3.27
20	Italy	3.26
21	Japan	3.22
22	Austria	3.20
22	Luxembourg	3.20
24	Greece	3.19
25	Australia	3.18
26	Czech Republic	3.15
27	Turkey	3.14
28	Egypt	3.10
29	Poland	3.09
30	Korea	3.07
31	Iceland	3.07
32	Ireland	3.05
33	New Zealand	3.04
34	Hungary	3.04
35	Spain	3.03
36	India	3.02
37	Chile	3.02
38	Norway	3.00
39	Indonesia	2.96
40	Estonia	2.94
41	Malaysia	2.91
42	Portugal	2.88
43	Slovenia	2.88
44	Croatia	2.84*
45	Botswana	2.79*
46	Costa Rica	2.77
47	Venezuela	2.75
48	Jordan	2.69
49	Thailand	2.69
50	Haiti	2.68*
51	Nigeria	2.65
52	China	2.61
52	Latvia	2.61
54	Philippines	2.61
55	Mauritius	2.60
56	Peru	2.53
57	Slovak Republic	2.50
58	Bangladesh	2.49
59	Uruguay	2.45
60	Tunisia	2.40*
61	Morocco	2.39*
62	Nicaragua	2.32
63	Bolivia	2.31
64	Sri Lanka	2.30
65	El Salvador	2.25
66	Panama	2.25
67	Namibia	2.25*
68	Ecuador	2.24
69	Bulgaria	2.22
70	Guatemala	2.22
71	Trinidad and Tobago	2.18
72	Colombia	2.17
73	Lithuania	2.15
74	Honduras	2.14
75	Jamaica	2.12
76	Russian Federation	2.07
77	Zimbabwe	2.07
78	Dominican Republic	2.05
79	Paraguay	2.03
80	Ukraine	1.97
81	Vietnam	1.74
82	Romania	1.54

MEAN 2.85

5.05 Quality of local IT training programs

Your country's training and educational programs for IT:

1 = lag far behind most other countries, 7 = are among the best in the world

Rank	Country	Value
1	Finland	6.33
2	Netherlands	6.27
3	United States	6.24
4	Sweden	6.22
5	Singapore	6.06
6	Iceland	6.00
7	Israel	5.96
8	Canada	5.68
9	India	5.58
10	Ireland	5.55
11	Taiwan	5.52
12	United Kingdom	5.48
13	France	5.41
14	Switzerland	5.39
15	Denmark	5.38
16	Austria	5.29
17	Norway	5.23
18	Estonia	5.13
19	Germany	5.12
20	Australia	5.12
21	Hong Kong SAR	5.08
22	Belgium	5.07
23	Hungary	5.03
24	Spain	4.96
25	Tunisia	4.90*
26	New Zealand	4.87
27	Costa Rica	4.84
28	Czech Republic	4.79
29	Korea	4.74
30	Namibia	4.56*
31	Chile	4.55
32	Slovenia	4.53
33	Italy	4.42
34	Philippines	4.41
35	Japan	4.41
36	Uruguay	4.39
37	Portugal	4.34
38	Thailand	4.34
39	Botswana	4.25*
40	Jordan	4.23
41	Malaysia	4.21
42	Latvia	4.18
43	Brazil	4.10
44	Jamaica	4.08
45	Greece	4.07
46	Trinidad and Tobago	4.04
47	South Africa	4.01
48	Luxembourg	4.00
48	Slovak Republic	4.00
50	Poland	3.93
51	Sri Lanka	3.91
52	Morocco	3.91*
53	Dominican Republic	3.91
54	Argentina	3.83
55	Zimbabwe	3.82
56	Egypt	3.75
57	Bulgaria	3.74
58	Venezuela	3.69
59	Turkey	3.69
60	Indonesia	3.63
61	Panama	3.61
62	Peru	3.61
63	Croatia	3.60*
64	Mexico	3.58
65	Ukraine	3.55
66	Lithuania	3.54
67	El Salvador	3.49
68	Colombia	3.45
69	China	3.39
70	Mauritius	3.31
71	Paraguay	3.16
72	Russian Federation	3.14
73	Guatemala	3.10
74	Nicaragua	3.02
75	Nigeria	2.94
76	Vietnam	2.87
77	Ecuador	2.77
78	Bolivia	2.64
79	Haiti	2.63*
80	Bangladesh	2.54
81	Honduras	2.52
82	Romania	1.96

MEAN 4.30

5.06 Cost of business telephone subscription (US$ per month)

Business monthly telephone subscription charge weighed against GDP:

Rank	Country	Value
1	Korea	0.020
2	Luxembourg	0.025
3	Slovenia	0.026
4	Slovak Republic	0.031
5	Singapore	0.031
6	Czech Republic	0.032
7	Tunisia	0.035
8	Mauritius	0.038
9	Finland	0.038
10	Thailand	0.039
11	Greece	0.040
12	Germany	0.040
13	Ukraine	0.041
14	Spain	0.044
15	Botswana	0.044
16	Israel	0.046
17	Turkey	0.046
18	Egypt	0.050
19	Denmark	0.051
20	Switzerland	0.052
21	Belgium	0.055
22	Hong Kong SAR	0.056
23	Australia	0.057
24	Norway	0.057
25	France	0.057
26	Iceland	0.059
27	Ireland	0.059
28	Portugal	0.059
29	Austria	0.060
30	Netherlands	0.065
31	Estonia	0.070
32	Taiwan	0.070
33	Costa Rica	0.071
34	Italy	0.073
35	Colombia	0.075
36	Poland	0.077
37	Sweden	0.078
38	Russian Federation	0.080
39	Bulgaria	0.087
40	Hungary	0.087
41	Romania	0.089
42	Japan	0.090
43	Vietnam	0.095
44	Canada	0.096
45	United Kingdom	0.100
46	Malaysia	0.102
47	China	0.106
48	Namibia	0.107
49	Chile	0.115
50	United States	0.122
51	Lithuania	0.127
52	South Africa	0.128
53	Paraguay	0.130
54	Sri Lanka	0.132
55	Latvia	0.140
56	Guatemala	0.148
57	New Zealand	0.149
58	Croatia	0.150
59	Indonesia	0.153
60	Brazil	0.157
61	Jamaica	0.159
62	Bangladesh	0.180
63	Panama	0.200
64	Uruguay	0.207
65	Honduras	0.220
66	Mexico	0.232
67	India	0.236
68	Jordan	0.256
69	Morocco	0.265
70	El Salvador	0.269
71	Zimbabwe	0.273
72	Argentina	0.274
73	Peru	0.283
74	Trinidad and Tobago	0.310
75	Dominican Republic	0.325
76	Ecuador	0.375
77	Venezuela	0.378
78	Bolivia	0.601
79	Philippines	0.707
80	Haiti	0.781
81	Nicaragua	0.823
82	Nigeria	0.903*

MEAN 0.16

Source: International Telecommunications Union Database, 2002

Government Readiness

6.01 Government prioritization of ICT

ICT are an overall priority for the government:

1 = strongly disagree, 7 = strongly agree

Rank	Country	Value
1	Singapore	6.24
2	Tunisia	6.08
3	Taiwan	5.98
4	Malaysia	5.86
5	Israel	5.78
6	Finland	5.73
7	Mauritius	5.69
8	India	5.58
9	Japan	5.51
10	Jamaica	5.50
11	Sweden	5.43
12	Ireland	5.38
13	Hungary	5.37
14	Jordan	5.35
15	United States	5.31
16	Korea	5.31
17	Estonia	5.31
18	China	5.27
19	Hong Kong SAR	5.26
20	Canada	5.25
21	Iceland	5.19
22	Thailand	5.09
23	Luxembourg	5.04*
24	Germany	5.02
25	Switzerland	5.01
26	Denmark	4.95
27	Spain	4.93
28	Sri Lanka	4.91
29	United Kingdom	4.88
30	Czech Republic	4.85
31	Chile	4.81
32	Portugal	4.73
33	Botswana	4.70
34	Vietnam	4.68
35	Latvia	4.68
36	Morocco	4.65
37	Netherlands	4.62
38	Austria	4.62
39	Belgium	4.61
40	Lithuania	4.59
41	Mexico	4.58
42	Philippines	4.56
43	France	4.52
44	South Africa	4.51
45	Australia	4.50
45	Brazil	4.50
47	Bangladesh	4.44
48	Slovenia	4.36
49	Namibia	4.35
50	Croatia	4.33
51	Norway	4.30
52	Italy	4.30
53	New Zealand	4.24
54	Uruguay	4.22
55	Colombia	4.19
56	Costa Rica	4.19
57	Greece	4.10
58	Trinidad and Tobago	4.03
59	Romania	4.03
60	Slovak Republic	3.95
61	Dominican Republic	3.82
62	Turkey	3.71
63	Russian Federation	3.69
64	Indonesia	3.67
65	Bulgaria	3.64
66	Poland	3.59
67	Egypt	3.55*
68	Ecuador	3.49
69	Peru	3.45
70	El Salvador	3.43
71	Nigeria	3.33
72	Nicaragua	3.27
73	Panama	3.16
74	Ukraine	3.15
75	Bolivia	3.09
76	Venezuela	3.04
77	Honduras	3.03
78	Paraguay	2.65
79	Zimbabwe	2.38
80	Argentina	2.31
81	Haiti	2.04
82	Guatemala	2.04

MEAN 4.43

6.02 Government procurement of advanced technology

Government purchase decisions for the procurement of advanced technology products are:

1 = based solely on price, 7 = based on technology and encourage innovation

Rank	Country	Value
1	Singapore	5.23
2	Israel	5.11
3	Taiwan	5.11
4	Tunisia	5.08
5	United States	4.89
6	Korea	4.81
7	Malaysia	4.74
8	France	4.70
9	Finland	4.68
10	China	4.67
11	Germany	4.67
12	Switzerland	4.63
13	Sri Lanka	4.53
14	Luxembourg	4.39*
15	Canada	4.32
16	Ireland	4.30
17	Iceland	4.30
18	Japan	4.29
19	United Kingdom	4.27
20	Sweden	4.25
21	Spain	4.16
22	Czech Republic	4.16
23	Morocco	4.14
24	Hungary	4.12
25	Vietnam	4.08
26	Netherlands	4.00
27	Estonia	3.95
28	Denmark	3.94
29	Trinidad and Tobago	3.90
30	Hong Kong SAR	3.89
31	Namibia	3.88
32	Austria	3.88
33	Australia	3.87
34	Italy	3.83
35	Thailand	3.83
36	Brazil	3.81
37	Belgium	3.80
38	Slovenia	3.79
39	New Zealand	3.78
40	Norway	3.74
41	Indonesia	3.73
42	South Africa	3.71
43	Portugal	3.70
44	Slovak Republic	3.68
45	Botswana	3.67
45	Dominican Republic	3.67
47	Jamaica	3.63
48	Lithuania	3.50
48	Nigeria	3.50
50	Chile	3.45
51	Russian Federation	3.43
52	Croatia	3.40
53	Latvia	3.38
54	Bulgaria	3.37
55	Poland	3.35
56	India	3.33
57	Greece	3.32
58	Costa Rica	3.26
59	Mexico	3.17
60	Uruguay	3.16
61	Colombia	3.16
62	Romania	3.10
63	Jordan	3.09
64	Mauritius	3.00
65	Philippines	2.97
66	Ukraine	2.92
67	Zimbabwe	2.89
68	Nicaragua	2.87
69	Venezuela	2.87
70	Egypt	2.85*
71	El Salvador	2.81
72	Peru	2.80
73	Argentina	2.69
74	Panama	2.64
75	Bangladesh	2.51
76	Ecuador	2.49
77	Turkey	2.47
78	Honduras	2.32
79	Haiti	2.28
80	Paraguay	2.27
81	Bolivia	2.25
82	Guatemala	2.18

MEAN 3.66

6.03 Competence of public officials

The competence level of personnel in the civil service is:

1 = lower than the private sector, 7 = higher than the private sector

Rank	Country	Value
1	Singapore	5.15
2	Sri Lanka	4.55
3	China	4.11
4	United Kingdom	4.04
5	Japan	4.00
6	Canada	3.85
7	Israel	3.80
8	Finland	3.79
9	Hong Kong SAR	3.74
10	Switzerland	3.68
11	Ireland	3.56
12	Denmark	3.53
13	Australia	3.46
14	Vietnam	3.46
15	New Zealand	3.46
16	Netherlands	3.45
17	Luxembourg	3.45*
18	Tunisia	3.41
19	Taiwan	3.36
20	Austria	3.33
20	Estonia	3.33
22	France	3.22
23	Sweden	3.21
24	Malaysia	3.13
25	Korea	3.10
26	United States	3.07
27	Latvia	3.06
28	Hungary	3.03
29	Norway	3.03
30	Iceland	3.00
30	Slovenia	3.00
32	Morocco	2.95
33	Botswana	2.94
34	Lithuania	2.93
35	Belgium	2.89
36	Bulgaria	2.83
37	India	2.79
38	Thailand	2.79
39	Spain	2.69
40	Czech Republic	2.67
41	Germany	2.67
42	Jamaica	2.61
43	Mexico	2.59
44	Trinidad and Tobago	2.57
45	Nicaragua	2.51
46	El Salvador	2.48
47	Bangladesh	2.44
48	Italy	2.43
49	Mauritius	2.41
50	Brazil	2.38
51	Jordan	2.38
52	Portugal	2.36
53	Croatia	2.33
54	Slovak Republic	2.30
55	Poland	2.30
56	Chile	2.26
57	Namibia	2.25
58	South Africa	2.23
59	Dominican Republic	2.23
60	Ukraine	2.23
61	Greece	2.22
62	Honduras	2.22
63	Russian Federation	2.20
64	Haiti	2.15
65	Costa Rica	2.14
66	Nigeria	2.13
67	Colombia	2.09
68	Indonesia	2.06
69	Egypt	2.01*
70	Philippines	2.00
71	Romania	1.99
72	Peru	1.98
73	Turkey	1.76
74	Bolivia	1.76
75	Uruguay	1.72
76	Zimbabwe	1.69
77	Panama	1.66
78	Ecuador	1.64
79	Paraguay	1.52
80	Guatemala	1.48
81	Venezuela	1.42
82	Argentina	1.35

MEAN 2.73

6.04 Government online services

Are government services (downloadable permit applications, tax payments, government tenders) available on the Internet in your country:

1 = not available, 7 = commonly available

Rank	Country	Value
1	Singapore	6.36
2	Iceland	6.19
3	Finland	5.83
4	Norway	5.81
5	Estonia	5.77
6	Hong Kong SAR	5.74
7	Sweden	5.68
8	Brazil	5.62
9	Canada	5.61
10	Denmark	5.56
11	United Kingdom	5.52
12	United States	5.43
13	Taiwan	5.39
14	Chile	5.34
15	Australia	5.30
16	Netherlands	5.18
17	Ireland	5.09
18	Austria	5.06
19	Spain	5.01
20	New Zealand	4.98
21	Portugal	4.76
22	France	4.67
23	Lithuania	4.52
24	Korea	4.52
25	Italy	4.47
26	Czech Republic	4.45
27	Hungary	4.39
28	Switzerland	4.24
29	Tunisia	4.22*
30	Poland	4.15
31	Argentina	4.13
32	Germany	3.95
33	Israel	3.92
34	Mexico	3.91
35	India	3.85
36	Belgium	3.71
37	Slovenia	3.66
38	Colombia	3.64
39	South Africa	3.61
40	Peru	3.59
41	Croatia	3.50*
42	China	3.50
43	Ukraine	3.49
44	Panama	3.48
45	Uruguay	3.44
46	Slovak Republic	3.40
47	Dominican Republic	3.33
48	Luxembourg	3.33
49	El Salvador	3.33
50	Namibia	3.30*
51	Jamaica	3.29
52	Latvia	3.29
53	Malaysia	3.28
54	Japan	3.19
55	Turkey	3.19
56	Thailand	3.17
57	Costa Rica	3.15
58	Botswana	3.09*
59	Greece	3.00
60	Guatemala	2.99
61	Bulgaria	2.95
62	Ecuador	2.93
63	Morocco	2.85*
64	Jordan	2.72
65	Russian Federation	2.59
66	Philippines	2.29
67	Nicaragua	2.28
68	Nigeria	2.18
69	Egypt	2.17
70	Vietnam	2.15
71	Mauritius	2.13
72	Paraguay	2.11
73	Bolivia	2.10
74	Indonesia	2.04
75	Honduras	2.02
76	Venezuela	2.00
77	Sri Lanka	1.92
78	Haiti	1.72*
79	Trinidad and Tobago	1.55
80	Bangladesh	1.46
81	Romania	1.20
82	Zimbabwe	1.18

MEAN 3.72

Individual Readiness

7.01 Use of online payment systems

Online Internet payment systems in your country are:

1 = not available, 7 = used by most people

Rank	Country	Value
1	Finland	6.19
2	Estonia	5.58
3	Sweden	5.52
4	Iceland	5.24
5	Canada	5.05
6	Norway	4.97
7	United States	4.94
8	Netherlands	4.91
9	Australia	4.85
10	Korea	4.84
11	New Zealand	4.80
12	Singapore	4.73
13	Denmark	4.72
14	Turkey	4.69
15	United Kingdom	4.64
16	Hong Kong SAR	4.55
17	Switzerland	4.52
18	Luxembourg	4.50
19	Germany	4.48
20	Belgium	4.43
21	Brazil	4.41
22	Ireland	4.32
23	Austria	4.29
24	Slovenia	4.18
25	France	4.14
26	South Africa	4.12
27	Latvia	4.10
28	Trinidad and Tobago	4.00
29	Tunisia	3.98*
30	Israel	3.91
31	Italy	3.89
32	Portugal	3.84
33	Japan	3.82
34	Philippines	3.82
35	Sri Lanka	3.80
36	Peru	3.79
37	Chile	3.70
37	Spain	3.70
39	Czech Republic	3.70
40	Taiwan	3.70
41	Panama	3.60
42	Slovak Republic	3.60
43	Venezuela	3.58
44	Croatia	3.47*
45	Mexico	3.44
46	Malaysia	3.42
47	Colombia	3.35
48	Argentina	3.34
49	Namibia	3.32*
50	Poland	3.30
51	El Salvador	3.30
52	Hungary	3.24
53	Costa Rica	3.21
54	Uruguay	3.18
55	Thailand	3.17
56	Botswana	3.17*
57	China	3.16
58	Nicaragua	3.09
59	India	3.09
60	Dominican Republic	3.08
61	Lithuania	3.06
62	Ukraine	3.02
63	Morocco	3.00*
64	Mauritius	2.93
65	Greece	2.88
66	Indonesia	2.83
67	Zimbabwe	2.82
68	Jamaica	2.82
69	Guatemala	2.81
70	Paraguay	2.76
71	Jordan	2.72
72	Russian Federation	2.58
73	Egypt	2.50
74	Bulgaria	2.42
75	Nigeria	2.40
76	Ecuador	2.23
77	Haiti	2.18*
78	Honduras	2.15
79	Bolivia	2.12
80	Bangladesh	1.81
81	Vietnam	1.69
82	Romania	1.18

MEAN 3.64

7.02 Number of radios (per 1,000 people)

Number of radio receivers in use for broadcasts to the general public per 1,000 people

Rank	Country	Value
1	United States	2117.53
2	Australia	1908.04
3	Finland	1622.56
4	United Kingdom	1431.98
5	Denmark	1349.33
6	Estonia	1095.69
7	Iceland	1081.08
8	Canada	1047.05
9	Korea	1032.81
10	Switzerland	1001.69
11	New Zealand	997.05
12	Netherlands	980.33
13	Slovak Republic	964.63
14	Japan	955.66
15	France	950.04
16	Germany	947.96
17	Sweden	932.26
18	Norway	915.06
19	Ukraine	888.61
20	Italy	877.91
21	Costa Rica	816.12
22	Czech Republic	802.59
23	Belgium	793.14
24	Jamaica	783.77
25	Austria	753.20
26	Taiwan	715.23*
27	Ireland	694.82
28	Latvia	694.61
29	Hungary	690.31
30	Hong Kong SAR	684.40
31	Argentina	681.21
32	Bolivia	675.94
33	Singapore	672.11
34	Uruguay	603.37
35	Turkey	573.34
36	Colombia	544.22
37	Bulgaria	542.58
38	Trinidad and Tobago	532.19
39	Israel	526.05
40	Poland	522.64
41	Lithuania	500.14
42	Greece	478.23
43	El Salvador	477.76
44	Brazil	433.30
45	Malaysia	419.99
46	Ecuador	417.52
47	Russian Federation	417.50
48	Honduras	412.49
49	Slovenia	405.35
50	Luxembourg	391.20
51	Mauritius	379.38
52	Jordan	372.27
53	Zimbabwe	362.28
54	Chile	354.25
55	Croatia	339.58
56	Egypt	339.31
57	China	339.00
58	South Africa	338.08
59	Romania	333.96
60	Spain	333.14
61	Mexico	330.11
62	Portugal	303.67
63	Panama	299.74
64	Venezuela	294.06
65	Peru	272.87
66	Nicaragua	270.25
67	Morocco	243.13
68	Thailand	235.12
69	Sri Lanka	207.52
70	Nigeria	199.69
71	Paraguay	181.91
72	Dominican Republic	180.72
73	Philippines	161.23
74	Tunisia	157.57
75	Indonesia	157.19
76	Botswana	154.60
77	Namibia	140.82
78	India	120.53
79	Vietnam	108.67
80	Guatemala	79.40
81	Haiti	55.39
82	Bangladesh	49.44

MEAN 590.82

Source: World Bank, World Development Indicators 2002

7.03 Number of television sets (per 1,000 people)

Number of television sets in use per 1,000 people

Rank	Country	Value	MEAN 356.65 → 1,000
1	United States	854.14	
2	Denmark	806.75	
3	Latvia	789.19	
4	Australia	737.54	
5	Japan	724.87	
6	Canada	715.30	
7	Finland	691.65	
8	Norway	668.90	
9	United Kingdom	652.54	
10	Portugal	630.43	
11	France	628.27	
12	Spain	591.13	
13	Estonia	590.61	
14	Luxembourg	589.17	
15	Germany	585.59	
16	Sweden	574.29	
17	Switzerland	548.30	
18	Belgium	541.29	
19	Netherlands	537.93	
20	Austria	535.87	
21	Uruguay	530.42	
22	New Zealand	522.08	
23	Iceland	508.90	
24	Czech Republic	507.61	
25	Italy	493.91	
26	Hong Kong SAR	493.46	
27	Greece	488.49	
28	Ukraine	455.84	
29	Turkey	449.01	
30	Bulgaria	448.83	
31	Hungary	436.50	
32	Lithuania	421.79	
33	Russian Federation	420.92	
34	Slovak Republic	407.03	
35	Poland	399.85	
36	Ireland	398.74	
37	Taiwan	393.38*	
38	Romania	380.70	
39	Slovenia	367.57	
40	Korea	364.26	
41	Brazil	342.61	
42	Trinidad and Tobago	339.93	
43	Israel	334.95	
44	Singapore	303.66	
45	Argentina	293.44	
46	China	293.36	
47	Croatia	292.87	
48	Thailand	283.80	
49	Mexico	283.17	
50	Colombia	282.03	
51	Mauritius	268.10	
52	Chile	241.73	
53	Costa Rica	231.17	
54	Paraguay	218.34	
55	Ecuador	218.25	
56	El Salvador	200.76	
57	Tunisia	198.21	
58	Jamaica	194.09	
59	Panama	193.73	
60	Egypt	189.05	
61	Venezuela	185.00	
62	Vietnam	184.76	
63	Malaysia	167.60	
64	Morocco	165.78	
65	Indonesia	149.46	
66	Peru	148.08	
67	Philippines	143.79	
68	South Africa	127.04	
69	Bolivia	118.86	
70	Sri Lanka	110.97	
71	Dominican Republic	96.68	
72	Honduras	95.61	
73	Jordan	83.95	
74	India	78.03	
75	Nicaragua	68.98	
76	Nigeria	67.63	
77	Guatemala	61.48	
78	Namibia	38.14	
79	Zimbabwe	30.41	
80	Botswana	24.66	
81	Bangladesh	6.98	
82	Haiti	5.40	

Source: World Bank, World Development Indicators 2002

7.04 Number of cable television subscribers (per 1,000 people)

Number of cable television subscribers per 1,000 people:

Rank	Country	Value	MEAN 86.39 → 400
1	Netherlands	387.81	
2	Belgium	372.86	
3	Switzerland	358.13	
4	Luxembourg	280.99	
5	Denmark	264.76	
6	Canada	259.41	
7	United States	252.13	
8	Germany	246.78	
9	Taiwan	200.09	
10	Sweden	199.31	
11	Israel	185.02	
12	Norway	183.57	
13	Finland	183.54	
14	Korea	177.42	
15	Ireland	176.93	
16	Argentina	163.05	
17	Slovenia	161.13	
18	Romania	157.66	
19	Hungary	157.60	
20	Japan	147.42	
21	Slovak Republic	139.69	
22	Bulgaria	130.09	
23	Uruguay	125.86	
24	Austria	123.37	
25	Jamaica	98.90	
26	Czech Republic	93.23	
27	Poland	92.61	
28	Portugal	92.27	
29	Estonia	90.33	
30	Lithuania	89.23	
31	Hong Kong SAR	78.56	
32	Russian Federation	78.49	
33	Latvia	76.73	
34	Trinidad and Tobago	69.95*	
35	Australia	68.02	
36	Singapore	63.47	
37	Egypt	62.63*	
38	China	61.14	
39	United Kingdom	56.89	
40	Ukraine	52.32	
41	Botswana	50.97*	
42	South Africa	49.86*	
43	El Salvador	49.71	
44	Mauritius	47.29*	
45	France	45.17	
46	Chile	44.92	
47	Venezuela	40.21	
48	Namibia	40.03*	
49	India	38.52	
50	Croatia	38.01	
51	Guatemala	28.46	
52	Ecuador	25.70	
53	Nigeria	24.68*	
53	Vietnam	24.68*	
55	Mexico	23.11	
56	Haiti	19.34*	
57	Costa Rica	19.07	
58	Paraguay	17.80	
59	Morocco	16.13*	
60	Dominican Republic	16.01	
61	Tunisia	15.94*	
62	Brazil	13.70	
63	Colombia	13.64	
64	Peru	13.62	
65	Turkey	13.44	
66	Philippines	13.07	
67	Spain	11.82	
68	Panama	11.41	
69	Bangladesh	10.84*	
70	Nicaragua	10.84	
71	Bolivia	9.60	
72	Honduras	7.71	
73	Malaysia	5.18	
74	Iceland	4.63	
75	New Zealand	4.39	
76	Thailand	2.47	
77	Greece	1.24	
78	Italy	1.05	
79	Sri Lanka	0.29	
80	Jordan	0.21	
81	Indonesia	0.15	
82	Zimbabwe	0.00	

Source: World Bank, World Development Indicators 2002

7.05 Number of mobile telephones (per 1,000 people)

Number of mobile telephones per 1,000 people

Rank	Country	Value	MEAN 292.69	1,000
1	Luxembourg	861.09		
2	Hong Kong SAR	809.16		
3	Austria	761.52		
4	Norway	750.89		
5	Italy	737.30		
6	United Kingdom	727.04		
7	Finland	720.37		
8	Sweden	717.19		
9	Taiwan	715.23*		
10	Israel	701.80		
11	Singapore	683.82		
12	Netherlands	669.92		
13	Portugal	664.93		
14	Ireland	657.53		
15	Switzerland	643.88		
16	Denmark	631.06		
17	Slovenia	612.08		
18	Spain	609.26		
19	Germany	585.97		
20	Iceland	571.06		
21	Korea	566.94		
22	New Zealand	563.33		
23	Greece	557.26		
24	Japan	526.20		
25	Belgium	525.13		
26	France	493.32		
27	Australia	446.94		
28	Czech Republic	424.25		
29	United States	397.91		
30	Estonia	387.02		
31	Hungary	301.68		
32	Canada	284.60		
33	Turkey	245.56		
34	Croatia	230.94		
35	Chile	222.23		
36	Venezuela	217.46		
37	Malaysia	213.18		
38	Slovak Republic	205.35		
39	South Africa	190.18		
40	Poland	174.05		
41	Latvia	165.54		
42	Argentina	163.37		
43	Mauritius	150.81		
44	Paraguay	149.35		
45	Panama	144.56		
46	Jamaica	142.45		
47	Mexico	142.37		
48	Lithuania	141.68		
49	Brazil	136.31		
50	Uruguay	131.91		
51	Botswana	123.30		
52	El Salvador	118.49		
53	Romania	111.93		
54	Trinidad and Tobago	102.91		
55	Bulgaria	89.73		
56	Philippines	84.37		
57	Morocco	82.61		
58	Dominican Republic	82.47		
59	Bolivia	69.61		
60	China	65.82		
61	Guatemala	61.19		
62	Jordan	58.31		
63	Colombia	53.33		
64	Costa Rica	51.97		
65	Thailand	50.42		
66	Peru	47.64		
67	Namibia	46.68		
68	Ecuador	38.13		
69	Honduras	23.94		
70	Zimbabwe	22.92		
71	Sri Lanka	22.73		
72	Russian Federation	22.21		
73	Egypt	21.42		
74	Nicaragua	17.80		
75	Indonesia	17.30		
76	Ukraine	16.22		
77	Vietnam	9.88		
78	Tunisia	5.84		
79	India	3.53		
80	Haiti	3.09		
81	Bangladesh	1.49		
82	Nigeria	0.26		

Source: World Bank, World Development Indicators 2002

7.06 Number of Internet users (per 100 people)

Number of Internet accounts per 100 people

Rank	Country	Value	MEAN 38.44	200
1	Singapore	196.80		
2	Korea	170.30		
3	Taiwan	149.70		
4	Slovenia	108.44*		
5	Greece	98.14*		
6	Japan	92.80		
7	Netherlands	88.19		
8	New Zealand	85.85*		
9	Sweden	84.43*		
10	Iceland	84.06*		
11	Israel	82.00		
12	Austria	81.97		
13	Canada	81.92*		
14	Finland	81.58*		
14	Ireland	81.58*		
16	Hong Kong SAR	78.90		
17	Malaysia	74.80		
18	Belgium	67.92		
19	United Kingdom	66.50		
20	Denmark	64.18*		
21	Spain	61.27		
22	Australia	61.24*		
23	Luxembourg	59.27*		
23	Norway	59.27*		
25	Italy	58.78		
26	Czech Republic	57.00		
27	Switzerland	53.81		
28	Germany	52.24		
29	Portugal	46.58		
30	France	42.93		
31	Chile	39.00		
32	United States	31.20		
33	Latvia	30.58*		
33	Lithuania	30.58*		
35	Uruguay	27.40		
36	Trinidad and Tobago	27.33*		
37	Thailand	27.20		
38	Slovak Republic	26.00		
39	Croatia	24.38*		
40	Botswana	23.90*		
41	Estonia	23.16*		
42	Mauritius	22.32*		
43	South Africa	20.03		
44	Philippines	18.40		
45	Hungary	18.00		
45	Poland	18.00		
47	Jamaica	17.76*		
48	Mexico	16.40		
49	Venezuela	15.60		
50	Turkey	15.48		
51	Brazil	14.00		
51	Bulgaria	14.00		
51	Colombia	14.00		
54	Dominican Republic	12.83*		
54	Tunisia	12.83*		
56	Panama	12.00		
57	Argentina	11.10		
58	Namibia	9.87*		
59	Guatemala	8.80		
60	Jordan	8.71*		
61	Peru	8.60		
62	China	7.90		
63	Honduras	5.80		
64	Ecuador	5.60		
65	Morocco	5.12		
66	Indonesia	5.10		
67	Costa Rica	5.00		
67	Romania	5.00		
69	Sri Lanka	4.80*		
70	Haiti	4.30*		
71	Russian Federation	4.00		
72	Bolivia	3.50		
72	India	3.50		
74	Nicaragua	3.00		
75	Nigeria	2.83*		
75	Zimbabwe	2.83*		
77	Bangladesh	2.50*		
78	Egypt	2.20		
79	Ukraine	2.00		
79	Vietnam	2.00		
81	Paraguay	1.70		
82	El Salvador	1.50		

Source: Pyramid

7.07 Number of narrowband subscriber lines (per 100 people)

Number of narrowband subscribers per 100 people

Rank	Country	Value	
			MEAN 66.29
1	Japan	152.20	
2	Taiwan	150.10	
3	Luxembourg	135.20*	
4	Denmark	130.56*	
5	Iceland	127.75*	
6	Singapore	127.20	
7	Korea	126.10	
8	Sweden	124.86*	
9	Canada	124.02*	
10	Israel	124.00	
11	Netherlands	110.41	
12	United Kingdom	106.37	
13	Finland	104.81*	
14	Germany	104.55	
15	France	103.48	
16	Spain	102.42	
17	Norway	102.04*	
18	Greece	101.98*	
19	Australia	100.91*	
20	Switzerland	98.80	
21	Belgium	97.51	
22	New Zealand	97.14*	
23	Italy	93.44	
24	Turkey	92.85	
25	Portugal	89.68	
26	Hungary	88.00	
27	Bulgaria	85.00	
28	Ireland	84.97*	
29	Uruguay	82.00	
30	Slovenia	79.88*	
31	Slovak Republic	78.00	
32	Croatia	76.60*	
33	Estonia	76.36*	
34	Austria	75.65	
35	Czech Republic	75.00	
36	Malaysia	74.70	
37	Poland	74.00	
38	Chile	72.00	
39	Lithuania	69.96*	
40	Latvia	67.20*	
41	Costa Rica	65.00	
42	Brazil	61.00	
43	Colombia	59.00	
44	Mauritius	56.91*	
45	Trinidad and Tobago	56.25*	
46	Hong Kong SAR	55.20	
47	Jamaica	51.32*	
48	Argentina	51.00	
48	Romania	51.00	
50	Panama	49.00	
51	Russian Federation	48.00	
51	United States	48.00	
53	Mexico	43.00	
54	Ukraine	42.00	
55	Egypt	40.50	
56	El Salvador	40.00	
57	Dominican Republic	37.01*	
58	Jordan	35.24*	
59	Botswana	35.20*	
60	Tunisia	34.77*	
61	China	34.00	
61	Ecuador	34.00	
61	Venezuela	34.00	
64	Namibia	30.65*	
65	South Africa	29.98	
66	Thailand	28.00	
67	Sri Lanka	27.27*	
68	Peru	27.00	
69	Zimbabwe	23.91*	
70	Haiti	22.47*	
71	Nigeria	21.77*	
72	Bangladesh	21.65*	
73	Bolivia	20.00	
73	Guatemala	20.00	
75	Morocco	17.87	
76	Vietnam	17.00	
77	Honduras	16.00	
78	Philippines	14.40	
79	India	13.70	
80	Nicaragua	13.00	
81	Indonesia	12.20	
82	Paraguay	10.00	

200

Source: Pyramid

7.08 Number of broadband subscriber lines (per 100 people)

Number of broadband subscribers per 100 people

Rank	Country	Value	
			MEAN 3.62
1	Korea	50.80	
2	Slovenia	26.57*	
3	Japan	17.20	
4	United Kingdom	17.04	
5	Hong Kong SAR	16.50	
6	Singapore	15.40	
7	Taiwan	14.10	
8	Netherlands	12.24	
9	Belgium	11.82	
10	Austria	11.76	
11	Sweden	11.17*	
12	Denmark	10.20*	
13	Finland	9.99*	
14	Ireland	9.99*	
15	Canada	9.17*	
16	Greece	8.22*	
17	Luxembourg	8.09*	
18	Norway	8.09*	
19	New Zealand	5.89	
20	United States	4.00	
21	Germany	3.11	
22	Switzerland	3.08	
23	Portugal	2.33	
24	France	1.48	
25	Spain	1.22	
26	Chile	1.00	
26	Croatia	1.00*	
26	Czech Republic	1.00	
26	Hungary	1.00	
26	Trinidad and Tobago	1.00*	
31	Australia	0.69*	
32	Italy	0.53	
33	China	0.50	
33	Sri Lanka	0.50*	
35	Malaysia	0.10	
36	Turkey	0.07	
37	Botswana	0.06*	
37	Estonia	0.06*	
37	Latvia	0.06*	
37	Lithuania	0.06*	
37	Mauritius	0.06*	
42	Israel	0.05	
43	Jamaica	0.04*	
44	South Africa	0.00	
44	Morocco	0.00	
44	Argentina	0.00	
44	Bangladesh	0.00*	
44	Bolivia	0.00	
44	Brazil	0.00	
44	Bulgaria	0.00	
44	Colombia	0.00	
44	Costa Rica	0.00	
44	Dominican Republic	0.00*	
44	Ecuador	0.00	
44	Egypt	0.00	
44	El Salvador	0.00	
44	Guatemala	0.00	
44	Haiti	0.00*	
44	Honduras	0.00	
44	Iceland	0.00*	
44	India	0.00	
44	Indonesia	0.00	
44	Jordan	0.00*	
44	Mexico	0.00	
44	Namibia	0.00*	
44	Nicaragua	0.00	
44	Nigeria	0.00*	
44	Panama	0.00	
44	Paraguay	0.00	
44	Peru	0.00	
44	Philippines	0.00	
44	Poland	0.00	
44	Romania	0.00	
44	Russian Federation	0.00	
44	Slovak Republic	0.00	
44	Thailand	0.00	
44	Tunisia	0.00*	
44	Ukraine	0.00	
44	Uruguay	0.00	
44	Venezuela	0.00	
44	Vietnam	0.00	
44	Zimbabwe	0.00*	

60

Source: Pyramid

7.09 Household spending on ICT (US$ per month)

Household spending per month

Rank	Country	Value		MEAN 27.05	60
1	United States	53.20			
2	Korea	46.02			
3	Singapore	45.50			
4	Japan	44.45			
5	United Kingdom	43.99			
6	Israel	43.78			
7	Slovenia	43.42*			
8	Luxembourg	42.43*			
8	Norway	42.43*			
10	Portugal	40.83			
11	Iceland	40.81*			
12	Denmark	40.61*			
13	Netherlands	39.82			
14	Nicaragua	39.74			
15	Australia	39.18*			
16	Canada	38.53*			
17	Venezuela	38.37			
18	Sweden	38.32*			
19	Finland	38.15*			
19	Ireland	38.15*			
21	Mexico	38.09			
22	Belgium	37.42			
23	Germany	37.05			
24	France	36.93			
25	Italy	36.84			
26	Argentina	35.48			
27	Hong Kong SAR	35.13			
28	Uruguay	34.67			
29	Chile	34.30			
30	Paraguay	33.34			
31	Greece	32.63*			
32	Panama	32.45			
33	New Zealand	31.96*			
34	Morocco	30.78			
35	Peru	30.71			
36	Austria	30.70			
37	Spain	30.61			
38	Guatemala	29.81			
39	Switzerland	29.65			
40	South Africa	29.07			
41	Philippines	27.62			
42	Bolivia	27.40			
43	Trinidad and Tobago	26.79*			
44	Bangladesh	26.58*			
45	Honduras	25.17			
46	Taiwan	24.44			
47	Croatia	23.66*			
48	Latvia	23.52*			
48	Lithuania	23.52*			
50	El Salvador	22.23			
51	Mauritius	22.09*			
52	Malaysia	20.89			
53	Jamaica	20.36*			
54	Botswana	20.35*			
55	Zimbabwe	20.22*			
56	Estonia	20.06*			
57	Brazil	19.84			
58	Dominican Republic	19.60*			
58	Tunisia	19.60*			
60	Poland	18.00			
61	Sri Lanka	17.47*			
62	Czech Republic	17.00			
63	Namibia	16.60*			
64	Costa Rica	16.57			
65	Thailand	15.89			
66	Nigeria	15.17*			
67	Hungary	15.00			
68	Jordan	14.87*			
69	Ecuador	14.04			
70	Vietnam	13.42			
71	Indonesia	13.24			
72	Slovak Republic	12.00			
73	Turkey	11.65			
74	Haiti	10.38*			
75	Egypt	10.00			
76	Colombia	9.56			
77	China	9.31			
78	Ukraine	8.00			
79	India	7.51			
80	Bulgaria	5.00			
81	Romania	4.00			
81	Russian Federation	4.00			

Source: Pyramid

Business Usage

8.01 Use of Internet for coordination with customers and suppliers

To what extent has the Internet improved your firm's ability to coordinate with customers and suppliers to reduce your inventory costs?

1 = no change, 7 = huge improvement

Rank	Country	Value
1	Finland	5.22
2	United States	5.01
3	Germany	4.81
4	Taiwan	4.71
5	Singapore	4.63
6	Korea	4.51
7	Canada	4.49
8	Estonia	4.48
9	Iceland	4.47
10	France	4.43
11	Hong Kong SAR	4.29
12	Netherlands	4.27
13	Spain	4.22
14	Czech Republic	4.21
15	United Kingdom	4.19
16	Japan	4.13
17	South Africa	4.13
18	Panama	4.11
19	Ukraine	4.08
20	Austria	4.05
21	Ireland	4.02
22	Belgium	4.00
22	Sweden	4.00
24	Australia	3.96
25	Switzerland	3.95
26	New Zealand	3.94
27	Italy	3.89
28	Chile	3.84
29	Bolivia	3.83
30	Slovenia	3.83
31	Vietnam	3.82
32	Dominican Republic	3.77
33	Poland	3.73
34	Norway	3.71
35	Thailand	3.71
36	El Salvador	3.70
37	Mexico	3.70
38	Indonesia	3.70
39	Costa Rica	3.68
40	Peru	3.65
41	Honduras	3.63
42	Botswana	3.61*
43	Jamaica	3.61
44	Slovak Republic	3.60
45	Tunisia	3.59*
46	Brazil	3.59
47	Malaysia	3.58
48	Romania	3.58
49	Morocco	3.57*
50	Jordan	3.56
51	Sri Lanka	3.55
52	Argentina	3.54
53	Croatia	3.53*
54	Ecuador	3.50
55	Latvia	3.48
56	Nicaragua	3.48
57	Denmark	3.47
58	Namibia	3.46*
59	Bangladesh	3.41
60	Portugal	3.40
61	Uruguay	3.39
62	Philippines	3.37
63	Israel	3.36
64	Venezuela	3.33
65	China	3.33
66	Egypt	3.30
67	Nigeria	3.27
68	Hungary	3.25
69	Guatemala	3.24
70	Haiti	3.22*
71	Lithuania	3.21
72	India	3.20
73	Colombia	3.18
74	Paraguay	3.13
75	Bulgaria	3.11
76	Trinidad and Tobago	3.08
77	Turkey	2.94
78	Mauritius	2.93
79	Russian Federation	2.75
80	Zimbabwe	2.75
81	Greece	2.47
82	Luxembourg	2.00

MEAN 3.70

8.02 Businesses using e-commerce (%)

Worldwide percentage of businesses using the Internet with Internet commerce sites

Rank	Country	Value
1	Sweden	0.64
2	Norway	0.61
3	Denmark	0.42
4	Germany	0.39
5	Korea	0.39
6	Luxembourg	0.36*
7	Netherlands	0.35
8	Iceland	0.34*
9	China	0.33
10	Honduras	0.33*
10	Sri Lanka	0.33*
12	Argentina	0.32
13	Spain	0.31
14	United Kingdom	0.31
15	Japan	0.30
16	Italy	0.30
17	Colombia	0.28
18	Australia	0.28
19	Switzerland	0.27
20	Singapore	0.27
21	Taiwan	0.26
22	United States	0.26
23	Ireland	0.25
24	Portugal	0.24
25	Bolivia	0.22*
26	Israel	0.22
27	Belgium	0.22
28	South Africa	0.22
29	Finland	0.21
30	Mexico	0.21
31	Hong Kong SAR	0.21
32	Austria	0.21
33	New Zealand	0.20
34	Dominican Republic	0.20*
34	Tunisia	0.20*
36	Uruguay	0.19*
37	Brazil	0.19
38	Chile	0.18
39	Trinidad and Tobago	0.18*
40	France	0.18
41	Czech Republic	0.18
41	Hungary	0.18
41	Poland	0.18
44	Malaysia	0.17
45	Croatia	0.16*
46	Venezuela	0.16
47	Peru	0.16*
48	Canada	0.15
49	Latvia	0.15*
49	Lithuania	0.15*
49	Mauritius	0.15*
52	Estonia	0.14*
52	Jamaica	0.14*
52	Botswana	0.14*
52	Panama	0.14*
56	Costa Rica	0.13*
57	Indonesia	0.13
57	Ukraine	0.13*
59	Bangladesh	0.13*
59	Vietnam	0.13
61	El Salvador	0.13*
61	Namibia	0.13*
63	Greece	0.12
64	Haiti	0.12*
65	Nicaragua	0.12*
65	Nigeria	0.12*
65	Zimbabwe	0.12*
68	Jordan	0.12*
69	Thailand	0.12
70	Ecuador	0.11*
70	Morocco	0.11*
70	Philippines	0.11
73	India	0.11
74	Bulgaria	0.11
75	Slovenia	0.10
76	Guatemala	0.08*
77	Egypt	0.08
77	Romania	0.08
79	Paraguay	0.08*
80	Turkey	0.06
81	Slovak Republic	0.05
82	Russian Federation	0.04

MEAN 0.20 — 0.80%

Source: The World Information Technology and Service Alliance

8.03 Use of Internet for general research

Please rate your company's position in use of Internet for general research versus international competitors in its largest business:

1 = behind other local companies, 5 = equal to the best in the world

Rank	Country	Value
1	Germany	3.92
2	United States	3.75
3	Netherlands	3.73
4	Finland	3.69
5	Switzerland	3.64
6	Turkey	3.57
7	United Kingdom	3.53
8	Australia	3.50
9	Israel	3.46
10	Brazil	3.45
11	Argentina	3.43
12	France	3.42
12	Italy	3.42
14	Denmark	3.41
15	South Africa	3.38
16	Sweden	3.38
17	Singapore	3.33
18	Poland	3.32
19	Taiwan	3.29
20	Austria	3.29
21	Portugal	3.23
22	Canada	3.22
23	Hong Kong SAR	3.20
24	Belgium	3.20
25	Norway	3.19
26	Czech Republic	3.19
27	Jordan	3.13
28	Estonia	3.12
29	Egypt	3.09
30	Iceland	3.07
31	Japan	3.04
32	Spain	3.00
33	Korea	2.99
34	Slovenia	2.98
35	Malaysia	2.92
36	Costa Rica	2.91
37	Botswana	2.90*
38	Philippines	2.89
39	Greece	2.89
40	Nicaragua	2.88
41	Mexico	2.84
42	Venezuela	2.83
43	Ireland	2.83
44	Croatia	2.82*
45	Mauritius	2.82
46	Morocco	2.80*
47	Bolivia	2.79
48	New Zealand	2.77
49	Nigeria	2.75
50	Uruguay	2.73
51	Hungary	2.73
52	El Salvador	2.71
53	Ecuador	2.70
54	Indonesia	2.70
55	Chile	2.69
56	India	2.67
57	Latvia	2.65
58	Trinidad and Tobago	2.63
59	Guatemala	2.62
60	Panama	2.62
61	Tunisia	2.60*
62	Thailand	2.60
63	Jamaica	2.57
64	Namibia	2.52*
65	Honduras	2.51
66	Peru	2.48
67	Paraguay	2.47
68	Haiti	2.43*
69	China	2.40
70	Bangladesh	2.39
71	Colombia	2.34
72	Russian Federation	2.33
73	Dominican Republic	2.33
74	Sri Lanka	2.27
75	Luxembourg	2.25
76	Slovak Republic	2.25
77	Lithuania	2.18
78	Ukraine	2.18
79	Romania	2.13
80	Zimbabwe	1.93
81	Bulgaria	1.90
82	Vietnam	1.79

MEAN 2.88

8.04 Sophistication of online marketing

Please rate your company's position in online marketing versus international competitors in its largest business:

1 = behind other local companies, 5 = equal to the best in the world

Rank	Country	Value
1	Germany	3.59
2	Finland	3.25
3	United States	3.24
4	Switzerland	3.12
5	Denmark	3.07
6	France	3.00
6	Luxembourg	3.00
6	Poland	3.00
9	Taiwan	2.97
10	Argentina	2.93
11	Singapore	2.91
12	Netherlands	2.90
13	Brazil	2.86
14	Sweden	2.85
15	United Kingdom	2.83
16	Austria	2.80
17	Hong Kong SAR	2.77
18	Canada	2.73
19	Japan	2.72
20	Portugal	2.70
21	Belgium	2.67
22	Italy	2.67
23	Iceland	2.60
24	Spain	2.60
25	Australia	2.59
26	Korea	2.51
27	Norway	2.48
28	Indonesia	2.45
29	Czech Republic	2.43
30	Israel	2.43
31	South Africa	2.42
32	Egypt	2.40
33	Slovenia	2.38
34	India	2.35
35	Mexico	2.34
36	Ireland	2.33
37	Latvia	2.31
38	Jordan	2.31
39	Nigeria	2.30
40	Chile	2.30
41	China	2.29
42	Thailand	2.28
43	Greece	2.26
44	New Zealand	2.26
45	Estonia	2.26
46	Bangladesh	2.24
47	Croatia	2.22*
48	Turkey	2.21
49	Paraguay	2.20
50	Botswana	2.19*
51	Malaysia	2.17
52	Haiti	2.16*
53	Russian Federation	2.13
54	Hungary	2.12
55	El Salvador	2.12
56	Uruguay	2.07
57	Costa Rica	2.04
58	Tunisia	2.04*
59	Trinidad and Tobago	2.03
60	Namibia	2.02*
61	Mauritius	2.00
61	Nicaragua	2.00
61	Philippines	2.00
61	Slovak Republic	2.00
65	Dominican Republic	1.97
66	Romania	1.96
67	Panama	1.96
68	Venezuela	1.95
69	Honduras	1.93
70	Morocco	1.88*
71	Ukraine	1.87
72	Sri Lanka	1.86
73	Guatemala	1.86
74	Lithuania	1.84
75	Ecuador	1.83
76	Bolivia	1.80
76	Colombia	1.80
78	Peru	1.77
79	Bulgaria	1.71
80	Vietnam	1.70
81	Zimbabwe	1.67
82	Jamaica	1.63

MEAN 2.35

8.05 Presence of wireless e-business applications

Does your company offer wireless e-business applications for suppliers or consumers:

1 = no, 7 = yes, applications are equal to the most sophisticated in the world

Rank	Country	Value
1	Germany	4.31
2	Iceland	4.20
3	Sweden	3.87
4	Spain	3.67
5	Switzerland	3.50
6	Canada	3.39
7	United States	3.39
8	Poland	3.33
9	Taiwan	3.30
10	Austria	3.28
11	Netherlands	3.27
12	Italy	3.26
13	Finland	3.25
14	Denmark	3.24
15	United Kingdom	3.19
16	Hong Kong SAR	3.17
17	Brazil	3.16
18	Czech Republic	3.12
19	Norway	3.10
20	Japan	3.08
21	Singapore	3.07
22	Korea	3.02
23	Belgium	3.00
24	France	3.00
25	Ireland	2.97
26	New Zealand	2.85
27	South Africa	2.82
28	Slovak Republic	2.75
29	Australia	2.73
29	Mexico	2.73
31	Israel	2.67
32	Argentina	2.61
33	Slovenia	2.58
34	Costa Rica	2.54
35	Croatia	2.51*
36	El Salvador	2.47
37	Zimbabwe	2.41
38	Trinidad and Tobago	2.39
39	Philippines	2.35
40	Luxembourg	2.33
41	Colombia	2.32
42	Nicaragua	2.28
43	Peru	2.26
44	Chile	2.25
45	Botswana	2.23
46	Portugal	2.22*
47	Ukraine	2.21
48	Nigeria	2.19
49	Tunisia	2.18*
50	Turkey	2.14
51	Jordan	2.10
52	Ecuador	2.10
53	China	2.06
54	Guatemala	2.05
55	Morocco	2.04*
56	Hungary	2.04
57	Honduras	2.03
58	Dominican Republic	2.02
59	Namibia	2.02*
60	Mauritius	2.00
61	Haiti	2.00*
62	Latvia	1.95
63	Panama	1.94
64	Paraguay	1.93
65	Estonia	1.92
66	Russian Federation	1.92
67	Egypt	1.91
67	Venezuela	1.91
69	Thailand	1.89
70	India	1.83
71	Uruguay	1.82
72	Vietnam	1.79
73	Malaysia	1.79
74	Indonesia	1.75
75	Bolivia	1.68
76	Bangladesh	1.68
77	Greece	1.67
78	Sri Lanka	1.62
79	Bulgaria	1.59
80	Jamaica	1.58
81	Lithuania	1.49
82	Romania	1.16

MEAN 2.48

8.06 Use of e-mail for internal correspondence (%)

What amount of your company's internal correspondence is done by e-mail:

1 = 0%, 7 = 100%

Rank	Country	Value
1	Sweden	5.84
2	Singapore	5.84
3	Argentina	5.83
4	United States	5.81
5	Belgium	5.79
6	Denmark	5.72
7	United Kingdom	5.70
8	Canada	5.68
9	Finland	5.67
10	Australia	5.64
11	New Zealand	5.62
12	Switzerland	5.52
13	Germany	5.50
13	Venezuela	5.50
15	Italy	5.47
16	Malaysia	5.46
17	Netherlands	5.45
18	Brazil	5.44
19	France	5.41
20	Hong Kong SAR	5.37
21	Mexico	5.37
22	Spain	5.36
23	Korea	5.28
24	Ireland	5.26
25	Iceland	5.19
26	Czech Republic	5.18
27	India	5.17
28	South Africa	5.15
29	Israel	5.08
30	Japan	5.08
31	Norway	5.00
32	Austria	4.97
33	Turkey	4.88
34	Chile	4.82
35	Estonia	4.70
36	Poland	4.67
37	Philippines	4.61
38	Taiwan	4.61
39	Costa Rica	4.55
40	Croatia	4.48*
41	Thailand	4.43
42	Botswana	4.41*
43	Ecuador	4.38
44	Indonesia	4.38
45	Peru	4.38
46	Portugal	4.27
47	Haiti	4.24*
48	El Salvador	4.23
49	Slovenia	4.21
50	Slovak Republic	4.20
51	Morocco	4.12*
52	Greece	4.05
53	Luxembourg	4.00
54	Colombia	3.97
55	Hungary	3.95
56	Latvia	3.89
57	Mauritius	3.88
58	Tunisia	3.79*
59	Panama	3.71
60	Guatemala	3.69
61	Nicaragua	3.63
62	Uruguay	3.53
63	Bangladesh	3.49
64	Namibia	3.43*
65	Nigeria	3.41
66	Bolivia	3.37
67	Zimbabwe	3.18
68	Paraguay	3.13
69	Honduras	3.05
70	Jamaica	2.98
71	Vietnam	2.87
72	Jordan	2.87
73	Dominican Republic	2.85
74	China	2.78
75	Bulgaria	2.72
76	Lithuania	2.72
77	Egypt	2.67
78	Trinidad and Tobago	2.66
79	Romania	2.65
80	Sri Lanka	2.33
81	Ukraine	2.25
82	Russian Federation	1.84

MEAN 4.37

8.07 Use of e-mail for external correspondence (%)

What amount of your company's external correspondence is done by e-mail:

1 = 0%, 7 = 100%

Rank	Country	Value
1	Singapore	4.91
2	Iceland	4.81
3	Venezuela	4.77
4	Finland	4.72
5	Israel	4.71
6	Korea	4.71
7	Estonia	4.59
8	Brazil	4.59
9	Ecuador	4.58
10	United States	4.53
11	Bangladesh	4.46
12	Argentina	4.43
13	El Salvador	4.40
13	Slovak Republic	4.40
15	Hong Kong SAR	4.37
16	Mexico	4.30
17	Belgium	4.29
18	Sweden	4.28
19	Malaysia	4.24
20	Czech Republic	4.21
21	Norway	4.20
22	Australia	4.16
23	Denmark	4.16
24	New Zealand	4.15
25	United Kingdom	4.15
26	Poland	4.15
27	France	4.14
28	Sri Lanka	4.14
29	Netherlands	4.09
30	Spain	4.09
31	Botswana	4.06*
32	Costa Rica	4.05
33	Morocco	4.02*
34	India	4.02
35	Guatemala	4.01
36	South Africa	4.00
36	Taiwan	4.00
36	Turkey	4.00
39	Chile	3.99
40	Croatia	3.98*
41	Peru	3.98
42	Canada	3.95
43	Japan	3.93
44	Indonesia	3.92
45	Bolivia	3.91
46	Italy	3.89
47	Thailand	3.87
48	Nicaragua	3.86
49	Slovenia	3.82
50	Panama	3.81
51	Mauritius	3.81
52	Tunisia	3.81*
53	Vietnam	3.79
54	Germany	3.79
55	Ireland	3.78
56	Jordan	3.78
57	Latvia	3.75
58	Switzerland	3.73
59	Haiti	3.73*
60	Paraguay	3.72
61	Austria	3.69
62	Uruguay	3.66
63	Greece	3.62
64	Nigeria	3.61
65	Dominican Republic	3.59
66	Philippines	3.59
67	Honduras	3.53
68	Egypt	3.50
69	Namibia	3.44*
70	Lithuania	3.38
71	Portugal	3.29
72	Colombia	3.26
73	Zimbabwe	3.25
74	Hungary	3.16
75	Jamaica	3.02
76	Ukraine	2.94
77	Trinidad and Tobago	2.94
78	Bulgaria	2.81
79	China	2.81
80	Luxembourg	2.33
81	Russian Federation	2.28
82	Romania	1.77

MEAN 3.88

8.08 Pervasiveness of company web pages

In your country, how common are Web pages by companies:

1 = rare, 7 = as common as in the world's leading countries

Rank	Country	Value
1	Finland	6.94
2	United States	6.85
3	Iceland	6.81
4	Sweden	6.77
5	Canada	6.76
6	United Kingdom	6.76
7	Switzerland	6.65
8	Netherlands	6.64
9	Australia	6.50
10	Germany	6.48
11	Norway	6.45
12	Denmark	6.41
13	Luxembourg	6.33
14	Hong Kong SAR	6.29
15	Austria	6.29
16	Japan	6.25
17	France	6.19
18	Korea	6.18
19	Israel	6.13
20	New Zealand	6.10
21	Brazil	6.03
22	Singapore	6.01
23	Belgium	6.00
24	Italy	5.95
25	Spain	5.83
26	South Africa	5.81
27	Czech Republic	5.73
28	Argentina	5.67
28	Taiwan	5.67
30	Tunisia	5.67*
31	Estonia	5.66
32	Ireland	5.65
33	Hungary	5.47
34	Slovak Republic	5.40
35	Venezuela	5.31
36	Namibia	5.28*
37	Poland	5.26
38	Slovenia	5.22
39	Turkey	5.19
40	Chile	5.14
41	India	5.06
42	Portugal	5.00
43	Uruguay	4.95
44	Botswana	4.93*
45	Mexico	4.93
46	Thailand	4.91
47	Philippines	4.83
48	Malaysia	4.76
49	Latvia	4.75
50	Panama	4.63
51	Morocco	4.54*
52	Jordan	4.52
53	Greece	4.45
54	Egypt	4.33
55	Costa Rica	4.31
56	Indonesia	4.29
57	Colombia	4.19
58	Croatia	4.18*
59	Dominican Republic	4.18
60	Trinidad and Tobago	4.17
61	Lithuania	4.11
62	Ukraine	4.10
63	Jamaica	4.00
64	Russian Federation	3.95
65	Sri Lanka	3.87
66	Bulgaria	3.74
67	Peru	3.66
68	Nigeria	3.63
69	Guatemala	3.62
70	China	3.61
71	Ecuador	3.56
72	El Salvador	3.53
73	Vietnam	3.44
74	Honduras	3.38
75	Zimbabwe	3.35
76	Nicaragua	3.34
77	Paraguay	3.22
78	Haiti	3.07*
79	Bolivia	3.01
80	Mauritius	2.94
81	Bangladesh	2.92
82	Romania	2.40

MEAN 5.00

Government Usage

9.01 Use of Internet-based transactions with Government

Please rate your company's position in Internet-based interactions with government versus international competitors in its largest business:

1 = behind other local companies, 5 = equal to the best in the world

Rank	Country	Value
1	Finland	3.00
1	Iceland	3.00
3	Denmark	2.89
4	Germany	2.88
5	United States	2.87
6	Taiwan	2.87
7	United Kingdom	2.86
8	Sweden	2.76
9	Singapore	2.74
10	Canada	2.70
11	Australia	2.64
11	Netherlands	2.64
13	Turkey	2.62
14	Argentina	2.54
15	Brazil	2.53
16	Norway	2.52
17	Switzerland	2.51
18	Hong Kong SAR	2.51
19	France	2.50
20	Estonia	2.48
21	Austria	2.47
22	Italy	2.44
23	Belgium	2.43
24	Mexico	2.42
25	Egypt	2.40
26	Korea	2.37
27	Chile	2.37
28	Spain	2.32
29	Thailand	2.32
30	Japan	2.31
31	Poland	2.31
31	South Africa	2.31
33	New Zealand	2.30
34	Latvia	2.29
35	Venezuela	2.25
36	Indonesia	2.24
37	Paraguay	2.21
38	Israel	2.21
39	India	2.21
40	Czech Republic	2.19
41	Botswana	2.19*
42	Ireland	2.18
43	Bangladesh	2.18
44	Hungary	2.16
45	Slovenia	2.15
46	Croatia	2.14*
47	China	2.14
48	Mauritius	2.11
49	Greece	2.06
50	Philippines	2.06
51	Haiti	2.05*
52	Malaysia	2.04
53	Portugal	2.03
54	Nigeria	2.02
55	Slovak Republic	2.00
56	Lithuania	1.93
57	El Salvador	1.88
58	Uruguay	1.88
59	Panama	1.87
60	Costa Rica	1.87
61	Tunisia	1.85*
62	Sri Lanka	1.82
63	Peru	1.79
64	Russian Federation	1.79
65	Morocco	1.78*
66	Trinidad and Tobago	1.77
67	Jordan	1.75
68	Namibia	1.74*
69	Ecuador	1.71
70	Colombia	1.71
71	Jamaica	1.70
72	Zimbabwe	1.69
73	Nicaragua	1.67
74	Luxembourg	1.67
74	Ukraine	1.67
76	Dominican Republic	1.66
77	Guatemala	1.63
78	Bolivia	1.56
79	Vietnam	1.55
80	Bulgaria	1.53
81	Honduras	1.49
82	Romania	1.10

MEAN 2.17

9.02 Government online services

Are government services (downloadable permit applications, tax payments, government tenders) available on the Internet in your country:

1 = not available, 7 = commonly available

Rank	Country	Value
1	Singapore	6.36
2	Iceland	6.19
3	Finland	5.83
4	Norway	5.81
5	Estonia	5.77
6	Hong Kong SAR	5.74
7	Sweden	5.68
8	Brazil	5.62
9	Canada	5.61
10	Denmark	5.56
11	United Kingdom	5.52
12	United States	5.43
13	Taiwan	5.39
14	Chile	5.34
15	Australia	5.30
16	Netherlands	5.18
17	Ireland	5.09
18	Austria	5.06
19	Spain	5.01
20	New Zealand	4.98
21	Portugal	4.76
22	France	4.67
23	Lithuania	4.52
24	Korea	4.52
25	Italy	4.47
26	Czech Republic	4.45
27	Hungary	4.39
28	Switzerland	4.24
29	Tunisia	4.22*
30	Poland	4.15
31	Argentina	4.13
32	Germany	3.95
33	Israel	3.92
34	Mexico	3.91
35	India	3.85
36	Belgium	3.71
37	Slovenia	3.66
38	Colombia	3.64
39	South Africa	3.61
40	Peru	3.59
41	Croatia	3.50*
42	China	3.50
43	Ukraine	3.49
44	Panama	3.48
45	Uruguay	3.44
46	Slovak Republic	3.40
47	Dominican Republic	3.33
47	Luxembourg	3.33
49	El Salvador	3.33
50	Namibia	3.30*
51	Jamaica	3.29
52	Latvia	3.29
53	Malaysia	3.28
54	Japan	3.19
55	Turkey	3.19
56	Thailand	3.17
57	Costa Rica	3.15
58	Botswana	3.09*
59	Greece	3.00
60	Guatemala	2.99
61	Bulgaria	2.95
62	Ecuador	2.93
63	Morocco	2.85*
64	Jordan	2.72
65	Russian Federation	2.59
66	Philippines	2.29
67	Nicaragua	2.28
68	Nigeria	2.18
69	Egypt	2.17
70	Vietnam	2.15
71	Mauritius	2.13
72	Paraguay	2.11
73	Bolivia	2.10
74	Indonesia	2.04
75	Honduras	2.02
76	Venezuela	2.00
77	Sri Lanka	1.92
78	Haiti	1.72*
79	Trinidad and Tobago	1.55
80	Bangladesh	1.46
81	Romania	1.20
82	Zimbabwe	1.18

MEAN 3.72

9.03 Government success in ICT promotion

Government programs promoting the use of ICT are:

1 = not very successful, 7 = highly successful

Rank	Country	Value	1	MEAN 3.79	7
1	Singapore	5.76			
2	Tunisia	5.63			
3	Finland	5.63			
4	Israel	5.50			
5	Taiwan	5.27			
6	Malaysia	5.14			
7	Korea	5.07			
8	India	5.00			
9	Estonia	4.86			
10	Iceland	4.85			
11	Canada	4.83			
12	Sweden	4.79			
13	China	4.70			
14	Ireland	4.69			
15	United States	4.68			
16	Portugal	4.67			
17	Jordan	4.55			
18	Hungary	4.47			
19	Switzerland	4.38			
20	Brazil	4.36			
21	Belgium	4.33			
22	Vietnam	4.32			
23	Mauritius	4.31			
24	Sri Lanka	4.26			
25	Morocco	4.22			
26	Austria	4.18			
27	Thailand	4.13			
28	Hong Kong SAR	4.12			
29	Australia	4.12			
30	Germany	4.10			
31	Luxembourg	4.09*			
32	Denmark	4.05			
33	Botswana	3.93			
34	Chile	3.89			
35	Namibia	3.86			
36	Netherlands	3.86			
37	France	3.85			
38	Costa Rica	3.84			
39	Trinidad and Tobago	3.83			
40	Slovenia	3.82			
41	Philippines	3.81			
42	Colombia	3.80			
43	South Africa	3.79			
44	Dominican Republic	3.79			
45	Czech Republic	3.78			
46	Latvia	3.77			
47	Japan	3.75			
48	Spain	3.75			
49	New Zealand	3.64			
50	Italy	3.64			
51	Romania	3.60			
52	Norway	3.58			
53	Greece	3.56			
54	Mexico	3.49			
55	Lithuania	3.45			
56	United Kingdom	3.43			
57	Jamaica	3.42			
58	Croatia	3.29			
59	Uruguay	3.22			
60	Poland	3.16			
61	El Salvador	3.14			
62	Indonesia	3.13			
62	Nigeria	3.13			
64	Slovak Republic	3.11			
65	Turkey	3.06			
66	Egypt	3.05*			
67	Panama	2.95			
68	Peru	2.95			
69	Russian Federation	2.95			
70	Bulgaria	2.84			
71	Bangladesh	2.79			
72	Venezuela	2.75			
73	Ecuador	2.65			
74	Ukraine	2.59			
75	Nicaragua	2.58			
76	Bolivia	2.56			
77	Guatemala	2.44			
78	Zimbabwe	2.38			
79	Honduras	2.32			
80	Paraguay	2.30			
81	Argentina	1.97			
82	Haiti	1.91			

List of Authors

Scott Beardsley

Scott Beardsley is a director in McKinsey & Company's Brussels office. He is a global leader of McKinsey's telecommunications practice, has led the European wireline practice for five years, and is currently leading a special initiative on broadband. Prior to joining McKinsey, Mr. Beardsley was an editor and marketing manager at the Sloan Management Review; he has also worked in strategic sales and product marketing for the semiconductor industry's Advanced Micro Devices and Analog Devices. Mr. Beardsley was recently honored as a Fellow at the Institut d'Administration et de Gestion at the Université Catholique de Louvain in Belgium for outstanding contributions to management, and is a guest lecturer at the Business School. He was a Henry S. Dupont III Scholar (highest honors) at the Massachusetts Institute of Technology (MIT) Sloan School of Management where he graduated with an MBA in corporate strategy and marketing, and he holds a BSc in electrical engineering, magna cum laude, from Tufts University where he was a Kodak Scholar, elected a member of Tau Beta Pi, and was president of Eta Kappa Nu.
e-mail: scott_beardsley@mckinsey.com.

Ingo Beyer von Morgenstern

Dr. Ingo Beyer von Morgenstern holds a PhD in process engineering from the Technical University in Munich and an MBA from INSEAD, Fontainebleau. After working in North America, he later joined McKinsey Munich in 1985. He leads McKinsey's European High Tech Practice and co-leads its Global High Tech Practice; in these positions he serves clients in computer and data communications, industrial electronics, and aerospace and defense on strategic, operational, and organizational projects. The main focus of his work is value creation, profit improvement, governance, and growth. He lectures regularly at the physics department of the Technical University in Munich.
e-mail: Ingo_Beyer_von_Morgenstern@mckinsey.com.

Lionel C. Carrasco

Lionel C. Carrasco's high-tech experience spans fifteen years and twelve countries. It includes the design and implementation of several large-scale systems in industries such as banking, insurance, transportation, retail, manufacturing, and oil. He held the positions of Senior Vice President of Product Development and Vice President of Business Development at Centura Software Company (formerly GUPTA). At Centura, Mr. Carrasco was responsible for defining and articulating the company product strategy. Among his accomplishments are the development of the microserver strategy and the release of the company's core products, such as an embedded database server and Web development tools. His work contributed to the turnaround of the company in 2001, increasing its share value from US$0.75 to US$18 per share. As chief information officer of the Mexican news agency Notimex, he implemented Latin America's first automated system for news and created digital delivery of news via low-cost satellite networks. Mr. Carrasco has also worked as an international consultant for the United Nations Educational, Scientific and Cultural Organization in several countries, providing advisory and investments evaluations, he and has been an active founder of three startup software companies in Mexico. Serving as virtual chief technology officer and advisory board member, Mr. Carrasco was actively involved in the design, development, and implementation of Study 24x7 and StartupPro in the Silicon Valley; he also chaired the SQL Task Force and the Java Card Forum. Mr. Carrasco also founded Alterbrain, a regional e-builder firm with operations in Mexico, Brazil, the United States, and Argentina, and helped in the implementation of several large information technology (IT) projects using Internet-based technologies in banking, airlines, insurance, and other industries. In 2001, Mr. Carrasco completed a merger with Latin America's largest IT consulting firm, Neoris, and in mid-2002, Neoris appointed Mr. Carrasco to manage the Financial Services Division and the company's e-Business and Enterprise Application Integration practices in Mexico. Currently, Mr. Carrasco is the head of the global accounts group and the senior vice president on innovation at the Neoris headquarters in Miami.
e-mail: lionel.carrasco@neoris.com.

Mazen E. Coury

An independent strategy consultant, specializing in media, telecommunications, and information and communication technology (ICT), Mazen Coury has specialized in issues relating to the Arab world. He has collaborated with many institutions in the area, including Economic and Social Commission for Western Asia, in defining new development strategies for the area. Mr. Coury worked for a few years as a senior consultant with Gemini Consulting's strategy group in London and Paris, where he advised several corporations in building new organizations, defining and implementing business plans, creating new business strategies, and diversifying corporate assets. In that capacity, he managed the strategy and rollout of several telecommunication operators in the Middle East, including the engineering and technology aspects of their systems. Prior to that, he worked as project finance banker with the Société Générale group in China and France, overseeing projects in infrastructure, technology, and telecommunications. His two-year assignment in China included focusing on infrastructure projects in emerging markets throughout East Asia. A French-Lebanese national, Mr. Coury holds an MBA degree in finance from Cornell University and the London Business School.
e-mail: mazencoury@wanadoo.fr

Arnoud De Meyer

Arnoud De Meyer is Akzo Nobel Fellow in Strategic Management and Professor of Technology Management at INSEAD, and is also currently deputy dean of INSEAD in charge of administration and operations.

Professor De Meyer's main research interests are in manufacturing and technology strategy, the implementation of new manufacturing technologies, and the management of research and development (R&D). From the beginning of his academic career he has concentrated on understanding how innovation could be managed more effectively.

Besides his role as an academic, Professor De Meyer has also applied many of the concepts he developed in the business world. He has acted as a consultant for a number of companies throughout Europe and Asia, and he has helped several entrepreneurs in the startup of new business ventures. He is an outside director of three high-tech companies, one of which produces custom-made modems. He is also a member of the board of Infocomm Development Authority of Singapore, and was recently appointed to the Economic Review Council.

Professor De Meyer is an electrotechnical engineer and has a doctoral degree in management from the State University of Ghent (Belgium). He has also studied as a visiting scholar at the AP Sloan School of Management of MIT (United States).
e-mail: Arnoud.de.Meyer@insead.edu.

Soumitra Dutta

Soumitra Dutta is the Roland Berger Professor of e-Business and Information Technology and Dean for Executive Education at INSEAD. He is also the faculty director of Elab@INSEAD, INSEAD's initiative in building a center of excellence in teaching and research in the digital economy in collaboration with leading international organizations such as Morgan Stanley, SAP, Roland Berger, and Intel. Prior to joining the faculty of INSEAD, he was employed with Schlumberger in Japan and General Electric in the United States. Professor Dutta obtained his PhD in computer science and his MS in business administration from the University of California at Berkeley.

His research and consulting have focused on breakthrough approaches to the interrelationships between innovation, technology, and organizational design. He recently co-authored the book The Bright Stuff: How Innovative People and Technology Can Make the Old Economy New (Financial Times/Prentice Hall, 2002). His previous books were Embracing the Net: Get.Competitive (Financial Times/Prentice Hall, 2001) and Process Reengineering, Organizational Change and Performance Improvement (Mc-Graw Hill, 1999). His current manuscripts are included in *The Global Information Technology Report 2002–2003: Readiness for the Networked Future* (Oxford University Press, January 2003). In addition, he has published more than fifty articles in leading international journals.

A fellow of the World Economic Forum, Professor Dutta has won several awards for research and pedagogy. His research has been showcased in the international media including CNN, BBC and CNBC. He has taught in and consulted with leading international corporations across the world.
e-mail: Soumitra.Dutta@insead.edu.

Luis Enriquez

Luis Enriquez is an associate principal in McKinsey & Company's London office. He has extensive experience serving cable, mobile, and fixed operators in the telecommunications industry in the United States, Europe, and Latin America. He is one of the practice's global regulatory experts, and has led McKinsey's regulatory knowledge initiative. Prior to McKinsey, Mr. Enriquez worked extensively in regulation both in the United States and Latin America, and assisted Eastern European governments with liberalization and European Union accession issues. Mr. Enriquez holds a bachelor of arts in economics magna cum laude from Harvard University and did doctoral work in economics at the University of California at Berkeley.
e-mail: Luis_Enriquez@mckinsey.com.

José María Figueres-Olsen

José María Figueres-Olsen is a managing director of the World Economic Forum, where he heads the Center for the Global Agenda and oversees the development of the Center's Annual Meeting in Davos, Switzerland. Under his leadership, the Center has greatly expanded its offerings for the members and constituents of the World Economic Forum, actively engaging actors from business, politics, academia, and civil society in examining, understanding, and addressing many of the key issues that affect the world.

During his political career he served in positions of leadership, including that of president of Costa Rica from 1994 until 1998. During his presidency, he ushered the incorporation of the principles of sustainable development into Costa Rica's development platform, while stressing the importance of maintaining and enhancing sound macroeconomic and human development policies. In the international arena, he was the proponent of the Central American Alliance for Sustainable Development, signed by regional heads of state in late 1994. Prior to becoming president, he served as director of the Costa Rican Railways, as well as Minister of Trade and Minister of Agriculture for Costa Rica.

Former President Figueres has a keen interest in issues pertaining to the environment and access to information technology in the developing world. Outside of his official duties at the World Economic Forum, he currently holds leadership roles in major international organizations and initiatives. Among his multiple appointments, he serves as the personal representative of the United Nations Secretary General on issues pertaining to technology and the digital divide, as well as senior advisor of the Global Environment Facility of The World Bank. Additionally, he chairs the United Nations Information and Communication Technologies Task Force and is a board member of the Digital Nations Consortium, a project launched by the Media Lab at MIT.

A recipient of numerous major awards and distinctions, he is a graduate of the United States Military Academy at West Point and the John. F. Kennedy School of Government at Harvard University, where he was a Mason Fellow.
e-mail: Jose-Maria_Figueres@weforum.org.

Rossana Fuentes-Berain

Rossana Fuentes Berain is the World Economic Forum Media Leader. She is Managing Editor of Foreign Affairs en Español, Professor at Instituto Tecnológico Autónomo de México (ITAM), and Poynter Fellow in Journalism at Yale University. In her journalism career she has been a managing editor at REFORMA and El Financiero, and she is currently an advisor to the editor in chief of El Universal. She has a BA from the Universidad Autonóma Metropolitana, and an MA from the University of Southern California.
e-mail: rfuentes@itam.mx.

Amit Jain

Amit Jain is the research program manager for the Global Information Technology Project with the World Economic Forum at INSEAD. He has worked at INSEAD on various research projects in information and communication technology and knowledge management, and has been the technical director of INSEAD Online, INSEAD's e-learning effort. Prior to joining INSEAD, he worked with Schlumberger in the Middle East, and has pursued several entrepreneurial opportunities in information technology. Mr. Jain obtained his MBA from INSEAD, and a bachelor of technology degree in mechanical engineering from the Indian Institute of Technology.
e-mail: Amit.Jain@insead.edu

Mike Jensen

Mike Jensen is an independent consultant with fifteen years' experience in more than thirty countries in Africa assisting in the establishment of information and communications systems. A South African based in the East Cape, he sent his first e-mail twenty years ago while studying rural planning and development in Canada.

He subsequently returned to South Africa to work as a journalist at the Rand Daily Mail in Johannesburg in 1983. When the paper closed, he moved back to Canada and in 1986 he co-founded the country's national Internet service for NGOs, called, coincidentally, The Web. After helping to set up a similar Internet service provider (ISP) in Australia in 1989, he returned to South Africa where he works with international development agencies, NGOs, and governments, assisting them in the formulation, management, and evaluation of their Internet projects.

Mr. Jensen is a trustee of the African IT Education Trust, a board member of the South African ISP for NGOs (SangoNet), and is a former member of the African Conference of Ministers High Level Working Group, which developed the African Information Society Initiative (AISI) in 1996. He manages a popular website on the status of the Internet in Africa (http://www3.sn.apc.org/africa)
e-mail: MikeJ@sangonet.org.za.

Bruno Lanvin

At the World Bank, Bruno Lanvin is the manager of the Information for Development Programme (infoDev), a multidonor program focusing on extending digital opportunities for all (see http://www.infodev.org). So far, infoDev has financed more than 170 projects in some eighty-five countries around the world. In 2000, Mr. Lanvin was appointed Executive Secretary of DOT Force, the G-8 initiative launched by the Okinawa Summit of July 2000 to bridge the digital divide (see http://www.dotforce.org). The World Bank recruited him in September 2000 to be senior advisor for e-commerce and e-government. Prior to these appointments, he was Head of Electronic Commerce in the United Nations Conference on Trade and Development (UNCTAD) in Geneva. Mr. Lanvin has spent twenty years in the United Nations system and has occupied various senior positions, including management from 1999 to 2000 of UNCTAD's component of the United Nations "Development Account," which was devoted to e-commerce and development. In this position he organized a series of regional and interregional workshops on e-commerce, allowing more than 2,000 representatives from governments and enterprises to exchange experiences and best practices in the area of e-commerce. A frequent keynote speaker and participant in international conferences on the "new economy," he has published a large number of articles and books on ICT and development. He was the main drafter, team leader, and editor of Building Confidence: Electronic Commerce and Development, published in January 2000 (http://www.unctad.org/ecommerce). Bruno Lanvin has worked in more than sixty countries. He holds a BA in mathematics and physics from the University of Valenciennes (France), an MBA from Ecole des Hautes Etudes Commerciales (HEC) in Paris, and a PhD in economics from the Université of Paris I (La Sorbonne) in France. His mother tongue is French, and he speaks and writes English and Spanish; he also has a working knowledge of Italian, Portuguese, and Russian.
e-mail: blanvin@worldbank.org.

Pamela C. M. Mar

Pamela Mar oversees China activities and relationships for the World Economic Forum. She is responsible for the annual China Business Summit and for relations with Chinese companies, ministries, and other institutions. She is program manager for the East Asia Economic Summit, and helps to manage related initiatives and publishing projects in East Asia.

Ms. Mar has authored several articles, including "Corporate Governance in Transition Economies: A Case Study of Two Chinese Airlines" (Journal of World Business, 2001). She has also co-authored opinion articles and analysis appearing in international media, including the Asian Wall Street Journal, Far Eastern Economic Review, South China Morning Post, the Singapore Business Times and Straits Times, the New Straits Times, and Jakarta Post. Among her forthcoming publications are Recreating Asia: Visions for a New Century and a chapter on China's IT competitiveness in the Global Information Technology Report 2002–2003.

Prior to joining the Forum, Ms. Mar was a weekly columnist and book reviewer for Business Day newspaper and the Planning and Projects Manager at the Population and Community Development Association in Bangkok. She has also worked as a senior analyst and business development specialist with Star TV (Hong Kong) and as an associate in venture capital at the First Eastern Investment Group in Hong Kong.

Ms. Mar graduated from Yale University with highest honors, and with distinctions in both philosophy and East Asian studies; and holds a masters of management degree with honors from the London School of Economics.
e-mail: Pamela_Mar@weforum.org.

Roberto Martinez Illescas

Roberto Martinez Illescas is the director of Centro de Capital Intelectual y Competitividad. A specialist in public policy, planning, and regional economic development, he has worked as the World Bank and UNDP as a consultant. He has held high-ranking positions in the finance and communication ministries of the Mexican government as well as in the Mexican Federal Communication Commission. He has a BA from El Colegio de Mexico and graduate degrees from the London School of Economics and the John F. Kennedy School of Government at Harvard.
e-mail: robmar@alumni.ksg.harvard.edu.

Helmut Meitner

Dr. Helmut Meitner, Partner at Roland Berger Strategy Consultants since 2000, is responsible for functional IT and e-business issues as well as for IT industry. After obtaining degrees in computer science and business administration, he worked as a researcher at the University of Stuttgart and later as a consultant at the Fraunhofer Institute for Industrial Engineering (IAO) in Stuttgart, managing European IT development and consulting projects. He also acted as an expert on IT matters for the European Commission. Since joining Roland Berger Strategy Consultants in 1995, he has performed numerous IT and e-business projects in a range of industries (mainly financial services, consumer goods, retail, and transportation).
e-mail: Helmut_Meitner@de.rolandberger.com

Mark Melford

Mark Melford is a principal with the Communications, Media and Technology Group of Booz Allen & Hamilton, based in the London Office. His main interests are in "knowledge" industries, the ICT sector, and the promotion of entrepreneurship and innovation.

Mr. Melford has particular expertise in policy development for European and Gulf Cooperation Council governments, and has been a consultant to the Downing Street Policy Unit, the U.K. Treasury, and the Office of the e-Envoy, and has sat on the Scottish Office task force on the Knowledge Driven Economy.

Mr. Melford holds an MBA from INSEAD and an honors degree in general engineering from Cambridge University.
e-mail: Melford_Mark@bah.com.

N.R. Narayana Murthy

Mr. N.R. Narayana Murthy founded Infosys in 1981 along with six other software professionals. Mr. Murthy is presently the chairman of the board and chief mentor of Infosys. He served as the chairman and chief executive officer of Infosys since the company's inception until March 30, 2002.

Mr. Murthy is a member of the Prime Minister's Council on Trade and Industry (India), the Asian Executive Board at the Wharton Business School, the Board of Councilors at the University of Southern California School of Engineering, and the Cornell University Council. He is also a member of the Board of Advisors for the William F. Achtmeyer Center for Global Leadership at the Tuck School of Business. He is also a director on the Board of the Reserve Bank of India.

Mr. Murthy has won several awards, such as the Nikkei Asia Award, the Wharton School Dean's Medal, and the 2001 Freedom Prize by the Max Schmidheiny Foundation (St. Gallen), and has been named one of the "25 most influential global executives" by Time Magazine and CNN. He has also been featured in Business Week's "The Top Entrepreneurs" (1999) and "The Stars of Asia" (for three successive years— 1998, 1999, and 2000).

Mr. Murthy has a bachelor's degree in electrical engineering from the University of Mysore and a master's degree from the Indian Institute of Technology (IIT), Kanpur.

Infosys (NASDAQ: INFY) is an IT consulting and service provider, providing end-to-end solutions for global corporations. Today, Infosys is highly respected, acknowledged by its clients, employees, vendor-partners, investors, and by society –at large to be a dynamic, and innovative company.
e-mail: NMurthy@infosys.com.

Stefan Mytilineos

Stefan Mytilineos holds a degree in aeronautical engineering from the University of Bristol and an MBA with distinction from INSEAD, Fontainebleau. He has been with McKinsey's Business Technology Office for three years serving clients in the financial services and telecommunications and energy sectors on a variety of business and technology issues. He has led various knowledge initiatives within McKinsey on the impact of technology on business. Before McKinsey, Mr. Mytilineos worked in the IT department of a major investment bank leading the development of one of the bank's first Internet applications. He is originally from Greece, and apart from his native Greek he speaks English and French.

e-mail: stefan_Mytilineos@mckinsey.com

Fiona Paua

Fiona Paua is an economist with the Global Competitiveness Programme at the World Economic Forum. Previously, she was Vice President and the Country Head of Research for Citibank Philippines and a financial analyst at Goldman Sachs in the United States, Hong Kong, and Singapore. She has also served in various capacities at several institutions including the World Bank, the United States Agency for International Development, and ICT policy-related projects at Harvard University. She is the co-founder of b2bpricenow.com, winner of the 2001 Development Marketplace Award of the World Bank. Ms. Paua is a graduate of Dartmouth College and Harvard University.

e-mail: Fiona.Paua@weforum.org.

Dirk Reiter

Dirk Reiter is a senior partner at Roland Berger. Since completing his studies in electrical engineering in 1989, he has managed large-size transformation projects—first at Hewlett Packard, and, since 1993, in various functions at Roland Berger Strategy Consultants.

Mr. Reiter's focus is on strategy, process organization, sales and marketing, and e-business. He also specializes in the IT, media, and telecommunications industries, and is head of the international InfoCom Competence Center at Roland Berger Strategy Consultants. One of his key activities is involvement in strategic transformation projects; that is, supporting companies in their transition from the "old" to the "new" economy. This includes developing right-sizing strategies, cost-cutting programs, and efficiency-improvement campaigns. Mr. Reiter is also member of Roland Berger's Management Committee Germany.

e-mail: dirk_reiter@de.rolandberger.com.

Frank-Jürgen Richter

Frank-Jürgen Richter is director of the World Economic Forum, in charge of Asian affairs. His portfolio of responsibilities includes direct responsibility for the yearly East Asia Economic Summit. The East Asia Economic Summit was initiated to facilitate the exchange of experiences and expertise between leaders in business, government, and civil society in the interests of economic and social development in East Asia. Dr. Richter was educated in business administration, economics, and mechanical engineering in Germany, France, Mexico, and Japan. Prior to his career at the Forum, he had a distinguished career with multinational corporations in Asia and Europe. For almost a decade, he lived, studied, and worked in Tokyo and most recently in Beijing; in Beijing he developed and managed European multinational company's China operations. An active scholar, he has authored and edited several books on Asian economies and international business. He is an applied management scientist whose primary interests are international management and economic development, with strong secondary interests in political economy and geopolitical issues. Understanding economic institutions in general, and firm-level organizations in particular, is central to his research and rhetoric. His interests range from strategic management and human resource management to corporate governance, corporate social responsibility, and public-private partnerships. His books, numerous articles in professional journals, and opinion articles in the financial and regional press such as the Asian Wall Street Journal, Far Eastern Economic Review, Straits Times, and the South China Morning Post reflect this range of interests. Dr. Richter has focused on Asia and the financial crisis of 1997 to 1998 that affected Indonesia, Korea, Malaysia, Philippines, and Thailand, and that was responsible for Japan's economic fall as well as China's economic rise. He co-authored Recreating Asia: Visions for a New Century (Wiley, 2002) with Pamela Mar, and is currently working on a forthcoming volume, China: Enabling a New Era of Changes (Wiley, 2003). His books include fifteen further publications on Asia, including edited volumes for Palgrave-Macmillan. His most recent book with Palgrave-Macmillan is The Knowledge Economy in India (co-edited with Parthasarathi Banerjee), where he analyzes the influence of globalization and liberalization and the impact of technology on India's economy, while explaining India's economic fundamentals in a clear and concise manner.

e-mail: Frank-Jurgen.Richter@weforum.org.

Carsten H. Rossbach

Carsten H. Rossbach is a senior project manager with Roland Berger Strategy Consultants. As an expert within Roland Berger's international InfoCom Competence Center, he has worked in numerous ICT and media-related projects since 1997. Within these areas he has consulted in strategy, innovation, and cost management issues for providers of IT and telecommunications services, ranging from small and innovative niche players to large incumbents. The second focus of work is in ICT application strategy issues for corporations on the demand side, covering a variety of industries including media and financial services. Mr.

Rossbach holds a degree in business administration after having studied in Koblenz, Brussels, and Houston.

e-mail: carsten_rossbach@de.rolandberger.com.

Sukumar S.

Mr. Sukumar is Head of the Corporate Planning department at Infosys. He has served in this role since April 1999. The Corporate Planning department, reporting to the CEO of the company, is mandated with the role of managing the strategic and operations planning functions of the organization. As part of this, the department facilitates and manages key planning events, ensures adequate data support for decision making and also facilitates implementation of strategic initiatives within the company.

His areas of interest include applications of system dynamics to business problems and implementation subtleties of the Balanced Scorecard technique.

He has a bachelor's degree in mechanical engineering from Bangalore University and a postgraduate diploma in management from the Indian Institute of Management Bangalore (IIMB).

e-mail: SukumarS@infosys.com.

Constantijn van Oranje-Nassau

Constantijn van Oranje-Nassau is an associate at the Booz Allen Hamilton London office. In this capacity he researched and benchmarked ICT developments and related policies in a variety of countries on behalf of the British government. Prior to joining Booz Allen, Mr. van Oranje-Nassau worked for four years at the European Commission in the private office of the Commissioner for Foreign Affairs, where he was responsible for ICT, R&D, and innovation-related issues. He holds a degree in law from Leiden University and an MBA from INSEAD in Fontainebleau.

e-mail: Van_Oranje-Nassau_Constantijn@bah.com.

Jürgen Wunram

Dr. Jürgen Wunram holds a PhD in mathematics from the University of Hamburg. He first worked as a systems and software engineer in the Columbus space station program at DASA in Bremen and then joined McKinsey in 1992. Dr. Wunram is a principal in the Hamburg Office and a member of the High Tech Practice in Europe. He has served clients in the IT, automotive, and aerospace industries.

Dr. Wunram is leading the Digital Transformation initiative, a research initiative on how companies are leveraging digital technologies to drive performance improvements across enterprise by transforming core business processes and reconfiguring their value network.

e-mail: Juergen_Wunram@mckinsey.com.

Christine Zhen-Wei Qiang

Christine Zhen-Wei Qiang is an economist at the Global ICT Department at the World Bank. Her main responsibilities include ICT policy and strategy development, design and preparation, and supervision of information infrastructure projects. She has written and published a number of articles on ICT and development, with a focus on policy. She was the author of the ICT chapter in China and the Knowledge Economy: Seizing the 21st Century (World Bank, 2001) and co-authored the chapter "Liberalization, Investment and Beyond—An ICT Reform Agenda for Universal Access and the Networked Economy" in Issues in Telecommunications Development III (ITU, forthcoming) and "Investment and Growth of the Information Infrastructure: Summary Results of a Global Survey" (Telecom Policy, 2000). Ms. Qiang holds a PhD in economics and an MSE in computer science and Eengineering from the Johns Hopkins University.

e-mail: cqiang@worldbank.org